Fodor's

National Parks
of the East THIRD
EDITION

PLUS SEASHORES, FORESTS
AND WILDLIFE REFUGES

Fodor's Travel Publications, Inc.
New York • Toronto • London • Sydney • Auckland
www.fodors.com/

Third Edition

917.4
FOD
3rd ed.

ISBN 0–679–03508–7

Fodor's National Parks of the East

EDITOR: Anastasia Redmond Mills

Editorial Contributors: Steven Amsterdam, Neal Burdick, Paul Calhoun, John Filiatreau, Tara Hamilton, David Harford, Sylvia Higginbotham, Susan Ladd, Willard Lewis, Karl Luntta, Diane Marshall, Robert S. McCord, Chris Mikko, Eddie Nickens, Dick Pivetz, Michael Pretzer, Carolyn Price, Kay Scheller, William Scheller, Jill Schensul, M.T. Schwartzman, Sarah Scott, W. Lynn Seldon Jr., Donna L. Singer, Jonathan Sisken, Dennis Steele, Carol Thalimer, Dan Thalimer, Bruce Walker, Jeffrey R. Young

Editorial Production: Tracy Patruno

Maps: Eureka Cartography, *cartographer*; Steven Amsterdam, *map editor*

Design: Fabrizio La Rocca, *creative director*; Guido Caroti, *cover design*

Production/Manufacturing: Mike Costa

Cover Photographs: landscape, David Muench/Corbis; egret, Roger Tidman/Corbis

Special Sales

PRINTED IN THE UNITED STATES OF AMERICA

10 9 8 7 6 5 4 3 2 1

CONTENTS

INTRODUCTION

Kay and William G. Scheller

or most Americans, the words "national park" summon up an image of majestic western landscapes, of vistas too expansive to fit anywhere but beneath the big sky of the high prairie, the Rockies, the Sierra Nevada, or the desert Southwest.

It's true that Yellowstone was America's—and the world's—first national park, set aside in 1872. But as the 20th century progressed, the nation's lawmakers, abetted by private-sector preservationists and philanthropists, began to realize that the eastern states contained their own wonderful variety of scenic and ecological treasures. The national parks, forests, seashores, and other preserves of the East also benefited from a growing sense of urgency among those who would save them: In the nation's most densely populated regions, the danger of development overwhelming irreplaceable natural treasures had to be met by a swift and generous response.

It was in that spirit that John D. Rockefeller, Jr., and several of his wealthy Bar Harbor neighbors donated much of the land for Maine's Acadia National Park in 1919; and

that writer Horace Kephart spearheaded the drive to set aside Great Smoky Mountains National Park in 1934. A civic sense of stewardship led Boston's Appalachian Mountain Club (AMC) to urge protection of New Hampshire's north country as far back as the 1870s, some 40 years before the federal government designated the White Mountain National Forest; and inspired President John F. Kennedy to secure the windswept dunes of his beloved Cape Cod as a national seashore in 1961.

The century of government and private effort that has gone into creating the East's treasury of public lands has resulted in an astounding variety of protected places. Preeminent are the national parks themselves, places set aside because of their natural beauty, geological significance, or ecological integrity in the face of civilization's encroachments—all criteria important to preservationists as far back as the 1872 founding of the park system. But the eastern national parks are only part of the story. Included within this guide are also four national forests, beneficiaries of a different sort of federal protection (and managed not by the Interior Department's National Park

Service but by the Forest Service under the Department of Agriculture).

While national parks focus almost entirely upon access and interpretation of outstanding natural sites for visitors, national forests are mandated as mixed-use facilities. The national forest system—founded in 1891 and vastly expanded under the forward-thinking leadership of President Theodore Roosevelt and his great Forest Service chief Gifford Pinchot—seeks to preserve forest lands for their role as watersheds and for their timber resources, as well as for public recreation.

Within some national parks and national forests are federally designated wilderness areas, large tracts of pristine acreage where no logging, road building, permanent structures, or motorized recreation is permitted. When the first expanses of American wilderness were officially protected, all of the eligible land was in the West, since a prime criterion was that it show no traces of human interference. Since virtually every square mile east of the Mississippi had been cleared for settlement or at least logged for timber or the creation of farmland, eastern parklands and second-growth forests didn't qualify—until the Eastern Wilderness Act of 1964 permitted designation of areas that had reverted to their original, untrammeled condition. In places such as New Hampshire's White Mountains and New York State's Adirondacks (protected within a state park that easily dwarfs all of the national parks in the East), you can visit trackless wilderness

domains that have shed all traces of the crosscut saw and the plow.

There are six national seashores highlighted in these pages, comprising some of the most beautiful and ecologically sensitive areas along America's Atlantic and Gulf coasts. Perhaps no category of parkland or public reserve is more fragile and in need of preservation than these, since overbuilt or otherwise damaged shoreline is often lost forever. The most fascinating aspect of the seashores is that unlike the mountain preserves—Great Smoky Mountains National Park, say, or Vermont's Green Mountain National Forest—where the seemingly immutable landscape is the product of the unfathomably slow workings of geological time, the world of sand dunes and shape-shifting barrier islands is very much a work in progress, where last year's nor'easter may have had as much influence on the lay of the land as any event since the ice age.

The two national wildlife refuges described in these pages, Georgia's Okefenokee and Virginia's Chincoteague, occupy another special niche in America's inventory of protected lands. Here, the accommodation of human visitors takes second place to the welfare of birds and animals. This doesn't mean we aren't welcome but that the refuges are just that—refuges, where threatened species or resting migratory birds are always foremost when it comes to land management decisions and the development of facilities. Needless to say, they are terrific places for observing wildlife.

Human interaction with the land is much more the focus at the one national recreation area that we've profiled—New Jersey's Delaware Water Gap—and along our two parkways, the Blue Ridge in Virginia and North Carolina, and the Natchez Trace, which winds through Mississippi, Alabama, and Tennessee. Created in the 1930s as part of President Franklin Roosevelt's New Deal program of providing public employment, these long, rambling byways provide automobile access to some of the South's most impressive vistas and a broad sampling of historic sites.

Variety, then, is the key idea behind the selection of parklands in this guide, and the array of recreational opportunities they offer. The parks range in terrain from the barren summit of New Hampshire's Mt. Washington, home to some of the world's most ferocious weather, to the teeming grasslands and hardwood swamps of the Florida Everglades; from the sea-lashed dunes of Cape Cod to the primordial stillness of Pennsylvania's old-growth Allegheny National Forest.

Each of the parks seems to suggest its own special means of discovery. Cape Cod National Seashore is a walk along the beach before breakfast, as big Atlantic rollers dispel in foam at the foot of dawn-reddened dunes. The Blue Ridge Parkway is a long, unhurried drive along a mountain crest ablaze with rhododendron and azalea. The Adirondacks are a canoeist's dream, a forested mountain redoubt riddled with endlessly meandering paddling waters. White Mountain National Forest is a trek above treeline from one friendly AMC hut to another; while Arkansas's Hot Springs National Park is, among many other things, a relaxing mineral bath.

Of course, you can visit any of these parks and find your own pace, your own path, your own special way to interpret and enjoy what has been so carefully preserved. Just remember as you explore that what was wisely secured yesterday has to be kept secure for tomorrow. All of the places in this book are specimens of a healthy natural environment. They are living—sometimes even entire—ecosystems. Treat them as such at the campsite, on the trail or waterway, or along the road, and America's historic investment in its grand open spaces will pay dividends for generations to come.

ACKNOWLEDGMENTS

e would like to thank all those who helped to ensure the accuracy of this book. Special thanks go to the following people, who are mostly employees of the U.S. National Park Service:

Acadia: Wanda Moran. **Adirondack:** Bob Wilson. **Allegheny:** Kathe Frank, Janeal A. Hedman, John Palmer. **Assateague:** John Schroer. **Big Cypress:** Marian Wack. **Biscayne:** Gary A. Bremen. **Blue Ridge:** Phil Noblitt, Ina Parr. **Cape Cod:** Frank Ackerman. **Cape Hatteras:** Warren Wrenn. **Cape Lookout:** Laurie Heupel. **Catoctin:** Mel Poole. **Chincoteague:** Larry Points. **Delaware Water Gap:** Randy W. Turner. **Everglades:** Deborah Nordeen. **Fire Island:** David Griese. **Great Smoky:** Nancy Gray. **Green Mountain:** Dennis Roy. **Gulf Islands:** Ruby Boyd. **Hot Springs:** Earl Adams. **Natchez Trace:** Leslie Blythe. **Okefenokee:** Maggie O'Connell. **Ouachita:** Cheryl G. Chatham. **Shenandoah:** Karen A. Michaud. **Voyageurs:** Carol Maass. **White Mountains:** Colleen Mainuille.

While every care has been taken to ensure the accuracy of the information in this guide, the passage of time will always bring change, and consequently, the publisher cannot accept responsibility for errors that may occur.

All prices and opening times quoted here are based on information supplied to us at press time. Hours and admission fees may change, however, and the prudent traveler will avoid inconvenience by calling ahead.

Fodor's wants to hear about your travel experiences, both pleasant and unpleasant. When a campground, hotel, or restaurant fails to live up to its billing, let us know and we will investigate the complaint and revise our entries where the facts warrant it.

Send your letters to: Editor, National Parks of the East, Fodor's Travel Publications, 201 East 50th Street, New York, NY 10022.

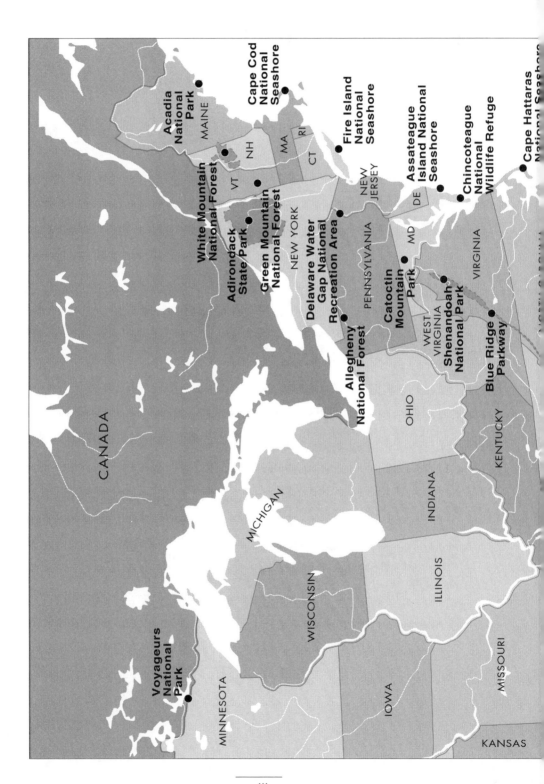

Acadia National Park

Cape Cod National Seashore

Fire Island National Seashore

Assateague Island National Seashore

Chincoteague National Wildlife Refuge

Cape Hatteras National Seashore

MAINE

NH

VT

MA

RI

CT

NEW JERSEY

DE

MD

White Mountain National Forest

Green Mountain National Forest

Adirondack State Park

Delaware Water Gap National Recreation Area

NEW YORK

PENNSYLVANIA

Catoctin Mountain Park

Allegheny National Forest

WEST VIRGINIA

Shenandoah National Park

Blue Ridge Parkway

VIRGINIA

OHIO

KENTUCKY

CANADA

MICHIGAN

WISCONSIN

INDIANA

ILLINOIS

IOWA

MISSOURI

KANSAS

MINNESOTA

Voyageurs National Park

**NATIONAL PARKS AND
SEASHORES OF THE EAST**

Cape Lookout
National Seashore

Biscayne
National Park

Great Smoky
Mountains
National Park

SOUTH
CAROLINA

Okefenokee
National
Wildlife
Refuge

GEORGIA

FLORIDA

Everglades
National Park
and Big Cypress
National Preserve

ALABAMA

The Natchez
Trace Parkway

Gulf Islands
National
Seashore

MISSISSIPPI

Hot Springs
National Park

Ouachita
National
Forest

ARKANSAS

LOUISIANA

TEXAS

OKLAHOMA

TENNESSEE

N

Essential Information

VISITOR INFORMATION For general information on U.S. national parks, contact the Office of Public Inquiries, **National Park Service** (Box 37127, Washington, DC 20013-7127, tel. 202/208–4747). Or try their **Web site:** www.nps.gov. For information on national forests, contact the **Forest Service** (United States Department of Agriculture, Box 96090, Washington, DC 20090, tel. 202/205–1760). For detailed information on the individual parks and forests (weather, special events, campsite availability), contact each location directly (*see* individual chapters). When you arrive at a park, stop by one of the visitor centers and pick up a free map and literature. Some visitor centers have exhibits, slide presentations, and brief films that will help you understand the area. In addition, the following regional offices of the U.S. National Park Service provide general information on parks in their areas.

Mid-Atlantic region: National Park Service (N.E. Field Area, U.S. Customs House, 200 Chestnut St., 3rd floor, Philadelphia, PA 19106, tel. 215/597–7013).

Midwest region: National Park Service (1709 Jackson St., Omaha, NE 68102, tel. 402/221–3431).

National Capital region: National Park Service (1100 Ohio Dr. SW, Washington, DC 20242, tel. 202/619–7005).

North Atlantic region: National Park Service (15 State St., Boston, MA 02109, tel. 617/223–5001).

Southeast region: National Park Service (75 Spring St. SW, Atlanta, GA 30303, tel. 404/562–3100).

SPECIAL TOURS A variety of associations offer naturalist-led tours that may include hiking, biking, camping, and/or canoeing. Some offer special educational programs, seminars, workshops, and field trips. These tours can be rugged and ambitious or relaxed and luxurious. Here's a sampling of what you'll find.

Backroads (801 Cedar St., Berkeley, CA 94710-1740, tel. 510/527–1555 or 800/462–2848, www.backroads.com) runs walking and cycling tours to several of the eastern national parks, including the Blue Ridge Parkway, Cape Hatteras, and Natchez Trace.

Earthwatch (680 Mount Auburn St., Box 9104, Watertown, MA 02272, tel. 800/776–0188, www.earthwatch.org) recruits volunteers to be short-term assistants to scientists on research expeditions, some of which are conducted in or near national parks. Volunteers do anything from observing the wild horses on Assateague Island to documenting dolphin pods and behavior from boats off the eastern coast of Florida.

National Wildlife Federation (8925 Leesburg Pike, Vienna, VA 22184, tel. 703/790–4000 or 800/822–9919, www.nwf.org/nwf/) runs weekend and weeklong seminars (nature hikes, classes, workshops) in areas of natural beauty, including some national parks.

The **Sierra Club** (85 2nd St., 2nd floor, San Francisco, CA 94109, tel. 415/977–5500, www.sierraclub.org) has offered skiing in the Adirondacks and canoeing in the Everglades, among other trips. On many trips, participants help preserve the environment by projects like revegetation and trail maintenance.

Wild Horizons Expeditions (5663 West Fork Rd., Darby, MT 59829, tel. 406/821–3747), a guide and outfitter that is licensed by the National Park Service, offers customized wilderness trips every year within various national parks.

Outward Bound U.S.A. (Rte. 9D, R2 Box 280, Garrison, NY 10524, tel. 800/243–8520) conducts educational wilderness programs designed to foster self-esteem and self-reliance in individuals age 14 and up. Trips are 8, 14, or 22 days long; semester courses are also available.

WHEN TO GO Summer is without question the busiest time of the year to visit most national parks and seashores, so be prepared to deal with full parking lots and traffic jams. If you must travel during this time, go early or late in the season to avoid the mid-summer peak; spring and fall are ideal. In winter some northern parks close certain roads because of heavy snowfall. Others have just as much going on as they do in summer: In Voyageurs, for example, winter is prime time for snowmobiling, ice fishing, and cross-country skiing.

Keep in mind that even in summer the weather can vary—especially in the mountainous parks. Temperatures can rise into the 90s during the day and drop into the teens or lower at night. Also, the climate often changes with elevation. Within a matter of minutes, a blue sky and brilliant sunshine can erupt into an extravaganza of hail and lightning. A key to enjoying your time in the parks is always keeping warm clothing and rain gear handy, no matter how promising the day.

The parks and the areas around them all host a variety of seasonal festivals and events. For information about specific goings-on and dates, *see* Seasonal Events *in* individual park chapters.

CAR RENTALS Renting a car to drive to and around the national parks is easy, provided you are over 25 (21 in some states) and have a valid driver's license and a major credit card. Rates vary from state to state, company to company, and season to season. Generally, the smaller the car, the lower the rate, but ask about promotions. Be aware that over-the-phone quotes do not include the collision damage waiver (CDW), personal accident insurance, or tax. To save money, check with your insurance agent to see whether your personal coverage includes rental cars, and find out if your credit-card company insures car rentals that are charged to your card. The CDW covers travel in all U.S. states but not necessarily in Canada. If you plan to cross borders, ask the agency if you will be covered. If you want to leave the car at a location different from the one where you picked it up, you will most likely have to pay an additional drop-off charge, which can be a couple of hundred dollars, depending on your route. Always ask in advance.

Many companies charge a flat daily or weekly rate with unlimited mileage; others charge by the mile over a certain number of miles. The rates for a subcompact vehicle with unlimited mileage start at about $30 or $35 a day and about $195 a week.

Once you find the best rate, make a reservation over the phone. If you're picking the car up at an airport, have your arrival time handy when you call. Record the reservation number, the name of the agent to whom you spoke, and the time and date of your call. Be sure to verify that the company will honor your credit card.

Among the major national car-rental firms are **Alamo** (tel. 800/327–9633), **Avis** (tel. 800/331–1212), **Budget** (tel. 800/527–0700), **Dollar** (tel. 800/421–6868), **Hertz** (tel. 800/654–3131), and **National** (tel. 800/227–7368).

RENTING AN RV The same rules for renting a car apply when you rent an RV: You must be over 25 (21 in some states) and have a valid driver's license and credit card. No special license or driving skills are required. In fact, driving an RV is much like driving a car, thanks to automatic transmissions and power brakes. The difficult part is handling a vehicle of that size (a motor home can be anywhere from 20 to 34 ft long), especially getting in and out of parking spaces and backing up. Many veteran RVers avoid going into reverse. Most rental agencies provide a brief (30-minute to one-hour) familiarization course in which drivers can get acquainted with the operation of the RV. All the technical equipment—the propane system for heating and cooking, the water tanks, the waste-disposal system, and the generator—is fully explained when you arrive at the rental office. Once you're on your way, stay in the slow lane, and go easy when braking and accelerating. Try to avoid driving at night.

You must reserve far in advance if you plan to rent an RV in summer. Also, prices are highest during these months.

Depending on the size of the vehicle you rent, you will be charged from $125 to $175 a day during high season. That may include unlimited mileage, or it may include a set number of free miles, and you will have to pay more for each additional mile. Most RVs use regular, unleaded gasoline, and it can be expensive: The gas tanks usually hold from 40 to 79 gallons, but RVs only get 8 or 9 miles to the gallon. Add to that the campground fees—roughly from $6 to $25 per night—and an RV vacation may not be as inexpensive as you had hoped.

First-time motor-home renters can call 888/467–8464 to receive a free video on RVing. To locate a rental agency, look under "Recreation Vehicles—Renting and Leasing" in the yellow pages for the dealer nearest you. You can also order a directory of RV-rental agencies called *Who's Who in RV Rentals,* published by **RV America** (tel. 703/591–7130); it costs $10, including first-class delivery. The largest nationwide RV-rental firm is **Cruise America** (tel. 800/327–7778).

Many roads in eastern national parks are narrow and winding. Some have restric-

tions on large vehicles. If you are driving a large RV or pulling a trailer, be sure to call the park in advance of your trip to find out about road restrictions.

ENTRY FEES Many national parks have an entrance fee, ranging from $3 to $20 per vehicle and good for seven consecutive days. In addition to entry fees, most of the national parks charge fees at their drive-in campgrounds. These cost from $5 a night for tenters to $12 a night for RVs. Senior travelers, travelers with disabilities, and frequent park goers can take advantage of the **Federal Recreation Passport Program,** which includes a number of passes that waive entrance fees for the cardholder and an accompanying carload of passengers.

For travelers 62 years and older, the **Golden Age Passport** is good for life, and available at national parks upon arrival. The passport costs $10, a one-time fee. You must have proof of your age and U.S. citizenship or permanent residency status; a driver's license or birth certificate is fine. In addition to free admission to the parks, the pass gives the holder a 50% discount on park facilities and services (excluding those run by private concessionaires).

The **Golden Access Passport** is free and available to those with permanent disabilities. The passport can be obtained at a park entrance with proper proof of a disability; it is good for life. Holders of this pass get in to the parks free and receive a 50% discount on all park facilities and services (excluding those run by private concessionaires).

The **Golden Eagle Pass** costs $50 and entitles the cardholder and an accompanying party to free admission to all parks for the calendar year. It is neither refundable nor transferable and does not cover additional park fees such as those for camping and parking. The Golden Eagle Pass can be purchased in person or by mail, by sending $50 to any of the National Park Service headquarters or regional offices (*see* Visitor Information, *above*).

Those planning to visit one specific park repeatedly should consider a **Park Pass,** available for $10 to $40 depending on the park. It gives the pass holder and accompanying party free admission to that park for the calendar year. The pass can be purchased in person or by mail from the specific national park at which it will be honored. It is neither transferable nor refundable.

In addition to higher entry and campground fees, budget cuts may result in the discontinuation of certain recreational programs offered at the parks at press time.

MONEY Carry credit cards, traveler's checks, and some cash when visiting the national parks. Many hotels and restaurants take all major bank traveler's checks, and major credit cards—American Express, Master-Card, Visa—are honored at car-rental agencies, most hotels, and some restaurants.

The following credit-card abbreviations are used throughout this guide: AE, American Express; D, Discover; DC, Diners Club; MC, MasterCard; V, Visa.

If you need cash quickly, you will probably have to drive into the nearest town or city to find an automated teller machine (ATM). Cirrus and Plus cards are widely accepted. Although we list ATM locations in every chapter, it's wise to check with your credit-card company or bank before you leave home to find out where there is an ATM near your destination that will accept your card. Also ask what the fee is for obtaining cash from a machine (it varies from bank to bank).

TRAVELING WITH CHILDREN There's no better way to teach children about nature than by visiting the national parks. As a family you'll find trails to follow, lakes to swim in, routes to bicycle on, and all sorts of animals and birds and geologic wonders to look at. In addition, some parks offer guided horseback rides, campfire programs, and ranger-led naturalist walks that are geared to children. Some parks have special child-care programs in which parents leave their children for the day. In addition, most

motels, hotels, and lodges near national parks are child-friendly; some even have kitchenettes for those who need to prepare food at home.

Packing. Don't expect to find baby supplies in the parks. In addition to diapers, formula, and any special foods your child may require, you may want to consider packing airtight fresh milk cartons, which don't need refrigeration, or powdered milk and distilled water. Be sure your first-aid kit is complete: You can't expect to run easily to the pharmacy to have prescriptions filled. And always carry your pediatrician's phone number.

Getting There. If you're planning to rent a car, consider taking along your child's own safety seat, since renting one may cost up to $5 per day. Safety seats can also be used in airplanes, although you'll have to pay an adult fare if your child uses his or her own seat. You might have your children pack their own "car bags," with crayons, coloring books, and toys to play with en route.

To find out more about traveling with children, contact the following agencies:

Rascals in Paradise (650 5th St., Suite 505, San Francisco, CA 94107, tel. 415/978–9800 or 800/872–7225) is a travel agency specializing in family travel.

"Have Children Will Travel" (Box 152, Lake Oswego, OR 97034, tel. 503/699–5869) is a quarterly newsletter covering travel tips, educational adventures, and vacation ideas for families. A one-year subscription costs $29.

TRAVELING WITH PETS Pets are allowed in developed areas of the national parks, including drive-in campgrounds and picnic areas, but they must be kept on a leash at all times. With the exception of guide dogs, pets are usually not allowed inside buildings, on most trails, on beaches, or in the backcountry. They also may be prohibited in areas controlled by concessionaires. Some of the parks have kennels, which charge about $6 a day, but before you decide to bring a pet to a national park, call to find out about specific restrictions.

TIPS FOR TRAVELERS WITH DISABILITIES The parks are meticulously accommodating to travelers with disabilities. Visitor centers provide information in braille, large print, and tape-recorded formats. At some visitor centers and park museums, free wheelchairs are available; ramps are strategically placed throughout the parks. The **Golden Access Passport** entitles those who are permanently disabled to free access to all U.S. national parks (*see* Entry Fees, *above*).

For people with disabilities, *Easy Access to National Parks* (Wendy Roth and Michael Tompane, Sierra Club Books, 1992) is indispensable.

A handful of nonprofit organizations take mixed-ability groups on guided adventure trips to some of the parks. These include **America Outdoors** (Box 1348, Knoxville, TN 37901, tel. 423/524–4814), **Outward Bound** (309 Walker Ave. S, Wayzata, MN 55391, tel. 800/243–8520), **People and Places** (3909 Genesee St., Cheektowaga, NY 14225, tel. 716/631–8223), and **Shake-A-Leg** (200 Harrison Ave., Newport, RI 02840, tel. 401/849–8898).

The following organizations provide travel advice and services for travelers with disabilities:

Information Center for Individuals with Disabilities (Fort Point Pl., 1st floor, 27–43 Wormwood St., Boston, MA 02210, tel. 800/462–5015) provides a list of travel agents who specialize in tours for people with disabilities.

Moss Rehabilitation Hospital Travel Information Service (tel. 215/456–9600, TTY 215/456–9602) is a free phone service providing travel information for people with disabilities.

Society for the Advancement of Travel for the Handicapped (SATH) (347 5th Ave., Suite 610, New York, NY 10016, tel. 212/447–7284) is a nonprofit organization that provides comprehensive travel information

for people with disabilities. The $45 annual membership free includes the quarterly SATH newsletter.

TIPS FOR OLDER TRAVELERS If you have any special dietary or medicinal needs, be sure to carry your own supplies when visiting the national parks. The **Golden Age Passport** entitles those over 62 to free admission to all U.S. national parks (*see* Entry Fees, *above*).

The **American Association of Retired Persons** (601 E St. NW, Washington, DC 20049, tel. 202/434–2277) offers several cost-cutting programs for the older traveler, including discounts on hotels, motels, car rentals, and sightseeing attractions. AARP membership is open to those 50 and over; annual dues are $8 per person or couple.

Mature Outlook (Box 9390, Des Moines, IA 50306, tel. 800/336–6330), a travel club for people over 50, offers hotel and motel discounts and a bimonthly newsletter. Annual membership is $19.95 (covers a single person or a couple).

National Council of Senior Citizens (8403 Colesville Rd., Suite 1200, Silver Spring, MD 20910, tel. 301/578–8800 or 888/373–6467) is a nonprofit group that offers members a multitude of travel discounts. Annual membership is $13 per person or per couple 50 years or older.

WHAT TO READ Many of the national parks have bookstores that sell field guides, maps, and other publications on the history, geology, plants, and wildlife of their specific area.

Three bibles for identifying plant and animal life are part of the Peterson Field Guide Series: *Eastern Birds (East of the Rockies), Wildflowers of Northeastern and North Central North America,* and the classic *Wildflowers.* The Audubon Society Field Guide Series (Knopf) puts out *Familiar Birds: North American East; Familiar Trees of North America: Eastern Region;* and *Familiar Wildflowers of North America: Eastern Region.* Two other good sources of information are *Wild Plants of America: A*

Select Guide for the Naturalist and Traveler (John Wiley & Sons), by Richard M. Smith; and *The Traveling Birder* (Doubleday), by Clive Goodwin.

The most detailed topographical maps of the national parks are those published by the **United States Geological Survey (U.S.G.S.)** (Box 25286, Denver Federal Center, Denver, CO 80225, tel. 303/202–4700 or 800/435–7627). Printed on plastic, U.S.G.S. maps are waterproof and tearproof—ideal for hiking trips. **Trails Illustrated** (Box 4357, Evergreen, CO 80437, tel. 303/670–3457 or 800/962–1643) also offers a line of topographical maps printed on plastic.

Free information kits for each and every national park can be ordered by calling the **National Park Service** (tel. 800/365–2267). Kits include a map, information on accessibility, important phone numbers, and a list of facilities and activities.

MORE INFORMATION THROUGH FODOR'S On the Web, check out Fodor's site (www.fodors.com) for information on major destinations around the world and travel-savvy interactive features. The Web site also lists the 80-plus stations nationwide that carry the Fodor's Travel Show, a live call-in program that airs every weekend. Tune in to hear guests discuss their wonderful adventures—or call in to get answers for your most pressing travel questions.

VISITING THE PARKS

OPENING AND CLOSING TIMES The buildings within national parks, including visitor centers, are generally open daily from 9 to 5, but these times do vary from park to park and season to season. Most park buildings are open every day of the year except Christmas. Natural areas of the parks are usually open 24 hours a day, 365 days a year, but fees are generally collected only during peak seasons and hours. If the fee station is closed you may enter the park free, but consider making a donation to help maintain the park.

STAYING HEALTHY AND SAFE The three leading causes of death in the parks are, in order, motor-vehicle accidents, drownings, and falls. Use common sense: Keep your eyes on the road while driving, assess water temperature and currents before taking the plunge, and stay on trails to avoid falling from cliffs. If you find yourself in an emergency situation, call 911; there are telephone booths at the visitor centers and other locations throughout the parks. Some of the parks have their own emergency numbers as well.

Before you go, be sure to pack a first aid kit, including a first-aid manual, aspirin, adhesive bandages, butterfly bandages, sterile gauze pads (2"×2" and 4"×4"), 1"-wide adhesive tape, an elastic bandage, antibacterial ointment, antiseptic cream, antihistamines, razor blades, tweezers, a needle, scissors, insect repellent, Calamine lotion, and sunscreen.

Altitude Sickness. One of the most common problems for hikers is altitude sickness, which results when a hiker ascends to heights over 8,500 ft without being properly acclimated. The symptoms include headache, nausea, vomiting, shortness of breath, weakness, and sleep disturbance. If any of these occur, it's important to retreat to a lower altitude. If you have a history of heart or circulatory problems, talk to your doctor before planning a visit to areas at high altitudes.

Animal Bites. Some animals, especially rodents, carry dangerous diseases. If you are bitten by a wild animal, it's important to see a doctor as soon as possible. Many animal bites require a tetanus shot and, if the animal could be rabid, a rabies shot.

Broken Bones. If you break a leg or arm on the trail, it is best to keep the broken area as still as possible and elevated while someone goes for help. If help is far away, make a splint from a branch, and strap it on with a bandanna or article of clothing.

Frostbite. Caused by exposure to extreme cold for a prolonged period of time, frostbite is marked by the numbing of ears, nose, fingers, or toes; white or grayish yellow skin is a sure sign. Frostbite victims should be taken into a warm place as soon as possible, and wet clothing should be removed. The area should then be immersed in warm—not hot—water or wrapped in a warm blanket. DO NOT rub the frostbitten area, as this may cause permanent tissue damage. When the area begins to thaw, the victim should exercise it, to stimulate blood circulation. If bleeding or other complications develop, get to a doctor as soon as possible.

Giardia. Invisible organisms that live in unpurified water cause campers severe stomach sickness. Though drinking water is available at many campgrounds, you'll have to purify spring or stream water if you plan on hiking into the backcountry. Water purification tablets come in packages with directions. The most widely used brand is Potable Aqua, which is made by Wisconsin Pharmacal and sells for about $5.50 for 50 tablets (good for 50 quarts of water). However, iodine can build up in the body and are not recommended for long trips; a better option is to filter water through a water-purification pump available at camping equipment stores. Boiling water is the least favorite method since it takes time and uses fuel, but if it is the only method available to you, use it; bring the water to a boil for at least five minutes, longer at high altitudes.

Hypothermia. Hypothermia, a potentially fatal decrease in body temperature, occurs even in relatively mild weather. Symptoms are chilliness and fatigue, followed by shivering and mental confusion. The minute these signs are spotted, get the victim to shelter of some kind and wrap him or her in warm blankets or a sleeping bag. Ideally another member of the party should get in the sleeping bag with the victim for added warmth. If practical, it's best for both people to be unclothed, but if clothing remains on, it must be dry. High-energy food and hot drinks also aid recovery. To avoid hypothermia always carry warm, dry clothing, avoid immersion or exposure to cold water or rain, and keep energy levels up by eating high-calorie foods like trail mix.

Lyme Disease. Lyme disease is a potentially dehabilitating and/or fatal disease carried by deer ticks, which thrive in dry, brush-covered areas. When walking in woods, brush, or through fields in areas where Lyme disease has been found, wear tick repellent and long pants tucked into socks. When you undress, search your body for deer ticks—which are no bigger than a pinhead—and remove them with rubbing alcohol and tweezers. Watch the area for several weeks. Some people develop a bull's-eye-like rash or flulike symptoms; if this happens, see your physician immediately. Lyme disease can be treated with antibiotics if caught early enough.

Plant Poisons. If you touch poison ivy, poison oak, or poison sumac, wash the area immediately with soap and water. A variety of ointments, such as Calamine lotion and cortisone cream, may relieve itching.

Snake Bites. Snakes will do everything to avoid you, but in the event you have a run-in and are bitten, it's necessary to act quickly. If it's a harmless snake, ordinary first aid for puncture wounds should be given. If it is poisonous, the victim should remain as still as possible, so as not to spread the venom through the body. He or she should lie down, keeping the wound area below the rest of the body, and another person should seek medical help immediately.

Sprains. If you're planning to do a lot of hiking, by all means break in your shoes or boots before you leave home. Wear boots that have good ankle support. Once you're out and about in the wilderness, it's always important to watch your step. Sprains can happen easily, especially on loose rocks and slippery paths.

Sunburn and Heat Stroke. Take great care in protecting yourself from the sun—even when it's cloudy or there's snow on the ground. Keep in mind that at higher altitudes, where the air is thinner, you will burn more easily, and that sun reflected off the snow, off sand, and off water can be especially strong even on overcast days. Apply sunscreen liberally before you go out, and wear a visored cap or sunglasses. Many scientists fear that overexposure to UV rays may cause increased rates of skin cancer and cataracts.

If you are exposed to extreme heat for a prolonged period, you run the risk of heat stroke (also known as sunstroke), a serious medical condition. It begins quite suddenly with a headache, dizziness, and fatigue but can quickly lead to convulsions and unconsciousness or even to death. If someone in your party develops any of the symptoms, have one person go for emergency help; meanwhile, move the victim to a shady place, wrap him or her in wet clothing or bedding, and try to cool him or her down with water or ice.

FIRE PRECAUTIONS When it comes to fire, never take a chance. Keep the following pointers in mind. Don't build fires when you're alone. Build small fires. Always build campfires in a safe place (away from tinder of any kind). Use a fireplace or fire grate if one is available. Clear the ground around the fireplace so that wind cannot blow sparks into dry leaves or grass. Throw used matches into the fire. Never leave a fire unattended. Always have a pot of water or sand next to a campfire or stove. When finished, be sure the fire is out cold (meaning you can touch it with your bare hands). Never cook in your tent or a poorly ventilated space.

PROTECTING THE ENVIRONMENT More than ever, our national parks are being discovered and rediscovered by travelers who want to spend their vacations appreciating nature, watching wildlife, and taking adventure trips. But as the number of visitors to the parks increases, so does stress on wildlife and plant life. Tourism can drum up concern for the environment, but it can also cause great physical damage to parks. Many of the trails and roadways in our national parks are overused and abused.

Do not leave garbage on the trails or in campgrounds. If you hike into the backcountry, carry your trash out with you. Bury human waste at least 100 ft from any trail, campsite, or backcountry water source. Some parks and many environmental organizations are starting to advocate packing out even human waste. Do not wash dishes or clothing in lakes and streams. If you must use soap, make sure it is biodegradable, and carry water in clean containers 100 ft away from its source before using it for cleaning. A free brochure titled "Leave No Trace" supplies more information on protecting the environment; to obtain a copy, call 800/332–4100.

Animals. As human development shrinks wildlife habitats, animal encounters are increasingly common in national parks. To avoid attracting bears, racoons, and other scavengers, all campers should animal-proof their food supplies. Animal-proof containers are available at most developed campsites, but backcountry campers must hang food in a bag or container at least 15 ft above ground and as far away from the trunk of the tree as possible. If you see a dangerous animal, back away slowly without turning your back to the animal or bending down. Try and look big and scary to a bear—stand next to other people, waves your arms, yell.

Some animals, especially rodents, carry dangerous diseases. If you are bitten by a wild animal, see a doctor as soon as possible. Many animal bites require a tetanus shot and, if the animal is rabid, a rabies shot.

Have respect for the animals you encounter: Never sneak up on them, don't disturb nests and other habitats, don't touch animals or try to remove them from their habitat for the sake of a photograph, don't stand between animal parents and their young, and never surround an animal or group of animals. You can also help to protect endangered species by reporting any sightings. (For more information on endangered species in the national parks, write: Chief, Wildlife and Vegetation Division, National Park Service, Box 37127, Washington, DC 20013.)

Dunes. In national parks that include barrier islands, you should walk on marked pedestrian dune crossovers and paths, not on the dunes themselves. Continual climbing of a dune system will cause erosion and weaken the protection of the natural primary dune system. Also refrain from picking dune grasses because they preserve the dunes.

A free brochure titled "Leave No Trace" supplies more information on protecting the environment; to get a copy call 800/332–4100.

VOLUNTEERING IN THE PARKS Air pollution, acid rain, wildlife poaching, understaffing of rangers, and encroaching development are among the threats to many national parks. These problems are being addressed by the National Park Service, but you can play a role by donating time or money. The National Park Service's Volunteers in the Parks program welcomes volunteers to do anything from paperwork to lectures on environmental issues. To participate, you must apply to the park where you would like to work.

To make financial contributions to the parks, contact the **National Park Service, Budget Division**, Box 37127, Washington, DC 20013. You can also make a donation to the **National Parks Foundation** (1101 17th St. NW, Suite 1102, Washington, DC 20036–4704), which is a nonprofit organization that supports the park service with supplementary assistance programs.

HIKING Three things should be taken into consideration when choosing hiking trails suitable to your physical condition and the amount of weight you plan to carry: (1) How long is the trail? (2) How steep is it and how quickly does the elevation increase? (3) How acclimated are you to the altitude at the start and finish? All hikers, especially solo hikers, should give their intended route, length of trip, and return date to a park ranger before setting out on a multiday, backcountry trip.

CAMPING Most automobile campsites in the national parks are offered on a first-come, first-served basis. If you are traveling during the peak summer months, be sure to arrive as early in the day as possible or make reservations at a nearby public campground. At some campgrounds in some parks (Acadia, Assateague Island, Cape Hatteras, Great Smoky Mountains, and Shenandoah) you can make free camping reservations prior to your visit through **Mistix** (tel. 800/365–2267); you may call no sooner than eight weeks in advance, up to the day before your planned arrival. At some National Forest Service campgrounds you can make reservations ($7.50 per reservation) through the **U.S. Forest Reservations** (tel. 800/280–2267).

Essential camping equipment includes a ground cloth, sleeping bag, sleeping pad, lantern, flashlight, and extra clothes for cold nights; you may also choose to bring a tent, a stove, fuel, matches in a waterproof case or lighter, cooking utensils and dishes, and scouring pad.

Most campgrounds in the national parks are equipped for RVs, although the majority have only the basic facilities. Electrical hookups, water pumps, and disposal stations are available only at a handful of stations. For more information, contact the **Association of RV Parks and Campgrounds** (8605 Westwood Center Dr., Suite 201, Vienna, VA 22182-2231, tel. 703/734–3000).

DINING The restaurants you are most apt to find in or near the national parks are casual places serving everything from pizza, sandwiches, and burgers to pasta, steak, and fish. America's move toward healthy diets has certainly affected restaurants throughout the East, with salad bars and low-cholesterol entrées found almost everywhere. Your craving for Chinese, Italian, or other ethnic cuisines can often be satisfied in larger cities outside the parks (although you may have to drive several miles to get there). Fast-food chains are present near some parks.

Within the parks themselves there are plenty of picnic areas complete with tables and fire grates.

Prices for meals (per person, excluding drinks and taxes) at restaurants listed in this book are as follows: $$$, over $25; $$, $10 to $25; $, under $10. Restaurants are listed in descending order according to price category; within price category, they are listed in alphabetical order.

LODGING In addition to campgrounds in and near the national parks, you can choose from a range of accommodations, from chain hotels and motels with modern appliances to rough and rugged wilderness camps with kerosene lamps instead of electricity. Cabins with housekeeping facilities are one of the most popular types of lodging. There are also small, family-owned bed-and-breakfasts and grand old established hotels.

If you're traveling during the high season—roughly between Memorial Day and Labor Day—it's advisable to make reservations three or four months in advance. At some of the most desirable hostelries, guests are known to make reservations for the next summer as they check out.

Also, bear in mind that prices are higher in summer. In fact, they sometimes drop as much as 25% when the season comes to a close.

Prices for lodgings (for two people in a double room) listed in this book are as follows: $$$, over $85; $$, $50 to $85; $, under $50. Lodgings are listed in descending order according to price category; within price category, they are listed in alphabetical order.

Acadia National Park
Maine

By Sarah Scott

Updated by Kay and William Scheller

ach year people travel down the coast of Maine in droves (in Maine one travels "down" the coast in an easterly direction), following the winding seaside routes in search of ocean views and traditional fishing villages. For many, Acadia National Park is their ultimate destination. About two-thirds of the way down the coast, primarily on Mount Desert Island, which is connected to the mainland by a short causeway, Acadia's 40,000 acres boast some of the most spectacular and varied scenery on the eastern seaboard: a rugged coastline of surf-pounded granite and an interior graced by sculpted mountains, quiet ponds, and lush deciduous forests. Cadillac Mountain, at 1,530 ft the highest point of land on the eastern seaboard, dominates the park.

In 1604, the French explorer Samuel Champlain saw the peaks of Acadia rising out of the sea and named the island L'Isle des Monts-Déserts, the Island of Barren Mountains. Today, the island is anything but deserted: With 3 million visitors annually, it's one of America's most visited national parks. Walking, hiking, biking, paddling, and driving amid extraordinary and diverse natural beauty are the draws here.

Acadia is open and used year-round, but it's most popular in the summer. That's when tourists descend upon the island, as much for the sights of tony Bar Harbor, where you'll find most of the accommodations, restaurants, and shops, as for the park. Although a shuttle bus was started in 1995 to relieve the summer traffic, cars remain the primary mode of park transportation. Many attractions lie along the 27-mi Park Loop Road, which encircles a significant section of the park, but there are plenty of opportunities to leave the car behind and explore Acadia on foot.

Though it's rugged, Acadia is also a land of graceful stone bridges, horse-drawn carriages, and the elegant Jordan Pond Tea House. This sense of gentility stems no doubt from Mount Desert Island's long history as a summer resort for society families—Rockefellers, Vanderbilts, and Morgans among them—who began vacationing here in the late 1800s. In fact, Acadia National Park was established by a group of concerned summer residents who purchased much of the island and donated the land to the federal government; the process was finalized in 1919. The extensive carriage road system is the legacy of John D. Rockefeller, Jr., who wanted to ensure that automobiles could never overrun the park's interior. The carriage roads are wide gravel roads that wind through the interior of the park, crossing numerous stone bridges and traveling through woods and across streams. As the name implies, they were originally built for use by horse-drawn carriages. Today they are enjoyed by walkers and bikers as well as equestrians.

ESSENTIAL INFORMATION

VISITOR INFORMATION Contact the **National Park Service** (Acadia National Park, Box 177, Bar Harbor 04609, tel. 207/288–3338).

Maps and information are available from mid-April to the end of October at the park's main **visitor center** (Rte. 3, Hulls Cove, just before entrance to Park Loop Rd.), which is open summer, daily 8–6; spring and fall, daily 8–4:30. The **Thompson Island Information Center** (tel. 207/288–3411), just before you drive onto Mount Desert Island, is open May–mid-October, daily 8–8 in summer and 10–6 in spring and fall. It keeps an up-to-date log of available accommodations. When these seasonal centers are closed, the park headquarters at Eagle Lake maintains an **information center** (Rte. 233, tel. 207/288–3338) that is open daily 8–4:30. The park's **Web site** is www.nps.gov/acad.

The following four chambers of commerce can provide area visitor information such as lodging and dining outside the park. **Ellsworth Chamber of Commerce** (163 High St., Ellsworth 04605, tel. 207/667–5584 or 207/667–2617). **Bar Harbor Chamber of Commerce** (93 Cottage St., Box 158, Bar Harbor 04609, tel. 207/288–5103 or 800/345–4619). **Southwest Harbor Chamber of Commerce** (Main St., Rte. 102, in old clapboard building on left as you drive south, tel. 207/244–9264 or 800/423–9264). **Northeast Harbor Chamber of Commerce** (tel. 207/276–5040).

FEES Some areas require no entrance fee, but a ranger will collect a park entrance fee north of Sand Beach on the Park Loop Road. There are various fee plans, depending on the length of your stay and the number in your party. Call ahead or visit one of the information centers to determine the best plan for you. Passes (a one-day pass costs $5 per vehicle; a four-day pass is $10) are available at the entrance station on the Park Loop Road.

PUBLICATIONS In addition to the park's free newspaper, *Acadia Beaver Log,* numerous publications, maps, and guidebooks are available from both the **Eastern National Association** (Acadia National Park, Box 177, Bar Harbor 04609) and the park's main visitor center in Hulls Cove (*see* Visitor Information, *above*).

Some great books are *Mount Desert and Acadia National Park,* by Sargent F. Collier, an informal but thorough history of the park; *A Walk in the Park,* by T. A. St. Germain, Jr., with maps and text on what may be the most popular activities in Acadia; *A Pocket Guide to the Carriage Roads of Acadia National Park,* by Diana F. Abrell, a small booklet with maps and information on the carriage roads; *Activity Guide to Acadia National Park,* by Carol Peterson and Meg Scheid, geared toward teachers and parents; and *Native Birds of Mount Desert Island and Acadia National Park,* by Ralph H. Long.

GEOLOGY AND TERRAIN Most of Acadia is on Mount Desert Island, the third-largest island off the coast of the continental United States. Bisected by Somes Sound, a dramatic fjord carved by a glacier that melted 10,000–12,000 years ago, the island has two "lobes." The park extends over both of them, but the most popular sights— Sand Beach, Cadillac Mountain, and the Park Loop Road—are on the eastern lobe. Additional sections are on Isle au Haut, a much smaller, heavily forested island in Penobscot Bay, about 12 mi southwest of Mount Desert (as the crow flies), and reached by boat from Stonington; Schoodic Peninsula, farther down east on the mainland; and tiny Baker Island, reached by boat from Mount Desert Island.

Mount Desert began to form about 500 million years ago when ancient rivers deposited sediments on the ocean floor, forming the first bedrock. The last glacier, which advanced and retreated several times over New England, is responsible for the island's current appearance: the 17 glacially rounded mountains; such water basins as Eagle Lake and Echo Lake, which were carved out by the glacier; and huge boulders on the sides of Cadillac and South Bubble mountains, which the glacier transported over long distances and deposited randomly. Although most of Acadia's shoreline is rugged pink granite, the sea has shifted tons of sand and crushed shell into one location to create the curving Sand Beach on the island's eastern side.

FLORA AND FAUNA Acadia is heavily forested, with a mix of deciduous and coniferous trees including alder, sugar maple, northern white cedar, aspen, white pine, spruce, and fir. On the windswept, rocky mountaintops, shrubs such as highbush blueberry, mountain holly, and creeping juniper thrive. In the low-lying marshes, many of which were created when beavers flooded areas of land, you'll find such common plant species as water lilies and cattails. You can identify a wide range of flora at the **Wild Gardens** (*see* Exploring, *below*), where more than 400 plants are labeled and displayed.

Marine mammals commonly spotted in Acadia's waters include harbor seals, porpoises, and finback and minke whales, and, occasionally, humpback and right whales. Several companies offer whale-watching excursions off Mount Desert Island (*see* Guided Tours *in* Exploring, *below*). On shore, the most commonly seen animals are the white-tailed deer and snowshoe hare, although coyotes, weasels, beavers, and several species of rodents, turtles, snakes, and salamanders are also abundant. Dozens of types of birds inhabit the park, too, from great blue herons and hawks to herring gulls and common eiders. Acadia sponsors a Peregrine Reintroduction Program, aimed at bringing back the peregrine falcon, a species nearly extinct in the eastern United States by the mid-1960s. In 1991 a pair of peregrines nested on the cliffs of Champlain Mountain in Acadia, and ever since, this area has been closed off from early spring through mid-August. Since 1991, 30 peregrine chicks have hatched in Acadia at three different locations.

WHEN TO GO Acadia is lovely during any of New England's distinctly different seasons. Although summer is by far the most popular, it's by no means the only time to enjoy the park. From mid-May to late fall, Bar Harbor is swarming with tourists; expect higher lodging prices. On the other hand, summer is the best time to take advantage of shopping, dining out, and touring on Mount Desert Island; the town of Bar Harbor virtually shuts down in winter. Because the park is heavily trafficked in summer, you might try the fall foliage season or winter to avoid crowds. Opportunities to cross-country ski, snowshoe, and snowmobile are plentiful, and camping is available year-round (although backcountry camping is not permitted in Acadia). Call **Blackwoods Campground** (tel. 207/288–3274, or 207/288–3338 for park headquarters in winter) for fee information. Some roads are left unplowed in winter (but remain open to skiers and snowmobilers), including the road to the summit of Cadillac Mountain.

Because of its island setting, Acadia is both cooler in summer and more moderate in winter than is the mainland. Average summer temperatures are in the mid-70s, although windless summer days can drive the thermometer into the 90s. Rain and fog are frequent at this time: After the Pacific Northwest, the Maine coast receives more annual precipitation than any other U.S. area, so be prepared for sudden weather changes. In fall, temperatures drop into the 40s and 50s and rainfall increases slightly. Winter temperatures dip into the 20s and below; the average monthly snowfall is 12 to 17 inches. Spring rolls in around late April, delivering highs in the 50s. Several trails, particularly those at higher elevations, are covered with ice and snow until this time.

SEASONAL EVENTS July: Bar Harbor's **Downeast Dulcimer and Folk Harp Festival** (tel. 207/288–5103), which usually takes place over three days in mid-July, includes concerts and workshops. The **Wooden Boat Show** is held mid-July at the Hinckley Great Harbor Marina in Southwest Harbor (tel. 207/359–4651). **July–August:** For several weeks during these two months, the **Arcady Music Festival** (Arcady Music Society, Box 1265, Southwest Harbor 04679) brings excellent weekly classical music performances to the Bar Harbor area (tel. 207/288–5015 or 207/288–3151). The **Bar Harbor Music Festival** (tel. 212/222–1026 off-seaon; 207/288–

9987 in summer) presents 10 classical and jazz concerts, most of them held in local churches or inns, but one is always held in the amphitheater at Blackwoods Campground.

WHAT TO PACK Pack a warm sweater and windbreaker to fend off stiff ocean breezes. Appropriate hiking and walking footwear is a must, especially for clambering over the rocky shore. Running shoes are fine for walking on the carriage roads, but hiking boots are better for any of the park's trails, many of which require steep climbs. It's always wise to bring sunscreen and a water bottle. In winter, waterproof footwear, warm headgear, mittens, and layers of warm clothing are essential.

GENERAL STORES The major grocery store in Bar Harbor is **Don's Shop 'n Save** (86 Cottage St., tel. 207/288–3621), which is open in summer Monday–Saturday 7 AM–9 PM and Sunday 9–6; it has shorter hours the rest of the year. For gourmet- and health-food supplies, try the **Alternative Market** (99 Main St., tel. 207/288–5271), which sells exotic coffees and high-end groceries and is open in summer, daily 7:30 AM–11 PM, and in fall and spring, daily 7:30–6. On the western side of the island, try **Southwest Food Mart** (Rte. 102, Southwest Harbor, tel. 207/244–5601), which is open summer, daily 8–8, and in fall and spring, daily 8–7. **Sawyer's Market** (Main St., Southwest Harbor, tel. 207/244–3315), a small family-run store with high-quality foods, is open in summer Monday–Saturday 5:30 AM–8 PM, Sunday 9–5, and in fall and spring, daily 5:30 AM–6 PM.

ATMS In Bar Harbor, try the **Bar Harbor Banking and Trust Company** (82 Main St.). **First National Bank of Bar Harbor** (102 Main St.) is down the street. **Bar Harbor Banking and Trust** also has offices and an ATM on Main Street in Southwest Harbor and on Main Street in Northeast Harbor.

ARRIVING AND DEPARTING Most visitors arrive by car, which is by far the easiest way to travel here.

By Bus. Vermont Transit (tel. 800/552–8737) runs one bus daily in summer from Bangor to Bar Harbor. **Downeast Transportation** (Box 914, Ellsworth 04605, tel. 207/667–5796) has year-round bus service between Ellsworth and several locations on Mount Desert Island.

By Car and RV. Most visitors arrive from the south, from which there are two main routes to the park. After taking I–95 north to Bangor (47 mi from the park), cut east on U.S. 395, then take Route 1A to Ellsworth, the largest mainland city near the park. From Ellsworth, follow Route 3 to Mount Desert Island. A more scenic route is to get off I–95 in Brunswick, 115 mi southwest of Ellsworth, and follow coastal U.S. 1 to its junction with Route 3.

Rental cars are available at the Bar Harbor airport from **Budget** (tel. 207/667–1200 or 800/527–0700) and **Hertz** (tel. 207/667–5017 or 800/654–3131).

By Plane. The **Bar Harbor/Hancock County Airport** (Rte. 3, Trenton, tel. 207/667–7432) is the closest airport to Acadia. **Colgan Air** (tel. 207/667–7171 or 800/272–5488 for reservations) provides daily service to and from Boston. **Airport Shuttle** provides service to Mount Desert Island from the Bangor International Airport by advance reservation only (tel. 207/223–4070 or 800/974–0702).

By Train. There is no train service to this part of Maine.

EXPLORING

Dozens of popular sights, most with parking, are scattered along park roads, making it tempting to see the park primarily by car. Many people do just that, and the park seems overcrowded with vehicles at times. To really see the best parts of Acadia, and enjoy a little solitude, you will want to abandon the car for a bike or a pair of hiking boots; numerous easy walking trails and the beautiful system of carriage roads make this possible for people of all fitness levels. Biking and more rigorous hiking on mountain trails are other wonderful ways to see the park.

The sections of the park linked by the Park Loop Road get very crowded, but they are among the most spectacular sections of Acadia and should not be missed. You can easily spend one to three days exploring the sights just along this 20-mi paved road, which begins near the Hulls Cove Visitor Center on Route 3. It's two-way for a few miles until it crosses Route 233 and becomes one-way for a large section. The road winds past the entrances to the **Wild Gardens** and **Nature Center** in Sieur de Monts Spring. The nature center has vegetation from different island ecosystems. Admission to both is free.

The road then follows the shoreline, providing excellent views of Frenchman Bay, and finally reaches a cluster of attractions, including Sand Beach, Thunder Hole, and the Otter Cliffs, which drop precipitously into the sea. The road eventually loops back up, away from the shore, and becomes two-way again, cutting through the wooded, mountainous interior of Acadia. Attractions along this span include the Jordan Pond House (*see* The Best in One Day, *below*) and the Bubbles, where a huge boulder perches atop a high cliff on South Bubble Mountain. Just before the end of the loop, a side road branches off the Park Loop Road and climbs 3½ mi to the summit of 1,530-ft Cadillac Mountain, from which the view of Acadia and the surrounding seas is unmatched.

You can drive the Park Loop Road in a day, but the perfect trip requires at least a day of exploring by car plus several more days for the relatively uncrowded interior. You can rent a bicycle in Bar Harbor (*see* Biking *in* Other Activities, *below*) and bring it into the park for an extended ride on the park roads or carriage roads. Hiking (*see* Nature Trails and Short Walks *and* Longer Hikes, *below*) is another great way to experience the park, and the options are limitless: from climbing to the summit of Cadillac to exploring the less-trafficked western side of the island.

If you have three or four days in Acadia, try getting off the beaten path and visiting parts of the park that aren't on Mount Desert Island. One of the most beautiful is **Isle au Haut** (meaning "High Island"), an island accessible by boat from the fishing village of Stonington on Deer Isle. It requires some backtracking from Mount Desert to get to Stonington, so this excursion is best saved for the end of your trip to Acadia. Remote and heavily wooded, Isle au Haut is magical; few hikers cross paths on its 18 mi of trails. Although a small year-round community exists on Isle au Haut, there is no auto ferry to the island, and space on the mail boat is limited. Tickets are sold on a first-come, first-served basis, though access is rarely denied. For information on Isle au Haut and for camping reservations, contact the National Park Service (*see* Visitor Information *in* Essential Information, *above*); for boat schedules, call **Isle au Haut Ferry Company** (tel. 207/ 367–5193). The round-trip fare is $24 on weekdays, $28 on weekends.

Baker Island is a small, undeveloped island off Mount Desert to which park staff lead excursions (*see* Guided Tours, *below*). **Schoodic Peninsula** is a bold, granite peninsula famous for the impressive surf that pounds its shore. Reach Schoodic by taking U.S. 1 north from Ellsworth to West Gouldsboro, then taking Route 186 to Winter Harbor and following signs to the park.

THE BEST IN ONE DAY Stop first at the Hulls Cove Visitor Center to see a short orientation video and obtain maps and brochures about the park. Make sure to pick up a map of the carriage roads, which should not be missed. If you'd like to start the day with a short, brisk walk, take the trail that begins at the far end of the visitor center parking lot to Witch Hole Pond. Or, begin your drive on the Park Loop Road. To truly appreciate the coast between Sand Beach and Otter Cliffs, leave your car at the beach parking lot and walk down **Ocean Trail,** a flat 1.8-mi trail that parallels the Park Loop Road. For a short but rigorous hike, try the trail that begins just across the road from

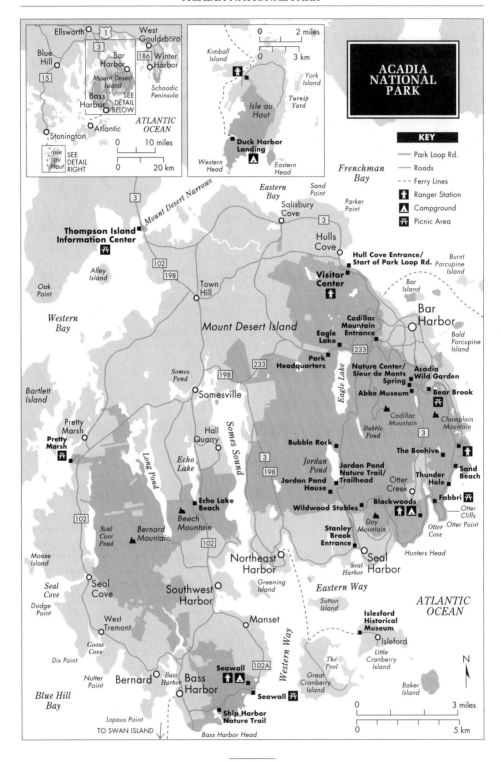

ACADIA
NATIONAL
PARK

KEY

— Park Loop Rd.
— Roads
--- Ferry Lines
🏠 Ranger Station
⛺ Campground
🏕 Picnic Area

Ellsworth 1 West Gouldsboro

Blue Hill 3 186 Winter Harbor

15 Bar Harbor

Mount Desert Island

SEE DETAIL BELOW

Bass Harbor

ATLANTIC OCEAN

Stonington Atlantic

Schoodic Peninsula

Isle au Haut SEE DETAIL RIGHT

0 10 miles
0 20 km

Kimball Island

York Island

Turnip Yard

Isle au Haut

Duck Harbor Landing

Western Head   Eastern Head

0 2 miles
0 3 km

Frenchman Bay

Eastern Bay

Sand Point

Salisbury Cove

Parker Point

3

Hulls Cove

Hull Cove Entrance/ Start of Park Loop Rd.

Burnt Porcupine Island

Thompson Island Information Center

102

198

Alley Island

Oak Point

Town Hill

Visitor Center

Bar Island

Bar Harbor

Bald Porcupine Island

Western Bay

Mount Desert Island

Eagle Lake

Cadillac Mountain Entrance

233

Park Headquarters

233

Nature Center/ Sieur de Monts Spring

Abbe Museum

Acadia Wild Garden

Bear Brook

Somes Pond

198

Somesville

Eagle Lake

Bartlett Island

Pretty Marsh

Pretty Marsh

Hall Quarry

Long Pond

Echo Lake

Somes Sound

Bubble Rock

Bubble Pond

Cadillac Mountain

Champlain Mountain

The Beehive

3

Jordan Pond

Jordon Pond Nature Trail/ Trailhead

Thunder Hole

Sand Beach

198

Jordon Pond House

Otter Creek

Fabbri

Otter Cliffs

Echo Lake Beach

Beech Mountain

Wildwood Stables

Blackwoods

102

Seal Cove Pond

Bernard Mountain

102

Stanley Brook Entrance

Day Mountain

Otter Cove   Otter Point

Moose Island

Northeast Harbor

Seal Harbor

Seal Harbor

Hunters Head

Seal Cove

Seal Cove

Dodge Point

Southwest Harbor

Greening Island

Eastern Way

ATLANTIC OCEAN

West Tremont

Manset

Sutton Island

Islesford Historical Museum

Goose Cove

Dix Point

Western Way

The Pool

Isleford

Little Cranberry Island

Nutter Point

Bernard

Bass Harbor

Bass Harbor

Seawall

102A

Great Cranberry Island

Baker Island

Blue Hill Bay

Seawall

Ship Harbor Nature Trail

Lopaus Point

TO SWAN ISLAND

Bass Harbor Head

N

0 3 miles
0 5 km

Sand Beach and makes a 1-mi loop over the **Beehive,** a 520-ft outcropping of granite that offers a wonderful view of Sand Beach and the ocean. If you're afraid of encountering heights and climbing, however, pick another hike—this one entails several steep climbs that require the use of iron rungs for foot- and handholds. Another beautiful short hike in this area is the 1.4-mi **Great Head Trail** loop, accessible from the eastern end of Sand Beach.

After spending the morning exploring this magnificent stretch of Acadia's coastline, continue to the **Jordan Pond House** (*see* Dining, *below*), famous for its view of the Bubbles, two dramatically rounded peaks characteristic of Acadia's geology. Teatime here is a century-old tradition; stop in for some popovers with strawberry jam and homemade ice cream. Or opt instead to walk the nearby self-guided **Jordan Pond Nature Trail** (*see* Nature Trails and Short Walks, *below*) or explore some carriage roads, many of which intersect near Jordan Pond. **Wildwood Stables,** down the road from the Jordan Pond House, has daily horse-drawn carriage rides in the summer (*see* Horseback Riding *in* Other Activities, *below*).

Finish your day by driving up the **Cadillac Mountain Road,** 7 mi round-trip. On the summit are a large parking lot, a gift shop, and interpretive plaques explaining various aspects of Cadillac and its history. More important, you can savor the magnificent view of islands and sea beneath the setting sun.

ORIENTATION PROGRAMS A 15-minute orientation video is shown every half hour at the visitor center in Hulls Cove. With astounding footage of Acadia's scenery, the video includes the natural and human history of Mount Desert Island and acquaints you with things to do in the park, emphasizing Acadia's dual nature—extremely trafficked in spots, yet ripe with the opportunity for solitude.

GUIDED TOURS Rangers lead a variety of tours; ask at the visitor center (tel. 207/288–3338) or obtain a copy of *Acadia Beaver Log*

for times and themes. Some terrific land tours are "Mr. Rockefeller's Bridges Walk," a 1.5-mi walk over carriage roads and stone bridges, which takes about 2½ hours; and "At the Summit," a one-hour program atop Cadillac Mountain during which participants study the glaciation that shaped the park and discuss Acadia's natural and cultural history. Both tours are free.

Park naturalists also interpret trips aboard several commercial boats; make reservations with the private companies that own them. The **Baker Island Cruise** (tel. 207/276–3717) is a 4½-hour excursion that departs from Northeast Harbor. The **Islesford Historical Cruise** (tel. 207/276–5352) takes visitors on a 2¾-hour trip to the village of Islesford on Little Cranberry Island, which is just off Mount Desert Island but is not part of Acadia. The park operates a small historical museum here; admission to the museum is free.

A few private companies operate summer tours inside the park. **Oli's Trolley** (tel. 207/288–9899) runs 2½-hour narrated trolley-bus tours of Bar Harbor and the highlights of the park. **National Park Tours** (tel. 207/288–0300) narrates bus tours along the Park Loop Road and to some of the area's mansions. For information on the many boat cruises around the island, contact the **Bar Harbor Chamber of Commerce** or the **Southwest Harbor Chamber of Commerce** (*see* Visitor Information *in* Essential Information, *above*). **Whale Watcher, Inc.** (tel. 207/288–3322 or 800/508–1499) operates nearly two dozen sightseeing trips daily, including two-hour cruises of the bay on a topsail schooner ($17.50), a two-hour nature sightseeing cruise ($15), and three- to four-hour whale-watching trips ($28). The company is next to the town pier in Bar Harbor. **Acadian Whale & Sea Bird Watcher Companies** (52 West St., tel. 207/288–9794 or 800/421–3307) offers whale-watching trips ($29) and puffin cruises to Petit Manan Island, the nesting place of numerous species of birds ($20). The boats leave from the Golden Anchor Inn pier in town. Combination tickets are available.

SCENIC DRIVES AND VIEWS The 20-mi **Park Loop Road** can be driven in about an hour without stops, but who would want to drive the whole stretch without pulling over to admire the views? You can spend at least a day exploring the sights along this road. The trip to the top of **Cadillac Mountain** is a must, with the most spectacular views in the early morning or late afternoon. Traffic on the Park Loop Road is heaviest between 10 AM and 2 PM.

Another excellent scenic loop is on the western half of Mount Desert Island. Take **Route 233** off the Park Loop Road and head west past the park headquarters and Eagle Lake. This road connects with **Route 198** and eventually **Route 102,** making a 40-mi loop around the western lobe of the island. The scenery here is less dramatic than on the eastern lobe, but there are several points of interest on Route 102 and Route 102A, which makes an additional loop along the shore. Some of these stretches are inside the park boundaries, but most of the road winds through residential areas. In addition to passing through the small towns of Somesville, Seal Cove, Bass Harbor, and Southwest Harbor, you can stop to enjoy the views at the Pretty Marsh Picnic Area, Seawall Campground and Picnic Area, the Ship Harbor Nature Trail, and the Bass Harbor Head lighthouse, all of which are easily explored on foot from parking areas. **Echo Lake** on Route 102, which has a beach area and lifeguard, provides some of the best swimming in the park.

For dramatic views of Somes Sound, take **Sargent Drive** from Route 3/198, near Northeast Harbor. This narrow, 5-mi road follows the eastern shore of the sound. No buses or RVs are allowed.

HISTORIC BUILDINGS AND SITES Though no historic buildings here are open to the public, two museums provide glimpses into Acadia's history. The privately run **Robert Abbé Museum at Sieur de Monts Spring** maintains a collection of Native American antiquities and has special exhibits on the culture of Maine's Native Americans. *Just off Park Loop Rd., tel. 207/288–3519. Admission: $2. Open July–Aug., daily 9–5; slightly shorter hrs May–June and Sept.–Oct.*

The **Islesford Historical Museum** has exhibits on island and maritime history. Take the mailboat to the island or one of the park-service tours (*see* Guided Tours, *above*). *Little Cranberry Island, tel. 207/ 288–3338. Admission free. Open July–Aug., daily; check visitor center for hrs.*

For a look into 400 years of local history, including photographs, documents, and artifacts, stop by the **Bar Harbor Historical Society,** downstairs in the library. *Jesup Memorial Library, Mount Desert St., Bar Harbor, tel. 207/288–4245. Open mid-June– mid-Oct., Mon.–Sat. 1–4.*

A host of "hands-on" exhibits at both locations of the **Mount Desert Oceanarium** teach visitors about the sea and its denizens. The Living Room has more than 20 tanks of coastal sealife. *Rte. 3, Thomas Bay, Bar Harbor, tel. 207/288–5005 and Clark Point Rd., Southwest Harbor, tel. 207/ 244–7330. Open mid-May–late Oct., daily 9–5 (may close at 4 in spring and fall; call to verify).*

Jackson Laboratory, the world's largest mammalian genetics research institution, also provides the largest variety of high-quality mice to researchers around the globe. At the Summer Visitor Program, Mondays and Wednesdays from 3 to 4 PM, staff scientists talk about ongoing projects (a tour of the facility is not offered). *600 Main St., Bar Harbor, tel. 207/288–6046. Admission free. Program held June–Sept.*

More than 200 hand-carved birds by local resident Wendell Gilley are displayed alongside the works of several other American carvers at the **Wendell Gilley Museum.** An artist-in-residence gives demonstrations. *Corner of Main St. and Herrick Rd., Southwest Harbor, tel. 207/244–7555. Open Sept.–June, daily 10–4; July–Aug., daily 10–5.*

NATURE TRAILS AND SHORT WALKS There are two self-guided nature trails in the park.

The **Jordan Pond Nature Trail** begins and ends near the Jordan Pond House, making a smooth 1-mi loop along the shore and through nearby fields and wooded areas. Interpretive pamphlets provide information on natural and park history at selected points along the loop, which takes about 45 minutes to complete. The **Ship Harbor Nature Trail**, a 1.3-mi loop, covers slightly more hilly ground; it begins off Route 102A on the island's western lobe, not far from the Seawall Campground. This trail cuts through the woods to the shore and follows a section of pink granite shoreline along an inlet filled with striking deep-green water. Pamphlets are also available for this trail, which takes close to an hour to hike.

Another short hike is the 1.2-mi round-trip **Bubble Rock Trail**, accessible from the Park Loop Road at the north end of Jordan Pond. The trail climbs over steep grades and level areas to the top of South Bubble Mountain, where the famous Bubble Rock, a huge glacial erratic the size of a mini-van, perches on a slant at the edge of a cliff. The view of Jordan Pond below is outstanding. A slightly longer trail in this same area is the **Jordan Pond Shore Path**, a moderately strenuous, 3.3-mi loop that essentially follows the pond's shoreline.

Those looking for a very easy stroll—and who wouldn't mind eating an ice-cream cone while taking it—should take the one-mi **Bar Harbor Shore Path**, which follows the ocean's edge right along the harbor in town, winding past several impressive oceanfront mansions. The short walk begins near the town pier.

LONGER HIKES Acadia is better known for short to moderate-length hikes than for long ones, simply because the lay of the land is not conducive to extensive hikes or backcountry expeditions. By combining several shorter trails, however, one can hike for miles.

One of the longest trails is the strenuous **Cadillac Mountain South Ridge Trail,** which begins just south of the entrance to Blackwoods Campground. The 7.4-mi

(round-trip) trail heads north and climbs steadily through the woods, eventually cutting above the treeline to the summit of Cadillac. This isn't a loop, so prepare for a long day of hiking unless you have a car waiting for you at the summit parking area.

A more moderate route to the top of Cadillac is the 4.4-mi **North Ridge Trail**, which includes some steep grades and level stretches through woods and over rocky areas. The trail begins at the North Ridge Cadillac parking area, on the Park Loop Road just after it becomes one-way; this, too, is not a loop.

A good loop to do in a less-trafficked part of the park is the 7-mi climb over **Sargent and Penobscot mountains,** from the trailhead off Route 198/3, 3 mi north of Northeast Harbor. The trail climbs over the exposed rocky peaks, which are 1,373 and 1,194 ft respectively, providing ocean views and a good workout. The park staff gives this hike a strenuous rating.

A somewhat shorter hike is the ascent up **Champlain Mountain,** which is 3.2 mi round-trip. Hikers park their cars on Route 3 near the Tarn, a small reservoir, and hike on a gently switchbacking, stone-lined path through a young birch forest. The trail gains elevation quickly but fairly effortlessly to a small summit known as Huguenot Head and becomes more rigorous as it climbs to Champlain Mountain, elevation 1,058 ft. Some hand-over-hand bouldering is required near the top. The Champlain Mountain trail connects with several others at the summit, including the fabled **Precipice Trail,** which is extremely exposed and not recommended for timid climbers. The panoramic view at the top of Champlain includes a fine vista of the ocean and looming Dorr Mountain to the west.

A beautiful hike near Southwest Harbor and Seawall Campground is the ascent of **Beech Mountain.** Two trails depart from the south shore of Long Pond (not to be confused with the Long Pond near Seal Harbor). One follows the lakeshore for a distance, then climbs steeply up to the summit on a loose, rocky trail. There is an old observation tower at the summit, which is 839 ft above sea level. To descend to the same parking area, a slightly longer and definitely more beautiful trail winds down the mountain through rich forest strewn with interesting large boulders. The hike is roughly 3 mi round-trip.

OTHER ACTIVITIES Biking. Acadia is a wonderful place to cycle, with routes as varied as the bikers who come here. If you choose to ride on the paved park roads—especially the Park Loop Road—it's best to do so either in the early morning or early evening, when the traffic is lighter. The hilly Park Loop Road is a little treacherous, thanks to the steady flow of auto traffic, but the scenery is marvelous. In general, however, park rangers recommend leaving the paved roads and exploring the carriage road system. The bike routes on these bumpy and rocky gravel roads are almost limitless, but you need a mountain bike or hybrid for most of them (two loops are maintained for narrow-tire bikes). Some carriage roads are relatively level, requiring only ordinary athletic prowess. Others wind up and around the smaller mountains in Acadia and can be quite rigorous. The park staff will help you select an appropriate route.

A good place to take off for a variety of carriage-road bike routes is from the visitor center in Hulls Cove; the trail system begins at the far end of the parking lot. From here, bikers can ride a short distance to link up with the 3.3-mi **Witch Hole Pond Loop,** which is surfaced with fine gravel and maintained especially for bicycles. A carriage road connects with this loop and leads south to a 5.8-mi loop around **Eagle Lake.** The carriage-road system connects the park's northernmost and southernmost parts, so ambitious riders can begin at the visitor center and work their way south, past Eagle Lake and Jordan Pond.

Bikes can be rented in Bar Harbor from **Bar Harbor Bicycle Shop** (141 Cottage St., tel. 207/288–3886), **Acadia Outfitters** (106 Cottage St., tel. 207/288–8118), and **Acadia Bike and Canoe** (48 Cottage St., tel. 207/288–9605). Average rates are $15 for a full-day rental, $10 for half a day.

Bird-Watching. Acadia attracts more than 300 species of sea, shore, and land birds. Ship Harbor Nature Trail, the Wonderland Trail near Bass Harbor on the western part of the island, Otter Point near Otter Cliffs, and Sieur de Monts Spring are known for prime bird-watching. In winter, several species of sea ducks can be spotted off Acadia's shores, including common eiders, buffleheads, red-breasted mergansers, and white-winged scoters. Peak birding is from late May through September, when birdsong fills the woods of Acadia. Contact the **visitor center** (tel. 207/288–5262) for information about naturalist guided three-hour bird walks along different nature trails.

Boating. The many lakes and ponds of Mount Desert Island are ideal for canoeing, and the waters around Acadia are filled with yachts and tour boats, as well as working fishing and lobster boats, throughout the summer. Boats are not rented inside the park. Rent a canoe at **National Park Canoe Rentals** (Pond's End, Mount Desert, tel. 207/244–5854) and launch it just across the road on Long Pond—the longest lake on an island in the United States (4½ mi). National Park offers free lessons, canoes rigged for fishing, fishing licenses, roof racks if you want to transport, and sunset trips led by a naturalist. Another option is **Acadia Bike and Canoe** (48 Cottage St., Bar Harbor, tel. 207/288–9605). The average price of a full-day rental is $28.

Options for plying the waters around Mount Desert Island range from taking a schooner or whale-watching cruise (*see* Guided Tours, *above*) to trying your hand at sea kayaking, an increasingly popular sport in Maine. The waters here are known for their dangerous currents, however, so hook up with a tour company if you lack experience. **Coastal Kayaking Tours** (Bar Harbor, tel. 207/288–9605, 800/526–8615 outside

Maine) operates half-day, full-day, and three-day overnight outings and also rents kayaks. **National Park Sea Kayak Tours** (Bar Harbor, tel. 207/288–0342) is another good outfit.

Carriage Rides. If you want to go horseback riding, you'll have to bring your own horse; there are no rentals in the park. However, **Wildwood Stables** (tel. 207/276–3622), near Jordan Pond, offers a variety of horse-drawn carriage rides on the carriage roads from June 15 to Columbus Day. Wildwood leads three one-hour rides daily ($12 per person) with 10 people in a carriage, plus a two-hour evening ride to the summit of Day Mountain ($15 per person).

Fishing. Freshwater fishing in Acadia rates from fair to poor, but that shouldn't discourage anyone from canoeing around one of Mount Desert's ponds in search of land-locked salmon, lake trout, brook trout, or smallmouth bass. People ice fish in Acadia as well.

Rock Climbing. Acadia's granite makes for some excellent rock climbing. Popular locations are on the Bubbles, the south face of Mt. Champlain (the Precipice), and Otter Cliffs, where climbers negotiate routes high above the pounding surf. Unfortunately, the best book on climbing routes in Acadia, *Guide to East Coast Rock Climbs,* by John Harlan, is out of print, but a desk copy is kept at the visitor center, and climbers are welcome to take notes from it. The park does not provide any guide services or gear. Permits are required for groups; call Resource Management (tel. 207/288–5463). Two local companies, **Acadia Mountain Guides** (Bar Harbor, tel. 207/288–8186 or 207/288–0342) and **Atlantic Climbing** (Bar Harbor, tel. 207/288–2521), provide instruction and guides.

Skiing. In good conditions cross-country skiing on more than 43 mi of Acadia's carriage roads is a magical experience. A wonderful but strenuous ski is up the 1.1-mi Day Mountain Trail, a carriage road that winds around this 583-ft mountain near Blackwoods Campground. Going up is a

workout, but the trip down makes up for the climb, as do the ocean views at the top. The loop around Eagle Lake (*see* Biking, *above*) is another excellent ski route and is easily reached near the parking lot on Route 233. Ski rentals are available at **Cadillac Mountain Sports** (26 Cottage St., Bar Harbor, tel. 207/288–4532).

Snowmobiling. In winter, the entire Park Loop Road is left unplowed (except for a 2-mi stretch between Sand Beach and Otter Cliffs) and is open to snowmobilers. A short stretch of carriage road along the eastern shore of Eagle Lake is also open, but carriage roads are otherwise off-limits. The speed limit is 35 mph, towing people on skis or sleds is prohibited, and adult supervision of drivers under the age of 14 is required.

Snowshoeing. You can snowshoe anywhere in the park, but the carriage roads and unplowed roads are recommended over the steeper hiking trails or the Cadillac Mountain Summit Road, which gets icy. For rentals, try **Cadillac Mountain Sports** (*see* Skiing, *above*).

Swimming. The best swimming in Acadia is at **Echo Lake,** on the western part of the island. It has a large beach, changing rooms, and a lifeguard. There is also a lifeguard at **Sand Beach,** which is a spectacular spot with good surf—but the water is freezing. Swimming is not allowed in the other lakes and ponds of Acadia because they are sources of drinking water for surrounding communities. The one exception is the north end of Long Pond.

CHILDREN'S ACTIVITIES Several of the park's ranger-led programs are geared toward children ages 5–12; reservations are required for these programs (tel. 207/288–5262). Acadia also sponsors a Junior Ranger program. By following the activities outlined in a booklet (available for $1.50) and attending two naturalist programs, participants earn a Junior Ranger badge.

EVENING ACTIVITIES The park service offers evening programs in the amphitheaters at the Blackwoods and Seawall campgrounds. The one-hour programs cover such topics as Acadia's geology, the carriage roads, shore ecology, and park history. Check the *Acadia Beaver Log* or call the **National Park Serice** (tel. 207/288–3338) for a schedule. Park rangers also offer an astronomy program.

DINING

If you love seafood, you'll be in heaven on Mount Desert Island, whether in a down-home sandwich shop or elegant restaurant. If you don't like seafood you're sure to find something to suit your palate among the dozens of restaurants in Southwest Harbor and Bar Harbor, the latter being home to most of the island's dining establishments. Most restaurants are closed from November through Memorial Day.

INSIDE THE PARK **Jordan Pond House.** This park landmark has been serving delicious food since the 1870s. The original structure burned in the late 1970s, and the present-day gray-shingled house overlooking Jordan Pond is quite contemporary, with high, angular ceilings, massive windows, and a large stone center-chimney fireplace. Although both lunch and dinner are served here in season, the restaurant is best known for its afternoon tea on the lawn, a long-standing tradition at which popovers, strawberry jam, and homemade ice cream are served. Otherwise the menu (the same for lunch and dinner) is basic and unexciting, with such items as prime rib, steamed lobster, crabmeat au gratin, and baked haddock. *Park Loop Rd., tel. 207/276–3316. AE, D, MC, V. Closed mid-Oct.–mid-May. $$–$$$*

NEAR THE PARK **Café Bluefish.** One of the smaller and quieter restaurants in Bar Harbor, Café Bluefish has a charming atmosphere with dark wood booths, antique furniture, soft lighting, jazz playing in the background, and a selection of books and old *Life* and *National Geographic* magazines. Cajun barbecued shark, exquisite poached salmon with sherried mustard sauce, and herbed salmon strudel are some of the creative seafood dishes served. Desserts, such as an irresistible white and dark chocolate confection and fresh fruit crisps, are also excellent. Salads are not included with the price of the entrée, making this restaurant a little overpriced. *122 Cottage St., Bar Harbor, tel. 207/288–3696. MC, V. No lunch. $$$*

George's. In an 1850s farmhouse a block off Main Street, George's offers some of the most inventive dining in town and is considered one of the best area restaurants by locals. Decorated in terra cotta and shades of peach with tapestries and art adorning the walls, George's has several dining rooms and seating on the quiet outdoor terrace overlooking the garden. George recommends the lobster strudel, prepared with white sauce, cheese, and fresh herbs. Other specialties include a nightly lamb special, charcoal-grilled salmon and wild swordfish, and muscovy duck breast served with seasonal fruits. The fixed-price menu is popular. *7 Stephens La., Bar Harbor, tel. 207/288–4505. AE, D, DC, MC, V. No lunch. Closed Nov.–mid-June. $$$*

Opera House. This restaurant-cum-listening room is the top choice among local opera lovers. The walls of the dimly lit dining room are covered with photos and illustrations of opera stars, and opera sets the tone of every meal. The menu is long and elaborate, featuring such dishes as chateaubriand Ponselle, tenderloin of beef stuffed with lobster tails and served with a creamy crabmeat sauce, and Cornish game hen stuffed with wild rice. Light breakfasts featuring muffins, coffee, and New Orleans–style *beignets* (doughnuts) are also served. It's not appropriate for families with small children. *27 Cottage St., Bar Harbor, tel. 207/288–3509. AE, D, DC, MC, V. No lunch. Closed mid-Oct.–mid-May. $$$*

Reading Room. Both guests and nonguests frequent the large, oceanfront dining room at the Bar Harbor Inn (*see* Lodging, *below*). With crystal chandeliers, a grand piano, and conspicuous flower arrangements, the elegant Reading Room offers great harbor views. Breakfast and dinner, as well as a buffet Sunday brunch, are served inside; lunch is outside on Gatsby's Terrace under bright yellow umbrellas. For dinner try the house special—lobster pie—or filet mignon. A down east lobster bake is served on the outdoor terrace every day from 11:30 to dusk. *Bar Harbor Inn, adjacent to municipal pier, tel. 207/288–3351. AE, D, DC, MC, V. Closed mid-Nov.–mid-Apr. $$$*

Redfield's. This small restaurant in Northeast Harbor is raved about by innkeepers and other restaurateurs all over the island. The menu changes daily, but one might expect dishes such as sesame-dipped salmon with tahini ginger sauce, lobster cakes with saffron mayonnaise, or lightly smoked loin of lamb with black olive, roasted garlic, and caper confit. Owner-chefs Maureen and Scott smoke their own meats and seafood and make everything from scratch. A small, brightly lit spot with only seven tables, Redfield's has plain white walls, tables, and chairs, with bright Impressionist oil paintings on the walls. There is an extensive selection of French, Italian, and dessert wines. Desserts might include mocha java sorbet or white-chocolate mousse wrapped in a chocolate crepe. The wine and tapas–coffee bar opens at 4 PM. *Main St., Northeast Harbor, tel. 207/276–5283. Reservations essential. Closed weekdays in winter. AE, MC, V. $$$*

The Claremont. Southwest Harbor's finest restaurant is at the Claremont Hotel (*see* Lodging, *below*), where you'll dine in a slightly worn room with wonderful views of Somes Sound. The menu changes weekly, but prime rib with Yorkshire pudding on Saturdays is a house tradition. Other dinner specialties include citrus-roasted salmon served on a bed of spinach; roasted rack of lamb with juniper berry and raspberry sauce; and sautéed duck breast in a champagne, cranberry, and green peppercorn sauce. *Claremont Rd., Southwest Harbor, tel. 207/244–5036. Jacket and tie. No credit cards. Closed mid-Oct.–mid-June. $$–$$$*

Galyn's Galley Restaurant. This cavernous, two-story restaurant, across from Agamont Park, has a bar upstairs and a few tables streetside. The dining room has wooden floors and paneling, a brick fireplace, and stained-glass panels; cheerfulness is favored over character. Seafood sandwiches, burgers, and salads are the main fare at lunch; dinner specials include prime rib and fresh seafood. *17 Main St., Bar Harbor, tel. 207/288–9706. AE, D, MC, V. Closed just before Christmas–Feb. 1. $$*

Mama DiMatteo's. Mama DiMatteo's decor resembles a solarium, with skylights, hanging plants, green walls, and lots of natural wood. A local favorite that's open all year, this is a good spot for families. Specialties include fresh pastas, smoked chicken ravioli, shrimp *Calabrese* (sautéed with prosciutto, capers, and black olives and served in a tomato-wine sauce over rotini). A smaller-portion menu is available until 6 PM, and pizzas and salads are also served. There is an extensive wine list. *34 Kennebec Pl., Bar Harbor, tel. 207/288–3666. No lunch. AE, D, MC, V. $$*

Miguel's. Although it sits on a quiet side street in Bar Harbor, Miguel's Mexican restaurant is anything but quiet on Friday and Saturday nights. Open year-round, Miguel's attracts local college students as well as families to its large bar and dining area decorated with southwestern tapestries, cactus plants, and lanterns. Renowned for excellent frozen margaritas and locally brewed beer on tap, Miguel's also dishes up blue-corn crab cakes, shrimp fajitas, and *tofitas*—a vegetable fajita with marinated grilled tofu. *51 Rodick St., Bar Harbor, tel. 207/288–5117. Reservations not accepted. MC, V. Closed Mon. and Nov.–early Apr. No lunch. $$*

Nakorn Thai. With big windows and white walls, Nakorn Thai is open and light and very simple: red tablecloths, posters of Thailand, and not much else for ambience. Appetizers include tempura, spring rolls, soups, and Thai salads. Main dishes range from *pad thai* noodles to spicy seafood dishes such as the seafood combo with scallops, shrimp, squid, crab, and lobster meat sautéed with snow peas, carrots, and mushrooms in a ginger sauce, and fish à la Bangkok—a deep-fried fish fillet topped with green curry and a coconut milk sauce. *30 Rodick St., Bar Harbor, tel. 207/288–4060. D, MC, V. Reservations not accepted. Closed late Oct.–Mar. No dinner Sat. Closed Sun. $$*

Parkside Restaurant. In downtown Bar Harbor, the Parkside is on a busy corner across from the village green. White trellises, white wicker furniture, and hanging plants create a light, airy atmosphere. The restaurant is lively and noisy, its terrace packed with bons vivants sipping frosty drinks and dining on fresh shellfish marinara with lobster, shrimp, mussels, crab, and scallops or veal *portafino* (with garlic, olives, tomatoes, capers, lemon, and mushrooms). *185 Main St., Bar Harbor, tel. 207/288–3700. AE, D, MC, V. Closed late Nov.–mid-May. $$*

Thurston's Lobster Pound. Tiny Bass Harbor looks much the way many of Maine's tiny fishing villages did before they were discovered by tourists. Diners can sit under the restaurant's bright yellow awning and watch lobstermen deliver their dinner to the dock. Lobsters, clams, and corn are cooked in outdoor steamers. There are also chowders, hamburgers, hot dogs, sandwiches, and delicious homemade pies (don't miss the raspberry pie or blueberry cake when the berries are in season). If you want a picnic, they'll pack everything to go. *Steamboat Wharf Rd., Bernard, tel. 207/244–3320 or 800/235–3320. Reservations not accepted. MC, V. Closed late Oct.–Memorial Day. $–$$*

Keenan's. Some of the island's best food is served out of a tiny shack at a bend in the road on the outskirts of Bass Harbor. Diners sit at formica tables and chow on shrimp *étouffée* (in a brown sauce with garlic and green seasonings); baked haddock stuffed with shrimp; tenderloin stuffed with spinach and feta; crab cakes; succulent

baby back ribs; and spicy Cajun gumbos packed with shrimp, lobster, and hot sausage. Outside, the restaurant's mascot—a black Newfoundland named Rufus—watches over a wood-fired cooker as it steams crabs, clams, lobsters, mussels, and corn. *Corner of Rte. 102A and Flatiron Rd., Bass Harbor, tel. 207/244–3403. Reservations not accepted. No credit cards. No lunch. $–$$*

Epi Pizza and Subs. Fancy it ain't, but this is Bar Harbor's hometown pizza joint and the food is good. Just order at the cash register, find a table, and wait for your food. The restaurant is neat, with tile walls, wall mirrors, and red-and-black tables and lamps. A couple of video games in the back keep kids happy. Aside from pizza, you can get grinders, calzones, spaghetti, lasagna, and salads. The restaurant opens at 10 AM, so you can plan a picnic. *8 Cottage St., Bar Harbor, tel. 207/288–5853. Reservations not accepted. No credit cards. Closed Jan. $*

OFF THE ISLAND **Bangkok Restaurant.** Chef Air imports all of his Thai ingredients (from Thailand via Boston) to assure diners of a truly authentic meal at this small, friendly spot in the Colonial Motel. He'll make the food as spicy (or bland) as you wish. House specialties include sirloin tips and vegetables in a Thai sauce, spicy fish fillet, *pad thai,* and Tom Yum seafood for two (spicy and sour soup with shrimp, scallops, and squid or haddock in lemongrass broth). *Rte. 3, Bar Harbor Rd., Ellsworth, tel. 207/667–1324. D, MC, V. No lunch Sun. $*

Le Domaine. Chef-owner and Cordon Bleu graduate Nicole Purslow is carrying on the tradition of elegantly simple French country cooking begun here by her mother more than 50 years ago. The restaurant is in a red-shingled, white-shuttered, seven-bedroom inn that, appropriately, has the feel of a farmhouse in Provence. The same feeling extends to the dining room, a cozy spot with wooden floors, a large fireplace, and lots of fresh flowers. Nicole makes maximum use of the vegetables and herbs in her garden and emphasizes robust dishes made with super-fresh ingredients. The 5,000-bottle wine cellar is entirely French, as is the superb selection of after-dinner drinks. *Box 496, Rte. 1, Hancock 04640, tel. 207/ 422–3916 or 800/554–8498. Reservations essential. AE, D, MC, V. Closed Nov.–Apr. No lunch.*

PICNIC SPOTS Almost any site in Acadia has picnicking potential, from Sand Beach to the summit of Cadillac. The park operates five official picnic areas with tables and grills: Pretty Marsh and Seawall on the western part of the island; Bear Brook, Thompson Island, and Fabbri on the eastern part. Each offers its own brand of scenery, from the tidal mud flats at Thompson Island to the exposed rocky beach at Seawall. The Thompson Island Picnic Area is just after the bridge to Mount Desert, and supplies can be picked up in Ellsworth or Trenton, a small town on Route 3. For the Bear Brook and Fabbri picnic areas, both along the Park Loop Road, you should shop in Bar Harbor. Seawall, on Route 102A across from the Seawall Campground, is close to Southwest Harbor's grocery store, and supplies for Pretty Marsh, on the westernmost part of Mount Desert, are sold at the small grocery store in Somesville.

LODGING

You'll have dozens of choices including motels, beach-side cottages, small family-run bed-and-breakfasts, inns, and resort hotels. Many of the best accommodations are in and around Bar Harbor or Southwest Harbor; others are scattered around the island, on back roads, and on Route 3 between Ellsworth and Mount Desert. If you're arriving during the peak season of July 1 to Labor Day, when rates are at their highest, reserve a room at least a couple of weeks ahead. Many accommodations close in winter. If you do arrive without reservations and need help finding a place, try one of the Bar Harbor Chamber of Commerce offices. The one at the **Bluenose Ferry Ter-**

minal (Rte. 3, tel. 207/288–3393) is open daily 9 AM–11 PM. The **main office** (93 Cottage St., tel. 207/288–5103) is open weekdays 8–4. Also try the **Thompson Island Information Center** (tel. 207/288–9702), open daily in season 8–8.

ON THE ISLAND **Asticou Inn.** One of the oldest and most renowned hotels on the island, the Asticou is the lodging of choice in Northeast Harbor. Built in 1883, the Asticou is a rambling, gray-shingled, old-style resort hotel. In the main inn there are three long floors of rooms, most of them small and very simply furnished with filmy white curtains, trademark yellow window shades, painted white furniture, and floral bedspreads. Two outlying shingled cottages have suites and larger rooms, and three modern "topsider" cottages contain two units each. There are claw-foot tubs in some bathrooms but no TVs in any room. Public areas include a huge deck overlooking the sweeping lawn and harbor, a writing room, lounges, and an elegant dining room with yellow walls that are intricately painted with floral designs. Breakfast, lunch, and dinner are served in the main inn. In early June the nearby Asticou Azalea Gardens should not be missed. *Northeast Harbor 04662, tel. 207/276–3344 or 800/258–3373. 26 rooms, 21 suites. Facilities: dining room, bar, pool, tennis, babysitting, children's programs. D, MC, V. $$$*

Breakwater 1904. The Breakwater is the best place to experience Bar Harbor's Gilded Age. The 1904 Tudor oceanfront mansion, on a quiet side street, has many interesting details like hundreds of tiny, leaded-pane windows, needlepoint rugs, and a specially commissioned billiard table. Public areas include the living room, parlor, dining room, billiard room, and a second-floor sitting room opening onto a veranda. The decor of the six guest rooms, each about 500 square ft, lives up to expectations, with plush rugs, canopy beds, chaise lounges, and huge walk-in closets. Four of the six rooms have direct ocean views. Two carriage houses are rented by the week in season, and for shorter periods off-season. Complimentary afternoon tea and afternoon hors d'oeuvres are served daily. Bar Harbor is a short stroll away on the Shore Path, which runs right by the Breakwater. *45 Hancock St., Bar Harbor 04609, tel. 207/288–2313, 800/238–6309 for reservations, fax 207/288–2377. 6 rooms. Facilities: dining room, bar, billiards. Full breakfast. AE, MC, V. Closed Nov.–Mar. $$$*

Claremont Hotel. Built in 1884, the Claremont is the oldest summer hotel on Mount Desert Island. Its setting, atop a hill overlooking Somes Sound, and the graceful four-story hotel itself evoke the charm of an earlier era, as do the quiet grounds with a private dock and a croquet court. The hotel feels a little damp and rickety, and the public areas are decorated with an undistinguished jumble of wicker and upholstered furniture and marine paintings. The rooms, accessible off long corridors, have bright floral or pastel bedspreads and wallpaper. About half have ocean views and many have modern bathrooms; all have telephones. Beds are four-poster, brass, or wicker. There are also 12 modern housekeeping cottages and 7 large rooms in two outlying guest houses. One of these, the Phillips House, is a short walk from the main hotel and has a cozy public area with a huge stone fireplace, walls of bookcases, and a grand piano. *Claremont Rd., Box 137, Southwest Harbor 04679, tel. 207/244–5036 or 800/244–5036, fax 207/244–3512. 43 rooms. Facilities: TV in public room, dining room, dock, tennis, croquet, bicycles, boating. No credit cards. Closed late Oct.–late May. $$$*

Inn at Canoe Point. An elegant 1889 Tudor-style summer cottage, the Inn at Canoe Point is right on Frenchman Bay. A long gravel driveway shaded by huge white pines, cedars, and birches winds down to the secluded inn, where there is a small sandy beach. In addition to an elegant front hall with a grand piano, a large library, and a public room with a fireplace, the inn has a master suite furnished with antiques and four other rooms. All have ocean views

except the Anchor Room, which has direct access to a deck that looks out onto the water. The Garret Room is a suite with a bedroom overlooking the water and a sitting room with a pull-out couch. Most popular is the Garden Room, with its huge picture window overlooking both the garden and ocean. Breakfast is served on the deck in fine weather or in the cozy public room. *Box 216, Canoe Point on Rte. 3, Bar Harbor 04609, tel. 207/288–9511, fax 207/288–2870. 4 rooms, 1 suite. Full breakfast. D, MC, V. $$$*

Lindenwood Inn. Comfortable elegance best describes innkeeper Jim King's latest undertaking—a handsome compound overlooking Southwest Harbor. The main house, a magnificently restored turn-of-the-century sea captain's home, is filled with artwork Jim collected in his travels. The rooms are spacious and the furnishings tastefully contemporary. Many have private decks. Also in the compound are an 1860 house with six lovely rooms; housekeeping suites with TVs and fireplaces; and guest cottages (available by the week), where children are welcome. All of the cottages have TVs, kitchens, and decks, and many of the rooms and cottages have harbor views. A full breakfast is served to room guests in the dining room, which, six evenings a week in peak season, serves up some of the area's finest food (TV weatherman Willard Scott asked *Gourmet* to get the inn's recipe for seafood chowder). *118 Clark Point Rd., Southwest Harbor 04679, tel. 207/244–5335 or 800/307–5335. 20 rooms, 3 cottages. Facilities: pool, hot tub, dock. $$–$$$*

Atlantic Oakes-by-the-Sea. A large resort hotel and conference center, Atlantic Oakes is on Route 3 adjacent to the Nova Scotia ferry terminal and just a mile from town. Atlantic Oakes comprises the Willows, a 1913 summer home; a large main building added in 1991; and several outlying motel-style buildings dating from the mid-'70s. The best rooms are in the Willows, also referred to as the mansion, an eight-room white clapboard building whose rooms have floral wallpaper, reproduction furniture, ceiling fans, and private decks overlooking Frenchman Bay. The incongruous newer building, whose public areas recall those of an airport terminal, has rooms with floor-to-ceiling windows, private balconies, and dark-wood furniture, with brass fixtures. The hallways and stairwells in this building are institutional. Rooms in the outlying buildings are rather stuffy, with rugs and furnishings that have seen better days. Lobster bakes, a mile down the road in Hulls Cove, are open to the public and cost $22. *Rte. 3, Bar Harbor 04609, tel. 207/288–5801 or 800/336–2463, fax 207/288–8402. 150 rooms. Facilities: indoor and outdoor pools, hot tub, tennis court. Full breakfast. AE, MC, V. $$–$$$*

Bar Harbor Inn. An inn since the 1950s and a yacht club before that, the inn sits directly on lovely Bar Harbor. The shingled main building (which has the smaller of the inn's accommodations) houses the Reading Room restaurant (*see* Dining, *above*), has a large lobby with fireplace and wing chairs, and offers rooms with either ocean or pool views. The Oceanfront Lodge, a separate dwelling built in 1985, has larger rooms with private balconies and ocean views. Decorated with floral prints, these are more up-to-date, with oversize beds and ceiling fans. Guests can use a local health club. *Newport Dr., Bar Harbor 04609, tel. 207/288–3351 or 800/248–3351, fax 207/288–5296. 153 rooms. Facilities: restaurant, bar, breakfast room, room service, pool, hot tub. Continental breakfast. AE, D, DC, MC, V. $$–$$$*

Briarfield Inn. This 1887 house in downtown Bar Harbor was refurbished using columned bookcases, moldings, diamond-pane and beveled-glass windows, and antique furniture salvaged from old churches and other buildings. Each room has Victoriana: crocheted bedspreads, mosquito-net canopies on canopy beds, and the owner's collectibles. In the front hall, upstairs hallways, and the parlor, shelves and cupboards house dozens of china teacups, figurines, and objets d'art. A side porch is home to one of the world's few elephant museums, with its impressive collection of carvings, statues, and figurines. The Briarfield is, in a word or two, quirky but comfortable. There are no phones in rooms. *60 Cottage St., Bar Harbor 04609, tel. 207/288–5297 or 800/228–6660. 17 rooms. Facilities: mountain bikes. Continental breakfast. AE, MC, V. Closed Dec.–Mar. $$–$$$*

Edgewater Motel & Cottages. Beautifully situated right off Route 3, this wonderful place on Salisbury Cove is a great place to get away from the bustle of downtown Bar Harbor. Each of the eight spacious, tastefully appointed waterfront rooms in the two-story motel has a sitting area; five have decks, and four have kitchens and fireplaces. The 11 cottages vary in size and proximity to the water, but all have decks and kitchens. Apartment II, a stone's throw from the water, has a huge fieldstone fireplace and porch. There's lots of room for kids to run around, and a private beach. *Box 566, Bar Harbor 04609, tel. 207/288–3491. 8 motel units, 4 apartments, 11 cottages. Facilities: beach, boating. Continental breakfast in spring. Closed mid-Oct.–Mar. $$–$$$*

Inn at Southwest. This large Victorian (1884) in downtown Southwest Harbor has been an inn for more than 100 years. Downstairs public areas, which include a parlor and a small breakfast nook, are carefully decorated in the Victorian style with burgundy wallpaper, hanging glass lamps, watercolor paintings, and antiques. The rooms, some of which have harbor views, are equally well done, with down comforters and antique Bar Harbor wicker rockers. A wraparound porch is used frequently by guests for reading or eating breakfast. There are no phones or TVs in rooms. *Main St. (Rte. 102), Box 593, Southwest Harbor 04679, tel. 207/244–3835. 9 rooms. Full breakfast, afternoon snack. MC, V. Closed Nov.–early May. $$–$$$*

Maples Inn. Built in 1903, the Maples Inn is on a quiet, tree-lined street in Bar Harbor, just a few minutes' walk from shops and restaurants. The ambience of the public areas, which consist of a guest living room and a breakfast area, is homey rather than elegant, and the whole inn smells pervasively of the delicious baked goods served by the innkeepers. The six guest rooms, all named after trees, are light and sunny with queen-size beds and floral or nautical borders. The Red Oak room is popular in summer because of its private third-story deck, known as the Red Oak Tree House. Guests can expect personalized welcome letters on their beds when they arrive, and warm hospitality. Afternoon tea is served at four on the front porch, weather permitting, where there's a collection of antique rockers. Some of the recipes from the delicious breakfasts have been featured in culinary magazines. There are no phones or TVs in rooms. *16 Roberts Ave., Bar Harbor 04609, tel. 207/288–3443. 6 rooms. D, MC, V. Closed Jan.–Mar. $$–$$$*

Park Entrance Oceanfront Motel. As its name suggests, this motel is opposite the Route 3 entrance to the park, about 2½ mi from downtown. The large, oceanfront complex comprises three long buildings facing out over a huge lawn and the ocean. The rooms, many of which have sliding glass doors leading out to the lawn or a small balcony, are decorated with basic motel materials: fake wood paneling, hanging prints, and unexciting upholstered furniture. Although the rooms are nothing special, the recreational facilities—like picnic area with grills and kitchenettes in some rooms—make this a great place for families. *Rte. 3, RR 1, Box 180B, Bar Harbor 04609, tel. 207/288–9703 or 800/288–9703, fax 207/288–9703. 58 rooms. Facilities: pool, hot tub, croquet, horseshoes, volleyball. MC, V. Closed Nov.–late Apr. $$–$$$*

Black Friar Inn. The Black Friar is a funky little B&B on a side street in Bar Harbor. Built in 1905 and restored in 1980, the house has colorful decorative touches, such as the orange and terra-cotta trim and the painted columns near the front door, the several stained-glass panels, and a green-glass lamp shaped like a bunch of grapes. The rooms are small—three are garrets—and are decorated individually, some with handmade lace bedspreads and pillowcases, wooden bedsteads with mirrors in the headboards, and antique chairs and stools with needlepoint cushions. The bathrooms echo the Victorian decor, with large old porcelain washbowls, tin ceilings, and dark-wood floors and paneling. The Black Friar may feel a little cramped, but the warm ambience created by furnishings, mantels, and other woodwork salvaged from Mount Desert Island summer cottages and churches makes up for it. The pub (for guests only) is especially pleasing with its paneled walls, red-leather benches, fireplace, and wall paintings of monks. Breakfast is included. *10 Summer St., Bar Harbor 04609, tel. 207/288–5091. 4 rooms with bath, 3 rooms with detached bath. No phone or TV in rooms. Facilities: pub. MC, V. Closed Dec.–Apr. $$*

Acadia Hotel. Just across from the village green, this small hotel is not the island's most peaceful spot. Though the management is extremely friendly and the hotel is quite appealing on the outside, with natural-wood clapboards, green shutters, and a new wraparound porch, it is unremarkable inside—with only a small desk area downstairs and 10 rooms on the first and second floors. The rooms, renovated for the 1997 season, have floral wallpapers; two have whirlpool tubs. This hotel is best if you're planning a short stay and wish to spend plenty of time downtown, although there is a wraparound porch, balcony, and pergola to wile away the hours. *20 Mount Desert St., Bar Harbor 04609, tel. 207/288–5721. 10 rooms. MC, V. $–$$*

Harbor View Motel and Cottages. Harbor View is in downtown Southwest Harbor and has a variety of rooms, including seven cottages, two groups of older rooms, two efficiencies, and a newer building that houses the office and nine rooms. The rooms in the newer section are the best, with pine wainscoting and sliding glass doors onto private decks overlooking the harbor. Some of these are actually a bedroom and a sitting room separated by an archway of glass panels. The top-floor efficiency apartment has a large modern kitchen, a whirlpool tub, a private bedroom, and a large living room with peaked ceilings and huge, geometrically shaped windows overlooking the water. The older rooms, part of the original motel, are cramped, and although some have been renovated in the last five years, others are rather shabby, with gaudy curtains, old shower stalls, and little room to maneuver. Breakfast is included in July and August. *11 Ocean Way, Box 701, Southwest Harbor 04679, tel. 207/244–5031. 29 rooms. D, MC, V. Closed Nov.–May. $–$$*

Aurora Motel. Conveniently located in Bar Harbor, the Aurora Motel is a good budget option year-round. The 40-year-old motel has large, clean rooms with bright blue rugs and bedspreads; several have pull-out couches. Color TV, coffeemakers, and phones are amenities not found in some nearby properties. *51 Holland Ave., Bar Harbor 04609, tel. 207/288–3771 or 800/841–8925. Facilities: air-conditioning. D, MC, V. $*

Rose Eden Cottages. Of the many lower-end motels and cottages on Route 3, this exclusively nonsmoking complex is one of the best. The neat, little white cottages sport bright red doors and shutters and window boxes filled with geraniums. The oldest cottages are about 30 years old but have been recently upgraded with new showers and kitchens, and all are pleasantly decorated with colorful spreads, white-ruffle curtains, and either bright wallpaper or white walls with stenciling. The newer cottages, set farther back from the highway, are larger and have knotty-pine walls and floors and wicker furniture. About 7 mi from Bar Harbor, Rose Eden Cottages is an economical and pleasant option away from the downtown hubbub and a ½-mi walk to a public sand beach. Facilities include cables TVs and a picnic area with grills. *Rte. 3, RFD 1, Box 1850, Bar Harbor 04609, tel. 207/288–3038. 10 cottages. D, MC, V. Closed mid-Oct.–late Apr. $*

OFF THE ISLAND **Black Duck on Corea Harbor.** Far removed from the hustle and bustle of Bar Harbor, yet only a few miles from the Schoodic section of the park, this charming nonsmoking B&B overlooks the harbor in one of Maine's prettiest—and least developed—fishing villages. There are four guest rooms and two waterfront cottages, and the inn is furnished in an eclectic mix of antiques and Oriental rugs. Miles of craggy coastline invite exploration. Should you wish to get married, one of the owners is a licensed notary public. *Box 39, Crowley Island Rd., Corea 04624, tel. 207/963–2689. 4 rooms, 2 with shared bath. 2 cottages. Full breakfast. MC, V. $$–$$$*

Sullivan Harbor Farm. Built by a local shipwright almost two centuries ago, this B&B overlooking Frenchman's Bay and Mount Desert is homey, unpretentious, and comfortable. There are three tidy guest rooms and an efficiency apartment in the house, and two cottages close by. "Cupcake," airy and spacious, has two bedrooms, working fireplaces in each room, and accommodations for up to six. "Milo," by a stream, has two working fireplaces and sleeps four comfortably. Innkeepers Joe and Leslie also operate a smokehouse and serve their prize-winning cold-smoked Atlantic salmon to guests at breakfast. There's a small beach across the way that's perfect for gathering mussels, and canoes and kayaks are available. *U.S. Rte. 1, Sullivan Harbor 04664, tel. 207/422–3735. 2 rooms with bath, 1 room shares bath, 1 apartment, 2 cottages. Facilities: boating. Full breakfast. MC, V. $$*

White Birches. Away from the bustle of Route 1, this motel sits up on a hill overlooking its own nine-hole, par-34 golf course (guests pay $10 before 4 PM, $5 after 4 PM for unlimited use). Rooms range from small but adequate to sumptuously furnished but reasonably priced. The Executive Rooms are the newest and nicest but lack air-conditioning and are close to busy Route 3. The best bet is a standard room with air-conditioning or one away from the highway. The restaurant serves good, moderately priced food all day, but the daily breakfast buffet for under $5 is a real bargain. *Rte. 3, Box 743, Ellsworth 04605, tel. 207/667–3621. 67 rooms, 2 suites. Facilities: restaurant, golf course. AE, D, DC, MC, V. $$–$$$*

CAMPING

For a directory of private campgrounds, write: **Maine Campground Owners Association**, 655 Main St., Lewiston 04240, tel. 207/782–5874.

INSIDE THE PARK Blackwoods Campground. This is the only park campground open year-round. The sites are all in a heavily wooded area, but a footpath leads down to the rocky shore not far away. Facilities from about mid-November to April are limited to picnic tables, fire rings, pit toilets, and a hand pump for water. In summer, Blackwoods has rest rooms with cold running water but no showers. RVs up to 35 ft long can be accommodated; there's a dump station but no utility hookups. *Off Rte. 3, 5 mi south of Bar Harbor, tel. 207/288–3274. 220 tent sites, 50 RV sites, 30 sites for vans and pop-ups. Mid-June–mid-Sept.: Reservations should be made at least several months in advance. Sites cost $16 nightly. Mid-May–mid-June and mid-Sept.–mid-Oct.: First-come, first-served basis. Sites cost $14 nightly. Winter rates vary. D, MC, V. $*

Duck Harbor Campground. On remote Isle au Haut, campers may stay in one of five lean-tos at Duck Harbor Campground, near the water, which has picnic tables, fire rings, a hand pump for drinking water, and a pit toilet. Write the park to request a reservation form, and plan to submit it on, or shortly after, April 1. During off-peak periods, the boat drops campers at the town landing and there is a 5-mi hike to the campground. In summer, the mail boat stops at Duck Harbor. The cost to reserve a site is $25. *Acadia National Park, Isle au Haut Reservations, Box 177, Bar Harbor 04609, tel. 207/288–3338 to request a reser-*

vation form, which must be accompanied by a $25 check. 5 lean-tos. Closed late-Oct.–early May. No credit cards. $

Seawall Campground. Across the street from the oceanfront Seawall Picnic Area, Seawall Campground operates on a first-come, first-served basis. The walk-in sites provide more privacy than the other wooded sites, although all are attractive. Arrive here as early in the morning as possible; campsites are in high demand. Station hours are 8:30 AM–8 PM. Seawall has rest rooms with cold running water but no showers and can accommodate RVs up to 35 ft long. There's a dump station but no utility hookups. Drive-up sites cost $14; walk-in sites are $10. *Rte. 102A, 4 mi south of Southwest Harbor, tel. 207/288–3338. 65 tent sites, 104 walk-in tent sites, 45 RV sites. MC, V. Closed late Sept.–mid-May. $*

NEAR THE PARK Bass Harbor Campground. Just ½ mi from the Bass Harbor lighthouse, this quiet campground has some wooded sites. There's a heated in-ground pool, tent and camper rentals are available, and no dogs are allowed. The cost of sites is based on two adults (no extra charge for children) and is $18 for a tent site and $22 for a site with hookups. *Rte. 102A, Box 122, Bass Harbor 04653, tel. 207/244–5857. 90 tent sites, 40 RV sites. Facilities: pool, playground, coin laundry. Closed Oct.–early June. $*

Echo Lake Camp. If you want to camp, but not totally rough it, this Bar Harbor facility, owned by the Appalachian Mountain Club, may be the perfect solution. Guests sleep in tents with board floors on beds with mattresses, pillows, and bedding. Tents accommodate from two to three or from four to six. In season, there's a minimum one-week stay. Reservations should be made by April 1. There are rowboats, canoes, and kayaks available. The camp is only open nine weeks in summer. *Just off Rte. 102, Mt. Desert Island (for an application, write Mrs. Lillian Buck, 360 Main St., Wethersfield, CT 06109), tel. 617/523–0636, Appalachian Mountain Club. Accommodations for 85* guests. *Facilities: dining room, kitchen, library, recreation room, boating. No credit cards. $*

Lamoine State Park. Just a few minutes from Bar Harbor, Lamoine State Park offers a less-crowded camping alternative. The 55-acre park has a picnic area and boat launch but no hot showers. *Rte. 184 off Rte. 3, tel. 207/667–4778. 61 sites. MC, V. Closed mid-Oct.–mid-Apr. $*

Mount Desert Narrows Camping Resort. On Route 3, this campground has 25 acres. Amenities include three bath houses, video games, pool table, small movie theater, an entertainment pavilion, shuttle service to Bar Barbor, car rentals, and canoes. Sites cost $20–$37. *RR 1, Box 2045, Bar Harbor 04609, tel. 207/288–4782. 100 tent sites, 240 RVs sites. Facilities: pool, basketball, playground, boating. Closed Nov.–Apr. D, MC, V. $*

Narrows Too Camping Resort. On Route 3 in Trenton, about 10 mi northwest of Bar Harbor in the direction of Ellsworth and 2½ mi down the road from Mount Desert Narrows Camping Resort, this campground on the water has tent sites in a field and some RV sites with ocean views. The pool is heated, and there are showers, car rentals, hookups, a dumping station, and a shuttle-bus service into Bar Harbor. It costs $19 for a four-person tent in-season; $27 for basic hookup; $37–$40 for oceanfront hookup; $3 charge for each extra child, $5 for extra adult. Reservations are advised at least a month in advance for peak season. *RR 1, Box 193B, Trenton 04605, tel. 207/667–4300. 19 tent sites, 120 RV sites. Facilities: pool, miniature golf, badminton, basketball, horseshoes, volleyball, coin laundry. Closed mid-Oct.–Memorial Day. $*

Adirondack State Park
New York

By Neal Burdick

Updated by Kay and William Scheller

dirondack State Park is almost too big, and too complicated, to grasp. Consider first its size. At 6.1 million acres, it's the largest U.S. park outside Alaska, occupying most of the interior of the northern third of New York State. It has more acreage than any three national parks in the lower 48 combined. You could fit New Jersey in it and have room left over for Rhode Island. It takes in all or parts of 12 counties, two area codes, and more than 200 zip codes.

Consider also its location. It's within a day's drive of every eastern seaboard city between Washington, D.C., and Boston; a few hours from Montréal; and a few more from Detroit. Yet some of the most remote patches of wilderness east of the Rockies are here.

Finally, consider its diverse attributes. Most people associate the park with the Adirondack Mountains, but these peaks make up only a fraction of the landscape. The Adirondacks are at once a wilderness park and a popular resort. Tumbling rivers, secluded ponds, and the rugged shoreline of Lake Champlain, "the sixth Great Lake," are full of opportunities for fishing and boating. You'll find cross-country ski trails, crafts fairs and horse shows, scenic roads, tranquil communities, plant life rarely seen south of the tundra, and the rink where the U.S. hockey team toppled the Russians in the 1980 Winter Olympics.

The Adirondack park, although a state park—the only one in this book—clearly merits inclusion. However, it differs in several important ways from most public lands. Only about 47% of the park is public property; the rest is owned by individuals, corporations, clubs, or municipalities; you can't set foot in these sections without the owners' approval. Lake George's motel-packed main drag is just as much a part of the park as the Five Ponds Wilderness Area's soaring pines. There are no user fees and no "entrances," other than occasional road signs marking boundaries. Park services are relatively limited. There are just two official visitor centers, and they're both in the middle of the park, more or less.

A glance at the park's topsy-turvy history sheds dim light on some of these conundrums. Sidestepped by the westward migration, the Adirondack region was not carefully explored until the mid-1800s. Pike's Peak, Colorado, was tackled before climbers reached the Adirondacks' highest peak, Mt. Marcy. And the source of the Nile was discovered before the source of the Hudson River—again, near the peak of Mt. Marcy. Once people settled the region, the sacking of its dense forests transformed New York into the nation's leading lumber state. White pines were turned into ship's masts, spruce into paper pulp, and hardwoods into either furniture or charcoal—necessary to the success of the region's secondary enterprise, iron mining.

It was predicted that the resulting deforestation would wreak havoc upon the Erie Canal, New York's commercial lifeline, whose water level depended heavily upon the Adirondack watershed. In 1885, state business leaders and solons, on the advice of America's pioneer conservationists, instituted one of the country's first measures of enlightened conservation. The legislature established the Adirondack Forest Preserve, declared it state-owned, and disallowed the removal of trees. The purpose was clear: Protect the state's business interests.

Resentful timber cutters scoffed at the preserve law, inspiring the legislature to create a second layer of protection in 1892, called the Adirondack Park. The original forest preserve and much of the private land around it fell within this new designation. With loggers still disregarding these measures, however, an amendment was added to the state constitution in 1894, declaring the state-owned forest preserve portions of the park "forever wild" and rendering it unconstitutional to take down a tree on preserve lands. Subsequent alteration, such as construction of the highway to the top of Whiteface Mountain, has required state voter approval. No other wilderness area in the world enjoys such protection.

The park has grown to its present size through additions over the years. Since 1971, development on private land has been controlled by the Adirondack Park Agency.

Park and forest preserve—the distinction is important. The park comprises all land, including private, within the lopsided circular boundary called "the Blue Line." The forest preserve is the state-owned public land within the park, spread out among dozens of individual fragments. It is identified by small, usually yellow signs marked with the words FOREST PRESERVE along with that area's use classification: "Canoe Area," "Wild Forest," or "Wilderness."

ESSENTIAL INFORMATION

VISITOR INFORMATION One of the many unique things about this park is that its population centers are inside it, not along its fringes. Principal centers, all with visitor accommodations and information centers, are Lake George in the southeastern quadrant; Old Forge in the southwest; Cranberry Lake in the northwest; and Lake Placid, Saranac Lake, and Tupper Lake in the north central.

For information specifically on the park, contact either of two state-operated **Visitor Interpretive Centers:** the main one, near Paul Smiths (12 mi north of Saranac Lake on Rte. 30, Box 3000, Paul Smiths 12970, tel. 518/327–3000), and its smaller subsidiary in Newcomb, on Blue Ridge Road, 25 mi west of Exit 29 on I–87 (Box 101, Newcomb 12852, tel. 518/582–2000). Each center is staffed by paid naturalists and volunteers and has handouts, an orientation film, lectures, and displays. They're open daily 9–5.

Their **Web site:** www.northnet.org/adirondackzic.

The **New York State Department of Environmental Conservation** (DEC; 50 Wolf Rd., Room 111, Albany 12233, tel. 518/474–2121) and its regional offices and public campgrounds, which exist throughout the region, distribute camping permits and information on backcountry use. Backcountry campers staying three or more days need permits; there are no other restrictions beyond those outlined in DEC brochures.

Their **Web site:** www.northnet.org/nysdec.region5.

The **Adirondack Mountain Club** (ADK; 814 Goggins Rd., Lake George 12845, tel. 518/668–4447), a nonprofit outing and education organization and the state's oldest hiking club, runs an information center at its headquarters just inside the park. It's at Exit 21 on I–87, near Lake George, and is open from mid-May through mid-October, Monday through Saturday 8:30–5; off-season, weekdays 8:30–4:30. **High Peaks Information Center** (end of Loj Rd., off Rte. 73, 9 mi south of Lake Placid, tel. 518/523–3441) is at the principal trailhead in the heart of the High

Peaks, a 6-million-acre section of the park that contains more than 40 mountains higher than 4,000 ft. The center is open daily 8–7, sometimes a bit later on weekends. It provides information on current weather and trail conditions and sells guidebooks, maps, and camping supplies.

For information on local attractions, lodgings, and restaurants, contact the many **chambers of commerce** throughout the North Country. The biggest ones are in Lake George (Rte. 9 S, tel. 518/668–5755), Lake Placid (Olympic Center, Main St., tel. 518/523–2445 or 800/447–5224), Saranac Lake (30 Main St., tel. 518/891–1990 or 800/347–1992), Tupper Lake (60 Park St., tel. 518/359–3328), and Herkimer County (Main St., Mohawk, tel. 315/866–7820).

The **Adirondack Regional Chamber of Commerce** (136 Warren St., Glens Falls 12801, tel. 518/798–1761) is another excellent source of information. The **Adirondack Information Center** (between Exits 17 and 18 off I–97 in Glens Falls) is open daily 9–5.

FEES There are no backcountry camping or entrance fees.

PUBLICATIONS By far the superior comprehensive guide to the park is the 388-page second edition of *The Adirondack Book: A Complete Guide* by Elizabeth Folwell, published by Berkshire House Publishers (Box 297, Stockbridge, MA 01262, tel. 413/243–0303 or 800/321–8526) as part of its Great Destinations series. The third edition will be out in the fall of 1998. The **Adirondack North Country Association** (183 Broadway, Saranac Lake, NY 12983, tel. 518/ 891–6200) publishes the best road map of the park. **Adirondack Maps Inc.** (Keene, NY 12942, tel. 518/576–9861) has a series of highly detailed maps, some for specialized purposes such as canoeing. For natural history, try the *Adirondack Wildguide,* by Michael DiNunzio, published by the Adirondack Conservancy (Box 65, Keene Valley, NY 12943, tel. 518/576–2082) and the Adirondack Council.

The **Adirondack Mountain Club** (*see* Visitor Information, *above*) publishes several guidebooks on specific park activities: seven on hiking, two on canoeing, one on rock climbing, one on winter use, and two "samplers": *Day Hikes for All Seasons* and *Backpacking Trips.* U.S. Geological Survey topographical maps, showing trails and shelters (called "lean-tos" in the Adirondacks), accompany each of the hiking guides. The magazine *Adirondac* is published six times per year. Another fine magazine is the full-color bimonthly *Adirondack Life* (Box 97, Jay, NY 12941, tel. 518/946–2191).

GEOLOGY AND TERRAIN The Adirondack region is the only mountainous area in the eastern United States not part of the Appalachians. Instead, it's a southern appendage of the vast Canadian Shield, a base of firm granite underlying much of central Canada. Unlike the Appalachians, which are a series of long ridges, the Adirondack region is a tilted dome, with its highest elevations in the mountains of the east-central portion (imagine the dome of the U.S. Capitol canted so that its peak is well off center toward the east-northeast). Exposed rock in the Adirondacks is among the oldest in the world, having been dated at about 1.1 billion years old—nearly twice the age of the Appalachians. The landscape you see throughout the park was shaped by several periods of heavy glaciation, the most recent just 10,000 years ago.

Most of the highest peaks occupy the east-central part of the park. On the far east the range drops rather precipitously into Lake Champlain. The highest point, Mt. Marcy, at 5,344 ft, is only 25 mi west of Lake Champlain, which is a mere 95 ft above sea level. Within a short radius of Mt. Marcy are all 42 of the high peaks: those mountains whose elevation exceeds 4,000 ft. The highest of these, all within a few miles of Lake Placid, are rugged and rocky, with sharp profiles. The lower ones are more rounded, with forested summits. Many of the latter are officially trailless, although unmarked "herd paths" often lead to the summits.

To the south, west, and north, the dome slopes away more gradually, characterized by gently rolling upland forests and wetlands. Elevation averages 1,000 to 2,000 ft, with the odd peak exceeding 3,000 ft. Here is the true wilderness of the park: miles of rarely traversed forest, broken frequently by ponds, streams, and bogs. It can feel as though you're in the Yukon, when in fact you're never more than 30 mi from civilization.

FLORA AND FAUNA The park's astounding variety of animal life ranges from "Champ," a cousin of the Loch Ness Monster, who may or may not live in Lake Champlain, to moose and timber rattlesnakes. Plant life includes enormous, ancient white pines and hardy mosses and lichens clinging tenaciously to the rocks of high summits.

The Adirondacks straddle an unmarked, indistinct boundary between North America's temperate-zone forests and its northern, or boreal, habitat. The temperate forests are characterized by pines, ashes, and oaks, the boreal forests by birches, maples, spruces, and firs. These regions mingle throughout the Adirondacks, creating a vast arboretum and an especially colorful display of fall foliage.

All but a tiny fraction of the park was once heavily logged, so most of the forests are at least second-growth, and few of the trees are older than 100 years. Some antediluvian specimens do stand, but if the loggers didn't get to them you can imagine how inaccessible they are.

A hike to one of the higher peaks, or a drive to the top of Whiteface, will take you through diverse vegetation zones. As you gain altitude, you'll see increasingly smaller trees until, on the rocky, windswept summits, there are almost none at all. Generally, a gain of 1,000 ft in elevation is comparable to traveling 300 mi north; therefore, on the highest summits you're in a subarctic ecosystem.

While the existence of a true timberline in the Adirondacks is endlessly debated, these highest summits encompass a treeless world marked by such rare plants as Lapland diapensia. On the summits, you're likely to run into volunteers who will urge you to stick to the trails so as not to damage these delicate residents.

Much Adirondack wildlife is typical of that in eastern woodlands: Chipmunks raid picnic grounds, and black bears (harmless unless famished or cornered) hang around campsites. The significant whitetail-deer population presents a concern to drivers, especially in the evening.

Among species not found farther south are two that for many visitors define the Adirondack wilderness experience: the moose and the loon. Moose, having been wiped out by hunters 125 years ago, are returning as herds farther east outgrow their ranges. The loon, with its haunting cry and aura of mystery, is a common if reclusive denizen of backcountry ponds.

The bald eagle has also been reintroduced. These magnificent creatures, while not numerous, are sometimes seen perched in tall trees along lakeshores or soaring on thermal currents above cliffs.

The Adirondacks, long known for sportfishing, have lately felt the effects of overharvesting and acid rain. You can still catch trophy-size fish in a few places; however, you'll never get anyone to tell you where these places are.

WHEN TO GO Ten of the 13 major U.S. storm tracks pass over the Adirondacks, so the weather has a way of making itself known. Lousy spells are tough to predict, but they seldom last long. The first frost traditionally hits around Labor Day, the last around Memorial Day. The all-time coldest temperature in New York State (−52°F) has been measured in the park; semi-official lows of −60°F have been reported. On the other end of the scale, the temperature has never officially reached 100°F in the region.

Though it is a park for all seasons, most visitors come in summer, the only season when many tourist attractions are open.

Summer temperatures range from 80°F daily highs to 55°F nightly lows; humidity is sometimes a problem. The towns Lake George and Lake Placid (which actually surrounds Mirror Lake, despite its name) bear the brunt of summer's gridlock; they're especially crowded in July and August. The visitor centers can steer you away from overcrowded destinations.

By Labor Day the crowds thin, but the weather remains hospitable, with daytime highs in the 60s. Foliage is as bright as any in New England, usually peaking in late September or early October. After that the thermometer plummets, usually to below freezing at night.

Winter sees great fluctuation in temperature. Highs are about 20°F, and lows of 0°F are common—although cold spells with highs below 0°F and lows of -40°F alternate with rare thaws that may see daytime highs in the mid-40s. This is the season for winter sports: The deepest snows in the east make for excellent downhill and cross-country skiing and snowmobiling.

Few people other than anglers come in the spring, partly because there isn't one. Snow, or its effects, can last through May—later in the high country. Summer kicks in soon after. Locals refer to the time in between as "mud season."

These generalizations about the weather apply to the lowland areas of the park. High peaks often see severe winter conditions from Labor Day through late June, and snow has been known to fall on their summits in all 12 months.

SEASONAL EVENTS Lake Placid, with its world-class winter sports facilities, hosts sporting events throughout the year—you can even watch ski jumping on the Fourth of July. Other activities include freestyle-skiing championships, bobsled races, the best college hockey in the country, and figure-skating and ice-dancing competitions. Call 518/523-2445 or 800/462-6236 for schedules.

Late January–early February: Winter festivals in many communities feature snow sculpture contests, broomball games, snowmobile or cross-country ski races, and a parade. The most famous is the **Saranac Lake Winter Carnival,** held the first two full weekends in February, when you can enter a giant ice castle, one of the few still built with ice actually cut from a nearby lake (tel. 518/891-1990). Lake Placid's 90- and 120-meter **ski jumping competition** is held the first two full weekends in February (tel. 800/462-6236). **First weekend in May:** The **Hudson River Whitewater Derby** at North Creek (tel. 518/251-2612) in the south-central part of the park brings some of the world's best canoeists and kayakers to test the rampaging spring runoff. **Early July:** Lake Placid's **"I Love New York" Horse Show** (tel. 800/462-6236) draws top U.S. show jumpers; next door, ski jumpers and freestyle skiers practice on artificial snow off the 70- and 90-meter Olympic ski jumps. **Second weekend in July: Woodsmen's Days** in Tupper Lake (tel. 518/359-3328) celebrate the region's logging heritage with competitions in ax-throwing, chain-saw sculpture, log rolling, and more. **Early August:** Westport's **Essex County Fair** (tel. 518/962-8383) is a classic of its kind. It's small enough to be accessible, and the setting—in a gingerbread-Victorian town on one of Lake Champlain's scenic little bays midway along the eastern edge of the park—is postcardlike. **First weekend in October:** The event billed as the **World's Largest Garage Sale** (tel. 518/623-2161) takes place in Warrensburg, in the southeastern corner of the park. One caveat: The traffic it generates would overflow the world's largest garage.

WHAT TO PACK If you're going to stay in motels and go to amusement parks, you needn't haul along anything other than the usual vacation garb. The one exception might be warm jackets and sweaters; evenings and rainy days can be quite cool, even in midsummer. High-country hikers should prepare year-round for a sudden deterioration of weather by packing a warm sweater and hat, foul-weather gear, first-aid equipment, fire starters, flashlights, and good maps. If camping overnight, bring a water filter or purification pills; *Giardia* contamination, which causes the dreaded "beaver fever," a persistent and unpleasant intestinal affliction, is common up here. Do not drink water directly from streams or lakes, even in the backcountry. Illness, sometimes severe, and death can result.

ARRIVING AND DEPARTING You'll need a car once you get here, so you might as well arrive in one. Train, bus, and plane service are available into or near the park, but car rentals inside the park are few and far between.

By Bus. Adirondack Trailways (tel. 800/858–8555) runs daily between New York City and the Adirondacks. This local service stops virtually everywhere, including Lake George, Keene Valley, Lake Placid, and Saranac Lake. There's also daily service to Tupper Lake and Lake George to Ticonderoga in late spring and summer. **Greyhound** (tel. 518/434–8095 or 800/231–2222) has daily service from Albany to Montréal, with stops in Glens Falls and Plattsburgh, the park's southern and northern gateway cities, respectively.

By Car. Principal highway access is on I–87, also called the Northway. The main link between New York City and Montréal, it runs between the mountains and Lake Champlain, along the eastern edge of the park, for 90 scenic mi. Other main routes are, from the Midwest or Boston, I–90; from northern New England, I–89 to the Lake Champlain ferry crossings at Grand Isle, Burlington, and Charlotte, Vermont; from Ontario and the northern Midwest, Highway 401 in Ontario to the St. Lawrence River toll-bridge crossings in Alexandria Bay, Ogdensburg, and Massena, New York; from points south of New York State, I–81 and I–88.

New York City is about four to five hours from the park boundary and about five or six hours from Lake Placid. From I–87, take Exit 21 for Lake George, Exit 23 for Warrensburg, Exit 29 for the Newcomb Visitor Interpretive Center, or Exit 30 for Lake Placid, Saranac Lake, and the Paul Smith Visitor Interpretive Center.

Other times to Lake Placid from major cities are: Montréal, 2 hours (plus possible border delays); Buffalo, 6 hours; Boston, 6 hours; Philadelphia, 8 hours; Detroit, 10 hours; Washington, D.C., 11 hours.

Main roads in the park are mostly two-lane and in good to excellent condition. Outside the occasional hamlet, when there isn't a log truck chugging along in front of you, it's possible to cruise along at 55 mph with little trouble. Principal north–south roads are Routes 9N, 22, and 9, all in the eastern corridor and listed in order of their scenic appeal and historic interest, and Route 30, which splits the park in two from Amsterdam to Malone. The wild western part of the park has no major north–south roads. Main east–west roads are Route 28, which arcs from Warrensburg up to Blue Mountain Lake and back down to Utica; Route 8, which zigzags from Lake George to Utica; and Route 3, which runs from Plattsburgh to Watertown via Saranac Lake, Tupper Lake, and Cranberry Lake.

Daily except Saturday, you can rent a car at the airport from **Hertz** (tel. 800/654–3131). Peripheral cities with major airports and a full range of car rentals are Albany and Syracuse, New York, and Burlington, Vermont.

By Plane. Adirondack Airport, near Saranac Lake, Tupper Lake, and Lake Placid, has flights to and from Albany on **Commutair** (tel. 800/428–4322), a puddle-jumper subsidiary of US Airways Express. At press time, there were three round-trip flights on weekdays, one on Sunday, none on Saturday.

Peripheral cities with major airports are Albany and Syracuse, New York, and Burlington, Vermont. US Airways also provides commuter service to Watertown International Airport and Plattsburgh's **Clinton County Airport** (tel. 800/639–4777).

By Train. Amtrak (tel. 800/872–7245) operates one train daily through the eastern part

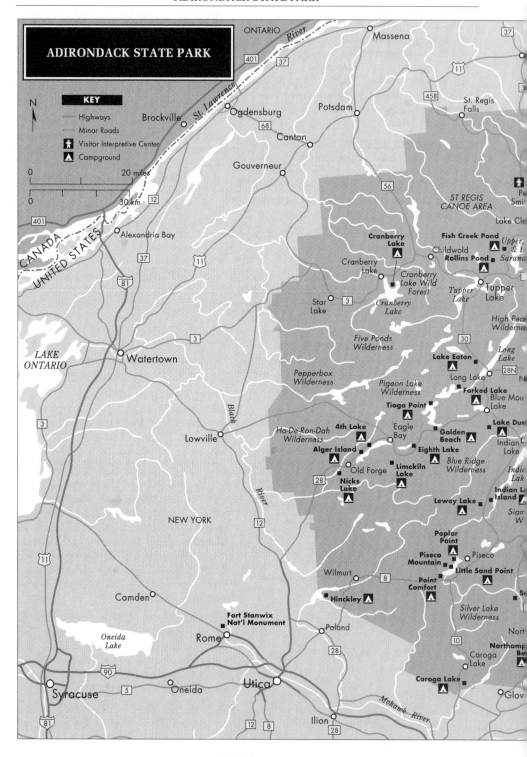

ADIRONDACK STATE PARK

KEY
- Highways
- Minor Roads
- Visitor Interpretive Center
- Campground

N

0 ——— 20 miles
0 ——— 30 km

401

CANADA
UNITED STATES
LAKE ONTARIO

ONTARIO
St. Lawrence River
Massena
401 37
458
St. Regis Falls
Brockville
Ogdensburg
68
Potsdam
Canton
Gouverneur
Alexandria Bay
37
11
81
56
ST REGIS CANOE AREA
Lake Cle
Pe
Smi
37
Cranberry Lake
Fish Creek Pond
Upper & L
Childwold
Rollins Pond
Saran
Cranberry Lake
Cranberry Lake Wild Forest
Star Lake
3
Cranberry Lake
Tupper Lake
Tupper Lake
High Pea Wilderne
Watertown
3
Five Ponds Wilderness
30
Lake Eaton
Long Lake
Pepperbox Wilderness
Pigeon Lake Wilderness
Long Lake
28N
N
Forked Lake
Blue Mou Lake
Black River
Tioga Point
Ha-De-Ron-Dah Wilderness
4th Lake
Eagle Bay
Golden Beach
Lake Du
Lowville
Alger Island
Old Forge
Eighth Lake
Blue Ridge Wilderness
Indian Lake
Indic Lak
28
Limekiln Lake
Nicks Lake
Lewey Lake
Indian L Island
Sian W
NEW YORK
12
Poplar Point
Piseco
Piseco Mountain
Little Sand Point
Wilmurt
8
Point Comfort
Silver Lake Wilderness
Camden
Hinckley
Fort Stanwix Nat'l Monument
Poland
Nort
Oneida Lake
Rome
28
10
Northamp Be
Caroga Lake
90
Caroga Lake
Syracuse
5
Oneida
Utica
Glov
81
Mohawk River
Ilion
12 8
28

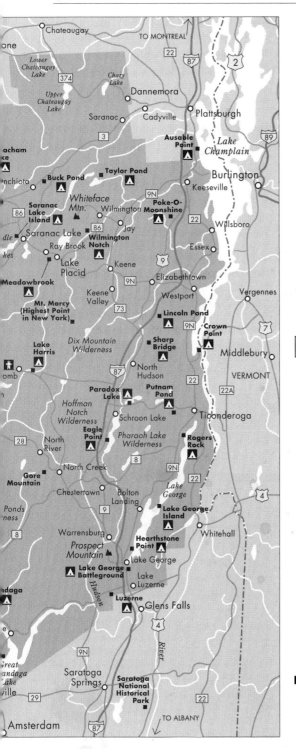

of the park. The *Adirondack* connects Washington, D.C., and Montréal, with stops including New York City (Penn Station), Albany, and Saratoga Springs. This route, at times carved out of sheer cliffs plunging into Lake Champlain, is one of the most scenic train rides in America. It's best to disembark in Westport; you can arrange ahead for a shuttle to Lake Placid or nearby towns through **Lake Placid Sightseeing** (tel. 518/523–4431). The New York City–Westport fare is $45 one-way. The *Ethan Allen Express* connects Washington, D.C., to Rutland, Vermont, with stops including Philadelphia, New York City, and Saratoga Springs. The *Empire* operates between Washington, D.C., and Toronto, with stops including New York City, Schenectady, and Saratoga Springs. **Whiteface Ski Center** offers complete packages from several northeastern cities (tel. 800/333–3454).

EXPLORING

It's impossible to explore the entire park in a short period—it's bigger than Vermont, remember. Some parks have loop roads that orient you to their wonders in a few minutes; even if such a road existed in the Adirondacks, it would take about 10 hours, nonstop, to circumnavigate. Your best bet is to pick a small part of the park and get to know it. It may be the High Peaks around Lake Placid, or the resort and dude ranch country of Lake George, or the wilderness lakes and ponds of the northwest backcountry; but familiarizing yourself with small sections at a time will be more satisfying than trying to comprehend it all in one bite. Getting to know the Adirondacks thoroughly could involve several days in museums if your interest is in human history, or several days on the trails and canoe routes if you wish to understand the natural history.

THE BEST IN ONE DAY It'll be a very long day, but if it's all you have, enter the park heading north on I-87, taking Exit 30 to Lake Placid via Routes 9 and 73. Between here and Lake Placid you'll navigate a couple of dramatic deep passes (called "notches" in the Adirondacks), drive through the picturesque hamlets of Keene and Keene Valley, and view such high peaks as Whiteface (4,867 ft), Algonquin (5,114 ft), and Marcy (5,344 ft). In Lake Placid, do some window-shopping and have lunch at the Artist's Cafe (*see* Dining, *below*).

From Lake Placid take Route 86 through Saranac Lake to Paul Smiths, then turn right onto Route 30 for the visitor center in under a mile. After a brief orientation stop here, take Route 30 south through Tupper Lake, Long Lake, and Indian Lake. This is the core of the Adirondacks, where logging and hunting are more common pursuits than retailing and skiing. You'll also be in the most well-watered part of the park, where ponds and lakes pop up around almost every turn.

In Indian Lake, take Route 28, which gradually descends along the banks of the upper Hudson River, past signs advertising whitewater rafting and rustic-furniture making. You'll reach I–87 at Warrensburg, about 45 mi south of where you exited I–87 earlier in the day. Drive this tour in late June; you'll need all the daylight you can get.

ORIENTATION PROGRAMS The **Visitor Interpretive Centers** and the **Adirondack Mountain Club** (*see* Visitor Information *in* Essential Information, *above*) conduct educational programs year-round, appropriate to each season. Topics range from animal-track identification to minimum-impact camping, from park history to beginning snowshoeing. The **Adirondack Museum** (tel. 518/352–7311), in Blue Mountain Lake near the center of the park, and the **Adirondack Center Museum** (tel. 518/873–6466), in Elizabethtown in the eastern section, also have seasonal lectures and demonstrations (*see* Historic Buildings and Sites, *below*).

GUIDED TOURS **North Country Tours** (Box 210, Lake George 12845, tel. 800/743–6278) offers one- to four-day bus tours, popular especially with senior citizens. **Lake Placid**

Sightseeing (Hilton Plaza, Lake Placid 12946, tel. 518/523–4431) provides bus and van tours ($20) of historic and sports sites around Lake Placid.

Hop aboard the 50-passenger pontoon mail boat at **Bird's Boat Livery** (Rte. 28, Raquette Lake, tel. 315/354–4441) for a tour of Raquette Lake ($8) by a member of the family that has been providing mail service since 1942. The boat leaves the dock Monday–Saturday at 10:15 in July and August and tours run about 2½ hours. Pack a lunch.

If you plan on roughing it, the following services can provide guides. For fishing or canoeing, winter backcountry ski tours, or whitewater rafting try **Jones Outfitters** (37 Main St., Lake Placid 12946, tel. 518/523–3468) or **Middle Earth Expeditions** (HCR01, Box 37, Rte. 73, Lake Placid 12946, tel. 518/523–9572). For hiking, fly fishing, and canoe tours, contact **Tahawus Guide Service** (Brookside La., Ray Brook 12977; mailing address: Box 424, Lake Placid 12946; tel. 518/891–4334). For white-water rafting, try **Hudson River Rafting Co.** (1 Main St., North Creek 12853, tel. 800/888–7238). A directory of licensed guides, most of whom work in the Adirondacks, is available from the **New York State Outdoor Guides Association** (Box 4704, Queensbury 12804, tel. 518/798–1253).

SCENIC DRIVES AND VIEWS The best views of mountains are along **Route 73** from Exit 30 off I–87 to Lake Placid; **Route 86** from Jay—which has a classic covered bridge—past Whiteface Mountain to Lake Placid, Saranac Lake, and Paul Smiths; **Route 9N** from Elizabethtown to Keene; and **Route 28N** from Long Lake to Newcomb.

The best views *from* mountains are along the **Prospect Mountain Veterans Memorial Highway** (open May–Oct., $5 per car), which offers commanding views of Lake George; and along **Whiteface Mountain Veterans Memorial Highway** near Lake Placid (open mid-May–mid-Oct., $8 per car and driver, $4 per passenger, kids under 6 free), which runs to just below the summit of the fifth-highest Adirondack peak. Here, take the mountain elevator to the actual summit, where you'll have a 360° view of the park, the Champlain and St. Lawrence valleys, Vermont, and even Montréal, Canada.

The best lake drives are **Route 9N,** from Lake George to Ft. Ticonderoga, from which you'll see the length of Lake George; **Route 22** from Ticonderoga to Willsboro, from which you'll see Lake Champlain and its valley, as well as several historic towns; **Route 374** from Chateaugay to Plattsburgh, from which you'll see the Chateaugay lakes, Chazy Lake, and Lake Champlain, as well as long-distance panoramas of the Adirondack peaks and Vermont's Green Mountains; **Route 3** to **Route 30** to **Route 28,** past Saranac, Tupper, Long, Blue Mountain, and Indian lakes; and **Route 28** from Blue Mountain Lake to Old Forge to see the Eckford and Fulton chains.

You'll see pastoral river valleys and villages from **Route 9N** and **Route 73,** between Keeseville and Keene Valley in the northeastern quadrant of the park. **Route 3,** from Tupper Lake to the western edge of the park; **Route 56,** from Sevey's Corner on Route 3 to the park's northern boundary; **Route 30,** just about anywhere; and **Stillwater and Big Moose roads,** from Eagle Bay to the park's western boundary near Lowville, all offer miles and miles of dense woods. About half of the latter trip is on unpaved road, but a ride on these roads gives the truest sense of Adirondack wilderness.

HISTORIC BUILDINGS AND SITES   Preserved homes of many prominent early Adirondack citizens are open to the public, often under the auspices of local historical societies.

Ft. Ticonderoga, off Route 22 in the southeastern quadrant of the park, is beautifully restored to its Revolutionary War grandeur. It's the site of one of America's legendary moments, when Ethan Allen and his Green Mountain Boys took the fort from the British, without a shot, "in the name of the Great Jehovah and the Continental Congress." Other nearby fort remnants, in Lake George and on Lake Champlain's Crown Point, recall the 17th and 18th centuries, when the Champlain–Hudson corridor was North America's principal battleground, a legacy recounted in James Fenimore Cooper's *The Last of the Mohicans. Rte. 74, Ft. Ticonderoga, tel. 518/585–2821. Admission: $8. Open early May–late Oct., daily 9– 5 (July–Aug. until 6).*

John Brown's Farm, near Lake Placid, is where the famous abolitionist's "body lies a-molderin' in his grave." He and his associates tried unsuccessfully to establish a community of freed slaves here in the 1850s. The grounds are open year-round, the buildings from late May through late October, free of charge. *John Brown Rd., south of town off Rte. 73, across from horse-show grounds, tel. 518/523–3900.*

In Saranac Lake, stop by the **Robert Louis Stevenson Cottage,** where the famed British novelist wrote much of *The Master of Ballantrae.* In search of respite from tuberculosis, he wound up enduring the unusually harsh winter of 1887–88 here. *Stevenson La., off Pine St., tel. 518/891– 1990. Donation: $1. Open July–mid-Sept., Tues.–Sun. 9:30–noon and 1–4:30.*

The Gilded Age saw the construction of so-called Great Camps in the Adirondacks. These were actually multibuilding retreats established by some of the giants of industry and commerce of that era. Several survive, and one, **Sagamore,** is open for guided tours as well as overnight stays (*see* Lodging, *below*) and hosts numerous programs throughout the season. At Raquette Lake, near the center of the park, it was owned by the Vanderbilts for 50 years. It's accessible via 4 mi of dirt road. *Off Rte. 28, tel. 315/354–5311. Admission: $7. Open July 4–Labor Day, daily, and Labor Day–Columbus Day, weekends, for 2-hr historical tours at 10 AM and 1:30 PM; reservations advised.*

The **Adirondack Museum,** a magnificent 22-building complex, is by far the best such facility in the park. It contains a top-notch art gallery, one of the largest collections of freshwater boats in America, dioramas and exhibits on human settlement and natural history, photo archives, and several period structures. Lectures and demonstrations are given, too. *Blue Mountain Lake, tel. 518/ 352–7311. Admission: $10. Open Memorial Day–mid-Oct., daily 9:30–5:30.*

Exhibits of logging, conservation, pioneer living and related aspects of the region's history, as well as lectures on these subjects, are also presented at the **Adirondack Center Museum.** Its 19th-century formal garden offers a pleasant change of pace. *Main St. (U.S. 9), Elizabethtown, tel. 518/ 873–6466. Admission: $3.50. Open May– Oct., Mon.–Sat. 9–5, Sun. 1–5.*

Marcella Sembrich, founder of the vocal departments of the Juilliard School in New York and the Curtis Institute in Philadelphia, was with New York's Metropolitan Opera Company for its first season in 1883. The **Marcella Sembrich Opera Museum,** in her converted studio, displays operatic memorabilia she collected until her death in 1935. *Lake Shore Dr., Bolton Landing on Lake George, tel. 518/644–9839. Admission: $2. Open mid-June–mid-Sept., daily 10–12:30 and 2–5:30.*

At the **Six Nations Indian Museum** in the north-central part of the park, Native American founder and curator Ray Fadden discusses native cultures and gives tours of his personal collection of artifacts. Fadden, who also conducts lectures and gives demonstrations, is part and parcel of the museum. *Buck Pond Campsite Rd., Onchiota, tel. 518/ 891–2299. Admission: $2. Open July–Aug., Tues.–Sun. 10–6; Memorial Day–June and Sept. by appointment only.*

NATURE TRAILS AND SHORT WALKS There are literally hundreds of these throughout the Adirondacks. Each visitor center has a network of signed trails that can be hiked, skied, or snowshoed in 30 minutes to three hours. Trails radiating from the **Adirondack Mountain Club's Adirondak Loj trailhead/ High Peaks Information Center** (*see* Visitor Information *in* Essential Information, *above*) offer a range of distances and difficulties.

The 5-mi round-trip **Hurricane Mountain Trail** offers some of the best summit views for the least effort. Begin on Route 9N between Keene and Elizabethtown, 3.6 mi east of its split from Route 73. The panorama incorporates dozens of other mountains, the Champlain Valley, and Vermont. Blueberries are free for the picking in August.

Another easy climb is the 2-mi round-trip **Bald Mountain Trail,** which takes you through deciduous and then spruce-fir forest to an open summit with great views of nearby lakes and distant mountains. Begin on Rondaxe Road, .2 mi off Route 28, 4.5 mi north of the tourist information center in Old Forge.

The **Cathedral Pines Trail** is on Route 28 near the state's Eighth Lake Public Campsite, near Raquette Lake. Though only .1 mi long, it is an enchanting walk through soaring old-growth white pines, the likes of which are rarely seen in the East.

The **Charles Lathrop Pack Demonstration Forest Nature Trail,** on U.S. 9, just north of its junction with Route 28 north of Warrensburg, loops for about 1.5 mi through mixed forest past a wide variety of flora.

The 1.5-mi **Warren County Parks and Recreation Nature Trail** passes 29 marked points of ecological interest along the Hudson River. Pick up a pamphlet, which explains what you're seeing along the trail, at the trailhead on River Road, 2.5 mi north of Route 9 at Warrensburg's center.

To take the two most dramatic river-related hikes you must pay admission, since they're operated as tourist attractions by private companies. At **Ausable Chasm** in the northeastern corner of the park, after passing through the souvenir-stocked entrance building, you can walk a .75-mi trail down into the spectacular gorge known for its fascinating rock formations that were gouged out by the Great Ausable River some 500 million years ago. At the end of the trail you climb into a boat piloted by an experienced and knowledgeable guide for an exciting .75-mi ride down the churning river; boats depart whenever enough people arrive to fill them, which usually is every few minutes. The last leg of the adventure is a bus ride back to the starting point. *U.S. 9, 2 mi north of Keeseville, tel. 518/834–7454 or 800/537–1211. Admission: $12.95. Open Memorial Day–mid-Oct., daily 9:30–5 (July–Aug. until 6).*

The trek through **High Falls Gorge** is a self-guided, half-mile, round-trip walk on bridges and paths past three waterfalls plunging 700 ft into a rock-strewn gorge; it should take about 45 minutes. Taped commentary along the way explains what you're seeing, and there's a restaurant when you finish. *Rte. 86 between Wilmington and Lake Placid, tel. 518/946–2278. Admission: $4. Open Memorial Day–Columbus Day, daily 8:30–4:15 (July–Aug. until 4:45).*

LONGER HIKES The hundreds of miles of Adirondack trails are carefully maintained by the state DEC. The visitor centers have excellent information on longer hikes, as do several useful books (*see* Publications *in* Essential Information, *above*). Touch-screen computers at the visitor centers can recommend hikes of varying duration. If you plan to venture into the high country, check forecasts before you set out. Life-threatening weather occurs year-round, and there can be snow on the summits in the High Peaks in any month.

An easy 7-mi round-trip on the **Phelps Trail** proceeds through the Johns Brook Valley to **Johns Brook Lodge** (no phone; call the Adironack Mountain Club, tel. 518/523–3441, for information), a rustic hut run by the Adirondack Mountain Club. Begin this hike at the Garden, a parking area 2 mi off Route 73 in Keene Valley; follow the signs for the trail to Mt. Marcy. The trail undulates through pleasant, mixed, mature forest, crossing several small brooks before hugging the bank of Johns Brook for the last half-mi to the lodge.

In the Lake George area, the strenuous 16-mi round-trip **Tongue Mountain Trail** will afford you splendid views of Lake George, considered by many the most beautiful lake in America, thanks to its steep forested shores, the many islands that dot its surface, and the mountains that ring it. Begin at the Clay Meadow trailhead on Route 9N, 13 mi north of Lake George village. There is a less demanding hike that departs from the same trailhead and hugs Lake George's Northwest Bay shoreline for 5.5 mi.

With magnificent views from the summit, the 11-mi hike along **Rocky Peak Ridge** in the High Peaks section of the park is very popular. It begins with a steep, 2.9-mi climb up Giant Mountain, the 12th-highest peak in the Adirondacks, and passes by Marie Louise Pond, the third-highest body of water in the state. There's a parking area bordering Chapel Pond. High Peak's 12-mi **Algonquin Mountain Loop** leads to the 5,411-ft summit, an arctic ecosystem dominated by rare and fragile plant life; observe it closely, but do not stray from the marked trail. The loop also includes Avalanche Lake and Marcy Dam. Begin the hike at Adirondak Loj (*see* Lodging, *below*). **Mt. Marcy** is the highest and most popular peak in the park; consequently, its trails are the most trampled. There are better, less crowded trails, but if you must climb Marcy, the easiest of three routes begins at the Adirondack Mountain Club's High Peaks Information Center at the end of Loj Road, off Route 73, east of Lake Placid. The round-trip is 15 mi.

Among less demanding climbs with great views are **Ampersand Mountain,** a 5.5-mi round-trip from Route 3, 8 mi west of Saranac Lake; **St. Regis Mountain,** a 5-mi round-trip from just near the Paul Smiths Visitor Interpretive Center; and **Pharaoh Mountain,** a 6-mi round-trip from the Crane Pond trailhead 6.5 mi east of Schroon Lake, Exit 27 off I–87.

If you're a serious long-distance hiker, try tackling the **Northville-Placid Trail,** a 132-mi footpath that bisects the park north–south. "End-to-enders" usually take 10 to 15 days, camping in lean-tos. You can hike segments of this relatively level trail, which crosses three major roads: Route 8 near Piseco, Route 30 near Blue Mountain Lake, and Route 28N near Long Lake. The **Adirondack Mountain Club** (*see* Visitor Information *in* Essential Information, *above*) has a guidebook devoted exclusively to this trail.

OTHER ACTIVITIES **Biking.** Though designated wilderness areas are off-limits to mountain bikes, more than 1,000 mi of old logging roads and abandoned railroad beds lure cyclists. The park's main roads are also excellent for bicycling, with wide shoulders and relatively little traffic. **High Peaks Cyclery/Adirondack Bicycle Tours** (331 Main St., Lake Placid, tel. 518/523–3764) rents bikes and arranges guided and self-guided tours. The **Adirondack Mountain Club** (tel. 518/668–4447) and the **Adirondack North Country Association** (tel. 518/891–6200) provide a list of mountain-bike trails on the park's state lands. The Association also supplies a free scenic road map of the Adirondack North Country.

Boating. Larger lakes (George, Placid, Long, Cranberry, and the Fulton chain) have marinas and liveries that rent canoes and motorboats. Try **Island View Marina** (23 Lakeshore Dr., Hague, tel. 518/543–8888) for Lake George; **Captain Marney's Boat Rentals** (3 Victor Herbert Dr., Lake Placid, tel. 518/523–9746) for Lake Placid; and **St. Regis Canoe Outfitters** (Floodwood Rd., Lake Clear, tel. 518/891–1838) for St. Regis Lake. Sailing is popular on Lake Champlain, which has the advantages of a large water surface and plenty of wind. Ice-boating enthusiasts convene on Lake George. Canoeists favor the network of ponds in the St. Regis Canoe Area, which is off-limits to motorized vessels; the Bog River southwest of Tupper Lake; and the Raquette River between Tupper Lake and Long Lake (actually a widening of the river).

Bobsledding and Luging. If you really want to get your blood flowing, try North America's only public bobsled-and-luge runs, built at the Mt. Van Hoevenberg complex (*see*

Cross-Country Skiing and Snowshoeing, *below*) for the 1980 Winter Olympics. You can bobsled even in summer, when conditions are right, screaming down the serpentine bobsled runs with a professional driver. This is available for those ages 13 and older Wednesday–Sunday 10–12:30 and 1:30–4, July through Labor Day weekend; the cost is $20. Winter details may change but have been $30 per person per ride; call for hours.

You're mostly on your own when you do a luge run, the closest thing to supersonic sledding. This is only available on winter weekends 2–4 and costs $15. For the ultimate thrill, take the $100 per person, 1-mi, 1-minute bobsled ride. For up-to-date winter information on both adventures, call the **Olympic Regional Development Authority** (tel. 518/523–1655). They're definitely not for the timid.

Cross-Country Skiing and Snowshoeing. Most Adirondack hiking trails, except those in the High Peaks, are great for novice snowshoers and cross-country skiers. The **Paul Smiths Visitor Interpretive Center** trails are ideal for cross-country skiing; there's also a trail designated for snowshoeing at the Newcomb center. The trail network at the **Adirondak Loj** (tel. 518/523–3441) is the best way to check out the High Peaks backcountry; parking is $6 per day and rentals, trail information, and instruction are available.

You don't have to be an expert to tackle the trails the 1980 Olympians used at **Mt. Van Hoevenberg** (Rte. 73 east of Lake Placid, tel. 518/523–2811); the center is open daily 9–4:30 in season, and tickets are $12 ($10 after 1 PM). Nearby on Route 73 is the **Cascade Ski Touring Center** (tel. 518/523–9605), with a network of trails for those with less than first-class ability; equipment can be rented at the lodge. Tickets are $7. The 33-mi **Jackrabbit Trail,** maintained by the Adirondack Ski Touring Council (Box 843, Lake Placid 12946, tel. 518/523–1365), connects Keene, Lake Placid, Saranac Lake, and Paul Smiths; named for "Jackrabbit" Johannsen, a pioneer of recreational Nordic skiing, it challenges those with experience and endurance but has several spurs to roads that put it within the ability of intermediate skiers.

Outside the Lake Placid area, there are two outstanding cross-country skiing and snowshoeing centers: **Garnet Hill Lodge** (Thirteenth Lake Rd., North River, tel. 518/251–2821 or 800/497–4207), with 37 mi of groomed trails, and **Lapland Lake** (RD 2, Box 2053, Northville, tel. 518/863–4974), with 27 mi of groomed trails.

The **Adirondack Mountain Club** (814 Goggins Rd., Lake George, tel. 518/668–4447) organizes snowshoeing trips, provides maps and guidebooks, and rents equipment. **Syd & Dusty's Outfitters** (corner Rtes. 9 and 149, Lake George, tel. 800/424–0260) rents snowshoes (as well as backcountry and telemark skis).

Downhill Skiing. The biggest yet still pleasantly undeveloped (no condos or souvenir stands on the slopes) area is **Whiteface** (tel. 800/462–6236), near Lake Placid. **Gore Mountain** (tel. 518/251–2411 or 800/342–1234), near North Creek, has a gondola and is popular with families. Smaller local areas include **Big Tupper Ski Area** (tel. 518/359–7902 or 800/824–4754), just outside Tupper Lake, and **McCauley Mountain** (tel. 315/369–3225), near Old Forge. All areas have snowmaking capability.

Fishing. Famous trout streams include the East and West branches of the Ausable River, reachable from Routes 9N and 86, respectively; the Boquet River, south of Elizabethtown off U.S. 9; the South and Middle branches of the Saranac River, accessible from Route 3; the Little Salmon, Salmon, Little Trout, and Trout rivers in Franklin County; and the Chateaugay River off Route 374. Tupper Lake and the Saranac Lakes are noted for northern pike and bass, and the rivers that run into Lake Champlain see fall-spawning runs of landlocked Atlantic salmon. Lake Colby, Upper Saranac Lake, and Lake Clear, all in the Saranac Lake vicinity, also yield creels of salmon, as does Lake George.

There are plenty of fishing guides in the Adirondacks; just look in the Yellow Pages of any local telephone directory. In the High Peaks area, **Jones Outfitters** (37 Main St., Lake Placid, tel. 518/523–3468) can supply guides. One of them, Bob Hudak (tel. 518/523–3577), also works independently, taking parties of up to three people on single- and multiple-day trips on rivers in the northeastern quadrant of the park. In Saranac Lake, Brian McDonnell of **McDonnell's Adirondack Challenges** (tel. 518/891–1176) goes after brook trout, lake trout, and bass on canoe trips lasting anywhere from a day to a month, on backcountry ponds within an hour of Saranac Lake. Working with 15 other guides, he keeps the guide-to-client ratio at 1:3. Francis Betters of the **Adirondack Sport Shop** (Rte. 86, Wilmington, tel. 518/946–2605) will introduce you not only to good fishing in the High Peaks but to good tall tales. The **Warren County Department of Tourism** (tel. 518/761–6366 or 800/365–1050) can supply a list of guides in the Lake George area. **Sportfishing Charters** (tel. 518/793–7396) operates guided five-hour trips on Lake George from April through November.

The **DEC** has several fishing hot lines that provide up-to-date information on conditions. Call 518/891–5413 for the Lake Placid region and 518/623–3682 for Lake George. Be sure to get a license at any Town or City Clerk's office.

Horseback Riding. In the High Peaks area, **Wilson's Livery Stable** (Bark Eater Inn, Keene, tel. 518/576–2221) has guided trail rides, tours, and lessons year-round. The hub of equestrianism in the park, however, is Warren County. Head west out of Lake George toward Lake Luzerne on Route 9N and you'll pass dude ranches, rodeos, and stables enough to make you think you're in Wyoming, including **Ridin Hy Ranch Resort** (Sherman Lake, Warrensburg, tel. 518/494–2742) and **1000 Acres Ranch Resort** (465 Warrensburg Rd., Stony Creek, tel. 518/696–2444).

Rafting. The upper Hudson River, famed for the volume of logs it once carried out of the mountains, is better known today for the number of rafters it floats downstream each spring and summer. Several outfitters in the North River–North Creek area along Route 28 offer guided trips. Try **Whitewater Challengers** (tel. 800/443–7238), **Wildwaters Outdoor Center** (tel. 518/494–7478 or 800/867–2335), and **Hudson River Rafting Co.** (tel. 800/888–7238). The last also runs trips on streams on the periphery of the park, such as the Black River, near Watertown.

Rock Climbing. The High Peaks region is a mecca for climbers in the East; such names as Wallface, Poke-o-Moonshine, and Chapel Pond are legendary. The **Adirondack Mountain Club** (Adirondak Loj, Loj Rd., North Elba, tel. 518/523–3441) sponsors climbing workshops at Adirondak Loj, a rustic lodge named by a 19th-century advocate of phonetic spelling. For guided expeditions try **Adirondack Rock and River Guide Service** (Alstead Hill Rd., Keene, tel. 518/576–2041) and **Alpine Adventures** (Keene, tel. 518/576–9881), which also mounts ice and mountaineering trips.

Rock Hounding. Siamese Ponds Wilderness Region in western Warren County has an extensive network of passageways and valleys through rock formations carved by glaciers during the Ice Age. For information contact the **Gore Mountain Region Chamber of Commerce** (tel. 518/251–2612).

Snowmobiling. Old Forge, in the southwestern quadrant of the park, and Cranberry and Star lakes, in the northwest, are hubs of snowmobiling. Old Forge is known especially for its miles of marked trails and heavy snowfall. The **Old Forge Tourist Information Center** (tel. 315/369–6983) and **Cranberry Lake/Star Lake Chamber of Commerce** (tel. 315/848–2512) have information on rentals and guided tours. Snowmobiles must be registered in New York State.

Tubing. Hudson River Rafting Company (Main St., Lake Luzerne, tel. 800/888–7238) operates two-hour floats down the Sacandaga River daily from mid-June to Labor Day and weekends in spring and fall. They provide the tubes and the transportation (riders must be at least 12 years old).

CHILDREN'S PROGRAMS Other than programs at the visitor centers covering such topics as wildflower and animal-track identification, there is little in the park specifically geared toward kids. The Adirondacks are, however, home to several examples of that childhood nirvana: the theme park. **Santa's Workshop** (tel. 518/946–2211) is just before the Whiteface Memorial Highway tollbooth (when you're traveling east) near Wilmington; it's open mid-June–early fall. You'll be entertained by Santa and the reindeer, and there are rides, shows, and "workshops," where you can watch local craftspeople at work. Lake George's **Great Escape Fun Park** (tel. 518/792–3500), open Memorial Day–Labor Day, is New York State's largest theme park, with live shows, water rides, roller coasters, and all the rest.

EVENING ACTIVITIES The performing and visual arts thrive in the Adirondacks, especially in summer. **Pendragon Theater** (148 River St., Saranac Lake, tel. 518/891–1854) stages contemporary drama. The **Lake Placid Center for the Arts** (Saranac Ave., Lake Placid, tel. 518/523–2512) presents theater, music, dance, film, and art exhibits. Both are open year-round. The **Lake Placid Sinfonietta** (tel. 518/523–2051), a small professional orchestra, performs in July and August, often in a bandshell overlooking Mirror Lake. The **Adirondack Lakes Center for the Arts** (tel. 518/352–7715) in Blue Mountain Lake presents crafts workshops, classical-music concerts, folk festivals, and plays June through November.

DINING

There are literally hundreds of options, from fast-food outlets (the ubiquitous golden arches loom over several Adirondack towns) and coffee shops to sophisticated restaurants presided over by Continental chefs, and ethnic eateries—Chinese, Mexican, Greek. And we won't even attempt to discuss all the options near the park. The following suggestions hardly even scratch the surface; you can learn more from chambers of commerce and tourist offices, and by keeping your eyes and ears open in the various communities.

CENTRAL ADIRONDACKS **Big Moose Inn.** You find a lot of Adirondack flavor at this chef-owned, off-the-beaten-track restaurant (which serves three meals a day in season) and cocktail lounge overlooking the lake that was the scene of the murder on which Theodore Dreiser based his famous novel *An American Tragedy*. A fireplace warms things up when the weather's chilly, and tables are set up outside when it's fine. Homemade breads, soups, and desserts, as well as prime rib, veal, and lamb dishes, are the draws. Specialties include Australian cold-water lobster tails and rack of lamb, marinated in herbs, Dijon mustard, and garlic. The restaurant also serves pasta and vegetarian dishes. *5 mi from Rte. 28 on Big Moose Rd., Eagle Bay, tel. 315/357–2042. AE, MC, V. Call for off-season hrs. Closed Apr. and weekdays Nov.–Dec. 25. $$$*

Friends Lake Inn. Wine lovers won't want to miss this elegant inn-restaurant (*see* Lodging, *below*)—the wine cellar, with more than 14,000 bottles and 1,200 selections, is among the largest in upstate New York. Cuisine in the elegant, candlelit dining room leans toward new American, with specialties including grilled breast of duckling with a sauce of wild mushrooms and tart cherries, tenderloin au poivre finished tableside, veal and venison linguini, a variety of fresh fish, and daily seasonal specials and vegetarian options. Chef David Martin highlights natural flavors and keeps sauces uncomplicated to maintain a balance between food and wine. Cap off a delicious dessert with one of the many fine cognacs, ports, or liqueurs (smoking is permitted in the bar, and there's a selection of cigars available for purchase). A light bistro menu is also available nightly in the bar. *Friends Lake Rd., Chestertown, tel. 518/494–4751. AE, MC, V. No lunch weekdays or weekends when ski center is not open. $$$*

Eckerson's. Long lines testify to the popularity of this roadside restaurant. Like many other structures in the Adirondacks, the building has little to distinguish it, but the evident pleasure of people enjoying good food, made and served without frills, is unmistakable. Try the Angus prime rib, New York strip steak, or filet mignon. *Rte. 28, Eagle Bay, tel. 315/357–4641. AE, D, MC, V. $$*

Old Mill Restaurant. The huge mill wheel that dominates the front of this restaurant on Old Forge's main street recalls the building's original function. No one seems to mind the dark, somewhat gloomy interior, especially once the substantial, thoroughly American food arrives: steaks; seafood simply prepared; chicken breast stuffed with Swiss cheese, spinach, vermouth, and garlic; and home-baked bread. In summer, dining is outdoors and very relaxed. *Rte. 28, Old Forge, tel. 315/369–3662. Reservations not accepted. MC, V. Closed late-Oct.–Dec. 26 and late-Mar.–Mother's Day. $$*

Van Auken's Inn. The inn, with 12 guest rooms, occupies a restored historic building fronted by large white columns and two levels of porches; the dining room recalls the region's lumbering days with its 19th-century decorated tin ceilings, hardwood floors, and walls punctuated by oil paintings. The Taylor family, which owns the inn, is dedicated to good food, and the menu ranges from steak au poivre and roast duck in raspberry sweet-and-sour sauce to roast pork tenderloin in raspberry-pepper sauce. *Off Rte. 28, behind Thendara train station on Forge St., Old Forge, tel. 315/ 369–3033. MC, V. Closed Apr. and 3rd wk of Oct.–Nov. $$*

Lumberjack Inn. On the walls are 15-ft crosscut saws with teeth that would scare a shark, and other relics from the bygone glory days of logging. Beyond the history display, this place is renowned for its Paul Bunyanesque breakfasts, with enough platter-size flapjacks and fixin's to fortify you for a hard day of vacationing. Breakfasts, lunches, and dinners are comparably filling. *76 Main St., Tupper Lake, tel. 518/359–2910. Reservations not accepted. No credit cards. Closes 2 PM Thurs. in winter. $$*

LAKE GEORGE AREA **Algonquin.** Guests of this restaurant, a local favorite for more than 30 years, arrive by boat as often as by car. The paneled Pub Room downstairs, which has heavy wood beams overhead and a slate floor under foot, serves burgers, sandwiches, and other light fare. Topside, the dining room, has pastel walls and elegant windows and is the perfect setting for meals based on excellent beef and seafood dishes: filet mignon Danish style (with blue cheese and Bermuda-onion sauce) and Greek shrimp (with a sauce of fresh tomatoes, scallions, feta cheese, and sherry). The front tables in both rooms have splendid views of the lake; weather permitting, there's dining and entertainment outdoors on the decks. *Lake Shore Dr., Bolton Landing, tel. 518/644–9442. Reservations essential for Topside. AE, D, DC, MC, V. $$$*

Mario's. Many local food lovers call this the best Italian restaurant between Albany and Montréal. Outside, it's a sizable, white-clapboard building of no particular distinction; inside, it's a stucco-wall Italian villa full of red velvet, archways, and imitation Renaissance statues and paintings. Try the osso buco, veal scaloppine Marsala, or shrimp scampi alla Mario, served in garlic wine over rice or fresh pasta. *469 Canada St., Lake George, tel. 518/668–2665. AE, DC, MC, V. No lunch. $$*

Pumpernickel's. For some fine German-American fare, try this tidy establishment at the Bolton Pines Motel, about 5 mi from the main drag (and the congestion) of Lake George proper. German international cooking is featured for breakfast and dinner, with a New York deli and German beers to boot. Daily specials span the spectrum and might include grilled boneless chicken breast, stuffed shrimp scampi, haddock

Provençale, or New York strip steak. *Rte. 9N, Bolton Landing, tel. 518/644–2106. AE, MC, V. No lunch. Closed Mar.–Apr.; open weekends only mid-Sept.–mid-June. $$*

Jake's Round-Up. The only problem with this place is that once your kids have been here they won't want to go anywhere else. Nor, perhaps, will you. It's fun, the food is great, the portions big, and the prices moderate. Furnishings are primarily Old West (including cowboy-theme pinball machines and a mechanical horse the kids can ride) but, like the food, hold a number of surprises. The menu is an eclectic mix of Mexican, southwestern, barbecue, comfort food, and more sophisticated treats, with offerings like tacos, enchiladas, baby back ribs, "Better than Grandma's killer pot roast," garlic-roasted eggplant, honey Dijon garlic-roasted salmon, filet mignon, and daily specials ranging from osso buco to Louisiana cornmeal fried catfish. There's also a kid's menu—if you can get them to sit still long enough to eat. *23 Main St., Rte. 9, Glens Falls, tel. 518//761–0015. MC, V. No lunch Sun.–Wed.; no dinner Mon. $–$$*

Garrison Kooom Cafe. This little off-the-main-drag place with the oddly spelled name has the best buys in a pricey tourist town: generous portions of soup, sandwiches, or salads for lunch, and an assortment of moderately priced dinner items. Jukeboxes at booths and college banners on the walls create a casual atmosphere. This is one of the few places in Lake George that are open all year. *Beach Rd., Lake George, tel. 518/668–5281. MC, V. $*

OLYMPIC REGION **Charcoal Pit.** The main dining room of this chef-owned restaurant has a fireplace, hanging plants, high ceilings, walls full of paintings, and big windows on two sides. The veal and seafood are particularly well done, and the menu draws on Italian, Greek, and French culinary traditions. You might order veal Marsala, Greek shrimp, or *coquilles St. Jacques à la Parisienne* (sea scallops sautéed in butter and garlic, finished with white wine and heavy cream). Also worth trying is the beef: The restaurant serves a variety of cuts, from a 6-ounce filet mignon to a 12-ounce New York–cut boneless sirloin. *Rte. 86 near Cold Brook Plaza, Lake Placid, tel. 518/523–3050. AE, D, DC, MC, V. Closed weekdays Nov. and Apr. $$$*

Lodge at Lake Clear. For more than 30 years the Hohmeyer family has been serving delicious German food in the restaurant of their 1888 inn. The atmosphere is a merry hodgepodge of family collectibles, an old piano, antique decorative glasses, and hunting trophies. Dinner, featuring traditional as well as new German cuisine, includes a choice of three fixed-price meals, depending on the number of courses you want. The five-course feast includes offerings such as a herring in wine sauce or marinated artichoke appetizer, German-style marinated cucumber salad, soup, a choice of four entrées, and dessert (go for the blueberry-apple strudel). A lighter menu is served in the less formal rathskeller. *Routes 86 and 30, Lake Clear, tel. 518/891–1489. MC, V. Reservations essential. Restaurant closed Tues. in summer and fall.*

Alpine Cellar. Sauerbraten, rouladen, schnitzels, fresh fish, and steaks are a few of the specialties at this German-American restaurant on the lower level of a small, European-style motel. The cocktail lounge, with more than 100 brands of beer, has the feel of a Bavarian hofbrauhaus. *Wilmington Rd., Lake Placid, tel. 518/523–2180 or 800/257–4638. AE, D, DC, MC, V. No lunch. Closed late Mar.–mid-May and late Oct.–mid-Dec. $$*

Great Adirondack Steak and Seafood. This restaurant is at once sophisticated and rustic, with its wood paneling and scattering of antiques and collectibles; the view of Mirror Lake and the mountains behind it is spectacular. The menu is basically American, but ethnic dishes such as jerk chicken add interest. The lively bar is in its own small room, away from the dining area. *34 Main St., Lake Placid, tel. 518/523–1629. Reservations not accepted. AE, D, DC, MC, V. $$*

Artist's Cafe. This popular spot on Lake Placid's Main Street has an enclosed lakeside deck and a cozy dining room and bar. Paintings by local artists, all for sale, hang on the walls. At lunch there are hearty soups, quiches, and imaginative sandwiches; at dinner there's steak, seafood, pasta, and a children's menu. This café also serves breakfast in summer and winter. *1 Main St., Lake Placid, tel. 518/523–9493. Reservations not accepted. AE, D, DC, MC, V. $*

Casa del Sol. Travelers who know the Southwest will be surprised to find this bright, funky Mexican outpost so far east; the tiny bar is mobbed on Friday night during the off-season and daily in summer. Although the kitchen exercises restraint with the spice bottle, the food is unquestionably authentic. Try the *mole poblano* (boneless chicken breast served with rice and beans and doused with mole sauce, here made with peanut butter, raisins, and chili powder); haddock prepared Veracruz style, with tomatoes and olives and served with rice and salad; or the lobster-stuffed chile *rellenos. Rte. 86, Lake Flower Ave., Saranac Lake, tel. 518/891–0977. Reservations not accepted. No credit cards. $*

Noon Mark Diner. You may find a Mercedes next to a pick-up truck in the parking lot and a coil of climbing rope on the coat rack; this unpretentious, year-round three-meals-a-day place caters to all, from the upper crust of the nearby swank Ausable Club to locals to college outing clubbers. It offers a traditional American menu topped off by great pies and take-out baked goods in clean surroundings. *Main St. (Rte. 73), Keene Valley, tel. 518/576–4499. Reservations not accepted. No credit cards. $*

LODGING

Chain motels rub elbows with swank resorts in the Lake George and Lake Placid regions (you can find about 325 places to stay within a half hour of Lake George), and elsewhere there's an abundance of locally owned motels, cabin colonies, bed-and-breakfasts, and, yes, a few dude ranches. There are even a couple of pet motels. B&Bs are your best bets for economy, especially during peak travel periods (which include ski season in the Lake Placid region). A great many lodgings, even around Lake Placid, are not open year-round. *The Adirondack Book: A Complete Guide* (*see* Publications *in* Essential Information, *above*) provides more information.

CENTRAL ADIRONDACKS **Copperfield Inn.** The cathedral ceilings and tall, slender columns in the lobby add to the elegance of this hotel, which was built in 1990. The guest rooms combine European style and American practicality—you can take a telephone call while relaxing in a marble bath. It is a short walk from the Hudson River, where there's fishing, canoeing, and rafting, and is not far from golfing and antiques shopping. The hotel provides a free shuttle service to nearby Gore Mountain, where there is downhill and cross-country skiing. *224 Main St., North Creek 12853, tel. 518/251–2500 or 800/424–9910, fax 518/251–4143. 24 rooms. Facilities: restaurant, bar, grill, in-room VCRs, pool, tennis, exercise room, boating. AE, D, DC, MC, V. Closed late Oct.–Dec. 1. $$$*

Friends Lake Inn. Many guest rooms in this handsomely restored, 1880s nonsmoking farmhouse have wonderful views of the surrounding lakes and mountains. Most rooms have antique furnishings, colorful quilts, and Waverly print wall coverings and curtains. Many have queen-size pencil poster beds. Two deluxe "Adirondack Suites" have stone fireplaces, whirlpool tubs, and locally handcrafted furniture. Room 3 has its own living room and a private deck. B&B rates include a full country breakfast; MAP rates include breakfast and dinner in the elegantly appointed main dining room (*see* Dining, *above*). *Friends Lake Rd., Chestertown 12817, tel. 518/494–4751. 16 rooms. Facilities: restaurant, bar, outdoor hot tub, hiking, beach, boating, cross-country skiing, library. AE, MC, V. $$$*

Sagamore. The only Great Camp open to the public (*see* Historic Buildings and Sites *in* Exploring, *above*), the Sagamore (not related to the Sagamore in Bolton Landing) has a two-night minimum stay on weekends. Rooms are double occupancy (twin beds, bathroom down the hall), and the rate includes three buffet meals a day, served in the dining hall overlooking the lake. If you have your heart set on staying here in high season, sign up for one of the educational programs—participants are the first to get overnight accommodations. *Box 146, Raquette Lake 13436, tel. 315/354–5311. 30 rooms with shared bath. Open May–Oct. Facilities: dining room, bowling, croquet, hiking, beach, boating. $$$*

Dun Roamin Cabins. Although this cottage complex may look from the outside like a relic of the '30s, knotty-pine paneling, carpeting, and up-to-date furnishings create an entirely different effect inside. The cabins (two with fireplace, two with full kitchen, four with efficiency kitchen), especially those with a fireplace, are cozy and welcoming. This property is on one of the region's snowmobiling networks, and public hiking and cross-country ski trails are next door. Ice fishing is another option. In summer there's boating—the resort moors its craft at a nearby marina. And there are lawn games, grills, and picnic tables. *Rte. 9, Box 535, Schroon Lake 12870, tel. 518/532–7277. 9 cabins. MC, V. $$*

Garnet Hill Lodge. In winter, guests come here for the skiing: The hotel's cross-country ski trails are among the best in the country. The main lodge, built in 1936, is a large log cabin whose big common room is dominated by a striking fireplace made from stone quarried nearby. Except for one vintage summer cottage, outlying buildings and the lodge are decorated in knotty-pine paneling (frequently seen in area hotels). The kitchen, one of the best in the region, serves American cuisine and (although not year-round) a magnificent Saturday-night buffet that includes fresh poached Atlantic salmon, roast beef, turkey, and a house favorite, onion pie. Dining is also available on the porch, which has a wonderful view of Thirteenth Lake and the Adirondack Mountains. In summer you can take a boat or canoe out on the lake or go for long hikes in the surrounding woods. *Thirteenth Lake Rd., North River 12856, tel. 518/251–2821 or 800/497–4207, fax 518/251–3089. 25 rooms, 20 cottages. Facilities: restaurant, 2 tennis courts, boating, mountain bikes. MC, V for rooms only. $$*

Blue Spruce Motel. Tall spruces stand guard over this compact motel near the village center. Guest rooms are standard but have an unusual sparkle design in the ceiling. Some are connected, and one is an efficiency. The motel is next door to one of the best restaurants in Old Forge, the Old Mill (*see* Dining, *above*). There's plenty of parking for snowmobile and boat trailers. *Main St., Box 604, Old Forge 13420, tel. 315/369–3817. 13 rooms. Facilities: pool. AE, MC, V. $*

LAKE GEORGE AREA **The Sagamore.** On its own 70-acre island on Lake George, this Victorian grand resort opened its doors in 1883. On the National Register of Historic Places, it's the perfect place for those who want every amenity at their fingertips: luxurious accommodations, a European-style spa with four hot tubs, a nearby 18-hole championship Donald Ross–designed golf course, an indoor-outdoor heated year-round swimming pool, indoor and outdoor tennis courts, boats, windsurfing, sailing, parasailing, and more. In winter there's cross-country skiing and a shuttle service to several nearby downhill ski areas. There are several restaurants, and, in summer, there are lunch and dinner lake cruises aboard a 72-ft yacht. The lodge buildings have fireplaces, face the lake, and are great for families with kids. *Box 450, Bolton Landing 12814, tel. 518/644–9400 or 800/358–3585. 350 rooms. Facilities: 7 restaurants in summer (3 or 4 the rest of yr), health club, pool, 7 tennis courts, beach, windsurfing, sailing, cross-country skiing, children's programs. AE, D, DC, MC, V. $$$*

Canoe Island Lodge. Complete with its own private island, this elegant spot along 30-mi-long Lake George is a private retreat that has been carefully preserved. The main lodge, last refurbished in the 1960s, has oak paneling, a large fireplace, a scattering of handmade braided rugs, and comfortable sofas, which give it an Early American look. Rooms are in log cabins and cottages (all with carpets, modern bath, and TV). If you feel like a little privacy, head for the island facing the complex; it's .75 mi, or five minutes, by hotel shuttle. You can water-ski or take a cruise along the lake in the hotel's 40-person cruise boat. The restaurant serves American fare, and box lunches are provided. *Lake Shore Dr., Box 144, Diamond Point 12824, tel. 518/668–5592, fax 518/668–2012. 72 rooms. Facilities: dining room, cocktail lounge, 3 tennis courts, boating. No credit cards. Closed mid-Oct.–mid-May. $$$*

Merrill Magee House. This gracious Greek Revival inn on the National Register of Historic Places lives up to its self-description: the "Little Jewel of the Adirondacks." There's a family suite with two bedrooms, a sitting room, and a bath with an enormous claw-foot tub. The Peletiah Richards Guest House right behind the inn has 10 uniquely decorated, Victorian-style rooms, each with its own fireplace. The Carringtons—owners and innkeepers—are originally from England and welcome guests with English-style hospitality. The award-winning dining room serves lunch and dinner daily, and Sunday brunch in season. The inn has Victorian gardens, a screened porch, fireplaces in common rooms, and an Olympic-size pool. *2 Hudson St., Warrensburg 12885, tel. 518/623–2449 or 888/664–4661. 10 rooms, 1 suite. Facilities: restaurant, pub, pool, hot tub. Full breakfast. AE, MC, V. $$$*

Colonial Manor Motor Inn. The trim, well-tended look of the buildings and a convenient location make the Colonial Manor appealing. It has cottages and motel units, and children under 12 stay free. The pool faces the street, but lawns, trees, and a playground are at the rear. *Rte. 9, Box 528, Lake George 12845, tel. 518/668–4884. 35* *rooms, 25 cottages. Facilities: pool, hot tub, playground. AE, D, DC, MC, V. $$*

Briar Dell Motel. The pleasant motel rooms and cabins of this property, one of the smaller resorts on the steep shoreline of Lake George, are all on the lake. A motel with a private beach, boats, and dockage and at such a modest price is unusual so close to Lake George village. *Shore Dr., R.R. 2, Box 2372, Lake George 12845, tel. 518/668–4819. 22 rooms. Facilities: beach, boating. D, MC, V. Closed Columbus Day–Memorial Day. $*

Travelodge. The front units of this inn have one of the area's premier views—north down the length of Lake George. Rear units overlook the outdoor pool, playground, picnic area, and Prospect Mountain. Breakfast is served in the coffee shop, which also has a view. *Rte. 9N at I–87 Exit 21, Lake George 12845, tel. 518/668–5421 or 800/239–0586. 102 rooms. Facilities: coffee shop, pool, playground, recreation room. AE, D, DC, V, MC. Closed off-season; call for dates. $*

OLYMPIC REGION **Lake Placid Holiday Inn.** If views are what you're seeking, this is the place for you. Set high on a hill above the village, this well-appointed resort offers arresting panoramas of Main Street, Mirror Lake, and five mountain ranges. It's an easy walk to Lake Placid's trendy shops and practically next door to the ice arena, site of the skating events of the 1980 Winter Olympics, including the fabled U.S. hockey victory. Competitions and shows go on there year-round. All rooms have a coffeemaker, refrigerator, and microwave; many have a balcony; and some have whirlpool baths and fireplaces. *1 Olympic Dr., Lake Placid, tel. 518/523–2556 or 800/874–1980, fax 518/523–9410. 200 rooms, 12 suites, 2 condominiums. Facilities: 2 restaurants, bar, 5 tennis courts, health club, saunas, indoor pool, putting green. AE, D, DC, MC, V. $$–$$$*

Mirror Lake Inn. Perhaps the top of the line in the Adirondacks, this antiques- and chandelier-filled inn looks and feels as though it has perched on its slope above the shore of Mirror Lake since the 1920s. The excellent Conwell Dining Room's elegant atmosphere, Swiss Alps view, and classy appointments justify the steep prices. *5 Mirror Lake Dr., Lake Placid 12946, tel. 518/523–2544, fax 518/523–2871. 129 rooms. Facilities: restaurant, heated outdoor pools, tennis court, beauty salon, spa, exercise room, beach, ice-skating, meeting rooms. AE, DC, MC, V. $$–$$$*

Bark Eater Inn. In the 1800s this was a stagecoach stop. Now it's a delightful B&B in three buildings in a scenic setting, with riding (*see* Horseback Riding, *above*) and easy access to the longest ski touring network in the Adirondacks, via the Jackrabbit Trail (*see* Cross-Country Skiing and Snowshoeing, *above*). The inn's name comes from the English translation of "Ratirontacks," the Iroquois' word for their enemies the Algonquins; "Ratirontacks" also gives us "Adirondacks." *Alstead Hill Rd., Box 139, Keene 12942, tel. 518/576–2221. 6 rooms with bath, 7 rooms share 2 baths; 2 3-bedroom suites. Facilities: horseback riding, hiking, cross-country skiing. AE, MC, V. $$*

Hotel Saranac. From the outside this is an imposing six-story red brick hotel, but once you step inside, you find yourself in an ornate palazzo-style main lobby complete with high ceilings, pillars, and paintings on the walls. The upstairs decor is even more sumptuous: The second-floor Grand Hall is an exact replica of the Grand Salon of the Davanzati Palace in Florence, Italy. The hotel is operated as a training ground for Paul Smiths College's hotel-management students: Occasional goofs by neophytes in the hospitality business are more than made up for by their warmth and enthusiasm. The pleasant dining room is one of Saranac Lake's social centers; it serves three meals daily, prepared by the aspiring chefs of the college. A lighter menu of munchies and salads is available in the Boathouse Lounge, where the decorative theme is the Adirondack guide boat, a traditional wood craft that is broader in the beam than normal canoes. The hotel's location in downtown Saranac Lake is convenient: You'll find hiking trails on Mt. Baker, only five blocks away; swimming, sunbathing, and fishing on the lake, only 3¼ mi from the hotel; and skiing a short drive by car. *101 Main St., Saranac Lake 12983, tel. 518/891–2200 or 800/937–0211, fax 518/ 891–5664. 92 rooms. Facilities: restaurant, bar. AE, D, DC, MC, V. $$*

Schulte's Motor Inn. Alpine-style stucco-and-wood buildings with peaked roofs and balconies make this compact motel attractive. Country fabrics, bright colors, and modern appointments carry the cheerful theme indoors. Two cottages have fireplaces. *Cascade Rd., Rte. 73, Lake Placid 12946, tel. 518/523–3532. 30 rooms, 15 cottages. Facilities: coffee shop, pool, playground. AE, MC, V. $*

Johns Brook Lodge. Inaccessible by car, this remote hike-in facility operated by the Adirondack Mountain Club is at a major junction 3.5 gentle uphill mi from Keene Valley on the Mt. Marcy trail and is comparable in many ways to the huts of the White Mountains. College-age crew members provide sumptuous family-style breakfasts and dinners as well as trail lunches, advice, and Band-aids for blisters. Wool blankets and pillows are provided, but most people bring sleeping bags. Hikes of all lengths and difficulties begin at the lodge, and there are some spectacular swimming holes. There are no showers or flush toilets. *Adirondack Mountain Club, Box 867, Lake Placid 12946, tel. 518/523–3441 (no phone on site). 2 10-person bunkrooms and 2 4-person private rooms, 2 year-round self-service cabins, 3 self-service open shelters. MC, V (card number must be given at time of reservation; cards not accepted in person at the lodge). Closed fall–spring, except some fall weekends. $*

CAMPING

There are private campgrounds throughout the Adirondacks. The **New York State Department of Environmental Conserva-** **tion** (tel. 518/457–2500 for information; 800/456–2267 or TTY 800/622–1220 for reservations) operates 41 public campgrounds around the park, and they are the most reliable. Some of these are at historic sites; some are on islands in the larger lakes, such as Lake George and Indian Lake. Most are open from May through Labor Day, some longer to accommodate hunters and leaf-peepers. Most also have a table and grill at each site, a beach, running water, and adequate lavatories, but not all have showers, and none has hookups (most private campgrounds have them, however). There is a fee of $7.50 for each advance reservation, but it's often easy to get a spot without prearrangement. DEC campground rates are $9–$16 nightly, or $3–$5 for day use; MasterCard and Visa are accepted if you are booking through the 800 number above, but no credit cards are accepted at the sites.

The DEC also maintains primitive campsites (usually with no facilities other than a privy, and some not even that) along major canoe routes such as Bog River/Lake Lila and the St. Regis Canoe Area. Local forest rangers, listed in phone books, are the best source of information about these sites.

Cranberry Lake. In the western part of the park, Cranberry Lake has picnic tables, fire grates, flush toilets, and showers. A trail leads from the campground to Bear Mountain, a 3-mi round-trip hike with a splendid view of the lake just past the summit. *242 Lone Pine Rd., tel. 315/848–2315. 172 sites. Facilities: beach.*

Fish Creek Pond. This campground, 12 mi east of Tupper Lake, has a recreation program, boat rentals, a boat launch, showers, picnic tables, and a beach with a bathhouse. *Rte. 30, tel. 518/891–4560. 355 sites. Facilities: beach, boating.*

Lake George Islands Campground. There are three campgrounds, each with fireplaces, picnic tables, and pit toilets. The sites are accessible only by boat. There is no shuttle boat, but there are plenty of marinas nearby that offer rentals. Glen Island has 213 sites and is accessible from

Bolton Landing; Long Island has 90 sites and is accessible from Cleverdale; and Narrow Island has 86 sites and is accessible from Hulett's Landing. *Glen Island: tel. 518/644–9696; Long Island: 518/656–9426; Narrow Island: 518/499–1288. 389 sites. Closed mid-Sept.–mid May.*

Meacham Lake. Rarely crowded, Meacham Lake has showers, a recreation program, some beautiful wooded campsites, and one of the largest sandy beaches in the park. *Rte. 30, Duane, tel. 518/483–5116. 224 sites. Facilities: beach.*

Rogers Rock. On the shore of Lake George, Rogers rock has flush toilets and showers, fireplaces, picnic tables, boat launch, and lots of French and Indian War history. *Rte. 9N, Hague, tel. 518/585–6746. 314 sites. Facilities: beach.*

Rollins Pond. About 12 mi east of Tupper Lake and near the St. Regis Canoe Area, the Paul Smiths Visitor Interpretive Center, and several favorite hiking areas, this campground has showers, boat rentals, and a boat launch. Although somewhat less developed than other area campgrounds, Rollins Pond can become an RV megalopolis, complete with gridlock, in summer. *Rte. 30, tel. 518/891–3239. 290 sites.*

Wilmington Notch. Near Lake Placid, Wilmington Notch is the site of a dramatic waterfall and gorge on the West Branch of the Ausable River and is near Whiteface and the other High Peaks. There are showers and picnic tables. *Rte. 86, Wilmington, tel. 518/946–7172. 54 sites.*

Allegheny National Forest
Pennsylvania

By Carolyn Price

Updated by David K. Harford

ention Pennsylvania, and the horse-and-buggy charm of Lancaster County or the stone bank barns of an Andrew Wyeth painting come to mind. It would probably be a revelation even to some of the state's residents that in the northwest corner of their state—an area traditionally associated with oil refineries and coal mines—lies an area of woodland romance. Allegheny National Forest comprises more than half a million acres.

Like all other National Forests, Allegheny has multiple uses: It provides wood products, recreation, wildlife habitat, and watershed protection. Allegheny is largely a second-growth forest that regenerated after intense timber harvesting between 1880 and 1920. Today it has one of the richest stands of black cherry and hardwood trees in the world.

The terrain is gouged by three river corridors: the Allegheny, the Clarion, and the Tionesta. The 27-mi Allegheny Reservoir, on the upper Allegheny River, presents a gleaming waterscape of 7,783 acres in Pennsylvania (and another 4,297 in New York), with 90 mi of shoreline. A hunter's delight? An angler's dream? You bet. But Allegheny National Forest is also a family camper's and hiker's haven.

Because of the forest's privileged location (a third of the nation's population lives within a day's drive of its boundaries), its year-round recreational opportunities, and its vast expanse of woods and waterways, more and more adventurers are discovering the wide range of activities the region has to offer. Summer visitors fish, hike, swim, canoe, camp, ride horses, bike, and birdwatch; autumn devotees drive through the brilliant foliage of black cherry and red oak; winter travelers tour by snowmobile and cross-country skis. The cool, dark hardwood forests (packed with black cherry, maple, oak, ash, beech, and hemlock) contain almost 200 mi of pedestrian trails, more than 100 mi of maintained all-terrain vehicle (ATV) trails, and more than 350 mi of trails open to snowmobiles.

Crisscrossing the alternately flat and rolling plateau are some 500 mi of trout streams, some stocked with wild brown, native brook, and rainbow trout. Muskellunge (muskie) can be landed in any of the three rivers. Wildlife watchers will appreciate the many human-made impoundments and waterfowl at Buzzard Swamp and the self-guided interpretive trail at Little Drummer Historical Pathway.

Recreational facilities include three overlooks, four beaches, six boat launches, 11 picnic areas, and 16 developed campgrounds—five of which can only be accessed by boat or foot. More than 8,000 acres of designated federal wilderness make it possible for backpackers who bristle at the thought of "developed" recreation to attain true seclusion.

ESSENTIAL INFORMATION

VISITOR INFORMATION Contact the **supervisor's office** of the Allegheny National Forest (222 Liberty St., Box 847, Warren 16365, tel. 814/723–5150, TTY 814/726–2710). The forest's **Web site** is www.penn.com/~anf. Two ranger stations are on forest grounds: **Bradford Ranger District** (Kinzua Heights Star Rte., Box 88, Bradford 16701, tel. 814/362–4613, TTY 814/927–8881) and **Marienville Ranger District** (Rte. 66, Marienville 16239, tel. 814/927–6628).

FEES There are no entrance fees. However, there are eight day-use areas that charge $3 per car.

PUBLICATIONS First and foremost, shell out $4 for the **administrative map** of the Allegheny National Forest, your principal resource when planning driving or hiking excursions. It's published by the Forest Service and indicates campsites, trails, boat launches, picnic areas, and every recreational facility available within the forest's boundaries. There are 33 **topographical maps** that cover the forest. You can order them by mail from the supervisor's office (*see* Visitor Information, *above*). Including tax they cost $4.24, plus $2.50 postage. You may pay by MasterCard or Visa or make checks or money orders payable to ENFIA (Eastern National Forest Interpretive Association).

In addition, free maps and **brochures** with information on camping, canoeing, hiking, hunting, fishing, trail biking, cross-country skiing, snowmobiling, and off-road vehicle driving are available from forest headquarters and ranger stations, and the park's Web site (*see* Visitor Information, *above*).

The supervisor's office on Liberty Street in Warren carries a number of interesting publications on the forest's cultural and natural history and recreational opportunities. The *Allegheny National Forest Hiking Guide,* by Bruce Sundquist, Carolyn Weilacher Yartz, and Jack Richardson (Sierra Club, $8), is indispensable for hikers. *The Death and Rebirth of the Seneca,* by Anthony F. C. Wallace (Vintage, $12.95), chronicles the history of the Seneca nation. (The Allegheny Forest covers historical Seneca lands.) You

can order these books from the supervisor's office or the park's Web site (*see* Visitor Information, *above*). Add 6% tax, plus $2.50 shipping and handling.

GEOLOGY AND TERRAIN The Allegheny Forest includes two basic types of terrain. The Allegheny Plateau is flat, with heavily forested areas packed with hardwoods. It is distinguished from the Allegheny Mountains by the general absence of steep slopes and by high, rolling land rather than dramatic ridges and deep valleys. The plateau is gashed by fish-filled streams and waterways. The second type of terrain comprises the river corridors of the Allegheny, Tionesta, and Clarion, which include broad pastoral valleys and steep-sided hills. The Kinzua Dam, built as a flood dam on the Allegheny in 1965, created the 27-mi Allegheny Reservoir.

The more challenging sections of the forest, from a hiker's point of view, are in the west; the best snowfall is in the east; and the highest elevations are in the east. There are plenty of roads but also sizable wilderness areas; Hickory Creek Wilderness alone occupies 8,663 acres.

Evidence of the area's economic importance is reflected in the forest's timber harvesting and its many roads and wells. The local lumber industry harvests millions of board feet of black cherry, maple, ash, and oak annually. Fully 93% of the subsurface rights are owned by individuals and companies for oil drilling.

FLORA AND FAUNA The Allegheny is home to four forest types: Allegheny Hardwoods (black cherry, ash, yellow poplar), Northern Hardwoods (beech, sugar maple, hemlock), Upland Hardwoods (red maple, black birch), and Oak (red, white, chestnut, and black). You may also run into little clearings with apple trees planted by turn-of-the-century homesteaders and shrubs and trees bearing berries planted by the Forest Service. These trees provide excellent nutrition for many resident wildlife species, including bear and deer.

In many areas, deer populations are higher than the forest vegetation can support. Deer browsing on seedlings, acorns, and shrubs affects the diversity and quantity not only of understory tree species but also of small mammals, songbirds, and wildflowers. In these areas, you'll see understory characterized by species deer do not like to eat, mostly lush, green fern (especially New York fern and hay-scented fern) or striped maple. Areas being reforested are fenced to keep deer from browsing on the new seedlings until the young trees have grown beyond their reach.

From early June through July, you're sure to notice the showy mountain laurel blossoms, typical of open hardwood forests. Pennsylvania's shade-tolerant state flower flourishes happily in this region. Drive through the Bradford Ranger District in late May and early June for some of the best views.

The list of mammals is long (49 species have been reported), with the white-tailed deer the most prominent.

The Forest Service is proud of how successfully it has managed bears here. Fifty years ago the numbers were in the single-digit range; now close to 300 are harvested through hunting annually, and the bear population is estimated to be around 1,000. Despite this increase, black bears are shy and secretive; they frequent recreation areas only when they get wind of garbage cans full of campers' leftovers.

Beavers are multiplying in number and may be observed in the low-gradient streams around Buzzard Swamp. They continue to flourish in areas like Sugar Run and Willow Bay as well as the Branch Salmon Creek in the Marienville district. Appropriately enough, Beaver Meadows Campground near Marienville also reports quite a few spottings.

Wild turkeys are quite common and sought-after during hunting season. Serious birders (there are 87 varieties of birds common to the region) should head for Buzzard Swamp, just south of Marienville, or Owl's Nest (home of Little Drummer Historical Pathway), just west of Ridgway, where impoundments create an ideal habitat for a variety of waterfowl. Bald eagles may be viewed near the Allegheny Reservoir or on the Allegheny River at Tionesta. The best time to view is in the spring before the leaves appear on trees. Warblers—including scarlet tanagers, morning warblers, and black-throated blue and black-throated green warblers—are common, especially during their spring migration. Migrating raptors glide through in the fall months.

One of the nicest things about camping at Allegheny National Forest is the relative absence of pests and poisonous vegetation. A few rattlesnakes have been spotted, but because of the higher altitudes and cooler temperatures their numbers are low. Poison ivy, typically associated with drier climates, is not happy in these damp, shaded woodland areas.

WHEN TO GO The busiest season lasts from late June to September, when nights have warmed up enough for overnight campers and daylong hikes through lush woods can be topped off with a fishing stop or a dip in the reservoir. But the other seasons have their attractions, too. Spring brings fishing season in April. Fall foliage is spectacular, even if you merely tour along forest roads by car. Winter visitors are usually treated to an abundant snowfall from December through February, making cross-country skiing and snowmobiling conditions good. If you don't mind the cold spring nights (they extend well into June), camping can be wonderful then simply because there aren't many people around.

SEASONAL EVENTS **February:** Chapman State Park, a 20-minute drive from Warren, sponsors a **Winter Carnival** the first weekend of February, with sleigh rides, ice skating, toboggan races, and other winter sports. **June: Forest Fest,** the third weekend in June, includes naturalist-led tours, boat rides, evening programs, children's entertainment, crafts displays, and dozens of recreational activities. **July:** Come to the **Independence Day Festival** in Warren on the Fourth of July for fireworks, an arts-and-crafts show, and a midday parade. **August:** On the third weekend in August, learn about the tribal history of northwestern Pennsylvania and take in a parade, food, and crafts at the **Native American Festival** in Tionesta. **September:** The **Pennsylvania State Championship Fishing Tournament** in Tidoute, the nation's oldest tournament, has been attracting anglers for more than 30 years.

WHAT TO PACK Pack a metal container suitable for boiling water or, at least, bring a water purifier, especially if you're doing backcountry touring. Consult the salesperson at the place of purchase: You need a purifier with a screen fine enough to filter out *Giardia lamblia,* a parasitic flagellate protozoan that can cause intestinal disorders.

The forest lies on a storm pathway from the Midwest to the Northeast, so bring rain gear no matter what the season. Water-repellent boots are especially important even when showers abate, since heavy dew accumulates year-round and makes for wet vegetation. Up until late June or early July, nights remain cool, so pack long underwear if you're an overnight visitor.

Finally, consider a small backpacking stove and waterproof matches if you're camping overnight. With all the rainfall, firewood—although ubiquitous—gets wet, and you may need a backup system for dinner preparations.

GENERAL STORES If you're approaching from the east via Route 59, stop at **Costa's True Value Hardware** (323 Water St., Smethport 16749, tel. 814/887–5542) for fishing and hunting supplies. **Love's Canoe Rental and Sales** (3 Main St., Ridgway 15853, tel. 814/776–6285), right on the southeastern edge of the forest in Elk County, carries camping equipment, mountain bikes, and all the hunting, fishing, and cross-country ski gear you'll need. **Allegheny Outfitters** (Box 1681, Warren 16365, tel. 814/723–1203) carries camping equipment, arranges boat trips on the river for which it is named, and leads canoeing and backpacking tours.

ATMS In recent years ATMs have sprung up in the region quicker than a copse of trees. Almost all the small towns and certainly the larger towns like St. Mary's, Warren, and Bradford have ATMs in banks, grocery stores, malls, convenience stores (try the numerous Uni-Mart and Sheetz convenience stores especially). Call the area's largest bank, National City Bank (tel. 800/352–0186), for a location of an ATM near you or for their free brochure listing addresses of all their ATMs in the region.

ARRIVING AND DEPARTING The easiest—and usual—way to arrive is by car. Allegheny National Forest lies no more than a few hours from Buffalo, New York (100 mi); Erie, Pennsylvania (60 mi); and Pittsburgh, Pennsylvania (140 mi). If you hail from New York City or Washington, D.C., you're still within a day's drive.

By Bus. There aren't any bus stations nearby, but **Greyhound Lines** (tel. 800/231–2222) does drop off and pick up passengers in Bradford, the northern gateway to the forest region.

By Car and RV. Approaching from the south, whether from Pittsburgh, Philadelphia, or Washington, D.C., you can make use of I–80, then jog north via U.S. 219, Route 36, or Route 66. If you're departing from the New York or New Jersey area you might opt for the slower U.S. 6, a designated Great Army of the Republic National Recreational Trail, which winds through the northern Alleghenies, and enter the forest via Kane in McKean County.

By Plane. Bradford Regional Airport (tel. 814/368–5928) is served by US Airways (tel. 800/428–4322). You can rent cars from the National (tel. 800/227–7368) branch on its premises. Bradford lies near the northeast corner of the forest in McKean County; a short 10- to 15-minute drive will deposit you within forest boundaries.

By Train. The nearest passenger train station is in Erie, about 60 mi northwest of the forest. Call **Amtrak** (tel. 800/872–7245) for schedule and fare information.

EXPLORING

Most visitors drive the roadways to view fall foliage or springtime's flowering mountain laurel. With its many roads, the forest offers easy access to almost any location outside of designated wilderness. To view wildlife or observe vegetation more closely, however, you'll do better on foot or in a boat.

THE BEST IN ONE DAY Don't miss the **Tionesta Scenic Area** on U.S. 6; it's a 6-mi drive from Ludlow. What you'll see is a 2,000-acre old-growth forest packed with centuries-old hemlock and beech—the largest tract of old-growth timber in the East. If you've never seen what a twister can do to woodlands, walk to the overlook to view the destruction that a single tornado wrought in the spring of 1985 (*see* Nature Trails and Short Walks, *below*). Summer visitors who want to boat or swim gravitate to the **Allegheny Reservoir,** but the pristine beauty of its shoreline warrants a trip any season of the year (*see* Scenic Drives and Views, *below*). Birders should head toward **Buzzards Swamp** or **Owl's Nest** to observe waterfowl in a wetlands environment.

ORIENTATION PROGRAMS There are no orientation programs here, but all the information about camping or recreational facilities that you'll need is available at the ranger stations (*see* Visitor Information *in* Essential Information, *above*).

GUIDED TOURS The Forest Service doesn't offer any formal guided tours. **Allegheny Outfitters** (Box 1681, Warren 16365, tel. 814/723–1203) arranges boat trips on the river for which it is named and leads canoeing and backpacking tours.

SCENIC DRIVES AND VIEWS One of the prettiest byways in the country, **U.S. 6** travels through Allegheny National Forest for 29

paved miles. You can hook up to this route, also known as the Grand Army of the Republic National Recreation Trail Highway, right outside of Warren in the northwest portion of the forest, and then move southeast to Sheffield, where the road doglegs east to Kane and then jogs northeast outside the forest limits.

No one should leave before driving by the **Allegheny Reservoir.** The following route, beginning and ending in Warren, will take you on a loop. Starting in Warren, travel east on the scenic U.S. 6, then hop onto Route 59, heading east (the entryway is just outside the Warren city limits). Follow 59 to Kinzua Dam; Route 59 will intersect with Route 321 south. Take this road to Forest Road 262 just past Red Bridge Recreational Area. Turn north and enjoy the Longhouse Scenic Drive back to the Kinzua Dam. The last miles of this loop are known as the Longhouse National Scenic Byway.

NATURE TRAILS AND SHORT WALKS It's important to note that Forest Service policy prohibits the use of saddle, pack, or draft animals on hiking or cross-country ski trails.

There are nearly 200 mi of pedestrian trails in Allegheny National Forest, 86.7 of which belong to the North Country National Scenic Trail (NCNST), which runs all the way from upstate New York to the Dakotas. Most of the trails are heavily wooded, with species like black cherry, pine, oak, hickory, beech, and hemlock shading a bright green understory of dense fern cover. You'll see deer along most of the trails.

Safety Tips. Some trails are used by hunters in the late spring and fall, so hikers should wear fluorescent or brightly colored clothing during these seasons. The pump water in the developed campgrounds and recreation areas is potable, but you should never drink straight from a stream—always boil or purify water.

The **Hearts Content Scenic Interpretive Trail** is a 1.25-mi loop in the Bradford Ranger District. Start at the trailhead in the

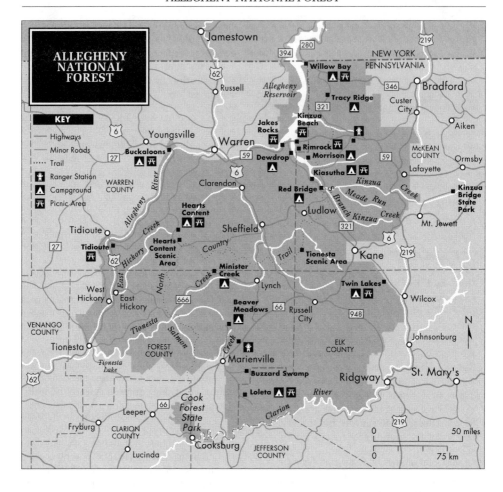

picnic area of the Hearts Content Recreation Area. You will travel through a dense forest of beech, hemlock, and white pine. This is an old-growth area, all of it either purchased by or given to the federal government in the early 20th century, and some of its trees have been around for more than four centuries. Small mammals (rabbits, chipmunks, raccoons) inhabit the area, but deer aren't as numerous in an old-growth forest like this one, with limited browse, as they are in the rest of Allegheny.

Also in the Bradford Ranger District, but east of Route 948, lies the **Tionesta Scenic Area Interpretive Trail.** Really two loops that share some common ground, these self-

guided tours are marked with diamond-shaped blazes on tree trunks and venture through old-growth forests of 400-year-old hemlock, 300-year-old beech, black cherry, and sugar maple. For the most part you'll be walking a plateau, but the course includes some sharp descents into stream-filled valleys. The longer (1.5-mi) foot trail requires only a leisurely, hour-long jaunt. The shorter (.5-mi) trail doesn't take more than 20 minutes. It begins and ends at the same points as the longer trail (look for signs on Forest Road 133E to find the trailhead), but it follows a north fork shortly after the first bridge crossing and cuts back quickly to the end of its course. The longer path continues farther west, to converge with a section of the North Country National Scenic Trail, before it swings back to the same terminus. You'll find dramatic evidence here of the tornado that in the spring of 1985 toppled one-third of the trees in the 2,000-acre Tionesta Scenic Area.

LONGER HIKES Minister Creek Trail, a 6.6-mi stretch traveling north to intersect with the North Country National Scenic Trail before circling back to the original trailhead, takes off from the Minister Creek Campground in Forest County. Right after crossing the Warren County border, the trail forks and becomes a loop encompassing various branches of Minister Creek, where fishing for native brookies is popular. Ascents onto shale plateaus, descents into valleys, and rocky overlooks characterize the terrain. Look for off-white markers.

The 11.1-mi loop of the **Hickory Creek Trail** starts at the Hearts Content Recreation Area and travels west into rolling, forested backcountry, then dips south and east as it returns, traversing several creeks and streams as it runs roughly parallel to the more southerly Middle Hickory Creek. The northern half of the loop winds through woodlands of black cherry, hemlock, oak, and beech in which sunlight and noise are so excluded that an otherworldly atmosphere prevails. The more exposed forests of the southern division have less even terrain than the northern half. The trail markers are faded yellow blazes on the trees. No motors or mechanized traffic is allowed here; visitors can hike, fish, or photograph in quiet seclusion.

The **Morrison Trail** in the Bradford Ranger District consists of two contiguous loops marked with off-white blazes that share a 1.3-mi segment and together provide 10.8 mi of backpacking pleasure. The western portion of this trail runs along the eastern brow of Kinzua Creek near the Allegheny Reservoir. Because of frequent steep grades, hiking this trail is challenging, and the Forest Service strongly advises that you use a buddy system. You'll be rewarded with fine views of the reservoir, waterfalls, and flow-ering meadows in springtime. Wildlife sightings are frequent: grouse, turkey, black bear, and—you guessed it—whitetail deer.

Also in the Bradford Ranger District is the **Johnnycake/Tracy Ridge Trail**—two contiguous loops, the larger looking on the map like a round-bottomed basket about to wobble over onto its side. If you hike the larger loop (you must hike part of the smaller one to reach it), you'll cover 10.3 mi of terrain much like the Morrison Trail's (*see above*), so be prepared for a workout. You'll also incorporate about 5 mi of the North Country National Scenic Trail (marked with blue diamond blazes) as you travel along the eastern rim of the Allegheny Reservoir. The smaller loop, which lies to the east and includes an interpretive trail on its southern leg, encircles Tracy Ridge Campground, which sits at a 2,245-ft elevation. Follow the off-white markers.

The big daddy of them all, the **North Country National Scenic Trail,** marked with blue diamond blazes, chalks up some 86 mi within the forest's boundaries. Many of the above trails converge with or lead to branches of the NCNST. Request the national forest's pamphlet and map (*see* Publications *in* Essential Information, *above*), and you can choose from 10 sections of its course, from 2- to 13-mi stretches.

OTHER ACTIVITIES ATVs. Motorized trail bikes and all-terrain vehicles can use the 100-plus mi of ATV trails now in place at Allegheny National Forest. Using an ATV on any other trail not marked for ATV use is prohibited. The season begins the Friday before Memorial Day weekend and lasts until September 20. You must have an ATV registration from either Pennsylvania or your home state; if, however, your home state doesn't have a reciprocity agreement with Pennsylvania, you must obtain a Pennsylvania registration from the state's Department of Environmental Resources (Snowmobile/ATV Unit, Box 8553, Harrisburg 17105, tel. 717/783–9227). The registration fee is $20 for two years and is not a user's fee for traveling on state-owned land. The speed limit is 25 mi per hour, but drivers should stay below 15 mi per hour on most trails, since these vehicles don't have great traction on gravel. Contact forest headquarters (*see* Visitor Information *in* Essential Information, *above*), which will send you a stack of brochures, including maps that cover each ATV trail in the forest.

Biking. Mountain biking is particularly fine in the fall, when arching corridors of brilliant foliage light up the roadways. The numerous Forest Service roads, whether gravel or dirt, are perfect surfaces for touring. Purchase a Forest Service administration map and chart your own course. Gated forest roads provide excellent riding opportunities with wide, hardened surfaces and no competition with traffic. Love's Canoe Rental and Sales (3 Main St., Ridgway 15853, tel. 814/776–6285) carries many different bike models.

Bird-Watching. *See* Flora and Fauna *in* Essential Information, *above.*

Boating. Power boating is permitted on the Allegheny and Tionesta reservoirs; there are no limits on motor size. There are five launch sites on the Allegheny Reservoir alone. Motorboats, rowboats, canoes, and pontoon boats can be rented at the 300-slip Kinzua-Wolf Run Marina (tel. 814/726–1650), 4 mi east of Kinzua Dam on Route 59. You can purchase bait, tackle, and lunch-type fare here as well. Alcohol possession is prohibited on the Allegheny Reservoir and Tionesta Lake and subject to citations.

Canoeing. The going is mostly easy on the Allegheny, Tionesta, and Clarion rivers (except for a few rapids on the Clarion) and on the Allegheny and Tionesta reservoirs. The 60-mi course of the Clarion is recommended for intermediate canoers before mid-May, when water levels begin to drop and less experienced paddlers can dip in. All these waterways are rich with scenic stopping points; you'll have no trouble finding a place to camp overnight, fish, or view wildlife. Many developed canoe-in camp-

sites are available, and there are canoe liveries in Warren, Kane, Tionesta, West Hickory, Ridgway, Cooksburg, and Clarington. A marina at the south end of the Allegheny Reservoir also rents canoes. Contact the supervisor's office (*see* Visitor Information *in* Essential Information, *above*) for a brochure that shows canoe launches and ranger stations and gives brief descriptions of boat campgrounds. Call the **Western Pennsylvania Conservancy** (tel. 412/288–2777) for maps of the Allegheny River or the Clarion River. **Allegheny Outfitters** (Box 1681, Warren 16365, tel. 814/723–1203) leads canoe trips.

Cross-Country Skiing. Conditions are less predictable here than in other parts of the Northeast, so call ahead. If you don't own your own skis and poles, you can rent from plenty of rental shops in the area, among them **Love's Canoe Rental and Sales** (3 Main St., Ridgway 15853, tel. 814/776–6285). The **Westline Inn** (*see* Lodging, *below*) also rents equipment.

Fishing. Anglers on the Tionesta Creek, the Allegheny River, and the Allegheny Reservoir find muskies, walleye, smallmouth bass, and—in record numbers—brown trout and northern pike. If you're in the reservoir area (accessible from Warren via Route 59), try Sugar and Hodge Run bays. Bring your boat or rent one; launches are plentiful around the perimeter of the 27-mi reservoir. Many streams on the Allegheny River are stocked with trout by the Pennsylvania Fish and Boat Commission; the opening day for their harvest is in mid-April. If you venture south of Kinzua Dam all the way to Tionesta, you'll discover walleye in abundance. There are two accessible fishing piers on the Allegheny Reservoir: Elijah and Web's Ferry. Other accessible fishing piers are at Irwin Run (Clarion River), Tionesta Creek (Sheffield), and Twin Lakes in the Marienville district. A **fishing hot line** (tel. 814/726–0164) will keep you abreast of current conditions on the Allegheny Reservoir and south of it along the river's course. Fishing licenses ($12 and up) can be purchased at sporting-goods outlets.

Horseback Riding. Bring your own horses and camp if you wish, but be aware that all hiking trails and cross-country ski trails are closed to horses. Otherwise, you have more than 1,000 mi of Forest Service road and more than 600 mi of OGM (oil, gas, and minerals) roads to choose from. The **Flying "W" Ranch** (Rte. 666, Star Rte. 2, Box 150, Tionesta 16353, tel. 814/463–7663) in Forest County east of Tionesta is a top-notch operation with a stable of some 50 horses and guides who lead trail rides through the forest. The ranch also rents rooms and serves meals for moderate rates and is the scene of a large three-day rodeo every July.

Snowmobiling. More than 350 mi of trail are open to snowmobilers. Many are segments of roadway that don't get plowed December 20–April 1. Another 100-plus mi are groomed, and one part of these maintained stretches is dubbed the Allegheny Snowmobile Loop, which, while loosely fitting loop status, does contain three breaks. Make sure to get the Allegheny National Forest Region Outdoor Recreation Map from the tourist promotion agencies or any Forest Service office. Available by December each year, it is an annually updated map of the trail system for snowmobilers.

Swimming. The sandy shoreline of Kinzua Beach is perfect. A $3 day-use fee gives visitors access to shower facilities and some 100 picnic sites. You'll find a large, grassy beach and picnic area at **Kiasutha Recreation Area,** 10 mi northwest of Kane. **Twin Lakes Recreation Area,** 8 mi southeast of Kane, has day-use swimming areas on both grassy and sandy shoreline.

CHILDREN'S PROGRAMS No specific children's programs are scheduled by the Forest Service, but this is decidedly a family vacation spot, and young ones will find plenty to do sportswise. Several of the developed campgrounds have playgrounds, and many private operations just outside forest boundaries cater to the young set. Within the Allegheny National Forest, campgrounds particularly nice for

children are Twin Lakes, Kiasutha, Red Bridge, and Willow Bay. All have playgrounds and easy hiking trails; Twin Lakes and Kiasutha also have beach facilities. Call the forestry office in Warren (tel. 814/723–5150) to check for any events of interest to children that may be scheduled by non-forestry groups in or around the Allegheny National Forest.

One private enterprise stands out. The **Knox, Kane, Kinzua Railroad Train Excursion** (Box 422, Marienville, PA 16239, tel. 814/927–6621) is a steam-and-diesel locomotive that chugs through 100 mi of the Allegheny National Forest. It's the only train that travels over the Kinzua Railroad bridge, originally built in 1882 and now listed on the National Register of Historic Places.

EVENING ACTIVITIES In summer, various campgrounds offer Saturday evening lectures on a fairly regular basis. Employees of the Forest Service, Pennsylvania Game Commission, or the Cradle of Forestry in America Interpretive Association speak or present slides on such topics as wildflowers and resident animal life.

DINING

Everything's casual. Elegance may be minimal, but you can count on fresh, inexpensive, and frequently homemade fare that includes some of the nation's best pies and down-home victuals. The only food concession on forest grounds is the Kinzua-Wolf Run Marina's Docksider's Cafe, a full-service restaurant; its hours vary greatly according to the season. You may want to bring a picnic lunch if you're an all-day visitor or else try out one of the nearby family restaurants. Don't worry about reservations at any of the following, except perhaps for dinner at the Westline Inn.

NEAR THE NATIONAL FOREST **Bucktail Inn.** If nothing else, look at the colorful lamp shades and try the homemade desserts. Banana cream, lemon, apple, blueberry, and cherry pies are baked on the premises each morning. The dinner menu—hearty and down-home—has such items as steaks, seafood, pork chops, meat loaf, and roast beef. Entrées are usually accompanied by potatoes, and a trip to the relish table is included. Breakfast and lunch are also served. *S. Forest St., Marienville, tel. 814/927–8820. MC, V. Closed Mon. $$*

Carnegie's. Outside the northeast corner of the Allegheny National Forest, Carnegie's is one of the area's newest dining spots. Two enterprising young men converted Bradford's large former library building into a two-story restaurant that serves everything from snacks and sandwiches to steaks and seafood dinners. This is a relaxing establishment with lustrous ornate woodwork and walls that are lined with old books in keeping with the building's bibliotecal history. *27 Congress St., Bradford, tel. 814/362–9717. AE, D, MC, V. Closed Sun. May–Oct.; Oct.–May open 2 PM–8 PM only. $$*

Westline Inn. A rustic old inn offering drinks, rooms, and meals, this is one of the most attractive dining spots in the area. You can dine on the patio or in an antiques-laden room; the building dates to the 1800s and was home to what some claimed was the world's smallest railroad, only 3 mi long. Shrimp, rainbow trout, and crepes are top choices. Or better yet, go to the tank and pick the fish of your choice. There's a delicious seafood buffet the first Friday of every month. *Off Rte. 219, on Forest Rd. 321, Westline, tel. 814/778–5103. Reservations essential. AE, D, MC, V. No lunch Mon.–Thurs. $$*

Five Forks. Lucky diners here sit on the spacious deck that overlooks the Allegheny River and watch eagles soaring in the sky and black bear and deer wandering in the woods. The best $5.50 you can spend is for the lunch buffet here, a dozen different entrées offered Monday through Friday. *Rte. 62, 2 mi south of Tionesta, tel. 814/755–2455. D, MC, V. $*

Flying W Dude Ranch. Three buffet spreads a day (breakfast, at $5.99, is partic-ularly popular) plus a full menu draw more than cowboys to this authentic dude ranch. The large, rustic-style dining room with hardwood floors has great views of the forest. *Rte. 666, Star Rte. 2, Box 150, Tionesta, tel. 814/463–7663. D, MC, V. Closed weekdays May–Memorial Day and Labor Day–Oct.; closed Nov.–Apr. $*

Pennsy Restaurant. Fresh and homemade are the words the folks at the Pennsy live by. Seek out their celebrated homemade breads, pies, sweet rolls, sausages, and Sunday specials like roast turkey, stuffed pork chops, and prime rib. You can get a hearty lunch for between $5 and $7. *157 N. Broad St., Rte. 219, Ridgway, tel. 814/772–9935. No credit cards. No lunch Mon. No dinner. $*

PICNIC SPOTS Consult the administrative map (*see* Publications *in* Essential Information, *above*) for exact locations of all the forest's picnic areas. Some of the most scenic ones are on or near the Allegheny Reservoir just off Route 59.

LODGING

The little towns and cities on the forest's edge are the kind that still take pennies in parking meters. (In Ridgway or Kane a dime will buy you an hour's reprieve.) You're not going to find stainless steel highrises or luxury resorts. Warren, home of the forest headquarters, is renowned for its tree-lined streets and Victorian homes. It has a Holiday Inn and a Super 8 motel, but most of the options operate on a smaller scale.

NEAR THE NATIONAL FOREST **Glendorn.** Just outside the northeast section of the Allegheny National Forest, this sprawling 1,280-acre estate built with oil money has hefty rates (starting at $345) that include lodging and all meals and activities. Many of the buildings are made of logs or stone and have fireplaces and carpeting. Skeet and trap shooting are among the myriad activities available. *1032 W. Corydon St.,*

Bradford, tel. 212/696–4566 or 800/843–8568 (reservations), fax 212/689–1598. 3 rooms and 1 suite in lodge, 2 suites in 1 cabin, 5 1-bedroom cabins, 1 3-bedroom cabin. AE, D, MC, V. Facilities: restaurant, pool, lake, massage, 3 tennis courts, archery, health club, hiking, fishing, bicycles, cross-country skiing, billiards. $$$

Faircroft Bed and Breakfast. This charming 1800 homestead on a 75-acre tract of land is right next to the National Forest. Hosts John and Lois Shoemaker are natives of the area and have a wealth of information for visitors. There's a common room with a TV, a nice screened porch, and a pond that is great for ice skating in the winter. You haven't had breakfast until you taste one of Lois's Swedish offerings—make sure you are hungry. Box 17, Montmorenci Rd., Rte. 948, 2 mi from Rt. 219, Ridgway 15853, tel. 814/776–2539. 3 rooms. AE, D, MC, V. $$

Holiday Inn. This modern inn puts you just 10 mi away from Kinzua Dam. 210 Ludlow St., Warren, tel. 814/726–3000 or 800/446–6814. 112 rooms. Facilities: bar, restaurant, indoor pool, no-smoking rooms, sauna, exercise room, recreation room. AE, D, MC, V. $$

Old Charm Bed & Breakfast. The first B&B in St. Mary's is in the former home of the Straub family, founders of Straub Brewery, which is close by and open for tours six days a week. A full breakfast comes with a stay in the antiques-filled rooms. A gift shop selling baskets and other local crafts is on the ground floor. The National Forest is less than 30 minutes away. 444 Brusselles St., St. Mary's 15857, tel. 814/834–9429, fax 814/834–9274. 6 rooms. AE, D, MC, V. $$

Westline Inn. Totally surrounded by Allegheny National Forest, this is backwoods lodging at its best. The comfortable rooms are not elegant, but some have big brass beds. There are no phones or TVs in the rooms (there's a phone booth outside). A large indoor hot tub awaits guests. The Westline is not for folks wanting to be pampered, but those looking for a laid-back good time will be happy. Sometimes noise from the bar below drifts upstairs. Off Rte. 219 (Box 137), Westline, tel. 814/778–5103. 2 rooms with bath, 4 rooms share baths. Facilities: restaurant, bar, hot tub. AE, D, MC, V. $$

Christmas Inn. It's Christmas 12 months a year at this inn that's owned by Bob and Connie Lovell, who also own America's First Christmas Store, which is a few blocks from their inn. Guest rooms, all with original woodwork of oak, curly maple, or mahogany, have some year-round Christmas paraphernalia. Guests are given coupons for breakfast at the nearby Smethport Diner, a small country diner that's earned national acclaim. The Allegheny National Forest is 20 mi away. 911 W. Main St. (U.S. Rte. 6), Smethport, tel. 800/841–2721 or 800/653–6700. 7 rooms. AE, D, MC, V. $

Super 8. Rooms here are simple and clean and many have comfortable recliners. A free Continental breakfast is offered each morning in the lobby. 204 Struthers St., Warren 16365, tel. and fax 814/723–8881 or 800/800–8000. 56 rooms. Facilities: no-smoking rooms. AE, D, MC, V. $

CAMPING

Half the campsites at developed areas can be reserved for the summer season while the other half are first-come, first-served. **Reservations** (tel. 800/280–2267) can be made 5 to 240 days in advance. Camping is permitted year-round at some recreation areas, but after the summer season (Memorial Day–Labor Day) some recreation areas close completely and others shut down certain facilities. Flush toilets and showers, for instance, are turned off in winter. Daily charges are $7–$16 for individual sites, $40 for group sites.

Allegheny National Forest provides 16 **developed campgrounds** with more than 700 sites. The recreation area with the largest capacity, Tracy Ridge, has 119 campsites; the smallest, Minister Creek, only six. Ten other campgrounds are on the Allegheny Reservoir. Five of these are "primitive type"—accessible only by boat or hiking trail. They provide pit toilets, rock ring fireplaces, and wells with hand pumps on them; no fee is charged. Of the remaining five, four are developed shoreline sites with gravel pull-in areas for trailers, and one is on the Allegheny plateau.

Campgrounds are in sheltered, shady areas surrounded by hardwoods or conifers. You may be able to see or hear your neighbors in summer, when camping activity is at its peak. A campground "host" lives on the premises. Generally, you can count on the bare minimum of a picnic table, a fire ring, and a parking space large enough for one vehicle, plus latrines (vault toilets) and drinking water from a hand pump. Campgrounds in some areas provide tent pads for each site and a dump station. Dewdrop, Kiasutha, Red Bridge, Loleto, and Twin Lakes recreation areas have flush toilets, pressurized water fountains, and hot showers; some have a playground and a concrete boat launch. Group sites are available for $40 per day at Buckaloons, Tracy Ridge, and Twin Lakes recreation areas. Contact the supervisor's office for the "Recreation Areas Facilities and Schedules" brochure.

In this dense forest you're obviously not going to have to worry about **firewood.** However, the supply gives out if the weather doesn't hold, and it rains with some frequency. So accumulate what you need for the length of your stay when you arrive, or come with your own supply.

Backcountry camping. Backcountry camping opportunities are ample and require neither a permit nor a fee. Unlike on most other public land, camping is permitted in nearly all areas of the Allegheny National Forest. There are, however, some **restrictions.** There is no camping: on the shores and within 1,500 ft inland of the timberline around the Allegheny Reservoir, except in the developed areas designed for camping; at Jakes Rocks or Rimrock areas or on the main access road to these areas; within 1,500 ft on either side of the center line of Allegheny Reservoir Scenic Drive or Longhouse National Scenic Byway; on either side of the main channel of Kinzua Creek from Red Bridge up to Mead Run; at Tionesta Scenic Area or Tionesta Research Area; along Loleta grade between Loleta Recreation Area and Forest Road 592 from Memorial Day to Labor Day; in the Duhring Area near Spring Creek.

Camping is not permitted in excess of 14 continuous days at any site. You may also not relocate within 1,500 ft of a site just occupied.

All persons camping in undeveloped areas should use a cook stove or build a safe fireplace, keep a clean camp (pack out what you pack in), and make sure any fire is fully extinquished before leaving camp. If latrines are needed, they should be provided in a suitable area to assure the health and sanitation of your family and others who will follow. Latrines should be dug 100 ft from streams.

RVs. Electricity, sewage, and water hookups are not generally available, though Buckaloons, Willow Bay, Loleta, and Twin Lakes recreation areas do provide some sites equipped with electricity. There are trailer dump stations at Buckaloons, Dewdrop, Kiasutha, Red Bridge, Tracy Ridge, Twin Lakes, Loleta, and Willow Bay recreation areas.

Assateague Island National Seashore and Chincoteague National Wildlife Refuge

Maryland, Virginia

By Carolyn Price

Updated by Bruce Walker

isitors to this narrow, 37-mi-long barrier island off the coast of Maryland and Virginia confront a highly stylized landscape: low, flat stretches of beach, forest, and marsh with a weathered palette of sand- and sun-bleached hues. Shore areas are painted with the whites, silvers, and fawns of beach and berm, the pale shades of dune and parched golden beach grass. In the forest, colors turn to evergreen and fragrances to resin; loblolly pines shoot high over a tangled understory of greenbrier, fern, and flowering serviceberry. And the marsh, with its cordgrasses and mudflats, is as silent and enigmatic to the uninitiated as its hidden biotic activity is frantic and nonstop.

The camouflage conceals surprises. Estuarine action goes on beneath swampy wraps. Shorebirds nest on eggs the color of seashells. Bashful species forage after sunset. But there are bold displays of life, too: shaggy feral horses scrounging for cordgrass; loons crying their sharp, territorial tremolos; and, on summer nights, millions of the protozoa known as *Noctiluca scintillans* studding the ocean with microscopic fireworks as the waves crash on the shore.

It's also a place of year-round human activity, from the summer cyclists and bikinied "june bugs" (the locals' term for summering students) to the winter hunters and anglers. About 2 million visitors arrived in 1995 to camp, canoe, swim, hunt, fish, surf, birdwatch, walk the beach, and observe the celebrated wild horses that populate the island. This could have become another Ocean City—a swaggering strip of neon and entertainment—but the residents of neighboring townships voted construction out and preservation in. As a result, the Assateague Island National Seashore, established in 1965, and the Chincoteague National Wildlife Refuge, established in 1943, share (along with Assateague State Park, not covered in this book) the nearly 40,000 acres of the island and its surrounding waters. The national seashore, on the northern end of the island in Maryland, is maintained for recreational use by the National Park Service; the refuge, to the south, manages and protects wildlife on the Virginia shore under administration of the U.S. Fish and Wildlife Service.

ESSENTIAL INFORMATION

VISITOR INFORMATION Contact the **Assateague Island National Seashore** (Rte. 611, 7206 National Seashore La., Berlin, MD 21811, tel. 410/641–3030 or 410/641–1441) for information on camping, fees, and recreational activities on the northern, or Maryland, portion of the island. The **Chincoteague National Wildlife Refuge** (Box 62, Chincoteague, VA 23336, tel. 757/336–6122), south of the seashore boundaries across the state line in Virginia, has its own set of rules and regulations.

Three visitor centers are at your disposal: the Barrier Island Visitor Center in Maryland and the Chincoteague Refuge Visitor Contact Station and Toms Cove Visitor Center in Virginia. All offer free brochures and sell a host of publications, and you can get cheerfully dispensed information at each site from a refuge naturalist or park ranger.

FEES Every vehicle entering the national seashore is charged $5; upon payment you receive a paper pass, good for seven days, that should be displayed prominently on your dashboard. Pedestrians and cyclists pay $2 per person.

Pedestrians and cyclists are admitted free to Chincoteague National Wildlife Refuge; drivers pay $5 per carload for a pass good for seven consecutive days.

Frequent visitors to the national seashore can purchase a $15 annual entrance pass. The refuge's equivalent comes in the form of a Duck Stamp, which can be obtained for $15 at most post offices, some sporting goods stores, and at the refuge itself. You may also obtain the federal Duck Stamp through the mail, by sending $15.50 (which includes postage and handling) to the U.S. Postal Service, Philatelic Sales Division, Washington, DC 20265. The refuge also offers a $12 annual pass.

The Maryland and Virginia portions of the island honor three of the authorized entrance passes: the annual Golden Eagle Passport ($50), the lifetime Golden Age Passport (available to those 62 years or older for a one-time fee of $10), and the lifetime Golden Access Passport.

ORV (off-road vehicle) owners must fill out an application for a permit and submit $60 in payment by mail or in person. The permit is valid for 13 months, from January 1 through January 31 of the following year.

PUBLICATIONS The 127-page *Assateague Island Handbook* ($6.95) is your best bet for an overview of Assateague's natural history and terrain. Produced by the National Park Service, the book has color photographs of plant and animal life and eight pages devoted to the highly publicized wild horses.

Pick up a copy of *The Life of Assateague,* a handy 5- by 7-inch paperback by Bill Perry, for a guide to the three short nature trails, each devoted to different ecosystems, on the island's northern end. There are black-and-white photographs and pen-and-ink renderings of sundry flora and fauna.

Assateague—Island of the Wild Ponies, a 32-page children's photo-essay book by Larry Points and Andrea Jauck, two long-time National Park Service naturalists, shows and tells you everything about the lives of the island's most famous residents. It is available at the visitor centers.

Dr. Stephen P. Leatherman's *Barrier Island Handbook* is a valuable study of island environments and their evolution; it also analyzes the effect of human and vehicular traffic on islands like Assateague.

At the top of the list for ornithologists are *A Field Guide to the Birds of Eastern and Central North America,* by Roger Tory Peterson, and *The Birder's Handbook,* by Paul R. Ehrlich, David S. Dobkin, and Darryl Wheye. The latter, at almost 800 pages, isn't for carrying around in the field, but it's one of the best resources on bird biology and behavior. Peterson's classic text, on the other hand, is a general, portable, user-friendly accompaniment for walks and is especially useful for its field identification tips.

Birdlife at Chincoteague and the Virginia Barrier Islands, by Brooke Meanley, a biologist who specialized in ornithology and spent many years in the Chesapeake Bay region, is a 100-odd-page paperback with black-and-white photographs. It gives a nice overview of bird populations on the North American barrier islands, from Assateague in the north to the southerly Fishermans Island.

Misty of Chincoteague, by Marguerite Henry, practically put Chincoteague and its wild horses on the map. It remains a children's classic and is very good reading. If your child prefers the factual, try the Center for Marine Conservation's wonderful 113-page paperback *The Ocean Book;* it's full of experiments, crossword puzzles, riddles, and educational activities for all ages.

Finally, take advantage of the multitude of free brochures available at every visitor center. They cover all areas of interest and activity on the island, from the resident populations of mammals and birds to opportunities for shelling, shellfishing, hunting, and camping. A color map of the island and basic rundown of seasonal sports, also free, will be mailed to you on request.

GEOLOGY AND TERRAIN Assateague Island is about 6,000 years old. Evidence of its makeup points definitively to the Appalachian Mountains, eroded fragments of which traveled down the Delaware River valley and settled on the continental shelf. Assateague started out as a peninsula of Delaware. Through the action of winds and waves, the island grew longer and longer, like a slightly decurved Pinocchio's nose composed of sand. These sands shift constantly, and regular visitors will note a decidedly different shoreline from one season to the next. During this century alone, the southern tip has extended more than 2 mi, and the northern reaches have sidled hundreds of feet westward.

FLORA AND FAUNA Wild horses are among the largest animals at Assateague; they're certainly the most publicized. Stalwart creatures with thick skin and stout silhouettes, they consume a salty diet of cord and beach grass, which makes for a plump profile as well as a shorter life than those of domesticated types. They arrived with 17th-century English settlers, who used them for agriculture and transportation, as well as an occasional food source. Today there are about 150 of them at the refuge; another group calls the seashore home. The horses on the refuge are confined to a certain area so are not free, but neither are they tethered: They wander the wilderness areas or linger, in very small numbers, near roads or camping sites. *Please do not interact with these creatures.* Several are killed each year by cars as they try to get food from humans on roadways. Appealing as they may seem, the horses will bite and kick; children, especially, should keep their distance. An overlook spanning Black Duck Marsh on the Woodland Trail at the refuge is a good place to view grazing bands of from 2 to 10.

Other frequently sighted mammals are the white-tailed deer and the smaller, exotic sika elk; the latter, with a dark stripe down its back and white spots on its sides, was imported from Asia in the early 20th century. The maritime forest surrounding the Woodland Trail on the Virginia end is a good place to observe both species; for sika, in particular, try the Lighthouse Trail within the shrub habitat areas.

Many of the other land mammals are elusive. The opossum, brown bat, meadow jumping mouse, raccoon, and red fox are all nocturnal. The Delmarva fox squirrel, an endangered species carefully managed and monitored by the refuge, does most of its stuff in the early morning and late afternoon. The river otter, though shy, may be seen in the bay or in impoundments during the day if you keep your distance. Educational exhibits along the Woodland Trail edify walkers on wildlife.

With Assateague Island's position on the Atlantic flyway, its proximity to miles of open sea, and its rich food supply in the form of grasses, bulrushes, and aquatic creatures, both migratory and resident bird populations prosper. The Christmas Count (*see* Seasonal Events, *below*) on Chincoteague usually documents more than 150 species. Nesting colonies of willets, oystercatchers, laughing gulls, herons, egrets, terns, and ibises abound; warblers, clapper rails, and black ducks breed consistently; and large concentrations of migratory birds winter along the coastal strands. Due to the endangered status (technically it's threatened, not endangered) of the piping plover—a little, sand-colored shorebird—the Seashore and the Refuge often seal off parts of the island, including the entire southern hook, during nesting season.

As for flora, the beach, forest, and marsh each nourish distinctive forms. The dune area, though markedly devoid of vegetation, does support some hearty, low-lying plants with powerful root systems (*Hudsonia,* American beach grass). Loblolly pine, a species not found north of the Delmarva

Peninsula, dominates the island's landscape but contorts into gnarled roots and branches seaside, where sand and wind stunt its growth. In the woodland areas, however, it climbs to heights of 80 to 100 ft.

The salt marshes and meadows are filled with salt marsh cordgrass (which the horses eat in great quantity), seashore salt grass, and salt meadow cordgrass. Wetlands also sustain a rich supply of three-square rush, a crucial nourishment for the migratory waterfowl that winter here. Aster, rose pink, bayberry, wax myrtle, and many common ferns stand out against the otherwise uniform hues of the field and forest.

A word on the pests that show up around late May and don't retreat until autumn: Mosquitoes are the most pesky. The greenhead, or American horsefly, lands but gives its victim three or four seconds before it bites, so at least you have a chance of swatting it. The very persistent stable fly is gray and looks like the common housefly but bites when it lands. This one has a penchant for ankles. The only other annoyance—but a serious one—is the tick that carries Lyme disease. Stay on trails to avoid it; it also helps to wear long trousers and long sleeves.

WHEN TO GO Assateague Island is a year-round destination. The best weather is in late spring and fall, but winds can be unpredictable during these seasons, and nighttime temperatures drop. In May, the average temperature is almost 70°F, but the water temperature is still only in the high 50s. The crowds (and insects) arrive in the summer, when you can count on ocean temperatures climbing to the mid-70s. Stick some industrial-strength insect repellent in your beach bag if you want to explore nonbeach habitats.

If you're a birder, come during the migratory waterfowl season between September and December or the spring shorebird season. In September, both air and water temperatures are usually in the 70s, and biting insects have dwindled. December averages 40°F temperatures, but unpredictable winds and precipitation make long underwear essen-

tial. Those who like solitude and pristine surroundings may prefer the winter, despite occasional storms.

SEASONAL EVENTS **Easter weekend:** The **Chincoteague Easter Decoy Festival** celebrates the talents of about 150 local artists who exhibit their works and submit them for viewing and sales. **May: International Migratory Bird Celebration** has plenty of family activities like bird walks, birdhouse and feeder building, and art contests. **July:** After two weeks of food and fireworks at the Chincoteague Volunteer Firemen's Carnival, visitors watch the herds of wild horses cross the Assateague Channel and mount the shores of Chincoteague Island during the **Firemen's Annual Pony Swim and Auction,** held the last Wednesday and Thursday in July, a tradition dating from 1925. **Oct.:** Oysters come in many guises—raw, steamed, fried, or frittered—at the annual **Oyster Festival** in Chincoteague, held every Columbus Day weekend. **Nov.:** Come to the **Waterfowl Week** during Thanksgiving week and you'll get a crack at observation points on the refuge's northern end that are not open the rest of the year. Refuge representatives present guided walks and lectures on wildlife. **Dec.:** Participants in the annual **Christmas Count,** held over Christmas week and sponsored by the National Audubon Society, document the populations of birds sighted within a 15-mi area of Chincoteague.

PETS The best advice is not to bring them. No pets of any kind are allowed in the Refuge, even if they stay in your car. Dogs are allowed, on leashes no longer than 6 ft only, on much of the national seashore. But hot beach sand can be hard on paws, and sand-laden winds may sting the eyes of even hardy breeds.

WHAT TO PACK Between mid-May and September, bring insect repellent. You may need long trousers and long sleeves in marshy areas. Bring a windbreaker and rain gear no matter what the season. You don't necessarily need hiking boots (trails are easy and beachfront doesn't require them);

but if you're going out in marshy areas, consider packing high-top waterproof footwear. If you're doing any shellfishing, bring wading shoes; flip flops aren't suitable. Since only one food concession operates on the island—and offers little more than hot dogs and sodas—pack a lunch if you're a day-tripper.

GENERAL STORES The **Assateague Market** (7643 Stephen Decatur Hwy., tel. 410/641–3380) is open March–April, weekdays 7–7, weekends 7 AM–10 PM; May–October, daily 7 AM–10 PM. It sells everything from subs and beer to firewood and beach rafts and rents fishing, crabbing, and beach equipment. **Bucks Place** (corner of Rtes. 376 and 611, tel. 410/641–4177) is open April–May and September–October, daily 7–dark; June–August, daily 6 AM–midnight. It sells an array of camping supplies—propane stoves, steamers, sleeping bags, crab traps, bait, and tackle—and the staff cheerfully dispenses information on local campsites and area restaurants.

Since there are no food concessions on the Virginia end within the Refuge, you might want to pick up a lunch on your way in: Try **J&B Cold Cuts** (3571 Main St., Chincoteague, tel. 757/336–5500) or **Steve's Mini Market** (Maddox Blvd., Chincoteague, tel. 757/336–1958).

ATMS On the Virginia end, go to the **Marine Bank** (6395 Maddox Blvd., tel. 757/336–6539) or the **Shore Bank** (6350 Maddox Blvd., tel. 757/336–3144) in Chincoteague; they're only about 2 mi from the entrance to the Refuge. At the Maryland end you'll have to shoot north for Ocean City; Coastal Highway, the main drag of this resort town, has unlimited choices.

ARRIVING AND DEPARTING Traveling between the entrance to the National Seashore in Maryland and the entrance to the wildlife refuge in Virginia, a distance of approximately 57 mi, requires about 1½ hours on the road. The Maryland entrance is 259 mi from New York City and 135 mi from Baltimore; the Virginia entrance is 166 mi from Washington, D.C., and 177 mi from Philadelphia.

The best way to get here is by car; any other transportation involves a combination of modes that will run you ragged or broke.

By Bus. The closest terminal is in Ocean City, Maryland, 10 mi north of Assateague Island. Two **Greyhound** (tel. 800/231–2222) buses run there daily from Wilmington, Delaware, at noon and 3:30 PM ($28.75 one-way). You'll need to rent a car or hire a taxi for the last leg of the trip.

By Car and RV. The bridge to the National Seashore begins about 10 mi south of Ocean City, Maryland, on Route 611. It takes about three hours to drive here from either Washington or Baltimore. Use the Chesapeake Bay Bridge; then make your way east on Route 50, or take the more scenic passage across the Delmarva Peninsula via Routes 404 and 113. From Wilmington, you can come directly down Route 13 through Dover to Route 113 South (though you might have fewer traffic headaches by jogging a bit west to the lovely Route 213, then picking up either Route 50 or Route 404). The latter option takes quite a bit longer, but the eastern shore of the Chesapeake Bay through Kent County is blessed with the coastal plain and long stretches of farmland that have made the area famous.

By Plane. The nearest airport is in Salisbury, Maryland, 30 to 45 minutes from the national seashore entrance and about an hour to the front gates of the Refuge. US Airways (tel. 800/428–4322) is the only carrier that serves this small airport. (Book on an advance-reservation special or you'll pay a fortune for your fare.) You can rent a car at the airport from **Avis** (tel. 800/331–1212), **Hertz** (tel. 800/654–3131), or **National** (tel. 800/227–7368); there is no municipal bus service, and a cab ride to either park entrance will run you $50–$60. By car from Salisbury, take the billboard-infested Route 50 for the most direct approach to the National Seashore entrance, or follow Route 12 to the Virginia coast.

By Train. While it's not the most convenient possibility, it's possible to travel by **Amtrak** (tel. 800/872–7245) to Wilmington,

Delaware, then walk over to the **Hertz** offices across from the station and rent a car for the rest of your journey.

EXPLORING

The two entrances to the seashore boundaries are about 1½ hours apart, so decide where you're going to station yourself for the day rather than shuttling back and forth. Then get out and walk or ride a bike (you can rent bikes in the town of Chincoteague). These forms of transport allow you to absorb the setting much more fully than if you're huddled in a car or a tour bus. It's easy to park at the major trailheads, and changing facilities and rest rooms are ample near the major parking areas.

THE BEST IN ONE DAY Again, get out of the car and use your feet. Try the trails recommended under Nature Trails and Short Walks (*see below*) if you want to combine exploring wildlife areas or various island ecosystems with sunbathing or enjoying beach activities. *See* the walk outlined in Longer Hikes, *below,* for a more vigorous trek.

To see the more pristine segments of the shore, you can walk the beachfront 7 mi north of the park or, on the Virginia end of the island, the 12½ mi of beach north of the Toms Cove Visitor Center to the state line. For bay (as opposed to surf) activities, the bayside day-use area on the Maryland end offers a beautiful, unobstructed view of Chincoteague Bay, where you can windsurf for 20 mi to the south, as well as a wonderful picnic spot with tables and one of the best locations for clamming in the summer.

ORIENTATION PROGRAMS Stop for information at the Barrier Island Visitor Center on the Maryland end, or at the Refuge contact station if you enter via the southern portion. A seasonal schedule of events, including interpreter-led walks, videos, demonstrations, and children's activities, should help you plan the day's itinerary. The walks vary from 45 minutes to 2 hours and are an excellent introduction to the Seashore and Refuge. Educational videos play hourly at the Refuge visitor contact station. On the Virginia end, the National Park Service offers beach-oriented activities.

GUIDED TOURS Ranger-led tours, lectures, and nature walks are free and are announced on bulletin boards at the Barrier Island Visitor Center in Maryland and both the Chincoteague Refuge Visitor Station and the Toms Cove Visitor Center in Virginia.

A private operation, **Assateague Island Tours** (tel. 757/336–6155) is the only concessionaire within the boundaries of the Chincoteague National Wildlife Refuge; it maintains a booth at the Chincoteague Refuge Visitor Center. A 1½-hour safari tour ($7), available April–November, takes you on a bus trip through the heart of the Refuge. A Chincoteague Island historical tour is also available.

SCENIC DRIVES AND VIEWS The Wildlife Loop in the Refuge is open to vehicular traffic daily 3 PM–dusk. Ocean lovers need only seek out the coastline for 30 or so mi of amusement. The best view of Chincoteague Bay is probably on the northern end at the bayside day-use area. For opportunities to view wildlife, *see* Flora and Fauna *in* Essential Information, *above, and* Nature Trails and Short Walks *and* Longer Hikes, *below.*

NATURE TRAILS AND SHORT WALKS All the trails on the island are relatively short; only the Refuge's Wildlife Loop (*see below*) exceeds 3 mi. The trails cover flat terrain, paths are well maintained, and trailheads are clearly marked. Walkers and cyclists should stay on them so as not to trample the sand-trapping vegetation that stabilizes dunes or to disturb habitats crucial to the survival of wildlife. Moreover, you're far more likely to pick up disease-carrying ticks off the trail.

Assateague. Three nature trails on the Maryland end of the island—none more than .5 mi long—wander through three different ecosystems. Their trailheads are all within easy walking distance of both the oceanside and bayside campgrounds; the **Life of the Dunes** and **Life of the Forest** trails start right off Bayberry Drive, and the **Life of the Marsh** loop begins about .25 mi northwest of the intersection of Bayberry and Bayside drives. Pick up the booklet *The Life of Assateague* (*see* Publications *in* Essential Information, *above*) on your way into the park, and follow its commentary on local vegetation and animal life as you amble along the flat, sandy pathways. The text's numbered format corresponds to strategically posted signs.

Chincoteague. The Refuge passes out free maps, indicating the locations of trails and nature walks, at both visitor centers. The **Woodland Trail** (1.6 mi) is a short, paved loop appropriate for pedestrians and cyclists as well as people in wheelchairs. The maritime forest is on view here, and visitors can look forward to sighting migrating songbirds, possibly the endangered Delmarva squirrel, and both the native white-tailed deer and the sika elk. Freestanding exhibits dot the trail. While a chance to view the horses isn't guaranteed, interested visitors should stop at the overlook for vistas that include this animal's grazing compartments.

The **Black Duck Trail** is less than .5 mi long and really serves as a connector between the Woodland Trail and the Wildlife Loop, with no trailhead as such. It's for foot, bike, and wheelchair traffic only. The paved path is an interface between two managed impoundments where ducks, geese, swans, and various shorebirds gather.

The little **Lighthouse Trail** is only .25 mi long and covers such unique barrier island habitats as shrub, forest, and dune. A boardwalk is carefully elevated over natural terrain; bikes are not allowed. There is also some steep grade up the side of old sand dunes. The lighthouse is still operated by the Coast Guard.

Swan's Cove Trail is partly paved, partly graveled. The trail starts at the Toms Cove Visitor Center parking lot, and passage is

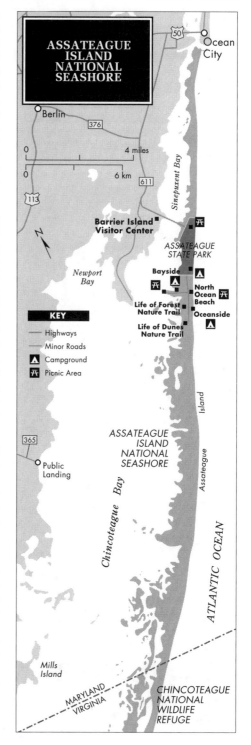

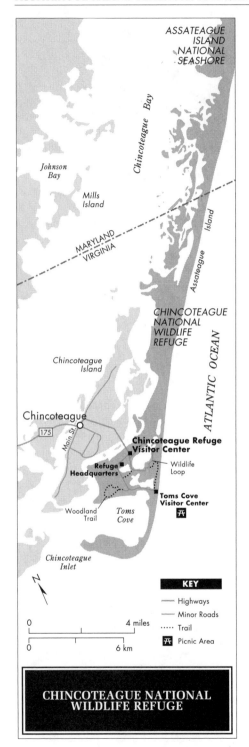

ASSATEAGUE
ISLAND
NATIONAL
SEASHORE

Chincoteague Bay

Johnson
Bay

Mills
Island

MARYLAND
VIRGINIA

Assateague Island

CHINCOTEAGUE
NATIONAL
WILDLIFE
REFUGE

Chincoteague
Island

ATLANTIC OCEAN

Chincoteague

175

Main St.

**Chincoteague Refuge
Visitor Center**

**Refuge
Headquarters**

Wildlife
Loop

**Toms Cove
Visitor Center**

Woodland
Trail

Toms
Cove

Chincoteague
Inlet

N

KEY

—— Highways
—— Minor Roads
····· Trail
🎋 Picnic Area

0   4 miles

0   6 km

**CHINCOTEAGUE NATIONAL
WILDLIFE REFUGE**

permitted to pedestrians and bicyclists only—no mopeds allowed. The 1.25-mi trail parallels the shoreline (though you don't see the Atlantic because the sand dune is high), then bends westward to hook up neatly with the longer Wildlife Loop. Wading birds are commonly sighted here.

The **Wildlife Loop** is a 3.2-mi ellipse, open all day to pedestrians and bicyclists; from 3 PM until dusk, vehicular traffic is also permitted. Begin your walk at the parking lot adjacent to the Chincoteague Refuge Visitor Center, or use one of the smaller trails— Black Duck or Swan's Cove—as a warm-up before heading directly into the loop. The Wildlife Loop crosses over coves, traverses loblolly forests, and borders grass-filled marsh.

LONGER HIKES The beach is where strong walkers can get a workout. Even at low tide, the sand is soft, and walkers end up nearly doubling their actual walking distance because their foot muscles flex an extra 20° to 30° in negotiating the malleable surface. If you're not in great shape, watch out for shinsplints. Or walk backward if you're not too self-conscious. According to park rangers, it minimizes the damage to unpracticed muscle groups.

For a longer walk through numerous ecosystems, habitats, and terrains, park in the lot north of the Toms Cove Visitor Center. Take Swan's Cove Trail to its terminus, and then turn right onto the Wildlife Loop and continue over Snow Goose Pool until you hit an intersection. If you were to turn left here, you'd still be on the loop; but by turning right (bicycles are not permitted beyond this point) you can walk parallel to the shoreline past the first dune crossing (closed to all traffic, including pedestrian) to the second dune crossing. Take this crossing, which is marked D DIKE, all the way to the sea, and walk back to your car along the beach; you can go barefoot from here, if it's warm enough, and pick up shells along the way. You'll have covered about 7 mi, but it will feel like more after walking on the sand. Strong walkers can do the distance easily in an afternoon.

OTHER ACTIVITIES **Back-Road Driving.** Four-wheel-drive vehicles have been scooting up and down the beach on the island's eastern rim for decades. The 12-mi stretch open to off-road vehicles (ORVs) on the Maryland end fills up by 9:30 each weekend morning between Memorial Day and Labor Day.

ORV drivers should call the Seashore or Refuge and request an application for an ORV permit and the brochure entitled "Off-Road Vehicles." Permits cost $60 a year and may be obtained through the mail or in person on either end of the island. The brochure includes a clear map of both the Virginia and Maryland ORV zones, which run north and south along the beach, and indicates the locations of air pumps, emergency telephones, and dune crossings. Trucks must stay on the ocean side of the post areas and adhere to the existing track, for the sake both of the environment and transmissions. The speed limit of 25 mi per hour is strictly enforced. All regulations regarding ORV use (including vehicle size and equipment requirements) are specified in the brochure.

The Maryland Seashore controls ORV traffic by imposing a limit of 145 vehicles; the Virginia end takes only 48 at a time. Bad news for privacy-seekers: Trucks lined up on the shore in the summer may not sit more than 3 or 4 yards apart from each other. During the piping plover's nesting season (March 15–August), the Refuge Hook is closed to all traffic, and the number of ORVs allowed drops to 18. In the event that plovers nest in a four-wheel-drive area in Maryland, the park then seals off the area and .5 mi to the south and north.

Biking. The beach is strictly off-limits; on the Maryland end, use the 3-mi paved path marked for bicycles along Bayberry Drive; in Virginia, pedal around the Wildlife Loop, the Woodland Trail, or Swan's Cove Trail. All are flat, well-maintained routes that present no serious aerobic challenge, and surfaces are paved or sandy with strewn gravel. The Wildlife Loop is best before 3 PM, when the road opens to vehicular traffic.

Go to the south end of the island for rentals. (You won't need anything fancy.) **Piney Island Country Store** (7085 Maddox Blvd., Chincoteague, tel. 757/336–6212) rents bikes for $2 an hour, $7 a day, or $3 and $10, respectively, for one with a child carrier.

Rainy Day Canoes rents bikes from the concession stand at the end of Bayside Drive on Assateague. The rates are $4 an hour, $8 for 4 hours, or $12 for 24 hours.

Bird-Watching. More than 300 species have been spotted on Assateague Island. Although one hears sad tales of endangerment with ever-increasing frequency, the good news is that in the Maryland Seashore both the osprey and brown pelican appear to be recovering from their DDT-inflicted troubles. A brochure available on both ends of the island gives a rundown of the predominantly migratory bird population and tells you when each species is most likely to be sighted. Bring a field guide and binoculars; the serious birder should pack a spotting sight. Check the bulletin boards at the visitor centers for upcoming ranger-led bird walks.

Boating. If you launch from the national seashore, boat motors must not exceed 7.5 horsepower. Canoers launch into Chincoteague Bay from Old Ferry Landing, within a mile of the campgrounds, and venture south to choose from four bayside canoe-in camping sites (off-limits to motorboats). Each site is marked by a sign showing a silhouette of two boaters in a canoe. The closest is 2 mi away, the farthest 13. The sites are open year-round but are most welcoming in the spring and fall; summer mosquitoes drive even the island's horses away. The only permissible landing point in Virginia is at the southernmost tip of the island, called Fishing Point.

Canoe rentals are available at **Rainy Day Canoes** (Rte. 589, Racetrack Rd., Berlin, MD, tel. 410/641–5029) for $20 a day and a

$50 deposit. They also have a concession at the national seashore. **Barnacle Bill's** (3691 S. Main St., Chincoteague, VA, tel. 757/ 336–5188) carries bait, tackle, ice, and maps as well as charter boats.

At the Chincoteague National Wildlife Refuge, boats are allowed to land only at Fishing Point on the Hook (September– March 14).

Fishing. People do fish in the bay (by boat only) on the Maryland end around the first three buoys, but conditions aren't great. In the Refuge, fishing and crabbing are permitted in Toms Cove, Swan's Cove adjacent to Beach Road, and a few other seasonally assigned areas.

Shellfishing. Several succulent bivalves— quahog clams, oysters, ribbed mussels—and the blue crab populate the waters around the island. Oyster season is September 15– March 15 only; clams must measure an inch in width to be kept; crabs of less than 5 inches from point to point must be thrown back, and no crab fishing is permitted from January through March. More than one collapsible crab pot qualifies you as a commercial fisherman, and you will require a license. Ask for the blue "Shellfishing in Maryland" brochure at the Barrier Island Visitor Center: It specifies maximum catches for the day and provides a map showing the best sites for each species. Shellfishing is also allowed near the refuge at Toms Cove, but watch for NO TRESPASSING signs marking oyster beds leased to local watermen.

Surf Fishing. Anglers flock here for flounder, croaker, spot, kingfish, weakfish, black drum, red drum, striped bass, bluefish, northern puffer, and shark. You can fish 24 hours a day if you want, but the rule specifies that all members of your party must be participating. In Virginia an overnight fishing permit is required. Late spring and fall are the optimum seasons, but in summer there are regularly scheduled demonstrations by park experts. The Toms Cove Visitor Center in the Chincoteague National Wildlife Refuge is an official weigh station.

Horseback Riding. *Maryland:* Riding is allowed in the National Seashore October 9–May 14; in the summer and early fall, mosquitoes and flies plague humans and horses alike. If you are traveling with a group that includes five or more horses *or* you intend to stay overnight, you need a permit from the Office of the Superintendent before you arrive. The Horse Group Site, on the ocean side, accommodates no more than 12 units (any combination of motor homes, horse trailers, and tents with vehicles), no more than 25 people, and no more than 25 horses; the overnight charge for the entire site is $25. *Virginia:* Riding is allowed on the oversand vehicle area of the Refuge and the road leading to it.

Shelling. At the national seashore you'll find everything from spiraling whelks and tough little periwinkles to the smooth, concentric sculpture of the surf clam. You may take out no more than one gallon of shells per beach visit. A park checklist available at the Barrier Island Visitor Center describes 30-odd bivalves and gastropods.

Surfing. Daredevils venture out in wet suits weeks before most mortals would consider dipping their toes. Each year designated areas are set aside for surfing; swimming and other beach activities are prohibited there. Ask at the visitor center when you arrive.

Swimming. Between Memorial Day and Labor Day, the North Beach in Maryland and the Toms Cove area of the Refuge offer lifeguarded stretches of beach. At Assateague there is a bathhouse next to the day-use parking lot, where you can shower and change; toilets and potable water are also available. On the Virginia end, two bathhouses with similar facilities sit right off the beach at Toms Cove.

Windsurfing. The bay is ideal when the wind is up. Launch from the bayside day-use area on the Maryland end, and you'll have 20 mi to play in.

CHILDREN'S PROGRAMS **Assateague.** The Barrier Island Visitor Center houses a 500-gallon aquarium, a 110-gallon touch tank populated by harmless marine creatures, and a beachcomber room with hands-on museum displays. Aquarium feedings are held regularly with a young audience in mind. Check the weekly schedule posted at the center for talks or walks that children would enjoy. Many of the park brochures are written in simple prose that will stimulate a child's curiosity. There is also a typed sheet for children, the "Visitor's Center Explorer."

Chincoteague. In summer, the Refuge center offers programs specifically for children, including "Junior Refuge Manager" and "Junior Birder" programs.

EVENING ACTIVITIES Evening programs vary with the season. The Refuge auditorium on the Virginia end offers nighttime lectures and illustrated programs. The Barrier Island Visitor Center in the north schedules weekend evening talks May through October. In summer, National Park Service rangers host outdoor campfire programs several evenings each week.

DINING

Fresh seafood and shellfish are the draw here—crab cakes, fresh flounder, softshell crabs, and Chincoteague oysters. Plenty of fast-food eateries and deli markets operate in Chincoteague (there's a McDonald's immediately outside the Refuge entrance).

INSIDE THE PARK Only one small concession operates on the island, on the Maryland end, on state park grounds east of the state park entrance. Apart from cheeseburgers and ice cream, the menu is limited. It's a good idea to pack your own lunch.

NEAR ASSATEAGUE **Captain's Galley II.** This spruced-up waterfront property on the commercial fishing harbor in West Ocean City has a large seating capacity, and boats are granted free docking privileges for the evening. Fresh seafood, including crab cakes made with Maryland back-fin crabmeat, is the byword. Entrées run $10–$20. *12817 Harbor Rd., West Ocean City, MD, tel. 410/213–2525. Reservations not accepted. AE, D, MC, V. $$*

NEAR CHINCOTEAGUE **Bill's Seafood Restaurant.** Decoys sit atop the window valances, and wooden booths line the walls. Come as early as 5 AM: French toast and sausage will set you back only $3. Dinners feature local seafood—crab cakes, stuffed jumbo flounder—but chicken and steaks are also options. *4037 Main St., Chincoteague, VA, tel. 757/336–5831. AE, D, DC, MC, V. $$*

Village Restaurant. White tablecloths, candles, and pink napkins dress up this dining room and lounge. Fried Chincoteague oysters and softshell crabs top a menu interspersed with nonmarine selections like stuffed veal and calves' liver. There's a long wine list. *6576 Maddox Blvd., Chincoteague, VA, tel. 757/336–5120. AE, D, MC, V. $$*

Maria's Family Restaurant. Maria's is divided into three spaces: a family-style dining room with a big brick fireplace, a quick-stop shop with carryout menu for pizza and subs, and a recreation room next door with video games, pool tables, pinball machines, and piped-in rock. The menu ranges from Italian (manicotti, veal parmigiana) to Eastern Shore (chowder, seafood platters); service is very pleasant. *6506 Maddox Blvd., Chincoteague, VA, tel. 757/336–5040. AE, D, MC, V. $*

PICNIC SPOTS The Maryland end has two designated picnic areas, one on the ocean and one bayside; there is a third near the Toms Cove Visitor Center on the Virginia end. These are exposed day-use sites, furnished with picnic tables and grills only, and no overhead coverings. If you're on the northern end and want to see the water, pick the bayside site; the sand dunes off the ocean site obstruct all views of the sea.

LODGING

Outside of campsites, there are no accommodations at the National Seashore or the Refuge. You can always stay in Ocean City, Maryland, but unless you're into Las Vegas kitsch or miniature golf, we suggest the more appealing Berlin, Maryland, and Chincoteague, Virginia. Do consider a bed-and-breakfast: Rooms aren't always cheap, but the owner/manager's lowdown on local shops and watering holes adds to the value. Book well ahead for the smaller establishments. The fewer the units, the more likely they are to be full.

NEAR ASSATEAGUE **Chanceford Hall.** The town of Snow Hill sits inland on the Pocomoke River, halfway between the national seashore and the wildlife refuge. This bed-and-breakfast, in the heart of historic Snow-hill, was constructed in three stages, beginning with the Georgian front section in 1759. Some 230 years later it was restored and turned into a showplace. The Colonial-style mantels, in cool Williamsburg greens and blues, match the moldings, and there are down comforters on the lace-canopy beds. The house has seven working fireplaces and furniture crafted by the owner. *209 W. Federal St., Snow Hill, MD 21863, tel. 410/632–2231. 4 rooms, 1 suite. Facilities: pool, bicycles, air-conditioning. No credit cards. $$$*

Atlantic Hotel. The historic district in Berlin, Maryland (7 mi from the Seashore), got a boost when a group of local investors renovated and opened the town's Victorian centerpiece, the Atlantic Hotel (built in 1895). The guest rooms line a wide corridor and are decorated with Oriental and floral rugs, tasseled draperies, and Tiffany-style lamps, as well as antique beds. The Victorian touches extend to the piano bar and pricey restaurant downstairs, where you may partake of the Continental breakfast included in the room rate. There's a two-night minimum on summer weekends. *2 N. Main St., Berlin, MD 21811, tel. 410/641–3589 or 800/814–7672, fax 410/641–4928.*

16 rooms. Facilities: restaurant, piano bar. AE, MC, V. $$–$$$

NEAR CHINCOTEAGUE **Watson House Bed & Breakfast.** You can't miss this light-green Victorian. Each room is appointed with modest country furnishings, potted plants, and wicker. A lavish breakfast is included in the rate, as is afternoon tea. The innkeepers also own the property next door, the Inn at Poplar Corner. Poplar Corner has four rooms, all with whirlpool baths and showers. *4240 Main St., Chincoteague, VA 23336, tel. 757/336–1564 or 800/336–6787, fax 757/336–5776. 6 rooms. Facilities: air-conditioning, bicycles. MC, V. $$$*

Refuge Motor Inn. Within walking distance of the Refuge, this two-story motel has a sauna, hot tub, indoor pool, and exercise room, sundeck, picnic tables, and outdoor grills, and offers evening cruises. The decorations are innocuous, with ducks and Canada geese on the wallpaper and shower curtains. Rent a bike to pedal to the Refuge. *7058 Maddox Blvd., Box 378, Chincoteague, VA 23336, tel. 757/336–5511 or 800/544–8469, fax 757/336–6134. 70 rooms, 2 suites. Facilities: indoor pool, hot tub, refrigerators, sauna, exercise room, playground, coin laundry. AE, D, DC, MC, V. $$–$$$*

Beach Road Motel. This motel is five minutes from the Refuge, in downtown Chincoteague near restaurants and night spots. The standard rooms are moderately priced in summer but drop to as low as $38 after Labor Day. All units have an earth-tone decor and include cable TV and small dining tables and chairs. The grounds have grills and picnic tables. *6151 Maddox Blvd., Chincoteague, VA 23336, tel. 757/336–6562 or 800/699–6562. 23 rooms. Facilities: pool, refrigerators. AE, D, MC, V. $–$$*

Mariner Motel. Rooms at this motel, a mile from the Refuge entrance, have cable TV. Continental breakfast is included. *6273 Maddox Blvd., Chincoteague, VA 23336, tel. 757/336–6565 or 800/221–7490, fax 757/336–5351. 92 rooms. Facilities: 2 restaurants, pool, playground, coin laundry, meeting rooms. AE, D, MC, V. $*

CAMPING

Tent campers should bring 18-inch-long stakes: Sandy soil and strong winds render pegs useless. Lock food supplies in car trunks at night. The wild horses can tear off the tops of Styrofoam coolers, rip through tents, and leave your camp looking like a tornado hit it. Don't leave leftovers on picnic tables, either. Food storage regulations are strictly enforced.

The maximum length allowed for a camper/motor home is 36 ft. Most vehicles have a 48-hour storage area for both freshwater and sewage treatment, and they'll do fine here. There's a water fill-up station that can fill storage tanks, and a dump station as well. No electric, sewer, or water hookups are available.

While no camping is permitted in Virginia on the Refuge, there are lots of private campgrounds in Chincoteague. Call or write the **Chincoteague Chamber of Commerce** (Box 258, Chincoteague, VA 23336, tel. 757/336–6161) or call the **Virginia State Travel Service** (tel. 757/824–5000).

Campers on the Maryland end pay $12 a night for a site May 15–October 15, when reservations can be made up to five months in advance. During the rest of the year, sites cost $10 but are doled out on a first-come, first-served basis.

You can reserve a site in person (no later than the day before your arrival), by mail (Assateague National Seashore, Rte. 611, 7206 National Seashore La., Berlin, MD 21811) or by phone (tel. 619/452–8787 or 800/365–2267, TTY 800/274–7275). Credit cards (D, MC, V) are accepted, as is payment by check received at least 10 days before you arrive. Campers may use sites for up to 14 days May–October, and for no more than 30 days during the entire calendar year. Drinking water, chemical toilets, cold showers, and sanitary dumps are available.

The National Seashore offers oceanside and bayside sites. The 104 **oceanside sites** are open year-round and feature drive-in sites for RV and tent camping and walk-in sites for tents only. Each individual site includes a picnic table and standing grill (no ground fires); bring your own firewood or propane stove. The sites are vulnerable to strong winds, which are common.

The 48 **bayside sites** are open spring through fall, with drive-in pads suitable for tents, trailers, and RVs. None are shaded. There are no electrical or water hookups. Fire ring grills (no other fires allowed) are provided. Again, bring your own firewood.

Backcountry camping is permitted at Assateague in Maryland, but the use of an overnight site and parking require a parking permit, and a $5 backcountry camping permit that must be obtained the day you arrive. MISTIX, which administers "frontcountry" campsites May 15–October, does not cover backcountry sites. The leader of each backcountry camping party must obtain permits in person at the campground registration office, off Bayberry Drive, by midafternoon on the day of arrival. Your chances of nailing a site on a summer weekend are 50-50; it's easier before Memorial Day and after Labor Day.

There are ocean- and bayside backcountry sites. Transportation by motor vehicle to any backcountry camp is prohibited. The two **oceanside sites,** open year-round, are hike-in only; the nearest is 4 mi from parking. The signs on the beach are hard to see. Chemical toilets and picnic tables are provided, but drinking water is not. There are emergency telephones at dune crossings 7 and 12.

The four **bayside sites** are open year-round, but biting insects make summer uncomfortable. All four are tent-only, hike-in or canoe-in. There's a seven-day limit. **Assateague State Park** (tel. 410/641–2120 or 410/641–2918), next door, has hot showers and costs more.

Biscayne National Park
Florida

By Herb Hiller

Updated by Diane P. Marshall

ristine, magical, subtropical Florida exists in Biscayne National Park as it exists nowhere else today except in the imagination. The coral reef to the south has become increasingly troubled by turbidity, and a new management plan for the Florida Keys National Marine Sanctuary (mostly to the south and west) seeks to reverse damage from local conditions, such as nutrient overload in shore waters caused by inadequate sewage treatment, among other problems. But though you can see Miami's towers from many of the park's 44 islands, Biscayne is virtually undeveloped and large enough for escaping everything that Miami and the Upper Keys have become. Here, preserved on 181,000 mostly watery acres, along the northernmost reach of what for many Americans remains paradise, the reef is healthy.

Biscayne was established in its present form in 1980. One of the newest parks in the national system, it marks a turning point for the state—from runaway development to preservation of the one-of-a-kind realms that, since being promoted a little more than a century ago, have made Florida a favorite vacation land. The park is largely underwater, and its islands remain unbridged— conditions that have always attracted adventurers. These days, to be sure, the adventuring is on the milder side, the sort that appeals to snorkelers and divers, hikers, campers, and anglers.

In 1992 Hurricane Andrew slapped the park with winds in excess of 150 mph that mowed down the jungle canopy and sheared the park's coastal mangroves. Surging seas tumbled deep-water corals at the edge of the Gulf Stream. Park headquarters and the visitor center were badly damaged. The new facilities that replaced these in summer 1997 are bigger and more comprehensive. Camping and informal ranger-led tours on weekends have resumed on Elliott and Boca Chita keys and hiking trails have reopened on these and Adams Key.

But Hurricane Andrew's damage was nothing compared to the ruin that loomed only 30 years ago. Pressed by developers eager to promote the next Miami Beach, the county government had incorporated the bay realm as the municipality of Islandia; there were plans to link these northernmost keys by a 20-mi causeway from the foot of Key Biscayne to the head of Key Largo.

Instead, history blinked. As alarm grew that the beauty of the upper keys and the surrounding waters might be lost forever, one of South Florida's folk heroes, then-Congressman Dante B. Fascell, arranged for the purchase of the islands and the bay portion by the federal government. In 1968 most of the present-day park was designated as Biscayne National Monument. Six years later the boundary was adjusted to connect with the northern boundary of John Pennekamp Coral Reef State Park. In 1980 Congress upgraded Biscayne's status to national park.

Today Biscayne attracts more than a half-million visitors a year. Boatless visitors come mainly during the cooler months, especially January through April, when mosquitoes are less active. A concessionaire at the Convoy Point Visitor Center provides boat service to the reefs for divers, snorkelers, and glass-bottom viewers, but service to the islands only by prior arrangement. As 95% of the park is water-based, most visitors have their own boats and come in the calmer, drier months, which are better for boating and reef-viewing. The side-by-side mainland cities of Homestead and Florida City, newly revived since Hurricane Andrew, provide anything else that visitors might need. Boating the shallow waters of the bay can be risky, and getting pulled off the bottom is costly. Biscayne is for people who know what they're doing—and whose idea of a good time is somewhat more demanding than plopping down at a resort.

ESSENTIAL INFORMATION

VISITOR INFORMATION **Biscayne National Park** (Box 1369, Homestead 33090–1369, tel. 305/230–7275, fax 305/230–1190) is open daily 8–5:30. The visitor center is open weekdays 8:30–4:30 (until 5 June–Aug.), weekends 8:30–5. The park's **Web site** is www.nps.gov/bisc.

Pets are limited to a special area at Convoy Point and Elliott Key.

FEES No fees are charged for admission or for access to the islands, but there is a $15 charge to berth private vessels overnight at the Elliott Key and Boca Chita Key docks. The park concessionaire charges for trips to the coral reefs and to the park's islands (see Guided Tours, Boating, and Diving and Snorkeling in Exploring, below).

PUBLICATIONS Literature beyond the official park brochure is limited. *Biscayne: The Story Behind the Scenery,* by L. Wayne Landrum, the park's former chief ranger, provides beautiful pictures and adequate descriptions of the principal zones of interest, but it overlooks the story of how the park was saved for the public. It costs $5.95. Free (though with advertising) is *Everglades & Biscayne National Parks,* published by

American Park Network (100 Pine St, Suite 2850, San Francisco, CA 94111, tel. 415/788–2228). This booklet contains more practical information (such as advice on taking pictures), but it's slanted toward Everglades. Both are available at the park.

GEOLOGY AND TERRAIN The park occupies the southern portion of Biscayne Bay, below Miami and north of the bridged Florida Keys. Its area combines four distinct zones of water and land formed during the last Ice Age, some 10,000 years ago. From shore to sea, the zones are mangrove forest along the coast; Biscayne Bay, a shallow nursery for marine life; the undeveloped upper Florida Keys; and the coral reefs. The park is 95% below water and ranges from 4 ft above sea level to 10 fathoms, or 60 ft, below.

The topography was formed as glaciers alternately advanced, absorbing water, and retreated, releasing water, thereby gently cradling the formation of life in the shallows. Freshwater released by the glacier in its last retreat combined with the lagoon contained by the outer reefs along the edge of the Gulf Stream, creating the brackish basin that remains today.

During interglacial periods, when the climate was warmer and the sea level higher, a chain of patch reefs grew in the shallow sea. These reefs were formed by the interaction of corals and algae in a process only slightly different from what goes on today. Corals and algae both extracted chemicals from the sea, which they converted to calcium carbonate and which over centuries became compacted into limestone. (Erosion of this limestone was the primary source of South Florida's beaches.) Then, as seawater was reabsorbed by advancing glaciers, lowering the level of the sea, the limestone formations emerged above the surface, attracted plant life, and became what we know as the Florida Keys.

Reef building continues today, though the process is microscopic. Branching corals add about 3 inches a year, while a hard coral may take 50 years to reach the size of a basketball. The corals are actually colonies of tiny, soft-bodied polyps that catch drifting plankton with outstretched tentacles. They use the calcium to build skeletons, which form the shapes so attractive to snorkelers and divers. The clustered corals form reefs, attracting a huge and diverse population; sea life lodges in every hole and crack.

The reef-building process is as geographically limited as it is slow, because the corals tolerate only the narrowest range of conditions. Seawater must be clean, bright, and just the right temperature and depth. Conditions at Biscayne remain salubrious, though the reefs are ever threatened by pollution from the mainland, the grounding of ships, and fisherfolk and recreational divers who drop anchor on them and otherwise do harm by touching or removing portions of them.

FLORA AND FAUNA Biscayne's corals range from the soft, flagellant fans, plumes, and whips found chiefly in the shallower patch reefs to the hard brain corals, elkhorn, and staghorn forms that can withstand the heavier wave action and depths along the ocean's edge. But some of the forms that predominate on each set of reefs are also found on the other.

More than 200 species of fish inhabit the reefs, from flamboyant angelfish, wrasses, and neon gobies to ordinary moray eels. Some, like the grunts, dart about in schools of hundreds, swimming with balletlike precision. Sharp-beaked parrot fish can be seen—even heard—munching on coral, from which they extract algae and coral polyps. (They're the only creatures allowed to molest the corals.)

This marine life depends heavily on the park's plant life, particularly the red mangrove trees that line the mainland shore of the bay and the islands and have roots that arch low above the shallow waters. The roots filter out pollutants from the shore while providing a safe habitat for microscopic sea life and an incubator for young shrimp and fish, which feed here before venturing into the fish-eat-fish reefs and depths beyond.

Most of the islands are covered with dense tropical forests formed from seeds borne here on the north-flowing winds and currents of the Caribbean. These hardwood forests, called hammocks, include such species as the buttonwood, gumbo-limbo, Jamaican dogwood, lignum vitae, mahogany, pigeon plum, poisonwood, red and black mangrove, strangler fig, torchwood, and wild lime. The forest on Boca Chita Key has similar native species thanks to a recently completed revegetation program.

Walking along trails through the keys, you are likely to see other natives such as zebra butterflies, the rare Schaus swallowtail butterfly, and golden orb spiders. Raccoons, rabbits, and various rodents live here (they are not to be fed). Bird life includes brown pelicans, white ibis, blue herons, snowy egrets, and other wading birds, as well as bald eagles, ospreys, and peregrine falcons. In spring and fall you may see a few migratory species as well.

HUMAN HISTORY The pre-Columbian Tequesta, the first known inhabitants of the area, seem to have collected the abundant seafood, fashioned their canoes from trees of the hammocks, and crafted implements from shells.

The Spanish nominally controlled these islands for 300 years, beginning in the early 16th century. Before Florida's acquisition by the United States in 1821, the islands had become hideouts for pirates who raided merchant ships in the offshore straits. Among the last of these was Black Caesar. One version of his legend is that he was a 6½-ft-tall African who intercepted slave ships and set the slaves free on uninhabited islands on both sides of the straits. The name Caesar Creek (between Adams Key and Old Rhodes Key) bears witness to his exploits—as may a yet-undiscovered 24 tons of silver he is said to have buried just before the U.S. Navy captured him in 1822.

Wreckers followed pirates. Ostensibly, they salvaged cargo and crew from ships that ran aground on the reefs. But many ships were lured to their doom by venal wreckers who flashed false navigational lights luring ships onto the very reefs they sought to avoid. Records verify 499 wrecks between 1848 and 1858 alone, with a combined loss valued at $16.3 million. The situation changed after the government began building aids to navigation; by 1900, wrecking was no longer profitable.

Later inhabitants grew pineapples, limes, tomatoes, and yams; smuggled liquor during Prohibition; and carved out playtime hideaways for the wealthy. Mark Honeywell, of the company best known for its heating system controls, owned Boca Chita Key from 1937 to 1945. His most notable legacy, a 65-ft decorative tower, was built as a lighthouse but was never approved by the Coast Guard.

Adams Key was the site of the Cocolobo Club, where rich and famous visitors included Presidents Harding, Hoover, Roosevelt, Johnson, and Nixon. Elliott Key, the park's largest island, was once the site of Camp Recovery, a county detox center for alcoholics.

One of the most colorful chapters of the pre–national park era will end only in 1999, when state-issued leases expire on the remaining homes in Stiltsville, just below Key Biscayne. The park plans to renew none of them. Starting in the early '30s, the rustic houses here were built on pilings. At one time 14 occupied the tidal flats, but most of them have been lost to hurricane and fire; only a few remain.

The Ragged Keys, just north of Boca Chita Key, are still privately owned.

WHEN TO GO The park is open year-round. Mosquitoes, however, can be as much a problem on the islands as they are on the mainland during South Florida's long summer. Most of the region's 65 or so inches of rain falls during this time of year, typically in brief but drenching afternoon showers. Hurricanes, too, are a summer and fall phenomenon. Thus, it's best to visit the islands between November and April; the reefs, however, are best viewed in summer. Temperatures in winter drop to the 50s and 60s (in extreme cases, the low 40s) at night and rise to the high 60s and low 70s by day. Humidity is especially high in summer, along with temperatures in the 80s and low 90s.

SEASONAL EVENTS **Late-Aug.:** Over the last consecutive Wednesday and Thursday in August, the park holds a **Lobster Mini-Season,** during which lobsters can be harvested. **Mid-Oct.:** The **Columbus Day Regatta** brings thousands of boats onto the bay for debauchery as much as for sport.

WHAT TO PACK Biscayne is a water park, so you'll want swimsuits, T-shirts, shorts, hardy footwear or water shoes, sunscreen, and maybe jeans and a long-sleeve shirt and hat if you burn easily. (Here, most people do. The summer sun is especially hot.) Binoculars are useful, as are mosquito repellent in summer and a backpack if you plan to hike much of the 7-mi trail on Elliott Key. None of the islands provides food facilities, and only Elliott Key has potable water. Snorkelers and divers will want to bring their gear or rent what they need from the park's concessionaire, the **Biscayne National Underwater Park Company** (tel. 305/230–1100). There is nothing to dress up for in the park.

GENERAL STORES The nearest grocery store is **Cole's Bait and Tackle Shop** (Homestead Bayfront Park, tel. 305/230–3090), which is open daily 7–7 and is just across the canal from Biscayne National Park (less than a mile by car). The shop stocks sandwiches that can be microwaved, soft drinks, coffee, and beer—stuff to get by on. (You must pay the $3.50 park admission to get to the store.) The nearest supermarkets and convenience stores are in Homestead, 9 mi west. The concessionaire at Biscayne National Park's Convoy Point sells candy bars as well as snacks and sandwiches.

ATMS Sites in Homestead, 9 mi west of the park, include **Barnett Bank** (850 Homestead Blvd. [U.S. 1], tel. 305/825–3376); **Coconut Grove Bank** (777 N. Krome Ave., tel. 305/245–6666); and **First National**

Bank of Homestead (1550 N. Krome Ave.; 1750 N.E. 8th St., tel. 305/247–5541).

ARRIVING AND DEPARTING Other than by boat, which is how most visitors arrive, you can enter Biscayne National Park by car, charter bus, and bicycle. The park is an uninteresting place to hike to. The entry is 9 mi east of Homestead and 9 mi south and east of Exit 6 (Speedway Blvd./S.W. 137th Ave.) off the Florida Turnpike.

By Bus. Greyhound/Trailways makes three trips daily from Miami International Airport and the Miami depot (4111 N.W. 27th St., Miami, tel. 305/871–1810) to the Homestead Bus Station (5 N.E. 3rd Rd., tel. 305/247–2040). Fare is $10 one-way, $19 round-trip. A cab from there costs $20–$25.

By Car. The drive is about an hour from the airport. Take LeJeune Road south from the airport to Route 836, and head west to either Route 826/874 or the Florida Turnpike; get on and head south to Exit 6. Two toll stations on Route 826/872 require 25¢ and 75¢ (more for RVs.). There are three tolls on the turnpike.

By Plane. The nearest airport is Miami International. Several car rental agencies have desks in the airport, and another dozen or so have offices immediately south of the airport on or just off LeJeune Road.

By Train. The nearest **Amtrak** station is at 8303 N.W. 37th Avenue, near Hialeah. Dade County Bus (tel. 305/638–6700) No. 42 Coconut Grove departs the station for the airport, where you can rent a car or take Greyhound to Florida City (*see* By Bus, *above*). It's another 9 mi east. The trip takes less than 30 minutes. Fare is $1.25. The fare machine accepts dollar bills.

EXPLORING

Biscayne is a great place if you want to dive, snorkel, canoe, camp, watch birds, and learn about marine ecology. The nearest accommodations are 9 mi to the west—they're commercial all the way. There are no restaurants and no bucolic cycling trails. The park concessionaire provides dive trips, canoe rentals, and drop-offs for island camping. With your own boat you can explore, laze on the water, camp on the beach, head down to the lower Florida Keys, fish, snorkel, and dive.

THE BEST IN ONE DAY Most visitors come to snorkel or dive; most have their own boats. If you don't have access to a boat of your own, it's best to schedule a trip with the park concessionaire, **Biscayne National Underwater Park Company** (tel. 305/230–1100). Divers should plan to spend the morning on the water, the afternoon exploring the Convoy Point Visitor Center. Snorkel trips (and one-tank shallow dive trips) depart in the afternoon, leaving the morning to stop by the visitor center. With your own boat, you can set your own schedule to see the visitor center, dive, and visit Elliott Key to hike the trails. Be sure to apply mosquito repellent, as well as sunscreen, regardless of time of year.

ORIENTATION PROGRAMS The Convoy Point Visitor Center has a museum with hands-on exhibits and dioramas, a weather station, a 50-seat auditorium that shows videos, a ranger information area, a bookstore, rest rooms, and vending machines. The Discovery Room has exhibits that teach you about issues relating to the park. The wraparound porch affords visitors gorgeous views of mangroves, Biscayne Bay, and the Miami skyline. This is the only area of the park accessible without a boat. There are special events throughout the year open to the public, as well as environmental educational programs for groups and schools.

GUIDED TOURS Biscayne National Underwater Park Company (Box 1270, Homestead 33030, tel. 305/230–1100), the park's authorized concessionaire, operates daily 9–5:30 from an office in the visitor center. Year-round, the company runs a 53-ft glass-bottom boat, *Reef Rover IV,* for sightseeing on the reefs. Though schedules vary depending on weather and demand, trips generally depart daily at 10 AM and last about three hours; the cost is $19.95. Advance reservations are essential. Go/no-go decisions are made two hours before scheduled departure times. It's a good idea to call. This same company also has a 45-ft catamaran used for snorkeling and diving tours. Call for more details.

TRAILS AND HIKES The best land exploring is on Elliott Key, which has free slips for 64 boats and offers campsites, drinking fountains, rest rooms with freshwater showers, and a swimming area with marker buoys north of the harbor. Elliott is the largest of the keys (more than 7 mi long), with a trail running nearly its whole length and a shorter loop trail, with a boardwalk, of slightly more than a mile from bay to ocean and around. The 7-mi trail is known as the Spite Highway. When the government announced its intention to purchase the keys for park use, quashing the developers' dream of an offshore resort, the owners of the island began bulldozing the land to preclude public use. They quit under pressure—but not before destroying many inland areas of ecological and scenic importance. The "highway," which was once 120 ft wide, has been steadily filling back in from both sides; it has become a more scenic, more canopied trail.

OTHER ACTIVITIES Bird-Watching. The park is a bird sanctuary, with more than 170 species sighted around the islands. Expect to see flocks of brown pelicans patrolling the bay—suddenly rising, then plunging beak first to capture prey in their baggy pouches. White ibis probe exposed mud flats for small fish and crustaceans. Large colonies of little blue herons, snowy egrets, and other wading birds nest seasonally in the protected refuge of the Arsenicker Keys, where visitors are not allowed ashore. Jones Lagoon, south of Adams Key, between Old Rhodes Key and Totten Key, is another good spot. It's approachable only by canoes, kayaks, and inflatables.

More rarely seen are the American peregrine falcon, which migrates through the park; the bald eagle, which can sometimes be seen in coastal or inland areas; and the wood stork, a large white wading bird with a black head and black wing linings.

Boating. Canoes can be rented from the park concessionaire (*see* Guided Tours, *above*) at $8 an hour, $22 for a half-day, or $25 for a full day. The nearest source for sailboat rentals is Miami, at **Castle Harbor Sailing** (3400 Pan American Dr., Dinner Key Marina, Coconut Grove, tel. 305/858–3212). Rentals start at $26 an hour ($84 for a half-day, $130 for a full day) for a 23-ft Pearson Ensign day sailor and run to $350 for a full day for a 41-footer. Captained boats are also available. It's about a four-hour sail to Elliott Key. **Club Nautico** (2560 S. Bayshore Dr., Monty's Marina, Coconut Grove, tel. 305/858–6258) has the closest powerboat rentals. Rates start at $120 for two hours, $199 for a half-day, and $299 for a full day for a 20-ft Horizon.

There is no channel into Elliott Key harbor. The harbor entrance can be less than 3 ft deep at low tide. University Dock, 2 mi to the north, contains a marked anchorage area, dock, and sandy beach. There are no other facilities here. Note that waterskiers are required to stay out of the anchorage area and at least 100 ft from other boats and docks.

Diving and Snorkeling. Pick your reef or wreck and follow these steps: Anchor at least 300 ft from any other anchored boat; drop your hook in a sand patch and not on the corals (the lightest bottom in the clear water is sand); fly your dive flag whether you're diving or snorkeling; slip on your gear, and you're overboard. Beginning divers will want to explore any of the nearly 100 patch reefs 2–3 mi east of Old Rhodes and Elliott keys (among the most popular are Dome, Elkhorn, Schooner, and Star Coral reefs). An easy boat ride from Caesar Creek, all stand in less than 6 ft of water; use charts for navigation. The outer reefs attract a wider variety of sea life, including the larger snapper and grouper and the migratory game fish that range

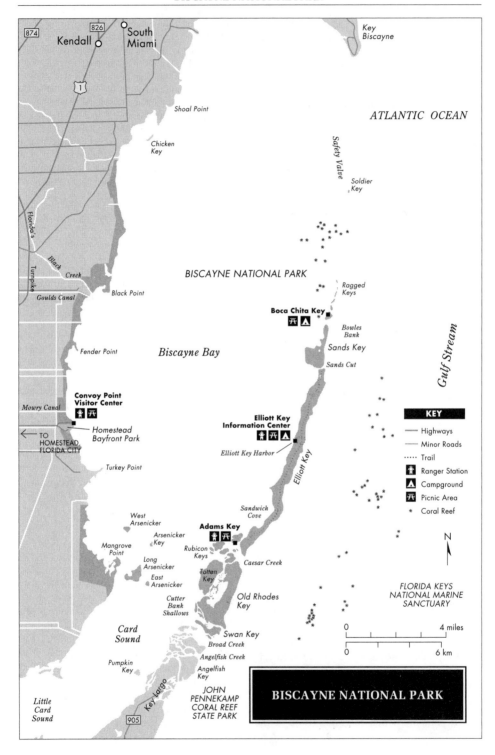

874 | Kendall ○ | 826 | ○ South Miami | Key Biscayne

1

Shoal Point

ATLANTIC OCEAN

Chicken Key

Safety Valve

Soldier Key

Florida's

Black Creek

BISCAYNE NATIONAL PARK

Turnpike

Goulds Canal

Black Point

Ragged Keys

Boca Chita Key

Bowles Bank

Sands Key

Fender Point

Biscayne Bay

Sands Cut

Gulf Stream

Convoy Point Visitor Center

Mowry Canal

Homestead Bayfront Park

Elliott Key Information Center

← TO HOMESTEAD FLORIDA CITY

Elliott Key Harbor

KEY

——— Highways

Turkey Point

Elliott Key

——— Minor Roads

········ Trail

Ranger Station

Campground

Picnic Area

* Coral Reef

West Arsenicker

Sandwich Cove

Arsenicker Key

Adams Key

Mangrove Point

Rubicon Keys

Long Arsenicker

Caesar Creek

FLORIDA KEYS NATIONAL MARINE SANCTUARY

East Arsenicker

Totten Key

N

Cutter Bank Shallows

Old Rhodes Key

Card Sound

Swan Key

0   4 miles

Broad Creek

0   6 km

Pumpkin Key

Angelfish Creek

Angelfish Key

Key Largo

JOHN PENNEKAMP CORAL REEF STATE PARK

BISCAYNE NATIONAL PARK

Little Card Sound

905

through the Gulf Stream. Barracuda and sharks are everywhere, but neither is likely to trouble you if you're not spearfishing. Legare Anchorage, east of Sands Key and north of Elliott Key, is off-limits to divers.

The park concessionaire (see Guided Tours, above) operates two sightseeing boats for snorkeling and dive trips. You'll need a reservation. Schedules vary with weather and demand; departures for the two-tank dive trips are generally Wednesday, Friday, Saturday, and Sunday at 8:30; for snorkel trips and one-tank shallow-dive trips, daily at 1:30. Trips usually last four hours. All snorkelers pay $27.95 per person, including mask, fins, snorkel, and vest. Divers pay $35, with equipment rental extra for those who haven't brought their own. Full equipment rental is $37. In-the-water trips generally give snorkelers and divers two hours on the reef. Since go/no-go decisions are made only two hours before scheduled departure times, it's a good idea to call ahead. Reservations are advised. Show up at least 45 minutes before departure or your reservation will be canceled.

Fishing. On the flats look for bonefish, permit, and tarpon, available year-round, as are the fish found around the reefs: snapper, grouper, and grunt. Deep-water catches may include billfish, bluefish, mackerel, and sailfish—all migratory and typically found in winter (though billfish and sailfish often show up in summer, too)—and dolphin, typically found in summer and ranging from schoolies to 60–70 pounders. Deep-water fish tend to be found wherever their food—flying fish and ballyhoo—are. Boating conditions vary widely in the Gulf Stream. Sometimes a 30-footer can't get out, but other times you can take a canoe out. Everything depends on how the wind is blowing. Your best bet is to bring up the Weather Channel on your radio or TV to learn the sea and wind conditions for the coming day. The National Oceanic and Atmospheric Administration (NOAA) gives additional information on marine VHF radio.

Swimming. The only designated swimming area is just north of the harbor on Elliott Key. There's open ocean swimming with surf, depending on winds, on the east side of Elliott Key. Neither the northern nor the eastern site has lifeguards. You can swim almost anywhere in the park. Put out a dive flag so other boaters know you're in the water.

DINING

No food is available inside the park other than the snacks sold by the Convoy Point concessionaire. There are **picnic areas** on Elliott Key, Adams Key, and Boca Chita Key, and at Convoy Point.

NEAR THE PARK Your best bets for nearby dining are Florida City and Homestead, both 9 mi west of the park. Key Largo is less than 20 mi south of Florida City and has dozens of restaurants in varied price ranges.

Chez Jean Claude. Since 1990, this 60-seat restaurant in a '30s Mediterranean-style house has specialized in the Alsatian and French regional cooking of its owner-chef. The decor inside features French art prints, white table covers, and fresh flowers in each of three intimate rooms. The prix-fixe menu features rack of lamb, fresh seafood, several homemade linguine dishes, beef Burgundy, filet mignon, and aged steaks. Desserts include chocolate rum truffle cake, peach melba, key lime pie, and German apple torte. To get here from the park (about 15 minutes), drive west on S.W. 328th Street to Krome Avenue; turn right to the restaurant. This is the best restaurant near the park. *1235 N. Krome Ave. (corner of N.E. 13th St.), Homestead, tel. 305/248–4671. Reservations essential. AE, MC, V. No lunch. Closed Mon. $$–$$$*

Mutineer Restaurant. Former Sheraton Hotels builder Allan Bennett built this upscale roadside restaurant with its indoor-outdoor fish and duck pond when Florida City was barely on the map (1980). Bilevel dining rooms are divided by sea scenes in etched glass; there are striped velvet chairs, stained glass, and a few portholes, but no excess. The Wharf Lounge, behind its solid oak doors, is imaginatively decorated with a magnified aquarium and nautical antiques, including a crow's nest with stuffed crow, a gold parrot, and a treasure chest. The big menu lists 18 seafood entrées plus another half dozen daily seafood specials, as well as game, ribs, and steaks. Favorites include barbecued baby back ribs, whole Dungeness crab, and snapper Oscar (topped with crab-meat and asparagus). There's live music Thursday–Saturday evenings. *11 S.E. 1st Ave. (corner U.S. 1 and Palm Dr.), Florida City, tel. 305/245–3377. Reservations essential. AE, D, DC, MC, V. $$*

Richard Accursio's Capri Restaurant and King Richard's Room. The best Italian food near the park has been served here, between Florida City and Homestead, since 1958. The place feels like a Rotary-meeting site (which it is): clubby in its darkness, with captain's chairs and banquettes. Locals show up to indulge in the special-ties, which include pizza with light, crunchy crusts and ample toppings; mild, meaty conch chowder; mussels in garlic or marinara sauce; pasta shells stuffed with ricotta cheese in tomato sauce; yellowtail snapper Française; and key lime pie with plenty of real key lime juice. From 4:30 to 6:30, six early-bird entrées are offered for $8.95, including soup or salad and potato or spaghetti. *935 N. Krome Ave., Florida City, tel. 305/247–1544. Reservations essential. AE, MC, V. Closed Sun. $–$$*

Angie's Cafe. The breakfasts and lunches at this 90-seat homespun tropical roadside restaurant are local, fresh, and cooked to order. In the morning you might get corned beef hash and eggs, Angie's Italian sand-wich (fried egg, melted cheese, and Italian ham on an English muffin), or a special with an egg, pancake, and strip of bacon or sausage. Lunch favorites include the Italian salad, grouper sandwich, and the "crabby crabber" (crab legs, fresh spinach, and Monterey Jack grilled on rye). The restau-rant is on U.S. 1, just before the road nar-rows on its way to the Keys. *404 S.E. 1st Ave. on U.S. 1, Florida City, tel. 305/245–8939. Reservations not accepted. No credit cards. No dinner. $*

El Toro Taco. The Hernandez family makes some of the best Mexican food you can find—quite an accomplishment in this com-munity with a large Mexican population. Salt-free tortillas and nacho chips are made with Texas corn cooked and sometimes ground themselves. The cilantro-dominated salsa is mild; if you like more fire, mix in minced jalapeño peppers. Specialties in-clude chili *rellenos* (green peppers stuffed with chunks of ground beef and topped with three kinds of cheese) and chicken fajitas marinated in Worcestershire sauce and served with tortillas and salsa. Breakfast, lunch, and dinner are served. *1 S. Krome Ave., Homestead, tel. 305/245–8182. Reser-vations not accepted. BYOB. D, MC, V. $*

Potlikker's. This southern country-style restaurant takes its name from the broth left over after the boiling of greens. Plants hang from open rafters in the lofty pine-lined din-ing room. Among the specialties are lemon-pepper chicken breast with lemon sauce, fresh-carved roast turkey with homemade dressing, and at least 11 vegetables served with lunch and dinner entrées. Try the 4-inch-tall frozen key lime pie; it tastes great if you dawdle while it thaws. *591 Washington Ave., Homestead, tel. 305/248–0835. Reser-vations not accepted. AE, MC, V. $*

Tiffany's. Descendants of a pioneer family designed this charming tearoom-restaurant amid a complex of specialty shops to resemble a Miami pioneer homestead. For breakfast try Belgian waffles with fresh strawberries and whipped cream or apple-cranberry topping. Lunch dishes include crabmeat au gratin, asparagus supreme (rolled in ham with hollandaise sauce), and Caesar salad with chicken or seafood. Save room for the strawberry whipped-cream cake or the harvest pie (filled with apples, cranberries, walnuts, and raisins and topped with caramel and walnuts). *22 N.E.*

15th St., Homestead, tel. 305/246–0022. Reservations essential. MC, V. No dinner. Closed Mon. $

LODGING

NEAR THE PARK There is no lodging other than island camping within the park; you can stay in Homestead, Florida City, or Key Largo, which is less than 20 mi south of Florida City.

Best Western Gateway to the Keys. This two-story motel, which sits well back from the highway, has spacious closets, a heat lamp in the bathroom, and complimentary Continental breakfast. Standard rooms come with either two queen-size beds or one king-size. More expensive rooms come with a wet bar, fridge, microwave, and coffeemaker. Otherwise it's a standard modern motel (e.g., floral prints and twin reading lamps). 1 Strano Blvd., Florida City, 33034, tel. 305/246–5100, fax 305/242–0056. 114 rooms. Facilities: pool, hot tub, coin laundry. AE, D, DC, MC, V. $$

Days Inn. This motel at the end of the Florida Turnpike is almost on par with the Hampton Inn (see below). The rooms are stylish, with floral bedcovers and armoires. Vacationers who want quiet, comfort, and good rates will be happy here. During races at the nearby Motorsports Complex, room rates double and triple. 51 S. Homestead Blvd. (U.S. 1), Homestead 33030, tel. 305/245–1260, fax 305/247–0939. 110 rooms. Facilities: restaurant, bar, no-smoking rooms, pool, coin laundry. AE, D, DC, MC, V. $$

Hampton Inn. This two-story motel just off the highway has clean rooms and guest-friendly policies, including free Continental breakfast and free local calls. All rooms have at least two upholstered chairs, twin reading lamps, and a desk and chair. This motel has a diving-package deal with the park. 124 E. Palm Dr., 33034, tel. 305/247–8833 or 800/426–7866, fax 305/247–6456. 123 rooms. Facilities: pool. AE, D, DC, MC, V. $$

National 6. The chief advantage of this plain, two-story, gray-and-white motel is that it's next to the Tropical Everglades Visitor Center. People pick it mostly for that reason and typically stay one night, on the way to or from the Keys. The rooms, done in pickled wood paneling with blue carpet, are not noteworthy. 100 U.S. 1, Florida City 33034, tel. 305/248–4202 or 800/626–8357. 160 rooms. Facilities: pool, coin laundry. AE, D, MC, V. $$

Super 8. These standard rooms in a pair of one-story buildings would hardly rate notice anywhere else. In Florida City, however, many other choices are either more expensive or not affiliated with a chain; additionally, these rooms are quiet. Avoid rooms 148–151 and 101–104, nearest the road. 1202 N. Krome Ave., Florida City 33034, tel. 305/245–0311, fax 305/247–9136. 52 rooms. Facilities: coin laundry. AE, D, DC, MC, V. $–$$

Rodeway Inn. This one-story, U-shape motel stands directly across from the Pioneer Museum. The rooms are clean, if basic, and are done in brown and tan. Some have fridges, for which there's no extra charge. The place is utterly commercial, with much paved parking space inside the U. It's your best bet for cheap doubles (as low as $36) in the summer. 815 N. Krome Ave., Florida City 33034, tel. and fax 305/248–2741. 45 rooms. Facilities: no-smoking rooms, pool, coin laundry. AE, D, MC, V. $–$$

CAMPING

The only two places at present where you may camp within the park are at Elliott Key and Boca Chita Key, both accessible only by boat. There is no charge for tent sites, which are available on a first-come, first-served basis. Freshwater showers are available; potable water is available on Elliott Key only. Permits are not required.

Boca Chita Key Campground. This primitive camping area has no designated sites. Saltwater toilets, picnic tables, grills, and nature trails are among the facilities. There's no fresh water. You can visit the nonworking lighthouse, which is open periodically—usually on weekends. There's a small harbor and a sea wall with places to tie up your boat ($15 docking fee). *8 mi off shore from the park's visitor center, tel. 305/230–7275, fax 305/230–1190.*

Elliott Key Campground. Rather than designated sites at this island campground, there's an open camping area for you to pitch your tent. Since you can only reach the island by boat, this campground is never full. You can hike the short nature trails, swim, sunbathe on the small beach, and watch an automated audiovisual program about the ecosystem. Facilities include drinking water, rest rooms, cold showers, picnic tables, a ranger station, and a boat harbor with 50 slips. There's a $15 docking fee per night. *7 mi off shore from the park's visitor center, tel. 305/230–7275, fax 305/230–1190.*

Miami/Homestead KOA. This park has sod and gravel RV and trailer sites up to 40 ft wide, with full hookups and pull-throughs. Facilities include a recreational hall, fire pit, and liquid propane gas. There are also two air-conditioned cabins. *20675 S.W. 162nd Ave., Miami 33187, tel. 305/233–5300, fax 305/252–9027. 275 sites, 2 cabins. Facilities: pool, hot tub, coin laundry. AE, D, MC, V. $*

Southern Comfort RV Resort. This campground has 350 RV sites with full hookups, 70 pull-throughs, a barbecue area with a full-service bar, a recreation pavilion, liquid propane gas, 24-hour coin laundry, shuffleboard, organized activities December–March, cable TV, and a store. It's 6 mi from Everglades National Park and 7 mi from Biscayne National Park. *345 E. Palm Dr., Florida City 33034, tel. 305/248–6909, fax 305/242–1345. 350 sites. Facilities: bar, pool, coin laundry. MC, V.*

The Blue Ridge Parkway
Virginia, North Carolina

By Paul Calhoun

Updated by W. Lynn Seldon, Jr.

his 469-mi-long scenic corridor traverses the spine of the southern Appalachian Mountains from Shenandoah National Park, in Virginia, to Great Smoky Mountains National Park, on the North Carolina–Tennessee border. It has much in common with the parks at its northern and southern limits—notably the motor-vehicle access to hiking, camping, and picnicking opportunities; cultural and historical attractions; and modern lodgings nestled in some of the most striking mountain scenery in the East.

At the heart of the parkway is the road itself, a 469-mi ribbon of two-lane blacktop that winds through rural, mountainous backcountry that would otherwise be nearly inaccessible. Created as the first rural national parkway, the roadway still encourages relaxing driving; there are endless through-the-window sightseeing opportunities and well-placed, paved overlooks where you can safely stop for a lingering look at grandeur. Stopping on the roadway's shoulder is legal if not encouraged, but motorists should choose their spots with an eye for safety and minimizing damage to the grassy border. Be prepared for the quick stops of fellow travelers and roaming wildlife. Although the speed limit is 45 mph in most places (35 mph in some stretches), the twists and turns and alluring views drop the average speed closer to 30 mph. Relax and enjoy the scenery; take an alternate route if you're in a hurry.

The Blue Ridge Parkway is a ride-awhile and stop-awhile recreational motor road connecting the Great Smoky Mountains and Shenandoah National parks. Born in 1933 as a Great Depression–era public works effort, the parkway was begun in 1935 and finished in 1987. The aim was to link both the parks and to fight the area's dire unemployment. Today the parkway attracts more than 20 million visitors and generates $2.2 billion of revenue per year for North Carolina and Virginia.

The Blue Ridge's attraction is its elevated views of the wooded mountains and valleys that typify the Southern Highlands: modest peaks cloaked in a lush, leafy canopy of oak, hickory, and maple, with an occasional evergreen highlight of hemlock, spruce, or fir. With the exception of North Carolina's 6,684-ft Mt. Mitchell, the highest mountain east of the Mississippi, only a few Blue Ridge summits peak above 4,000 ft, but the Blue Ridge Parkway does reach its highest point at Richland Balsam, which is 6,047 ft. Enveloping this expanse is the bluish haze that allegedly gave the Blue Ridge its name. Originally a product of moisture given off by the forest, today's haze is frequently infiltrated by airborne pollution that occasionally restricts views and has damaged some of the high-elevation foliage.

More than six decades and 600 million visitors after it first opened, the parkway attracts a steady but uncrowded flow of weekday visitors from April through September; highest visitation is on summer weekends and during October's peak fall foliage, which usually occurs the second or third week of the month. In particularly popular areas, such as Virginia's Mabry

Mill (Milepost 176.1), the traffic can sometimes resemble a big-city traffic jam; such instances typically occur in October. The parkway is the most-visited area in the National Park System. Few travel the road in winter, and sections are frequently closed due to ice and snow.

The natural and cultural resources of the southern Appalachian Mountains are preserved and interpreted on and off the Blue Ridge Parkway at the fascinating modern Folk Art Center near Asheville, North Carolina, among other places. Tunnels are interspersed with mountaintop drives, and "leg-stretcher" trails can lead to longer hikes. Overlooks open up the valleys and ridges in a spectacular fashion. Campgrounds, picnic areas, visitor centers, lodges, and restaurants allow leisurely travel.

The protected domain bordering the parkway has an average width of only 800 ft. Despite the relative narrowness of the corridor, many places offer short walks, and there are even a few extended hikes. The feeling of wilderness is more illusion than reality, but the typical walker on the average trail will never feel near the bustle of civilization.

ESSENTIAL INFORMATION

VISITOR INFORMATION For information on the parkway, including advice on camping and on-parkway dining, lodging, and sightseeing, contact the **Blue Ridge Parkway Association** (Box 453, Asheville, NC 28802) or the park headquarters (400 BBT Bldg., 1 Pack Sq., Asheville, NC 28801, tel. 704/298–0398) for 24-hour recorded information. The park's **Web site** is www.nps.gov/blri.

Visitor centers at Humpback Rocks, Peaks of Otter, Museum of North Carolina Minerals, and Craggy Gardens are open May through October.

For information on accommodations, restaurants, and local sights, contact the **North Carolina Division of Travel and Tourism** (430 N. Salisbury St., Raleigh, NC 27611,

tel. 919/733–4171 or 800/847–4862). Their **Web site** is www.visitnc.com. Also try the **Virginia Division of Tourism** (1021 E. Cary St., Richmond, VA 23219, tel. 804/786–4484 or 800/932–5827) for a free guidebook. Their **Web site** is www.virginia.org.

FEES There are no entrance fees on the parkway.

MILEPOSTS Mileposts—small gray concrete markers with black mileage indicators—are numbered from north to south on the parkway. Most parkway literature (and this chapter) refers to locations in terms of miles from the parkway's northern junction with the Skyline Drive, at the U.S. 250 crossover at Rockfish Gap on Afton Mountain. Milepost 216.9 is the Virginia–North Carolina state line.

PUBLICATIONS *The Blue Ridge Parkway Directory,* a color, 38-page, magazine-size annual guide, is available free from the Blue Ridge Parkway Association (*see* Visitor Information, *above*). You can get a color, pocket-size strip map, "Blue Ridge Parkway," from park headquarters or at visitor centers and district ranger's offices. They also give out the "Blue Ridge Parkway Bloom Calendar," a pamphlet telling where and when to spot the myriad varieties of wildflowers blooming on the parkway. *Parkway Milepost,* a parkway newspaper, is available free at parkway visitor centers; it provides seasonal news about parkway events and attractions, natural history, and regulations.

One of the best books on the parkway, especially if you're looking to stop and stretch your legs a little, is *Walking the Blue Ridge: A Guide to the Trails of the Blue Ridge Parkway,* by Leonard M. Adkins, who has actually walked each of these trails with a measuring wheel to ensure accuracy.

GEOLOGY AND TERRAIN The southern Appalachian Mountains are ancient by any standard; some rocks are an estimated 1.2 billion years old. Over the aeons the mountains were uplifted and shifted by changes in the earth's crust, then weathered and worn into their present configuration during the past 100 to 200 million years. The southern Appalachians have only a handful of peaks reminiscent of the towering, rock-studded mountains of the West; most of that lofty presence eroded long ago and now makes up the soil of the coastal plains of the Atlantic Ocean and Gulf of Mexico. Exceptions occur, such as Sharp Top, at Peaks of Otter (Milepost 86), which has an unusually sharp peak of aged, coarsely crystalline rock, and Flat Rock (Milepost 308.3), a quartzite outcrop that provides a stunning vantage point overlooking North Carolina's Grandfather Mountain and the Linville Valley.

Most of the roadway follows the backbone of the Blue Ridge, providing lofty views of surrounding lowlands and distant mountain peaks; the southern 114 mi wind through North Carolina's Black Mountains, Craggies, Pisgahs, and Balsams before ending in the Great Smokies. To the east of the parkway is the fertile, gently contoured terrain of the Piedmont section of Virginia and North Carolina. To the west are the rugged mountains that form the western rampart of the southern Appalachians; in Virginia, from Waynesboro to Roanoke, the southern section of the famed Shenandoah Valley lies between the southern Appalachians and the Piedmonts.

FLORA AND FAUNA Having been softened and worn down by the elements and the ages, the mountains provide fertile footing for a wide variety of vegetation. Particularly famous is the parkway's display of fall foliage and, thanks to strict rules against collecting, the spring and summer proliferation of wildflowers.

Except for the dark green spruce and fir blanketing the high elevations of the Black Mountains and the Mt. Mitchell area (Milepost 340–355), most of the parkway foliage is typical of the deciduous oak-hickory blend common to the region. Interspersed throughout are dogwood, sourwood, tulip poplar, black gum, sassafras, red maple, hemlock, and Virginia and white pine.

Bursting forth in May and June, flame azalea and catawba rhododendron are the splashy stars of the parkway's wildflowers; more furtive blooms can be spotted throughout the season. The wetland-dwelling skunk cabbage appears in February, and the colorful bull thistle is common along the roadside and in lowland pastures from June to the first killing frost. In between, some 110 other species are notable enough to be included in the "Blue Ridge Parkway Bloom Calendar" (*see* Publications, *above*).

Although wild animals abound along the parkway, they tend to be harder to spot and more wary of human approach than in the adjoining Shenandoah and Great Smoky Mountains national parks.

The Virginia white-tailed deer, a common roadside grazer in the parks, is less often seen along the parkway, its place taken by the woodchuck, known colloquially as the groundhog. Likewise, the black bear is a reclusive parkway denizen. Joining the woodchuck as common daytime sightings, especially along nature trails, are squirrels and chipmunks. At night you might see foxes, raccoons, opossums, and skunks; bobcats are fairly common after-dark travelers, but seeing one is a once-in-a-lifetime treat.

More than 100 species of birds appear along the parkway during the spring migration, and more than 200 additional species visit year-round (*see* Other Activities *in* Exploring, *below*). During the fall raptor migration, several birds-of-prey species glide southward along the mountain ridgeline, a seasonal event that attracts an ever-increasing number of birders. The parkway's two poisonous snakes, the timber rattler and copperhead, are rare; there is also a wide variety of nonpoisonous snakes, lizards, frogs, and salamanders.

WHEN TO GO The parkway is most crowded on summer weekends and during October's fall-foliage season (usually during the second and third weeks of the month). Because of unpredictable weather and limited options for accommodations, winter is the parkway's quietest season; unexpected cold fronts and snowfalls can strike from October to April. Spring can arrive from March through May, varying with elevation and late-winter weather patterns. Although it is farther north, Virginia usually experiences warm weather before North Carolina because of the latter's higher elevations. Summer temperatures are usually 10° to 15° cooler than in the nearby lowlands, ranging from the 40s to 90s.

SEASONAL EVENTS **Summer:** On Sunday evenings in summer, **Roanoke Mountain Campground** (Mill Mountain Spur Rd., 1 mi from parkway at Milepost 120, tel. 540/857–2458) hosts miniconcerts and demonstrations of traditional Southern Highlands music; they're generally held at 7 PM. **July: Linville Falls Music Festival** celebrates traditional mountain music and dance at the Linville Falls Campground (Milepost 316.4). **August:** In late August, **Brinegar Day** (tel. 910/372–8568) at Brinegar Cabin (Milepost 238.5) in historic Doughton Park features crafts demonstrations. **October: Fall harvest activities** (tel. 540/745–9661) at Mabry Mill (Milepost 176.1) on weekends in October include crafts demonstrations, apple butter–making, and old-time music.

WHAT TO PACK Year-round, bring sunscreen, sunglasses, a hat or cap, rain gear, and comfortable walking shoes. Long-sleeve shirts and light jackets are often needed, even in July and August. Most of the parkway is relatively pest free, but pack insect repellent to ward off ticks and the few chiggers, mosquitoes, or gnats you might encounter. It's a good idea to bring your own drinks and snacks; concessions are far apart and offer a limited assortment. You might also bring a couple of aerosol tire-inflator cans, should you get a flat you don't want to change on the spot.

GENERAL STORES Development along the parkway is kept minimal to contribute to its wilderness appeal. Stores are plentiful in nearby towns and cities, but on-parkway general stores are many miles apart. The camp store at **Peaks of Otter** (Milepost 86, tel. 540/586–1614) sells snacks and camping supplies and is open early April–late May, daily 9–6:30, and early June–late October, daily 9–7. **Doughton Park** (Milepost 241.4, tel. 910/372–4744) has a combination gift shop, variety store, and service station open early May–late October, daily 8–6. **Crabtree Meadows** (Milepost 339.5, tel. 704/675–4236) has similar facilities but a better selection of goods than the Doughton Park store; it's open early May–late October, daily 10–6. **Pisgah Inn**'s full-service camp store (Milepost 408.6, tel. 704/235–8228) has a service station and Laundromat and is open early April–late November, daily 8–8.

Other than full-service restaurants (*see* Dining, *below*), several other parkway food-and-rest stops carry limited general-store supplies: **Whetstone Ridge** (Milepost 29, tel. 540/377–6397) has a restaurant and gift-crafts shop open May, September, and October, weekdays 9–5, an hour later on weekends; June–late August, weekdays 8:30–6, an hour later on weekends. **Otter Creek** (Milepost 60.8, tel. 804/299–5862) has a restaurant and gift-crafts shop open April, May, and Labor Day–November, daily 9–7; June–Labor Day, daily 8–8. **Mabry Mill** (Milepost 176.1, tel. 540/952–2947) has similar facilities open May, September, and October, daily 8–6; June–late August, daily 8–7. **Northwest Trading Post** (Milepost 258.8, tel. 910/982–2543), the largest gift-crafts shop on the parkway, sells snacks; it's open mid-April–late October, daily 9–5:30.

There are just three gas stations along the 469-mi route: In addition to at Doughton Park and Pisgah Inn (*see above*), you can get gas at **Peaks of Otter** (Milepost 86, tel. 540/586–1233), which is open May and September, weekdays 9–5:30, weekends 8–7; June–August and October, weekdays 8–7, weekends 8–8. In an emergency, ask for gas at the Peaks of Otter Lodge desk (tel. 540/586–1081), which is open 24 hours.

ATMS There are no ATMs on the parkway; there are several in towns and cities near the parkway. In Virginia, try the **First**

Union National Bank (Towers Mall, Roanoke, tel. 540/563–7000): Take U.S. 220/I–581 north toward Roanoke; take the Colonial Avenue/Wonju Street exit; turn right at the stoplight, then left into Towers Mall. In North Carolina try the Biltmore branch of First Union National Bank (1 Angle St., Asheville, tel. 704/251–7251): Take I–40 west and follow the signs to the Biltmore House/Estate; the bank is across from the Biltmore entrance.

ARRIVING AND DEPARTING There is no rail or air service to the parkway itself, but several communities near the parkway are accessible by air, rail, or bus.

By Bus. Greyhound Lines (tel. 800/231–2222) serves Charlottesville (310 W. Main St.) and Roanoke (26 Salem Ave.) in Virginia, and cities that are convenient to sections of the parkway farther south. Once there, however, you'll need to rent a car to reach the parkway.

By Car and RV. The parkway is accessible to any motor vehicle, although the steep climbs may challenge larger RVs. From Charlottesville, take I–64 west to Exit 99 to the parkway's northern entrance at Rockfish Gap; driving time is approximately 30 minutes.

You can rent a car at the Charlottesville-Albemarle Airport from Avis (tel. 804/973–6000), Budget (tel. 804/973–5751), or Hertz (tel. 804/973–8349).

By Plane. Charlottesville-Albemarle Airport (201 Bowen Loop, Charlottesville, VA, tel. 804/973–8341), 8 mi north of Charlottesville on U.S. 29, is closest to the parkway's northern access and is served by American Eagle (tel. 800/433–7300), Comair/Delta (tel. 800/354–9822), United Express (tel. 800/241–6522), and US Airways Express (tel. 800/428–4322). You can rent a car at the airport (see By Car and RV, above) or take a taxi (Yellow Cab, tel. 804/295–4131), which costs $100 one-way, to the closest parkway lodging, Peaks of Otter (Milepost 86). There is no public transportation to the parkway.

By Train. Charlottesville, Virginia, has the closest train station (600 E. Water St.); it's served by Amtrak (tel. 800/872–7245). There is no public transportation from the station to the parkway. Cab fare (Yellow Cab, tel. 804/295–4131) to the car-rental agencies at the airport (see By Car and RV, above) is about $20, or about $75 to Peaks of Otter.

EXPLORING

The parkway's major appeal is to motor tourists, although there are opportunities for hiking, camping, and bicycling. Cyclists must follow certain rules (see Other Activities, below).

THE BEST IN ONE DAY Stop to enjoy the most inviting overlooks, take a couple of walks, visit one or two of the more popular attractions, and you've gotten about as much out of the parkway as one day will allow. Seeing the best of the entire roadway calls for at least two days, and preferably three or more.

Must-see stops in the Virginia section of the parkway are the historical exhibits and hiking opportunities at Humpback Rocks (Milepost 5.8), Peaks of Otter (Milepost 86), Rocky Knob (Milepost 169), and Mabry Mill (Milepost 176.1). Worth the detour, if you have the time, are the view from the foot of Roanoke's towering Mill Mountain Star (on the spur road that intersects the parkway at Milepost 124.5) and the expansive picnic area and walking opportunities at Smart View (Milepost 154.5) and Ground Hog Mountain (Milepost 189).

In North Carolina, be sure to see Doughton Park (Milepost 241.1), Linville Falls (Milepost 316.4), Crabtree Meadows (Milepost 339.5), Craggy Gardens (Milepost 364.6), Mt. Pisgah (Milepost 408), and Waterrock Knob (Milepost 451.2)—all of which have wondrous walking, picnicking, and sightseeing opportunities. Also well worth the stop is Linn Cove Viaduct (Milepost 305), the inventive, structurally elegant bridge

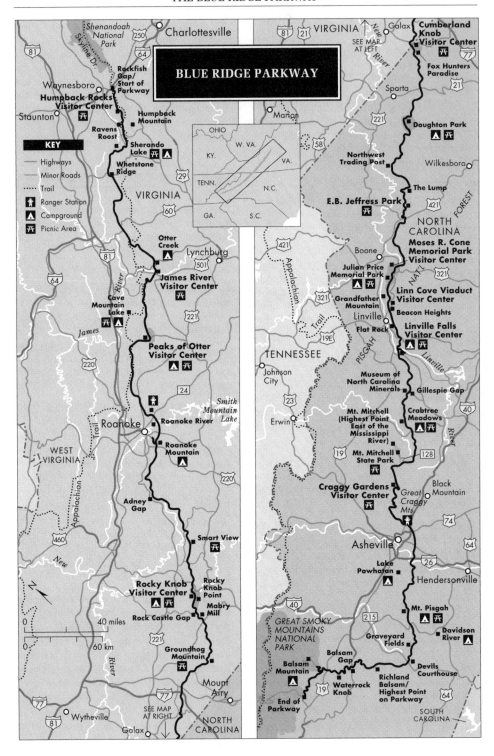

KEY
— Highways
— Minor Roads
····· Trail
🏚 Ranger Station
🔺 Campground
🏕 Picnic Area

BLUE RIDGE PARKWAY

that enables the parkway to continue uninterrupted.

ORIENTATION PROGRAMS There are no visitor-center slide shows or introductory movies along the parkway; there are informative seasonal programs conducted at campground and visitor-center amphitheaters from May through October. To find the topic, time, and locations of upcoming programs, read the *Parkway Milepost* (*see* Publications *in* Essential Information, *above*) or look for the blue sheets on bulletin boards at visitor centers, district ranger's offices, picnic areas, and campgrounds.

GUIDED TOURS There are no commercial guided tours on the parkway; there are numerous high-quality, very informative, ranger-led walks and programs. Typical presentations include nature lore, storytelling, and night prowls. Attendance averages 10 to 30, although some activities, such as mountain music, often have an audience approaching 150. Consult *Parkway Milepost* (*see* Publications *in* Essential Information, *above*).

From April through October, **bus trips** are available 10–5 every hour on the hour from the Peaks of Otter camp store (Milepost 86, tel. 540/586–1614) to a parking area 500 yards from the summit of Sharp Top. The cost is $2.50 round-trip, $1.50 one-way—choose the latter if you enjoy the thought of walking down but don't want to tackle the strenuous, 1.5-mi hike up the famous peak. The 500 yards from the bus stop to the peak are moderately challenging, but if you're used to walking uphill you shouldn't have a problem.

SCENIC DRIVES AND VIEWS The parkway is a scenic drive from end to end, with 469 mi of outstanding scenery and eye-catching views at nearly every turn. The following lists include some of the most popular roadside vantage points.

Virginia. Ravens Roost (Milepost 10.7): This spot allows a bird's-eye view of the Shenandoah Valley, Torry Mountain, and other Allegheny peaks to the west. **Otter Lake** (Milepost 63.1): This small lake has a densely wooded shoreline and an especially scenic area near the dam. **Peaks of Otter** (Milepost 86): The sparkling waters of modest-size Abbott Lake rest in the shadow of towering Sharp Top, one of the parkway's most-visited attractions. **Roanoke River Gorge** (Milepost 114.9): View the wooded river canyon from the 165-ft-high parkway bridge, or pull over and take the 10-minute walk to a pedestrian overlook. **Smart View** (Milepost 154.5): The small pond and open meadows on a mountaintop plateau allow a typical glimpse of Virginia farm country. **Rocky Knob** area (Mileposts 167–174): This is a famed 10-mi stretch of varied scenic views, from 3,572-ft Rocky Knob Point to the wild and rugged Rock Castle Gorge.

North Carolina. Fox Hunters Paradise (Milepost 218.6): This elevated vantage point is where hunters once listened to the hounds chasing their quarry in the valley below. **Doughton Park** area (Mileposts 238.5–244.7): At this open expanse of bluegrass downs, you can view an isolated mountain homestead. **The Lump** (Milepost 264.4): Take in the towering view of the Carolina foothills to the east. **Moses H. Cone Memorial Park** (Milepost 292.7): This historic 3,500-acre estate has miles of scenery, picnicking, hiking, camping, and fishing. **Julian Price Memorial Park** (Milepost 295): Adjoining Cone Memorial Park, here are an additional 4,200 acres of scenery and outdoor activities. **Linn Cove Viaduct Information Center** (Milepost 304.4): View the 1,243-ft-long viaduct, where creative engineering enabled the parkway to span uninterrupted a section of particularly rugged terrain on the rocky slope of Grandfather Mountain. **Linville Falls Visitor Center** (Milepost 316.3) and **Linville River Parking Area** (Milepost 316.4): Exhibits tell a story about this massive waterfall, and a short trail takes you to it. At the parking area you'll see one of the parkway's largest stone arch bridges, with three 80-ft spans. **Mt. Mitchell State Park via Route 128** (Milepost 355.8): Stop to see the highest peak in the East; you can drive nearly to the top on Route 128 for a short walk to the observation tower. **Craggy Gardens Visitor Center** (Milepost 364.4): These gardens are scenic year-round but especially so in mid-June, when they're cloaked in purple rhododendrons. **Mt. Pisgah** (Milepost 408.6): Panoramic views are had from 5,000-ft elevations at this spot, once part of a 100,000-acre estate George W. Vanderbilt purchased in the late 1800s; it is the nucleus of Pisgah National Forest. **Richland Balsam Overlook** (Milepost 431.4): Here you'll find towering views from the highest point on the roadway.

◼ HISTORIC BUILDINGS AND SITES Johnson **Farm** at Peaks of Otter (Milepost 85.9) is a preserved mountain farmstead, typical of communities that existed in the Blue Ridge region in the 1920s and 1930s. It is reached via a moderate 2.1-mi loop trail from the Peaks of Otter Visitor Center.

Mabry Mill (Milepost 176.1), arguably the most popular single attraction on the Virginia span of the parkway, was run by E. B. Mabry from 1910 to 1935. Blacksmithing demonstrations are given in summer.

Moses H. Cone Memorial Park (Milepost 292.7) and **Cone Manor House** (Milepost 294) compose a historic estate that encompasses some 3,600 scenic acres, with miles of carriage trails for horseback riding and walking, and picnicking, hiking, camping, and fishing opportunities.

Julian Price Memorial Park (Milepost 295), the former summer retreat of life-insurance pioneer Julian Price, adjoins Cone Memorial Park with an additional 4,200 acres of scenery and outdoor activities.

◼ NATURE TRAILS AND SHORT WALKS Several excellent short walks are just off the parkway. If you're a serious hiker, pick up *Walking the Blue Ridge* (*see* Publications *in* Essential Information, *above*), which gives an extensive list of where to walk and what you'll see.

The parkway offers hikers and walkers of all skill levels more than 100 varied and

intriguing trails in North Carolina and Virginia. Meandering alongside and crossing the scenic motor road, the trails provide a close-up look at some of the most beautiful wilderness in the country. Many trails wind their way through unique biological and geological environments, while others lead to historic sites with stories of how people have shaped our heritage. Many parkway trails continue onto Forest Service and private land. Please respect all these lands and treat them with care. The trails below give a nice sampling of the parkway's offerings; times and mileages are round-trip.

Otter Lake Trail (Milepost 63.1, .8 mi, 30 min). This is a moderate leg-stretcher around the wooded shoreline of small Otter Lake; it's very convenient to the roadway, with only occasionally tricky footing.

Abbott Lake Trail (Milepost 85.7, 1 mi, 30 min). From the parking lot at Peaks of Otter Lodge, this easy loop springs through an open meadow and around the lake, offering stunning views of Sharp Top.

Roanoke River Trail (Milepost 114.9, .7 mi, 25 min). This short but scenic trail to a pedestrian overlook allows views of a steep-sided section of the Roanoke River valley.

Rocky Knob Picnic Loop Trail (Milepost 169, 1.3 mi, 45 min). This is an easy meander around the scenic picnic area, taking you through rhododendron and hemlock forest.

Craggy Gardens (Milepost 364.6, 2 mi, 1 hr). Highlights of this moderately challenging, self-guided nature trail from the visitor center to the picnic area are the cloaking presence of trailside rhododendron and the view from the observation platform on Craggy Flats.

Graveyard Fields Loop Trail (Milepost 418.8, 2.2 mi, 1½ hrs). This moderately easy loop to an area of fallen tree trunks, victim of a 1925 fire, also runs to Yellowstone Falls. There, aptly, the landscape reminds one of the Rocky Mountains.

Devil's Courthouse (Milepost 422.4, .9 mi, 45 min). Take this short but moderately strenuous hike through spruce and fir forest to see the "courthouse," a huge rock outcropping with a 360° view into South Carolina and Georgia, and toward the Balsams.

Waterrock Knob Trail (Milepost 451.2, 1.1 mi, 55 min). A short, moderately strenuous climb from the parking area through red spruce and Fraser fir to the highest trail elevation on the parkway, this climb yields a four-state view and a panoramic vista of the Great Smoky Mountains.

LONGER HIKES Although the parkway offers only limited backcountry territory, it does have access to a number of moderately strenuous hikes and a few quite challenging ones. Times and mileages are round-trip.

Starting from the Humpback Gap parking area, the **Appalachian Trail to Humpback Rocks** (Milepost 6, 4.3 mi, 2 hrs) heads uphill and doesn't ease up until it reaches the saddle at the top of the mountain; from here it is .3 mi to the rocks and the stunning views over the valley. This relatively short hike definitely gets the blood flowing; it's not easy. The trail is poorly marked where it reaches the rocks at the top of the mountain; pay particular attention so you're able to retrace your steps to the parking area.

Sharp Top Trail at Peaks of Otter (Milepost 86, 3 mi, 2 hrs), the most popular trail on the parkway, starts at the camp store at the base of Sharp Top and climbs to 1,400 ft. Steep in some places and moderate in others, it requires an overall strenuous effort to reach the view of the lodge, lake, and distant Blue Ridge Mountains from the rock outcroppings at the summit. There is seasonal bus access to the .5-mi loop near the peak (*see* Guided Tours, *above*); hikers are not allowed to walk on the road.

The **Rock Castle Gorge Trail** (Milepost 167.1, 10.6 mi, all day) starts innocently enough at the entrance to the Rocky Knob campground, but after you walk 3.3 mi and descend to the backcountry camping area in the gorge, you begin to understand why

this pathway was given National Recreational Trail status. And you still have a 7.3-mi ascent back out of the gorge on the return trail. Your rewards for this truly rugged backcountry experience are views of thick mountain foliage and a splashing stream.

You can hike a short stretch of the **Tanawha Trail** (Milepost 305.2, 13.5 mi, all day), or you can try to do the whole run in one day—the latter option is not for the faint of heart. In its entirety, this trail—with elaborate bridges and wooden staircases— runs from the **Beacon Heights** parking area (Milepost 305.2) to **Julian Price Memorial Park** (Milepost 297.2). It is easiest hiked from south to north, and other good access points include the **Stack Rock** parking area (Milepost 304.8) and **Linn Cove** information center (Milepost 304.4). Part of the trail's appeal is its intricate engineering; its natural beauty derives from views of the southeast face of **Grandfather Mountain,** the falls on **Stack Rock Creek,** and the tunnels through lush growth of mountain laurel and rhododendron.

There are other excellent nearby hiking opportunities. **Appalachian Trail** (Box 807, Harpers Ferry, WV 25425, tel. 304/535–6331). **Mt. Mitchell State Park** (Rte. 5, Box 700, Burnsville, NC 28714, tel. 704/675–4611). **Shining Rock Wilderness Area** (District Ranger, U.S. Forest Service, 1001 Pisgah Hwy., Pisgah Forest, NC 28768, tel. 704/877–3265).

OTHER ACTIVITIES Arts and Crafts. Parkway Craft Center is in Moses Cone Memorial Park (Milepost 294, tel. 704/295–7938). You can buy crafts and watch demonstrations at the **Folk Art Center** (Milepost 382, tel. 704/298–7928). **Northwest Trading Post** (Milepost 258.8, tel. 910/982–2543) is the largest crafts shop on the parkway.

Biking. Accomplished cyclists will delight in the scenery and challenge of the parkway; inexperienced riders may be intimidated by the narrow shoulders, heavy summer weekend and October foliage traffic, and distances between food outlets and services. Climbs and descents vary from 600 ft to 6,000 ft. Mountain bikes are ideal for such steep terrain, but all bikes are restricted to paved areas. During times of limited visibility—at night and in tunnels—bikes must have a white light on the front and a red light or reflector on the back. Wear gloves and a helmet. The Blue Ridge Parkway Association (*see* Visitor Information *in* Essential Information, *above*) distributes a printout of major climbs and descents.

Bird-Watching. You can see more than 100 species along the parkway during the spring migration, and another 200 species annually. The fall raptor migration is a favorite attraction along the Virginia span, where these birds of prey have a major flyway along the Blue Ridge. Popular viewing spots include the **Ballroom Terrace,** a covered viewing platform at the Waynesboro/Afton Mountain Holiday Inn (Exit 99 off I–64 at the parkway's northern terminus, tel. 540/942–5201) and **Harvey's Knob** (Milepost 95.3). Although not on a flyway, North Carolina's **Waterrock Knob** (Milepost 451.2) is popular for raptor scanning.

Boating. Price Park Lake (tel. 919/372–4499), in Julian Price Memorial Park (Milepost 297.1), rents rowboats and canoes. It's open May 8–31 and September 11–October 31, weekends 10–6; June–September 6, daily 8:30–6.

Fishing. Anglers trying their luck along the parkway must obey the rules of the state in which they are fishing; further restrictions include specially designated areas, a ban on live bait, and a parkway prohibition against fishing from a half hour after sunset to a half hour before sunrise. Lures in designated "special waters" are restricted to single-hook artificials only, and in some cases artificial flies only. Licenses are available at off-parkway sporting goods stores and the Peaks of Otter Lodge. Under a reciprocal agreement, Virginia and North Carolina licenses are honored in all parkway waters. Price Park Lake (*see* Boating, *above*) is stocked with trout.

Hang Gliding. Two Virginia areas are open to hang gliding: **Ravens Roost** (Milepost 10) and **Roanoke Mountain** (Milepost 120.3). Both are cliff-launch locations. A free special-use permit is required; apply in person at the district ranger's office .1 mi north of Route 24 (Milepost 111) near Roanoke and bring proof of a Hang 3 (advanced) rating.

Horseback Riding. A popular spot is an 18-mi span of trail near **Roanoke** (Mileposts 109–121); you'll need your own horse. For information, contact the district ranger's office (tel. 540/857–2485). At **Moses Cone Memorial Park** (Milepost 294.1), one- and two-hour rides are conducted from April 15 to December 1 by **Blowing Rock Stables** (tel. 704/295–7847) at a cost of $20 per person for one hour, $35 for two hours. Reservations are recommended and novices are welcome; no riders under age 9 are allowed.

Rock Climbing. Individuals need permits to climb, so the best bet is to arrange to climb with a group. Call **Ravens Roost's** (Milepost 10) Asheville headquarters (tel. 704/271–4779, ext. 209) for information. The **district ranger's office** (tel. 540/377–2377) can provide names and numbers of local climbing clubs. The most popular North Carolina climbing location is **Devil's Courthouse** (Milepost 421), near the intersection of Route 215 and the parkway, but some areas of this site were closed in late 1995 to prevent further damage to rare plants. No one knows if they'll be reopened. Contact a regional climbing club for the scoop. There are no commercial outfitters on the parkway.

Snowshoeing and Cross-Country Skiing. These are popular activities when weather allows, despite there being no touring centers or rental shops on the parkway. In North Carolina, head for the **Heintooga Spur Road** (Milepost 458.2), south of Asheville. Contact the **district ranger's office** (tel. 704/456–9530) for conditions and advice. In Virginia, try the **winter recreation area** (Mileposts 121–136) between U.S. 220, south of Roanoke, and U.S. 221 at Adney Gap. Contact the **district ranger's office** (tel. 540/982–6490); if you get three beeps indicating that your call has reached the ranger's pager, key in your phone number. **Moses Cone Memorial Park,** which may be accessed from U.S. 221 at Blowing Rock, has 25 mi of trails. The parkway itself is open to skiers or snowshoers only when gates at both ends of a section are closed.

Swimming. No swimming is allowed on parkway property.

CHILDREN'S PROGRAMS Children are welcome at seasonal interpretive programs and tours (*see* Orientation Programs *and* Guided Tours, *above*), but they must be accompanied by an adult. *Parkway Milepost* (*see* Publications *in* Essential Information, *above*) and the blue sheets on bulletin boards at visitor centers, district ranger's offices, picnic areas, and campgrounds list scheduled activities for kids.

EVENING ACTIVITIES After-hours attractions for parkway visitors include seasonal interpretive programs and tours (*see* Orientation Programs *and* Guided Tours, *above*). *Parkway Milepost* (*see* Publications *in* Essential Information, *above*) and the blue sheets on bulletin boards at visitor centers, district ranger's offices, picnic areas, and campgrounds list times and locations.

DINING

There are two full-service restaurants and six informal eateries right on the parkway, and overall, their food and service are very good by national park standards. They offer traditional Southern Highlands fare, such as ham, beef, and fish. Only Peaks of Otter and the Pisgah Inn serve alcoholic beverages. In the north, three options are clustered within 50 mi; from Peaks of Otter (Milepost 86) south, it is 65 to 100 mi between restaurants. Dress everywhere is casual, although a dressed-for-dinner look is appropriate at the full-service restau-

rants. A short drive from the parkway will take you to restaurants with more gourmet and ethnic specialties.

ON THE PARKWAY **Peaks of Otter Restaurant.** This attractive, gray, board-and-batten building on a shore of small Abbott Lake has good food and trails leading up to famous Sharp Top, making it perhaps the favorite place for most parkway drivers to eat and walk it off. The dining room, with its iron chandeliers, potted plants, and rustic wood paneling, grants dazzling views of the lake and the rocky peak of Sharp Top, which towers over it. Regional residents have been known to drive a couple of hours for a special meal here—feasting on baby back ribs, roast turkey, trout, or red snapper. Tackle the climb up Sharp Top and you can justify the feature dessert: Peaks ice cream pie. There is also a convenient lunch counter adjacent to the dining room where you can have a full breakfast or a burger for lunch, and there's a camp store at the base of the trail where you can get snacks or ice cream. *Milepost 85.9, Blue Ridge Pkwy., VA, tel. 540/586–1081 or 800/542–5927. MC, V. $–$$*

Pisgah Inn. Traditional Southern Highlands dishes come with a stunning panoramic view of the southern Blue Ridge. This is another eatery where attention to detail, fresh vegetables, and chef's specials attract travelers and regional residents alike. You can get delicious fresh mountain trout at any meal. *Milepost 408.6, Blue Ridge Pkwy., NC, tel. 704/235–8228. MC, V. Closed late Nov.–early Apr. $–$$*

Bluffs Coffee Shop. This popular spot serves typical Highlands food, including homemade desserts. Breakfast, lunch, and dinner (till 7:30) are served. *Doughton Park, Milepost 241.1, Blue Ridge Pkwy., NC, tel. 910/372–4744. Closed Nov.–Apr. $*

Crabtree Meadows. With a design and menu similar to those of Virginia's Whetstone Ridge and Otter Creek (*see below*), Crabtree Meadows is great if you want a quick but hearty meal or you're a camper with no desire (or ability) to cook for yourself. The country menu offers lunch and dinner entrées of ham, chicken, corn cakes, catfish, and sandwiches. Service concludes at 6 PM, so dinners must be early. *Milepost 339.5, Blue Ridge Pkwy., NC, tel. 704/675–4236. AE, DC, MC, V. Closed Nov.–Apr. $*

Mabry Mill. The buckwheat-and-corn cakes, country ham, biscuits, and strawberry cobbler at this cedar board-and-batten restaurant are nearly as famous as the oft-photographed gristmill itself. But you may have to wait to try them during peak season, as the restaurant has limited seating and unlimited appeal. The most popular dining spot is the enclosed porch; there is also a paneled and wallpapered counter area with 12 stools. *Milepost 176.1, Blue Ridge Pkwy., VA, tel. and fax 540/952–2947. AE, DC, MC, V. Closed Nov.–Apr. $*

Otter Creek. This clone of the Whetstone Ridge facility (*see below*) differs in its low-elevation setting with a view of scenic Otter Creek. *Milepost 60.8, Blue Ridge Pkwy., VA, tel. 804/299–5862. No credit cards. Closed mid-Nov.–Mar. $*

Whetstone Ridge. One of the restaurant-cum-gift-shop facilities along the northern section of the parkway, Whetstone Ridge has a sandwich counter and a small dining room. Specialties include buckwheat pancakes, open-face roast beef sandwiches, fried chicken, baked ham, and blackberry cobbler; there's also a striking view over the Shenandoah Valley. *Milepost 29, Blue Ridge Pkwy., VA, tel. 540/377–6397. No credit cards. Closed Nov.–late Apr. $*

NEAR THE PARKWAY **Old Mill Room.** In an 1830s-era, water-powered gristmill that was moved and reassembled at the elegant Boar's Head Inn, guests dine under exposed wood beams and a huge Spanish chandelier. The menu is Continental, but the sauces and seasonings carry a distinctly French accent. Excellent choices include locally raised lamb and veal, and fresh fish. The wine list is extensive. *Boar's Head Inn, U.S. 250 W, Charlottesville (3 mi west of town, 30 mi east of Blue Ridge Pkwy. via U.S. 250), VA, tel. 804/296–2181 or 800/*

476–1988. Reservations essential for dinner. AE, D, DC, MC, V. $$$

Buck Mountain Grille. The casual, airy interior and sophisticated menu belie the Grille's 1950s-era roadhouse exterior. Very popular locally and regionally, its food is prepared from scratch and includes vegetarian dishes, seafood, chicken, and steaks. The ice cream cakes are sublime. *5006 Franklin Rd., Roanoke (on U.S. 220 just south of Roanoke, across from the Blue Ridge Pkwy. exit at Milepost 121.4), VA, tel. 540/776–1830. AE, DC, MC, V. Closed Mon. $$*

Captain Sam's Landing. This seafood restaurant with nautical decor has antiques, a wooden deck, and a patio. There's a shrimp feast one week each month, and chicken and steak are always on the menu. *2323 W. Main St., Waynesboro (on U.S. 250, 10 min from the south entrance to Skyline Dr.), VA, tel. 540/943–3416. Reservations not accepted weekends or during shrimp feast. AE, DC, MC, V. No lunch. Closed Sun. except during shrimp feast. $$*

Woodberry Inn. The three dining areas in this Tudor-style lodge rich in antiques and reproductions can accommodate 84 guests. Dining is casual, with a varied menu that includes steaks, baked and fried chicken, sautéed shrimp, and an acclaimed shrimp cocktail. *Rte. 758 E, Blue Ridge Pkwy. (.1 mi from parkway on Rte. 758/Woodberry Rd., 2 mi north of Mabry Mill at Milepost 174), VA, tel. 540/593–2567 or 800/763–2567. AE, D, MC, V. Closed Nov. 5–Mar. $$*

PICNIC SPOTS Picnicking along the parkway is a great way to savor the scenery. In addition to at the sites listed below, picnicking is also permitted on the grassy shoulder of the parkway and at overlooks. Note: Fires (including charcoal in grills) are allowed only in designated picnic areas.

The 12 developed sites, each with tables, cooking grills, drinking water, and rest rooms, are as follows: **Humpback Rocks** (Milepost 5.8). **James River** (Milepost 63.8). **Peaks of Otter** (Milepost 86). **Smart View** (Milepost 154.5). **Rocky Knob** (Milepost

169). **Cumberland Knob** (Milepost 217.5). **Doughton Park** (Milepost 238.5). **E. B. Jeffress Park** (Milepost 272). **Linville Falls** (Milepost 316.4). **Crabtree Meadows** (Milepost 339.5). **Craggy Gardens** (Milepost 364.6). **Mt. Pisgah** (Milepost 408.6). Peaks of Otter, Doughton Park, Crabtree Meadows, and Mt. Pisgah have camp stores and/or snack shops. Peaks of Otter and Smart View are particularly popular for summer and fall-foliage picnicking; Rocky Knob and Craggy Gardens are known for their vibrant spring bloom.

LODGING

There are four lodgings along the parkway and countless more nearby. Three-season, on-parkway options range from housekeeping cabins to rustic-looking but modern lodges with full-service restaurants; only Peaks of Otter Lodge (Milepost 85.9) is open year-round. Vacancies are rare in October and almost as scarce on major holidays and summer weekends; to be safe, make your reservations as far in advance as possible. Off-parkway options include inexpensive chain motels, B&Bs, and elegant country inns.

ON THE PARKWAY **Pisgah Inn.** This board-and-batten mountain inn is nestled in the outstandingly scenic area that was part of the 100,000-acre estate George W. Vanderbilt purchased in the late 1800s. The property was the site of the first forestry school in the country and the nucleus of Pisgah National Forest. The 51 guest rooms are clustered in three separate two-level, motel-style units; all have TVs (but no phones) and patios or balconies with stunning views of the southern Blue Ridge. There's also a crafts shop on the premises. *Milepost 408.6, Box 749, Waynesville, NC 28786, tel. 704/235-8228, fax 704/648-9719. 50 rooms, 1 suite. Facilities: restaurant, coffee shop, no-smoking rooms. MC, V. Closed late Nov.–early Apr. $$–$$$*

Peaks of Otter. This gray-stained, board-and-batten complex has 59 rooms in three separate two-story motel-style units, plus three suites in the main lodge. The view across Abbott Lake to the rocky peak of Sharp Top is one of the parkway's most famous. All rooms have either patios or balconies, and all face the lake. Only the lodge suites have phones and TVs. *Milepost 85.9, Box 489, Bedford, VA 24523, tel. 540/586-1081 or 800/542-5927 in VA, fax 540/586-4420. 59 rooms, 3 suites. Facilities: restaurant, bar, snack bar, hiking, fishing. MC, V. $$*

Rocky Knob. These rustic housekeeping cabins were built with concrete floors and squared logs by the Civilian Conservation Corps in the 1930s; they were sided and renovated into modern lodgings in the 1950s, but they still don't have baths (there is a central bathhouse with showers). Flooring is modern sheet vinyl; all utensils and linens are supplied; the cold-water-only kitchens have combination sink-stove-refrigerator units; and there are no TVs or phones. The cabins are in a quiet area at the head of Rock Castle Gorge and are popular with travelers wanting to economize by self-catering or to avoid the crowds at the larger lodges. *Milepost 174.1, VA, tel. 540/593-3503. 5 cabins. Facilities: coin laundry. AE, DC, MC, V. Closed Labor Day–Memorial Day. $*

NEAR THE PARKWAY **Cataloochee Ranch.** This rustic, ranch-style resort has two lodges and seven cabins on 1,000 acres adjacent to Great Smoky Mountains National Park. The view from the 5,000-ft elevation is worth the visit alone, but there are plenty of other reasons to come: There are many recreational activities available on site and there's a public golf course and a ski area nearby. The buildings are of squared logs and stone; guest rooms are likewise rustic but modern, with handmade quilts. All meals are included in the room rate. *Rte. 1, Box 500F, Maggie Valley, NC 28751 (on U.S. 19, 8 mi north of Blue Ridge Pkwy.), tel. 704/926-1401 or 800/868-1401, fax 704/926-9249. 13 rooms, 7 cabins. Facilities: restaurant, hot tub, tennis court, hiking, horseback riding, fishing, meeting rooms. AE, MC, V. Closed Nov.–Dec. 26 and Mar. $$$*

Waynesboro/Afton Mountain Holiday Inn.
This three-story, white-brick hotel stands at
the northern tip of the Blue Ridge Parkway,
where the roadway joins the Skyline Drive.
The outstanding attraction is the soaring
view over Rockfish Valley (36 rooms have a
full view and another 36 a partial view).
The covered Ballroom Terrace is a popular
spot for watching the fall raptor migration.
There's a golf course nearby. *Junction of
I-64 (Exit 99) and U.S. 250 atop Afton
Mountain, Box 849, Waynesboro, VA
22980, tel. 540/942-5201 or 800/465-4329,
fax 540/943-8746. 118 rooms. Facilities:
restaurant, bar, indoor pool, meeting
rooms. AE, D, DC, MC, V. $$*

Woodberry Inn. This luxury lakeside inn
comprises a main lodge and 16 rooms in two
separate buildings. Rooms have wainscot-
ing, handmade bedspreads, TVs, phones,
and individual climate control. Four are
secluded but farther from the lake. Some
have drive-to-the-door parking; others have
porch views of the lake. Opportunities for
golf and tennis are nearby, and there's an
antiques and art gallery on site. *Box 908,
Meadows of Dan, Rte. 758E, Blue Ridge
Pkwy. (.1 mi from parkway on Rte. 758/
Woodberry Rd., 2 mi north of Mabry Mill at
Milepost 174), VA 24120, tel. and fax 540/
593-2567 or tel. 800/763-2567. 16 rooms.
Facilities: restaurant, lake, hiking, fishing.
AE, D, MC, V. $$*

Apple Valley Motel. This brick motel
harkens to the days before interstates, but it
has been renovated and is nicely maintained in a secluded setting convenient to
the parkway. Despite its private surroundings, it is less than 2 mi from major shopping centers and only 5 mi from downtown
Roanoke, the largest city along the parkway.
*5063 Franklin Rd., Roanoke, VA 24014 (on
U.S. 220, just south of the Blue Ridge Pkwy.
exit at Milepost 121.4), tel. 540/989-0675.
18 rooms. AE, D, DC, MC, V. $*

Super 8. The signature beige-stucco exterior and dark trim alert you that this is a
Super 8. It sits in a modern retail district
between Charlottesville and the regional

airport. Carpeted guest rooms have cable
TV and phones; shopping and dining are
close by. *390 Greenbrier Dr., Charlottesville, VA 22901 (1 block off U.S. 29, 5 mi
north of the city and 9 mi south of the
Charlottesville-Albemarle Airport), tel. 804/
973-0888, fax 804/973-2221. 66 rooms.
AE, D, DC, MC, V. $*

CAMPING

The parkway has nine developed campgrounds, which are listed below. They have
both tent and RV sites but no water or electrical hookups. Each site has its own cooking grill and picnic table. All campgrounds
have rest rooms (but not showers) and RV
sewage stations, seasonal ranger-led interpretive programs, and hiking trails. Most
have telephones nearby. Campgrounds are
generally open early May through late October. Winter camping is sometimes available, weather permitting; contact parkway
headquarters in advance. Campers are limited to a total of 14 nonconsecutive days
between June 1 and Labor Day, 30 days for
the calendar year. Reservations are not accepted nor are they usually needed, though
you should come early on summer holiday
weekends and during October's peak fall
foliage. Pets are allowed, but they must be
on a leash no longer than 6 ft. Fees at all of
the parkway campgrounds are $10 per site
per night for up to two adults, $2 per extra
adult. Children under 19 are free.

The only two **backcountry camping** areas
on the parkway are North Carolina's
Doughton Park (Milepost 238.5) and **Rock
Castle Gorge** in Virginia's Rocky Knob area
(Milepost 169). You'll need a backcountry
permit, which you can get free from park
headquarters and district ranger's offices.
A free permit, which you have to get in
advance from regional ranger stations, is required for backcountry camping (*see* Visitor Information *in* Essential Information,
above).

Otter Creek. At the parkway's northernmost and lowest-elevation (800 ft) camp-

ground, the sites are laid out on 552 acres in two loops along Otter Creek and within a short walk of small but scenic Otter Lake. Closest to the creek and the restaurant are Loop A (RV) sites 1 and 11–25, and Loop B (tent) sites 1–17 and 41; tent sites 18–32, on the outside of Loop B, are the most secluded. There's a pay phone near the restaurant. *Milepost 60.9. 45 tent sites, 24 RV sites. Facilities: restaurant. $*

Peaks of Otter. On 4,150 acres in the shadow of Sharp Top and within a stone's throw of Abbott Lake, this is one of the parkway's most popular—and crowded—campgrounds. Closest to the lake are Loop A (tent or RV) sites 1–16, and Loop T (RV) sites 21–46. Most secluded are Loop A sites 19–42 and Loop B sites 1–28. There's a pay phone at the entrance station. *On Rte. 43, ½ mi east of Milepost 86. 86 tent sites, 62 RV sites. $*

Roanoke Mountain. This 1,142-acre campground is surprisingly secluded, despite its proximity to one of the most exclusive neighborhoods in Roanoke. It's only a 4-mi drive from downtown and has many cultural and historic attractions. Most sites offer privacy, especially Loop A (tent) sites 18–60 and all 30 Loop B (RV) sites. A pay phone is at the entrance station. *On the Mill Mountain Spur Rd., 1 mi from Milepost 120.4. 74 tent sites, 30 RV sites. $*

Rocky Knob. This large (4,200 acres), four-loop, exceptionally scenic campground is especially rich in scenery when mountain laurel and rhododendron bloom in May and June. Loop T offers RV camping only; Loops A, B, and C accommodate tent or RV campers. All sites are secluded; Loops C and T have a slight edge over the others in terms of scenery and privacy. *Milepost 167.1. 81 tent sites, 28 RV sites. $*

Doughton Park. The largest (6,430 acres) of the parkway campgrounds, this site is laid out in two separate loops: 25 large RV/trailer sites and 110 small RV/tent sites. The large RV sites are well spaced and private, particularly sites 8–12; sites 87–96 have the most privacy of those in the small RV/tent loop. There is a pay phone across from the small RV/tent loop entrance. *Milepost 239. 110 tent sites, 25 RV sites. $*

Julian Price Memorial Park. This rhododendron-cloaked campground offers great diversity: The Tanawha Trail runs near the five loops on the west side of the parkway, and Price Lake is a short walk from Loop A on the east side of the parkway. For the most privacy, try either Loop B (RV/tent) sites 22–44 or Loop F (RV) sites 1–129. The campground has 3,900 acres; there's a pay phone at the main entrance station on the west side of the parkway. *Milepost 297. 129 tent sites, 68 RV sites. $*

Linville Falls. Along the spur road to the campground is a parking area with a view of a bend in the Linville River; the camping area itself is between the road and another bow in the river. From the nearby visitor center a number of short trails (.5–1 mi) provide breathtaking views of the Linville Falls and gorge areas. The campground has 996 acres; there's a pay phone at the entrance station. *On the spur road at Milepost 316.3. 50 tent sites, 20 RV sites. $*

Crabtree Meadows. The smallest (253 acres) of all the parkway campgrounds, Crabtree Meadows has outstanding scenery and a .9-mi hike to Crabtree Falls. Trail access is from Loop A at the main entrance parking area or from between sites 9 and 11. For the most privacy, head to Loop A, sites 7–17, or Loop C, sites 44–69. A pay phone is at the camp store. *Milepost 339.5. 71 tent sites, 22 RV sites. $*

Mt. Pisgah. The parkway's southernmost, highest-elevation (5,000 ft) campground is in the shadow of Big Bald Mountain, with spruce and fir replacing the typical oak- and hickory-dominated forest. Loop C, sites 78–102, and Loop A, sites 14–30, are most private. There are 690 acres; the pay phone is at the lodge. *Milepost 408.6, tel. 704/235-9109. 70 tent sites, 70 RV sites. $*

Cape Cod National Seashore
Massachusetts

By Karl Luntta

rom its surface we over-
looked the greater part of the
Cape. In short, we were tra-
versing a desert with the view of an autum-
nal landscape of extraordinary brilliancy, a
sort of Promised Land, on the one hand,
and the ocean on the other . . . A thousand
men could not have seriously interrupted
it, but would have been lost in the vastness
of the scenery as their footsteps in the sand.

—Henry David Thoreau, *Cape Cod*

Thoreau, the naturalist and writer, visited
Cape Cod several times between 1849 and
1857. In the florid passage above, he refers to
the Wellfleet Bluffs area, now part of Cape
Cod National Seashore. While "Promised
Land" may be hyperbole, his description
still holds a great deal of truth. Today, the
Seashore comprises some 40 mi of smooth
beaches, tidal flats, sand dunes, forests, and
marshes, much of it unsullied by human
development.

Cape Cod National Seashore was authorized
in August 1961, under the administration of
President John F. Kennedy, for whom Cape
Cod was home and haven. The first park to
be established around residential and commercial areas, it stretches through the towns
of Chatham, Orleans, Eastham, Wellfleet,
Truro, and Provincetown on the Lower Cape.
(Cape Cod can be compared in shape to an
upraised arm, with the Upper Cape as the
shoulder, the Mid-Cape as the biceps, and
the Lower Cape as the forearm and fist.)

The seashore figures conspicuously in
Cape Cod's history. An estimated 3,000
ships have met their doom on the sandbars,
rocks, and pounding breakers this side of
the peninsula—the first recorded wreck
was the *Sparrowhawk*, a British vessel that
went down near Nauset Beach in 1626. So
horrendous were the sailing conditions here
that in 1872 Congress organized the U.S.
Life Saving Service with nine stations along
the Cape. The Service evolved into the
U.S. Coast Guard, which still maintains stations on the Cape, though not on Seashore
beaches. Today, the bulk of Cape Cod National Seashore's acreage embraces this
eastern Atlantic coast. Known as the Outer
Beach, these beaches are the best on the
Cape—some even say they are the best on
the East Coast. Miles of dunes and beaches
stand guard against the often brawny surf
of the open Atlantic, resulting in tidal flats,
coves and marshes, and rivers and rivulets,
each a small microcosm of Cape Cod's natural curiosities.

Though the ocean and beaches may be the
Seashore's most popular attraction, other
park facilities are well worth exploring.
They include 11 mi of bicycle trails and 25
mi of both ranger-guided and self-guided
hiking trails; two visitor centers; five lighthouses; and preserved swamps, forests,
and a cranberry bog. Surf fishing on the
beaches and freshwater fishing are allowed,
as is shellfishing in designated areas. Access to seashore beaches and trails is easy:
Paved roads are the norm. Sections of Truro
and Provincetown shores allow off-road
vehicles.

Within park boundaries are more than 600
private residences of striking architectural
diversity (some of which are open to the

public for touring), as well as several privately owned motels, campgrounds, and businesses. Thirty park-owned sites and structures are listed on the National Historic Register of Historic Places.

ESSENTIAL INFORMATION

VISITOR INFORMATION Cape Cod National Seashore (Park Headquarters, 99 Marconi Site Rd., Wellfleet 02667, tel. 508/349–3785, ext. 200) is open weekdays 8–4:30. **Cape Cod Chamber of Commerce** (Rtes. 6 and 132, Hyannis 02601, tel. 508/362–3225). **Salt Pond Visitor Center** (Rte. 6, Eastham 02642, tel. 508/255–3421) is open late June–Labor Day, daily 9–5; fall and spring, daily 9–4:30; January–February, weekends 9–4:30. **Province Lands Visitor Center** (Racepoint Rd., Provincetown 02662, tel. 508/487–1256) is open mid-April–mid-November, daily 9–5.

The park's **Web site** is www.nps.gov/caco/.

FEES At town-owned and private facilities that fall within park boundaries, fees for parking vary. At Seashore-operated beaches, daily entrance fees are $1 for walk-ins and cyclists, and $7 for cars. A seasonal pass costs $20. Children 16 and under enter free. Fees are collected only late June–Labor Day, 9–5 (although beaches remain open until midnight). Pay at the entrances to beach parking lots. Trails and roads within Seashore boundaries are not subject to fees.

A $60 permit fee, good for the season, is required for off-road vehicles. Self-contained RVs, which are allowed overnight stays in specified areas, require a seasonal fee of $100. These fees are payable at the Oversand Vehicle Station in Race Point.

PUBLICATIONS Most visitor information centers (*see* Visitor Information, *above*) distribute free maps, guides, trail descriptions, and regulations. The Salt Pond and Province Lands visitor centers operate small bookstores selling books, maps, videos, puzzles, postcards, and other Seashore paraphernalia.

Many books have been written about the area, but Thoreau's classic travel journal *Cape Cod* best captures the sublime beauty of the Cape's natural endowments. *The Outermost House* is naturalist Henry Beston's 1928 log of the year he spent on Coast Guard Beach. *The Life Savers of Cape Cod*, by J. W. Dalton, is a 1902 account of the historic U.S. Life Saving Service, forerunner of the U.S. Coast Guard. The comprehensive *Guide to Nature on Cape Cod and the Islands*, edited by Greg O'Brien, explores Cape birds, seashores, wetlands, weather, and more. *A Guide to the Common Birds of Cape Cod* was written by Peter Trull, a senior field naturalist with the Cape Cod Museum of Natural History. The concise *Cape Cod*, by Robert Finch, is the official park handbook, complete with excellent color photographs and helpful diagrams.

GEOLOGY AND TERRAIN Of Cape Cod National Seashore's 43,569 acres, 27,398 are owned and administered directly by the National Park Service. The rest fall into public and private sectors. This mix of private and public ownership gives the seashore an unusual feel; just minutes away from a briny marsh flushed by ocean tides, you'll come across a small residential section, making it difficult to assess whether or not you are within park boundaries. But along the 40-mi stretch from Chatham to Provincetown, or on one of the trails operated by the park, there's no mistaking it: You're on protected land.

Cape Cod is the world's largest glacial peninsula. The whole of the Cape, as well as the islands of Martha's Vineyard and Nantucket, was formed 21,000 years ago as sheets of ice up to 2 mi thick descended from the frigid north into what is now New England. Over time, the glacial advance slowed due to the more temperate, more southern climes. As the ice melted, sea levels rose—today's level is about 400 ft higher than during glacial times—and receding glaciers gouged great holes in the earth, which in turn fused with underground springs to become kettle ponds, more commonly known as bogs and freshwater ponds. The aptly named Salt Pond, for example, was once a freshwater kettle pond before the sea finally broke through to connect it with the larger Nauset Marsh.

Rock debris and glacial till (sand and clay) pushed south by the great sheets of ice were left behind after the glaciers retreated, forming much of the terrain as we now know it. Observe, for example, the moraines—small hills formed from glacial deposits—along Cape Cod Bay and Buzzards Bay on the Upper Cape, and outwash plains, the flat or gently sloping surfaces most common in the Mid- and Lower Cape.

Throughout the seashore you'll find small dunes covered with scrubby beach grass, forests of pitch pine and scrub oak, pungent saltwater marshes, and great boulders (Doane Rock at the Salt Pond Visitor Center is the largest glacially deposited rock visible on Cape Cod); all have their origins somewhere farther north.

The wind and ocean have most profoundly affected the terrain of the seashore. Changing tides and the fury of storms have taken sand and shore from one place and deposited them in others. Roughly 3 ft of shoreline are lost along the Atlantic coastline annually; the cliffs that dominate the coastline are falling into the sea. Erosion is starkly evident at Marconi Station Site, which, dismantled in 1920 because of cliff erosion, has all but disappeared. Sand, however, is rapidly redeposited farther north, yielding underwater sandbars, and eventually sandspits and sandbars that break the water's surface. Province Lands, at the very tip of the Seashore, is relatively new, formed about 5,000 years ago. It continues to expand westward as sand is deposited from the south.

FLORA AND FAUNA The habitats of Cape Cod National Seashore exist only with permission from the ocean. This is strikingly evident in the marshy wetlands where the sea meets fresh water. From here, in an almost laboratorylike environment, springs much of the plant and animal life that supports the seashore.

Whale-watching is a popular summer activity. Stellwagen Bank, a feeding ground for the mammals, sits to the north of Race Point, the Seashore's northernmost tip. Though whale-watching companies operate out of Barnstable and Provincetown (see Whale-Watching in Other Activities, below), on clear spring and summer days, you might spot finbacks, minkes, humpbacks, and pilot whales, as well as white-sided and white-beaked dolphins off Race Point. From November to May, harbor seals migrate south from breeding grounds along the Maine and Canadian coast and can be seen in groups at points all along the seashore, notably Race Point, Coast Guard Beach, and Great Island.

Along the more quiescent intertidal flats (the often muddy area between the high point and low point of tides) live hermit crabs, spider crabs, snails, and several varieties of shrimp and sea worms. Whelks, including the knobbed whelk, which can grow up to 16 inches, are also found here. Clams, such as quahogs (pronounced ko-hogs), steamers, and razor clams, make their home in mudflats and sandy flats. The wide-bodied surf clam is most common along the beach. Fiddler crabs, easily recognized by their one oversize claw, can be found in several environments, from sandy beaches to grass-covered dunes. Occasionally, a jellyfish washes up on shore; they're most common in the warmer waters of Nantucket Sound. Among local species are sea-wattle jellyfish and the large Portuguese man-of-war. Most jellyfish tentacles have small, stinging cells that emit toxins; though in most cases the toxins are not fatal, they can irritate the skin. Steer clear of them, even if they appear to be dead or dying on the beach.

More than 300 species of birds, from large seabirds to woodland and wetland birds, make their home for at least part of the year on Cape Cod. In the 19th century, hundreds of species were decimated by hunters; in this century, many have returned. The tern, relative of the gull, including the common, roseate, and least tern, can be spotted in summer. Nauset Marsh, near the Salt Pond Visitor Center, hosts the largest tern colony in New England. Signs are posted in tern breeding areas; avoid disrupting them. Other summer birds include the threatened piping plover, also protected during its breeding season. Swallows, bobolinks, and mockingbirds are found along the shore and around Fort Hill, where views of Nauset Marsh and Nauset Beach are spectacular. Herons, along with several types of egrets, are common marshland dwellers.

In spring and summer, warblers, blackbirds, catbirds, flycatchers, sparrows, orioles, titmice, chickadees, tanagers, and robins are commonly seen. Seagoing birds include gannets and cormorants (spring–fall), and gulls (year-round). In winter, several types of freshwater and seagoing ducks, including mergansers, scaup, scoters, eiders, buffleheads, goldeneyes, and mallards, are found in seashore waters. Hawks, ospreys, vultures, and other birds of prey are less common.

Though the seashore is not brimming with large land mammals, white-tailed deer do appear frequently. Opossums, rabbits, raccoons, foxes, squirrels, muskrats, and many of the usual woodland rodents are common throughout the seashore. The coyote, once thought to be eliminated on Cape Cod, has also made recent appearances.

The dominant flora found in the seashore are pitch pine and several types of oak. The pitch pine is one of the earliest inhabitants of the Cape and plays an enormous role in mitigating the erosion of the Outer Cape. The most common oaks are the scrub oak, black oak, and white oak. Also widespread is the American holly, most often associated with the red winter berries popular at Christmas. Red cedar is found inland; red maple, brilliant in spring and fall, is found along the Red Maple Swamp Trail near Fort Hill. Cedar found along the Atlantic White Cedar Swamp Trail near the Marconi Station Site was once more abundant, but deforestation has reduced its distribution. Beech, also once common but now virtu-

ally absent from the area, can be seen on the Beech Forest Trail in Province Lands, along with black birch and eastern hemlock. Near ponds and swamp areas, you'll see tupelo, inkberry, swamp azalea, wild sarsaparilla, sweet pepperbush, and laurel. Beach grass, beach pea, and beach heather are common on windswept dunes, as are beach plum and bayberry bushes. Wildflowers pepper marshes and ponds.

Poison ivy grows in almost every habitat. Dog ticks and deer ticks are also found in grassy areas. Deer ticks carry the spirochetal bacteria that cause Lyme disease. Though insect repellents are helpful, be sure to tuck in your trouser cuffs and shirttails. Wear light-colored clothing so ticks can be easily spotted, and check your entire body after time spent outdoors. The height of the tick season is May through July, but infection can occur year-round.

WHEN TO GO Cape Cod National Seashore is open year-round, with a busy summer season. Trails and beaches are accessible year-round, but such facilities as bathhouses, as well as many hotels and restaurants, close in winter. Route 6, the major thoroughfare from Orleans to Provincetown, is a two-lane roadway and from June through Labor Day it's prone to gridlock. On weekends and holidays, Seashore beach parking lots sometimes fill before 10 AM.

Summer temperatures on Cape Cod average 71°F–78°F from June through August; they rarely exceed 80°F or fall below 55°F. Shoreline temperatures are usually several degrees cooler, particularly in the evening. Rainfall is heaviest in summer, with an average of 3½ inches in August. The Seashore's ocean waters are, at 50°F–60°F, among the coldest on the Cape (the shallow waters of Cape Cod Bay and Nantucket Sound are about 10°F warmer). August through October is hurricane season, when the Cape gets its fair share of major storms.

Some consider the Seashore most appealing in the spring and fall. Spring on the Cape is a short season, with cool temperatures, overcast skies, and mystical foggy mornings. Fall is pleasant, with bright foliage and mild temperatures perfect for hikes along the marshes and beaches. The ocean is warmest from late August through early to mid-October. Fall temperature highs range from 51°F to 70°F, lows from 35°F to 56°F.

Winter, due to moderating ocean breezes and the relative warmth of Gulf Stream waters, is more temperate on Cape Cod than on the mainland. Snow is common but rarely amasses. However, this is the season of nor'easters, vicious blizzards and gale-force winds that are potentially more dangerous than hurricanes. For 24-hour local weather information, call (tel. 508/790–1061) or **Todd Gross's 24-Hour Weather Line** (tel. 508/976–5200). Gross is a Boston-based meteorologist; his weather line costs 65¢ per minute.

SEASONAL EVENTS **May:** Hundreds of sailboats compete in the **Figawi Race,** held every Memorial Day weekend since 1972. **June:** The **Hyannis Harborfest** (tel. 508/775–2201), a weekend festival that takes place in early June, includes live music, jugglers, clowns, boat races, food vendors, and activities for children. In late June, Provincetown celebrates its Portuguese heritage with the annual **Portuguese Festival,** three days of revelry featuring band concerts, traditional foods, sidewalk sales, and more. **July:** The **Barnstable County Fair** (Rte. 151, East Falmouth, tel. 508/563–3200), begun in 1844, is Cape Cod's biggest summer event. The six-day affair features livestock and food judging; horse, pony, and oxen pulls; arts-and-crafts demonstrations; stage entertainment; carnival rides; and some truly artery-clogging food. The traffic can be horrendous, but the fair is worth the trip. **August:** Parades, street musicians, and vendors crowd the streets of Provincetown during **Carnival Week,** held in late August. **August–early September:** The **Harwich Cranberry Harvest Festival** (tel. 508/432–1600) comprises 10 days of festivities, including a country-western jamboree, an arts-and-crafts show, a parade, fireworks, pancake breakfasts, and an antique-car show.

WHAT TO PACK Take along a bathing suit and towel for lying on the beach; long-sleeved shirts and trousers for hiking; and insect repellent, a hat, and sunscreen for both activities. Also, pack whatever gear you'll need for your bicycle. Cameras, camcorders, and binoculars are allowed. You'll find drinking water at bathhouses throughout the park, but you might want to carry some for use on the trail. The only snack bar on Seashore property, at Herring Cove Beach, is likely to be crowded in summer. Consider carrying lunch or snacks in with you. There are four picnic areas within the Seashore.

What not to pack: The six Seashore-maintained beaches have "protected beach" areas; all are under the surveillance of park lifeguards. Surfboards, face masks, snorkels, and scuba gear; stoves or grills that require propane, white gas, or charcoal; fires; and pets are not allowed in these areas. Rafts, rubber tubes, and other inflatables, as well as glass containers, are not allowed on any Seashore beaches. Metal detectors are prohibited anywhere within the Seashore.

GENERAL STORES **Eastham Superette** (Rte. 6, between Fort Hill and the Salt Pond Visitor Center, tel. 508/255–0530) sells a full line of groceries, supplies, and wine and liquor. It's open Monday–Saturday 7 AM–9 PM, Sunday 7:30 AM–9 PM, and remains open until 10 on busy weekends. The two **Cumberland Farms** outlets (Rte. 6, Wellfleet, tel. 508/349–3719; 100 Shank Painter Rd., Provincetown, tel. 508/487–9668) sell groceries and supplies (but no alcohol) and are open daily 6 AM–11 PM.

ATMS **Eastham:** Fleet Bank (Brackett Rd.). **Wellfleet:** Cape Cod 5 Bank (Main St.). **Provincetown:** Seamen's Bank (221 Commercial St.; Shank Painter Rd. at A&P Supermarket). **Cape Cod Bank & Trust** (Lopes Square at MacMillan Wharf).

ARRIVING AND DEPARTING Town and seashore roads can be accessed from points along Route 6 between Orleans to Provincetown. Visitor centers and beach and trail entrances are well marked. You'll first encounter the Salt Pond Visitor Center; the Province Lands Visitor Center is at the park's northern tip.

By Bus. Plymouth and Brockton Street Railway (tel. 508/746–0378 or 508/775–5524) provides daily service from Boston's Logan Airport to Hyannis ($15 one-way). From Hyannis, the bus continues to Provincetown ($9 one-way), making additional local stops. Public transportation is virtually nonexistent inside the park.

By Car and RV. From the Sagamore and Bourne bridges, your entry points to Cape Cod, the 40- to 45-mi drive to the Salt Pond Visitor Center takes less than an hour on most days; tack on an additional 30 minutes on busy summer days. If you travel across the Sagamore, stay on Route 6. From the Bourne Bridge take Route 28 north to Route 6. Follow Route 6 to the visitor center. For a more scenic jaunt, exit Route 6 after the Bourne Bridge and head north to Route 6A, which follows Cape Cod Bay's shoreline. Both Routes 6 and 6A join at the Orleans traffic circle, about 3 mi before the Salt Pond Visitor Center.

For car rental at the Barnstable Airport, try **Avis** (tel. 508/775–2888 or 800/831–2847) or **Budget** (tel. 508/771–2744, 800/527–0700, or 800/848–8005). At Provincetown Municipal you'll find **Budget** (tel. 800/848–8005), which is staffed only during summer high season. You can also rent cars from **U-Save** (tel. 508/487–6343) at the Providence Airport. Call well ahead to reserve a car in summer.

Bargain Rent-a-Car (13 Main St., tel. 508/771–1298) is about 2 mi from the train station. **Trek Rent-a-Car** (233 Barnstable Rd., tel. 508/771–2459) is two blocks from the train station.

Town Taxi (tel. 508/771–5555).

By Plane. Barnstable Municipal Airport (tel. 508/775–2020) is roughly 50 mi from Provincetown and about 25 mi from the Salt Pond Visitor Center in Eastham. It's served by Cape Air (tel. 508/771–6944 or 800/352–0714), Colgan Air (tel. 508/775–7077 or 800/272–5488), Delta's Business Express (tel. 800/345–3400), Island Airlines (tel. 508/775–6606 or 800/698–1109), US Airways (tel. 800/428–4322), and Northwest Airlink Business Express (tel. 800/225–2525). The **Provincetown Municipal Airport** (tel. 508/487–0241) is within the Seashore boundaries. It's served by Cape Air (tel. 508/771–6944 or 800/352–0714). You'll want a car once you're here (*see* By Car and RV, *above*).

By Train. Amtrak (Main St., Hyannis, tel. 800/872–7245) offers limited weekend summer service from Providence, Rhode Island.

EXPLORING

Public transportation within Seashore boundaries is limited to shuttle buses that run to Coast Guard Beach from its inland parking lot. Exploring must be done by car, by bicycle, or on foot—a combination of all three works best. Cars are allowed access to beach and trail parking, as well as to several scenic roads.

Bicycles are not allowed on hiking trails, nor is hiking allowed on bicycle trails. You can see the major sites—the dunes at Province Lands, the trails of Great Island, the Atlantic White Cedar Swamp Trail at Marconi Station Site, Nauset Marsh, and Coast Guard Beach—in less than a week. Two or three days are sufficient to get a good sense of the Seashore's habitats and terrain.

THE BEST IN ONE DAY Start out early, especially in summer. Visit the Salt Pond Visitor Center, where you can gather a few brochures and watch *Sands of Time,* a 12-minute movie shown every half hour 9:30–1 and at 2, 3, and 4. You can also browse through a small museum with exhibits on the history of whaling, and more. A knowledgeable staff is on hand to answer questions. Plan one to two hours to hike the 1-mi Nauset Marsh Trail (*see* Nature Trails and Short Walks, *below*), which winds

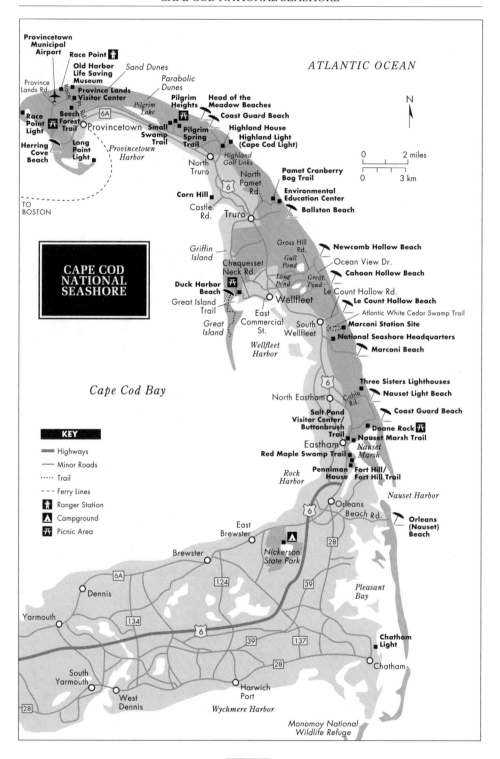

around Salt Pond and Nauset Marsh and offers plenty of opportunity to study the seashore's ecological splendor. Backtrack to the visitor center and take a short drive to Nauset Light Beach (*see* Swimming *in* Other Activities, *below*), where you can see a working lighthouse and go for a swim.

Lunch in Wellfleet, a picturesque town with cafés and antiques shops aplenty. Take Route 6 to Truro (about a 20-minute drive), where you can relax at Pilgrim Heights and walk the .25-mi Pilgrim Spring Trail (*see* Nature Trails and Short Walks, *below*). The spring is said to be the site where the Pilgrims first found fresh water in New England.

Drive 10 mi to Province Lands and stop at the visitor center for information on local trails and beaches. Race Point (*see* Swimming *in* Other Activities, *below*), the northernmost point on Cape Cod, is a prime spot for whale-watching in summer. If you've got your bike and a little energy, ride the Province Lands Trail (*see* Biking *in* Other Activities, *below*), a 5.25-mi trail that loops in and out of the dunes and passes Great Pond.

ORIENTATION PROGRAMS The Salt Pond Visitor Center shows rotating 10-minute orientation films daily from late June through Labor Day. Among the films, which concentrate on the history and geography of the seashore and surrounding areas, are *Sands of Time, Voice of Cape Cod, Thoreau's Cape Cod,* and *Wooden Ships, Men of Iron.* Show times are posted at the visitor center. The Salt Pond amphitheater stages several presentations, including slide shows and special programs for children (*see* Children's Programs, *below*). Call or write ahead for the seasonal schedule.

GUIDED TOURS Numerous local tours led by rangers are arranged at both Salt Pond and Province Lands visitor centers. Schedules vary, depending more upon tides than times. It's best to write ahead for the current schedule or call on the day you wish to visit. Most tours are free, but tickets are limited. Among the tours offered are the Fort Hill Walk, a 1.5-mi hike through the Fort Hill area of Eastham; the Pilgrim Lake Dunes Walk, a 1.5-mi walk around Pilgrim Lake and the parabolic dunes of Truro; the Tidal Flats Walk, a two-hour hike around the tidal flats of Great Island in Wellfleet (wear sneakers or boots); and the Nauset Marsh Canoe Trip, a 1.5-mi canoe trip through the marsh, for which a small fee is charged. Dozens of additional treks are led in spring, summer, and fall. Lecture programs, like Cape Cod Whales, a one-hour talk about the local presence of whales, are also offered.

Several private organizations operate specialized tours: The **Massachusetts Audubon Society's Wellfleet Bay Wildlife Sanctuary** (Box 236, South Wellfleet 02663, tel. 508/349–2615) offers naturalist-led natural history walks throughout the Seashore. Call ahead to reserve; fees vary. The **Cape Cod Museum of Natural History** (Rte. 6A, Brewster 02631; tel. 508/896–3867 or 800/479–3867) operates one or two hiking tours per month in summer. The naturalist-led tours explore seashore trails; some even venture off the trails. The hikes last two to six hours, are moderately strenuous, and cost $5–$10. Daylong trips are $15–$25. At the **Center for Coastal Studies** (59 Commercial St., Box 1036, Provincetown 02657, tel. 508/487–3622), a small, nonprofit group dedicated to the study and preservation of Cape Cod's coastal environment, naturalists conduct hikes through the dunes, salt marshes, beaches, and tidal flats of Provincetown. **Art's Sand Dune Tours** (tel. 508/487–1950 or 508/487–1050) has been giving narrated tours of the Provincetown dunes and coast for more than 50 years. The 1¼-hour trip costs $9 with a four-person minimum; a sunset tour costs $10.

SCENIC DRIVES AND VIEWS Several dozen roads wind into and out of Cape Cod National Seashore; many are access roads to trails, beaches, and visitor centers, whereas others are town roads that lead through residential centers. Scenic vistas and, in fact, the park's more compelling acreage are best seen by bicycle or on foot.

Along **Route 6,** which borders and at times bisects the park from Eastham to Province-town, haphazard development vies with small-town charm and the open pitch-pine forests and dunes of the Lower Cape. The 5-mi stretch from Eastham to Wellfleet is congested as a result of the motels, gas stations, and convenience stores that flank it. But along this stretch you'll also pass entrances to the Salt Pond Visitor Center and the park headquarters, at the Marconi Station Site. You can turn off for the town of **Wellfleet** and **Great Island,** a Seashore property with a 4-mi hiking trail past marshes. **Scenic Ocean View Drive** in Wellfleet, between Le Count Hollow Road and Gross Hill Road, passes by four Wellfleet town beaches.

North of Wellfleet, Route 6 narrows a bit and the congestion and roadside development give way to large forests of pitch pine, with the ocean never much more than 2 mi to the east and the bay never more than 2 mi to the west. You'll pass **Highland Light,** also called Cape Cod Light, the first lighthouse built on the Cape (*see* Historic Buildings and Sites, *below*).

Clearly visible from Route 6 is **Pilgrim Lake,** a quiescent and brackish body of water ringed by immense dunes. Beyond the lake, the dunes reach the road, and blown sand can be hazardous in windy weather. **Race Point Road** and **Province Lands Road** cover the Province Lands section of the Seashore and pass the great dunes. At the Province Lands Visitor Center, climb to the observation deck and take in one of the Seashore's most breathtaking views—a panoramic sweep of Province-town, dunes, and ocean.

HISTORIC BUILDINGS AND SITES As the site of the Pilgrims' first New World landing in 1620, the area along the Seashore has a rich and singular history. Several historic buildings are on Seashore property, and many more are in towns. Check with the Cape Cod Chamber of Commerce (*see* Visitor Information *in* Essential Information, *above*) and

local chambers of commerce for information on historic sites and artifacts. The Seashore-operated buildings and sites below do not charge admission.

The mansard-roofed Second Empire **Captain Edward Penniman House** (circa 1868), in the Fort Hill area of Eastham, was once the home of a wealthy whaling captain, evidenced by the back gate, which is framed by a startling whale jawbone. Guided tours are conducted regularly, and "open house" hours are often announced. Check the Salt Pond Visitor Center for details.

The **Atwood-Higgins House** (circa 1675) in Wellfleet is a classic full Cape–style house (compact and rectangular, with steep gable roof and central chimney) on rolling acreage. Guided tours are arranged by reservation only; pick up tickets and the shuttle bus from the Salt Pond Visitor Center.

The **Marconi Wireless Station Site** is just that—a site, not a building—and not even all of the original site, at that. On the same road as the park headquarters, this is where the Italian wireless-communications pioneer Guglielmo Marconi built his extraordinary transmitting station at the turn of the century. The station used four 210-ft wooden towers, equipped with 25,000-volt transmitters, to send radio waves across the Atlantic. The first successful messages, transmitted in Morse code, traveled to England on January 18, 1903, when President Theodore Roosevelt sent his "most cordial greetings and good wishes" to Edward VII. The station operated for 15 years, but with the wind and ocean eroding 3 ft of cliff each year, it was doomed. The station was dismantled in 1920; half of the original site has since fallen into the sea. Today you'll see a small model of the station, artifacts, and a memorial to Marconi. This is one of the narrowest parts of Cape Cod; from an observation platform you can see the Atlantic on one side and Blackfish Creek and Cape Cod Bay on the other.

The tiny **Three Sisters Lighthouses,** looking a bit like playhouses, are now on Cable Road at Nauset Light Beach. Built in 1892, the three were once working lighthouses on the nearby beach but were removed due to beach erosion and replaced by wooden structures and later by today's steel tower. Ranger-led tours are conducted through the Salt Pond Visitor Center.

Old Harbor Life Saving Station, on Race Point Road just beyond the Province Lands Visitor Center, was once part of the old U.S. Life Saving Service. The building was plucked from an eroding beach in Chatham and transported here by barge in 1977. Now a museum, the station houses artifacts from the early days of 20th-century lifesaving, as well as plaques describing the history of the service and the shipwrecks along this shoreline. Hours vary, so call the Province Lands Visitor Center for details.

Highland Light (turn off Rte. 6 onto Highland Rd. in Truro), also known as Cape Cod Light, is not under Seashore protection but is worth a special mention. The first lighthouse on this site opened in 1798, here in the Truro Highlands, one of the more treacherous stretches of beach on the East Coast. The oldest lighthouse on Cape Cod, this 66-ft version was built in 1857 and is now automated. Thousands of ships—and lives—have been lost offshore. Until 1996, the lighthouse was in danger of falling into the sea due to erosion of the 120-ft cliff on which it stood. However, through redirection of federal and state funds as well as small local fund-raising efforts, the U.S. Army Corps of Engineers was able to move the lighthouse some 300 ft back from the cliff. Though the lighthouse is closed to the public, nearby you'll find the **Highland Golf Course,** which operates as a park concession and was built in 1892, and the **Highland House Museum,** the site of an old Truro inn, now home of the historical society museum.

NATURE TRAILS AND SHORT WALKS Each of the Seashore's nine walking trails has trailhead boxes with free pamphlets explaining the trail's notable characteristics.

The 1.5-mi **Fort Hill Trail,** which passes through Red Maple Swamp, begins and ends at the parking lot of the Captain Edward Penniman House. Follow the signs on Route 6 in Eastham. This is a fairly easy trail with some mild slopes, fitted with log steps, and a boardwalk. The swamp is particularly vibrant in fall, when the maples turn shades of red and gold. Year-round, this is one of the Seashore's premier bird-watching areas. Watch for the stilt-legged and elegant great blue heron. Allow at least an hour for the trail.

The **Buttonbush Trail** is relatively short, about .25 mi, and unique in that it is designed for people with vision impairments; the trail has Braille text on plaques, large-print trail markers, and a guide rope. Access the trail from the Salt Pond Visitor Center in Eastham.

The 1-mi **Nauset Marsh Trail,** which begins at the Salt Pond Visitor Center, is one of the Seashore's most enticing. The trail passes Salt Pond before it comes upon Nauset Marsh. At Nauset Marsh, stop at the overlook and spend some time observing the marsh and the ocean beyond. The bird life here is rich and varied, though so are the odors emanating from the decaying salt grasses. On the return trip you'll pass an old farmstead. Allow at least an hour for this walk.

Start at Marconi Station Site for the 1.25-mi **Atlantic White Cedar Swamp Trail,** a loop that entails a walk over some steep stairs, sandy areas, and a boardwalk.

The .5-mi **Cranberry Bog Trail** includes some log steps and a boardwalk. Take North Pamet Road in Truro to the Environmental Education Center parking lot. This is swampland. Once covered by red maple, it became a working cranberry bog in the late 19th century and eventually fell into disuse.

The **Small's Swamp** trail begins at Pilgrim Heights in Truro. A .75-mi trail, it rambles over moderate grades with some log steps. "Small" refers to the settler, Thomas Small, who built a farm here in the 1860s. Native Americans inhabited the land before Small, and artifacts of that time are displayed.

The .25-mi **Pilgrim Spring** trail requires moderate climbing. It swings by the spot where the Pilgrims allegedly first dipped their lips upon landing, and can be accessed at Pilgrim Heights in Truro.

The .5-mi **Beech Forest Trail,** off Race Point Road on the way to the Race Point Visitor Center, has steep steps and lots of sand. It loops around two small kettle ponds and allows a fascinating look at one of the last remnants of pre-Pilgrim-era forest.

LONGER HIKES The longest hikes are along the 25-mi length of the Atlantic coastline between Coast Guard Beach and Race Point. Bring water and food, and be prepared to complete the walk in one day. Rangers are quick to remind you that walking a mile in sand is like walking 2 mi on solid ground.

A more moderate alternative is to hike any stretch between Coast Guard Beach and Marconi Beach. This distance is less than 5 mi one way and offers expansive views of the marsh and Nauset Light.

The 4-mi **Great Island Trail** runs the length of a small spit of land at the Seashore's western side, on Cape Cod Bay. Great Island was once an island, but the southward current of the bay shifted sand over time to connect it to the mainland. It was home to Native American Wampanoags before it became a whale-watching outpost for whalers and people who fish. To find the trail, follow signs to Wellfleet center, turn left onto Commercial Street, right at the town pier onto Kendrick Road, and then left onto Chequesset Neck Road.

OTHER ACTIVITIES **Biking.** All public seashore roads are open to cyclists, but heavy summer traffic can make for an unpleasant, if not dangerous, ride. It's better to stick to the Seashore's three trails, which cover about 11 mi total. The trails are moderate to easy, for the most part paved, and very crowded in summer. All trails are two-way, and obstacles, such as blown sand, can pop up unexpectedly. Go slowly, and when braking, use both rear and front brakes.

The **Nauset Trail** covers a bit more than 1.5 mi from the Salt Pond Visitor Center, past Nauset Marsh, and on to Coast Guard Beach. Access points can be found at the visitor center and at the Doane Rock picnic area. The **Head of the Meadow Trail** in Truro covers about 2 mi of easy path from the Head of the Meadow Beach parking area, past a great salt meadow and Pilgrim Lake, and on to High Head Road. The 7.3-mi **Province Lands Trail** is challenging, dipping and looping through sand dunes, past kettle ponds, through the Beech Forest, and on to Race Point. Enter at the Race Point Beach parking area, the Beech Forest parking area, Province Lands Visitor Center, or the Herring Cove Beach parking area.

Idle Times (Rte. 6, Eastham, tel. 508/255–8281; Rte. 6, Wellfleet, tel. 508/349–9161), offers 3- to 10-speed adult mountain bikes. Rentals cost $12 for four hours, $16 for a 24-hour period, and $60 for a week. Children's bike rates run about $4–$15 less. At **Arnold's** (329 Commercial St., Provincetown, tel. 508/487–0844), 10- to 21-speed mountain bikes can be rented for $2.50–$3.50 per hour, $10–$15 for a day, and $50–$65 a week. Children's bikes rent for $2.50 per hour or $10 per day. Arnold's also rents tandem bikes for $10 per hour or $22.50 per half-day. **Ptown Bikes** (42 Bradford St., Provincetown, tel. 508/487–8735) rents mountain bikes at $10 per half-day and $65 per week and single-speed "beach cruisers" (basic, one-speed bike with high handle bars, saddle seat, and fat balloon tires) at $10 per half-day and $40 per week.

Bird-Watching. The place to start is the **Salt Pond Visitor Center,** where you can inquire about the ranger-led tours "Birds of the Beach" and "Early Bird Walks." **Nauset Marsh** is a particularly popular spot for year-round bird-watching, with its terns, great blue herons, and other marsh birds. Check with the **Massachusetts Audubon Society's Wellfleet Bay Wildlife Sanctuary** (*see* Guided Tours, *above*) for seashore bird-watching activities.

Boating. You're free to bring your own motorboats, canoes, and kayaks and launch them at appropriate town landing areas and piers. Each town enforces its own bylaws regarding boating in freshwater ponds, maximum horsepower allowed, and water-skiing.

Jack's Boat Rentals (Gull Pond, tel. 508/349–7553; Rte. 6, Wellfleet, tel. 508/349–9808) rents pedal boats, sea cycles, and kayaks at $35 per 24-hr period for a double; canoes at $30 for 24 hours; sailboards at $35 for 24 hours; and Sunfish at $60 for 24 hours. They also offer windsurfing and sailing lessons, lead kayak tours, and rent beach chairs, umbrellas, boogie boards, and more. **Flyer's Boat Rental** (131A Commercial St., Provincetown, tel. 508/487–0898 or 800/750–0898), open May through Columbus Day, rents small (16 ft) motorboats. Rentals start at $18 per hour (two-hour minimum) and $90 per day. Flyer's also rents a number of different types of sailboats, including Sunfish, starting at $16 per hour, and 19-ft sailboats, starting at $25 per hour. Ask Flyer's about sailing lessons, fishing trips, and shuttles to Long Point at the very tip of Cape Cod.

Fishing. A license is required for all freshwater fishing. There are, however, only a few places on seashore property accessible to freshwater fishing enthusiasts. Gull Pond, Great Pond, and Long Pond, all in Wellfleet, are populated by trout, bass, pickerel, perch, and bullheads, all of which are subject to size and quantity limits. Non-commercial shellfishing areas and seasons are strictly regulated by town ordinances. Local town halls issue licenses, which often require a fee. Surf casting is allowed outside of protected beach areas and at town beaches, where you're likely to catch bluefish, striped bass, or fluke. No licenses are required, but minimum legal lengths for certain fish should be observed; ask any fishing-supply shop for such requirements.

The **Goose Hummock Shop** (Rte. 6A, Orleans, tel. 508/255–0455) sells fishing gear and provides freshwater fishing licenses and free tide charts. **Nelson's Bait & Tackle** (43 Race Point Rd., Provincetown, tel. 508/487–0034) sells bait, tackle, and licenses and provides free tide charts.

Off-Road Driving. Several miles of all-terrain-vehicle (ATV) corridors, primarily from High Head in Truro to Race Point in Provincetown, are open to ATVs. Sections close down periodically due to the nesting patterns of endangered birds, beach erosion, or inclement weather; call the **Oversand Vehicle Information Line** (tel. 508/487–3698) for status reports. You can get an ATV permit from the Race Point Ranger Station (mid-April–Nov. only); operators are required to view a short educational video. The seasonal fee for ATVs is $60.

Swimming. Cape Cod National Seashore's six beaches—Coast Guard, Nauset Light, Marconi, Head of the Meadow, Race Point, and Herring Cove—are characterized by rugged surf, lofty cliffs, and wide expanses of sandy shore. The water is cold and the undertow strong, but you won't find better places to sunbathe and dip. Facilities include rest rooms and parking, and some beaches have showers and picnic tables. Beaches "officially" open mid-June and close around Labor Day. They are closed midnight–6. Parking lots fill up by mid-morning on summer weekends; plan your visit accordingly.

Interspersed among Seashore beaches are more than a dozen town-operated beaches, most with rest rooms and picnic tables. Parking at town beaches is a challenge; fees vary from one town to the other, and some turn back nonresidents. Nauset Beach, in Orleans, at the southernmost section of the Seashore, is one of the best town beaches.

Whale-Watching. Narrated whale-watching boat tours are highly recommended; they run from about late spring through mid-fall. Although they make several trips daily, reservations are advised. The average cost of a tour during peak season is $18. In Provincetown, try **Portuguese Princess Whale Watch** (tel. 508/487–2651 or 800/442–3188 in New England), **Dolphin Fleet**

(tel. 508/349–1900 or 800/826–9300), or **Ranger V** (tel. 508/487–3322 or 800/992–9333).

CHILDREN'S PROGRAMS **Children's Hour** at Salt Pond Visitor Center, for children five and older, features scavenger hunts and sea stories (parents must be present). A Junior Ranger Program is also offered for children 8–12. Call ahead for schedules or reservations.

At the Province Lands Visitor Center, **Sea, Surf, and Sand: A Children's Discovery** takes kids through an hour of beachside activities, including sea-creatures exploration. The hour-long **Sharing Nature with Children** lets kids play environmental games with adults.

EVENING ACTIVITIES Salt Pond's **Evening Program,** usually held at 8, presents slides and other visual displays at the Salt Pond amphitheater. The Province Lands center conducts a **Sunset Beach Walk,** a family activity that includes storytelling around a campfire.

DINING

Cape Cod is named for a fish, so you shouldn't be surprised to find that seafood in all forms—from fish-and-chips to Wellfleet oysters—is fresh and abundant. Dozens of seafood restaurants can be found within Seashore boundaries, others in the towns that border the park. All are privately operated. The tonier, more expensive restaurants are in town centers, particularly Provincetown; along Route 6 you'll find family-style seafood joints and fast-food eateries.

NEAR THE PARK **Chillingsworth.** A short distance from the Seashore, this elegant eatery offers award-winning French and nouvelle cuisine complete with an outstanding wine list. The frequently changing prix-fixe dinner menu includes five courses and features such entrées as venison with celery root purée and fried pump-

kin, or sweetbreads and foie gras with wild mushrooms and ham, asparagus, and smoky sauce. *2449 Main St. (Rte. 6A), Brewster, tel. 508/896–3640. Reservations essential. AE, DC, MC, V. Closed late-Nov.–Memorial Day; Mon. June–mid-Oct.; weekdays rest of yr. $$$*

Lobster Pot. As you might have guessed, lobster, excellent chowders, and seafood are specialties at this homey, albeit noisy, family-owned restaurant. The homemade breads and desserts are also good. Though it's crowded in summer, the wait is worth the views of Provincetown Harbor and MacMillan Wharf. *321 Commercial St., Provincetown, tel. 508/487–0842. Reservations not accepted. AE, D, DC, MC, V. Closed Jan. $$*

Michael Shay's. Provincetown devotees will recognize the site of this restaurant as the old Basil's. The decor is simple, as is the cuisine—a combination of Continental and classic American coastal fare. Lobster, scallops, and a piquant sweet clam pie, as well as vegetarian lasagna and a well-stocked salad bar make this a good stop. The restaurant serves breakfast, lunch, and dinner, seven days a week, year-round. *350 Bradford St., Provincetown, tel. 508/487–3368. Reservations essential at dinner. D, MC, V. $$*

The Moors. Anchors, ship's planks, and nautical debris are the main ornamentation inside and out. Specialties are seafood and Portuguese cuisine, including soup made from *chourico* and *linguiça* (two types of spicy Portuguese sausage). And—a blessing in Provincetown—parking is available. *5 Bradford St., Provincetown, tel. 508/487–0840. Reservations essential. AE, D, DC, MC, V. Closed Thanksgiving–Mar. $$*

Land Ho! This busy, landmark Orleans restaurant is famous for its extensive newspaper lending rack and its ceiling cluttered with signs and license plates. The food is hearty and simple: Fish-and-chips, burgers, sandwiches, chowders, and soups are the staples, and they're good. *Rte. 6A, Orleans,* *tel. 508/255–5165. Reservations not accepted. MC, V. $–$$*

Box Lunch. A local chain, Box Lunch is great for a take-out picnic lunch. The "Rollwich," sandwich ingredients rolled in a pita, is this restaurant's main claim to fame. Try the Jaws Rollwich, a quarter-pound of roast beef, horseradish, mayo, and onions. Other rollwiches include the standard sandwich meats, lobster, egg salad, and vegetables. Order ahead for quickest service. Breakfast—rollwiches filled with eggs, sausages, and cheese—is also available. *Rte. 6, Eastham, tel. 508/255–0799; 50 Briar La., Wellfleet, tel. 508/349–2178; 353 Commercial St., Provincetown, tel. 508/487–6026. Reservations not accepted. No credit cards. $*

Poit's. With picnic-table seating and video games indoors and an ice cream hut and miniature golf outdoors, the restaurant's style has been pure kitsch since its 1954 opening. It has no service—you place your order, and the staff will give you a shout over the loudspeaker. But the food—fish-and-chips, fried clam plates, chowder, and lobster rolls—is unfailingly fresh and tasty, as evidenced by the crowds lined up outside. You can't miss it: just south of the Marconi Station Site in North Eastham. *Rte. 6, North Eastham, tel. 508/255–6321. Reservations not accepted. D, MC, V. Closed Sept.–Mar. $*

PICNIC SPOTS There are four park picnic areas: at Beech Forest Trail in Province Lands, Pilgrim Heights in Truro, the head of the Great Island Trail in Wellfleet, and Doane Rock near the Salt Pond Visitor Center. All are in shaded, wooded areas, with parking, rest rooms, and grills. Many town beaches have picnic tables as well.

Picnicking on Seashore beaches is allowed, but the use of glass is forbidden. Outside of protected areas, you can cook on a white gas, propane, or coal stove or grill. Regulations require that picnickers douse coal fires and remove fire remnants—do not bury the coals.

LODGING

You'll find a plethora of hotels, motels, inns, B&Bs, condos, and campgrounds open during every season except winter. The accommodations that are open in winter reduce their rates by as much as 50%. Rates begin to rise in May, peak from Memorial Day through Labor Day (reserve well ahead in summer, particularly for holiday weekends), and fall after Columbus Day. Several hotels, motels, hostels, and campgrounds operate within Seashore boundaries, some on private property and several as park concessions. The Seashore is long and thin—no accommodation is more than a few minutes from a beach.

NEAR THE PARK **Chatham Bars Inn.** About 25 minutes from the Salt Pond Visitor Center, this imposing inn is a stately vacation retreat that projects elegance, grace, and old money. In operation for more than 80 years, the hotel comprises 26 authentic bungalows and the Main Inn (which is fronted by an ocean overlook and veranda), plus a chintz-filled reception hall. Dinner (open to the public) is formal but relaxing—the view of Pleasant Bay and the Atlantic is near perfect. *297 Shore Rd., Chatham 02633, tel. 508/945–0096 or 800/527–4884, fax 508/945–5491. 152 rooms. Facilities: 2 restaurants, bar, pool, 3 tennis courts, exercise room, beach, library, children's programs. AE, DC, MC, V. $$$*

The Masthead. The best of several worlds converges at this informal hotel and resort, an eclectic collection of individually decorated rooms (some have antiques), small efficiencies, and cottages in several seaside buildings. A little more than a five-minute walk from downtown Provincetown, the property sits on a 450-ft private beach. *31–41 Commercial St., Provincetown 02657, tel. 508/487–0523 or 800/395–5095, fax 508/487–9251. 8 rooms (2 share bath), 6 apartments, 3 efficiencies, 3 cottages, 1 studio. Facilities: kitchenettes, beach. AE, D, DC, MC, V. $$–$$$*

Four Points Hotel. For those who find a certain comfort in staying at a familiar chain hotel, this Sheraton hotel is the perfect choice. It's slick and efficient without any pretenses. The rooms are decorated in a generic, eminently forgettable hotel style, but the location—just minutes from Fort Hill and Salt Pond—is a major plus. Poolside rooms are best. *Rte. 6, Eastham 02642, tel. 508/255–5000 or 800/533–3986, fax 508/240–1870. 107 rooms. Facilities: restaurant, bar-nightclub, 2 pools, hot tub, sauna, 2 tennis courts, health club. AE, D, DC, MC, V. $$–$$$*

Wellfleet Motel & Lodge. This comfortable, medium-size resort motel sits on 12 wooded acres on Route 6 between the Salt Pond Visitor Center and the Marconi Station Site. The property offers direct access to the Cape Cod Rail Trail (bike trail) and the Seashore, and the Audubon Society's Wellfleet Bay Wildlife Sanctuary is across the road. Accommodations are clean but sparse, with king- and queen-size beds, some two-room suites, and basic amenities. It's a good value. *Rte. 6, Box 606, South Wellfleet 02663, tel. 508/349–3535 or 800/852–2900, fax 508/349–1192. 65 rooms. Facilities: café, bar, indoor and outdoor pools, hot tub, recreation room. AE, DC, MC, V. $$–$$$*

Fairbanks Inn. This 1776 no-smoking redbrick inn, originally a sea captain's home and one of Provencetown's oldest structures, consists of a main house and several outbuildings filled with canopy beds, antiques, and Oriental rugs on wideboard pine floors. There's also a rooftop sundeck with grill. This is an excellent base for exploring the Seashore and Provincetown. Breakfast is included. *90 Bradford St., Provincetown 02657, tel. 508/487–0386 or 800/324–7265, fax 508/487–3540. 10 rooms with bath, 2 rooms share bath, 1 penthouse, 1 studio apartment with kitchen. AE, MC, V. $$*

Inn at Duck Creeke. Minutes from Route 6, the Seashore, and Wellfleet center, this circa-1815 inn looks out over 5 acres of salt marsh and a duck pond. The setting is informal and authentically antique; diverse and individually decorated rooms are situated in several buildings, including the old carriage house and saltworks. Next door is the inn's Sweet Seasons restaurant and Duck Creeke Tavern, the home of local jazz ensembles on hazy summer nights. The inn also operates the Bean Stock, a small coffee shop where they roast their own beans. Breakfast is included. *70 Main St., Box 364, Wellfleet 02667, tel. 508/349–9333, fax 508/349–0234. 17 rooms with bath, 8 rooms share 4 baths. Facilities: restaurant, pub, coffee shop. AE, MC, V. Closed mid-Oct.– early-May. $$*

Provincetown Inn. At the extreme west end of town, this rambling seaside hotel's charm is defined by its weathered, kitschy ambience. Though the hotel lobby is plastered with unseemly murals depicting Provincetown's history, the rooms, some of which are seaside, are clean and comfortable. Breakfast is included. *1 Commercial St., Provincetown 02657, tel. 508/487–9500 or 800/942–5388, fax 508/487–2911. 100 rooms. Facilities: restaurant, bar, pool, sauna. MC, V. $–$$*

HOSTELS

Little America AYH-Hostel. On a breezy dune by the Cranberry Bog Trail on North Pamet Road in Truro—the heart of the Seashore—sits this former Coast Guard station with a spectacular view of Ballston Beach and the surrounding dunes. *Box 402, Truro 02666, tel. 508/349–3889. 42 rooms. Facilities: kitchen, volleyball, beach. Closed mid-Sept.–late June. MC, V. $*

Mid-Cape AYH-Hostel. This hostel is less than 3 mi from the Salt Pond Visitor Center. *75 Goody Hallet Dr., Eastham 02642, tel. 508/255–2785. 50 beds in 8 cabins. Facilities: kitchen, volleyball. Closed mid-Sept.–mid-May. MC, V. $*

CAMPING

Cape Cod National Seashore does not allow tents on park property. Self-contained vehicles (a motor home or truck with attached shell and permanently mounted holding tanks for sewage and gray water) are allowed access to certain beaches, with a park permit, for 72 consecutive hours per visit. Park permits are $100 per season, and reservations are taken, in writing, for the Fourth of July and Labor Day weekends only. Otherwise, it's first-come, first-served, and only approximately 100 vehicles are allowed inside the park at any one time. Due to local ordinances, campfires may not be allowed on the camping sites.

NEAR THE PARK **Atlantic Oaks Campground.** Next to the Four Points Sheraton, this campground is less than a mile north of the Salt Pond Visitor Center. Primarily an RV camp, it offers limited tenting as well (no designated sites). The setting is a pine and oak forest, and you're minutes from the Seashore. There are bikes for rent and there's direct access to the Cape Cod Rail Trail. RV hookups, including cable TV, cost $32 per double; tent sites are $24. Showers are free. *Rte. 6, Eastham 02642, tel. 508/255–1437 or 800/332–2267. 100 RV sites, tenting area. Facilities: bicycles, playground, coin laundry. Closed Nov.–Mar. D, MC, V. $*

Horton's Park Camping Resort. This campground is in a great location—a heavily wooded area just a few hundred feet from the famous Cape Cod Light and from numerous Seashore beaches and activities. In addition to the facilities listed below, there are metered showers, a convenience store, and horseshoes. Tent sites average $18 for two, and RV sites with hookups for electricity, water, and sewage average $25. Additional adults are charged $7, kids under 3 stay free, and no dogs are allowed. Parking is $6 per day. Day visitors can visit the park for a small entrance fee and park-

ing fee. *Box 308, 71 S. Highland Rd., North Truro, tel. 508/487–1220 or 800/252–7705. 200 sites. Facilities: coin laundry, volleyball, playground. Closed mid-Oct.–Apr. MC, V. $*

Nickerson State Park. Cape Cod's largest and most popular camping site is on 2,000 acres teeming with wildlife, white pine, hemlock, and spruce forest, and jammed with opportunities for trout fishing, walking, or biking along 8 mi of paved trails; canoeing; sailing; motorboating; and bird-watching. Tent sites cost $6; RVs must be self-contained. Facilities include showers, bathrooms, picnic tables, barbecue areas, and a store. Maps and schedules of park programs are available at the park entrance. Campers are allowed year-round; tent camping is allowed April–September (but reservations for sites are accepted only Memorial Day–Labor Day). *Rte. 6A, East Brewster 02631, tel. 508/896–3491, reservations 508/896–4615. 418 sites. No credit cards. $*

Paine's Campground. Primarily for tenters (though it has a half-dozen RV hookups), Paine's is in an excellent location, about a 25-minute walk from the beach and a mile north of the Marconi Station. In 16 acres of forest and huckleberry trees, the camp is very private and separated into family, couples, and singles sites. Sites run $12 per person during July and August, less for off-season; children 6–18 are charged $3 per night and kids under 6 are admitted free. RV hookups are $4 extra per site per day. Dogs (must be leashed and must have rabies certification) are allowed for $3. A reservation fee of $5 is required, and showers are metered. The good-natured Paines have owned this campground for nearly 40 years. *Box 201, South Wellfleet 02663, tel. 508/349–3007 or 800/479–3017, fax 508/349–0246. 144 tent sites, 6 RV sites. Facilities: volleyball. MC, V. Closed mid-Sept.–mid-May.*

Cape Hatteras and Cape Lookout National Seashores

North Carolina

By Susan Ladd

istory, mystery, and myth pepper these islands like sea oats. The first settlers, remembered today as the Lost Colony, landed here in 1585, only to disappear shortly thereafter without a trace. Pirates plundered ships in these waters; it was here that the notorious Blackbeard met his end, cornered near Silver Lake Harbor at Ocracoke.

Those who endured drew their living from the sea, fishing and whaling, and setting out in small boats as the ocean raged to rescue sailors whose ships had foundered. They stayed for the same reason people flock here today: for the unparalleled beauty of the ever-changing coastal landscape. In its gentler moods the ocean casts pearly shells on the wide, flat beaches and laps at the sand. In moments of fury, it lashes and churns at the dunes, gouging out channels and reshaping the shoreline. The ocean is forever resculpting these banks; Bodie Island and Pea Island (for example) are islands no more.

Cape Hatteras and Cape Lookout offer two very different beach experiences. Cape Hatteras is a 70-mi strand of narrow islands connected to the mainland by a series of bridges and ferries and bisected by a modern road that allows easy access to the shoreline. When the National Seashore was established in 1953, the small towns along the island were permitted to remain, so accommodations, supplies, and recreational opportunities are always close at hand.

Cape Lookout, a 55-mi span of three unconnected islands, is essentially a beach wilderness—as close as you can get to experiencing the coast as the original colonists did. Because no bridge ever connected it with the mainland, it has remained undeveloped and relatively pristine. The only access is by boat, and the only accommodations are tents and primitive cabins.

Rich in history and natural beauty, Cape Hatteras National Seashore draws more than 2 million visitors annually; some 300,000 make their way by ferry to the desolate shores of Cape Lookout. These visitors range from family vacationers and garden-variety sun worshipers to bird-watchers, anglers, shell collectors, surfers, sailors, and divers. But the allure is always the chance to find a quiet strip of beach all your own.

ESSENTIAL INFORMATION

VISITOR INFORMATION For information on Cape Hatteras, contact the **Cape Hatteras National Seashore** (Rte. 1, Box 675, Manteo 27954, tel. 919/473–2111). You'll find up-to-date listings of events and activities at the visitor centers and ranger stations on Bodie, Hatteras, and Ocracoke islands. For more information on nearby towns, contact the **Outer Banks/Dare County Tourist Bureau** (Box 399, Manteo 27954, tel. 919/473–2138 or 800/446–6262) or the **Ocracoke Civic and Business Association** (Box 456, Ocracoke 27960, tel. 919/928–6711).

For information on Cape Lookout, contact the **Cape Lookout National Seashore** (131 Charles St., Harkers Island 28531, tel. 919/728–2250). The visitor center at Harkers

Island has information on the latest beach and weather conditions and ferry schedules. For further information on nearby towns, contact the **Carteret County Tourism Development Bureau** (Box 1406, Morehead City 28557, tel. 800/786–6962) or stop by the new **visitor center** on U.S. 70 in Morehead City.

FEES There are no fees to enter the national seashores.

PUBLICATIONS Ranger stations and visitor centers at both seashores have free publications on park attractions and activities.

To learn more about the forces that shape the barrier islands, read *Ribbon of Sand,* by John Alexander and James Lazell (Algonquin Books). Coastal author David Stick has written some of the best volumes on the history and lore of the Outer Banks, including *The Outer Banks of North Carolina* and *Graveyard of the Atlantic* (both University of North Carolina Press). All three are sold at the visitor centers on Bodie, Hatteras, and Ocracoke islands and at the Cape Lookout visitor center.

GEOLOGY AND TERRAIN The two national seashores are part of a long, thin strand of islands stretching 175 mi from the Virginia border to the tip of Cape Lookout. The islands, separated from the mainland by large shallow sounds, form a buffer between land and sea.

Two great ocean currents—the cold Labrador Current from the north, and the warm waters of the Gulf Stream from the south—converge offshore. In the dead heat of August, swimmers at Avon shiver deliciously in waters still only 72°F, while 90 mi south at Shackleford Banks, the water is a balmy 80°F. The currents converge at Diamond Shoals, just off the tip of Cape Hatteras, in turbulent, treacherous seas. The churning waters and shifting sands have claimed more than 2,000 ships since sailors first began exploring these waters, thus earning the name "Graveyard of the Atlantic."

The dynamics of land and sea have slowly but inexorably moved the barrier islands south and west. You can see evidence of the westward movement in the black peat moss uncovered in areas of the beach; this is where the marsh was thousands of years ago. The southward current has shifted the inlets. As the current enters an inlet, it deposits sand at the bottom of the island to the north and carves it away from the top of the island below. Oregon Inlet, just south of Bodie Island, provides the most dramatic example. It is moving away from the Herbert C. Bonner Bridge, and only constant dredging by the Army Corps of Engineers keeps the inlet open under the bridge.

Barrier islands consist essentially of dunes, forest, and marsh. The shifting dunes are anchored by vegetation with a special ability to withstand the salt spray and unrelenting wind. The small shrubs that take hold in the shelter provided by the dunes give rise, in turn, to the maritime forest. The marsh is the place where freshwater and salt water meet, an ideal incubator for many ocean residents.

FLORA AND FAUNA Not much can survive on the wind-whipped dunes. Sea oats, whose deep roots anchor the dunes, are so crucial to the stabilization of the Outer Banks that they're protected by federal law. Pennywort and prickly pear cactus also grow nearby.

Birds that can be seen along the shoreline include the tiny sanderling, the orange-beaked oystercatcher, the seagull, and the brown pelican—the last formerly endangered but now a common and welcome sight. The piping plover, a small, shy gray-and-white bird that feeds at water's edge, is very much endangered. Its tiny nests on the open beach are easily destroyed by humans, storms, and predators. The authorities occasionally bar sunbathers and vehicles from parts of the beach to protect plover nesting grounds.

Ghost crabs, which venture out of their burrows to skitter along the sand, pose the gravest danger to another endangered animal that comes here to nest in the summer: the loggerhead turtle. The massive loggerheads, weighing an average of 250 pounds, drag themselves to the shores of Cape Lookout and Cape Hatteras in the spring and dig large holes in the sand, where each female deposits more than 100 leathery, golfball-size eggs. But an estimated 98% of the hatchlings die on their way to the surf, mostly picked off by seagulls and ghost crabs. Rangers and volunteers do what they can, marking nests and moving them when necessary, and even patrolling the beaches at night to help the hatchlings make it to the sea.

Behind the protective barrier of the dunes, the maritime forest takes hold. Live oaks, sculpted by the wind, will grow no higher than the safety of the dune. Wax myrtle, yaupon holly, and cedar are a few of the trees you'll find at Buxton, Ocracoke, and Shackleford banks.

In the shelter of the forest live raccoons, rats, rabbits, river otters, and snakes. One of the rarest inhabitants is the Outer Banks king snake, smaller than a regular king snake and sporting different color bands. Cape Lookout has no unique species, but the early settlers introduced many animals to the islands. Survivors include nutria (a member of the beaver family) and ring-necked pheasants.

The marsh is home to a great variety of birds. Herons and egrets pick their way delicately through the grasses, and ducks glide along the water's surface. Whistling swans, snow geese, Canada geese, and 25 species of ducks winter here; sparrows, warblers, and terns can be seen during the spring and fall migrations. The marsh also provides a nursery ground for oysters, shrimp, clams, scallops, and many species of fish, some of which grow to maturity in the calm, mineral-rich waters before entering the ocean. More than 90% of the sea creatures we commonly eat spend part of their lives in the salt marsh.

WHEN TO GO Fall is the most popular season at Cape Lookout, largely because it's the best time for fishing. Many people find the heat, humidity, and mosquitoes too much to handle in the summer.

Cape Hatteras, which draws more of a family crowd, is busiest in July and August, when school is out and recreational opportunities reach their peak. But if you're more interested in solitude than a suntan, visit in spring or fall, when the weather is milder, the beaches are less crowded, and the insects are not as hungry.

From March through May, temperatures reach the 60s and 70s and rainfall is lowest; wildflowers bloom in the maritime forests and birds begin nesting. Sun worshipers flock in during June, July, and August, when temperatures average 80°F–84°F. The beach remains pleasantly warm in September and October, with highs in the 72°F–80°F range.

November and December, when temperatures are in the 56°F–64°F range, are a good time for shelling and fishing, and you'll often have the beach to yourself. The only two months to avoid are January and February, when temperatures average 38°F–53°F and the winds are most intense. Many businesses close down for these two months.

June 1 through November 1 is hurricane season, but it's a good idea to check the weather radio any time you visit the Outer Banks: Conditions can change rapidly, bringing severe storms with dangerous lightning.

SEASONAL EVENTS *Near Cape Hatteras.* **May and June:** The **Hang Gliding Spectacular** in May and the **Rogallo Kite Festival** in June are held at Jockey's Ridge in Nags Head to honor Kitty Hawk resident Frank Rogallo, who invented the flexible wing used in hang gliders today (tel. 919/441–4124). **June–August:** *The Lost Colony* (tel. 800/488–5012), America's longest-running outdoor drama, tells the story of the colony, founded near Manteo in 1587, that vanished without a trace. (The settlers' journey to the New World is re-created year-round aboard the *Elizabeth II,* a 16th-century sailing ship at Roanoke Harbor in Manteo; tel. 919/473–1144.) **December 17:** The **First Flight Commemoration,** held at the Wright Brothers Memorial in Kill Devil Hills, marks the brothers' first powered flight here in 1903 (tel. 919/441–7430).

Near Cape Lookout. **May:** The **Traditional Wooden Boat Show**, hosted by the North Carolina Maritime Museum in Beaufort, explores the enduring craft of boatbuilding in the area (tel. 919/728–7317). **June:** The **Beaufort Old Homes Tour** (tel. 919/728–5225) showcases the extensive historic district. **August:** The **Strange Seafood Exhibition** (tel. 919/728–7317), hosted by the North Carolina Maritime Museum, serves up unusual sea critters. **December:** The **Core Sound Decoy Festival** (tel. 919/728–1500) celebrates an aspect of carving that dates back seven generations in Harkers Island.

WHAT TO PACK The two most important items are sunscreen and insect repellent. The sun, reflecting off the water and white sand, can produce intense and painful burns. Shelter is scarce in most of the isolated beach areas. A hat is a must, and a beach umbrella is a good idea if you plan to make a day of it.

The need for insect repellent cannot be overemphasized. Park rangers joke that the mosquitoes must carry glass cutters, since they even seem to get into your car. Wooded areas are worse for mosquitoes, ticks, and biting flies; the seashore for sand fleas. Deet is probably the best-known insect repellent, but a less toxic and more fragrant alternative is Avon's Skin So Soft bath oil; Cutters has incorporated Avon's formula.

On Cape Lookout National Seashore, even a day trip requires more gear than a typical day on the beach, because there are no stores, water fountains, snack bars, or concessions of any kind. Bring everything you need, including plenty of fresh water, food, and protective shoes such as sneakers. Bring a trash bag, too, so that you can carry out everything you bring in.

GENERAL STORES **At Cape Hatteras.** The **Oregon Inlet Fishing Center** (just north of the Herbert C. Bonner Bridge, tel. 919/441–6301) is open late March–early November, daily 5 AM–7 PM. It stocks groceries, film,

suntan lotion, clothing, beach supplies, fishing supplies, boat equipment, and more. There's also a boat ramp and fishing charters. The **Lee Robinson General Store** (less than a mile from the ferry dock in Hatteras Village, tel. 919/986–2381) is open March–December, daily 8 AM–11 PM. It carries clothes, toys, groceries, and gifts in its wood-shingled building. The **Community Store** (on Silver Lake in Ocracoke, tel. 919/928–3321) is open spring–fall, Monday–Saturday 7 AM–9 PM, Sunday 8–8; winter, Monday–Saturday 7–6. It has been a mainstay in the community since 1918: You can sit in the rockers out front or stock up on groceries, hardware, office supplies, fishing gear, camping gear, or auto parts.

Near Cape Lookout. East'ard Variety Store (1 mi south of the ranger station on Harkers Island, tel. 919/728–7149) is open Sunday–Thursday 5:30 AM–10:45 PM, Friday–Saturday 5:30 AM–11:45 PM. This is the quintessential if-we-don't-have-it-you-don't-need-it store. You'll find beach supplies, groceries, commercial and recreational fishing gear, bottled propane gas, and plumbing, automotive, and mobile-home supplies and parts.

ATMS **At Cape Hatteras.** The nearest ATM location is the Centura Bank on Route 158, 2 mi from the park entrance at Whalebone Junction in Nags Head. There are dozens of ATMs in the area, including at a Centura Bank in Buxton and at the Variety Store in Ocracoke.

At Cape Lookout. The nearest ATM is at the Wachovia Bank on U.S. 70 in Beaufort, 17 mi from the ranger station at Harkers Island.

ARRIVING AND DEPARTING You can get close to both parks on public transportation, but to actually reach either one and explore the area properly you'll need a car.

By Car and RV to Cape Hatteras. The most practical access is via Manteo from the west or Nags Head from the north; the southern approach requires a 2½-hour ferry ride from Cedar Island or Swan Quarter to Ocracoke.

From Norfolk, Virginia, take U.S. 17 south to Elizabeth City, North Carolina, or Route 168 to Barco. Pick up U.S. 158 to Nags Head and proceed south to Whalebone Junction. Route 12 goes straight through the park. From Raleigh take U.S. 64 east 200 mi to Whalebone Junction, then pick up Route 12 south.

You can rent a car in Elizabeth City at **National** (tel. 919/335–1860 or 800/227–7368).

You can rent a car at Manteo's Dare County airport from **B&R Car Rental** (tel. 919/473–2600). Nearby taxi services include **Beach Cab** (tel. 919/441–2500) and **Outer Banks Limo Service** (919/261–3133).

You can rent a car at Norfolk's airport from **Avis** (tel. 800/331–1212), **Budget** (tel. 757/855–8035 or 800/527–0700), **Dollar** (tel. 757/855–1988 or 800/800–4000), **Enterprise** (tel. 757/853–7700), **Hertz** (tel. 757/857–1261 or 800/654–3131), or **Thrifty** (tel. 757/855–5900 or 800/367–2277).

By Car and RV to Cape Lookout. Most people visiting Cape Lookout will probably take the southern approach, catching the ferry from Harkers Island; to visit the park's northernmost island, you may catch a vehicle ferry from Atlantic on the mainland or a passenger ferry from Ocracoke Village in the Cape Hatteras National Seashore.

From Raleigh take U.S. 70 east 147 mi to Morehead City; continue on U.S. 70 to Otway, then turn right on Harkers Island Road. From Wilmington take U.S. 17 north 51 mi to Jacksonville, then Route 24 east 43 mi to Morehead City; pick up U.S. 70 east to Otway, then turn right on Harkers Island Road.

You can rent a car at **Hertz** (tel. 919/726–9200) or **Enterprise** (tel. 919/240–0218 or 800/736–8222), both in Morehead City.

Wilmington's New Hanover airport has rental-car desks for **Avis** (tel. 910/763–1993), **Budget** (tel. 910/762–9247), **Hertz** (tel. 910/762–1010), and **National** (tel. 910/762–8000).

By Bus to Cape Hatteras. The closest bus station is **Trailways** (tel. 919/335–5183 or 800/231–2222) in Elizabeth City, 60 mi to the north.

By Bus to Cape Lookout. The closest bus station is **Carolina Trailways** (tel. 800/231–2222) in Morehead City, 20 mi west of the park.

By Plane to Cape Hatteras. The closest airport is the **Dare County Regional Airport** in Manteo (tel. 919/473–2600), roughly 6 mi from Whalebone Junction; it is served by a small commuter airline, Southeast Airlines (tel. 919/473–3222). The closest major airport is **Norfolk International Airport** (tel. 757/857–3351), 90 mi to the north in Virginia.

By Plane to Cape Lookout. The closest airport is **Craven County Regional Airport** (tel. 919/638–8591) in New Bern, 56 mi northwest of Harkers Island. But locals warn that connections to New Bern from most major airports usually involve long layovers; they recommend flying into **New Hanover International Airport** (tel. 910/341–4125) in Wilmington, 108 mi south of Harkers Island.

By Train. The train station nearest to Cape Hatteras is in Norfolk, Virginia, 90 mi to the north. The train station nearest to Cape Lookout is in Rocky Mount, 140 mi northwest of Harkers Island. **Amtrak** (tel. 800/872–7245) serves both stations.

EXPLORING

Cape Hatteras is the more accessible of the two seashores. A two-lane highway, Route 12, cuts from one end to the other, broken only by the Herbert C. Bonner Bridge across Oregon Inlet and the modern ferry system that carries passengers and vehicles to Ocracoke Island. At periodic access ramps you can park and walk over the dunes to the beach. There are also numerous access ramps for four-wheel-drive vehicles.

The mostly undeveloped shore, fringed with sea oats, stretches more than 80 mi from end to end. You can drive all the way down and back in one day, but that doesn't leave time to linger. To really enjoy a visit, catch an early morning ferry to Ocracoke and spend the day. If you want to visit nearby historic sites, such as the Wright Brothers National Memorial and Fort Raleigh National Historic Site, set aside another full day. But don't get so caught up in attractions that you miss the joy of a solitary walk down deserted stretches of beach.

Cape Lookout presents more challenges to the visitor, and if your priorities are comfort and ease of travel, it's probably not for you. The seashore consists of three unconnected islands—Shackleford Banks, North Core Banks, and South Core Banks—and the only way to reach them is by boat. For ferry phone numbers to and from a variety of destinations, call the **Cape Lookout National Seashore** (tel. 919/728–2250) and press "1." Sand Dollar Transportation (tel. 919/728–6181) and Barrier Island Transportation (tel. 919/728–3575) run **passenger ferries** run from **Harkers Island.** In **Beaufort** try Island Ferry Service (tel. 919/728–6888) or Outer Banks Ferry Service (tel. 919/728–4129) to Shackleford Banks and to the southern tip of South Core Banks near the Cape Lookout Lighthouse. It's a 20- to 40-minute ride to the dock, a .25-mi walk to the lighthouse, and another 3 mi to the point.

The open beach stretches as far as your legs can take you, but to really explore the islands you need a four-wheel-drive. **Vehicle ferries** run from Davis to the midpoint of South Core Banks (Alger Willis Fishing Camps, tel. 919/729–2791) and from Atlantic to the southern end of North Core Banks (Morris Marina, tel. 919/225–4261).

It's a 40-minute drive from the ferry landing on North Core Banks to the village of Portsmouth at the island's northern tip. There's an unpaved road through the interior, but you'll find smoother traveling on the beach. If you want to visit Portsmouth but don't have a four-wheel-drive, you can take a 20-minute passenger ferry from Ocracoke (Rudy Austin, tel. 919/928–4361).

Many people visit the islands by **private boat,** dropping anchor on the shallow sandy bottom of the sound and wading ashore. But take care if you try this: The shifting sandbars of Core Sound have put many a boat in dry dock for repairs.

THE BEST IN ONE DAY **Cape Hatteras.** There are few structures as evocative as the three lighthouses along the Cape Hatteras National Seashore. Begin at the 1872 **Bodie Island Lighthouse** near the northern end. The 150-ft tower with wide horizontal stripes is set amid quiet marshlands and still has its original Fresnel glass lens. The candy-striped 1870 **Cape Hatteras Lighthouse,** farther south at Buxton, is, at 208 ft, the nation's tallest. Erosion has threatened the tower since 1935; the current plan is to move it inland. At certain times of the year, usually Easter–Columbus Day, visitors can climb the 268 steps to the top for the best view on the beach. From Buxton, head south to the town of Hatteras and catch the free ferry to Ocracoke; then drive to Ocracoke Village on the south end of the island, and turn left on Lighthouse Road to reach the **1823 Ocracoke Lighthouse.** Unlike the others, this one stands a mere 75 ft, its whitewashed sides bare of any design. The state's oldest operating lighthouse serves mostly as a guide to Silver Lake Harbor.

Cape Lookout. Catch an early ferry to the point at Cape Lookout. (Be sure to pack everything you'll need, including water.) From the dock, walk along the wooden boardwalk to the lighthouse and visit with the volunteer caretakers. The old keeper's quarters is also a visitor center, staffed from March through November. An exhibit is being mounted there featuring artifacts from the wreck of the *Olive Thurlow,* which was recently discovered submerged in the bight. Take the boardwalk to the dunes and, once on the beach, turn southward to the point, where the island ends. Along the dune line, look for the massive timbers of old shipwrecks that are covered and uncovered periodically by the shifting sands. Fishing and shelling here can be very good. (Each visitor may take two gallons of uninhabited shells out of the park each day.) You can continue around the point to the gun mounts—massive, partially submerged metal structures that served as submarine defenses during World War II.

GUIDED TOURS **Cape Hatteras.** Aerial tours are offered by **Kitty Hawk Aero Tours** (First Flight Airstrip, Kill Devil Kills, tel. 919/441–4460). **Water Works** (Milepost 16.5, Whalebone Junction, tel. 919/441–8875) offers airboat tours and dolphin-watch excursions. Tour the sounds and estuaries with **Kayak EcoTours** (Kitty Hawk Kites, Nags Head, tel. 919/441–4124 or 800/334–4777) or **Wilderness Canoeing** (Manns Harbor, tel. 919/473–3270).

Cape Lookout. Island Ferry Service (Beaufort, tel. 919/728–6888) offers two-hour nature and history tours of Shackleford Banks. Sailboat tours are offered by **Good Fortune** (Morehead City, tel. 919/728–7936) and **Lookout Cruises** (Beaufort, tel. 919/504–7245). Tour the harbor by paddleboat on the ***Crystal Queen*** (Beaufort, tel. 919/728–2527) and by motorboat on **Mystery Tours** (Beaufort, tel. 919/726–6783).

SCENIC DRIVES AND VIEWS A ferry is a delightful way to experience the islands and also the best means of getting from one national seashore to the other. If you want just a taste, try the free ferry from Hatteras to Ocracoke Island (tel. 800/293–3779). Cars are loaded on a first-come, first-served basis, so drive to the first open space. Ferries depart every hour in the winter, every half hour in the summer—when you may have to wait. The ride takes 40 minutes. Bird-watchers should bring binoculars to observe the many species that nest on the small sandbar islands that dot Pamlico Sound. If you want more, head to the south end of Ocracoke and catch the Cedar Island Ferry (tel. 800/293–3779): pedestrians $1, bicycles $2, cars and motorcycles $10. In the summer and fall, you must reserve ahead and be at the dock 30 minutes prior to departure.

There are two views to go out of your way for at **Cape Hatteras.** One is from the Her-

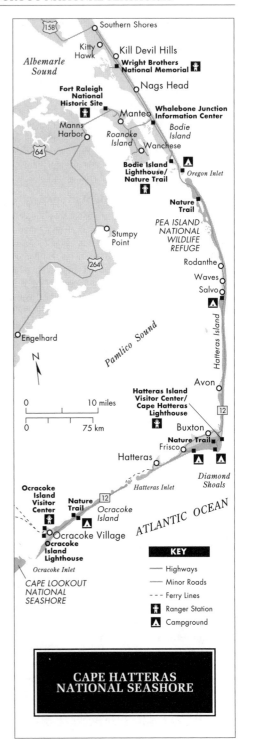

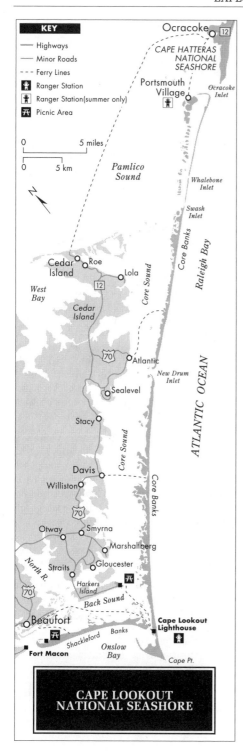

KEY

— Highways
···· Minor Roads
- - - Ferry Lines
Ranger Station
Ranger Station (summer only)
Picnic Area

0   5 miles
0   5 km

Ocracoke 12

CAPE HATTERAS NATIONAL SEASHORE

Portsmouth Village

Ocracoke Inlet

Pamlico Sound

Whalebone Inlet

Swash Inlet

Core Banks

Raleigh Bay

Cedar Island   Roe
Lola
West Bay
Cedar Island
12

Core Sound

Atlantic
New Drum Inlet
Sealevel

ATLANTIC OCEAN

Stacy

Core Sound

70
Davis
Williston
Core Banks

Otway   Smyrna
Marshallberg
Straits   Gloucester
North R.
70
Harkers Island
Back Sound
Beaufort
Shackleford   Banks
Fort Macon
Onslow Bay
Cape Pt.

Cape Lookout Lighthouse

CAPE LOOKOUT NATIONAL SEASHORE

bert C. Bonner Bridge: Drive slowly as you cross Oregon Inlet on this silver ribbon curving over the turbulent waters. At the crest you can see a beautiful cross-section of the barrier island, with marsh and sound on one side and the ocean and shoreline on the other. But the best view on the Outer Banks may be from the **Cape Hatteras Lighthouse.** Your knees will ache from climbing the 268 steps up to the wrought-iron balcony at the top, but you'll be able to see Diamond Shoals and the point of the island to the south. Walking around the balcony, you get a complete view of the village of Buxton, the interior of the island, and the shoreline stretching north. The lighthouse is only open at certain times of the year, usually Easter–Columbus Day. Check with the Park Service rangers for more details.

Scenic drives on **Cape Lookout** require a four-wheel-drive. From the ferry docks at Davis and Atlantic, you can strike out by beach or inland path. Once past the fishing camps, there's nothing but pure deserted island. The beach here changes every day; the dark timbers of ancient shipwrecks are uncovered periodically, as are the rusted remains of autos abandoned before the beach became a national seashore. Because so few people frequent these beaches, they're a sheller's paradise, as well as a great spot for bird-watching and nature study.

HISTORIC BUILDINGS AND SITES Cape Hatteras. The bones of the schooner *Laura A. Barnes* rest amid the dunes at Coquina Beach, just off Route 12 across from the entrance to the Bodie Island Lighthouse. The ship was bound for Georgetown, South Carolina, with an empty hold and no passengers when a nor'easter stripped its masts and ran it aground some 4 mi north in 1921. The crew was rescued, but the ship was unsalvageable. It was moved here in 1973.

U.S. Lifesaving Service stations were built every 7 mi along the Outer Banks to rescue passengers and crews of ships that foundered in the fierce seas. The 1874 **Chicamacomico Lifesaving Station,** on Route

12 in Rodanthe, was one of the first. The original, one-story station was converted to a boathouse when the two-story shingled station with lookout tower was built in 1911. Both still stand, along with outbuildings and cisterns dating from 1874 to 1911. *Open May–Oct., Tues., Thurs., and Sat. 11–5.*

There's a pocket of foreign soil on Ocracoke Island. To help protect shipping lanes during World War II, Great Britain sent anti-submarine craft; one of them, the H.M.S. *Bedfordshire,* was sunk by a U-boat 40 mi off Cape Lookout. When the bodies of four sailors washed ashore on Ocracoke Island, the people of the village buried them in a small plot and deeded the land forever to England. The Union Jack flies over this small, fenced **British Cemetery** maintained by the U.S. Coast Guard at Ocracoke. To reach it, take Route 12 to Ocracoke Village and turn right on British Cemetery Road.

Cape Lookout. On the northern tip of North Core Banks, the once-thriving **Portsmouth Village** was established in 1753 to aid the commercial shipping trade. By 1860, nearly 700 people lived there. But shipping eventually moved north and the population declined; the last residents left in 1971. Today the village is a beautifully preserved ghost town. A town genealogy, old photos of its residents, and other memorabilia are on display in the Salter/Dixon House. The site is staffed by Park Service volunteers March through November. The best way to reach Portsmouth is a 20-minute ride by ferry from Ocracoke Island; the village is a short walk from the dock. Allow at least a half-day to tour it.

NATURE TRAILS AND SHORT WALKS There are no formal trails in the Cape Lookout National Seashore, but the Cape Hatteras National Seashore offers a number of short, easy trails. The **Bodie Island Pond Trail** begins behind the Bodie Island Lighthouse. A boardwalk leads through hedges of bayberry hung with saw greenbrier to the marsh, where dense undergrowth gives way to salt-meadow cordgrass and cattails.

From the observation platform at trail's end, you can see snow geese in autumn, as well as egrets and herons.

The **Bodie Island Dike Trail,** which begins at the far end of the lighthouse parking lot, shows how human influence has changed the landscape. Dams and dikes built in the early 1900s to promote waterfowl hunting turned a section of the marsh into a freshwater pond. Artificial dunes constructed on the oceanfront in 1938 blocked salt spray and flooding, giving rise to the trees and shrubs that have overtaken the wetlands. It's a 30-minute walk to the spot where the trail meets Route 12; you can retrace your steps or walk back along the highway.

The **North Pond Interpretive Trail** at the Pea Island National Wildlife Refuge begins at a rest area a few miles south of the Herbert C. Bonner Bridge. The trail runs atop a dike between two ponds. There are several observation decks equipped with binocular viewers on the open areas around North Pond. It's an easy 15-minute walk to the end of the pond, but the dedicated birder can continue on the service road that winds 2.5 mi around the pond and ends at Route 12 about 2 mi from the rest area.

The **Buxton Woods Trail** takes visitors to one of the few remaining maritime forests on the Outer Banks. The .75-mi loop trail begins at a parking area off the road that leads to the Cape Point Campground. The terrain is surprisingly hilly, rising and falling over old dunes that once marked the beach. Thirty miles from the mainland, one is struck by the strangeness of birdsong coupled with the crashing of ocean waves.

The **Hammock Hills Nature Trail** on Ocracoke Island offers the best cross-section view of barrier island ecology. The .75-mi loop trail begins at a parking area across from the Ocracoke Campground on Route 12, within view of the dunes, and plunges into the maritime forest. Here you can see how plants adapt: Live oaks are sculpted and stunted by the salt spray; cedar will be thin and stripped on the ocean side, full and green on the protected sound side. The trail cuts through the forest to the marshland. From the observation platform here, you can see where the marsh meets the sound. The trail reenters the forest and loops back around to the parking lot. Keep an eye peeled for fast-moving (and nonpoisonous) black racer snakes.

LONGER HIKES Most of the marked trails in the national seashores are short, but in a sense the seashore is one very long walk. You can trek the entire length of the Cape Hatteras National Seashore on the **Cape Hatteras Beach Trail,** which begins at the Whalebone Junction Information Center and spans 75.8 mi of sound and seashore. Maps—which include comfort stations, campgrounds, and off-road vehicle (ORV) ramps—are available from the National Park Service at the Seashore headquarters in Manteo or any of the visitor centers.

OTHER ACTIVITIES Off-Road Driving. It is extremely important to follow the regulations in this fragile environment; driving on the dunes destroys the sea oats and other vegetation that hold the sand in place. Carry a shovel, tire-pressure gauge, first-aid kit, spare tire, tow rope at least 14 ft long, litter bag, fire extinguisher, flashlight, and bumper jack. Be sure to lower the pressure in all tires. Travel on the firm, wet portion of the beach located just below the high-tide mark.

At **Cape Hatteras,** there are more than 13 beach access ramps marked with four-wheel-drive signs for these vehicles only. Check the weather forecast and tide tables before you leave, and ask a ranger about current beach conditions. No permit is needed. At **Cape Lookout,** four-wheel-drives and all-terrain vehicles (ATVs) are the only way to travel on North and South Core banks. There is no fee to keep a vehicle on the islands while camping, but if you plan to leave a vehicle unattended on either island overnight, you must get a permit ($5 per week) at the Harkers Island headquarters of the national seashore.

Biking. The beautiful drive on **Cape Hatteras** from Whalebone Junction to Ocracoke Village is becoming more and more popular with cyclists. The roads are mostly straight and flat, so they don't require advanced skills. But the heavy summer traffic on Route 12 calls for caution. Lighter traffic and cooler weather make spring and fall better seasons for cycling. Manteo has a new bike trail that bisects Roanoke Island following U.S. 64. Biking is also the best way to see Ocracoke Island any time of year; you can tour the quaint village and easily reach any beach access area on the 13-mi span. Bicycling is not an option on **Cape Lookout**; there are no paved roads and mountain bikes are prohibited.

Bird-Watching. On the Cape Hatteras National Seashore, **Pea Island National Wildlife Refuge** is a birder's paradise. More than 265 species visit the refuge on a regular basis, and another 50 show up sporadically, with the greatest variety of species in spring and fall. The **Bodie Island ponds** are a good place to spot migratory shorebirds, as are the salt ponds at **Cape Hatteras Point.** The dikes at Pea Island and in the maritime woods at Buxton and Ocracoke are the best vantages from which to observe land-bird migration in the fall. Cape Lookout is home to great numbers of terns and black skimmers, which nest in colonies along the beach. Endangered piping plovers also nest here, and threatened eastern brown pelicans have made a dramatic comeback in the area.

Boating and Windsurfing. The wide, shallow sounds make for excellent sailing, windsurfing, and kayaking. One sound-side access area between Avon and Buxton, swept by sea breezes, is so popular with Canadian windsurfers that it's now known as **Canadian Hole (Le Trou Canadien).** The **Albemarle and Pamlico sounds** are ideal for sailboats and kayaks, too. Rentals are available at **Outer Banks Outdoors** in Avon (tel. 919/995–6060) or Nags Head (tel. 919/441–4124), **Fox Water Sports** in Buxton (tel. 919/995–4102), or **Hatteras Island Surf and Sail** in Waves (tel. 919/987–2296).

At Cape Lookout, kayaking is becoming a popular way to visit Shackleford Banks. You can rent kayaks and windsurfing equipment at **Island Rigs** (tel. 919/247–7787) in Atlantic Beach. Sailors and windsurfers can also rent at the **Sailing Place** (tel. 919/726–5664) on the Atlantic Beach Causeway.

Fishing. Anglers discovered these shores long before tourists. Fall and spring are the best times for surf and pier fishing; offshore fishing is best in summer, when blue marlin and other billfish are abundant.

At **Cape Hatteras,** one of the most popular spots for surf fishing is the mouth of **Oregon Inlet,** where red drum, striped bass, and large bluefish are plentiful. In summer, four-wheel-drive vehicles line this beach right up to the Bonner Bridge. Pier fishing centers on three locations: **Hatteras Island Fishing Pier** in Rodanthe (tel. 919/987–2323), **Avon Fishing Pier** (tel. 919/995–5480), and the **Frisco Pier** (tel. 919/986–2533). Daily entrance fees are $6. The **Oregon Inlet Fishing Center** (tel. 919/441–6301 or 800/272–5199), just north of the Bonner Bridge, offers Gulf Stream charters, inshore and inlet trolling charters, and specific charters for big bluefish.

At **Cape Lookout,** mackerel, mullet, sea trout, drum, and bluefish are among the prime quarry. Cape Lookout Point can be a good spot, as can the old gun mounts (*see* The Best in One Day, *above*), which provide a reeflike habitat for fish. Deep-sea fishing charters are available on the *Carolina Princess* (tel. 919/726–5479 or 800/682–3456) or *Continental Shelf* (tel. 919/726–7454 or 800/775–7450) at Morehead City or the *Capt. Stacy IV* (tel. 919/247–7501 or 800/533–9417) on the Atlantic Beach Causeway.

Hang Gliding. Cape Hatteras is a mecca for hang gliders because of windswept Jockey's Ridge, the tallest sand dune on the East Coast, which reaches anywhere from 110 to 140 ft. **Kitty Hawk Kites** (tel. 919/441–4124 or 800/334–4777), just across from the dune in Nags Head, provides rentals and instruction.

Horseback Riding. For trail rides in the maritime forest or on the beach at Cape Hatteras, contact **Buxton Stables** (tel. 919/

995–4659). **Seaside Stables** (tel. 919/928–3778) offers rides on the ocean or sound at Ocracoke. **White Sand Trail Rides** (tel. 919/729–0911) offers trail rides at Cedar Island near the Cape Lookout National Seashore.

Scuba Diving. The "Graveyard of the Atlantic" offers some of the best wreck diving in the world, including the World War II U-85 off Cape Hatteras and the U-352 off Cape Lookout. In addition, there are tankers, liberty ships, tugboats, and artifi-cial reef sites. Dive operators at Cape Hatteras include **Nags Head Pro Dive Center** (tel. 919/441–7594), **Sea Scan Dive Center** (tel. 919/480–3467), and **Hatteras Divers** (tel. 919/986–2557). **Olympus Dive Center** (tel. 919/726–9432) in Morehead City offers dive charters near Cape Lookout.

Swimming. Obviously, the opportunities are unlimited, but ocean currents can be dangerous and unpredictable. There are few lifeguards on the beaches of the Cape Hatteras National Seashore and none along the Cape Lookout National Seashore. You *will* find lifeguards at Coquina, Cape Point, Frisco, and Ocracoke beaches Memorial Day through Labor Day. In addition, Coquina Beach features a first-class day facility with handicapped-accessible showers, changing rooms, rest rooms, and pay phones.

CHILDREN'S PROGRAMS The Cape Hatteras National Seashore has a wide variety of programs for children available on request, including crab catching, cast-net fishing, wildlife discovery, cross-island walks, fishing with a ranger, soundside snorkeling, and refuge bird walks. Programs are held from mid-June to Labor Day; all are free, though some are limited to small groups.

The North Carolina Maritime Museum sponsors the **Cape Lookout Studies Program,** a series of natural history workshops at the former Coast Guard Station on Cape Lookout National Seashore. Workshops include dolphin biology and behavior, sea turtle conservation, and an introduction to the marine environment (tel. 919/728–7317).

DINING

Though there are technically no restaurants in either park, there are plenty to choose from close by, and it's not hard to find a good one—the challenge is narrowing the choices. Fresh seafood is the primary attraction; the flounder or shrimp you eat in the evening may well have been swimming in the Atlantic that morning.

NEAR CAPE HATTERAS **Chardo's.** This former fish house has been converted into one of the best Italian restaurants on the coast. Lace curtains, glass doors, and draped valances set the mood in the dining room, while in the dark, tiny bar, the tables are embossed with wine labels. The extensive menu includes fresh pasta, fish, veal, chicken, and grilled specialties. Salmon lovers should try the *tagliatelle al salmone*—the fish is tossed in brandy-tomato cream sauce with sun-dried tomatoes. Though the ambience is formal, folks in sport shirts are treated like royalty by the staff. *Milepost 9, U.S. 158 Bypass, Kill Devil Hills, tel. 919/441–0276. AE, MC, V. $$$*

Queen Anne's Revenge. Tucked back into a residential section of Roanoke Island, 10 minutes from Whalebone Junction, is this local favorite. Inside, juniper paneling, fresh flowers, and seascapes give it an airy, comfortable feel. The regular menu is extensive; favorites include the Hooker's Landing Special (a platter of fried fresh seafood) and scallops Queen Anne (sautéed with tomatoes, mushrooms, and peppers). There's usually a page of specials, too. Be sure to get "posh squash" as a side dish. *Old Wharf Rd., Wanchese, tel. 919/473–5466. Reservations not accepted. AE, D, MC, V. Closed Tues. Oct.–May. $$$*

Billy's Fish House. The old building sags on one side where the supports have settled into the sand of the harbor, and the floor has a pronounced tilt. But you get the feeling that if it ever did give way, most of the patrons would grab for one last hush puppy before they started paddling for shore. Billy May himself goes to the docks each day to handpick the seafood he serves, and it shows. The menu includes oysters, scallops, shrimp, flounder, and the local favorite, soft-shell crabs. *Rte. 12, Buxton, tel. 919/995–5151. Reservations not accepted. MC, V. $$*

Weeping Radish Brewery and Bavarian Restaurant. From the Bavarian-style building to the rousing polka music to the waiters in lederhosen, this place exudes a festive atmosphere. German pot roast, bratwurst and sauerkraut, and warm spicy potato salad are a few of the delights—you don't come here for seafood. The beer, brewed on site, is full and rich. *U.S. 64, Manteo, tel. 919/473–1157. MC, V. Closed 2 days each wk Jan.–Feb. $$*

NEAR CAPE LOOKOUT **Beaufort Grocery.** So named because it's in a converted grocery store, this restaurant is tucked away on a side street. The dining room is open and breezy, with white walls, light pine paneling, and ceiling fans. The lunch menu includes *gougeres* (herbed pastries stuffed with a variety of meats, cheeses, and salads) and homemade tuna, chicken, and shrimp salads. At night the white tablecloths come out; dinner entrées include grilled yellowfin tuna with marinated Chinese vegetables, and roast duck with raspberries. *117 Queen St., Beaufort, tel. 919/728–3899. D, MC, V. Closed Jan. $$*

Sanitary Fish Market and Restaurant. With a huge dining room and tables big enough to accommodate families and groups, this waterfront restaurant has been a Morehead City institution for more than 50 years. The extensive menu contains just about any seafood you can think of, fried or broiled, as well as grilled tuna and swordfish. Don't look for fancy sauces or exotic vegetables; the strength of this establishment is good, fresh seafood cooked simply, and lots of it. *501 Evans St., Morehead City, tel. 919/247–3111. Reservations not accepted. D, MC, V. $$*

Spouter's Inn. This dark and cozy waterfront restaurant is a good place for a romantic meal, but it also draws families and tourists. Glass doors open onto the dock to admit the seagoing crowd. The Seafood Supreme—baked grouper, crabmeat, and shrimp in cream sauce—is one dinner specialty, while the Out Island Sandwich, with shrimp, provolone, and sprouts, draws raves at lunch. Be sure to save room for the banana crepes. *218 Front St., Beaufort, tel. 919/728–5190. MC, V. $$*

PICNIC SPOTS At **Cape Hatteras,** one nice spot is the visitor center at **Ocracoke Island.** The deck overlooks Silver Lake Harbor, the Coast Guard station, and the ferry docks. Another pretty spot is the **Buxton Woods Picnic Area,** where tables are set in the shelter of the trees at the edge of the maritime forest.

Any meal on **Cape Lookout** is a picnic. There are shade shelters just behind the dunes. Shade shelters with picnic tables are also on the point at **Shackleford Banks** and just across from the visitor center on Harkers Island. There's also a picnic area by the keeper's quarters at the Cape Lookout Lighthouse.

LODGING

You can find almost any kind of accommodation near **Cape Hatteras.** The various towns all have hotels, motels, B&Bs, and rental cottages, but the widest selection is on the park's north end in Nags Head and Kill Devil Hills. Where to stay depends on your interests. For restaurants, attractions, and historic sites such as Fort Raleigh and the Wright Brothers Memorial, Nags Head and Kill Devil Hills are best. If you want to spend most of your time in the park itself, you might consider the more isolated Buxton. To experience a quaint coastal village, stay in Ocracoke.

The only accommodations within the park at **Cape Lookout** are primitive and isolated. Harkers Island, the closest point of entry, has a handful of small hotels and few other attractions. Families will probably be happier in Beaufort or Morehead City, which offer a wider selection of accommodations

and restaurants, as well as movies, shopping, and other amusements.

In both areas, make reservations at least six months in advance if you plan to visit during the summer. In the spring, fall, or winter, you can easily find a place to stay, often at half the summer rate.

CAPE HATTERAS **Nags Head Inn.** One of the newer oceanfront hotels, this plain, white, four-story structure has simple but large rooms, each with a desk between the beds and a table and chairs to the side. Seaside photos and muted shades of pink and blue make for a restful atmosphere. Streetside rooms lack both an ocean view and a balcony. The property is well located, dead center between the Wright Brothers Memorial and Whalebone Junction, and there's parking underneath. *4701 S. Virginia Dare Trail, Nags Head 27959, tel. 919/441–0454 or 800/327–8881. 100 rooms. Facilities: indoor and outdoor pools, hot tub. AE, D, MC, V. $$$*

Surf Side Motel. Just a mile from the park entrance at Whalebone Junction, the yellow stucco Surf Side comprises two highrises. Families like the main building, while couples gravitate to the annex, which has a honeymoon suite, private whirlpool tubs, and oceanfront efficiencies. All guests may stop by the cozy lobby, with its floral-print sofas and hanging plants, for morning coffee, or stretch out on the large wooden deck by the pool. The room decor varies widely, from country pine to dark Colonial furniture, and from light mauve and dusty blue to rich burgundy and navy. Breakfast is included. *Milepost 16 (Box 400), Nags Head 27959, tel. 919/441–2105 or 800/552–SURF. 76 rooms. Facilities: indoor and outdoor pools. AE, D, MC, V. $$$*

Comfort Inn. This is probably the prettiest chain hotel you'll ever see: It's patterned after the old lifesaving stations that dot the coast. The gray shingled building even has a crow's-nest lookout tower with a balcony. It's within walking distance of restaurants, shopping, and the beach. Continental breakfast is served in the spacious lobby, which has a TV, sofas, and rich teal draperies. The rooms are decorated in cool seaside tones. Choose a second-floor room for an ocean view. *Rte. 12 (Box 1089), Buxton 27920, tel. 919/995–6100 or 800/432–1441. 60 rooms. Facilities: pool. AE, D, DC, MC, V. $$*

Island Inn. This 1901 white frame hotel has a front porch with rocking chairs and a large wood-paneled lobby furnished with nautical relics. Like any other good historic inn, it also has a resident ghost (in Room 22). Many of the rooms are right out of Grandmother's house: antique beds with ornate headboards, wardrobes with mirrored panels, and Victorian photographs. (The charming atmosphere far outweighs the drawbacks— dripping faucets, cracked plaster, phoneless rooms.) The best rooms are in the crow's nest of the main hotel and have spectacular views of the village. The annex, built in 1981, has less personality, but it's adjacent to the pool. *Rte. 12 (Box 9), Ocracoke 27960, tel. 919/928–4351. 35 rooms. Facilities: restaurant, pool. D, MC, V. $$*

CAPE LOOKOUT Long before Cape Lookout was a park, anglers were coming to cast their lines on its isolated shores, and crude cabins and shelters went up amid the dunes to house them. These cabins continue to operate under two Park Service concessions. In some cases the rentals are wired for electricity, but you must supply the generator, as well as the food, utensils and dishes, linens—everything. The cabins are still patronized mostly by fisherfolk, but an increasing number of families are using them. They vary in size, sleeping from 4 to 12 people. Summer is the slackest time; fall is usually booked a year in advance.

Alger Willis Fishing Camps (Box 234, Davis 28524, tel. 919/729–2791) serves South Core Banks. Rates are $22–$132 per cabin per night. Ferry service (round-trip) costs $13 per passenger, $65 per vehicle.

Morris Marina Kabin Kamps (1000 Morris Marina Rd., Atlantic 28511, tel. 919/225–4261) serves North Core Banks. Rates are $100–$110 per cabin per night. Ferry service (round-trip) costs $13 per passenger, $65 per vehicle.

NEAR CAPE LOOKOUT **Beaufort Inn.** It's on the Beaufort Channel, tucked away from the crowded waterfront area but not so far away as to be inconvenient. Nautical paintings, model boats, and oil lamps decorate the warm, dark-paneled breakfast room; breakfast (the specialty of the house is Katie's breakfast pie) is complimentary. The rooms are formal, with dark Colonial furniture and valances on the windows, and private balconies with rocking chairs. There's also an outdoor deck on the waterfront. Little touches make the difference here: the antique washstand on the landing, the azaleas around the parking lot, and the friendly care provided by owners Bruce and Katie Ethridge. *101 Ann St., Beaufort 28516, tel. 919/728–2600 or 800/726–0321. 44 rooms. Facilities: hot tub, exercise room, bicycles. AE, D, DC, MC, V. $$$*

Inlet Inn. This modern hotel pays homage to the past with a private courtyard garden, a widow's-walk lounge, and transient boat slips. The inn overlooks the Beaufort waterfront and Carrot Island, and Beaufort's shops and restaurants are within easy walking distance. The rooms are oversize, with white walls, ceiling fans, and light-wood furniture. Those on the harborfront have French doors that open onto private porches with rocking chairs; on the third floor, they come with large window seats that afford a distant view of Cape Lookout. Breakfast is included. *601 Front St., Beaufort 28516, tel. 919/728–3600. 35 rooms. AE, MC, V. $$$*

Calico Jack's Inn and Marina. The motel on the waterfront at Harkers Island isn't fancy, but it is extremely convenient: The Cape Lookout ferry leaves from this marina, so all you have to do is get up and walk to the far end of the parking lot. The '50s-style motel has recently been renovated with new paint, carpeting, and furnishings, and it remains clean and well tended. *1698 Harkers Island Rd., Harkers Island 28531, tel. 919/728–3575. 24 rooms. MC, V. Closed mid-Dec.–Mar. $*

CAMPING

The two national seashores offer two distinctly different camping styles. If you prefer a manicured campground with picnic tables, bathhouses, and proximity to civilization, Cape Hatteras is the place to head. If it's the primitive, get-away-from-it-all experience you're looking for, you'll find it on Cape Lookout.

Cape Hatteras National Seashore has four campgrounds with more than 580 sites, all of which accommodate tents, trailers, and motor homes. All have modern rest rooms, potable water, unheated showers, grills, and picnic tables. No utility hookups are available, but there are dump stations near Oregon Inlet, Cape Point, and Ocracoke campgrounds. Though all the campgrounds except Frisco are on level ground, you'll still need longer tent stakes in the sandy soil.

Usually, between late May and early September, campsites cannot be rented for more than 14 days. Sites cost $12 per night at Cape Point, Frisco, and Oregon Inlet, $13 per night at Ocracoke. Reservations are available only for the Ocracoke Campground.

Cape Point Campground. Near the Cape Hatteras Lighthouse, this campground is popular with fisherfolk because of its proximity to the point. The huge, grassy compound has a fish-cleaning station and a large additional parking lot with boardwalks to the beach. *202 sites. Open Mar.–early Sept. $*

Frisco Campground. This is the only campground that's among the dunes—and grand dunes they are, with great views of the ocean and steady breezes. *127 sites. Open late May–early Sept. $*

Ocracoke Campground. This relatively isolated campground has sites set in a large loop parallel to the dunes. Make reservations six weeks prior to arrival. *Off Rte. 12. 136 sites. Open Mar.–early Sept. D, MC, V. $*

Oregon Inlet Campground. Because of its proximity to the area's excellent surf fishing and the Oregon Inlet Fishing Center, where many charter boats go out, this is the most popular campground. The sites are in three loops, each with its own comfort station and bathhouse. Anglers like Loop C, where there is a trail to the marina, but the most secluded is Loop A, which is closer to the dunes. *120 sites. Open Mar.–early Sept.*

Cape Lookout National Seashore offers primitive camping with no developed sites. You can pitch your tent anywhere you like as long as you don't disturb the vegetation and stay at least 100 yards from the Cape Lookout Lighthouse and Portsmouth Village. No permit is required. In the summer you'll want to find a spot among the dunes and close to the beach, where the wind will keep the heat and insects in check. Use a tent with mosquito netting and one that can withstand high winds, and use extralong wooden or plastic tent stakes. Driftwood campfires are allowed below the high-tide line only. Pets are prohibited. Be sure to bring everything you need with you, including water.

For a current list of campgrounds near Cape Lookout, contact the **Carteret County Tourism Development Bureau** (Box 1406, Morehead City 28557, tel. 800/786–6962).

Catoctin Mountain Park
Maryland

By Michael Pretzer

Updated by Dennis Steele

t's easy to overlook Catoctin Mountain Park, which sits astride the Blue Ridge system of the Appalachian Mountains in central Maryland. Unlike the other national parks in the region—Gettysburg National Military Park, Antietam National Battlefield, Monocacy National Battlefield, Harpers Ferry National Historical Park, and C&O Canal National Historical Park—Catoctin isn't tied to historical events or feats of engineering. No Indian wars were fought on the land; no towns or canals were built there. Civil War soldiers marched past the mountain without firing a shot.

Cunningham Falls State Park, immediately to the south, hogs the local attention. Catoctin, on the other hand, is downright secretive about what could be its most enticing feature. On the mountain's peak, at an elevation of 1,880 ft, stands Camp David. Developed for President Franklin D. Roosevelt as a secure and secluded retreat from Washington, D.C., Camp David has been a working getaway for presidents since the 1930s. It's the site where the Camp David Agreement—the Israeli-Egyptian peace pact brokered by President Jimmy Carter—was signed in 1978. But Camp David is off-limits to the public; don't think you'll see it or learn much about it from the park rangers or the volunteers at the visitor center. Only grudgingly will they even admit that Camp David is within the confines of Catoctin.

You would do yourself a disservice, however, if you bypassed Catoctin. It's a hospitable park that inspires feelings of peace and serenity even at its most crowded, and it will give you glimpses into Maryland's history. The 23 mi of trails within its 5,770 acres offer a variety of experiences. You can sample the gentle terrain of the well-worn mountain, or you can challenge yourself to a rigorous half-day hike that includes scrambling up rocky inclines. You can opt for a self-guided trail that introduces you to bygone mountain cultures, following in the footsteps of charcoal makers and moonshiners; or you can choose a nature trail that walks you through the environment that Catoctin's white-tailed deer find so appealing.

The word *Catoctin* derives from *Kittocton,* the name of an Algonquian tribe that is believed to have lived in the foothills south of Catoctin near the Potomac River. (Catoctin Mountain Park officials say the word probably meant "land of the big mountain"). The Monocacy River valley, to the east and the south of Catoctin Mountain, was home base for both the Algonquian and the Iroquois nations. They lived in harmony, but the Susquehannough, a tribe that had broken from the Iroquois and occupied the shores of Chesapeake Bay, continually harassed the Algonquian and Iroquois who lived near the perimeter of their territory. Eventually the Algonquian and Iroquois concentrated their encampments in the Monocacy valley; Catoctin Mountain became a neutral zone where the tribes could hunt and fish in peace but where no tribe lived permanently.

In the 1730s white settlers began moving into the valley, and the Indians departed.

The first residents of European stock were second-generation Americans and German immigrants, both lured by Lord Baltimore's offer of 200 acres of land for three years at no cost, to be followed by an annual rent of one cent an acre. By the middle of the century the first settlers had been joined by many others, including immigrants from Switzerland, Scotland, and Ireland.

Some of them took up charcoal manufacturing or logging. The charcoal makers sold to the Catoctin Iron Furnace, the remains of which can be seen off Route 806 just inside the southeast border of Cunningham Falls State Park. The loggers supplied the bark of oak and chestnut trees, sources of tannin, to tanneries in the Monocacy River valley. Other settlers established farms, traces of which—stone fences and cellar pits, for example—can still be seen in the woods.

Conservation was unheard of in the mountains during the 1800s, and the forest and the soil became depleted. The sawmills began to close at the turn of the century. The iron furnace converted from charcoal to coal in the 1880s and closed in 1903. The chestnut blight hit in 1904. Many of the mountain residents headed for the city, primarily to Baltimore.

In 1935 the 10,000 acres that today form Catoctin and Cunningham parks were purchased by the federal government, which planned to develop the Catoctin Recreational Demonstration Area as a park and then turn it over to the state of Maryland. The plan changed, however, when Roosevelt settled on part of Catoctin as his Camp Shangri-la. (When Dwight D. Eisenhower was president, he renamed the retreat Camp David in honor of his favorite grandson.) Catoctin was indeed developed as a recreational area, but to ensure security at Camp David, the federal government retained control of the park.

During Harry S. Truman's presidency, however, Maryland began to clamor for ownership. In 1954 the federal and state governments reached a compromise: The area was divided in half. The land north of

Route 77 stayed in federal hands as Catoctin Mountain Park; the land to the south of the highway went to Maryland as Cunningham Falls State Park.

Since becoming parkland, the 10,000 acres have reverted to hardwood forest. Today, the woodland is much like it was when the first European settlers arrived.

ESSENTIAL INFORMATION

VISITOR INFORMATION For detailed information about the park, contact the superintendent, **Catoctin Mountain Park** (6602 Foxville Rd., Thurmont 21788, tel. 301/663–9388). The visitor center is open year-round Monday–Thursday 10–4:30, Friday 10–5, weekends 8:30–5. The park **Web site** is www.nps.gov/cato.

For information on the state park, contact the park manager, **Cunningham Falls State Park** (14039 Catoctin Hollow Rd., Thurmont 21788, tel. 301/271–7574). For information on the area immediately surrounding the two parks, contact the **Catoctin Mountain Tourist Council** (Cunningham Falls State Park, Thurmont 21788, tel. 301/271–3285) or the **Tourism Council of Frederick County, Inc.** (19 E. Church St., Frederick 21701, tel. 301/663–8687 or 800/999–3613). For information on the Gettysburg area, north of Catoctin, contact the **Gettysburg Travel Council** (35 Carlisle St., Gettysburg, PA 17325, tel. 717/334–9410).

FEES There was no fee to enter Catoctin Mountain Park at press time. However, it is likely some fee structure for entry will be instituted in the future. Cunningham Falls State Park charges $3 per person, per day, between Memorial Day and Labor Day and on weekends in May and September. Weekdays the charge is $2. Both parks have fees for camping (*see* Camping, *below*).

PUBLICATIONS Maps, trail guides, and brochures are available at the visitor center, located at the intersection of Route 77 and Park Central Road about midway between the park's eastern and western borders. The center sells books about nature and the national parks, but only one is specifically concerned with Catoctin.

You can find maps and brochures about Cunningham Falls at the state park's administrative center (across Catoctin Hollow Rd. from the Hunting Creek Lake boat launch) and at the booths at the entrances to the lake and the camping areas. The park also has a visitor center in its Manor Area (off Rte. 15, about 2.5 mi south of the intersection of Rtes. 15 and 77).

GEOLOGY AND TERRAIN The Blue Ridge system of the Appalachian Mountains once had peaks as tall as the Rockies, but glaciers (during the Ice Age, glaciers came within 100 mi of Catoctin) and the forces of wind and water eventually wore the peaks into soft mountains. Today the peak of the aged Catoctin Mountain is 1,880 ft above sea level; the highest point that's accessible to the public is Hog Rock, at 1,671 ft. Hog Rock and similar outcroppings are primarily of Catoctin greenstone, which originated from the lava flows of 600 million years ago.

Owens Creek, a fishing brook, runs along the western and northern sides of the mountain. Big Hunting Creek, also a fishing brook, winds along its base to the south. Over the past centuries Big Hunting Creek has cut a valley, which was partially cleared to make way for Route 77. Big Hunting Creek slips back and forth across the border between the national and state parks. At Cunningham Falls it drops 78 ft in elevation over the course of 220 ft. It feeds into the man-made Hunting Creek Lake in the state park, then proceeds back into Catoctin. Both creeks flow in a southeasterly direction, ending at the Monocacy River, which flows south to the Potomac River.

FLORA AND FAUNA Catoctin Mountain Park is an eastern hardwood forest that has entered its mature, or climax, stage. Walk the trails and you'll discover sugar maple, chestnut, oak, hickory, and black birch trees. Near the creeks and in the valleys you'll see black locust, wild cherry, sas-safras, yellow poplar, hemlock, ash, and white oak.

The park's stands of American chestnut trees were decimated by the blight that struck the country in the early 1900s. For a time, a small section of the park near the Chestnut Picnic Area was used for research on the blight, but today you'll see only stumps, with an occasional sapling shooting up; a cure for the blight has yet to be found.

Spring is always a colorful season here, thanks to the wildflowers that carpet the park. Along the roadsides you'll see the ox-eyed daisy, garlic mustard, yarrow, chicory, and common strawberry. In the upland woods you'll find the wood anemone, bedstraw, common fleabane, and mountain laurel. In the lowlands, look for bloodroot, sweet cicely, miterwort, and blue violets. If you're lucky, you may uncover one of the park's seldom-seen flowers—cancerroot, say, or nodding trillium. You might even be as lucky as the hiker who, in 1993, became the first person to spot the rare Maryland cuckoo flower in the park.

Nearly 600 white-tailed deer are in the park. Barred, eastern screech, and great horned owls; the broad-winged hawk; downy and pileated woodpeckers; wild turkeys; and many other birds are plentiful in Catoctin, as are a host of small mammals, such as squirrels, woodchucks, and chipmunks. Two poisonous snakes, the timber rattlesnake and the copperhead, inhabit the park. Although they are poisonous, neither is deadly to healthy adults.

Brook, brown, and rainbow trout spawn in Big Hunting Creek and Owens Creek, and Big Hunting Creek below the lake is stocked with rainbows. As you might expect, rainbows are the most abundant species in Big Hunting; the brook trout is the rarest of the three.

WHEN TO GO Catoctin Mountain Park is used mostly as a weekend escape for Baltimoreans and Washingtonians. Fall is without a doubt the most popular season. On a

Saturday or Sunday in October, when the leaves on sugar maples and the other trees are most spectacular, Catoctin's parking lots, picnic areas, and campground have been known to fill up, leaving late-arriving visitors with nothing to do but drive slowly through and out.

Spring is popular, too, but the springtime colors are more subtle, and the weather less predictable. There's been snow in March, and rain is always a possibility.

SEASONAL EVENTS **March:** Cunningham Falls State Park (tel. 301/271–7574) holds its annual **maple syrup demonstrations** weekends in mid-March. Events include tapping trees, boiling sap, and eating pancakes and sausages drenched with syrup, as well as storytelling and interpretative programs. **Summer:** On some Saturday evenings in summer Cunningham Falls sponsors a series of concerts at Hunting Creek Lake, featuring folk, bluegrass, country-and-western, and other forms of American music; contact the park for specifics.

WHAT TO PACK The mid-Atlantic location makes for relatively mild weather. In mid-summer temperatures climb into the 80s or, occasionally, the 90s. Walking shorts and short-sleeved shirts will suffice during the day, but you may want trousers and long sleeves for the evening. The mountaintops will be windier and colder than the trail-heads, so take warmer clothes with you when you hike. Snow is a possibility between November and March, with storms most likely in January and February. In a hard winter, a couple of feet of snow cover the ground for as long as a month. You'll need warm, layered clothing for a winter visit.

For the most part the trails range in difficulty from easy to moderate, and you're unlikely to find yourself more than an hour away from a road, supervised campground, or trailhead. Sturdy walking or hiking shoes are recommended, although many hikers wear sneakers. Even on short hikes, take along water; it's not advisable to drink from the streams, as they may harbor the Giardia lamblia protozoan, which can cause diarrhea. Pack a pair of binoculars if you plan to bird-watch or to hike in search of vistas.

GENERAL STORES Thurmont, which lies about a mile beyond Catoctin's eastern border, has two supermarkets. **Jubilee** is in Thurmont Plaza along Route 806/550, a few blocks north of the town's main intersection. It's open Monday–Saturday 7 AM–10 PM, Sunday 8–8. **Food Lion** is in the Orchard Village Shopping Center, a development at the southern edge of town. From the intersection of Route 77 and U.S. 15, travel south on U.S. 15 less than a mile to the exit for Route 806. The supermarket is just up the hill to the right. It's open 24 hours daily.

There's a **camp store** in Cunningham Falls State Park, designed to serve the park's campers and visitors. It has limited supplies but a plentiful assortment of souvenirs.

ATMS There are three 24-hour banking facilities in Thurmont. One is at **Nations-Bank** at the intersection of Routes 77 and 806 in the center of town. **F&M Bank Center** is next to the Roy Rogers restaurant just east of Route 77's exit for Route 806. The third, a **Cirrus,** is adjacent to the Food Lion in the Orchard Village Shopping Center.

ARRIVING AND DEPARTING Catoctin Mountain Park is not a "destination" park. The typical length of stay is only two or three days, usually on a weekend. Even during a short visit, you'll probably want to travel outside the park. To do so you'll need a car. If you're traveling here by air or rail, head for Baltimore or Washington, where you can rent a car. Bus service will get you as close as Frederick, where you can also rent a car.

By Bus. Greyhound (tel. 800/231–2222) operates service to Frederick.

By Car and RV. From **Baltimore,** take I–70 west to Frederick, about 40 mi. In Frederick, get on Route 15 heading north; in Thurmont (another 20 mi), exit onto Route 77 heading west. The entrance to Catoctin is on the right in about 3 mi; the entrance to Cunningham Falls is ¼ mi farther on the left.

From **Washington,** take I–270 north to Frederick, about 40 mi. In Frederick take Route 15 north and continue as above.

From **Gettysburg,** Pennsylvania, take Route 15 south for about 15 mi; exit onto Route 77 in Thurmont and continue as above.

Hertz (tel. 301/662–2645) and **Budget** (tel. 301/816–6000) are both in Frederick.

Avis (tel. 410/859–1873) is at BWI Airport. **Thrifty** (tel. 410/783–0300) has an office a mile from the Amtrak station. In Union Station, **Budget** (tel. 202/289–5373) and **National** (tel. 202/842–7454) both have desks.

By Plane. The Baltimore-Washington region is served by three major airports. **Baltimore/Washington International Airport (BWI),** just south of Baltimore, and **Dulles International Airport,** west of Washington, have national and international flights. **Washington National Airport,** south of Washington, has national flights only. Among the major carriers at BWI are Continental, Southwest Airlines, and US Airways; at Dulles, American, United, and Northwest; at National, American, Delta, and US Airways. The major car rental companies can accommodate you at all three airports. The drive to Catoctin from any of them will vary between one and two hours—longer if local traffic conditions are poor. (Baltimore is less likely to be congested than Washington.) You can avoid rush-hour traffic by driving away between mid-morning and mid-afternoon.

By Train. Amtrak (tel. 800/872–7245) provides service to Pennsylvania Station in Baltimore, to BWI Airport Station, and to Union Station in Washington. All of the airport car rental companies are accessible from the airport train station.

EXPLORING

Catoctin has 23 mi of hiking trails, which range from the easy (accessible to wheelchair users) to the strenuous (steep and rocky). Some of the trails are educational, posted with interpretive signs for children and adults. Others are exhilarating, with eye-popping views and plenty of opportunities to see wildlife.

THE BEST IN ONE DAY One good thing about a small park: You can experience it intimately even if you're there for only a few hours. If you have a single day to spend in Catoctin, try to spend it on foot. Devote the morning to hiking. Most of the trails are short, so you'll want to string several of them together to form a loop. The trails are not marked with blazes, but the paths are quite visible, and all the trailheads and trail junctions have signs.

To reach many of the park's most scenic areas, walk the Blue Ridge Summit, Hog Rock, and Cunningham Falls trails—the 4.6-mi total will require just over three hours if you take time to enjoy the scenery. This loop trail begins at the visitor center and roughly parallels Park Central Road until you get to the Hog Rock Trail. Around the 1-mi mark you may want to take a brief side trip to the **Thurmont Vista,** which affords a view east toward the Monocacy River valley. After the trail turns westward, you'll be greeted by another vista, the **Blue Ridge Summit Overlook.** Cross Park Central Road and hook up with the **Hog Rock Trail.** If you're still feeling leisurely, pick up a printed guide at the trailhead and take the .5-mi Hog Rock Nature Trail loop. From Hog Rock, the highest point you can reach in Catoctin, hike down to Route 77; cross over the road to **Cunningham Falls,** the most popular natural attraction in the area. Return to the north side of Route 77 to catch the **Cunningham Falls Nature Trail;** in about a mile you'll be back at the visitor center. Drive to Chestnut or Owens Creek for a picnic lunch.

The season will dictate how you spend the afternoon. In the spring you may want to try fly-fishing in Big Hunting Creek (*see* Fishing *in* Other Activities, *below*). In the middle of summer you'll more likely want to head for the beaches of Hunting Creek

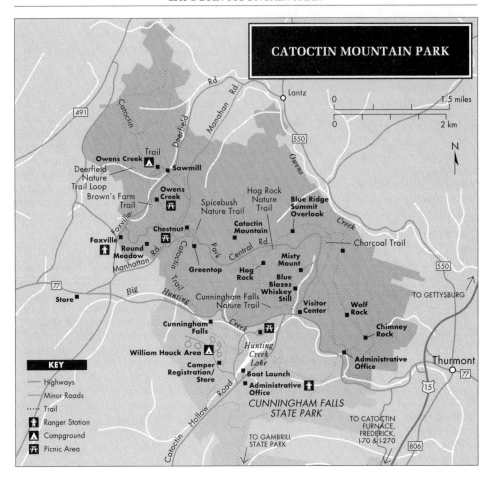

Lake (*see* Boating *and* Swimming *in* Other Activities, *below*). In the fall, you may want to take a second hike, a mile shorter than the morning one but more strenuous: the **Wolf Rock/Chimney Rock loop.** Start at the parking lot ½ mi north of the visitor center. Take the trail 1 mi to Wolf Rock. The trail climbs 400 ft and the rock outcroppings can be slippery. (Rappelling is allowed in the area, but only with a permit issued at the visitor center.) Continue up to Chimney Rock. After you catch your breath from the ascent and the view of the colorful countryside, head down the steep trail toward the administration building, then swing back to the parking lot. Allow about three hours to complete the loop.

ORIENTATION PROGRAMS AND GUIDED TOURS
There are no formal orientation programs or guided tours at Catoctin, but a variety of interpretive programs are offered year-round.

SCENIC DRIVES AND VIEWS Only one road, Park Central, winds through the park. It travels mostly east and west, between the visitor center at Route 77 and Foxville-Deerfield Road inside the park's western border. There are parking lots at the start of trails to three scenic views, **Blue Ridge Summit Overlook, Hog Rock,** and **Thurmont Vista.** Getting to each view requires a 15-minute hike.

HISTORIC BUILDINGS AND SITES At the end of the **Blue Blazes Whiskey Still Trail,** a .5-

mi self-guided walk, is an example of the type of still settlers used in the late 18th and 19th centuries to make corn whiskey. Many of the farmers operated stills to make alcohol, which they used in lamps and medicines.

The **Charcoal Trail** is a .5-mi loop that traces the process of cutting timber, drawing it to a hearth, and charring it. You'll see the remains of a charcoal pit along the trail.

At **Round Meadow** are the park's oldest and fourth-oldest buildings. The oldest, once the park's general store, is now its resource-management office. The blacksmith shop, which was constructed to help build the park in the 1930s, is open to the public; demonstrations of the blacksmith's trade are given on three Sundays during the summer.

Along Owens Creek near the entrance to Owens Creek Campground is an example of the **sawmills** once used by loggers in the area. The structure is made of stone and houses a vertical saw that turned logs into lumber.

The stone structure that housed the **Catoctin Furnace Iron Works** between 1774 and 1903 is at the southeastern edge of Cunningham Falls State Park, 3 mi south of Thurmont along Route 806. A .5-mi self-guided trail between the ironworks and the state park's Manor Area, accessible from Route 15, puts the region into historical perspective. Pick up a printed guide at the trailhead or at the Manor Area visitor center.

NATURE TRAILS AND SHORT WALKS The **Blue Blazes Whiskey Still Trail** describes the making of moonshine, and the **Charcoal Trail** highlights the important local industry of a bygone era (*see* Historic Buildings and Sites, *above*). The **Spicebush Trail,** a path accessible to people using wheelchairs, teaches forest ecology. A boardwalk off Foxville–Deerfield Road crosses Owens Creek and leads to a reconstructed **sawmill exhibit** near the campground.

The other three offer printed guides at their trailheads. **Hog Rock Trail,** named after the rock outcropping where farmers used to bring their hogs to feed on acorns and chestnuts, introduces you to 14 species of trees. **Deerfield Nature Trail,** 1.3 mi in length, details the habits and habitat of the white-tailed deer. **Brown's Farm Environmental Study Area Trail,** a .5-mi trail often used by school groups, points out relationships between human beings, animals, plants, and the land.

LONGER HIKES Most of Catoctin's trails are designed for the casual hiker, but there are some challenging ones for the more adventuresome. For a full day of hiking that will take you to the park's vistas and up its steepest trails, combine the Blue Ridge, Hog Rock, and Cunningham Falls trails loop with the Wolf Rock/Chimney Rock trails loop (*see* The Best in One Day, *above*). You'll cover 8.2 mi. With time for side trips and a stop at the falls, expect the trip to take between five and six hours.

An alternative is to hike into Cunningham Falls State Park—or beyond. The state park has four strenuous trails, each more than a mile long. The **Cliff Trail** is the shortest, at 1.5 mi round-trip, and arguably the most beautiful; it starts above the park's maple-syrup demonstration area and takes you through stands of hemlock and to rock outcroppings. **Old Misery Trail** switches back and forth and leads to some beautiful views; it's 4 mi round-trip but can be extended by continuing on the Cat Rock–Bob's Hill Trail. **Cat Rock–Bob's Hill** is a trail (7.5 mi one-way) between the parking lot across Route 77 from Catoctin's administration building and the state park's Manor Area. Cat Rock affords a 360° view in winter, and Bob's Hill, at an elevation of 1,765 ft, is the highest accessible point in Cunningham Falls. None of these trails are loops.

If you're itching to really stride out, take the **Catoctin Trail,** maintained by the Potomac Appalachian Trail Club. The trail runs 27 mi from Catoctin Mountain Park through Cunningham Falls State Park to Gambrill State Park. If you hike this trail, plan to start early; camping is not permitted along the way.

OTHER ACTIVITIES **Biking.** Cyclists are permitted to use the roads in the park, but there are no designated bike lanes, and shoulders are either narrow or nonexistent. No vehicles of any kind, including bicycles, may be taken on the trails.

Bird-Watching. Nearly 150 species of birds—from woodcocks to woodpeckers to wood warblers—have been sighted here. A brochure available from the visitor center lists all the species in the park.

Boating. There is no boating in the national park, but boaters are allowed to put craft into Hunting Creek Lake from the launch off Catoctin Hollow Road in Cunningham Falls State Park for a $2 fee. Only electric motors of less than one horsepower or 30 pounds of thrust may be used. Canoes may be rented at the boathouse on the lake for $5 an hour, two-person aqua-cycles for $6 a half hour or $11 an hour, six-person family-cycles for $12 a half hour or $21 an hour. The boathouse is open daily 10–5 between Memorial Day and Labor Day. Call the park manager's office (*see* Visitor Information *in* Essential Information, *above*) to inquire further.

Cross-Country Skiing. During the winter the gravel section of Manahan Road—a stretch of about 1.5 mi—and most of Park Central Road are left unplowed and made available for cross-country skiing. Skiing is allowed on hiking trails as well, but often the snowfall is insufficient to cover the rocky paths. The park does not groom the road or the trails for skiing.

Fishing. Big Hunting Creek is a challenge: The trout are easier to spot here than they are to catch. The creek was the first stream in Maryland to be reserved solely for fly-fishing and the first to be restricted by a catch-and-return policy. Before casting for the brook, brown, and rainbow trout, pick up the park's fly-fishing guide at the visitor center. Fly-fishing is also allowed at Owens Creek, where the catch-and-return restric-

tion does not apply. In Cunningham Falls State Park, fishing is permitted in Little Hunting Creek (catch-and-release, artificial lures only) and Big Hunting Creek (catch-and-release, artificial flies only), as well as Hunting Creek Lake (trout and bass). A fishing pier accessible to people using wheelchairs is located in the lake's boat-launch area. A Maryland fishing license and a trout stamp, which can be purchased at the camper registration office or the administrative office in the state park, are required for angling in either park. A license costs $10 for a Maryland resident, $20 for a resident of another state; the trout stamp is $5.

Horseback Riding. Horseback riding is allowed on 6 mi of trail in the national park from April 15 to December 1. The trail winds through woods, crosses creeks, and traverses mountainous terrain. Horse trailers may be parked in the lot across from the entrance to Camp Greentop. From the parking lot, take the trail marked with signs bearing a horseshoe symbol. A map and detailed riding regulations are available at the visitor center. Riding is also permitted on trails in the undeveloped areas of Cunningham State Park. There are no stables for renting horses near the parks, however.

Rope and Rock Climbing. Basic or beginning rock climbing with ropes is popular at Wolf Rock, which has a substantial stone outcropping with deep crevices. To climb, you must obtain a permit—no fee charged—from the visitor center; climbing helmets are required.

Swimming. In summer Cunningham Falls State Park marks off three areas of Hunting Creek Lake for swimming and puts lifeguards on duty there; it has two sandy beaches for sunbathing. Picnic areas, a snack bar, and showers are nearby. There's a daily fee of $3 per person to use the lake on weekends between Memorial Day and Labor Day. The fee is $2 per person on weekdays.

EVENING ACTIVITIES Between late May and the last weekend in September, the park's interpretive staff holds campfire sessions every Saturday evening at the Owens Creek Campground amphitheater. The topics cover the region's culture and the park's ecology. Check at the visitor center or with the campground host for specifics.

DINING

Although there are no restaurants within Catoctin Mountain Park, the state park has a snack bar by the lake that's open daily 10:30–5:30 in summer. There's a cluster of fast-food and chain restaurants in Thurmont, at Route 77's exit for Route 806. Nearby Gettysburg and Frederick, prime tourist spots in Pennsylvania and Maryland, respectively, offer an even greater variety, including fine-dining restaurants.

NEAR THE PARK **Dobbin House Tavern.** The 20-minute drive north will take you back 200 years. The stone Dobbin House, built in 1776, has been restored inside and out, with antiques similar to the original owner's furnishings, and is listed on the National Register of Historic Places. Colonial and Continental cuisines are served in six rooms with 18th-century decor by a waitstaff in period dress. Try the drunken scallops (sautéed with onions, garlic, and bacon and finished with white wine), the prime rib, or the roast duck. The adjacent Springhouse Tavern, with two working fireplaces, offers less formal dining in the atmosphere of an alehouse. *89 Steinwehr Ave., Gettysburg, PA, tel. 717/334–2100. AE, MC, V. No dinner at Springhouse. $$–$$$*

Tauraso's Ristorante and Trattoria. There are three dining areas: the saloon, with exposed brick and ductwork and a free-standing circular bar; a formal candlelit dining room with marble tables; and a garden with a fountain and wrought-iron tables. The menu includes Italian basics (including pizza from a wood-burning stone oven), New York strip steak, rack of lamb, and lots of seafood. *6 East St., Everedy Sq., Frederick, tel. 301/663–6600. AE, DC, MC, V. $$*

Herr Tavern & Publick House. About a mile and a half to the west of Gettysburg on Route 30W, just off Herr's Ridge Road, is the Herr Tavern & Publick House, two buildings that first opened in the early 1800s. They stand close to the site of the start of the Battle of Gettysburg and overlook the battlefield from Peace Light to Little Round Top. Fine dining in a country atmosphere can be found in the Herr Tavern Restaurant while lighter fare is offered in Hurricanes, the more casual of the two. Blackened prime rib, seafood jambalaya, pasta dishes, a vegetable medley, and a children's menu are offered in the tavern. Burgers, sandwiches, wings, and ribs are served in the laid-back tropical beach-club setting of Hurricanes. *900 Chambersburg Rd., Gettysburg, PA 17325, tel. 717/334–4332 or 800/362–9849. AE, MC, D, V. $–$$*

Muldoon's Grill. Not far from Gettysburg along Route 30W is Muldoon's Grill, a restaurant that is neither fancy nor historical. Instead it is a place where families can eat affordably and almost everyone will find something appetizing on the menu. The fare includes appetizers like potato skins with cheese and bacon, entrées like shrimp scampi, and more than 20 sandwiches and burritos. There is also a children's menu. Breakfast is served 7–11 AM. *401 Buford Ave., Gettysburg, PA, tel. 717/334–2200. AE, MC, V. $–$$*

Cozy Restaurant. In Thurmont it seems as if there's a billboard for the Cozy at every turn. The signs must be effective, for the restaurant, which has been in business since 1929, is usually bustling. It's decorated in an eclectic mix of country and Victorian, and it serves up serious down-home cooking. The main attraction is the buffet, where you can find everything from barbecued beef ribs to Alaskan snow crab. There's even a vegetarian buffet. On Friday and Saturday nights the restaurant lays out 100 different items, with an emphasis on seafood. It also has its own bakery. *103 Frederick Rd., Thurmont, tel. 301/271–7373. AE, MC, V. $–$$*

Mountain Gate Family Restaurant. Just down the road from the Cozy is Thurmont's other buffet ("family-style" is what they call it in Thurmont) restaurant. The parking lot is big, to accommodate tour buses, and the interior is bright and spacious. The menu features home-style cooking (such as roast turkey, pork chops, fried chicken), and there are lunch and dinner buffets. No one seems to dispute the Mountain Gate's claim of having one of the area's largest salad bars, and the restaurant is known for its homemade desserts. There's a breakfast buffet from 8 to 11 AM, but you can order breakfast any time any day, starting at 5 AM. *133 Frederick Rd., Thurmont, tel. 301/271–4373. D, MC, V. $–$$*

PICNIC SPOTS Picnic facilities are available at Chestnut and Owens Creek. Many of the sites at Chestnut are accessible to people using wheelchairs. Additional picnic sites can be found in the William Houck and Manor areas of Cunningham Falls State Park; the state park charges a fee during the summer and on some weekends in the spring and fall for use of the facilities in the William Houck Area.

LODGING

The only lodging within Catoctin Mountain Park is Camp David. Unless you're a head of state or a close friend of the president, you'll have to look to Thurmont, which has a limited selection of accommodations, or to the Gettysburg and Frederick areas, where lodging ranges from truck-stop motels to historic inns and bed-and-breakfasts to major chain hotels. The **Gettysburg Travel Council** (35 Carlisle St., Gettysburg, PA 17325, tel. 717/334–9410, fax 717/334–1166) and the **Tourism Council of Frederick County** (19 E. Church St., Frederick 21701, tel. 301/663–8687 or 800/999–3613, fax 301/663–0039) can assist you in selecting a place to stay.

NEAR THE PARK **Bluebird on the Mountain.** Ten minutes northwest of Catoctin Mountain Park is this bed-and-breakfast in a 1900 manor house. The rooms are sunny and airy, decorated with antiques, white linens and lace, and Oriental carpets; all have their own baths, although some are a couple of steps down the hall. Guests are invited to enjoy the outdoor hot tub and the gardens, complete with gazebo. A Continental breakfast, included in the rate, is served in your room or on the back porch. There are fireplaces in the suites, whirlpool baths in the suites and in one of the rooms, and golf, skiing, and antiques shops are nearby. *14700 Eyler Ave., Cascade, MD 21719, tel. 301/241–4161 or 800/362–9526. 3 rooms, 2 suites. AE, MC, V. $$$*

Brafferton Inn. A few steps from downtown Lincoln Square and in walking distance of Culp's Hill is one of Gettysburg's outstanding B&Bs. The stone structure was built in 1786 and fired upon during the Civil War: In 1863, as Union troops passed by, shots rang out and shattered the glass in a bedroom window; you can still see the bullet lodged in the mantel of one of its upstairs fireplaces. The original house, which is on the National Register of Historic Places, has rooms with fireplaces, brass beds, and a 19th-century maple canopied double bed; there are more guest quarters in the adjoining carriage house. All the rooms are furnished with antiques and Oriental carpets. A full breakfast is included in the rate. *44 York St., Gettysburg, PA 17325, tel. 717/337–3423, fax 717/334–8185. 8 rooms, 2 suites. MC, V. $$–$$$*

Cozy Inn. The inn and cottage complex, near the center of Thurmont and next to the Cozy Restaurant (*see* Dining, *above*), has been used by presidential families, Cabinet members, and the media. The rooms and suites (named after presidents) are decorated in traditional or Victorian style; some have fireplaces, whirlpool baths, waterbeds or canopy beds, and kitchenettes. A complimentary Continental breakfast is served Monday through Friday. *103 Frederick Rd., Thurmont 21788, tel. and fax 301/271–4301. 14 rooms, 2 suites, 5 cabins. Facilities: no-smoking rooms. AE, MC, V. $–$$$*

Rambler Motel. This motel at the northern edge of Thurmont has comfortable, clean rooms with traditional furniture built by local artisans. Each room has a cable TV and a telephone. All units are on the ground floor. A 24-hour convenience store and deli is next door. *Rtes. 15 and 550, Thurmont 21788, tel. 301/271–2424, fax 301/271–2425. 30 rooms. Facilities: air-conditioning, no-smoking rooms. AE, D, DC, MC, V. $–$$*

Super 8. The Super 8 in the southern part of Thurmont is one of the town's newer motels. All rooms have cable TV; some have waterbeds or microwaves and refrigerators. In the morning there's toast and coffee in the lobby. *300 Tippin Dr., Thurmont 21788, tel. and fax 301/271–7888, 800/800–8000 for reservations. 45 rooms, 1 suite. Facilities: no-smoking rooms. AE, D, DC, MC, V. $*

CAMPING

Camping in either park is allowed only in designated campgrounds. There are almost always sites available during the week throughout the year, but the campgrounds fill up rapidly on weekends, especially between late spring and fall.

Adirondack Shelters. The national park maintains two shelters for camping in the woods along the Catoctin Trail. To reach them, you must hike about 2 mi from the Owens Creek Campground. They are available on a first-come, first-served basis, but you must obtain a permit at the visitor center.

Camp Misty Mount. This group of rustic wood-and-stone cabins (for three to six people) and one lodge (for up to eight) is a National Historic District. Each cabin is furnished with metal cots and mattresses; you'll find a picnic table, a grill, and a fire circle outside—no cooking is allowed inside. Campers must provide bedding and

cookware. Flush toilets and hot showers are nearby, and a swimming pool is available from Memorial Day to Labor Day during limited hours. No pets are allowed. A dining hall and kitchen may be rented separately. *Off Park Central Rd., tel. 301/271–3140 (camp manager). 27 cabins, 1 lodge. MC, V. Open mid-Apr.–mid-May, weekends; mid-May–Oct., daily. $–$$*

Manor Campground. Within this campground operated by Cunningham Falls State Park, flush toilets and hot showers are centrally located; a visitor center, a picnic shelter, and trailheads are nearby. There are no hookups. A stay is limited to 14 days, pets are not allowed, and no reservations are accepted. *Off Rte. 15. 31 sites. Bathhouse closed Labor Day–Memorial Day. $*

Owens Creek Campground. The Catoctin Mountain Park campground provides a wooded setting for its sites, each of which has a picnic table and a fireplace or grill. There are flush toilets and hot showers. All sites are available on a first-come, first-served basis, and you self-register at the campground entrance by filling out a form and depositing a fee into a receptacle. *Foxville–Deerfield Rd., no phone. 51 sites. Open mid-Apr.–3rd Sun. in Nov. $*

William Houck Campground. The main campground in Cunningham Falls State Park has sites distributed over five loops by Hunting Creek Lake. Each site has a table, a grill, and a parking area. Flush toilets and hot showers are centrally located. Thirty of the campsites have electric hookups, but none have hookups for water. No pets are allowed and camping is limited to 14 days. There are also four rustic cabins here, each with a double bed and a bunk bed (bedding is not provided) and a porch; cooking must be done outdoors. Reservations ($5) for both camping sites and cabins may be made by phone or in person, weekdays 8:30–4. *Off Catoctin Hollow Rd., tel. 301/271–7574. 149 sites, 4 cabins. Open Memorial Day–Labor Day and weekends in May and Sept. $*

Delaware Water Gap National Recreation Area
New Jersey, Pennsylvania

By M. T. Schwartzman

Updated by Jill Schensul

inety minutes by car from both New York and Philadelphia is a dramatic valley formed by the Delaware River, the river that separates Pennsylvania from New Jersey, cutting the Kittatinny Ridge into twin peaks. The native Lenape (pronounced *len-uh-pee*) tribe's name for this ridge means "big mountain." Today the ridge crowns the Northeast's largest national recreation area, which encompasses more than 70,000 acres and stretches for 40 mi along both banks of the river. The park's boundary extends north nearly to the point where Pennsylvania, New York, and New Jersey meet and runs 1.5 mi south of the bend at Kittatinny Point. The lower part of the park surrounds New Jersey's Worthington State Forest.

In the 1800s city folk came for the fresh air and cool summers, staying weeks and even months at a time. Now, weekend outings are more popular among the park's 4 million annual visitors. They come not just to see but to do, for as the name suggests, the park's main draw is recreation. You won't find a steady stream of tour buses and cars going from overlook to overlook. The natural wonders here are best enjoyed outside your car. You can picnic along the shores of the river, scan the trees for migrating birds, photograph the dramatic landscape, explore picturesque historic sites, or canoe, fish, or even swim in the Delaware, which the Park Service calls one of the cleanest rivers in the East. Hikers can choose from more than 60 trails, including a 25-mi stretch of the Appalachian Trail. Some paths offer an easy stroll through the woods; others issue a challenge to climb the area's highest points.

Ironically, the federal government's original plan was to build a dam and reservoir at Tocks Island, 6 mi north of the gap. In 1965, to generate public support for the project, Congress established the Delaware Water Gap National Recreation Area with the reservoir as its centerpiece, but the park became the most convincing argument against building the dam: Its construction would have submerged 80% of the recreation area's land. In 1978 the Delaware was designated a Wild and Scenic River and put under Park Service control. In 1992 the Tocks Island Dam project was officially deauthorized, and in 1995 the recreation area celebrated its 30th anniversary, in its original state.

ESSENTIAL INFORMATION

VISITOR INFORMATION To find out about recreational opportunities, call the **Delaware Water Gap National Recreation Area** superintendent (Bushkill, PA 18324–9999, tel. 717/588–2451), weekdays 8–4:30. **Visitor centers** are at **Kittatinny Point** (tel. 908/496–4458) in New Jersey, which is open mid-April–October, daily 9–5, and November–mid-April, most weekends 9–4:30; at **Bushkill** (U.S. Route 209, tel. 717/588–7044), in Pennsylvania, which is open in summer daily 9–5 (other seasonal hours not determined as of press time); and at **Dingmans Falls** (tel. 717/

828–7802), also in Pennsylvania, which is open mid-April–October, daily 9–5, and November–December, weekends 9–4:30. Note that the Dingmans Falls center, trails, and falls overlooks are closed for renovation, scheduled to reopen spring 1999. The hot line for emergencies is tel. 800/543–4295. The park's **Web site** is www.nps.gov/dewa/.

For information on New Jersey's **Worthington State Forest,** contact the superintendent (HC 62, Box 2, Columbia, NJ 07832, tel. 908/841–9575).

For information on lodging and dining outside the park, and other local tourist facilities in the nearby Pennsylvania area, contact the **Pocono Mountains Vacation Bureau** (1004 Main St., Stroudsburg, PA 18360, tel. 717/424–6050 or 800/762–6667). For information on attractions, lodging, and dining on the New Jersey side, contact the **Skylands of New Jersey Tourism Council** (3117 Rte. 10 East, Denville, NJ 07834, tel. 800/475–9526).

FEES The fee for Smithfield and Milford beaches is $5 per vehicle per day; an annual pass is $25. Bridges between the Pennsylvania and New Jersey sides of the park have tolls of varying amounts.

PUBLICATIONS Pick up the **"Delaware Water Gap: Official Map and Guide"** at visitor centers and park headquarters, as well as **"Spanning the Gap,"** which covers current events and other timely and essential park information. Additional handouts cover boat and canoe access points, licensed canoe liveries, hiking and cross-country ski trails, hunting regulations, fishing, local campgrounds, Appalachian Trail regulations, and bald-eagle viewing.

Also for bird-watchers, a field checklist is available from the visitor centers or the **Pocono Environmental Education Center** (RR 2, Box 1010, Dingmans Ferry, PA 18328, tel. 717/828–2319, fax 717/828–9695).

The bookstores at the Kittatinny Point, Bushkill, and Dingmans Falls visitor centers (*see* Visitor Information, *above*) stock titles on the area's history, geology, and flora and fauna, as well as some for kids.

The Eastern National Association, in cooperation with the park service, maintains a mail-order list of trail maps, topographical maps, and children's titles and histories relating to the water gap. Of special interest to park visitors interested in the area's Colonial era are *Old Mine Road,* which tells the story of one of America's oldest highways, and *A Place Called Home,* a history of the Van Campen Inn—one of the park's oldest buildings. Contact park headquarters for an order form, or **Eastern National** (3 Main St., Layton, NJ 07851, tel. 973/948–0463). The **Walpack Historical Society** (Box 3, Walpack Center, NJ 07881, tel. 973/948–6671) sells reprints of *The Minisink,* a book chronicling the area from its prehistoric settlement to the Tocks Island Dam project.

GEOLOGY AND TERRAIN A water gap is a notch in the landscape created when a river crosses a mountain range, and the National Park Service calls this one the greatest in the world. How it formed is open to debate. Some scientists believe that the river was here before the mountains were, flowing along a flat coastal plain. Gradual folding in the earth's crust led to uplifting, but the river fought back, carving a gorge through the ridge that sought to block its path. Others contend that the mountains came first and that a shift in the river's course led to erosion of the ridge.

The Delaware Water Gap is a monument to water's power. The river follows a tight S-turn through the Kittatinny Ridge; to the west Mt. Minsi rises 1,463 ft, and to the east Mt. Tammany climbs to 1,527 ft—the remains of what may once have been a continuous highland that filled the 1,400-yard-wide gap.

The Kittatinny Ridge stretches diagonally across the park for 10 mi. Along its crest runs the Appalachian Trail. Visible from either side of the river, the ridge dominates the park's landscape north of the gap before veering to the east.

FLORA AND FAUNA The water gap's forest is a mix of softwood and hardwood, coniferous and deciduous. Periodic splashes of color punctuate its verdant tones: clusters of blooming dogwoods in May, rhododendron around the Fourth of July, and the biggest show of all in autumn.

The forest supports 43 known species of mammals. Hikers are most likely to encounter white-tailed deer, beaver, and an occasional black bear foraging through the woods. On the water, you may also see river otters. Among the 263 species of birds identified in the area are hawks and other raptors that make a semiannual migration through the park. As many as 10–15 bald eagles winter along the river.

WHEN TO GO The water gap's face reflects the seasons. In this mid-Atlantic climate, the changes are distinct and sometimes dramatic. January highs hover around freezing and nighttime lows drop into the teens. July days average in the upper 70s–lower 80s, but occasional heat waves can drive those figures into the 90s. Temperatures during the warm months bottom out in the mid-50s.

High season is whenever the weather is good. A dry spring lures hikers; a sunny summer brings swimmers, canoeists, boaters, and anglers to the river; and a cold and snowy winter draws cross-country skiers, snowmobilers, and those who want to ice-skate or ice-fish on the ponds and lakes. Ice-climbing challenges the adventurous and experienced. Bird-watchers may want to consider a trip in January or February, when bald eagles can be seen. The only true off-season is between fall foliage and winter's first snow, a rainy and muddy time that's not conducive to outdoor recreation. Because it's also hunting season, hikers should wear bright orange vests or jackets.

Still, summer is the busiest time at the park, and weekends are more crowded than weekdays. The farther into the park you hike, the fewer humans you are likely to meet, since most day-trippers stick to the short trails that lead to and from the parking areas.

SEASONAL EVENTS June: **Delaware River Sojourn** (tel. 717/828–2319), which takes place the second to the third Saturday in June, is a celebration of the river to increase awareness for the Delaware; the main event is an eight-day canoe trip. **Walpack Day** (tel. 973/948–6671), on the third Sunday in June, is the only day of the year that all the buildings of Walpack Center (*see* Historic Buildings and Sites *in* Exploring, *below*) are open to the public. **September:** On the weekend after Labor Day, **Celebration of the Arts** (tel. 717/424–2210) brings some 4,000 music fans to the tiny town of Delaware Water Gap, Pennsylvania, for an outdoor festival with live jazz and other performances Friday evening through Sunday afternoon. On the last weekend in September, the juried **Peters Valley Crafts Fair** (tel. 973/948–5200) attracts 13,000 people and 150 exhibitors. **October: Millbrook Days** (tel. 717/588–2451), on the first weekend of the month, celebrate turn-of-the-century rural life. **Van Campen Day** (tel. 973/948–6671), on the third Sunday of the month, re-creates the area's Colonial period with living history demonstrations and a Revolutionary War encampment.

WHAT TO PACK Be prepared for changeable conditions; bring T-shirts from spring through fall, but don't forget a sweater— June lows in the 40s have been recorded. If you plan to hike, bring sturdy shoes. Rock-strewn trails are common—and muddy during spring runoff. If you plan to bring your own canoe or tube, don't forget life preservers; the river can be deceptively deep and swift. The Park Service recommends that you wear a wet suit any time the water and the air temperatures add up to less than 100°F.

GENERAL STORES If you arrive from the east by way of I–80, you can stock up on cold cuts, soft drinks, and snacks—plus western boots at good prices—at the 24-hour **Columbia Service Complex** (tel. 908/496–4124), a convenience store and truck stop in the Country Pride Restaurant off Exit 4, 5 mi east of the park. If you're coming from points west and traveling up or down the Pennsylvania side of the river, you'll find groceries, tackle, and bait at the **Shawnee General Store** (tel. 717/421–0956). At the deli there, you can pick up a sandwich for later, or you can eat in either the little country store-style dining room or on the outdoor deck. Shawnee General Store is on River Road, just north of the Shawnee Inn, and is open daily 6:30 AM–7:30 PM, later on Saturday and during the summer.

ATMS There's an ATM at the **Columbia Service Complex** in New Jersey (I–80, Exit 4). On the Pennsylvania side, you'll find ATMs at **Mellon Bank** (U.S. 209, Marshalls Creek) and the **PNC Bank** (Foxmoor Village at U.S. 209, 3 mi south of the park border).

ARRIVING AND DEPARTING A network of interstates, federal highways, and state routes leads to, through, and around the park from every direction. Because driving is so easy, and public transportation limited, most visitors arrive by private vehicle.

By Bus. From New York City, **Martz Trailways** (tel. 800/637–9722) operates one local run daily with a stop in Delaware Water Gap, Pennsylvania, as well as several buses a day to the Stroudsburg station on Route 611, 5 mi from the water gap. From Philadelphia, **Greyhound Lines** (tel. 800/231–2222) runs two buses daily to Stroudsburg.

By Car or RV. The primary route from New York City, I–80 runs right through the Delaware Water Gap. On the New Jersey side, the highway hugs the river at the water's S-turn, and a toll bridge crosses the river within sight of the gorge. I–84 provides access to the park's northern reaches. In Milford you can connect with U.S. 209, which runs south through the park on the Pennsylvania side and intersects I–80. Two additional toll bridges span the river just south of Milford and at Dingmans Ferry.

Car rentals are available at the airports listed below. **Avis** (tel. 800/331–1212). **Budget** (tel. 800/527–0700). **Hertz** (tel. 800/654–3131). **National** (tel. 800/328–4567). **Payless** (tel. 800/729–5377 or 800/237–2804) is only at the Lehigh Valley airport.

By Plane. The closest commercial airports, both 40–45 mi away, are **Lehigh Valley International** (U.S. 22 and Airport Rd., Allentown, PA, tel. 610/266–6000), served by Continental, Delta, Northwest, United, and US Airways plus a number of regional and commuter lines, and **Wilkes-Barre/Scranton International** (Avoca, PA, tel. 717/457–3445), served by Delta, US Airways, and a few regional and commuter lines.

By Train. There is no train service to or near the park.

EXPLORING

Where you go will depend upon your interests. Historic sites lie mostly in New Jersey, beaches and snowmobile trails in Pennsylvania. Scenic roads line both sides of the river. You can drive between the main recreation sites and then explore deeper into the wilderness on foot or on the river itself. A day trip to the area should include a visit to the water gap, a picnic, a walk in the woods, and a drive along the scenic back roads. A two-day itinerary might add water sports or a longer hike.

THE BEST IN ONE DAY The place to start is at the park's centerpiece, the water gap. Stop in at the Kittatinny Point Visitor Center to pick up the free map and guide, and ask for a Terrace Talk (*see* Orientation Programs, *below*). Walk around to the back of the visitor center, and continue down to the riverbank for views of the gap. Then get back in your car and head across the bridge to Pennsylvania and north along River Road (*see* Scenic Drives and Views, *below*) toward one of the scenic waterfall walks (*see* Nature Trails and Short Walks, *below*). If you haven't packed a picnic, you can pick one up in the little river town of Shawnee and eat it when you get to the trailhead. After your walk, drive over the little bridge at Dingmans Ferry to New Jersey, and head south. Depending on what's open and your interests, visit the Peters Valley Craft Center (*see* Children's Pro-

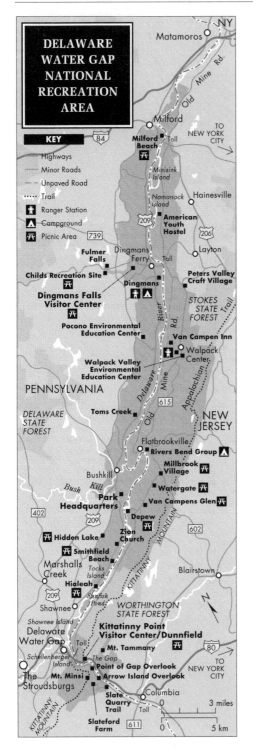

DELAWARE WATER GAP NATIONAL RECREATION AREA

KEY
- Highways
- Minor Roads
- Unpaved Road
- Trail
- Ranger Station
- Campground
- Picnic Area

grams, *below*), Van Campen Inn, or Millbrook Village (*see* Historic Buildings and Sites, *below*) before having dinner at the Walpack Inn (*see* Dining, *below*), where, if you're lucky, some deer will be dining, too, on the lawn beyond the restaurant's big picture windows.

ORIENTATION PROGRAMS Both visitor centers present slide-show introductions to the water gap, each with a site-specific component. At Kittatinny Point, rangers give free Terrace Talks—informal discussions on the geology and natural and cultural history of the area—on request from May to October, when staffing permits, and by reservation the rest of the year.

GUIDED TOURS For the most part, this is a do-it-yourself park. At Dingmans Falls, rangers lead a Walk to the Falls, usually at 11 and 2 on weekends May–October. At Slateford Farm, at the southern tip of the park, interpreters give guided tours of the grounds first worked in the 1800s. Tours generally run from noon to 5 late spring or early summer through late summer or early fall. Slateford Farm was closed at press time; reopening information was not available. Other ranger-led programs—talks, short interpretive hikes, hawk watches—are scheduled, mostly in summer, based on staff expertise and availability. Check with park headquarters or visitor centers for upcoming programs; sign-up may be necessary.

One Sunday a month at 2, the **Pocono Environmental Education Center** (*see* Publications *in* Essential Information, *above*) conducts naturalist-led walks on different nature-study topics, from finding fossils to watching warblers.

The only bus tour is the hour-long trip to some of the park's overlooks on the **Water Gap Trolley** (tel. 717/476–0010). You can pick it up at the stoplight in Delaware Water Gap. It costs $5 and runs daily 10–4 about every 1½ hours from late March to early November.

SCENIC DRIVES AND VIEWS One of the best ways to gain a sense of the park is simply to drive through it. More than 200 mi of roads wind through scenic valleys, over ridges, and past historic buildings.

Hugging the Delaware on the Pennsylvania side, **River Road** follows a curving, undulating path from I–80 up to U.S. 209 at the park boundary in Bushkill. Traveling upriver, you tunnel through woods and past farmlands, getting glimpses of the river along the way.

Along the New Jersey shore is the **Old Mine Road,** which traces its roots nearly to the beginning of American history. Built in the 17th century and stretching 104 mi between New York State and Pennsylvania, this was one of America's first commercial highways. Though most of the road is now paved, an unmaintained section at the water's edge appears much as it did in Colonial days. As you ride down this section's sometimes muddy surface, imagine Massachusetts delegate John Adams, who—legend has it—traveled the same route by stagecoach, stopping at the Van Campen Inn (*see* Historic Buildings and Sites, *below*) for the night before continuing to Philadelphia and the Continental Congress.

To get there, take the last exit off I–80W on the New Jersey side. Drive north alongside the river past Millbrook Village. At the bridge (Rte. 615), make a right, continue past Walpack Center (*see* Historic Buildings and Sites, *below*), and make a left at Peters Valley Craft Center. This leads you to the unpaved portion of Old Mine Road, which you can follow for about 5 mi. To return to the 20th century, make a right once you reach paved highway again, and make another right at the bridge. Follow this road back to I–80. The whole loop is about 50 mi.

For a 4-mi drive to some high vantage points along the river, take I–80 Exit 53 in Pennsylvania and follow Route 611 south through the historic town of Delaware Water Gap. Just down the road, Mt. Tammany stands high above the **Point of Gap** and **Arrow Island** overlooks.

HISTORIC BUILDINGS AND SITES Where the paved section of Old Mine Road meets Route 602 lies **Millbrook Village** (tel. 908/841–9531), 12 mi north of I–80. A gristmill was built here in 1832, and a community grew up around it and flourished until 1900 when people moved to other places for better jobs. The village has since been re-created to illustrate rural life of a century ago. Some original buildings remain, others were moved to the site, and still others were reconstructed, including a replica of the original mill, which was destroyed in 1922. The grounds are open daily until sunset; selected buildings are open daily in summer (Wednesday–Sunday in spring); and traditional crafts, such as blacksmithing and woodworking, are demonstrated on weekends.

One of the park's oldest buildings reflects the succession from Dutch to English rule during the Colonial period. On the unmaintained section of Old Mine Road (*see* Scenic Drives and Views, *above*), the **Van Campen Inn,** built in 1746, is a prime example of vernacular architecture—a local combination of traditional styles that reflects an area's history and culture. Look for the Dutch details, notably the curved wooden eaves, which contrast with the formal Georgian symmetry of the stone facade. The house is open May–October, Sunday 1–5 (tel. 973/729–7392).

If your idea of a ghost town includes tumbleweed and tombstones, **Walpack Center,** on nearby Route 615, will disappoint, but the cute little former town was genuinely abandoned during the 1970s in anticipation of the Tocks Island Dam project and the flooding that would follow. The buildings are kept up, painted in cream with green trim, and a few of them house offices or park staff, somewhat negating that frozen-in-time feeling. A single-lane country road leads from the post office at one end to a white steepled church at the other. You can wander the grounds, peeking in the abandoned buildings' windows, or visit the small museum operated by the Walpack Historical Society (tel. 973/729–7392) in the

First Rosenkrans House, open May–October, Sunday 1–5. All the other buildings are open only on Walpack Day (*see* Seasonal Events *in* Essential Information, *above*).

At the northern end of the park, in Montague, New Jersey, are two houses maintained by the Montague Association for the Restoration of Community History (tel. 973/293–7350). In addition to local art and historical exhibits, the **Neldon-Roberts Stonehouse,** on U.S. 206, offers summer folk art and crafts demonstrations; such topics as spinning and weaving, stained-glass making, surveying, and lace-making are explored. On Old Mine Road, the **Foster Armstrong House,** comprising a classic Dutch-style house built in 1790 with an 1820 addition, has exhibits on covered bridges and local lore. Courses on spinning, weaving, and quilting are offered year-round. Both houses are open Sunday 1–4.

NATURE TRAILS AND SHORT WALKS The Appalachian Trail (*see* Longer Hikes, *below*) forms the spine of the recreation area's primary trail network. Secondary paths lead between the Appalachian Trail and trailheads on the park roads. Alternative paths parallel the Appalachian Trail. There are also short trails around other natural and historic attractions.

Easy trails lead from visitor centers in both New Jersey and Pennsylvania. To find waterfalls, start at the **Dingmans Falls Visitor Center** (.8 mi off U.S. 209), where a mostly shady .5-mi loop leads through a ravine and past giant rhododendrons and hemlocks to Silver Thread Falls, an 80-ft spring-fed cataract, and on to Dingmans Falls, a thundering 130-ft cascade. You can hike this in 30–45 minutes.

Three more waterfalls—big, bigger, and biggest—are at the **George W. Childs Recreation Site** (3 mi off U.S. 209). Wooden steps and bridges lead to the bottom of the cataracts—Factory Falls, Fulmer Falls, and Deer Leap Falls. Paths follow both banks of woods-shaded Dingmans Creek, with crossing points at each falls. At Factory Falls, don't miss the ruins of a wool mill

built in 1825. Allow at least an hour to complete the 1.8-mi loop, which is steep and rocky at points.

If you want to climb very high in a very short distance, take the .5-mi **Table Rock Spur Trail** off the Appalachian Trail. You can start at Lake Lenape parking lot off Route 611 on Mountain Road outside Delaware Water Gap. The broken remnants of a paved road lead past water lily–filled Lake Lenape, where the going gets steeper. At the top, a right turn leads to a bare rock terrace. Beyond the treetops loom the twin peaks of Mt. Tammany and Mt. Minsi. Allow an hour for the 1-mi round-trip.

LONGER HIKES The **Appalachian Trail** enters the recreation area below the gorge and runs through the town of Delaware Water Gap, Pennsylvania. Signs guide hikers through the historic district to the river's edge. The trail picks up on the far bank at the Kittatinny Point Visitor Center and runs for 25 mi along the Kittatinny Ridge before exiting at Stokes State Forest. Along the way it parallels and connects with many of the water gap's most popular hiking paths.

Sunfish Pond, a 44-acre glacial lake, lies at the end of a 3.75-mi section of the Appalachian Trail. To get there, begin at the Dunnfield Creek parking area in Worthington State Forest, or follow the Appalachian Trail under I–80 from the Kittatinny Point Visitor Center. The route to the pond runs along the creek and past veils of water tumbling over fallen trees, then climbs to the top of the ridge. Sunfish Pond, in a clearing at the path's end, is encircled by another 1.5-mi loop. Look for newly chewed-through tree trunks—signs of the resident beavers. Hiking time on the 7.5-mi trek from the Dunnfield Creek parking area and back is four to five hours.

OTHER ACTIVITIES **Back-Road Driving.** Some ungated park roads that are not maintained lead to secluded sites within the park and are good choices for exploring in four-wheel-drive vehicles.

Biking. The Park Service recommends the paved sections of Old Mine Road in New Jersey for a moderately hilly bike tour. Mountain bikes are allowed in the park only on ungated roads, not hiking trails. Mountain bikes may be rented from **Starting Gate** (U.S. 209, midway between Marshalls Creek and Bushkill, PA, tel. 717/223–6215); rates are $10 for two hours, $20 all day; you can also rent in-line skates for $10 daily.

Bird-Watching. Raptors and other birds may be seen during their fall and spring migrations, and scavengers regularly feed on roadside carrion. Bald eagles visit during January and February. Midmorning or late afternoon, when the birds preen, is the best time to look for their white heads against the bare brown branches. Also look for the eagles over the river, as they swoop down to hook a fish with their talons. Eagle etiquette dictates that you keep your distance, so as not to stress the birds.

Boating. Forty miles of the Delaware River run through the park, and there are access points every 8–10 mi. Boating information and regulations and detailed maps are available at visitor centers and at park headquarters.

Canoeing, Kayaking, Rafting, and Tubing. Enthusiasts have been canoeing the generally gentle Delaware since at least 1876, and the native Lenape used it for fishing and transportation long before that. Spring is the best time for rafting the river, because the current is the swiftest and conditions for rapids are best. Summer is ideal for canoeing and tubing—the waters are calm and you don't need a wet suit. Outfitters include **Pack Shack Adventures** (88 Broad St., Box 127, Delaware Water Gap, PA 18327, tel. 717/424–8533 or 800/424–0955), which rents canoes, kayaks, rafts, and tubes; **Shawnee Canoe Trips** (River Rd. at the Shawnee Inn, Shawnee-on-Delaware, PA 18356, tel. 717/421–1500, ext. 1120, or 800/742–9633, ext. 1120, or 717/424–1139), which has canoes, rafts, and tubes; **Adventure Sports** (U.S. 209, 2 mi north of I–80, Box 175, Mar-

shalls Creek, PA 18335, tel. 717/223–0505 or 800/487–2628), which runs guided overnight trips ($145 per person) as well as renting canoes and rafts; and **Kittatinny Canoes** (Dingmans Ferry Bridge, Dingmans Ferry, PA 18328, tel. 717/828–2338 or 800/356–2852), which rents canoes, rafts, kayaks, and tubes. Equipment rental, which includes transportation upstream, is generally a few dollars more on weekends than weekdays. Canoes run $45–$55 for two people, kayaks $30–$36 per person, and tubes $13–$15. Rafts accommodate from 4 to 10 people and can cost anywhere from $17 to $27 per person, depending on outfitter and raft size. A complete list of licensed canoe liveries is available from the visitor centers or park headquarters.

Cross-Country Skiing. Winter visitors can cross-country ski along sparsely used park roads or on 13 mi of marked and maintained ski trails. The 5-mi **Slate Quarry Trail** (Slateford Farm, south of the water gap), in Pennsylvania, is good for beginners, and the 8-mi **Blue Mountain Lake Trail** (near Rte. 627), in the park's midsection on the New Jersey side, is more challenging. Cross-country ski rentals, guided tours into the park, and lessons are available from **Pack Shack Adventures** (*see* Canoeing, Kayaking, Rafting, and Tubing, *above*); daily rentals cost $12–$15 adults, $10–$12 children. The outfit also rents snowshoes and leads snowshoe hikes. Skis and snowboards may also be rented at the **Starting Gate** (*see* Biking, *above*); daily rental costs $15.

Fishing. The 20 natural lakes and ponds within the recreation area are home to panfish, bass, catfish, and pickerel. In the Delaware, anglers may catch American shad, smallmouth bass, walleye, eel, catfish, panfish, and muskellunge; rainbow, brook, and brown trout are found in the river's tributaries, such as the Flat Brook, in New Jersey, and Bushkill Creek, in Pennsylvania. Pennsylvania fishing licenses are available from the **Fish and Boat Commission** (tel. 717/657–4518) and cost $17 residents, $35 nonresidents; a three-day tourist license is $15, and a trout stamp is an additional $5.50. The **Division of Fish, Game, and Wildlife** (tel. 609/292–2965) is the source for New Jersey licenses: $16.50 residents, $25.25 nonresidents or $16.50 for seven consecutive days; trout stamps are $7.75 residents, $15.50 nonresidents. Because of a reciprocal agreement, you can fish in the river or from its banks with a license from either state.

Horseback Riding. Guided trail rides through the foothills begin at **Windrose Riding Center at Shawnee** (River Rd., ¼ mi north of I–80, tel. 717/420–1763); rides cost $20 for 45 minutes.

Model-Airplane Flying. The **Hialeah Air Park** (River Rd., ½ mi north of Smithfield Beach), maintained by the Roxbury Area Model Airplane Club (tel. 973/778–9236), is reserved for operators of radio-controlled model aircraft. There's usually somebody around on warm, sunny days, and you can watch as the pilots maneuver their planes into the air, making them perform aerobatic tricks, and then land. It's a sight you're not likely to see at most national parks.

Photography. The water gap, with its bookend peaks, is nature's perfect photographic composition. For unobstructed views and good angles, try the Point of Gap and Arrow Island overlooks (*see* Scenic Drives and Views, *above*). A wide-angle lens, tripod, and slow-speed film always yield the best landscape portraits. For a different view use a medium telephoto to isolate one or both of the peaks against the sky. To get a clear shot, try the bare rock terrace at the end of the Table Rock Spur Trail (*see* Nature Trails and Short Walks, *above*). Students in the photography classes at Peters Valley Craft Education Center (*see* Children's Programs, *below*) also spend time learning how to shoot the patterns and colors of nature in the park.

Rock Climbing. Both climbing up and rappelling down Mt. Tammany and Mt. Minsi have become popular sports, but specialized training and equipment are necessary. Instruction is available from **Pack Shack**

Adventures (*see* Biking, *above*); private lessons run $100, semiprivate $75 per person. Those climbing independently should stop in at a visitor center to get information and to notify park staff.

Snowmobiling. Two snowmobile trails start from Smithfield Beach: a 3-mi loop on the east side of River Road and a connecting 6-mi loop that heads over toward Hidden Lake Recreation Site.

Swimming. You can take a dip in the waters of the Delaware at the small, grassy areas at **Milford Beach,** near the park's northern end, and at **Smithfield Beach,** just above the water gap. Both are in Pennsylvania, both charge entry fees (*see* Fees *in* Essential Information, *above*), and both have bathhouses and picnic tables, as well as lifeguards who are on duty from mid-June through Labor Day. (Strong currents, sharp drop-offs, and changing conditions make many other spots unsafe for swimming, however, so check on prohibited areas before swimming unsupervised.)

Waterskiing. Two areas of river have been designated for waterskiing: **Smithfield Coppermine Pool** (a 2-mi stretch just downriver from Smithfield Beach) and **Price's Landing Pool** (½ mi of river between Schellenberger and Shawnee islands). At both these sites, from April through September, you can go up to 35 mph (compared to the 10-mph limit on the rest of the river). A 35-mph speed limit is posted riverwide the rest of the year.

CHILDREN'S PROGRAMS As part of its Junior Naturalist program, the Park Service lends out **Discovery Packs,** backpacks with simple tools and a booklet to help in exploring nature; they are available at both visitor centers. The resident artists at the **Peters Valley Craft Center** (19 Kuhn Rd., Layton, NJ 07851, tel. 973/948–5200) give workshops for kids in May in addition to opening their studios to the public and teaching adult workshops June–August. Converted from an old honeymoon resort, the **Pocono Environmental Education Center** (*see* Publications *in* Essential Information, *above*) sponsors a number of nature-oriented programs for kids. Weeklong summer day camps ($45–$85 per week or $12–$17 per day) have names like "Lifestyles of the Wet & Slimy" and run in July and August for children ages 3–12. In addition, there are weekend and weeklong vacation retreats for families year-round ($94–$164 per person), covering topics from astronomy to cemetery studies to wildlife. The **Walpack Environmental Education Center** (Box 134, Walpack Center, NJ 07881, tel. 973/948–5749), sponsored by the Eatontown, New Jersey, Board of Education, also offers students in elementary and intermediate schools a variety of programs, from 1½ to 5 days.

EVENING ACTIVITIES Rangers lead campfire programs at the Dingmans Campground in Pennsylvania and the Worthington State Forest Campground in New Jersey (*see* Camping, *below*); the Pocono Environmental Education Center offers evening programs about once a month year-round.

DINING

Commercial U.S. 209 does have places to eat, but a better bet is the small town of Delaware Water Gap, which, despite having only 700 inhabitants, has become a local culinary center. There are eight or so restaurants, a few of which go far beyond hiking fare. A handful of other eateries are tucked here and there around the park.

INSIDE THE PARK **Walpack Inn.** The only restaurant within the park's boundaries has been at this location since 1949. Lobster, teriyaki steak, and prime rib are all good choices. The Swedish brown bread is so popular it's sold by the loaf, and the fresh fruit pie is the dessert of choice. Dining is in a skylit greenhouse, facing the Kittatinny Ridge. Deer occasionally prance by in the open field outside—often enough that the restaurant's slogan, on the sign out front, is WE FEED THE DEER, AND PEOPLE, TOO. The rustic piano bar, adorned with mounted moose, bear, and deer heads, is worth the trip—if only for a drink beside the fieldstone fire-place. An elaborate brunch is served Sunday. *Rte. 615, ½ mi from Walpack Center Historic District, Walpack Center, NJ, tel. 973/948–9849 or 973/948–6505. MC, V. No lunch. Closed Mon.–Thurs. $$–$$$*

NEAR THE PARK **Brownie's.** The latest in a string of eateries that have occupied this site since the 1890s, this country pub serves burgers, sandwiches, steaks, and seafood all day, plus two or more dinner specials nightly. Fresh clams are steamed year-round, with clambakes on weekends in summer. The Famous Hot Wings live up to their billing, and the 16-ounce steak special will satisfy any hungry hiker fresh off the Appalachian Trail, two blocks away. *Main and Oak Sts., Delaware Water Gap, PA, tel. 717/424–1154. AE, MC, V. Closed Mon. $$*

Deerhead Inn. This tavern at the intersection of Main Street and the Appalachian Trail, built in 1869, has been known to townies as the home of jazz since the '50s. Early in the week, the fare is bar food and the clientele mainly locals, but by the weekend the menu and the crowd grow. People come to eat dinner—choosing from meat, vegetarian, and seafood entrées that take advantage of whatever's in season—and listen to live jazz Friday and Saturday evenings and Sunday starting midafternoon. If you stay for the jazz, you pay a music charge of $5–$10. A handful of inexpensive guest rooms are available and are used by the musicians or those who plan to hear them and stay late. *Main St., Delaware Water Gap, PA, tel. 717/424–2000. AE, MC, V. Closed Mon. No lunch. $$*

Gallery Café. Mediterranean meets Southwest in both decor and cuisine at this art-splashed, cathedral-ceilinged eatery. Owner Effie Rogers, who's from Greece, serves pastas, salads, a changing list of international burritos, a few chicken and seafood selections, and a half dozen macrobiotic items—all with an exclamation point after "fresh." Nibble on warm pita bread with apple butter; then choose from many wonderful concoctions that make liberal use of eggplant, radicchio, balsamic vinegar, feta cheese, and the like; and finish up with a home-baked dessert and cappuccino (yes, cappuccino in the shadow of the Appalachian Trail). Friday and Saturday nights a pianist plays. *760 Broad St., Delaware Water Gap, PA, tel. 717/424–5565. D, DC, MC, V. Closed Mon. $$*

Mimi's Streamside Cafe. In this lively joint up the road from the Shawnee Inn (*see* Lodging, *below*) on a stream that feeds the Delaware, there are really three establishments: the front bar, where rock music fills the air; the quaint main dining room; and the outdoor deck built around and under a big, old pine tree. Specialties include Pocono Mountain brook trout, beef tips, and chicken marsala. *River Rd., Shawnee-on-Delaware, PA, tel. 717/424–6455. AE, DC, MC, V. $$*

Stroudsmoor Country Inn. The restaurant at this turn-of-the-century inn (*see* Lodging, *below*), situated high on a hilltop, takes great pride in its theme menus. Weekdays is the soup-to-nuts meal, a five-course dinner with a choice of entrée. Friday evening brings the Italian Feast complete with strolling violinist, Saturday the Grand Buffet, and Sunday a champagne brunch and American harvest dinner. You will not leave hungry. *Stroudsmoor Rd. off Rte. 191 (6 mi from the park), Stroudsburg, PA, tel. 717/421–6431. AE, MC, V. $$*

Country Pride Restaurant. This 24-hour diner, part of the service complex off Exit 4 on I–80 in New Jersey, is a good place to fill up before or after a hike. The best values are the all-you-can-eat breakfast buffet and all-day dinner buffet; the regular menu offers still more choices. Every table has a telephone where you can make toll-free, collect, or credit-card calls. *I–80 at Exit 4, Columbia, NJ, tel. 908/496–4124. AE, D, MC, V. $–$$*

Ship Inn. New Jersey's first brew pub, the Ship Inn has a decidedly British flavor. Along with home brews, the inn serves more than a dozen British draught ales and hard cider and traditional pub fare such as shepherd's pie and tea and scones. *61 Bridge St., Box 497, Milford, NJ, tel. 908/995–7007 or 800/651–2537. AE, DC, MC, V. $–$$*

Trail's End Cafe. A sign across the street says GA 1100 MI. ME 900 MI. and indeed the Appalachian Trail is just a block away from this cozy storefront bistro that serves healthy food. At breakfast try their home-made granola or build your own omelet. Gourmet pizzas stand out at lunch. Brunch is served on Sunday. *Main St., Delaware Water Gap, PA, tel. 717/421–1928. No credit cards. Closed Mon.–Tues. No dinner Wed.–Thurs. and weekends. $–$$*

Water Gap Diner. This 24-hour spot ("only" 5 AM–11 PM in winter) offers a typical New York–style diner menu, heavy on the Italian and Greek fare and 20 specials daily. Thick slices of hot, home-baked challah bread are served on the side. *55 Broad St., Delaware Water Gap, PA, tel. 717/476–0132. AE, DC, MC, V. $*

PICNIC SPOTS One of the best is at the **Kittatinny Point Visitor Center,** in view of the water gap at the water's edge. At the **Dingmans Falls Visitor Center** and **George W. Childs Recreation Site,** the sound of rushing water serenades alfresco diners (*see* Nature Trails and Short Walks *in* Exploring, *above*). **Watergate Recreation Site** on the New Jersey side is a favorite of a gaggle of Canada geese, who make their warm-weather home in and around two ponds. **Millbrook Village** also offers an inviting picnic area under welcoming shade trees, in view of the picturesque white church (*see* Historic Buildings and Sites *in* Exploring, *above*). Picnic and barbecue supplies are available at nearby markets (*see* General Stores *in* Essential Information, *above*).

LODGING

From the late 19th century to the early 20th century, at least 25 resorts were built in and around the town of Delaware Water Gap,

Pennsylvania. Only one, the Glenwood, remains. As the Poconos west of the area have eclipsed Delaware Water Gap as a vacation center, the town remains better known for its antiques shops and jazz scene.

Within the national recreation area, only a youth hostel offers overnight accommodations. Lodging immediately bordering the park ranges from B&Bs and inns to motels and sprawling resorts. Rooms can be scarce on weekends.

INSIDE THE PARK **Old Mine Road Youth Hostel.** The sole indoor accommodation in the recreation area is a secluded two-story 1930s house at the end of a dirt road in the park's very northern reaches. Right on the river, it makes an ideal starting point for bike and canoe trips. The AYH-licensed hostel has homey dormitory-style sleeping and common rooms furnished with some handsome old furniture, braided rugs, and plants. Social activity centers on the wood-burning stove in the common room, and a fully equipped kitchen is available. *Box 172, Layton, NJ 07851, tel. 973/948–6750. 12 beds. No credit cards. $*

NEAR THE PARK **Shawnee Inn.** This rambling resort, the only one on the banks of the Delaware, dates from 1910. Though the decor in the inn is more motel than hotel, rooms are pleasant and clean, and a Victorian gentility prevails, from the immaculately manicured grounds to the expansive porch facing the Kittatinny Ridge. A handful of motel-style units also are on the grounds (as are modern, privately owned units). Request a room in the main inn with a river view. Golf packages and combination room-meal plans are available; a room without meals is an option midweek. *Shawnee-on-Delaware, PA 18356, tel. 717/ 421–1500 or 800/742–9633, fax 717/424– 9168. 84 rooms in inn, 19 rooms in motel building. Facilities: 3 restaurants, bar, 2 outdoor pools, indoor pool, tennis court, 27 holes of golf, driving range, miniature golf, putting green, basketball, boccie, exercise room, horseback riding, horseshoes, jog-*

ging, shuffleboard, volleyball, boating, playground, 2 recreation rooms. MAP. AE, D, DC, MC, V. $$$

Shepard House. A pansy-lined walk, electric candles in the windows, and a wraparound veranda beckon you to this circa-1910 three-story house just a block from the Appalachian Trail. The Forsythia Room has its own sitting room and a bay window with a writing table, while a round stained-glass window highlights the Wisteria Room. The Tea Rose Room is dressed in roses, and the spacious Queen Anne Room has a sitting area and two double beds. A picnic and barbecue area is out back. Ask the innkeeper if she's baked any of her fresh breads that day. Off-season rates are more moderately priced. *108 Shepard Ave., Box 486, Delaware Water Gap, PA 18327, tel. 717/424–9779. 1 suite, 2 rooms with bath, 4 rooms share 2 baths. No credit cards. $$$*

Ramada Inn. Predictably clean and comfortable, rooms here are also unexpectedly elegant with their mix of contemporary and antique reproduction furnishings. Second-floor rooms have balconies. Suites have a king-size bed, sofa, sitting area, and writing table. *Broad St., Box 270, Delaware Water Gap, PA 18327, tel. 717/476–0000 or 800/ 228–4897, fax 717/476–6260. 94 rooms, 10 suites. Facilities: restaurant, bar, indoor and outdoor pools, recreation room. AE, D, DC, MC, V. $$–$$$*

Stroudsmoor Country Inn. In a cluster of 17 buildings that includes a mini-village of a dozen country and Victorian shops, this classic turn-of-the-century inn on 200 acres sits high on a ridge 6 mi from the park. Rooms in the main inn mix period antiques with floral wall coverings and plush carpeting. Guests can relax hearthside in the lobby, the piano lounge, or the pub's horse-shoe bar. Rooms 9 and 15, the largest, have sitting areas; Room 17 has a canopy bed; and several rooms have four-posters. The slightly larger cottage accommodations have porches but lack the furnishings that lend character to the main building's rooms. A wood-clad natatorium is a delightful place for a dip. Breakfast is available for a $10 surcharge. *Stroudsmoor Rd. off Rte. 191, Box 153, Stroudsburg, PA 18360, tel. 717/421–6431 or 800/955–8663, fax 717/421–8042. 14 rooms in main inn, 14 cottage units, 2 suites. Facilities: restaurant (see Dining, above), piano bar, pub, meeting rooms, indoor and outdoor pools, hot tub. AE, MC, V. $$–$$$*

Daystop of Columbia. This two-story motel, with a view that's more interstate than water gap, is run by Days Inn and is part of the service complex off I–80 that includes the Country Pride Restaurant (*see* Dining, *above*) and a convenience store. Standard doubles are nicely appointed with exposed brick walls. *I–80 at Exit 4, Columbia, NJ 07832, tel. 908/496–8221 or 800/329–7466, fax 908/496–4809. 35 rooms. Facilities: restaurant, no-smoking rooms. AE, D, MC, V. $$*

Eagle Rock Lodge. This early 19th-century house, now a B&B, sits on 10½ riverfront acres just north of Shawnee's center. Sit on the 80-ft-long, screened-in porch and look out at the Delaware and the Kittatinny Ridge, or wander down a steep landscaped lawn to the river. Guest rooms are furnished in an eclectic mix of country antiques. Rooms 3, 5, and 6 in back have the best views of the river and ridge. The bathrooms have vintage tubs, not showers, and the porch provides the setting for full breakfasts. Families and other groups often book the whole lodge or rent a nearby three-room house. *River Rd., Box 265, Shawnee-on-Delaware, PA 18356, tel. 717/ 421–2139 or 516/248–4963 weekdays Labor Day–July 4. 5 rooms share 2 baths, 1 suite. Facilities: volleyball, badminton, croquet. AE. Closed weekdays Labor Day–July 4 except by special arrangement. $$*

Chestnut Hill on the Delaware. This 1860 B&B offers beautiful views and cozy rooms. Owners Linda and Rob Castagna are gracious hosts. *63 Church St., Box N, Milford,*

NJ 08848, tel. 908/995–9761. 3 rooms with bath, 2 share bath, 1 cottage. $$–$$$

CAMPING

Primitive camping is intended only for travelers along the river (in designated camping areas) or the Appalachian Trail on a multiday journey. No permits are required and no fee is charged, but there's a one-night limit. For other guidelines and restrictions concerning camping along the Appalachian Trail, contact park headquarters, the **NY/NJ Trail Conference** (232 Madison Ave., Box 2250, New York, NY 10016, tel. 212/685–9699), or the **Appalachian Trail Conference** (Box 807, Harpers Ferry, WV 25425-0807, tel. 304/535–6331).

Since backcountry camping is limited to through-hikers and -boaters, the best bet for those who drive to the park is one of the organized campgrounds, most of which are outside the park boundary. A list of campgrounds within a 40-mi radius is available from the visitor centers or park headquarters.

INSIDE THE PARK Dingmans Campground. On U.S. 209 in Dingmans Ferry, Pennsylvania, Dingmans has wooded sites for tents, trailers, and RVs on its high ground, plus partially wooded sites along the river for tents. Tent sites cost $12.50–$17, RV and trailer hookups $14.50–$17. Water and electrical hookups are available at 50 sites. There are two bathhouses with flush toilets and showers plus six pit toilets. *R.R. 2, Box 20, Dingmans Ferry, PA 18328, tel. 717/ 828–2266. 125 sites. Facilities: softball, volleyball, horseshoes, playground, basketball. MC, V. Closed mid-Oct.–mid-Apr. $*

Walpack Valley Campground. This privately held campground facing the Kittatinny Ridge in New Jersey's Walpack Valley is like a little town, since RV owners stay long enough to landscape their sites and even erect toolsheds and decks. Streamside overnight tent sites are available along the Flat Brook, which is stocked with trout spring and fall. Tent sites cost $15, RV sites $17. There are portable toilets but no showers. *Rte. 615, Walpack Center, NJ 07881, tel. 973/948–4384. 65 tent sites, 10 RV sites. No credit cards. Closed Dec. 16–Mar. 30. $*

Worthington State Forest Campground. There's camping for tents, trailers, and RVs in an open field along the Delaware River near the Douglas Parking Area as well as nicer tent sites at the river's edge. There are no hookups. You must obtain a permit in person or by mail from the forest superintendent (*see* Visitor Information *in* Essential Information, *above*). Sites with pit toilet cost $8; sites with bath and shower access cost $10 (up to six campers per site). *Old Mine Rd., Columbia, NJ 07832, tel. 908/841–9575. 69 sites. No credit cards. Closed Dec.–Apr. $*

NEAR THE PARK **Delaware Water Gap KOA.** A full-service resort, this KOA has wooded sites about 3 mi from the river. Tent sites are $24 (up to two campers), $27 with electric and water. There are two bathhouses with flush toilets and showers; tetherball and hayrides, among other activities, are available. *RR 6, Box 6196 Hollow Road, East Stroudsburg, PA 18301, tel. 717/223–8000 or 800/562–0375. 47 hookups, 6 tent sites, 43 pop-ups, 55 trailers, 4 cabins. Facilities: pool, miniature golf, horseshoes, basketball, volleyball, recreation room, coin laundry, children's programs in summer. D, MC, V. Closed Nov.–Mar. $*

River Beach Campsites. On the banks of the Delaware, this campground borders the recreation area's northern boundary. Some tent sites have water and others have electricity as well; RV sites have both plus cable-TV hookups. Canoes may be rented for trips to Dingmans Ferry, 12 mi downriver, and tube trips start 3 mi upstream and end at the campground. There are a store and two bathhouses with flush toilets and showers. Sites are $3–$6, depending on location, plus $9 per person. *U.S. 209 and Rte. 6, Box 382, Milford, PA 18337, tel. 717/296–7421 or 800/356–2852. 125 tent sites, 5 lean-tos, 30 RV sites. Facilities: coin laundry, boating, video games. AE, D, MC, V. Closed Dec.–Feb.*

Stokes State Forest. On the New Jersey side this state forest has three areas for tent camping and RVs: Steam Mill Camping Area (open weekends in season), Shotwell Camping Area, and Lake Ocquittunk. All are just outside the Recreation Area and near the Appalachian Trail. There are no bathhouses, dump stations, or hookups. Half of the sites are reservable; the other half are available on a first-come, first-served basis. Stop in at the main office for directions to the campgrounds. *1 Coursen Rd., Branchville, NJ 07826, tel. 973/948–3820. Steam Mill closed Nov.–Mar. No credit cards. Shotwell sites $10, Steam Mill and Lake Ocquittunk sites $8, reservations $7 extra. 77 sites. Flush toilets at Shotwell only.*

Everglades National Park and Big Cypress National Preserve
Florida

By Donna L. Singer

Updated by Diane P. Marshall

hink of the Everglades as a vast, shallow "river of grass" that covers much of the lower half of the Florida peninsula, fanning out from Lake Okeechobee and creeping southward to Florida Bay and the Gulf of Mexico. Of some 4.3 million acres of subtropical, watery wilderness, more than 1.5 million belong to Everglades National Park, a mere 35 expressway miles from downtown Miami. Visitors can move from open sawgrass prairie to dense hardwood hammock. Watery sloughs teem with fish, freshwater marshes are sprinkled with wildflowers, and coastal mangroves harbor nesting birds and sea turtles. The 100 keys of Florida Bay are home to pelicans, ospreys, and bald eagles; the Ten Thousand Islands of the Gulf Coast, to the gentle manatee. The park is also a last refuge for 14 officially listed threatened and endangered species.

The park is open year-round. The prime tourist season is winter, when temperatures are moderate, rainfall minimal, and mosquito activity low. Summer, with its high temperatures, torrential rains, and bugs, welcomes fewer visitors. Access is along one 38-mi road in the park, with several offshoot walking trails. Flamingo, on Florida Bay at the end of the road, is an outpost resort providing lodging, dining, convenience shopping, and a post office. The towns nearest to Flamingo are Homestead and Florida City.

On the Gulf of Mexico lies grandly named Everglades City, 55 mi as the eagle flies north-northwest of Flamingo (99 mi by Wilderness Waterway canoe trail, and 130 by shortest road connection). Once a county seat, the town today numbers fewer than 400 people but has stores, a smattering of lodgings, restaurants, and recreational outfitters. Most everything depends on visitors to the park.

Ancient Calusa shell mounds in the backcountry bear silent witness to the importance of the Glades in the lives of early Native Americans. Some canoe trails might date from the Seminole Wars (1818–55), when the U.S. government tried to forcibly relocate the region's Native Americans. Today, some members of the Miccosukee tribes still live as their ancestors did on the hardwood hammocks in the Glades; the Seminoles have a reservation in the Everglades, north of the park.

After thousands of birds were killed for their plumage and alligators were poached nearly to extinction for their hides, conservationists pushed efforts to save the Everglades and their inhabitants. In 1947 the southeastern corner became Everglades National Park; the Ten Thousand Islands area was added in 1957. Today Everglades is one of the country's largest national parks and is recognized by the world community as a Wetland of International Importance, an International Biosphere Reserve, and a World Heritage Site.

Yet even more awesome than the Everglades itself is the watershed, of which the Everglades is only part, that connects almost all of Florida from Orlando south to the Florida Keys—a distance of more than 200 mi across a slope of only 20 ft. The lakes south of Orlando collect their waters in the marshy origins of the Kissimmee River. The Kissimmee spills into Lake Okeechobee, and the lake in turn drains from its southeast rim into that shallow Everglades river of grass. The Everglades feeds these freshwaters into the salt waters of Florida Bay. The brackish soup stirred by this mix acts as a coastal nursery, sustaining a variety of marine life. Bay waters finally slosh east through channels between the Florida Keys, bathing the coral reefs at the fringe of the Atlantic in liquid sustenance.

But the system no longer functions as nature intended. The Kissimmee River no longer meanders and distributes impurities across its floodplain but has been channeled for the benefit of cattle and dairy farming. Its collected wastes flood into Lake Okeechobee. There, to protect coastal cities from seasonal flooding, to supply water for sugar farms along the lake's southern rim, and to provide a sink for agricultural waste and nutrient-laden runoff, the big lake has been beset with an elaborate diking and plumbing system. Okeechobee has been left forever dependent on an environment that for most of this century has steadily failed it.

This vast engineering around Lake Okeechobee disrupts the natural flow of water into the Everglades. Instead of following age-old seasonal patterns, the flow comes spigot-like, subordinate to needs of agriculture and coastal development. For the animal and plant life that evolved with the natural system, the engineered arrangement proves catastrophic. The Tamiami Trail across the Everglades set up a further barrier, so that even when water is released southward into the park, that water gushes rather than trickles.

The wrong amounts of water at the wrong time and in the wrong places and the influx of impurities have reduced the nesting bird population by more than 90 percent of its historic numbers. The increasingly saline bay at the hem of the Everglades has devastated shrimp fisheries. Algae blooms proliferate. Black bear are very rare in the area.

The Florida panther nears extinction. Exotic plants once imported to drain the Everglades and feral pigs released for hunting crowd out indigenous species. In 1994 the nonprofit group American Rivers ranked the Everglades among the most threatened rivers of North America. North in the system cattle and sugar prosper. South in the system fisheries decline and tourism stands at the brink of ruin.

Visitors who first view the Everglades today hardly appreciate the system's peril. Few people from elsewhere have ever seen such an abundance of birdlife as still survives. Park rangers honestly detail the rise and fall of the system in hopes of increasing awareness.

Luckily, priorities change, and new policies, still largely on paper, hold promise for the endangered Everglades system. Tourism and fishing interests, conservationists, and aggressive park management have pushed for improvement. Federal and state governments together have advanced environmental protection toward the top of water-management priorities. Construction has begun on several key projects to restore more natural water flow to the park. Work on a major portion of the Kissimmee River has begun in effort to reestablish a portion of its floodplain. The state has acquired the Frog Pond, some 1,800 acres of critical farmland to the east of the Everglades, and is reconfiguring a crucial flood-control canal in the same area in order to allow more natural flooding. Passage in 1994 of Florida's Everglades Forever Act mandates the creation of 40,000 acres of filtration marshes to remove nutrients from the Everglades Agricultural Area before these enter the protected wetlands. Although the future of Everglades National Park hangs uncertain in this time of transition, the signs are no longer unrelentingly bleak.

Some 40% of what is commonly called Big Cypress Swamp was established as Big Cypress National Preserve in 1974 to protect the watershed of Everglades National Park. A watery wilderness, Big Cypress is devoted to balanced land use in the name of preservation. Its success is dependent upon research and compliant visitors—the preserve's politically dictated policy is "use without abuse." Some activities allowed here but not in most other national parks include hunting, off-road vehicle use (airboats, swamp buggies, ATVs, ATCs, and street-legal 4×4s), and cattle grazing.

In August 1992, Hurricane Andrew carved a path of devastation through the Glades and Big Cypress. The winter of 1994–95 was the wettest on record, severely upsetting the mating cycle of the park's remaining wildlife. Facilities such as boardwalks, overlooks, and trails have been restored, but the hurricane destroyed hardwood hammocks that will take much longer to grow back.

ESSENTIAL INFORMATION

VISITOR INFORMATION **Everglades National Park** (40001 SR 9336, Homestead 33034, tel. 305/242–7700). The park's **Web site** is www.nps.gov/ever. **Tropical Everglades Visitors Association** (160 U.S. 1, Florida City 33034, tel. 305/245–9180 and 800/388–9669). The following are on-site visitor centers. **Ernest F. Coe Visitor Center** (tel. 305/242–7233). **Flamingo** (tel. 941/695–2945). **Royal Palm Visitor Center** (tel.305/242–7237). **Shark Valley** (tel. 305/221–8776). **Gulf Coast** (tel. 941/695–3311).

Information on Big Cypress National Preserve can be obtained at the **visitor center** (U.S. 41). Write or call **Big Cypress National Preserve** (HCR 61, Box 11, Ochopee 34141, tel. 941/695–4111) for brochures and maps. The preserve's **Web site** is www.nps.gov/bicy.

FEES The Everglades entrance fee, valid for seven consecutive days at all three park entrances, is $10 (Shark Valley $8) per private car, van, or motor home, or $5 (Shark Valley $4) per person on foot, bicycle, or motorcycle. Entrance to Big Cypress National Preserve is free; however, all off-road vehicles (such as airboats and swamp bug-gies) require permits, which cost $35 per year and can be obtained at the Oasis Visitor Center (midway between Miami and Naples on U.S. 41, Ochopee 34141, tel. 941/695–4111).

PUBLICATIONS An informative brochure with a detailed map of the preserve; excellent trail guides for hiking, biking, canoeing, and bird-watching; and informative booklets on flora and fauna, endangered species, and park preservation are free at the Everglades visitor centers or by writing the park (*see* Visitor Information, *above*). Videos, nautical charts, and other publications are available from the **Florida National Parks & Monuments Association, Inc.** (10 Parachute Key, No. 51, Homestead 33034, tel. 305/247–1216, fax 305/247–1225).

A must-read is the classic *Everglades—River of Grass* ($18.95), a witty and poetic history of the Glades by the pioneering conservationist Marjory Stoneman Douglas. For an informative account of the park's natural history, try the *Everglades Wildguide* ($5.95) by Jean Craighead George; this is the official National Park Service handbook. Wildlife biologist William B. Robertson, Jr.'s *Everglades—The Park Story* ($8.95) is a readable guide to flora, fauna, and history. Ornithologists will find *Florida's Birds* ($19.95) by Herbert W. Fell and David S. Maehr and the *Everglades National Park Bird Checklist/Habitat Guide* helpful (available in two versions: one free, the more detailed version $2.50). Helpful, too, is *Trees of Everglades National Park and the Florida Keys* by George Stevenson ($3.95). The trail-by-trail photo story *Let's Take a Trip—The Everglades* by Cheryl Koenig Morgan ($3.95) is geared toward kids. The *Guide to the Wilderness Waterway of the Everglades National Park* ($9.95) contains maps and helpful information for boaters and canoeists on the 100-mi inland Wilderness Waterway, which connects Everglades City on the Gulf of Mexico to Flamingo on Florida Bay. The history of Florida's Seminole Indians and their relationship to the Everglades is explored in Merwyn S. Garbarino's *The Seminole* ($9.95).

A selection of publications on Big Cypress National Preserve, including *Big Cypress Swamp and the Ten Thousand Islands* by J. Ripple ($24.95), a brochure with a detailed map of the preserve, and a video are all available at the visitor center or by writing the preserve (*see* Visitor Information, *above*). The Big Cypress National Preserve publishes the biannual *National Parks and Preserves of South Florida,* which contains information on Everglades and Big Cypress as well as Biscayne and Dry Tortugas national parks.

GEOLOGY AND TERRAIN The Everglades is really a shallow, freshwater river 50 mi wide and 6 inches deep that is slowly moving south. In summer, as much as 93% of the park is submerged in water. The park is a patchwork of six distinct ecosystems: vast expanses of freshwater saw-grass prairie interspersed with tropical hardwood hammocks (tree islands), pinelands, thickets of willows in deeper freshwater areas called "sloughs," cypress-tree islands, and coastal prairie and mangrove swamps. The Ten Thousand Islands region along the Gulf Coast is a labyrinth of passages, channels, tide-swept islets, mud shallows, and oyster bars where freshwater from the Barron River and salt water from the gulf intermingle in Chokoloskee Bay.

The gently sloping, mostly level landscape was once an ancient sea bottom. As the glaciers expanded, they consumed the shallow sea, and the land emerged; as they melted, the seas returned, again submerging the peninsula. This process occurred at least four times, forming the porous, spongelike limestone bedrock on which the Everglades rests.

The more than 2,400 square mi of the Big Cypress Swamp encompass marshlands, wet and dry prairies, hardwood hammocks, sandy islands of slash pine, estuarine mangrove forests, and strands of cypress trees. It rests on the same limestone aquifer as the Everglades. About a third of the preserve is covered with cypress trees, primarily the dwarf cypress; these edge the wet prairies,

line the sloughs, and form the cypress domes unique to the preserve. Looking like bubbles on the open landscape, cypress domes have tall trees in the center of an island, reaching to the deeper water of the slough, and shorter trees tapering to the edges of the island.

FLORA AND FAUNA The Everglades has become one of the last havens for such rare and endangered species as the American crocodile, Florida panther, manatee, brown pelican, southern bald eagle, and loggerhead turtle. Alligators sun themselves along riverbanks and ponds and at "gator holes," watery oases that alligators have excavated with their feet, tails, and snouts. Gator holes also attract other wildlife, such as raccoons, otters, snails, herons, and egrets. The more elusive, lighter-colored and narrow-snouted crocodile can be seen only around the mangrove swamps in the Florida Bay area. Look for the gentle sea cows, or manatees, in the mangrove swamps and in Chokoloskee Bay in the park's Ten Thousand Islands area. The nation's last Florida panthers roam the Everglades and Big Cypress but are extremely difficult to spot; consider yourself fortunate if you see their paw prints.

As for the park's abundant birdlife, 347 species have been identified. Among them are two found only in Florida's southernmost tip: the Cape Sable seaside sparrow and the great white heron (look for them in the Flamingo–Florida Bay area). Hundreds of herons, egrets, wood storks, and other water birds flock to the ponds, like Mrazek and Eco ponds near Flamingo, to feed. Look for the white ibis, with its long, curving bill, especially in February. The Anhinga Trail is a prime bird-watching area. Observe the anhinga drying its wings or diving for a fish, which it spears, flips in the air, then swallows whole. Or watch the peacock-hued purple gallinule, with its bright yellow legs, walk across lily pads in search of insects. Look for barred owls and the rare short-tailed hawk, as well as deer, marsh rabbits, and bobcats in the hardwood hammocks. From your car window you may see tall, great blue herons moving through the grasslands.

The most prevalent plant in the park's freshwater areas is saw grass, an ancient sedge, which sprawls over 8 million acres and is tough and difficult to penetrate. Its sharp barbs can easily slash bare skin and thin clothing. Several species of palm grow within the park, including the royal palm, which can be seen in its greatest numbers at the Royal Palm Visitor Center, and the rare paurotis palm, best seen from the Mahogany Hammock Trail. Such tropical trees as the gumbo-limbo and the massive mahogany grow harmoniously alongside the more familiar oaks; willows and slash pines are also found in the park. Among the most beautiful plants are the bromeliads and orchids, air plants that grow on trees. In Big Cypress Preserve, look for the few remaining great bald cypresses, some of which are 600–700 years old.

Remember that the animals are wild: Don't disturb them, feed them, or get too close. Alligators may look slow and awkward, but they are amazingly fast. Watch for poisonous snakes such as diamondback and pygmy rattlers, water moccasins, and coral snakes. Some plants, such as poisonwood and manchineel, are also dangerous. Check at the visitor centers for the latest precautions.

WHEN TO GO The parks really have two seasons: wet (the mosquito season) and dry (the tourist season). The ebb and flow of life has been controlled for centuries by this deluge-and-drought pattern. The dry winter months (from mid-November to mid-April) are the most popular time to visit, since the "skeeter meter" records bearable levels and the temperatures range from the 40s at night to the 80s during the day. Lower water levels make the trails drier and easier to navigate, and wildlife viewing is at its peak. In Everglades National Park ranger-led activities and special programs are in full flush during the winter—but so are the prices and the crowds (although there are no fees at any time of year for National Park Service programs).

The short "hump" seasons of spring and fall can be good times to visit. The summer season (from June to October) brings sudden daily torrents of rain—as much as 12 inches in one day, high humidity, intense sun, and temperatures in the 80s and 90s. The mosquito population burgeons. (The pamphlet entitled "The Mosquito and You" is worth picking up.) But if you arm yourself with insect repellent, sun protection, and rain gear, the summer season can have its upside. Crowds thin out and the less expensive, off-season lodging and service rates go into effect.

SEASONAL EVENTS The Miccosukee tribe holds two annual festivals at the Miccosukee Cultural Center and Indian Village on U.S. 41, the Tamiami Trail, about 25 mi west of Miami, near the Shark Valley entrance to Everglades. **Dec.–Jan.:** The **Indian Arts Festival,** from December 26 to January 1, is a weeklong celebration of Native American dance, crafts, and foods, featuring artisans from all over the country. **July:** The fourth weekend in July brings the **Everglades Music and Crafts Festival,** which focuses on American Indian heritage and celebrates the many cultures in the Miami area through music, crafts, arts, and food. Contact the Miccosukee tribe (Box 440021, Tamiami Station, Miami 33144, tel. 305/223–8380) for information.

WHAT TO PACK Bring casual, comfortable, loose-fitting clothes and hiking boots or sturdy walking shoes, and be prepared to get your feet wet (especially in summer) on the marshy hiking trails. If you plan to do a lot of hiking, cycling, or canoeing, pack socks, lightweight long pants, T-shirts to be worn under long-sleeved cotton shirts, and a rain slicker (a must for summer months). If you camp in the Everglades during the fall or winter, be sure to bring a jacket, a lightweight sweater, and a heavier sweater, as temperatures can dip to the mid-30s at night.

Regardless of the season, the south Florida sun is always strong, so bring sunglasses, a hat, and plenty of sunscreen (with at least SPF 15 if you burn easily). Be sure to pack lots of powerful mosquito repellent. Also, bring a canteen for summer hiking, biking, or canoeing.

GENERAL STORES The only general store within Everglades National Park is the **Flamingo Marina Store** (Box 428, Flamingo, tel. 941/695–3101, ext. 304), which is part of the Flamingo Lodge complex and is 38 mi from the Ernest F. Coe Visitor Center. The Marina Store is open daily 7–7 and sells groceries, camping supplies, souvenirs, bait, tackle, and fuel for boats and cars. Several general stores in Homestead and Florida City, only 11 mi from the park entrance, carry supplies for campers, boaters, and hikers.

Serving Big Cypress and the Gulf Coast portion of Everglades is **Glades Haven** (800 S.E. Copeland Ave./Rte. 29, Everglades City, tel. 941/695–2746), 24 mi from the Big Cypress National Preserve Visitor Center and directly opposite the Gulf Coast entrance to Everglades. Open daily 6 AM–9 PM, the store stocks groceries, camping and RV supplies, bait, tackle, fishing licenses, maps and charts, and also rents canoes. Next door is Glades Haven Recreational Resort (*see* Camping, *below*), a tent and RV campground.

ATMS The nearest automated teller machines are at banks in Florida City, Homestead, and Naples; there's an ATM at the Circle K in Everglades City.

ARRIVING AND DEPARTING Everglades National Park is virtually in Miami's backyard, and vacationers with limited time can sample the park on a one-day excursion from the city by car. There is no public transportation from Miami to Big Cypress or the Gulf Coast Everglades entrance. The best way to get to either park is by car or RV. From Homestead, which is 11 mi from the main Everglades entrance, you could bike or take a taxi. There is neither public transportation to the main park entrance nor within the park itself.

By Bus. Greyhound/Trailways makes three trips daily from Miami International Airport (Concourse E, lower level) and the Miami depot (4111 N.W. 27th St., tel. 305/871–1810) to the Homestead Bus Station (5 N.E. 3rd Rd., tel. 305/247–2040). The fare is $10 one-way, $19 round-trip. A cab from there to the Ernest F. Coe Visitor Center costs about $27.

By Car and RV. The main highways from Miami to Homestead and Florida City are Route 836 west to Route 826/874 south to the Homestead Extension of the Florida Turnpike (which ends at U.S. 1), U.S. 1, and Krome Avenue (Rte. 997/old U.S. 27). To reach the Ernest F. Coe Visitor Center at Everglades, 11 mi from Homestead, turn right (west) from U.S. 1 or Krome Avenue onto Route 9336 in Florida City and follow the signs to the park entrance. Flamingo is another 38 mi. To reach the Shark Valley entrance (a 45-minute trip from Miami), take U.S. 41 (Tamiami Trail) west.

To reach the park's western gateway, take U.S. 41 west for 77 mi, turn left (south) onto Route 29, and travel another 3 mi through Everglades City to the Gulf Coast Ranger Station. From Naples on the Gulf Coast, take U.S. 41 east for 35 mi, then turn right onto Route 29.

Big Cypress National Preserve Visitor Center is on U.S. 41, 50 mi west of Miami and 53 mi east of Naples.

By Plane. From Miami International Airport (tel. 305/876–7000) it's 34 mi to the Homestead–Florida City area, 83 mi to the Flamingo Visitor Center, and 60 mi to the Big Cypress National Preserve Visitor Center. **Super Shuttle** (tel. 305/871–2000) vans operate 24 hours a day between the airport and the Homestead–Florida City area, leaving from outside most baggage claim areas on the lower level. Depending on the destination, the cost is $33–$41 for the first person, and $12 for each additional person traveling together.

By Train. Amtrak (8303 N.W. 37th Ave., near Hialeah, tel. 305/835–1200 or 800/872–7245) serves Miami. You can catch a bus (Metrobus 42 Coconut Grove/$1.25) to the airport to pick up a car or the Grey-hound/Trailways bus (*see* By Bus, *above*) or a taxi from the station to get to Homestead and Florida City.

EXPLORING

A combined drive-hike is the best way to see the east-coast area of the Everglades. The only way to explore the mangrove islands and estuaries of the Gulf Coast region is by boat or canoe. Hiking trails, canoes, and off-road vehicles provide the best access to Big Cypress, since the roads cover only a small portion of the preserve. Keep in mind that Big Cypress is remote and has only limited services. Have a full tank of gas and plenty of food and water before you head out, since you won't find any there.

THE BEST IN ONE DAY **The Everglades.** We have two itinerary suggestions. Begin at the Ernest F. Coe Visitor Center (where you can pick up a map), then take the 38-mi drive on Rte. 9336 to Flamingo, stopping along the way to walk several short trails (each takes about 30 minutes) for an overview of the park's six ecosystems: the Anhinga Trail and the junglelike Gumbo-Limbo Trail at Royal Palm Visitor Center; the Pinelands Trail, where you can see the limestone bedrock that underlies the park; the Pahayokee Overlook Trail, which ends at an observation tower; and the Mahogany Hammock Trail with its dense growth. Have lunch at the Flamingo Resort, or picnic at Paurotis Pond, Nine Mile Pond, or Flamingo. After lunch you can take the Pelican backcountry cruise (two hours) or the Bald Eagle–Florida Bay cruise (90 minutes) from the Flamingo Marina, or rent a canoe and explore one of several short canoe trails in the area. Or you can take the two-hour Wilderness Tram along the Snake Bight Trail (winter only), or rent a bike and cycle that or one of the other short trails. The Flamingo Visitor Center has pamphlets on the canoe, hiking, and biking trails. To return, retrace your way.

The second itinerary starts at Shark Valley. Take the tram tour around the 15-mi loop (two hours), or rent a bike and travel Shark Valley Road. There's an observation tower midway on the loop, as well as two short nature trails. For lunch, cross over U.S. 41 to the Miccosukee Restaurant (*see* Dining, *below*) or bring a picnic. Continue west for 40 mi on U.S. 41, observing the birds and alligators along the Tamiami Canal. Turn left (south) onto Route 29 and travel another 3 mi to the Gulf Coast Visitor Center, where you can take a boat tour around the Ten Thousand Islands area. If you are based in Naples, you can take this trip in reverse order.

Big Cypress National Preserve. You can sample Big Cypress in one day by combining some driving, hiking, and guided touring in an off-road vehicle. Leaving from Miami on U.S. 41 (Tamiami Trail), turn left (south) onto Route 94, the 26-mi unpaved Loop Road Scenic Drive. Stop for a short walk along the Tree Snail Hammock Nature Trail. When the road reaches the Tamiami Trail again at Monroe Station, double back (turn right) to the Big Cypress National Preserve Visitor Center at Oasis, and enjoy a picnic lunch there. Return to Tamiami Trail, heading west again. Turn right into the H. P. Williams Roadside Park (Route 839), where the 17-mi Turner River Road/Birdon Road Trail begins. You can drive, hike, or bike this trail, which will eventually bring you back to Tamiami Trail near preserve headquarters. Conclude your tour with a swamp buggy or airboat tour from one of the concessionaires along Tamiami Trail, but keep in mind that portions of the Big Cypress have recently been off-limits to such vehicles. Call in advance to find out what kind of tours are available. If you are starting from Naples, simply reverse the order of the itinerary.

ORIENTATION PROGRAMS The Everglades' Ernest F. Coe Visitor Center offers a wide range of entertaining and interactive exhibits. Several films exploring flora and fauna are shown regularly, including one geared especially toward kids, and state-of-the-art computers trace park events and activities. The 15-minute film at the Oasis

Visitor Center is a great introduction to the flora and fauna of Big Cypress.

GUIDED TOURS Everglades National Park offers free ranger-led hikes, bicycle tours, bird-watching tours, and canoe trips; the number and variety of these excursions are greatest from mid-December through Easter, and some (such as the canoe trips) are not offered in summer. Among the more popular are a 50-minute walk around the Taylor Slough (departing from the Royal Palm Visitor Center); a 15-mi, two-hour tram tour focusing on the wildlife of Shark Valley; and a 90-minute "Early Bird Special" focusing on bird life (departing from Flamingo Visitor Center at 7:30 AM). You can get your feet wet on "Slough Slogs" through the saw-grass marshes (from Royal Palm Visitor Center and Shark Valley Information Center; wear long pants and lace-up shoes). The canoe trips leave from the Flamingo and the Gulf Coast visitor centers. For monthly listings of ranger-led tours and information on reservations, contact the park or visit its Web site (*see* Visitor Information *in* Essential Information, *above*).

TW Recreational Services (Flamingo Lodge Marina and Outpost Resort, Flamingo 33034, tel. 941/695–3101, ext. 180) offers about a dozen naturalist-guided tours in winter and about three in the summer of the Everglades. Most are boat trips into the backcountry or Florida Bay. Prices range from $10 to $37; reservations are essential.

Between November and April, **TRF Concessions** (Shark Valley Tram Tours, Box 1739, Tamiami Station, Miami 33144, tel. 305/221–8455) operates the popular two-hour tram tour ($8) at Shark Valley; reservations are essential December–March.

Everglades National Park Boat Tours (Rte. 29, Box 119, Everglades City 34139, tel. 941/695–2591 or 800/445–7724 in FL) offers several cruises from the Gulf Coast Visitor Center in Everglades City. The tours last 1¾ hours and cost $13.

Majestic Everglades Excursions (Box 241, Everglades City 34139, tel. 941/695–2777)

take in Everglades National Park and Ten Thousand Islands and sometimes include a stop at Watson Place, site of a turn-of-the-century wilderness plantation. The 3½- to 4-hour trips, on a 24-ft covered-deck boat, depart from Glades Haven, which is just shy of a mile south of the circle in Everglades City on SR 29 (Copeland Ave.). Tours ($65) are limited to six passengers and include brunch or afternoon snacks.

Although airboats and swamp buggies are not permitted in the park, plenty of concessions along U.S. 41 (Tamiami Trail) offer these rides into nonpark areas. One of the best is **Miccosukee Indian Airboat Rides** (adjacent to the Miccosukee Indian Village and Culture Center, U.S. 41, Box 440021, Miami 33144, tel. 305/223–1011). The cost is $7. The namesake owner of **Ray Cramer's Everglades Airboat Tours, Inc.** (U.S. 41, Coopertown, tel. 305/852–5339) grew up frogging, fishing, and hunting in the Everglades. On his excursions, he blends descriptions of area wildlife and vegetation with entertaining personal anecdotes. He offers day trips, but the best tours depart just before sunset, when the nocturnal animals come out. The 90-minute trip costs $42.60. Closer to the Gulf Coast try **Wooten's Everglades** (U.S. 41, Ochopee 34141, tel. 941/695–2781 or 800/282–2781), which offers both airboat and swamp buggy rides. An alligator and crocodile farm and a snake exhibit are part of the program. The 30-minute airboat and swamp buggy rides cost $12.50; admission to the farm is $6.

For personal guided tours through the Gulf Coast Everglades area and Big Cypress National Preserve, contact **North American Canoe Tours** (Ivey House, 107 Camellia St., Everglades City 34139, tel. 941/695–4666, fax 941/695–4155), which offers canoeing, bicycling, and hiking tours from November to April ranging in length from one to five days. Canoe and kayak rentals are available at $20 the first day, and $18 each additional day for canoes, and $35–$55 per day for kayaks; reservations are a must. **Swampland Airboat Tours** (Box 476, Copeland

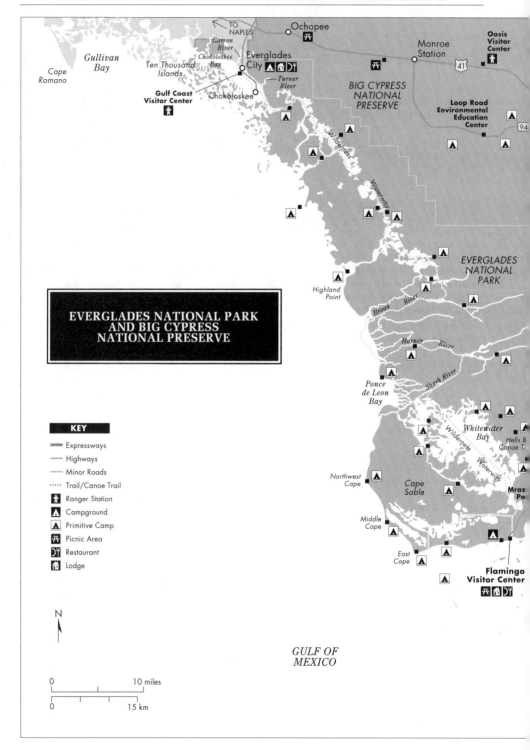

EVERGLADES NATIONAL PARK
AND BIG CYPRESS
NATIONAL PRESERVE

KEY

Expressways
Highways
Minor Roads
Trail/Canoe Trail
Ranger Station
Campground
Primitive Camp
Picnic Area
Restaurant
Lodge

Cape Romano
Gullivan Bay
Ten Thousand Islands
Barron River
Chokoloskee Bay
Everglades City
Gulf Coast Visitor Center
Chokoloskee
Turner River

TO NAPLES
Ochopee
Monroe Station
Oasis Visitor Center
BIG CYPRESS NATIONAL PRESERVE
Loop Road Environmental Education Center
94
41

EVERGLADES NATIONAL PARK

Highland Point
Wilderness
Waterway
Broad River
Harney River
Shark River
Ponce de Leon Bay
Whitewater Bay
Hells B Canoe T
Wilderness
Waterway

Northwest Cape
Cape Sable
Mraz Po
Middle Cape
East Cape
Flamingo Visitor Center

GULF OF MEXICO

N

0 ___ 10 miles
0 ___ 15 km

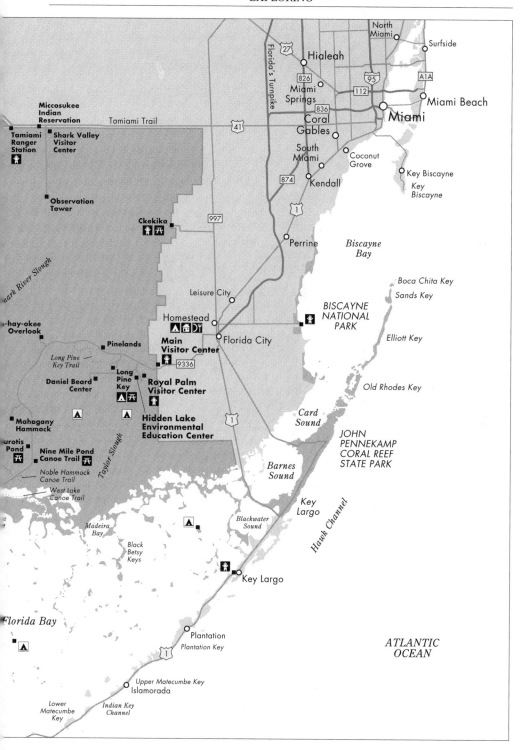

34137, tel. 941/695–2740) also offers personalized tours of the Everglades and Big Cypress, starting at $60 per hour for two or $25 per hour per person for three to six people; reservations are essential.

SCENIC DRIVES AND VIEWS The **Main Road to Flamingo** (Rte. 9336) from the Ernest F. Coe Visitor Center in Everglades traverses six distinct ecosystems in its 38 mi. You'll drive through pinelands, a sea of sharp-toothed saw grass with islands of dwarf cypress forests and the taller, denser hardwood hammocks of live oak, mahogany, and gumbo-limbo. Look for the ecotone, or transition zone, between saw-grass prairie and saltwater-loving mangrove forests as you get closer to Flamingo. Interpretive placards en route will help you understand this diverse wilderness. Be sure to stop at one of the ponds (Mrazek, Nine Mile, Eco) in the early morning or late afternoon to observe the hundreds of wading birds gathered to feed, and keep a sharp eye out for other wildlife.

The 80-mi stretch of the **Tamiami Trail** (U.S. 41) crosses the Everglades and Big Cypress Preserve. The canal that parallels the road attracts flocks of wading birds (especially in winter), and alligators are often spotted sunning themselves along the rocky banks. You will pass through a variegated landscape of wet prairies, sloughs and marshlands, and hardwood hammocks.

Though the 26-mi **Loop Road Scenic Drive** (Rte. 94) in Big Cypress is a single-lane road with lots of potholes, it's a good drive for viewing such hard-to-see animals as deer, otters, and wild turkeys, as well as wood storks and red-cockaded woodpeckers. The 17-mi **Turner River Road/Birdon Road Drive** is a U-shaped trail of graded dirt (rough riding), ideal for viewing the wildflowers that periodically flood the grass prairie (especially in the rainy season), slash pine islands, and bald cypress stands.

NATURE TRAILS AND SHORT WALKS The **Anhinga Trail** (.5 mi; 30 min) at the Royal Palm Visitor Center is one of the nation's best wildlife-viewing trails. A combination of pavement and boardwalk, it cuts through the Taylor Slough—a marshy river that's home to alligators, turtles, marsh rabbits, anhingas, herons, purple gallinules, and hundreds of varieties of fish. Scan the saw grass for the white jagged arms of the swamp lily.

The **Gumbo-Limbo Trail** (.5 mi), which originates at Royal Palm Visitor Center, meanders through a shaded hammock of royal palms, wild coffee, gumbo-limbo, lush ferns, and orchids. The colorful gumbo-limbo has been called the "tourist tree" because its peeling red bark resembles a visitor who's stayed out in the Florida sun too long.

The **Pahayokee Overlook Trail** (.25 mi; 15–30 min), 9 mi south of Royal Palm Visitor Center on the main road, ends at an observation tower, from which you can see a sweeping vista. Look for indigo snakes, vultures, and red-shouldered hawks among the wildlife in this area.

The **Mahogany Hammock Trail** (.5-mi loop), 7 mi south of Pahayokee on the main road, leads you into a cool, dark hardwood hammock. On this boardwalk trail you'll see the largest living mahogany tree in the United States, as well as huge mahogany and palm trees that were toppled like matchsticks by Hurricane Donna's 180-mph winds in 1960, and again by Hurricane Andrew in 1992. Look carefully in the trees for the tiny, jewel-hued Liguus tree snails.

The **West Lake Trail** (.5-mi loop) winds through a mangrove forest along the edge of a large, brackish lake. Here you can see the four types of mangroves—red, black, white, and buttonwood—that thrive in the saltier water near Florida Bay and protect the state's fragile coastline.

The **Bayshore Loop** (2 mi) begins at the rear of Loop C in the Flamingo campground and veers left at the trail junction to the bay. It takes you along the Florida Bay shoreline, where you can look for remnants of the old fishing village of the 1800s.

LONGER HIKES Longer hikes in the Everglades range from 4 mi and two to three hours round-trip to 14 mi and one to two days. All of the longer trails begin near Flamingo and lead into the coastal prairies of the southwestern section. The terrain is flat and the trails are relatively easy to navigate. **Snake Bight Trail** (4 mi round-trip) takes you through a hardwood hammock filled with dozens of tropical tree species to a bird-watcher's heaven on the end-of-the-trail boardwalk. Pick up this trail off the park's main road, just north of the Flamingo Visitor Center. The **Rowdy Bend Trail** (5 mi), along an overgrown old roadbed shaded by buttonwoods and across an open coastal salt prairie, begins at the Main Road just before Flamingo and joins with the Snake Bight Trail.

The **Coastal Prairie Trail** (15 mi) begins at the rear of Loop C in the Flamingo campground. The old road was used by wild-cotton pickers and fishermen when Flamingo was a fishing village in the 1800s. Here you'll find such salt-tolerant plants as cactus and yucca. Sections of this trail are submerged during the rainy summer season (and at other wet times), so check with the ranger at Flamingo for its status. You'll need a backcountry permit for overnight camping (*see* Backcountry Camping *in* Camping, *below*).

The only marked hiking trail in Big Cypress is a section of the **Florida Trail,** which begins at the Oasis Visitor Center parking lot and stretches 31 mi (one way) north to I–75 (Alligator Alley) or 8 mi south to the Loop Road Scenic Drive. Hikers should be prepared for ankle- to waist-deep wet areas. The trail is rocky in spots, and as a precaution against insects and snakes you should wear sturdy shoes that cover your feet completely. There are two primitive campsites along the trail, but no potable water. If you are hiking during one of the hunting seasons, wear bright colors and stay alert. This trail is for more experienced hikers. You can purchase a book on the Florida Trail at the visitor center, or contact the **Florida Trail Association** (Box 13708, Gainesville 32604, tel. 904/378–8823).

OTHER ACTIVITIES Bicycling. The best areas for cycling in the Everglades are Shark Valley and Flamingo. You can cycle in the Preserve along the 26-mi Loop Road Scenic Drive. The partly paved road is rough and has lots of potholes, but the up-close views of plant and animal life are worth the jolting. There are also hard-packed roads (designated as off-road vehicle trails) in the Bear Island area of the preserve north of I–75, through pinelands, hardwood hammocks, and freshwater sloughs. Check with the visitor center for maps of the trails that are best for bicycles. You can rent bicycles at Shark Valley for $3.25 per hour from **TRF Concessions** (*see* Guided Tours, *above*) and ride the 15-mi paved Loop Road; the trip takes two or three hours. (Bicycles are rented only until 3 and must be returned by 4.) **TW Recreational Services** (*see* Guided Tours, *above*) at Flamingo rents bikes for $2.50 per hour or $12 per day. Ask the rangers at the visitor center about trails, and inquire about water levels and insect conditions before you go. For a relatively easy ride take the Snake Bight Trail (3.2 mi) through a mangrove forest. A more strenuous trip is the Coastal Prairie Trail (*see* Longer Hikes, *above*).

Bird-Watching. Be sure to ask at the visitor centers for an up-to-date bird checklist, which notes the abundance and seasonal occurrence of each species. Winter is the optimum season, when many species cluster around the ponds and gator holes. During the summer heat, the best hours are sunrise and sunset. The **Anhinga Trail** is one of the best bird-viewing areas in the park. **Mrazek Pond,** just off the main road before Flamingo, and **Eco Pond,** between the Flamingo Visitor Center and the campgrounds, are excellent sites for water birds. The boardwalk along the coastal prairie at the end of the **Snake Bight Trail** (particularly at low tide) and the **Shark Valley Road** loop also offer good bird-watching. Head for the breezeway at the **Flamingo Visitor Center** at sunset to watch flocks of birds fly to the mangrove islands of Florida Bay. Telescopes and interpretive placards are there to help you identify the birds more easily.

In the **Ten Thousand Islands** region, you can see ospreys nesting on the mangrove islands or channel markers, white egrets dotting tree branches like balls of cotton, and the brown pelican.

In **Big Cypress National Preserve,** birds congregate in trees and along the banks of the canal that parallels U.S. 41 (Tamiami Trail). Along the **Loop Road Scenic Drive** and the **Turner River Road** you may see wood storks nesting, as well as a variety of other birds.

Boating and Canoeing. The best canoeing is in winter, when the rainfall is minimal, the mosquitoes tolerable, and the temperatures moderate. Canoe trails vary in length and in difficulty. Check with a ranger before departure for reports on water levels, weather predictions, and insect problems, and file a float plan with the ranger as a precautionary measure. You can obtain free trail maps at the visitor centers and buy navigational charts at the Flamingo Marina, Ernest F. Coe Visitor Center, or Gulf Coast Visitor Center. There's a $3 launch fee good for seven days on nonmotorized vessels.

Most canoe outfitters rent aluminum canoes—mainly 17-ft Grummans. Try the **Flamingo Marina** (Box 428, Flamingo 33090, tel. 941/695–3101, ext. 180 or 304). It's $27 for a full day, $22 for a half day and it's open daily 8–4 summer, 6–6 winter. **Everglades National Park Boat Tours** (Gulf Coast Ranger Station, Everglades City 33929, tel. 941/695–2591 or 800/445–7724 in FL) charges $21 for a full day, $17 for a half day and is open daily 8:30–5. **North American Canoe Tours** (*see* Guided Tours, *above*) is open November–April, daily 8–5.

The 99-mi inland **Wilderness Waterway** between Flamingo and Everglades City is open to motorboats as well as canoes, although powerboats may have trouble navigating the route above Whitewater Bay. There are six canoe trails available from the Flamingo area. They vary from the short **Noble Hammock Trail** (2-mi loop) through a maze of mangrove-lined creeks and ponds to the more challenging **Hells Bay** (5.5 mi one-way) and the lengthy **West Lake Trail** (7.7 mi one-way), known as an alligator and crocodile habitat. In the Gulf Coast area, canoeists enjoy exploring the nooks and crannies and mangrove islands of **Chokoloskee Bay,** as well as the many rivers near Everglades City. The **Turner River Trail** through part of the Everglades and Big Cypress provides a good day trip through mangrove, dwarf cypress, coastal prairie, and freshwater slough ecosystems.

Small powerboats can explore the shallow waters of Florida Bay, the waters around the Ten Thousand Islands, and the Wilderness Waterway and some canoe trails. The **Flamingo Marina** (*see above*) rents 10 small powered skiffs, 8 houseboats, and several private boats available for charter. The marina also has 50 boat slips and provides ample boat trailer parking and free launch access via two ramps, one for Florida Bay, the other for Whitewater Bay and the backcountry.

Fishing. Largemouth bass are plentiful in freshwater ponds, while snapper, redfish, and sea trout can be caught in Florida Bay. The mangrove shallows of the Ten Thousand Islands along the Gulf of Mexico yield tarpon and snook. Whitewater Bay is also a favorite spot. Note: The state has issued health advisories for largemouth bass and sea trout due to high mercury content. Signs are posted throughout the park. Lobstering and spearguns are prohibited. Freshwater fishing and saltwater fishing require separate Florida licenses. Saltwater licenses may be purchased at the Flamingo Marina and in Everglades City at the Town Hall on the traffic circle, or at Glades Haven store (*see* General Stores *in* Essential Information, *above*). A limited number of freshwater licenses are sold at Flamingo; they may also be purchased at Everglades City Town Hall or Glades Haven. Or contact the **Greater Homestead–Florida City Chamber of Commerce** (43 N. Krome Ave., Homestead 33030, tel. 305/247–2332) for information on where to purchase licenses in those towns. Possession limits vary, so request a copy of the parks' fishing regulations. Also, new mercury warnings have been issued in Everglades National Park and in the Big Cypress Preserve. Check with park rangers for particulars (*see* Visitor Information *in* Essential Information, *above*).

For U.S. Coast Guard–licensed fishing guides, try **Fishing on the Edge** (tel. 941/695–2322) or **Butler Guide Service** (tel. 941/695–4103).

Off-Road Vehicles. Everglades does not permit off-road or all-terrain vehicles, but Big Cypress does to a limited extent. All off-road vehicles, such as airboats, swamp buggies, and ATVs, must have a permit from the National Park Service. Information about trails, vehicle requirements, and regulations is provided with the permit (*see* Fees *in* Essential Information, *above*).

CHILDREN'S PROGRAMS There are no specific programs for children at either park. At the Flamingo Visitor Center, the ranger-led "Naturalist's Knapsack" allows kids to handle alligator skulls, flamingo feathers, and sea turtle shells during a 30-minute talk. Several books available in the gift shop list park activities suitable for children. For a monthly activity schedule, contact the Flamingo center (*see* Visitor Information *in* Essential Information, *above*).

At the **Miccosukee Indian Village** (Box 440021, Miami 33144, tel. 305/223–8380) on U.S. 41 next to the Shark Valley entrance to the Everglades, guides take you on a tour ($5) through the tribe's history, culture, and lifestyle, and you see demonstrations of doll making, basket weaving, bead-work, and alligator wrestling.

EVENING ACTIVITIES You can attend ranger-led evening programs at Flamingo, Shark Valley, and Gulf Coast visitor centers and the Long Pine Key campground during the winter season only. Contact the respective centers for schedules and topics (*see* Visitor Information *in* Essential Information, *above*). Shark Valley hosts the ranger-led Sunset Tram Tour (5:30 PM) and the Full Moon Tram Tour (6:30 PM) on various nights; both last 2½ hours, a fee is charged, and reservations are essential.

DINING

Casual but neat attire is the rule when dining in or near the park. While there are fast-food places and varied cuisines in Homestead and Florida City, the primary offerings are fresh seafood and Native American dishes—fried frogs' legs and tacos and burgers prepared with fry bread. South Florida specialties include dolphin fish (mahimahi), grouper, yellowtail snapper, stone crab claws, swordfish, conch chowder, conch fritters, fried alligator, and key lime pie. Many restaurants will pack a picnic for you, and several will prepare your catch with all the trimmings if you fillet it first.

INSIDE THE PARK **Flamingo Restaurant.** Big picture windows on the second floor overlook Florida Bay, revealing soaring eagles, gulls, pelicans, terns, and vultures; dine at low tide, and you get to see the birds flock to the sandbar just offshore. Look for pastas and a few grills. Service is limited to buffets in summer, though the snack bar at the marina store stays open all year to serve pizza, sandwiches, and salads, and you can always order a picnic basket. *1 Flamingo Lodge Hwy., tel. 941/695–3101, ext. 275. Dinner reservations essential. AE, DC, MC, V. $$*

EVERGLADES CITY **The Oar House.** Fishnets on paneled walls, a collection of hand-painted 19th-century oars, and etched glass create a casual atmosphere. Driving in over the bridge across Barron River, you can't miss the Oar House's teal exterior in this otherwise unglitzy little town. Glades favorites mark the menu: steaks, seafood, gator tail, and daily specials like country fried steak, pork fritters, and turkey with stuffing and gravy. *305 N. Collier Ave.,*

Everglades City, tel. 941/695–3535. Reservations not accepted. MC, V. $

Ivey House Restaurant. Tasty home-style meals are served every night at 6 to hotel guests. If you're not a hotel guest, you can call by 4 to make a reservation. The menu changes nightly, with a variety of meat and vegetarian selections. The $11.95 check buys you barbecue chicken with potatoes, a vegetable, tossed salad, pineapple upside down cake, and coffee or tea. On Mexican night (which varies week to week) the menu features chicken fajitas, tortillas, beans, rice, flan, and coffee or tea for the same price. *107 Camellia St., Everglades City, tel. 941/695–3299. Reservations essential. MC, V. Closed May–Oct. $*

HOMESTEAD–FLORIDA CITY For restaurants in Homestead and Florida City, *see* Dining *in the* Biscayne National Park *chapter.*

TAMIAMI TRAIL **Garden Court Restaurant.** The light and airy Garden Court opens into the lobby of the Port of the Islands Resort on one side and overlooks the pool on the other. Pink walls, faux bamboo furnishings, and floral prints remind of the tropics. The food—American and Continental, with local specialties—is good, the service impeccable. Start with the alligator fingers and proceed with the grouper. An outdoor bar and grill overlook the harbor. *Port of the Islands Resort, 25000 Tamiami Trail E, Naples, tel. 941/394–3101 or 800/237–4173. AE, DC, MC, V. $$*

Miccosukee Restaurant. The murals depict Miccosukee village life, and waitresses in colorful woven skirts serve such Miccosukee dishes as pumpkin bread, breaded catfish deep-fried in peanut oil, Indian fry bread (dough deep-fried in peanut oil), and an "Indian burger" (ground beef in fry bread). *Tamiami Trail opposite Shark Valley entrance to the park, tel. 305/223–8380, ext. 332. Reservations not accepted. MC, V. $*

PICNIC SPOTS **Everglades.** The picnic area at the **Flamingo Visitor Center** overlooks Florida Bay and its keys. Bird- and wildlife-watching are the main attractions at the

Paurotis Pond and **Nine Mile Pond** picnic sites (on the road from the Ernest F. Coe Visitor Center to Flamingo). There are sites with grills and rest rooms at the three campgrounds within the park: **Flamingo, Long Pine Key, Chekika.**

Big Cypress. There are two wayside picnic areas with grills, concrete tables, and benches along U.S. 41 (Tamiami Trail) as you drive west from the Big Cypress Visitor Center. None of them have rest rooms. At **Kirby Storter Roadside Park,** a short interpretive trail winds through a freshwater prairie and cypress stand adjoining the picnic site. The **H. P. Williams Roadside Park** has a picnic site along the Turner River. There is also a picnic area with grills at the **visitor center.** Supplies can be obtained in Homestead–Florida City or at the Flamingo Marina Store or Glades Haven (*see* General Stores *in* Essential Information, *above*).

LODGING

If you plan to spend several days exploring the Everglades, stay either in the park itself (at the Flamingo Resort or one of the campgrounds) or 11 mi away in the Homestead–Florida City area, where there are reasonably priced motels and RV parks. If you plan to spend only a day in the Everglades, you may prefer to stay in the Florida Keys or the Greater Miami–Fort Lauderdale area. Lodgings and campgrounds are also available on the Gulf Coast in Everglades City and Naples. Accommodations near the parks range from inexpensive to moderate and offer off-season rates during the summer months. For those who crave luxury and lots of extras, head for Miami or Naples; expect to pay more. For information, contact the Tropical Everglades Visitors Association (*see* Visitor Information *in* Essential Information, *above*).

INSIDE THE PARK **Flamingo Lodge Marina and Outpost Resort.** This rustic strip of civilization plunked into the wilds is for serious nature lovers. The accommodations—a two-story motel and cottages—are basic but attractive and well kept. The motel rooms, which face Florida Bay (but don't necessarily overlook it), have paneled walls, contemporary furniture, floral bedspreads, and bird prints. The cottages, which have kitchenettes, are in a wooded area where you can spy on ibis and heron through sliding glass doors. The setting and the amiable staff compensate for the lack of amenities. If you plan to stay in winter, make your lodging, restaurant, tour, and canoe reservations well in advance. *Box 428, Flamingo 33090, tel. 941/695–3101 or 800/600–3813. 101 rooms, 24 cottages, 1 2-bath suite. Facilities: restaurant, bar, pool, coin laundry. AE, D, DC, MC, V. $$*

EVERGLADES CITY **On the Banks of the Everglades.** This small no-smoking inn takes its name from the building it occupies, the former Bank of Everglades, built in 1923. Daughter and father Patty Flick Richards and Bob Flick renovated the building and created three spacious rooms, two suites, and three efficiencies with queen- or king-size beds and stylish coordinating linens, wall coverings, and draperies. Suites and efficiencies have private baths and kitchens; all accommodations have hair dryers and ironing boards. Rooms share a women's or men's bath. There's popcorn and movies shown on the VCR in the parlor at night. Continental breakfast is served in a former bank vault. *201 W. Broadway (mailing address: Box 455, 34139), tel. 941/695–3151 or 888/431–1977, fax 941/695–3335. 3 rooms, 2 suites, 3 efficiencies. AE, D, MC, V. $–$$*

Rod & Gun Club. The public rooms at this Florida landmark, with their dark wood walls and taxidermy and the wraparound screen porch overlooking the Barron River, take you back to the '20s and '30s, when U.S. presidents and the Barrymore clan hung out at this inn for hunting, fishing, and boating. Although the old guest rooms upstairs are no longer in use, there are several plain but spacious cottages with private rooms. The plumbing is old, so be prepared for drips. *200 Riverside Dr., 34139, tel. 941/*

695–2101. 17 rooms. Facilities: restaurant, bar, pool. No credit cards. $$

Ivey House B&B. Clean and friendly, Ivey House is run by the folks who operate North American Canoe Tours, David and Sandee Harraden. The shotgun-style cracker house was a popular boardinghouse for workers during the construction of the Tamiami Trail. Rooms have a modem connection so guests can log in if they wish. Typically, evenings are spent sitting around the living room, sharing the day's adventures and piecing together jigsaw puzzles. Breakfast is included. *107 Camellia St., Everglades City 34139, tel. 941/695–3299, fax 941/695–4155. 8 rooms with bath, 10 rooms share 5 baths, 1 2-bedroom cottage. Facilities: bicycles, boating, recreation room, library, coin laundry. MC, V. Closed May–Oct. $*

TAMIAMI TRAIL **Port of the Islands Resort & Marina.** An eye-catching pink-and-turquoise Spanish Mission style anchors this 500-acre resort just 12 mi from the Everglades' Gulf Coast entrance and 20 mi from Big Cypress's Oasis Visitor Center. The resort has its own cruise boat, and charter-fishing trips and trap and skeet shooting are also available. The high-ceiling lobby has a windowed tower and huge fireplace. Luxurious rooms, decorated in hues of seafoam, are in the hotel proper, an annex, and in courts around the pool; 23 have kitchenettes. Ask for one that overlooks the harbor (there's a 99-slip marina and marina store on the premises) or the pool. *25000 Tamiami Trail E, Naples 33961, tel. 941/394–3101 or 800/237–4173, fax 941/394–4335. 185 rooms, 5 suites. Facilities: restaurant, bar, grill, 2 pools, 6 tennis courts, exercise room, bicycles, boating, playground. AE, DC, MC, V. $$*

CAMPING

Everglades National Park has three developed campgrounds—Chekika, Flamingo, and Long Pine Key—for tents and RVs, plus primitive backcountry sites. The developed campsites have no hookups for water, electricity, or sewage, but do have modern rest rooms and showers, picnic tables, grills, tent and trailer pads, drinking water, and sanitary dump stations. The park accepts reservations for December 15–April 30 up to five months in advance. May–October sites are first-come, first-served. Pets are allowed in campgrounds and visitor center parking lots but must be restrained at all times. Your stay is limited to 14 days from December through March and to a total of 30 days per year. You can camp at all the sites for free in summer; the rest of the year, sites cost $14.

The Everglades has 48 **backcountry campsites**; two can be reached by land, the others only by water. Fifteen are chickee sites (raised wooden platforms with thatched roofs); the rest are beach and ground sites. Most have chemical toilets. Four chickee sites and nine ground sites are within an easy day's canoeing from Flamingo; five ground sites are within an easy day's canoeing from Everglades City. Backcountry camping permits are required for all overnight camping (except aboard boats) and may be obtained in person up to 24 hours before the day your trip begins from the **Flamingo Visitor Center** (Flamingo 33090, tel. 941/695–2945) or the **Gulf Coast Ranger Station** (Rte. 29, Everglades City 33929, tel. 941/695–3311). Permits are issued on a first-come, first-served basis; capacity and length of stay are limited; a fee will be charged based on group size. You can obtain the "Backcountry Trip Planner" from a visitor center, or write the Flamingo Ranger Station (Backcountry Reservations Office, 40001 SR 9336, Homestead 33034) for more information.

Chekika. This small, cozy, isolated campground, in a hardwood hammock surrounded by open prairie, has a nature trail and fishing lake. It's also the only site with hot showers. Check with park headquarters for availability. This campground sometimes closes due to high water in summer; check with park headquarters (tel. 305/242–7700). *S.W. 168th St., west of Krome Ave., tel. 305/251–0371. 20 drive-in sites.*

Flamingo. Flamingo, the largest, most popular campground, is along Florida Bay, with access to hiking and canoe trails and fishing in the bay. The marina and marina store, restaurant, and post office are nearby, too. Try to get a site in Loop A, where the two cold showers are. *End of park's main road, 38 mi SW of park entrance, no phone (call park headquarters, tel. 305/242–7700 for information). 235 drive-in sites and 60 walk-in sites.*

Long Pine Key. The pine forest and much of the network of nature trails here were destroyed by Hurricane Andrew; they have all been fully restored and are open for hikers and campers. Check with park headquarters to see what's available. *Off main park road, 6 mi southwest of park entrance, no phone (call park headquarters, tel. 305/ 242–7700 for information).*

Big Cypress National Preserve. For those interested in front-country camping, the eight primitive campsites in Big Cypress have no water or facilities. All allow tent camping; most accommodate RVs. For information, contact the Oasis Visitor Center (midway between Miami and Naples on U.S. 41, Ochopee 34141, tel. 941/695– 4111) or the Big Cypress Nature Preserve Headquarters (HCR 61, Box 11, Ochopee 34141, tel. 941/695–2000).

Burns Lake. A favorite among the park staff, Burns Lake, like the campgrounds at Monument Lake and Midway, has a small lake. Unlike the others, it's surrounded by woods, is more private, and is farther from the highway. A gravel path surrounds the lake, and the rest of the area is a mix of grass and rough scrub. There are no facilities or designated sites: Set up your tent in a large field. *Burns Rd., off U.S. 41, 12 mi west of Oasis Visitor Center, no phone (call the visitor center, tel. 941/695–4111, for information). Facilities: lake, hiking. Free.*

Dona Drive Campground. The park's most popular campground has picnic tables and the only dump station with potable water ($4 charge). Sites are available on a first-come, first-served basis. The $4 camping fee is payable by cash or check. *5 mi east of Rte. 29 off U.S. 41, no phone (call the visitor center, tel. 941/695–4111, for information). 10 drive-in sites. $*

Monument Lake Campground. Birds and wildlife visit the small lake next to the field where you set up camp in undesignated sites. Rest rooms, which were under construction at press time, will have nonpotable water. *U.S. 41, 4 mi west of Oasis Visitor Center, no phone (call the visitor center, 941/695–4111, for information). Facilities: lake, pay telephone. Free.*

RVs. Since there are no RV hookups in Everglades National Park, RVers may prefer sites outside the park. The parks discussed below have rest rooms, shower/bath facilities, and liquid propane gas. For sites in the Homestead–Florida City area, *see* Camping *in the* Biscayne National Park *chapter.*

Glades Haven Recreational Resort. RV sites with full hookups are available at Glades Haven, just across the street from the Gulf Coast Visitor Center of Everglades. The resort has a marina and docks, a convenience store, and a deli. Tent sites are also available. *800 S.E. Copeland Ave./Rte. 29, Box 408, Everglades City 34138, tel. 941/695–2746, fax 941/695–3954. 60 sites. Facilities: coin laundry. AE, MC, V. $*

Outdoor Resorts at Chokoloskee Island. This campground lies 3 mi south of the Gulf Coast Visitor Center at Everglades City. RV sites with full hookups are available year-round; prices fluctuate depending on whether the site is on the water and with or without a dock. The campground has a convenience store, recreation hall, and kayak and canoe rentals, as well as some RV trailers and motel efficiencies for rent. *Box 39, Chokoloskee Island 34138, tel. 941/695–2881, fax 941/695–3338. 283 sites. Facilities: 3 pools, 3 hot tubs, 2 tennis courts, 2 coin laundries. MC, V. $*

Fire Island National Seashore
New York

By Jonathan Siskin

Updated by Steven K. Amsterdam

 slender 32-mi strip of land, Fire Island runs parallel to Long Island— a battered pawn in the South Shore's frequent battles against gale-force winds, fierce nor'easters, and constant beach erosion. Only 50 mi from Manhattan (about 1½ hours by car and ferry; closer to two by train, taxi, and ferry), Fire Island is synonymous in the minds of Manhattanites with summer shares, beach parties, and sun-worshiping. It is also home to a vibrant gay and lesbian community. But people often forget that much of this bastion of fun and frolic is a precious and wonderful national seashore. It contains the only federally designated wilderness area in New York State and is one of the few unspoiled stretches of seashore along the northeastern seaboard.

There is dispute over the origins of the island's name. Some say it's from the lore of pirates who built fires at night in order to lure cargo ships, their prey, to the shore. Another suggestion is that the island was named for posion ivy, a Fire Island native, which brings to mind scarlet leaves and a fiery itch.

In 1964 Congress named parts of Fire Island a national seashore. The beaches and parking lots of Robert Moses State Park occupy the westernmost 5 mi of the island, while those of Smith Point County Park cover 6 mi of land on the island's eastern tip. In between lies the rest of the national seashore, interspersed with 17 tiny communities, strips of private property that span the ¼-mi–½-mi from the Great South Bay (which separates the island from Long Island) to the restless Atlantic Ocean. These communities, many of which date from the turn of the century, were allowed to remain and to grow within designated confines after the island became part of the National Park System. Despite the constant erosion and evolution of this delicate wilderness, there are about 1,400 acres here to explore.

About 1.5 million people visit the island each summer, some to spend a day, others the whole season. Most visitors fall into the former category, coming for a weekend afternoon at the beach, to take nature walks, and to explore the island's wilderness areas. The absence of roads and cars on most of the island, though perhaps slightly inconvenient, makes it a terrific escape, especially for those fleeing the hustle and bustle of New York City. As it has just a few small hotels and limited camping facilities, you'll probably want to rent a house or cottage if you plan to stay more than two nights.

ESSENTIAL INFORMATION

VISITOR INFORMATION Contact the park superintendent at **Fire Island National Seashore** (120 Laurel St., Patchogue 11772, tel. 516/289–4810), who is available weekdays 8–4:30.

For information on ferries, dining and lodging, house and apartment rentals, and local sights, contact the **Fire Island Tourism Bureau** (49 N. Main St., Sayville 11782, tel.

516/563–8448), which is open Memorial Day–Labor Day, daily 9–5.

We list the island's four visitor centers from west to east. **Fire Island Lighthouse** (½ mi east of Robert Moses State Park, tel. 516/661–4876). **Sailors Haven** (by the ferry terminals, tel. 516/597–6183). **Watch Hill** (tel. 516/597–6455). **Smith Point West** (just west of Smith Point County Park, tel. 516/281–3010). All of these have trail guides, talks, and occasional evening programs. The hours of operation depend on staffing; the Lighthouse and Smith Point West are open during the week from the end of June to Labor Day and on weekends during the rest of the year; Sailors Haven and Watch Hill are only open in summer.

■ **FEES** There is no entrance fee regardless of where on the island you disembark or park. The only cost you will incur getting onto the island is the charge to park, board the ferry from Long Island, or dock your own boat. Sports-vehicle driver permits, which are good from mid-September through mid-June, are issued at Smith Point for a fee of $20. Sports vehicles are prohibited in summer.

■ **PUBLICATIONS** Contact the park headquarters for maps and brochures (*see* Visitor Information, *above*). Available at the ferry terminals and the general stores, two weeklies, *Fire Island Tide* and *Fire Island News,* have news and features on island life and events, and listings of services available to visitors.

■ **GEOLOGY AND TERRAIN** Composed largely of white-quartz sand mixed with mineral deposits of magnetite and garnet, Fire Island acts as a natural barrier, protecting part of the Long Island coast against the combined forces of heavy surf and strong winds. Without any protection itself, Fire Island is especially vulnerable to storms coming off the Atlantic.

The Fire Island National Seashore's wilderness area, a 7-mi stretch between Smith Point West and Watch Hill, looks not much different than it did to the Algonquian,

Sagtikos, and Shinnecock Indians who staged great hunts and spiritual rituals here, or to the settlers who arrived here from Europe 400 years ago.

The terrain's most notable feature is the complex series of sand dunes that rise behind the ocean beach. Heading north from the Atlantic, you encounter first the primary dunes, then, behind them, a row of secondary dunes. Shaped over the centuries by the combined action of winds and tides, these ever-shifting piles of sand are held together by plants and grasses. Beach grass traps the windblown sand and binds the dunes together. Extremely fragile, they may take years to form and can be destroyed in a single day by careless visitors. For this reason, signs around the island warn against leaving the boardwalk trails and walking on the dunes.

Another perennial concern is beach erosion, which is slowly changing the shape of the island. Each day more than 10,000 waves break on the shore, shoveling 500,000 cubic yards of sand westward each year. During high spring tides and winter storms, when wave action, tidal currents, and wind are especially potent, the danger of erosion increases. The beach is usually able to rebuild itself in summer, when the action of tides and waves is at a minimum, but some damage always remains. The sea also eats away at its share of houses.

■ **FLORA AND FAUNA** The roots of the beach grass, also called sea grass, are essentially the glue that holds the dunes of Fire Island together and stabilizes erosion. The greenish gray flowers of false beach heather grow above the dune line, along with beach shrubs, holly, phragmites, sassafras, bayberry, shadblow, stunted pitch pine, oak trees, and wild cherry trees. Beach peas, found primarily in the wilderness area, yield an edible vegetable that islanders recommend with pasta. The pretty, pinkish white blossoms of beach plums decorate the island in the springtime; in summer, the plant replaces its flowers with edible fruit. Salt-spray roses bear red and pink blossoms that islanders gather and dry in the fall to use for soothing rose-hip tea during the colder months. Reeds flourish in both freshwater and salt water, overwhelming other plant life.

A short distance from the Sailors Haven Visitor Center, you'll encounter the Sunken Forest, a primeval maritime hardwood forest hidden behind the dunes. More than a dozen different types of trees, plants, and shrubs grow here, including black oak, cattail, sassafras, holly, tupelo, ferns, and inkberry. The term "sunken" derives from the fact that, due to the force of winds driving the salty air over the top of the dunes, vegetation has been forced to grow horizontally instead of vertically. No tree is able to grow higher than the level of the dunes. The resulting low forest canopy is extremely dense, forming a shady habitat for rabbits, foxes, and deer. One drawback to this environment: It also makes a welcoming home to poison ivy.

Along the migratory route known as the Atlantic flyway, the island is a favorite destination for local bird-watchers in spring and fall. In the spring, populations of migratory waterfowl—including mallards—nest on the waters of the Great South Bay; these ducks breed on the island's sheltered waters, as do geese. Other members of the duck family that can be spotted here include black ducks, gadwalls, and blue-winged teals. Hawks can be observed on their way south in late September and early October.

The tidal marshes on the bay side of the island draw piping plovers, small, stocky, sandy-colored birds that resemble sandpipers. Named for their distinctive bell-like whistle, these birds are often heard before they are seen. Watch them jerk idiosyncratically along the beach, starting and stopping every few steps. Their presence, from their arrival at the end of March through their September departure, is treasured here—they are an endangered species. You'll also see plenty of common terns, elegant snowy egrets, stately green herons,

and black-crowned night herons; the last nest in the bayside forests. Four different kinds of gulls, as well as mourning doves and whippoorwills, summer here; soaring sparrow hawks occasionally pass overhead; and hairy woodpeckers are sometimes heard hammering away in forests.

The waters surrounding the island teem with marine life. Mussels are plentiful, and observant visitors wandering along the beach often notice starfish washed up on the sand. The ubiquitous horseshoe crab is difficult to miss. Closely related to ticks and scorpions, these crabs use their long spiked tails to navigate and their legs to grind food. While they are not aggressive with humans, you should avoid stepping on their sharp tails.

Fish abound in the waters surrounding the island, and the Great South Bay is a favorite spot for anglers in search of bluefish, flounder, and striped bass; surf casters go for bass as well as bluefish and mackerel. Sea trout can be caught anywhere.

It is not uncommon to see white-tailed deer meandering through the woods or even alongside boardwalk trails. They're cute and often friendly, to the point of eating from your hand, but keep your distance and don't feed them. Their overpopulation has become such a problem that they were recently given birth-control hormones. Rabbits, red foxes, raccoons, and colorful monarch butterflies inhabit the island as well. Less appealing are the island's three varieties of ticks: dog ticks, lone star ticks, and northern deer ticks (be especially wary of the last, as they are carriers of Lyme disease).

WHEN TO GO Fire Island is primarily a spring and summer destination, with peak season falling approximately between Memorial Day and Labor Day, although fall is popular, too. Summer rentals extend that season a few weeks in either direction. Beaches are especially crowded on weekends. Ferries continue to make crossings in the wintertime, but far less frequently and to fewer destinations.

Wind and proximity to the sea keep temperatures reasonable all summer; ferry crossings can even be a bit chilly. Fog and mist loom often in early morning and late afternoon.

In summer, daytime temperatures range from the 70s to 80s, falling back into the 60s and upper 50s at night. Spring is generally rainy.

SEASONAL EVENTS April: Participants in the **March for Parks Walk-a-thon** make the trek from Robert Moses State Park to Kismet. **Spring and summer:** Cherry Grove, Saltaire, Fair Haven, Davis Park, Point o' Woods, Kismet, and Ocean Beach host **theater productions and art exhibits** (contact the Fire Island Tourism Bureau, tel. 516/563–8448, or check the *Fire Island Tide* for more information), and at Watch Hill and Sailors Haven the national seashore sponsors **photography contests and sand-castle-building competitions.** July: Many communities celebrate the **Fourth of July** with parades. **August:** The **Barefoot and Blacktie Gala** in front of the lighthouse on the first Saturday in August always draws a partying crowd. **September:** The island's most outrageous event is the **Miss Fire Island Contest**, a fiercely competitive drag event held the second Saturday after Labor Day at the Ice Palace (tel. 516/597–6600), a nightclub in Cherry Grove.

WHAT TO PACK Sunbathing is the name of the game: Bring sunglasses, sunscreen, a hat, swimsuits, and towels. For Cherry Grove, and some other beaches, swimsuits are more optional. The rules are enforced town by town: You'll know when you get there what is allowed. You'll need a jacket, windbreaker, or sweater for ferry crossings and for evenings. Mosquitoes attack after sunset; long clothes, bug spray, and citronella candles can help you defend yourself. With poison ivy and ticks prevalent, it's wise to wear long sleeves, slacks, and socks when hiking. Lightweight hiking shoes are best for walking on sand or along the wooden boardwalks. No matter where you go, restaurants and food stores are usually close to the ferry landing, though all supplies are *significantly* cheaper on the mainland. At night you may want a flashlight for any treks that take you away from the lights of commerce.

GENERAL STORES While there are no large supermarkets on the island, there are several small, well-stocked general stores and groceries selling deli foods, soft drinks, some gourmet ingredients, juice, beer, and wine. **Davis Park:** Davis Park Harbor Store (tel. 516/597–6956). **Fire Island Pines:** Pines Pantry (tel. 516/597–6200). **Cherry Grove:** Joseph's (tel. 516/597–9210). **Ocean Bay Park:** Ocean Bay Park Market (tel. 516/583–8431). **Seaview:** Seaview Market (tel. 516/583–8482). **Ocean Beach:** Ocean Beach Trading (tel. 516/583–8440). **Fair Harbor:** Pioneer Market (tel. 516/583–8435). **Saltaire:** Saltaire Market (tel. 516/583–5522). **Kismet:** Kismet Market (tel. 516/583–8449). Food and supplies can also be bought prior to boarding the ferries in the Long Island towns of Sayville, Patchogue, and Bay Shore.

You no longer have to bring all your cash. Most of the general stores have ATMs or are equipped to accept ATM-card payment.

ARRIVING AND DEPARTING On sunny summer mornings multitudes of cars, ferries, and private boats carry visitors to the island, an overwhelming majority traveling from no farther than Long Island or New York City.

By Boat. Private boats are another possibility for transportation to the island. Docking fees, charged everywhere, vary according to the length of your boat and whether you require an electrical hookup. Anyone can dock at Watch Hill or Sailors Haven, whereas town residents have priority at Davis Park and Atlantique (*see also* Boating in Exploring, *below*).

By Car. To reach the west end of the island, take the Robert Moses Causeway to **Robert Moses State Park.** If you are coming from New York City or western Long Island, you can either travel east on the Long Island

Expressway (I–495) and then follow the Sagtikos Parkway south to Exit 53, or you can follow the Southern State Parkway east to Exit 40. Either route will lead you to the Robert Moses Causeway, which traverses Captree Island and brings you to the state park on the west end of the island, where you can leave your car in parking field Number 5 for a small fee. To reach the east end of the island, take the Long Island Expressway as far as the William Floyd Parkway; then go south, crossing the Narrow Bay, to **Smith Point County Park** (tel. 516/852–1313), where a parking fee is charged. There is no overnight parking at either location. Smith Point State Park closes at 10 PM and Robert Moses State Park closes at sunset. The drive from Manhattan to the island's western end is usually a little over an hour but could take up to two hours if you hit traffic.

There are no roads for driving on Fire Island. Park either at Smith Point, Robert Moses State Park, or the ferry terminals on Long Island at Patchogue, Sayville, and Bay Shore.

Car rental companies at MacArthur Airport are **Avis** (tel. 800/331–1212), **Budget** (tel. 800/527–0700), and **Hertz** (tel. 800/654–3131).

By Ferry. Ultimately, most people have to take a ferry to get to Fire Island. Ferries leave from Patchogue for Davis Park (Davis Park Ferry Co., West Ave., ½ block from Division St., tel. 516/475–1665) and Watch Hill (Davis Park Ferry Co., Brightwood St., tel. 516/475–1665); from Sayville for Cherry Grove, Fire Island Pines, and Sailors Haven (Sayville Ferry Service, 41 River Rd., tel. 516/665–3600); and from Bay Shore for Ocean Bay Park, Seaview, Ocean Beach, Atlantique, Dunewood, Fair Harbor, Saltaire, and Kismet (Fire Island Ferries, Inc., 99 Maple Ave., tel. 516/665–2115). During peak season (April or May until September or October), ferries run every hour or two. Ferries run only to Cherry Grove, Fire Island Pines, Ocean Beach, and Saltaire in winter, and only on a very limited basis (call in advance for schedule information). Fares are around $11 round-trip, and parking costs up to $10 a day.

In July and August, a ferry also runs between Kismet and Ocean Beach.

By Plane. If you are coming from outside the greater New York City area, consider that **MacArthur Airport** (tel. 516/467–3210), in Islip, Long Island, is less than 10 mi from Fire Island as the crow flies. It is served by American, US Airways, Business Express, Carnival, Northwest Airlink, and United Express. (You will likely have to make a connection at either LaGuardia or Kennedy Airport in Queens.) You can rent a car at the airport (*see* By Car, *above*).

By Train. The **Long Island Railroad** (LIRR, tel. 516/822–5477) has regular service from Manhattan's Penn Station to stations near each of the three ferry terminals. Trips cost more during peak hours, which are 6–10 AM westbound and 4–8 PM eastbound. To Bay Shore: 1 hour, $6.50 each way ($9.50 peak). To Sayville: 1 hour, 20 minutes; $6.50 each way ($9.50 peak). To Patchogue: 1 hour, 40 minutes, $7.25 each way ($10.75 peak). At the stations in Bay Shore, Sayville, and Patchogue, minivans are usually waiting to take you (for a few dollars) to the ferry terminal. To Robert Moses State Park: about 2 hours; $12 round-trip; take the LIRR to Babylon, then catch the S47 bus to the beach.

By Water Taxi. Water taxis run among the communities on the island. Fares vary; most trips cost around $4–$6 ($4 is the minimum fare). Although it is possible to take a water taxi across the Great South Bay to Long Island, the trip could run you $100 or so. It's best to call **South Bay Water Taxi** (tel. 516/665–7474 or 516/665–8885) in advance; even at the ferry stations, there is no guarantee that a water taxi will be waiting for you.

EXPLORING

Since the island has no roads for cars, you'll have to either traipse around the island on foot, shuttle around by water taxi, or use your own private boat. With ferry landings well apart, you'll also have to decide before you leave where you want to spend the day. Beach bums will probably head for one of the lifeguarded beaches near Watch Hill and Sailors Haven. The beach at Robert Moses State Park, accessible by car, is quite crowded. To tote your belongings from the pier to the beach, you can usually rent a red wagon at the docks.

The federal wilderness area can only be explored on foot. There is a 7-mi sand trail between the Watch Hill Visitor Center (tel. 516/597–6455) at the western end of the preserve and the Smith Point Visitor Center (tel. 516/281–3010) at the eastern end.

Although the national seashore, Robert Moses State Park, and Smith Point County Park are all public resources, bear in mind that tourists are not especially welcome in the island's communities. To maintain privacy and discourage day-trippers, some communities (particularly those toward the western end of the island) issue inexpensive tickets for minor infractions, such as walking shirtless on the boardwalk, drinking water from a container on the beach, or riding a bicycle after dark.

THE BEST IN ONE DAY To experience the island in a day, you'll have to take a lot of water taxis. Start at the **Smith Point Visitor Center** and take a tour of the virtually untouched **federal wilderness area.** Then go to Watch Hill, where you can catch a water taxi to **Sailors Haven** and take a guided tour of the primeval **Sunken Forest.** The 1.5-mi boardwalk trail through the forest explores the low, lush, and slanted flora that grows just below the top of the dunes—the most striking natural phenomenon on the island. The snack bar at Sailors Haven is a good bet for a tasty lunch of seafood, meat, or pasta. After your meal you might be ready to spend a lazy hour or two relaxing in the sunshine at Sailors Haven's lifeguarded beach. The current is always strong here so be cautious.

Catch another water taxi and end your day with a visit to the **Fire Island Lighthouse**

(tel. 516/661–4876), with its keeper's quarters and visitor center (*see* Historic Buildings and Sites, *below*). You'll need a reservation, so be sure to call in advance. For a terrific view, climb the nearly 200 steps to the top. Linger to watch a beautiful sunset over the water before hiring a water taxi to take you back to Sailors Haven to catch the ferry back to Sayville, or to your car at Smith Point County Park.

For a day on the beach, families with young children will find plenty of company near the family-oriented communities of Ocean Bay Park and Ocean Beach. Sailors Haven and Watch Hill attract couples and other families, gays gravitate to Cherry Grove and Fire Island Pines, and Davis Park and Fair Harbor draw the singles.

The **protected wilderness** between Smith Point West and Watch Hill is recommended for hikers. This 7-mi section of the island remains the least developed and is an ideal spot for day visitors who want to immerse themselves in nature and momentarily escape the trappings of civilization.

ORIENTATION PROGRAMS Ranger-led nature walks depart from the **Smith Point West Visitor Center** (tel. 516/281–3010) from mid-May to mid-October. Among the topics covered are Fire Island history (with a discussion about shipwrecks), shells, and edible plants.

The visitor center at **Watch Hill** (tel. 516/ 597–6455) offers canoe trips, fishing expeditions, bird-watching hikes, and nighttime star-gazing talks in summer.

The visitor center at **Sailors Haven** (tel. 516/597–6183), gateway to the Sunken Forest, also regularly conducts naturalist activities, including evening campfire programs at which rangers talk about astronomy, some of the island's ancient legends, and the storms that have struck the island over the years.

GUIDED TOURS Other than the brief orientation walks listed above, the Park Service conducts few comprehensive tours of the park. National seashore rangers give one-

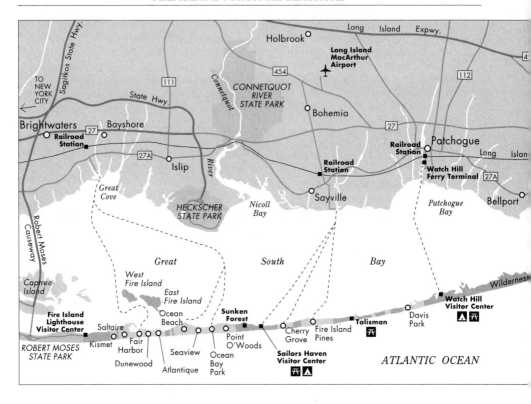

hour tours of the Sunken Forest. They will also guide you through the nature trails by Watch Hill, where you can see salt marshes, the new land being created by the tides, that serve as extremely fertile nurseries for marine life.

SCENIC VIEWS Visitors who climb the 192 steps to the top of the Fire Island Lighthouse (reservations required; tel. 516/661–4876) are rewarded with a spectacular view of the island and the surrounding area (on a clear day you can pick out the World Trade Center). Also, day-trippers shouldn't be in too much of a hurry to leave the island at the end of the day, because from any dock or pier the sunset is magnificent.

HISTORIC BUILDINGS AND SITES To help steer vessels away from the island, the first **Fire Island Lighthouse** was built in 1826. The lighthouse that stands today (½ mi east of Robert Moses State Park) was completed in 1858 and stood at the western end of the

island; since then, so much sand has shifted westward that the lighthouse is now about 5 mi east of the island's end. It houses a museum and has become a major tourist attraction; recently privatized, it has its own staff of rangers and exhibits on island history.

The **Fire Island Lighthouse Preservation Society** (tel. 516/321–7028) offers a glimpse into the lives of the dedicated lighthouse keepers who ran this station starting in the mid-19th century. The lighthouse closed in 1974 and was slated to be demolished, but a swell of popular support for its preservation altered these plans, and it was relit in May 1986. At the visitor center, rangers present history programs and guided tower tours. Admission is free, but donations are welcome.

The **William Floyd Estate** (tel. 516/399–2030), near Fire Island on Long Island in the town of Mastic Beach, was donated to

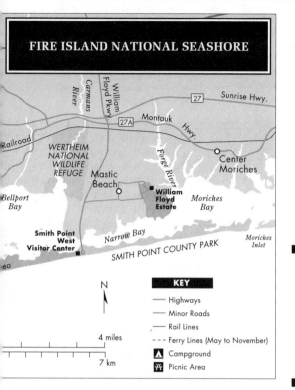

FIRE ISLAND NATIONAL SEASHORE

for all Fire Island nature trails.) Some of the sturdy holly trees that thrive in this unusual forest are more than 200 years old. You can walk the trail on your own or, during summer, take a ranger-led tour (see Orientation Programs, above).

The .75-mi loop from the **Watch Hill Visitor Center** takes you past beach plum and sassafras trees. Be on the lookout here for deer, foxes, and raccoons, which frequently scamper across the path.

The boardwalk trail near **Smith Point West** is nearly a mile long (one-way) and leads past massive sand dunes, cranberry bogs, and patches of pitch pine and bearberry.

LONGER HIKES A path called **Burma Road** runs through the federal wilderness area, but rangers do not recommend hiking it in its entirety because it is overgrown in many places and infested with ticks and poison ivy. Part of it is accessible, however. Stop at the **Watch Hill Visitor Center** (tel. 516/597–6455) or the **South Point Visitor Center** (tel. 516/281–3010) for more information.

OTHER ACTIVITIES **Biking.** Biking trails on the island are limited. Bikes are only permitted on freight ferries, which may be difficult to arrange for a short visit. You can rent bikes at **Ocean Beach Hardware** (tel. 516/583–5826) and pedal along a 3-mi cement path nearby.

Bird-Watching. This is serious bird-watching country: The tidal marshes on the bay side provide some of the finest waterfowl habitats in New York State. The nature trail around Smith Point, in particular, attracts bird-watchers intent on sighting some of the island's graceful herons, red-winged blackbirds, egrets, sandpipers, mallards, wild geese, and even an occasional snowy owl or lapwing tern. Spring and fall, when birds migrate, are the best time to watch; the lighthouse and Watch Hill are two popular vantage points during these seasons.

Boating. Nowhere on Fire Island can visitors rent boats; if you wish to get around this way, you will have to rent a boat on

the National Park Service in 1976 by a descendant of its namesake, and subsequently was placed under the administration of Fire Island National Seashore. William Floyd was a signer of the Declaration of Independence and one of the original members of the U.S. House of Representatives. Materials there trace the history of the Floyd family from 1724 to 1976. His house and bucolic 600-acre estate are a short drive from the Smith Point West Visitor Center (take Rte. 46 N and turn right on Neighborhood Rd.). Tours of the property are conducted on Friday, Saturday, and Sunday, from April through September.

NATURE TRAILS AND SHORT WALKS The 1.5-mi loop through the **Sunken Forest** allows great views of the forest canopy and the horizontal treetops. Begin near the Sailors Haven Visitor Center, where you can pick up a trail guide. (There are such pamphlets

Long Island or hire a water taxi (*see* Arriving and Departing *in* Essential Information, *above*). One of the most convenient marinas is in **Watch Hill** (nearly 200 slips, tel. 516/597–6644). A smaller but similarly convenient marina is in **Sailors Haven** (50 slips, tel. 516/597–6171). Electric power is available at both marinas and boats up to 50 ft are accommodated. There is also a marina at **Ocean Bay Park** (20 slips, tel. 516/924–4362) and a boat basin for day use at **Robert Moses State Park.** Anchorage is also available at Talisman, which is mid-island, between Watch Hill and Sailors Haven.

A few cruise operators sail to points around the island. A tourist favorite is the occasional luncheon cruise aboard the *Evening Star* (tel. 516/666–3601). Guests have lunch on the boat and then dock at Ocean Beach for two hours. There is dessert, coffee, and dancing during the leisurely return trip. Special deals are offered in conjunction with the Long Island Railroad (tel. 516/822–5477). The *Evening Star* also runs 3½-hour dinner cruises three or four times a week ($42 and up), and a three-hour Sunday brunch trip ($29). All cruises operate from May to the end of October and depart from the Bay Shore Marina. The *Bay Mist,* which leaves from the Watch Hill ferry terminal in Patchogue (tel. 516/475–1606), offers brunch, lunch, and dinner cruises throughout the year. The *Fishtale* sets sail from Captree Island for bay or ocean fishing charters (tel. 516/226–8882 days, 516/669–5343 evenings).

Fishing. In the Atlantic off the coast of the national seashore anglers can go after bluefish, mackerel, and striped bass, while winter flounder, blowfish, and fluke lurk in the shallow waters of the bay. Fire Island's grocery stores carry a limited selection of fishing supplies (*see* General Stores *in* Essential Information, *above*).

Swimming. From about Memorial Day until about Labor Day there are lifeguards on duty at Robert Moses State Park, Ocean Beach (no rest rooms), Sailors Haven, Davis Park, Watch Hill, and Smith Point County Park.

CHILDREN'S ACTIVITIES A special children's program for kids 3–10 features seaside tales and crafts, while a Junior Ranger program geared for the needs of older children is offered every Wednesday in summer. Visitor centers also have specific, ranger-led children's activities on Sunday.

EVENING ACTIVITIES Sailors Haven and Watch Hill visitor centers organize various events. A few times each summer, guest speakers are invited to the centers to instruct stargazers on the wonders of the night sky. Specialists from Long Island's Theodore Roosevelt Bird Sanctuary give occasional talks on the island's birds of prey. Other lecture topics include endangered species, the deer population, and beach erosion. Call the visitor centers or the national seashore headquarters for more information (*see* Visitor Information *in* Essential Information, *above*).

DINING

There are restaurants in every town on Fire Island, usually just a short walk from the ferry landings (but without addresses, since there are no roads). Seafood caught fresh daily is on most menus. Reservations are always advisable on weekends, and dress is always casual.

IN THE PARK There are park-sanctioned eating establishments in Watch Hill and Sailors Haven. At Watch Hill, Watch Hill Concessions runs a restaurant and bar (Seashore Inn), a snack bar, a pizza place, a general store, and a marina.

Seashore Inn. Watch Hill Concessions runs this restaurant where you may eat inside or on the large deck at umbrella-shaded tables that overlook the 188-boat marina. The menu is varied, heavy on seafood, but with a good selection of meat (try the duck) and pasta dishes. The attached **Watch Hill Snack Bar** enjoys the same vibrant Great South Bay sunsets and has a cheaper, pizza and burger selection. *In Watch Hill, tel. 516/597–6655. AE, MC, V. Closed Labor Day–mid-May.* $$

Sailors Haven Snack Bar. The breakfast menu is basic—eggs, pancakes, French toast—but lunchtime ranges beyond the expected burgers and hot dogs to salads, platters, and occasional specials such as spaghetti. Beer and wine are also available. The best part is the setting: a deck overlooking the marina and Great South Bay. *Sailors Haven Walk, tel. 516/597–6171. Closed mid-Oct.–Apr. $*

OUTSIDE THE PARK **Island Mermaid.** Great Italian dining is right on the dock in this family-oriented community. There's an antipasto table, seafood paella, baked chèvre, and lots of pasta. *480 Baywalk, Ocean Beach, tel. 516/583–8088. AE, MC, V. $$$–$$$$*

Casino Café. Part restaurant, part bar, this is one of the only places on the island where you can dine right on the ocean, and the lobsters, clams, and mussels are accordingly fresh. The specialties are baked clams and blackened swordfish. *Davis Park, tel. 516/597–6150. AE, MC, V. $$–$$$*

Flynn's Casino. Every Sunday afternoon, this landmark buzzes for the weekly "it's not over yet" party. On Tuesday, Wednesday, and Thursday evenings in summer, there's a deluxe hot and cold buffet, and a special boat runs from Captree Boat Basin for the event. The regular menu is à la carte, with burgers, steaks, fresh fish, and Flynn's special baked clams. The restaurant and bar sprawl onto the big deck. *Ocean Bay Park, tel. 516/583–5000. AE, DC, MC, V. Closed mid-Sept.–mid-May. $$–$$$*

Kismet Inn. Kismet is vintage Fire Island. The building that houses the bar and restaurant was built in 1925 and withstood the 1938 hurricane; restaurateur Larry Cole has owned the place for more than 30 years. Shrimp scampi, broiled bluefish, plus the blackboard specials—all extremely fresh—accompany the view of the distant lighthouse and the bay. There are breakfast and lunch menus to satisfy the walk-ins from the eastern end of Jones Beach, and rock, funk, and ska bands for the Friday- and Saturday-night crowds.

Oak Walk, Kismet, by Bay Shore ferry terminal, tel. 516/583–5592. AE, MC, V. Closed Nov.–mid-Apr. $$–$$$

Pines and Dunes Yacht Club. This section of the **Fire Island Pines Botel** (*see* Lodging, *below*) is the Pines' favorite gathering place due to its great harbor view and convivial atmosphere. Grilled salmon, broiled filet mignon, and chicken breast stuffed with shiitake mushrooms exemplify the culinary approach here. Despite all this, the burgers may be the most stellar items on the menu. *At the Dock, Fire Island Pines, tel. 516/597–6500. AE, DC, MC, V. $$–$$$*

Top of the Bay. Refreshing breezes sweep through this dockside building's second-floor dining room. In addition to a panoramic view of Great South Bay (best at sundown), it offers some of the island's more sophisticated dishes, many of them with a decidedly southwestern bent. Try blue cornmeal-crusted chicken with tomato-basil salsa. *Dock Walk, Cherry Grove, tel. 516/597–6699. AE, D, DC, MC, V. Closed last Sun. in Sept.–1st Fri. in May. $$–$$$*

Casino Bar. This singles beachfront spot draws a straight and gay crowd from all over the island for the Friday- and Saturday-night DJ and the Sunday band. There's dancing with a view, blender drinks, bar food, and liquor promotions all summer long. *Davis Park, tel. 516/597–9414. AE, MC, V. $$*

Michael's. This fixture of the Fire Island scene is right by the dock, which makes it a fine spot for people-watching. The food has been pumped up from the diner fare of years past, and now you can get plates of broccoli rabe with white beans and orechiette pasta or snapper with fresh herbs. The prices have been rethought as well, but the mood remains casual and the service is still pleasant. Michael's serves breakfast and lunch served in addition to dinner, and it's open 24 hours on Saturday. *Dock Walk, Cherry Grove, tel. 516/597–6555. AE, D, MC, V. $–$$$*

Cultured Elephant. This restaurant with gourmet pretensions and a deck on the dock is a bit cheaper than some of its high-tone competitors. Try the gazpacho, mako shark steak, or grilled swordfish. *Harbor Walk, Fire Island Pines, tel. 516/597–6010. AE, MC, V. Closed mid-Oct.–mid-May. $–$$*

Hurricane's. In the center of the homey **Fire Island Hotel and Resort** (*see* Lodging, *below*), this bar and restaurant sits deckside to the pool. There's a simple and inexpensive pub menu most times, with the option of fancier and pricier steak and lobster specials on weekend nights. *Cayuga Walk, Ocean Bay Park 11770, tel. 516/583–8000. AE, D, MC, V. $–$$*

Rachel's at the Grove. A funky local hangout, Rachel's has bar and beach food, like sandwiches and shish kebabs, and a pleasant deck right at the edge of the dunes. *On the Boardwalk, Cherry Grove, tel. 516/921–0303. No credit cards. $*

PICNIC SPOTS There are established picnic areas at Watch Hill, Talisman, Davis Park, and Sailors Haven. You can also picnic on the beach at the national seashore; if you want to eat on the beach in other areas, check local regulations first.

LODGING

There are just a handful of hotels on Fire Island, and most are not luxurious—the island prides itself on being rustic. Hotels are open from May through September or October; high season is June through August. The vast majority of visitors who aren't just day-tripping rent houses, cottages, or apartments, as partial shares or in full, by the month or the season; these are completely furnished, and some have linens and towels. Properties that are unrented as of March may become available for weekly rentals. Try the following real estate companies. **At the Bay Realty** (Cherry Grove, tel. 516/597–9797). **Dana Wallace** (Ocean Beach, tel. 516/583–5596). **Ethelind S. Realty** (Davis Park, tel. 516/597–9735). **Fire Island Land Company** (Cherry Grove, tel. 516/597–6040). **Larson Realty** (Kismet, tel. 516/583–9100). **Island Properties** (Pines, tel.

516/597–6360). **Red Wagon Realty** (Ocean Beach, tel. 516/583–8158). **Pines Harbor Realty** (Pines, tel. 516/597–7575).

ON THE ISLAND **Belvedere Guest House.** Corinthian columns, fountains, ceiling frescoes, and statues put this vaguely Venetian-style structure jutting high above surrounding buildings in a class by itself. Rooms are furnished with antiques, and some have terraces. A leisurely Continental breakfast on Sunday keeps some of the mostly gay clientele from ever venturing over to the beach. *Bay View Walk, Cherry Grove 11782, tel. 516/597–6448. 38 rooms, 22 with bath. Facilities: pool, hot tub, exercise room. AE, MC, V. $$–$$$*

Cherry Grove Beach Hotel. The largest swimming pool on the island is here, minutes from the ferry landing. A few deluxe rooms have VCRs and wet bars. Catering to a largely gay clientele, it's next to the Ice Palace disco, home of the renowned Miss Fire Island Contest. *Main Walk, Box 537, Sayville 11782, tel. 516/597–6600, fax 516/597–6651. 58 rooms. Facilities: pool. AE, D, MC, V. $$–$$$*

Fire Island Hotel and Resort. This former Coast Guard residence now consists of several motel-style buildings encircling a pool. It's clean, pleasant, family-run, and just a short walk from the ocean. The simply furnished rooms are outfitted with TVs, table, chairs, and private baths—a rarity in the seashore park. *Cayuga Walk, Ocean Bay Park 11770, tel. 516/583–8000. 50 rooms, 8 time-share units, 2 2-bedroom cabins. Facilities: pool, playground, coin laundry. AE, D, MC, V. $$–$$$*

Fire Island Pines Botel. Rooms in this three-story cinderblock hotel are small and no-frills, but you've got to appreciate the view: a harbor full of yachts (which explains the name). *Fire Island Pines 11782, tel. 516/597–6500. 25 rooms, 5 with bath; 2 suites. DC, MC, V. $$–$$$*

Four Seasons Bed & Breakfast. Down pillows and comforters, Egyptian cotton sheets, beachy decor, air-conditioning, and TVs in rooms set the tone at this rustic beach house—the only hotel on the island that's open year-round. A hearty breakfast of lox, bagels, fresh cinnamon buns, and juice (if you feel like squeezing it) prepares you for the day, whether you choose to lounge in the spacious living area, walk to the beach, or take off on a bike and explore. Room rates include breakfast and, from May through October, afternoon tea. On weekends, there's a barbeque. Fishing equipment, bicycles, and beach chairs are available to guests. *468 Denhoff Walk, Ocean Beach 11770, tel. 516/ 583–8295. 11 rooms, 3 with bath; 2 apartments; 1 cottage. Facilities: hot tub, bicycles. AE, D, DC, MC, V. $$–$$$*

NEAR THE ISLAND Since there are so few hotel accommodations on Fire Island, many visitors stay at hotels on Long Island and take ferries over for the day. Some hotels even offer special packages for people who plan to visit Fire Island.

Holiday Inn Ronkonkoma. This Holiday Inn, under the same ownership as New York City's luxurious Parker Meridien hotel, aspires to be the finest Holiday Inn in the country. With the Sayville ferry terminal just 7 mi away, this is the closest full-service hotel to Fire Island. Reasonably priced packages include Fire Island ferry tickets. MacArthur Airport is 1 mi away by shuttle bus and the property has a car rental desk. *3845 Veterans Memorial Hwy., Ronkonkoma 11779, tel. 516/585–9500 or 800/422–9510, fax 516/585–9550. 287 rooms. Facilities: restaurant, bar, indoor and outdoor pools, exercise room, meeting rooms. AE, D, DC, MC, V. $$*

Inn at Medford. This inn, near the Long Island Expressway and MacArthur Airport, caters to vacationers as well as a business crowd. The Patchogue ferry terminal is nearby—just take Route 112S into town and follow the signs—making for convenient day trips to Fire Island. A southwestern motif prevails, reflected in paintings, bedspreads, and tapestries. *2695 Rte. 112, Medford 11763, tel. 516/654–3000 or 800/ 626–7779, fax 516/654–1281. 76 rooms.*

Facilities: bar, pool, hot tub, sauna, health club, coin laundry. AE, D, DC, MC, V. $–$$

Summit Motor Inn. This no-frills economy lodge was built in the '60s and renovated in the '80s. It has the advantage of being just a mile from the Bay Shore ferry terminal, and 10 minutes from both the MacArthur Airport and the Brentwood station of the Long Island Railroad. *501 E. Main St., Bay Shore 11706, tel. 516/666–6000, fax 516/665– 7476. 42 rooms, 5 suites. AE, D, DC, MC, V. $*

CAMPING

Backcountry camping is allowed, away from the dunes and the beach. Required permits, which are free, are available at the ranger stations at Smith Point and Watch Hill.

Suffolk County residents and their guests may camp in county parks with a **Green Key Pass,** a three-year pass available at any county park when you show picture I.D. and proof of residence.

Watch Hill Campground. The national seashore's only official campground, Watch Hill has only 25 sites that are much in demand, and reservations, available by lottery only, are required. In February or March, submit your application (available by sending an SASE to the superintendent; *see* Visitor Information *in* Essential Information, *above*) for the drawing in April. No-shows are common, however, so if your number doesn't come up, you may be able to snag a site by calling the campground (after May 1) at the last minute. The maximum stay is five nights and there is a small administrative fee charged per reservation. Wood fires are not allowed anywhere on the island, so you'll need a camp stove. *Tel. 516/597–6633. 25 tent sites. $*

Smith Point County Park. The sites, on the barrier beach, are open year-round. Five sites are first-come, first-served, and 141 are by reservation only. *Tel. 516/852–1316; 516/ 244–7275 for reservations. 146 tent sites. $*

Great Smoky Mountains National Park

North Carolina, Tennessee

By Eddie Nickens

Updated by Carol and Dan Thalimer

ike a rumpled quilt thrown across the foot of the eastern United States, the Great Smoky Mountains sprawl across more than half a million acres of ancient terrain, the largest wilderness sanctuary in the East. The park is a patchwork of old-growth forest and high mountain meadow, its diverse habitats stitched by mountain streams and roaring rivers.

Encompassing nearly equal portions of Tennessee and North Carolina, the Great Smoky Mountains National Park is a land of superlatives. Here are the largest stands of old-growth forest in the eastern United States and the greatest mountains east of the Rockies, with 16 peaks that shoulder into the sky more than 6,000 ft above sea level. But often, words pay poor homage to a park whose beauty also lies in the details of bloodroot and bluet, trillium and Turk's cap lily. A United Nations International Biosphere Reserve and World Heritage Site, the park contains about 125 species of trees, more than 200 species of birds, even 27 different species of salamanders.

These rugged mountains were once sacred to the Eastern Band of the Cherokee, who in 1838 were brutally removed from their ancestral home by government action and forced to march to Oklahoma. Thousands died along the Trail of Tears, but small groups of Cherokee held out in the North Carolina high country, and in 1889 the 56,000-acre Qualla Indian Reservation was formed. It now shares part of the park's southern border.

The high mountains that attracted rugged pioneer settlers in the 18th and 19th centuries were discovered by the timber industry in the early 1900s. A librarian and writer named Horace Kephart documented the changing fortunes of the southern Appalachian mountain peoples in the classic *Our Southern Highlanders* and sparked a national movement to declare the Smokies a national park. On June 15, 1934, the park was officially established.

Today the interior is managed as a wilderness preserve: There are extensive camping facilities and interpretive programs, but few other services. The park is traversed by two main roads, a portion of U.S. 441 called the Newfound Gap Road and the Little River Road, which leads to Cades Cove. On the perimeter of the park the resort towns of Gatlinburg, Tennessee, and Cherokee, North Carolina, have extensive visitor facilities, while smaller towns around the park, such as Townsend, Tennessee, and Bryson City, North Carolina, have more limited services.

This melding of facilities and sights makes the park a popular place. There are more than 9 million recreational visits to the park each year, more than twice the number of visits to any other national park. The oft-cited statistic that the park is within two days' drive of half of the nation's population shouldn't deter visitors, for solitude is often found just a short hike from the blacktop. Step off the paved road and the true heart of the park opens itself. Here you'll find hollows and coves and ridges rarely seen by human eyes. In the space of a few dozen feet, quietness pervades, all sounds muffled by moss and fern, stream and forest. Birds call. Brooks trickle. Rain drips. Tiny unseen streams seep from the undergrowth. Welcome to Shaconage (Place of Blue Smoke), the land held sacred by the Cherokee, a land whose wildness is still celebrated today.

ESSENTIAL INFORMATION

VISITOR INFORMATION For information on the park, contact the superintendent, **Great Smoky Mountains National Park** (107 Park Headquarters Rd., Gatlinburg, TN 37738, tel. 423/436–1200). The park's **Web site** is www.nps.gov/grsm.

There are two main visitor centers and a third that mainly serves as a sales annex. The **Oconaluftee Visitor Center** is near Cherokee, 2 mi north of the main park entrance. It is open November–mid-March, daily 8:30–4:30, and mid-March–October, variable longer hours. The center's **Mountain Farm Museum** is a living history exhibition area where park interpretive staff demonstrate pioneer trades and skills in farm buildings moved from other areas of the park. Near the northern entrance to the park is the **Sugarlands Visitor Center,** 2 mi south of Gatlinburg on Newfound Gap Road. Here a 10-minute park-produced film, *Sanctuary,* is full of evocative footage and narrative, but short on nuts and bolts. The center is open November–mid-March, daily 8–4:30, and mid-March–October, variable longer hours. **Cades Cove Visitor Center** (Cades Cove Loop Rd.) is 12 mi south of Townsend, Tennessee, and is open from mid-March to November, daily 9–5, and has variable hours the rest of the year.

For information on lodging, dining, and local attractions, contact the following organizations. **Swain County Chamber of Commerce** (Box 509, Bryson City, NC 28713, tel. 704/488–3681). **Cherokee Visitor Center** (Box 460, Cherokee, NC 28719, tel. 704/497–

9195 or 800/438–1601, fax 704/497–3220). Their **Web site** is www.cherokee.nc.com. **Jackson County Travel & Tourism Authority** (18 N. Central St., Suite G, Sylva, NC 28779, tel. and fax 704/586–2155 or tel. 800/962–1911). **Gatlinburg Chamber of Commerce** (Box 527, Gatlinburg, TN 37738, tel. 423/430–4148 or 800/568–4748). **Townsend Visitor Center** (Smoky Mountain Visitors Bureau, 7906 E. Lamar Alexander Pkwy., Townsend, TN 37882, tel. 423/448–6134 or 800/525–6834).

FEES Admission to the park is free.

PUBLICATIONS Brochures, booklets, maps, and guides are sold at the three visitor centers. The 25¢ *Smokies Guide* newspaper, available at visitor centers and from the superintendent (*see* Visitor Information, *above*), publishes park news and schedules of special events and ranger-led activities. The ***Great Smoky Mountains Trail Map,*** sold in the park, gives details on all backcountry campsites and trail shelters.

The **Great Smoky Mountains Natural History Association** (115 Park Headquarters Rd., Gatlinburg, TN 37738, tel. 423/436–7318) sells a number of great publications and tapes through its catalog "Books & Things." Among the best are Rose Houk's *Exploring the Smokies,* an 80-page full-color book that details recreational and educational opportunities; *Mountain Roads & Quiet Places,* by Jerry DeLaughter, a detailed guide to the less-traveled back roads that burrow through dense forest and skirt tumbling rivers and streams; *Smoky Mountains Audio Tour,* a 120-minute double cassette of natural history commentary, interviews with park rangers and former residents, and Cherokee legends, all keyed to highlights along Newfound Gap Road; and, for the kids, Ed Dodd and Jack Elrod's *Mark Trail in the Smokies!,* a 48-page full-color comic-strip volume that educates children about local plants and animals.

GEOLOGY AND TERRAIN Some 200 million years ago the ancient continents of Africa and North America collided, crushing and grinding together over a period of tens of millions of years. A result of this sustained tension, the Appalachian Mountains were gradually thrust upward. A 2,000-mi belt of folded and faulted rock that stretches today from Maine to Georgia, the Appalachians were originally as high as the Rockies. Additional millions of years of wind and rain have whittled the mountains down to their present, more modest though still awe-inspiring size.

The Great Smoky Mountains are the crowning glory of the Appalachian mountain chain, rising 4,000 and 5,000 ft above the surrounding valley floors, flecked by rocky outcrops and crisscrossed by more than 700 mi of river and mountain stream. Even though glaciers never reached the Smokies, their effects were felt in the primordial Appalachians. Cyclical freezing and thawing sheared from the cliffs huge chunks of rock and sent them crashing into the valleys below. Today, trout swim in the deep pools below these house-size boulders, and park visitors squeal as they "tube" over small waterfalls formed by rocks that once capped mighty mountains.

The crest of the Great Smokies forms the Tennessee–North Carolina border, a high-altitude horizon punctuated by Thunderhead Mountain, Clingmans Dome, Charlies Bunion, and Mount Guyot. From Newfound Gap, the geographic center of the park, the Little Pigeon River falls toward the Tennessee gateway town of Gatlinburg, while the Oconaluftee River tumbles across North Carolina on its way to downtown Cherokee. On the southwestern border of the park a series of flood-control dams form a 30-mi chain of mostly undeveloped waters. This least-accessible corner of the park is one of its most spectacular regions.

FLORA AND FAUNA A visit to the Great Smokies is a visit to ecosystems found from Georgia north to Canada. In the lowlands are mixed deciduous-coniferous forests common to the South, but atop the high peaks are boreal forests like those of Canada. In between are the oak-hickory-red

maple forests common to Virginia and the hardwood stands reminiscent of the north woods. More than 1,500 species of vascular plants have been documented in the park.

Some 95% of the park is forested, and a quarter of that is considered old-growth—a 110,000-acre treasure that represents more than 80% of the remaining old-growth forest in the eastern United States. Many of those stands are in "cove hardwood forests," a type that most commonly grows in topographic flats and mountain hollows and is the result of millions of years of forest evolution. Huge trees form a dense canopy in the cove forests, shading an understory of mosses and ferns.

Other unusual plant communities are the park's grass and heath balds, treeless patches found on several Smokies mountaintops. Along the highest ridges in the park grows the southernmost example of the red spruce–Fraser fir forest. Nearly 75% of all spruce-fir forest found in the Southeast grows here, but these trees are far from protected from outside peril. The balsam woolly adelgid, an insect introduced by Europeans in the early 1900s, has killed more than 95% of the mature Fraser firs in the Smokies, and air pollution and acid rain are damaging large stands of red spruce. For the unprepared, the skeletons of firs and dying spruce lining the ridgetops at Clingmans Dome are a startling sight, and a sobering reminder that our lifestyles have implications far beyond our backyards.

Among the park's favorite creatures are its 500–700 black bears, which feed on berries, nuts, and animal carrion. For many, seeing a black bear is a highlight of a park visit, and whenever a bear lumbers up to the roadsides, so-called "bear jams" are inevitable. All bears, however, should be considered potentially dangerous and viewed from a distance. Feeding the bears turns them into "panhandlers," and they become prime targets for poachers or prime candidates for highway accidents.

As many as 700 hybrid wild hogs live in the park, down from populations of 2,000 earlier in the decade, with concentrations in the park's western reaches. The largely nocturnal hogs feed on just about everything, and their habit of "tilling" up the forest floor with their tusks has been linked to the destruction of rare plants and the contamination of streams. Perhaps the most intriguing animal in the park is the red wolf. Once common throughout the Southeast, an experimental population of *Canis rufus* has been released around Cades Cove and Tremont. These largely nocturnal predators average only 60–70 pounds and are very shy. Chances of spotting a red wolf are slight, but best bets are early and late in the day along field edges, where the wolves hunt small rodents.

White-tailed deer in Cades Cove are uncommonly cooperative when it comes to wildlife viewing. In the summer, white-spotted fawns are a common sight, while the months of late October and November bring the breeding bucks out of the deep woods.

WHEN TO GO Weather is both the park's beauty and its bane. The same fog that cloaks mountaintops in an eerie, otherworldly "smoke" also blocks the views. Icy weather that sheathes waterfalls in crystal closes roads. April showers bring May trilliums. Frequent visitors learn to embrace the seasonal changes and wear a good waterproof hat.

Elevations in the park range from 800 ft to 6,643 ft, so generalizations regarding weather are difficult. In the Smokies, every 1,000-ft gain in elevation is equivalent to traveling 400 mi north; average temperatures fall 3°F. It can be 10°F—15°F cooler at Newfound Gap than it is in the lowlands. Rainfall varies as well, from an average of 55 inches per year in the valleys to a drenching 85 inches per year at Clingmans Dome.

As in most other parks, visitation peaks in summer, but more and more visitors are discovering that spring in the Smokies rivals any other season. The months of April and May still find much of the park

unpeopled. March to May, low temperatures average 42°F; highs average 61°F. By mid-April daytime highs occasionally crest in the 80s. By summer, however, even the Smokies aren't immune to the region's stifling heat and humidity. August afternoons in the lower elevations peak in the 90s, with evening lows dropping to the comfortable mid- to upper 60s. When summer heat drives visitors to the mountains, one place is a cool head taller than the rest: Mt. LeConte, where no temperature above 80°F has ever been recorded (*see* LeConte Lodge in Lodging, *below*).

During September and early October, the humidity and crowds (especially on weekdays) disappear—a welcome respite before the onslaught of the fall color season. September highs are in the 70s, with cool nights and first frosts by the end of the month. A second peak travel season occurs in October, as the park's hardwood forests turn to their autumn colors. Entire hillsides erupt in explosions of yellows, reds, and oranges, punctuated by the daggerlike dark evergreens. It's a fantastic time to visit the park, but only if you're prepared for the crowds. By early November, daytime highs fall to the 50s and 60s. Soon it is winter, a generally moderate season, with daytime highs in the 50s and lows in the high 20s. At the highest elevations, bitter outbreaks of severe weather have been known to plunge temperatures below 0°F.

SEASONAL EVENTS Contact the visitor centers (tel. 423/436–1200) for details on the following festivals and events, which are dependent on funding and availability of staff. **June: Women's Day** at the Mountain Farm Museum near Oconaluftee celebrates the past and present contributions of women in southern Appalachia. The annual **Storytelling Festival** at Cades Cove in late June brings to life the rich southern Appalachian Jack tales and ghost stories. **July:** The **Fourth of July Pow-Wow** fills the Cherokee Ceremonial Grounds with Native American song, dance, and skills competitions. The annual **Quilt Show** in Cades Cove in late July presents traditional quilt-making skills and patterns. **September:** Mid-month, the **Mountain Life Festival** at Oconaluftee's Mountain Farm Museum focuses on the skills early pioneers needed to carve a life from the rugged mountains. **May and late September:** At the two **Old Timers' Days** at Cades Cove, expect mountain music with banjos, dulcimers, and harmonicas. **October:** Early in the month, **Sorghum molasses-making demonstrations** at Cades Cove fill the air with the heavy, sweet aroma of this Appalachian favorite. **Cherokee Fall Festival** at the Cherokee Ceremonial grounds also takes place early in the month. **December:** The **Festival of Christmas Past** at Sugarlands Visitor Center turns back time to Yuletide traditions of the pioneers, and the **Twelve Days of Christmas** sees Santa and friends caroling to the Oconaluftee Island Park.

WHAT TO PACK These are among the most rugged mountains of the eastern United States, and even easy trails have stretches of rough, rocky, rutted terrain. More important than any camera or camcorder is a good pair of lightweight hiking boots or trail shoes. And all that lush greenery grows with a price: There are frequent rain showers in the Smokies, so pack a lightweight rain jacket to layer over light clothing in summer and heavy wool sweaters in winter. Many trails require frequent stream crossings, so hikers should pack plenty of polypropylene-type sock liners and consider carrying a walking staff. Backpackers should also pack 40 to 50 ft of light rope to hoist packs at least 10 ft above the ground, out of the reach of bears. Instructions are printed on the back of the *Great Smoky Mountains Trail Map* (*see* Publications, *above*).

GENERAL STORES **North Carolina.** Grocery stores, fast-food outlets, and gas stations are clustered in Cherokee, Sylva, and Bryson City on the North Carolina side of the park. Stores are few and far between on Route 28 from outside of Bryson City to Fontana Village. The **General Store at Fontana Village Resort** (Fontana Dam, tel. 704/498–2211) stocks picnic supplies and a good selection

of trail maps. It's open weekdays 9 AM–10 PM, weekends 8 AM–10 PM.

One-half mile south of the park entrance on Newfound Gap Road, Cherokee's **Gas N Groceries** (tel. 704/497–5515) sells liquefied petroleum gas and a few staples. Hours are Sunday–Thursday 6 AM–11 PM, Friday and Saturday 6 AM–midnight (until 10 PM in winter). Just ¼ mi south of Gas N Groceries is the **Cherokee Food Mart** (tel. 704/497–5524), which has shelves of food, sandwich meats, and a good supply of frozen food; it also carries the kind of camping supplies easily forgotten—coffeepots, Coleman fuel, rain tarps—but no LP gas. It's open daily 5:30 AM–10 PM (until 9 PM in winter). The closest full-service grocery market to the park is the **Qualla Market** (U.S. 441, 1.5 mi south of park entrance, tel. 704/497–7597). Summer hours are weekdays and Saturday 7 AM–9 PM, and Sunday 10–6; November–May hours are weekdays 7 AM–8 PM, Saturday 8–7, and Sunday 10–6.

Tennessee. In Gatlinburg the **Mountain Market** (U.S. 441, 100 yards north of park entrance, phone unlisted) is open daily 7 AM–midnight. The store's old wooden floors hold up a small produce and fresh meats display, plus picnic staples and a well-stocked hardware section. Across the parking lot from Mountain Market is the **Parkway Market** (tel. 423/436–6364), which has similar goods and is open Sunday–Thursday 7 AM–midnight, Friday and Saturday 7 AM–1 AM. In Townsend, **Black Bear Market** (U.S. 321, ½ mi north of park, tel. 423/448–1515), open Sunday–Thursday 7 AM–11 PM, Friday and Saturday 7 AM–midnight, has cardboard boxes of local onions and potatoes, picnic staples, dry goods, and the early morning aroma of bacon frying on the small grill at which you can buy breakfast biscuits and lunch sandwiches. In addition, there's a petting zoo and often live music. There's a better selection of hardware and camping supplies, in addition to the usual picnic goods, at the **Little River Village Campground** (Rte. 73, just outside the park entrance, tel. 423/448–2241), which is open daily March–November, variable hours.

ATMS Automated teller machines are located throughout Cherokee to the south of the park, along the parkway in Gatlinburg to the north, and in Townsend near the Cades Cove area in the park's northwest region.

ARRIVING AND DEPARTING A car is essential to exploring the park, which is traversed by two main roads. **Newfound Gap Road** (U.S. 441) runs north–south across the middle of the park, connecting the two primary park entrances: Cherokee, North Carolina, and Gatlinburg, Tennessee. **Little River/Laurel Creek Roads** runs for 24 mi along a stream between the Sugarlands Visitor Center and Cades Cove. **U.S. 321** threads its way along the northern border of the park, connecting the Cades Cove–Townsend area with Gatlinburg and Cosby in the little-traveled northeastern corner of the park. **I–40** parallels the park's eastern border, with few interchanges. On the southern border of the park, four-lane highways ferry traffic from Waynesville west to Sylva, Dillsboro, and Bryson City. From Bryson City west to Fontana Village, Route 28 is a scenic, windy road with views of deep forest and wide-open lake.

By Bus. Greyhound Lines serves Knoxville (100 Magnolia Ave., tel. 423/522–5144) and Asheville (2 Tunnel Rd., tel. 704/253–5353).

By Car and RV. Driving is the most popular way of sightseeing in the park, with its 238 mi of paved road and more than 100 mi of gravel road. In summer, it's common to see cars and trucks pulled along the roadside, hoods open and radiators boiling over. It's a good idea to carry an extra gallon of coolant and an extra quart of brake fluid. Driving in the park requires that you pump your brakes, use lower gears, and be patient. There's always someone slower than you just around the next bend. Turn your headlights on in the fog, and remove sunglasses before entering tunnels.

From Knoxville and points north and west, follow directions from McGhee Tyson Airport (*see* By Plane, *below*). From points east, follow directions from Asheville Regional Airport (*see* By Plane, *below*). From points south, follow U.S. 441 north to the park entrance at Cherokee. The park is approximately one hour's drive from both Knoxville and Asheville.

By Plane. The nearest major airport is **McGhee Tyson Airport** (tel. 423/970–2773), 45 mi west of Gatlinburg and near Knoxville, Tennessee. From the airport take U.S. 129 south to Maryville, Tennessee, then U.S. 321 north to Townsend. From the **Asheville Regional Airport** (tel. 704/684–2226) in North Carolina, about 60 mi east of the park, take I–26 north to I–40 west, then U.S. 19 south to U.S. 441 north to the park's entrance at Cherokee. All major rental car companies are represented at both airports.

By Train. There is no direct train service to the park. The closest city served by **Amtrak** (tel. 800/872–7245) is Greenville, South Carolina, 160 mi away.

EXPLORING

Most visitors enjoy what one park publication calls a "windshield experience" of the Great Smokies: More than 16% of park visitors never turn the car ignition off during their visit, and the vast majority never venture farther than a few hundred yards off the road. Granted, the views from Newfound Gap Road are incomparable, and the less crowded scenic routes through the valleys are valuable for those with little time to spend or inclination to hike. Still, the Great Smokies reveal their secrets only to those who take the time to walk away from the crowds and into the heart of the forest, where all seems silent until the ears are retuned to the seeping of a spring, the chatter of a "boomer" squirrel, and then the full chorus of the living wilderness.

THE BEST IN ONE DAY Rise early for a one-day tour of this gigantic slice of wilderness. You'll need to depart **Gatlinburg** in the dark to make the 45-minute drive to Cades Cove by sunrise, but save your groans: There's scheduled nap time in this dawn-to-dusk itinerary.

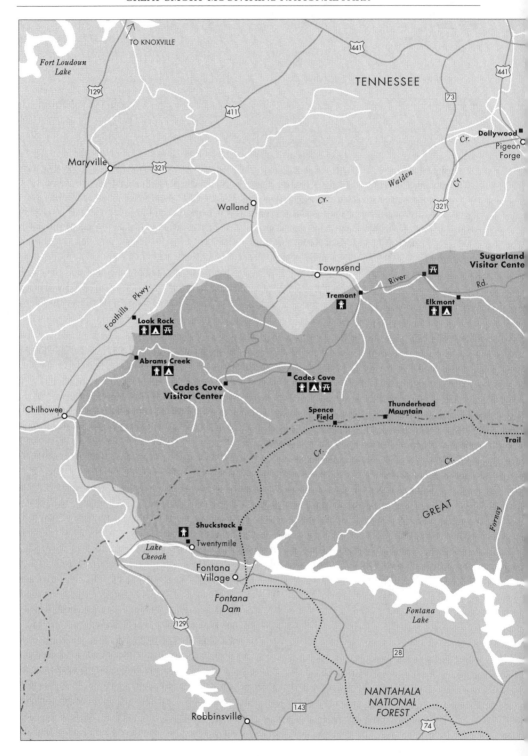

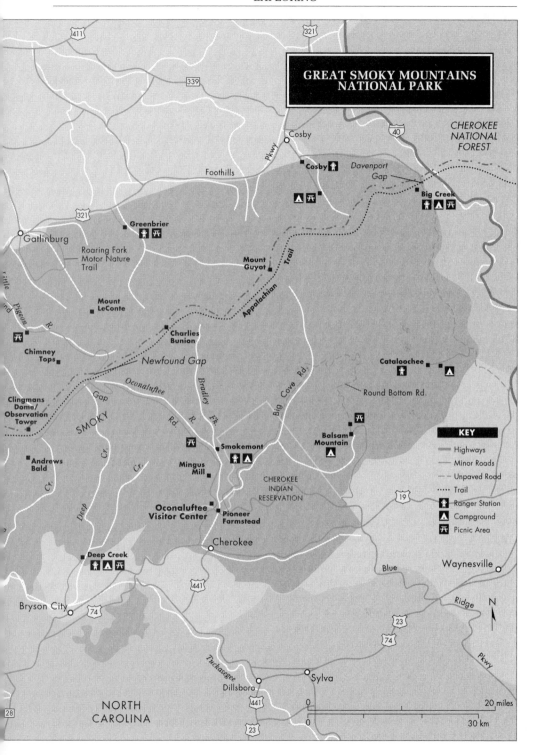

GREAT SMOKY MOUNTAINS NATIONAL PARK

CHEROKEE NATIONAL FOREST

Cosby

Cosby

Davenport Gap

Big Creek

Foothills

Greenbrier

Gatlinburg

Roaring Fork Motor Nature Trail

Mount Guyot

Appalachian Trail

Mount LeConte

Charlies Bunion

Cataloochee

Newfound Gap

Round Bottom Rd.

Oconaluftee

Chimney Tops

Clingmans Dome/ Observation Tower

Big Cove Rd.

SMOKY

Gap

Bradley Fk.

Balsam Mountain

Andrews Bald

Smokemont

Mingus Mill

CHEROKEE INDIAN RESERVATION

Oconaluftee Visitor Center

Pioneer Farmstead

Cherokee

Deep Creek

Blue

Waynesville

Bryson City

KEY

Highways
Minor Roads
Unpaved Road
Trail
Ranger Station
Campground
Picnic Area

Ridge

N

NORTH CAROLINA

Tuckasegee

Dillsboro

Sylva

Pkwy

0   20 miles

0   30 km

Cades Cove, in the far western reaches of the park, preserves the historic structures and open pastoral landscape of the region as it appeared at the turn of the century. The 11-mi loop road through Cades Cove can be very crowded, which is one reason for arriving at sunrise, except Wednesdays and Saturdays in the summer: The road is closed to cars until 10 AM. The other reason is the valley at dawn. The warm early light turns fields into seas of golden flame. Deer feed in the meadows. Drive slowly, stop often, and find an open pasture where you can take a long walk.

By midmorning find Missionary Baptist Church on the northern part of the Cades Cove loop. Directly across from the church pick up the gravel Rich Mountain Road; follow it 8 mi over the mountain, with fantastic views of the Cades Cove valley and the spine of the towering Smokies above, then out of the park. Turn right on U.S. 321 just outside Townsend; keep right where U.S. 321 turns south, load up on picnic supplies in Townsend, and then follow the road north back through the park entrance. Take a left on Little River Road and follow this scenic route to **Sugarlands Visitor Center,** 2 mi south of Gatlinburg. (Rich Mountain Road is closed in winter; at that time, continue around the loop road, take Laurel Creek Road from Cades Cove to Tremont, and continue straight on Little River Road, following the rest of this itinerary.)

From Sugarlands turn south on Newfound Gap Road and follow this primary Smokies thoroughfare toward its highest point at **Clingmans Dome.** Picnic along the way, perhaps at the Chimney Tops Picnic Area. From Chimney Tops continue south on Newfound Gap Road to Newfound Gap. About .2 mi south of the gap, turn right on the road to Clingmans Dome and follow the 7-mi scenic route to the parking lot. It's a .5-mi walk to the observation tower on a steep, serpentine asphalt walkway that switches back and rises above the treetops for a spectacular panoramic view.

After Clingmans Dome, you'll likely be in search of solitude. Continue south on Newfound Gap Road to Cherokee and turn right on U.S. 19 toward Bryson City. Once in town, follow the signs to the **Deep Creek** area of the park, 3 mi north of town. If there's time, rent an inner tube for a late afternoon float downriver. If not, find a nice smooth boulder, soothe your feet in the cool stream, and take a well-deserved nap. If all goes as planned, you'll be awakened by the flutelike calls of the wood thrush at dusk, with just enough time to find your way back to the car by dark.

ORIENTATION PROGRAMS The two main visitor centers present a variety of interpretive programs (*see* Visitor Information *in* Essential Information, *above*). Ranger-led hikes, slide shows, fireside talks, and living history demonstrations are offered by the score. Check the *Smokies Guide* (*see* Publications *in* Essential Information, *above*) and kiosks at visitor centers, ranger stations, and campgrounds for details. Ranger stations are at Greenbrier, Cosby, Big Creek, Cataloochee, Smokemont, Deep Creek, Twentymile, Look Rock, Abrams Creek, Cades Cove, Tremont, and Elkmont.

GUIDED TOURS Step-on bus tours depart from the Cherokee and Gatlinburg areas to Cades Cove, Newfound Gap, Clingmans Dome, and Roaring Fork. Rates are $13–$36, depending upon destination. **Mountain Tours Inc.** (Box 1134, Pigeon Forge, TN 37868, tel. 423/453–0864, fax 423/428–0068) is one tour company. **Smoky Mountain Tours** (Box 278, Gatlinburg, TN 37738, tel. 423/428–3014, fax 423/428–0068) also leads tours of the park.

Guided backpacking and flyfishing expeditions can be booked through **Old Smoky Outfitters** (511 Parkway, Gatlinburg, TN 37738, tel. 423/430–1936). Naturalist and writer **George Ellison** (Box 1262, Bryson City, NC 28713, tel. 704/488–8782) offers guided wildflower hikes, wildlife workshops, and southern Appalachian natural history seminars. The **Great Smoky Mountains Institute at Tremont** (9275 Tremont

Rd., Townsend, TN 37882, tel. 423/448–6709) offers three- and five-day courses in wildlife photography, Appalachian history, and natural history.

SCENIC DRIVES AND VIEWS The indispensable guide to scenic drives in the park is *Mountain Roads & Quiet Places* (*see* Publications *in* Essential Information, *above*). A copy of the brochure "Auto Touring" is available at visitor centers. These publications also tell you which roads are unpaved, closed in winter, or unsuitable for RVs.

The most popular auto tour in the park is the 11-mi **Cades Cove Loop Road,** which skirts the edge of a broad valley with open pastures and a preserved pioneer settlement. Cades Cove can be extremely crowded, but its pleasures are worth the trouble. If traffic sends your blood pressure skyward, pull the car off midway around the loop and hit the trail to Abrams Falls, a 5-mi round-trip.

The **Cataloochee Auto Tour** begins in a secluded valley where historic structures dot the hillsides. Take Exit 20 off I–40, drive .2 mi, turn right onto Cove Creek Road, an 11-mi windy, sometimes paved, sometimes gravel route that ferries you to the entrance to Cataloochee. You'll follow the right fork of Cove Creek through hardwood forests to Cove Creek Gap, the park boundary, where the road dips sharply for the descent of Cataloochee Divide. In the valley you'll pass restored and unrestored homes, churches, and schools (without the crowds prevalent at Cades Cove).

The 5-mi **Roaring Fork Motor Nature Trail** begins in Cherokee Orchard and follows a rushing creek through a young forest. A highlight of the loop is the Place of a Thousand Drips, where tiny underground seeps and springs turn a mountainside into an unusual sort of waterfall. The trail is always closed in winter.

Clingmans Dome Road clings to the crest of the Smokies for 7 mi, offering unparalleled views of ridges piled upon ridges. The road is closed in winter. A short walk along the Spruce-Fir Self-Guiding Nature Trail will get you away from the crowds (*see* The Best in One Day, *above*).

There are two sections of the **Foothills Parkway.** The western 17 mi of the alternate route, just outside the park boundaries, is known by Smokies insiders for its spectacular fall color. The eastern 6 mi connect U.S. 321 to I–40 and serve as a shortcut to Big Creek and Cataloochee. It's a shorter route than the western parkway and is closed in winter.

From Bryson City, **Lakeview Drive** is a 6-mi climb high above Fontana Lake. This is a prime spot for viewing fall colors. The road crosses numerous streams before dead-ending at Laurel Branch. Before returning to Bryson City, stretch your legs on the .75-mi walk through the tunnel.

HISTORIC BUILDINGS AND SITES The park's wealth of preserved pioneer settlements features white churches glistening jewel-like in distant valleys, working mills, and cabins whose varied dovetail corner-notches speak volumes about the heritage of their long-forgotten builders. There are 77 historic structures in the park, many clustered in **Cades Cove, Cataloochee,** and the **Mountain Farm Museum** at Oconaluftee Visitor Center.

About .75 mi north of Oconaluftee Visitor Center is the picturesque **Mingus Mill,** built in 1886. Even when Mountain Farm Museum is teeming with visitors, Mingus Mill is a good bet for a quiet walk around a restored historic site. Here you can listen to the sound of water dripping from the flume and get an explanation of how the mills work from a miller. *Near Cherokee, 2.75 mi north of the main park entrance, no phone. Admission free. Open mid-Apr.–Oct., daily 9–5.*

One of the park's best-kept secrets is the ruins of the tiny logging town of **Proctor.** Reachable only by boat, the crumbling remains of industrial sites, mill foundations, and a few standing structures along scenic Hazel Creek make a day trip to Proctor a private and personal glimpse of life in the Great Smokies long before it was a national park. For boat rentals or ferry service to Hazel Creek, contact **Fontana Village Resort** (tel. 704/498–2211 or 800/849–2258, fax 704/498–2345).

NATURE TRAILS AND SHORT WALKS Scores of short trails and interpretive walks beckon from nearly every curve in the park's roads. Designated **Quiet Walkways** are short strolls of .5 mi or less that meander from the main roads into deep forests or skirt laurel-lined streams. Parking areas for Quiet Walkways hold only two or three cars, so even in the most crowded areas of the park these accessible trails offer a quick route to peace and quiet. Watch for the signs.

None of the 11 self-guiding nature trails in the park is longer than 2.5 mi, except the 5-mi Alum Cave Bluffs Trail (*see* Longer Hikes, *below*). The paved 2.5-mi **Laurel Falls Self-Guiding Nature Trail** is a good introduction to the park's varied habitats and terrain. Three miles west of the Sugarlands Visitor Center, on Little River Road, the trail wends through laurel thickets, pine-oak forests, and a cove hardwood forest before tunneling through a ridgetop wood and down to Laurel Falls. It's a good choice for wildflower lovers who don't like to venture far from the road. Though the terrain on this trail is moderate, you soon learn that the lush vegetation that cloaks these mountainsides can hide very rugged country. If you're ready for a bigger challenge, continue past the falls for a steeper, more rugged .5 mi to an old-growth hardwood forest.

The .75-mi **Noah "Bud" Ogle Self-Guiding Nature Trail** is a different sort of interpretive walk. The trail skirts abandoned fields and apple orchards as you walk past the old Ogle homestead, a large log barn, and the stone foundation of the "weaner" cabin, where Ogle's sons each spent the first year of their newly married lives. The Ogles were one of the first families to settle in White Oak Flats, which is now Gatlinburg. The trailhead is on the Cherokee Orchard Road, 3 mi south of Gatlinburg via Airport Road.

The 4-mi round-trip hike to Andrews Bald via **Forney Ridge Trail** is a superb choice in May and June. From the Clingmans Dome parking area the trail first traverses a steep, rocky section, then meanders through a spruce-fir forest. Keep bearing left and you soon reach the bald, which soaks up the springtime sun, returning the energy in the form of early blooming wildflowers that poke their pastel blossoms through the mountain oat grasses. By mid-June, flame azalea and rose-purple catawba rhododendron light up the bald's shrubby edges.

If you like your mountain streams crashing over waterfalls, the **Deep Creek–Indian Creek Loop** fits the bill. The trail, just under 4 mi long, begins north of the Deep Creek Campground, 2 mi north of Bryson City. In less than a half-mile you come to Tom Branch Falls, which cascades over rock ledges that shatter the falling water into shimmering veils of mist. Another half-mile brings you to a fork in the trail; take the left fork and follow Deep Creek Trail. Cross the creek at the top of the trail, climb Sunkota Ridge, and pick up Indian Creek Trail back to the fork. Indian Creek Falls is visible near the stream's confluence with Deep Creek.

LONGER HIKES Veteran park visitors know that the more time spent on the trail, the better. But be honest about your hiking skills; don't attempt more than you are comfortable with. Trails in the Smokies can quickly get very steep and stay slippery for a day or two after a brief shower or heavy dew.

The area surrounding the popular 5-mi **Alum Cave Bluffs Self-Guiding Nature Trail** has been spared the logger's saw, and even today, the physical reminders of man's presence are kept to a minimum. The first 1.5 mi to Arch Rock are heavily forested with hemlock and yellow birch. Past Arch Rock, the trail gets steeper and climbs the dry mountain slopes above the creek, eventually breaking into open heath balds. The bluffs above are nearly 100 yards long. If you catch a second wind, continue on for the 2.5-mi climb to Mt. LeConte, home of the famous LeConte Lodge (*see* Lodging, *below*). In early June the rhododendron blooms along the trail are a highlight, but this trail doesn't fall under any best-kept-secret category. If the parking lot is packed, you may want to choose a different trail for solitude's sake.

The 8-mi round-trip hike to **Charlies Bunion** offers easy access, spectacular views, and relatively small elevation gain, which makes it a very popular trail. From the Newfound Gap parking area, take the Appalachian Trail east, where you'll walk on the spine of the Appalachian chain. All along are sweeping vistas of the Little Pigeon and Oconaluftee watersheds. About 2.7 mi down the trail is the Boulevard Trail; bear right, remaining on the Appalachian Trail, and continue to the best view of all, from the rocky knob of Charlies Bunion, perched atop sheer 1,000-ft cliffs.

The 8-mi round-trip **Ramsay Cascade Trail** offers a double bonus. First, you walk through the park's largest old-growth forest, a cathedral of tulip trees and Eastern hemlock trunks like giant temple columns. A bit farther on, the park's highest waterfall awaits: the 100-ft Ramsay Cascade. It's a strenuous pull, with an elevation gain of 2,375 ft in 4 mi, but worth every drop of sweat. The trailhead is in the Greenbrier area of the park, 6 mi east of Gatlinburg off U.S. 321.

In the wild, less-visited southwest corner of the park, there are peaks much higher than the 4,100-ft **Shuckstack,** but few offer its diversity of sights. There are two routes that are both challenging. One is the 4.5-mi one-way trip up **Twentymile Trail.** The other route is the 3.4-mi stretch of **Appalachian Trail** from Fontana Dam to Shuckstack, which has a 2,120-ft elevation gain. The blue-green waters of Fontana Lake and Lake Cheoah twinkle along the

valley floors, while the great ridgeline of the Smokies forms a high-altitude horizon, flecked with heath and grass balds. The trailhead at Fontana Dam is off Route 28, near Fontana Village, 50 mi west of Cherokee. Twentymile's trailhead is another 7 mi west.

APPALACHIAN TRAIL For 68 mi the famed **Appalachian Trail** (also called AT) bumps and grinds over the crest of the Great Smokies. Entering the park from the south at Fontana Dam, it climbs the 4,100-ft Shuckstack, then hops along ridgetops from Spence Field to Thunderhead Mountain to Clingmans Dome, and heads northeast until it exits the park at Davenport Gap near Big Creek. Sections of the trail near Newfound Gap are heavily traveled, but the remote southwest and northeast corners of the park offer a chance at great stretches of solitude.

Backcountry permits are required for overnight stays (*see* Camping, *below*). While the AT boasts the best views over the longest route, there is a price to be paid: Campers must stay in trailside shelters caged in with bear-proof cyclone fencing, so you'll share bunk space with strangers. Still, for many the best way to see the park is from the familiar white-blazed trail. For more information on the entire length of the trail, contact the **Appalachian Trail Conference** (Box 807, Harpers Ferry, WV 25425, tel. 304/535–6331).

OTHER ACTIVITIES Arts and Crafts Galleries. While cheap souvenir shops abound in the area, fine arts and crafts that meld utility and aesthetics are also an Appalachian hallmark. At the foot of the Arrowmont School of Arts and Crafts campus, **Arrowcraft** (576 Parkway, Gatlinburg, TN, tel. 423/436–4604) carries fine weaving, pottery, woodworking, and jewelry from Arrowmont artists and others. Tours of the **Arrowmont** campus (Box 567, Gatlinburg, TN, tel. 423/436–5860) are available by appointment. **Elizabeth Ellison Watercolors** (Main St., Box 1262, Bryson City, NC, tel. 704/488–8782) is a great find up a flight of narrow, creaky stairs above the 1920s Clampitt Hardware Store. Ellison's watercolors of native flora and landscapes often incorporate papers handmade from native plants such as yucca, iris, and mulberry. In the tiny historic hamlet of Dillsboro, **Oaks Gallery** (Riverwood Shops, Box 310, Dillsboro, NC, tel. 704/586–6542) carries the work of 90 area artists and craftspeople who work in clay, wood, stoneware, weaving, and other media. In the surrounding **Riverwood Shops** are working pewtersmiths and other artisans. In Cherokee, the **Qualla Arts & Crafts Mutual** (U.S. 441N/Box 310, Cherokee, NC, tel. 704/497–3103) is part museum, part gallery, owned and operated by Cherokee craftspeople. A best bet might be a Cherokee split-oak basket, accented with rivercane and honeysuckle.

Biking. Bicycles are not allowed on most trails or in the backcountry, and the park's narrow, windy roads are unsuitable for bicycles, but there are a few possibilities. From early May to mid-September the 11-mi Cades Cove Loop Road is closed to automobile traffic until 10 AM on Wednesdays and Saturdays. Rent cycles at the **Cades Cove Campground Store** (tel. 423/448–9034), which is open April–October. A 10-mi round-trip via the Deep Creek Loop is a good way to log bike time; mountain-bike rentals and route maps are available at **Nantahala Outdoor Center—The Bike Shop** (13077 Highway 19W, Bryson City, NC 28713, tel. 704/488–2175, ext. 158, or 888/662–1662).

Bird-Watching. More than 20 different kinds of warbler breed in the park, just a sampling of the more than 200 bird species in the Smokies. The excellent *Birds of the Smokies,* available from the Great Smoky Mountains Natural History Association (*see* Publications *in* Essential Information, *above*), is a pocket-size guide with checklists and tips.

Boating. Fontana Lake on the southwestern border of the park is a superb boating site,

with the surrounding mountains reflected in the clear blue-green waters. **Fontana Village Resort Marina** (*see* Lodging, *below*) rents johnboats, bass boats, and houseboats and offers launching facilities for private crafts.

Cross-Country Skiing. In winter, Roaring Fork Motor Nature Trail, the eastern portion of the Foothills Parkway, and Parson Branch, Rich Mountain, Clingmans Dome Road, and the Balsam Mountain Road to Round Bottom are closed to cars. Each allows cross-country skiing when the weather permits. Conditions vary widely. Rental equipment is not available in the park.

Fishing. The cold, pure waters of these mountains make for some of the Southeast's finest trout fishing. Rainbow and brown trout are common in most park streams, and the protected native brook trout frequents high headwater streams. There is no open season on brook trout, and only single-hook, artificial lures are permitted. To fish, you'll need a Tennessee or North Carolina license—either one covers the whole park. Guided fishing and fly-fishing instruction are available through **McLeod's Highland Fly Fishing** (191 Wesser Heights Dr., Bryson City, NC 28713, tel. 704/488–8975). **Old Smoky Outfitters** (511 Parkway, Gatlinburg, TN 37738, tel. 423/430–1936) also instructs and guides fishers. Fishing for lake trout, largemouth and smallmouth bass, muskellunge, and walleye is big sport in Fontana Lake and Lake Cheoah. Guided fishing trips can be booked through **Fontana Village Resort Marina** (*see* Lodging, *below*). There are more than 30 mi of stocked trout streams on the **Cherokee Indian Reservation.** Required tribal permits are $5 per day, available at most campgrounds in Cherokee. No other license is needed.

Horseback Riding. Guided horseback trips are offered by a number of outfitters. **Cades Cove Riding Stables** (4035 Lamar Alexander Pkwy., Walland, TN 37886, tel. 423/448–6286). **Davy Crockett Riding Stables** (505

Old Cades Cove Rd., Townsend, TN, tel. 423/448–6411). **Fontana Riding Stables** (*see* Fontana Village Resort *in* Lodging, *below*). **McCarter's Riding Stables** (1102 Steele Way, Gatlinburg, TN, tel. 423/436–5354). **Smokemont Riding Stables** (Box 72, Cherokee, NC, tel. 704/497–2373). **Smoky Mountain Stables** (729 Kear La., Gatlinburg, TN, tel. 423/436–5634). **Wonderland Stables** (3889 Wonderland Way, Sevierville, TN, tel. 423/436–5490 or 423/453–1111).

Indian Reservation. The 56,000-acre **Cherokee Indian Reservation** shares miles of the park's southern border. There are fine educational facilities that explain the history and culture of the Cherokee Indian, but much of the town of Cherokee is lined with "tomahawk shops" filled with plastic spears and stuffed bears. Children go bonkers over the main town drag, where they can have their picture taken with "street chiefs" in gaudy feathered headdresses beside tin tepees. The saddest sights are the caged bears. Pay not a penny to view these exploited creatures. Highlights of a visit to Cherokee include the wildly popular and impressive *Unto These Hills* outdoor drama; the historically accurate re-created **Oconaluftee Indian Village**; the **Museum of the Cherokee Indian,** where those even slightly interested in Native American culture can get lost for hours; and the **Qualla Arts & Crafts Mutual** (*see* Arts and Crafts Galleries *in* Other Activities, *above*). For further information, contact the **Cherokee Visitor Center** (Box 460, Cherokee, NC 28719, tel. 704/497–9195 or 800/438–1601).

Rafting. Numerous outfitters offer whitewater floats on nearby rivers. In addition to guided or unguided rafts, some outfitters rent "rubber duckies" or "funyaks," which are inflatable kayaks. The three outfitters we list are the best known. **Nantahala Outdoor Center** (13077 Hwy. 19 W, Bryson City, NC 28713, tel. 704/488–2175 or 888/662–1662). **Nantahala Rafts** (Gorgarama Park, Bryson City, NC 28713, tel. 704/488–2325 or 800/245–7700). **Rolling Thunder River Co.** (Box 88, Almond, NC 28702, tel. 704/488–2030 or 800/344–5838).

Railway Touring. Since 1988 the **Great Smoky Mountains Railway** (119 Front St., Box 397, Dillsboro, NC 28725, tel. 704/586–8811 or 800/872–4681) has been a don't-miss option during a park visit. These brightly painted diesel-electric and steam trains have enclosed cabooses and open cars. Choose between a Dillsboro departure and return, which includes a 3½-hour excursion along the Tuckaseegee River with a 45-minute layover in Bryson City; or a 4½-hour Bryson City departure- and return-excursion through the stunning Nantahala Gorge with an hour layover in the gorge. All-day "Raft & Rail" trips are a favorite. In addition, the railway offers romantic 2½-hour dinner train rides every Saturday night. Rates are $49.95 plus tax per person.

Swimming. Park officials "tolerate" swimming in the park's many streams and rivers, but it is not encouraged. Waters are swift and cold, and despite posted warnings, people climb waterfalls, and some have slipped and fallen to their deaths. If you choose one of the more popular swimming holes, be aware that there are hidden hazards. There are lots of paved pull-offs along **Little River Road** between Gatlinburg and Cades Cove. One great spot is **The Sinks. Deep Creek** is also popular (*see* Tubing, *below*). **Bradley Fork Creek** flows through Smokemont Campground, near Cherokee.

Tubing. Few outfitters rent inner tubes because they are less stable and therefore more dangerous than rafts. You may, however, pilot your very own inner tube down scenic **Deep Creek** as many times as you'd like. Commercial tubing centers are clustered at the park entrance at Deep Creek, 3 mi north of Bryson City. Most charge the same $5 for a tube with a wooden seat, $3 without, but vendors located farther away from the entrance charge a few dollars less. Deep Creek can be very crowded in July and August. Try it earlier in spring when there are fewer people and, due to the spring rains, faster water.

Wildlife Photography. The Smokies exact particular techniques from those wanting to put their treasures on film. Dark forests and fog fool light meters, while streams are sunlit only in the middle of the day. Tripods are required equipment if you want to photograph wildflowers or blur the water in a mountain river. Mecca for photography buffs in the Smokies is **Beneath the Smoke** (467 Parkway, Gatlinburg, TN 37738, tel. 423/436–3460), a gallery-store with a huge selection of prints, from backlit deer feeding in fog-shrouded meadows to black bear cubs clinging to trees to dew-dappled wildflowers. The store also has the most complete natural-history book selection around, with more than 4,000 titles, and offers free photography programs. Store personnel can handle technical questions and point you to the best overlooks for sunrise shots.

CHILDREN'S PROGRAMS From sing-alongs with interpretive staff to dozens of walks, talks, and tall-tale times, the park's rangers and interpretive staff offer enough children's programs to tire the most animated tyro; all are outlined in the park newspaper, *Smokies Guide,* or posted on kiosks at ranger stations, campgrounds, and visitor centers. The **Junior Ranger program,** run by the park service (tel. 423/436–1200), is for kids 8–12. Participants qualify for Junior Ranger status and the official badge when they've completed a natural history workbook, attended a special ranger-led activity, visited one of three Junior Ranger special areas, and picked up one bag of litter or turned in one bag of recyclables.

EVENING ACTIVITIES Several ranger-led activities explore the park after dark. Best bets are "Owl Calls and Wolf Howls" on summer nights June–August in Cades Cove, and the one-hour "Twilight Strolls" that depart from the Elkmont, Cosby, and Smokemont campgrounds each night May–Labor Day. Consult the *Smokies Guide* or kiosks at ranger stations, campgrounds, and visitor centers for details. All activities are dependent on funding.

DINING

Southern home-style cooking is the pride of the region, and meals at restaurants are often served family style, with heaping plates of vegetables and mountains of rolls and cornbread. Mountain trout is a favorite. There are no public dining facilities inside the park, but plenty are nearby.

NEAR THE PARK: NORTH CAROLINA **Lulu's Cafe.** If you need a break from the Smokies' traditional trout-ham-gravy food groups, try this gourmet American diner, considered by many locals the region's finest restaurant. Menu favorites include pasta primavera with garlic, herbs, sun-dried tomatoes, and pine nuts; and grilled Portobello mushrooms glazed with citrus basil sauce and served with pesto pasta and steamed vegetables. Come early on summer weekends. *612 W. Main St., Sylva, tel. 704/586–8989. Reservations not accepted. MC, V. $$*

The Chestnut Tree. This hotel restaurant is a consensus favorite for dining in Cherokee, even though it's on the highway bypass outside of town. On Friday it has a prime rib and seafood buffet, and on Saturday a mountain country buffet with fried chicken, roast turkey, pork chops, and country-style vegetables. Sunday brunch is a heavy meal, and the breakfast buffet is popular with families. *Holiday Inn, U.S. 19, Cherokee, tel. 704/ 497–9181. AE, D, DC, MC, V. No lunch. $–$$*

Dillsboro Smokehouse. A wide-open, wooden-floor dining room, its walls festooned with farm implements, sets the tone: This is the place for old-fashioned eatin'. Hickory-smoked pork, beef, ribs, chicken, and turkey are piled on the plates, served with no fewer than four side dishes at dinner (two at lunch). Order a box lunch for your trip on the nearby Great Smoky Mountains Railway. *267 Haywood St., Dillsboro, tel. 704/586–9556. Reservations not accepted. D, MC, V. $–$$*

NEAR THE PARK: TENNESSEE **The Burning Bush.** You can't beat the views: Velvet-antlered bucks graze in the forest beyond glass walls in two of the dining rooms. Inside, exotic finches call from large aviaries. Specialties include fillet of beef Rossini, a center-cut filet mignon sautéed in butter with mushrooms and Madeira sauce, and the small but tempting quail braised with brown sauce, peas, and mushrooms. *1151 Parkway, Gatlinburg, tel. 423/ 436–4669. Reservations essential in summer and fall. AE, D, DC, MC, V. $$–$$$*

Ogle's Buffet Restaurant. The name says it all: Sunday buffets include country ham, turkey, and chicken, while Friday-night seafood feasts feature five kinds of fish plus the requisite chicken and roast beef. The best seats in the house are in the glassed-in dining room that doubles as a walkway over the Little Pigeon River. *515 Parkway, Gatlinburg, tel. 423/436–4157. Reservations not accepted. AE, D, DC, MC, V. $*

Pancake Pantry. Its tall windows overlook Gatlinburg's finest shopping area and a line outside as long as 100 customers. Those who are waiting can admire the century-old brick exterior with copper highlights while they ponder which of the 24 varieties of pancakes to try. Austrian apple-walnut are a hit, and all are served with whipped butter and syrup or fruit compote and whipped cream. Ham and Swiss cheese sandwiches are specially boxed for picnicking in the park. *628 Parkway, Gatlinburg, tel. 423/436–4724. Reservations not accepted. No credit cards. $*

PICNIC SPOTS The Park Service maintains 10 developed picnic grounds (Big Creek, Deep Creek, Collins Creek, Balsam Mountain, Cosby, Greenbrier, Look Rock, Chimney Tops, Metcalf Bottoms, and Cades Cove), but any flat rock, flowering meadow, or streamside gravel bar makes for a fine place to spread a tablecloth. Along **Little River Road** between Sugarlands and Cades Cove are innumerable picturesque possibilities. Better yet is to load grub into a day pack and strike out for **Andrews Bald, Charlies Bunion,** or **Cataloochee.**

LODGING

Years ago, fine old lodges and inns were built to house visitors who arrived by train and bus. Many guests book rooms for the fall a year in advance. Large enough to provide privacy, but small enough to offer personality and personal service, these inns run the gamut from rustic to elegant. One word of caution: Any place that advertises "natural air-conditioning" is actually admitting to a lack of mechanical air-conditioning. Nights in the Smokies are generally comfortable throughout the year, but these hills aren't immune to stifling heat.

INSIDE THE PARK **LeConte Lodge.** The only overnight lodging in the park, this rustic mountaintop retreat is considered by many the highlight of their visit to the Smokies. There are five ways to get here, but all have one thing in common: hiking boots. The shortest route to the lodge is the 5.5-mi Alum Cave Bluffs Self-Guiding Nature Trail, a four-hour hike for a fit hiker. At the summit you'll find rooms in cabins or group sleeping lodges, with kerosene lanterns and heaters and bunk beds. Supplies are brought in by llama three times per week, and meals (dinner and breakfast are included in the room rate) are served family style. A fact-filled brochure is available with suggestions on gear and trail routes. Bed linens are provided and there are flush toilets, but there's no electricity, private baths, or showers. *250 Apple Valley Rd., Sevierville, TN 37862, tel. 423/429–5704. Capacity: 50. No credit cards. Closed late Nov.–mid-Mar. $$$*

NEAR THE PARK: BRYSON CITY, NORTH CAROLINA **Fryemont Inn.** Covered with the bark of huge poplar trees cut in the 1920s, this rustic lodge has rooms paneled with chestnut, gleaming hardwood floors, and large timbers that support a high vaulted ceiling in an open dining room. Small windows in each room open for an aromatic, evergreen-suffused breeze. The ambience is a bit more reserved than that at the Hemlock Inn (*see below*). In winter in the lobby, a fire roars from a stone fireplace large enough for 8-ft logs. If you're a light sleeper, ask for a room away from the stairs, kitchen, and dining room. Only the cottage suites have TVs and phones. Nonguests are welcome in the restaurant, which serves southern cooking. Breakfast and dinner are included in room rates. *1 Fryemont Rd., Box 459, Bryson City 28713, tel. 704/488–2159 or 800/845–4879, fax 488–8960. 37 rooms, 3 cottage suites. Facilities: restaurant, bar, pool. D, MC, V. Closed Nov.–3rd wk of Apr. $$$*

Hemlock Inn. While waiting for the dinner bell, guests gather on the flagstone porches of this mountaintop lodge to trade fish tales and tell of secret hiking spots. Perched high above three deep valleys on its own 44 secluded acres, the inn offers a real getaway. The only thing that separates you from the looming Alarka Mountains is a split-rail fence and a few bluebird boxes. There are no phones or TVs in the rooms, which are furnished with simple country accents and beds and tables made by area artisans. Breakfast and dinner (included in the room rates) are served family style at large tables with lazy Susans laden with seasonal vegetables. *911 Galbraith Creek Rd., Bryson City 28713, tel. 704/488–2885. 19 rooms, 4 cottages. D, MC, V. Closed Nov.–mid-Apr. $$$*

Folkestone Inn. This B&B is filled with fine Empire antiques, but you needn't worry about stuffiness. Hikers dry their boots by an enormous, ornate Victorian woodstove in the parlor while trading tall tales with the innkeepers. The English-cottage ambience is charming: The innkeepers brought from England painted porcelain doorknobs and English china on which a full breakfast is served. There are 4 landscaped acres with white benches by a field left unmown to attract birds, a stone bridge over a small brook, a croquet set waiting on the porch, and an English herb and perennial garden with a lattice arch. Upstairs rooms have pri-

vate balconies with views of the Alarka Mountains; downstairs rooms in the English basement are smaller but very cozy, with stone floors and walls, pressed-tin ceilings, and views of cattle in the neighboring fields. There are no TVs or phones in the rooms. The country setting, 3 mi from Bryson City and a scant .1 mi from the park entrance at Deep Creek, is a pleasing change from many area accommodations. *101 Folkestone Rd., Bryson City 28713, tel. 704/488–2730, fax 704/488–0722. 10 rooms. Facilities: croquet. D, MC, V. $$*

Lloyd's on the River. Between Cherokee and Bryson City, only 5 mi from each, this family-owned motor lodge caters to those searching to get away from frenetic downtown Cherokee. Double porches full of rocking chairs holding guests swapping family photos, a nicely landscaped L-shape pool, updated exteriors, and meticulous maintenance lend much charm to this motel with 1950s appeal. Rooms 1–14 have back porches overlooking the river. Loaded with personality, this is a super dollar value. *Box 429, Bryson City 28713, tel. 704/488–3767. 21 rooms. Facilities: pool. D, MC, V. Closed Nov.–Mar. $–$$*

NEAR THE PARK: CHEROKEE, NORTH CAROLINA

Best Western Great Smokies Inn. With its milled log-cabin exterior and stone floor, this is among the most attractive chain hotels in the area. Grounds meticulously landscaped with native plants keep the pool very private. Inside, attractive wallpapers and mountain art in each bright room are a welcome break from the usual chain-hotel decor. Some rooms have hot tubs. One block off the main drag through town, the hotel is next door to the tribal bingo facility and electric lotto-style gambling. *Follow U.S. 441 and turn north at Acquani Rd. Box 1809, Cherokee 28719, tel. 704/497–2020 or 800/528–1234. 152 rooms. Facilities: pool. AE, D, DC, MC, V. Closed Jan.–Feb. $$*

Newfound Lodge. This clean, comfortable hotel is only ¼ mi from the hub of Cherokee's activity, but it feels far more removed.

Private balconies overlook the Oconaluftee River, with a small, well-maintained riverside lawn lined with maple and river birch trees. You can fish from your porch, if you're hungry enough. *34 U.S. 441 N, Cherokee 28719, tel. 704/497–2746. 73 rooms. Facilities: pool. AE, D, MC, V. Closed Nov.–mid-Mar. $–$$*

NEAR THE PARK: DILLSBORO, NORTH CAROLINA

Squire Watkins Inn. Within one block of historic downtown Dillsboro, this secluded Queen Anne–style B&B has rooms filled with antiques, including iron or pineapple four-poster beds. Heirlooms from the innkeepers' families are in the large common areas, and a wide porch with swing and rockers overlooks 3 landscaped acres with towering white pines. For the best evening breezes, try the Dogwood or Rose room. Two Cape Cod–style housekeeping cottages with stone fireplaces and knotty-pine woodwork are nearby. You'd expect to pay far more for an inn of this quality. There are no TVs or phones in rooms. *Haywood Rd., Box 430, Dillsboro 28725, tel. 704/586–5244 or 800/586–2429. 4 rooms. No credit cards. $$*

Jarrett House. A regional landmark, this historic railway hotel with triple porches and a tin roof is right in the middle of the bustling tourist district. It's a nice change of pace, a B&B that won't break your budget. Floors creak and roll in the Victorian bedrooms. Light sleepers should request rooms off the street and away from the famous dining room, where the table is loaded up with southern-style veggies, like butter potatoes and harvest peas, served family style. Old hands save valuable stomach space for the real stuff: country cured ham and trout, fried in a light, peppery batter, served with head and tail attached, with "trout refills" a mere $1.50 extra. *100 Haywood St., Dillsboro 38725, tel. 704/586–0265 or 800/972–5623. 16 rooms. Facilities: restaurant. No credit cards. Closed mid-Dec.–mid-Apr. $*

NEAR THE PARK: ELSEWHERE IN NORTH CAROLINA

Balsam Mountain Inn. Guests seldom believe their eyes when they see this sprawling neoclassical inn. This old railroad hotel commands attention from the top of a small mountain in the Balsam range. Built in the early 1900s, with 10-ft-wide halls to accommodate steamer trunks and rooms for 100 guests, everything is big—except for the inn's ambience, which the owner manages to keep personal. Quilts, rockers, and bent willow-branch furniture fill the common rooms, while green wicker furniture and white iron beds lend an open, bright feel to the guest rooms, which have original art and antiques. Located 20 mi east of the park off U.S. 23/74, the inn isn't as nearby as many other lodges, but none of them can match its sprawling front porch or its 225 windows. *Seven Springs Rd., Box 40, Balsam 28707, tel. 704/456–9498 or 800/224–9498, fax 704/456–9298. 50 rooms. Facilities: restaurant, library. D, MC, V. $$$*

Fontana Village Resort. Built in the 1940s to house construction workers for the nearby Fontana Dam, this clustered community of cabins, cottages, a hotel, marina, and recreational facilities is a find. Far in the wild, untrammeled western reaches of the park, there is no finer family vacation spot in the Smokies; and if you hike or fish, you'll be happy you made the 1½-hour drive out of Cherokee. This is casual country. Rooms in the Fontana Inn are the typical motel offering; opt instead for one of the cozy cottages, which have fireplaces and kitchens. You'll be torn between utilizing as many of the area's considerable outdoor opportunities as possible, or perfecting your porch-rocking form—tough choices. *Rte. 28, Box 68, Fontana Dam 28733, tel. 704/498–2211 or 800/849–2258, fax 704/498–2345. 80 rooms, 100 cottages. Facilities: 3 restaurants, indoor pool, miniature golf, 4 tennis courts, exercise room, horseback riding, boating, fishing, bicycles, mountain bikes. AE, D, MC, V. $$$*

The Swag. This exquisite, rustic inn sits high atop the Cataloochee Divide overlooking a swag—a deep depression in otherwise high ground. From the 5,000-ft private peak, guests get a breathtaking 50-mi panorama of the Smoky Mountains. On 250 acres, the property shares a 1.5-mi boundary with and hiking trail access to the Great Smoky Mountains National Park. There are two main lodge buildings and three cabins assembled from several historic buildings. Each of the guest rooms is different, although they have in common rough wood walls, exposed beams, bare floors, and area rugs and are flawlessly furnished with local crafts. Rooms have either fireplaces or wood stoves, private decks, hair dryers, CD players, refrigerators, and coffeemakers; some have whirlpool baths. All meals are included in the room rate; this is a dry county, but you may bring your own alcoholic beverages. *Hemphill Rd., Waynesville 28786, tel. 704/926-0430, 704/926-3119, or 800/789-7672, fax 704/926-2036 in season; 212/570-2071 or 212/570-2086 off-season. 13 rooms, 3 cabins. Facilities: sauna, racquetball, 2 libraries. AE, D, MC, V. Closed Nov.–late May. $$$*

NEAR THE PARK: GATLINBURG, TENNESSEE

Best Western Fabulous Chalet Inn. In a quiet residential neighborhood a few blocks above the main downtown drag, this secluded mountain lodge is surrounded by rose gardens and stone terraces. Choose among rooms with views of Mt. LeConte and downtown Gatlinburg, rooms over the river, or rooms with a hot tub. Some larger rooms have two full bathrooms, and some have woodburning fireplaces; one- and two-bedroom town houses and private villas are available. Continental breakfast is included in the room rate in summer. *310 Cottage Dr., Gatlinburg, 37738, tel. 423/436-5151 or 800/933-8675, fax 423/430-9171. 80 rooms, 2 villas. Facilities: 2 pools. AE, D, DC, MC, V. $$-$$$*

Hippensteal's Mountain View Inn. Wide double porches run the entire length of this secluded mountaintop B&B. Built in 1990, it was designed by one of the Smokies' best-known watercolorists, Vern Hippensteal, and the lobby is a virtual gallery of his works. Rooms have an eclectic feel: There are painted iron beds, floral wallcoverings, fireplaces framed by white marble,

well-lighted reading chairs, and whirlpool baths. White wicker furniture is scattered about a large lobby with a fireplace. *Grassy Branch Rd., Box 707, Gatlinburg 37738, tel. 423/436-5761 or 800/527-8110, fax 423/436-2354. 11 rooms. AE, D, MC, V. $$$*

Midtown Lodge. Chalet-style town houses are a favorite here: Each has a large stone fireplace, a loft bedroom with king-size bed, and a full bathroom tucked under cathedral ceilings. Downstairs is a kitchen and sofa bed. Other options in this heart-of-downtown hotel include poolside rooms, luxury rooms, suites, and efficiencies. The hotel has a small gift mall, so there's plenty of bustle just outside the door. Rooms in the newer, quieter Tower Building are large and have microwaves, small refrigerators, and balconies overlooking the Little Pigeon River and the surrounding mountains. Some accommodations have whirlpool baths. *805 Parkway, Gatlinburg 37738, tel. 423/436-5691 or 800/633-2446, fax 423/430-3602. 133 rooms. Facilities: pool. AE, D, DC, MC, V. $$-$$$*

NEAR THE PARK: ELSEWHERE IN TENNESSEE

Inn at Blackberry Farm. One of the most outstanding small properties in the South, if not the country, this inn is an elegant retreat. A sprawling white house, a large guest house, and eight cottages crown a hilltop surrounded by natural beauty—lawns, meadows, forests, streams, and the Smoky Mountains—on a 1,100-acre estate near Walland, which is 17 mi west of Gatlinburg. Luxurious rooms have exquisite antiques and artwork. The main lodge and guest house have a great room with a fireplace and comfortable furnishings as well as a TV/VCR, library of videos, games, CDs, books, binoculars, and bird and wildflower guides. Guest rooms don't have TVs or telephones, but you will find fluffy robes, feather beds, and down comforters. Included in the room rate are three meals a day, afternoon tea, and sports. Conference facilities and a spa are scheduled to open in 1998. *1471 W. Millers Cove, Walland 37886, tel. 423/984-8166 or 800/862-7610, fax 423/681-7753. 26 rooms, 16 suites in 8 cot-*

tages. Facilities: pool, lake, hot tub, putting green, 4 tennis courts, boccie, croquet, hiking, horseshoes, jogging, Ping-Pong, shuffleboard, softball, volleyball, boating, fishing, bicycles, mountain bikes. AE, MC, V. $$$

Wonderland Hotel. Clinging to a freshly cleared mountainside 13 mi north of Gatlinburg, this sprawling lodge re-creates the rustic appeal of the time-worn original Wonderland Hotel, rough-sawn knotty-pine exterior and all. Some of the old lodge's rocking chairs and swings line the 165-ft porch, which has a spectacular view of Cove Mountain and a constant breeze, but the latest Wonderland incarnation has some weathering to do. An exposed cinderblock foundation doesn't help, and rooms are furnished with reproduction antiques that seem strangely out of character with the rustic interiors. There are no TVs or phones in rooms. *3889 Wonderland Way, Sevierville 37862, tel. 423/436–5490 or 423/428–0779, fax 423/429–4752. 29 rooms, 2 cabins. Facilities: restaurant. Closed early Dec.–early Apr., except New Year's Eve weekend. AE, D, MC, V. $$*

CAMPING

The wild backcountry of the park is an acclaimed backpacker's paradise: More than 800 mi of trails climb forested summits, cross open grassy balds, and plunge into mist-shrouded valleys. You can register for most sites at any visitor center or ranger station; other sites, including all Appalachian Trail shelters, are rationed due to heavy use and require telephone registration via the **Backcountry Reservation Office** (tel. 423/436–1231). Reserve these sites, daily 8 AM–6 PM, at least a month in advance. Free backcountry permits, available through the Backcountry Reservation Office, are required for overnight stays in the 100 backcountry campsites and 18 trail shelters.

INSIDE THE PARK There are 997 campsites at 10 Park Service campgrounds; sites cost $10–$15 per night. Some are large complexes; others are tiny little nooks scattered about a creek; still others are tucked under the boughs of high-elevation spruce-fir forests. Advance reservations for campsites are taken only at Elkmont, Cades Cove, and Smokemont campgrounds from mid-May through October, and for any group campsite. All other park campgrounds are operated on a first-come, first-served basis. There are no electrical hookups, water hookups, or showers at any of the Park Service campgrounds, but all have cold running water, fire grills, picnic tables, and flush toilets. For family-oriented activities and accessibility to ranger stations and interpretive programs, Cades Cove, Elkmont, and Smokemont campgrounds are your best bets. Big Creek, Cataloochee, and Abrams Creek offer the most solitude. Contact or stop by any of the park's visitor centers (*see above*) before you set out for the campgrounds listed below, none of which can be phoned directly.

Abrams Creek. Trailers are limited to 12 ft at this campground. *Off Hwy. 129 and the Foothills Pkwy W. 16 sites. Closed Nov.–late Mar. $*

Balsam Mountain. Remote Balsam Mountain has the highest elevation of the 10 campgrounds. There is wood for sale here. *Off Heintooga Rd. and the Blue Ridge Pkwy. 25 sites. Closed late-Oct.–mid-May. $*

Big Creek. This campground is in the northeast corner of the park. *Off TN 32. 12 tent sites. Closed Nov.–late Mar. $*

Cades Cove. There's a disposal station, wood for sale, and a small grocery store here. *Off Laurel Creek Rd. 159 sites main season, 45 off-season. Facilities: bicycles. $*

Cataloochee. This campground is in the eastern part of the park. *Off Cove Creek Rd. 27 sites. Closed Nov.–late Mar. $*

Cosby. This campground has a disposal station. *Off Hwys. 321 and 32. 175 sites. Closed Nov.–late Mar. $*

Deep Creek. Deep Creek is near superb creek tubing and hiking; there's a disposal station and wood for sale on the premises. *Off Deep Creek Rd. near Bryson City, NC. 108 sites. Closed Nov.–early Apr. $*

Elkmont. Elkmont is the closest of the campgrounds to Gatlinburg. Wood is sold here and there's a disposal station nearby. *Little River Rd. west of the Sugarland Visitors Center. 220 sites main season, 29 in off-season. Closed Dec.–late Mar. $*

Look Rock. This campground is in the northwest corner of the park. *Off Foothills Pkwy W. 92 sites. Closed Nov.–mid-May. $*

Smokemont. Smokemont is the closest campground to Cherokee. It has a disposal station and wood for sale. *Newfound Gap Rd., 5 mi north of Cherokee. 140 sites main season, 35 off-season. $*

NEAR THE PARK Commercial campgrounds are clustered at the primary park entrances at Cherokee in North Carolina, and Gatlinburg and Townsend in Tennessee.

Yogi-in-the-Smokies. This is one of several large, popular campgrounds that cater to RVs. Of the 250 sites, 22 have full hookups, 218 have water and electricity, and 10 are primitive. All sites are heavily wooded; some are on the river. There's a general store here. *Star Rte., Box 54, Cherokee, NC 28719, tel. 704/497–9151. 250 sites. Facilities: recreation room, playground, coin laundry. D, MC, V. Closed late Oct.–Mar. $*

Cherokee KOA Campground. This large KOA campground caters mainly to RVs. Of the 283 sites, 200 are RV sites, 75 are tent sites, and 8 are primitive. Sites are lightly wooded and shady. *Star Rte., Box 39, Cherokee, NC 28719, tel. 704/497–9711 or 800/825–8357. 283 sites, 150 camping cabins. Facilities: café, pool, hot tub, lighted tennis court, shuffleboard, volleyball, fishing, recreation room, playground, coin laundry. MC, V. Closed Dec.–Feb. $*

Ela Campground RV Park and Grocery. Halfway between Cherokee and Bryson City, on U.S. 19, Ela packs RVs in close, but it's a superclean, well-maintained camp-ground with friendly owners and 33 pull-through sites. Flower beds are maintained by the "seasonal residents." Bonuses are a mile-long walking trail, river access and tube rentals, an LP tank repair facility, and more than 1,000 movies for rent. The store's creaky wooden floors and board-and-batten exterior are reminiscent of an old country store. Inside is a game room and a popcorn machine, in addition to picnic and camping staples. Of the 216 sites, 156 are RV sites and 60 are tent sites. All sites are heavily wooded. *5100 Ela Rd., Bryson City, NC 28713, tel. 704/488–2410. 216 sites, 6 motel rooms. Facilities: pool, recreation room, playground, coin laundry. MC, V. $*

Little River Village Campground. If convenience to facilities is a factor, or the park campgrounds are full, the tent sites in the "Riverwalk" section of Little Village rival park campgrounds for a pleasing woods setting and privacy. Just .2 mi from the park entrance, this campground has clean bathhouses, picnic tables with cement decks, inner-tube rentals, and complete hookups for RVs. Of the 135 sites, 67 are RV sites, 35 are tent sites, and 33 are primitive. All sites are heavily wooded; some are along the river. *8533 State Rte. 73, Townsend, TN 37882, tel. 423/448–2241 or 800/261–6370, fax 423/448–6052. 135 sites, 4 cabins. Facilities: deli, pool, recreation room, playground, coin laundry. AE, D, MC, V. Closed Dec.–Feb. $*

Deep Creek Tube Center Campground. Halfway between Bryson City and the park's Deep Creek entrance, this campground is a pleasant full-hookup RV facility. Rent inner tubes and ride the creek for 2.25 mi back to the campground. Sites are lightly wooded and shady. Since the campground is small, reservations are strongly suggested. *1090 W. Deep Creek Rd., Box 105, Bryson City, NC 28713, tel. 704/488–6055. 26 sites, 3 cabins. Facilities: playground, coin laundry. D, MC, V. Closed Nov.–Mar. $*

Green Mountain National Forest
Vermont

By Tara Hamilton

Updated by Kay and William Scheller

lthough they possess neither the craggy pitch of New Hampshire's White Mountains nor the rugged wilderness expanse of New York's Adirondacks, Vermont's Green Mountains work their own potent magic. Surging and swelling rather than slicing and jutting, they are mountains of wisdom and subtle elegance, asserting a modest grandeur. The landscape and wildlife are as richly diverse as the mountains are old. Just beyond the next rise might be a great blue heron standing nimbly beside a shimmering pond, the engineering marvel of a beaver dam, a cool stand of towering eastern hemlock, or a pair of awkwardly beautiful moose.

The mountains, although themselves rounded and softened with age, display the stark contrasts of the seasons. The sumptuous verdant tones of summer illustrate how the mountains got their name, while autumn's harvest is a vibrant palette of color known worldwide. Winter, both exquisite and ruthless, can cover the forest floor with hushed, deep snows or strand you in a nasty blizzard. Spring flourishes with new growth and a brilliant display of wildflowers.

One of more than 155 national forests, Green Mountain is divided into northern and southern sections. Together they cover more than 350,000 acres and stretch across nearly two-thirds of the state's length. Over the past few centuries, the landscape has seen dramatic changes. In the mid-1800s, logging had reduced Vermont's forest cover to a mere 20%, and much of the cleared land was used for grazing sheep. By 1900, however, westward migration and a weakened economy left pastures abandoned and fields fallow. Gradually, through the natural succession of plant communities, the state has been reforested, and now 80% is woodland. Though the national forest is still used for timbering, the focus is primarily on recreational pursuits: camping, wildlife viewing, hunting, fishing, skiing, snowmobiling, and, of course, hiking.

The centerpiece of the national forest's extensive trail network is the Long Trail (LT), the oldest long-distance hiking trail in the country and the prototype for the Appalachian Trail (with which it coincides for about 100 mi). For 265 mi from Massachusetts to Canada, the LT balances on the north–south central ridgeline—the spine of the Green Mountains—traversing 142 mi of the national forest and connecting with 175 mi of side trails. It's maintained cooperatively by the United States Forest Service and the Green Mountain Club, a nonprofit organization founded in 1910 and devoted to maintaining this "footpath in the wilderness."

As national parks and forests continue to attract more and more outdoor enthusiasts, the Green Mountain National Forest has managed to maintain a sense of solitude and peacefulness in six wilderness areas, comprising almost 60,000 acres. The result of the National Wilderness Preservation Act of 1964, these areas differ from the rest of the forest in their designated purpose: to provide large blocks of mature and old-growth trees for wildlife in need of undisturbed habitat and to offer visitors, lured only by the song of the birds and a sense of adventure, a chance to experience the remoteness and beauty of the deep woods.

ESSENTIAL INFORMATION

VISITOR INFORMATION For information about the national forest, contact the forest supervisor, **Green Mountain National Forest** (231 N. Main St., Rutland 05701, tel. 802/747–6700, TTY 802/747–6765). For information on specific regions, contact the **Manchester Ranger District** (Rte. 11/30, R.R. 1, Box 1940, Manchester Center 05255, tel. 802/362–2307), **Middlebury Ranger District** (U.S. 7, R.D. 4, Box 1260, Middlebury 05753, tel. 802/388–6688), or **Rochester Ranger District** (Rte. 100, R.D. 1, Box 108, Rochester 05767, tel. 802/767–4261, TTY 802/767–4261).

The National Forest **Web site** is www .gorp.com/gorp/resource/us_national_forest/ vt.green.htm.

Contact the **Green Mountain Club, Inc.** (Rte. 100, R.R. 1, Box 650, Waterbury Center 05677, tel. 802/244–7037) for information on the Long Trail. The **Appalachian Trail Conference** (Box 807, Harpers Ferry, WV 25425, tel. 304/535–6331) has info about the Appalachian Trail. The **Vermont Department of Forests, Parks, and Recreation** (Agency of Natural Resources, 103 S. Main St., Waterbury 05671, tel. 802/241–3655) can tell you about state parks. Contact the **Vermont Chamber of Commerce** (Box 37, Montpelier 05601, tel. 802/223–3443) or **Vermont Department of Tourism and Marketing** (134 State St., Montpelier 05602, tel. 802/828–3237 or 800/837–6668) for other Vermont travel information.

FEES There are no entrance fees for the national forest, although state parks and some recreation areas within its boundaries do charge admission for day use. Fees are also charged at the following staffed shelters and tenting areas: Battell, Skyline

Lodge, Peru Peak, Lula Tye, Little Rock Pond, Griffith Lake, and Stratton Pond.

PUBLICATIONS An assortment of maps, pamphlets, and fact sheets covering an array of areas and topics—from day hikes and interpretive trails accessible to people who use wheelchairs to the latest moose management plan—is available from the forest service by mail or at any of the ranger district offices (*see* Visitor Information, *above*). Maps and brochures can also be obtained at state park visitor centers. For in-depth explanations of the myriad trails in the Green Mountains, pick up a copy of *Day Hiker's Guide to Vermont* or *The Long Trail Guide,* both put out by the Green Mountain Club (available in bookstores). *The Guide to the Appalachian Trail in New Hampshire and Vermont* is available from the Appalachian Trail Conference (*see* Visitor Information, *above*).

GEOLOGY AND TERRAIN In a number of episodes that occurred approximately 400 million years ago, massive continental and oceanic plates collided slowly but steadily, pushing up the earth's crust along a line roughly parallel to the East Coast. The result was the Appalachians, of which the Green Mountains are a part. The metamorphic rocks produced during the collision—greenstone, quartzite, gneiss, and the most common, schist—can be seen cropping out in numerous places, especially atop some of the higher peaks.

As a result of the east–west movement of the tectonic plates, the Green Mountains are oriented in three long, parallel north–south ranges. The first, or front, range includes the Hogbacks and Taconics in the western portion of the state. To the east, the second, or main, range has most of the taller peaks and is often thought of as Vermont's spine. The third range, including the Northfields and Worcesters east of Route 100, are in the state's middle-to-northern half and not within the national forest.

The Green Mountains' other great reshaping occurred during the most recent ice age, from 3 million to 10,000 years ago. Sheets of glacial ice up to 2 mi thick gouged and scraped at the mountains. When the glaciers retreated, they left behind a mishmash of boulders, rocks, pebbles, sand, and clay called till. The scouring action of the ice is largely responsible for the subtlety of the Greens: gentle, rounded peaks; broad, sloping valleys; and the sprinkling of mountain ponds and lakes.

FLORA AND FAUNA Most of the Green Mountains are covered by northern hardwood forests, in which sugar maple, American beech, and yellow birch predominate. Higher elevations, between 2,400 and 3,000 ft, are covered by a transitional forest that consists mainly of yellow and white birch and red spruce. Above 3,000 ft, red spruce and balsam fir dominate the landscape.

There is very little old-growth forest left in the Green Mountains due to the heavy logging and clearing of the 19th century, but just as forests have reemerged in the last 100 years, so too have several animal species previously driven from the state. Coyotes, pine marten, beavers, and moose have restaked their claim; in fact, moose have proliferated enough that a controversial hunting season was recently instituted. These species join the white-tailed deer, black bear, red fox, snowshoe hare, and bobcat as some of the national forest's larger mammals.

Also staging a comeback, with the help of a recovery plan formulated in 1979, is the peregrine falcon, endangered since the 1960s by the use of several "long-lived" pesticides, including DDT. Efforts to hatch and raise young peregrines in captivity and then release them in the wild have been successful; for the past several years small populations have been returning to the cliffs of Mt. Horrid each spring to nest (there's an observation site adjacent to Vermont Route 73).

The U.S. Forest Service subscribes to a management plan that includes various methods of logging for equally various purposes: providing a diverse wildlife habitat, maintaining open areas for viewing animals, enhancing berry-bush growth, and, of course, producing high-quality timber for profit, which in turn helps promote and protect local jobs. The grassy clearings and heterogeneous forests that result provide good habitats for a majority of the 323 wildlife species, which require a mix of nonwooded areas and young forests for many of their activities.

WHEN TO GO The best and most popular time for venturing into the woods on foot is mid-June through October. Excursions in mid-April to late May, also known as mud season, will likely result in serious confrontations with snowmelt mire. In fact, hiking is discouraged on many trails at higher elevations until Memorial Day to prevent excessive erosion. More likely to be the bane of a spring sojourn, however, are the bugs: Mosquitoes and blackflies can be downright ferocious until mid- or late June, enough to intimidate even the most seasoned backpacker.

Whether you're on foot or in your car, crowds are not usually an issue except during peak foliage season, when the number of "leaf peepers" can be more than a bit disconcerting and accommodations hard to come by. If you can withstand the hordes, though, the astounding explosion of colors makes this an exceptional time to visit.

With snowfall often beginning as early as late October and lasting into April, winters are long, but there's certainly no shortage of outdoor recreational opportunities. Cross-country and downhill skiing, snowmobiling and snowshoeing, and, for the heartiest of souls, winter camping are all exceedingly popular. The tranquillity of winter in the woods, though alluring, should be approached with prudence, given the possibility of hypothermia and frostbite.

SEASONAL EVENTS **Summer:** The **Vermont Department of Forests, Parks, and Recreation** helps sponsor an annual summer arts and entertainment series in state parks near the national forest (*see* Evening Activities *in* Exploring, *below*). **July:** The **Manchester Hildene Antiques Festival** (tel.

802/362–1788) is held on the grounds of the estate of Abraham Lincoln's son, Tod. **Late Aug.:** Killington and 40 surrounding towns host the **Killington Stage Race** (tel. 802/621–6887) for amateur and professional bicyclists.

WHAT TO PACK Although the Northeast may seem tame compared to the more rugged West, don't be lulled into complacency by the lack of towering peaks, grizzly bears, or unrelenting sun. The Green Mountains have their own temperament, and weather is weather no matter where you are. Unless you're only venturing on a very short hike, always carry provisions for cold and wet—even in summer. Bring good rain gear, and be sure to layer clothing made of wool, silk, or a synthetic material that wicks moisture well, such as polypropylene. In addition to standard hiking gear (e.g., sunscreen, pocketknife, maps), pack some high-energy food for extended excursions, and never hike without an adequate water supply (*see* Staying Healthy and Safe *and* Hiking and Camping Equipment *in the* Essential Information *chapter*). Sturdy walking shoes or hiking boots are a must, and if your plans include some porch sitting, bring a couple of good books.

GENERAL STORES In the south, the **Three Mountain Grocery** (Rte. 100), north of Jamaica, will fulfill food and other shopping needs, as will the larger grocery stores, pharmacies, and sport shops in Bennington, Manchester, Londonderry, and Wilmington. Bondville's **Winhall Market** (Rte. 30) carries choice meats, cheeses, and other picnic fixings. The **Newfane Country Store** (Rte. 30), in historic Newfane village, has been offering a wide range of high-quality goods, from Vermont-made food products to handcrafted gifts and toys, for 120 years.

Rimming the northern section of the forest, small mom-and-pop grocery stores in Pittsfield, Stockbridge, Rochester, and Hancock provide such basics as toothpaste and picnic supplies. Head for the **Warren Store** (just off Rte. 100) in Warren for savory baked goods, ingredients for a gourmet meal in the woods, or its good selection of wines and newspapers; the emporium upstairs rivals some big-city boutiques. For more serious shopping, Waitsfield and Middlebury proffer **Grand Union supermarkets** (Rte. 100 and U.S. 7, respectively) and a variety of sporting goods and hardware stores. If you're stocking up for camping or backpacking, stop in the **Bristol Market** (28 North St., Bristol) or the **Natural Food Coop** (1 Washington St., Middlebury) for bulk goods and other munchies.

ATMS You'll find cash machines in the following towns on or near the national forest: Bennington, Brattleboro, Wilmington, Manchester, Ludlow, Rutland, Brandon, Middlebury, and Waitsfield.

ARRIVING AND DEPARTING The most practical means of reaching your destination in the Green Mountain National Forest is by car. Most trailheads and campsites are a fair distance from public transportation, though buses access some trailheads near major crossroads.

By Bus. In addition to providing limited access to trailheads, **Vermont Transit Lines** (tel. 802/864–6811 or 800/451–3292; 800/642–3133 in VT) connects Bennington, Brattleboro, Burlington, Rutland, and other cities in Vermont with Boston, Springfield (Massachusetts), Albany, New York City, Montréal, and cities in New Hampshire. Call for information regarding particular drop-off points.

By Car and RV. Meandering their way along both the southern and northern sections of the Green Mountain National Forest, U.S. 7 and Route 100, on the western and eastern edges of the forest, respectively, make much of the area quite accessible. Several east–west roads cross the forest, some of which afford views worth the grumbling protests issued from your struggling vehicle. In the south, Route 9, otherwise known as the Molly Stark Trail, connects Bennington and Wilmington and passes by the trailhead for the George D. Aiken Wilderness. Route 140 passes through Wallingford, the northern boundary of the southern section, and accesses the White Rocks National Recreation Area. U.S. 4 heads from the New York border past Rutland, the southern boundary of the forest's northern section, and the Pico and Killington ski areas. Route 125 passes by the Robert Frost Interpretive Trail and near the Breadloaf Wilderness, while the Lincoln Gap Road and Route 17, heading over the Appalachian Gap, access northern areas of the national forest.

Enterprise (tel. 800/736–8222) will meet patrons at all Vermont Amtrak and bus stations. **Thrifty Car Rental** (tel. 802/863–5500) will also meet renters at Amtrak and bus stations.

Most major rental car companies have counters at Burlington International Airport, including **Avis** (tel. 802/864–0411 or 800/831–2847) and **Hertz** (tel. 802/864–7409 or 800/654–3131).

By Plane. Burlington International Airport (tel. 802/863–2874) is served by several major airlines, and smaller companies fly into the **Rutland, Springfield, Barre-Montpelier,** and **Stowe-Morrisville** airports. West of Bennington and convenient to southern Vermont, **Albany-Schenectady County Airport** in New York State is also served by several major carriers.

By Train. Amtrak's (tel. 800/872–7245) *Vermonter* runs from Washington, D.C., to St. Albans, Vermont, with numerous stops en route, including New York City; Hartford, Connecticut; Springfield, Massachusetts; and White River Junction and Burlington, Vermont. The *Ethan Allen* connects New York City and Rutland, Vermont, with stops including Albany and Saratoga Springs, New York.

EXPLORING

The forest is well served by a combination of state highways and national forest roads, but it's outside your car's confines that you can best appreciate the beauty of the place. With 512 mi of hiking trails winding through the forest, leg power is ultimately the best way to experience the Green Mountains.

THE BEST IN ONE DAY If you've only got one day to take it all in, you'll need a car and some energy. Start with a sumptuous breakfast at one of the many country inns or bed-and-breakfasts in southwestern Vermont. Then—preferably with picnic provisions stowed in a cooler—head east from Arlington on the Kelley Stand Road (also called the Arlington–West Wardsboro Road and Forest Road 6) for quick entry into the backwoods. At the 12-mi mark, turn right into the Grout Pond Recreation Area (*see* Nature Trails and Short Walks, *below*), where you'll find easy hiking trails and opportunities for fishing, taking a dip, or paddling a canoe. (You can rent in Arlington or at nearby Stratton Mountain Village.) If you'd like to see the forest without putting on hiking boots, try it on the back of a horse. Trail rides are offered at the Stratton Mountain Ski Area (*see* Horseback Riding *in* Other Activities, *below*).

After exploring the area, continue east to West Wardsboro and head north on Route 100. Take your time enjoying the mountain scenery and the villages of Jamaica, Peru (just off Rte. 100), and Weston. Take a break at the peaceful Weston Priory (.1 mi north of junction of Rtes. 100 and 155), a Benedictine monastery that welcomes respectful visitors. Time for lunch? Pick up picnic provisions at the general store in Peru or Jamaica or the cheese shop in Weston.

After lunch, continue north on Route 100 for a meandering 50-mi foray through the heart of central Vermont, stopping to gaze across any of the lakes or rivers along the way. Turn left on Route 125 in Hancock and, after 3 mi, right into the Texas Falls Recreation Area. There's a delightful 1.2-mi loop nature trail that meanders along Hancock Branch, which has gouged a small chasm out of the surrounding rock. Continue west on Route 125 up to the top of Middlebury Gap, where you can access the Long Trail. A .5-mi hike to the south brings you to Lake Pleiad, one of the highest lakes in the state.

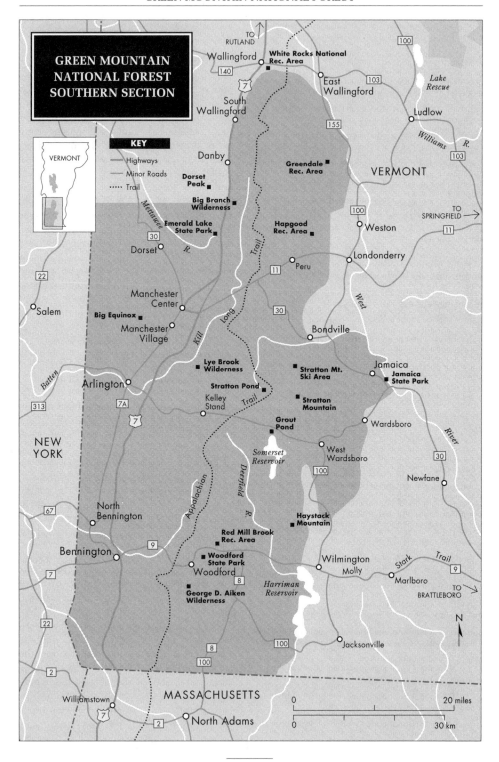

GREEN MOUNTAIN
NATIONAL FOREST
SOUTHERN SECTION

VERMONT

KEY

Highways
Minor Roads
Trail

TO
RUTLAND

Wallingford

White Rocks National
Rec. Area

140

7

South
Wallingford

East
Wallingford

103

Lake
Rescue

155

Ludlow

Williams R.

103

Danby

Dorset
Peak

Big Branch
Wilderness

Emerald Lake
State Park

30

Dorset

Mettawee R.

Greendale
Rec. Area

VERMONT

Hapgood
Rec. Area

100

Weston

TO
SPRINGFIELD

11

22

Salem

Manchester
Center

Big Equinox

Manchester
Village

Long Trail

Kill

Peru

11

30

Londonderry

West

Bondville

Batten

Arlington

313

7A

7

Lye Brook
Wilderness

Stratton Pond

Kelley
Stand

Trail

Stratton Mt.
Ski Area

Stratton
Mountain

Grout
Pond

Jamaica

Jamaica
State Park

Wardsboro

River

NEW
YORK

67

North
Bennington

9

Bennington

7

22

Appalachian

Somerset
Reservoir

Deerfield R.

West
Wardsboro

100

Haystack
Mountain

Red Mill Brook
Rec. Area

Woodford
State Park

Woodford

8

George D. Aiken
Wilderness

Harriman
Reservoir

Wilmington

Molly

30

Newfane

Stark Trail

Marlboro

9

TO
BRATTLEBORO

N

Jacksonville

8

100

100

2

MASSACHUSETTS

Williamstown

7

2

North Adams

0   20 miles

0   30 km

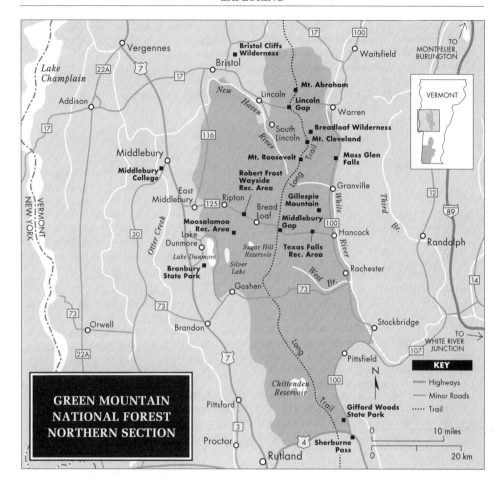

GREEN MOUNTAIN
NATIONAL FOREST
NORTHERN SECTION

Down the other side of the ridge, Route 125 passes through the historic Bread Loaf Campus of Middlebury College (*see* Historic Buildings and Sites, *below*) and past the Robert Frost Wayside and the Robert Frost Interpretive Trail (*see* Nature Trails and Short Walks, *below*). Here you can enjoy the gathering dusk while acquainting yourself with Frost's poems in the woods and fields that inspired him. Continue through the tiny hamlet of Ripton and on to East Middlebury, Middlebury, or Bristol for dinner in a fine restaurant and a well-deserved rest in one of the many B&Bs.

ORIENTATION PROGRAMS The **Vermont Youth Conservation Corps,** a nonprofit partner of the Department of Forests, Parks, and Recreation (*see* Visitor Information *in* Essential Information, *above*), sponsors **summer naturalist programs** at state parks, many of which are adjacent to the borders of the national forest. Programs include workshops or talks on such subjects as astronomy, natural history, and Native American and Early American crafts.

A few miles north of the national forest's northern section, the **Green Mountain Audubon Nature Center** (Huntington-Richmond Rd., R.D. 1, Box 189, Richmond 05477, tel. 802/434–4113) is bursting with great things to do, see, and learn and is a wonderful place to orient yourself, get comfortable in the woods, expand your knowledge, and pique your interest in the natural world. The center's 230 acres of diverse habitats are a sanctuary for wild things, and 5 mi of trails encourage the visitor, through trail maps and self-guiding materials, to explore and understand the workings of various natural communities. The center regularly offers events such as dusk walks, wildflower and birding rambles, nature workshops, and other community events and educational activities for both kids and adults.

GUIDED TOURS Hiking Holidays (Box 750, Bristol 05443, tel. 802/453–4816) runs hiking trips of varying lengths that combine learning about the natural world with the comforts and good food of cushy country inns. **Cycle Inn Vermont** (Box 243, Ludlow 05149, tel. 802/228–8799) will help you plan an inn-to-inn bicycling or walking vacation, making reservations and transporting baggage to any or all of their member inns. Tours generally last four to six days, and cyclists average 20–50 mi, but itineraries can be tailor-made. **Kedron Valley Stables** (*see* Other Activities, *below*) leads horseback trail rides. Contact **Green Mountain National Forest** (tel. 802/747–6700) for a complete list of outfitters and guided trips. You can request a free copy of "Vermont Traveler's Guidebook" from the **Vermont Chamber of Commerce** or the **Vermont Department of Tourism and Marketing** (*see* Vermont Information *in* Essential Information, *above*).

The **Vermont Department of Forests, Parks, and Recreation** (*see* Visitor Information *in* Essential Information, *above*) conducts guided nature walks and hikes as well as canoe and boat outings in the state parks.

SCENIC DRIVES AND VIEWS Following **Route 100** as it pokes in and out of the eastern edge of the national forest is as pleasurable as a country drive can get. You'll move through pastoral valleys, forested tunnel-like stretches, and quiet country villages of sparkling white houses with their obligatory green shutters. One particularly fine

section snakes through **Granville Gulf**: This "natural reservation" is free of human-built structures and is the origin of Mad River, which heads north, and White River, which runs south; it's also the origin of the 70-ft Moss Glen Falls.

As far as chin-dropping views go, it's hard to top those from the **Appalachian Gap,** the crest of **Route 17,** which connects the towns of Waitsfield and Bristol and skirts the forest's northern border. Crossing the Green Mountains' spine at the **Brandon, Middlebury,** and **Lincoln gaps,** also in the northern section, yields gorgeous serpentine drives. Due to the Lincoln Gap road's tight curves and steep grade, some might want to choose a less menacing route; it's closed at the Lincoln gap during the winter.

In the southern section, **Kelley Stand Road,** which reaches 2,726 ft on its beautifully subtle traverse of the forest, and **Forest Road 10** between Danby and Peru, immerse you in the solitude of the wilderness as much as is possible without your even getting out of the car.

HISTORIC BUILDINGS AND SITES On the hillside of Mt. Moosalamoo near Lake Dunmore is **Ethan Allen's Cave,** a huge hollowed-out boulder that is reputed to have been used as a hideout and storage spot by Vermont's favorite son and his Green Mountain Boys during the land-grant disputes between Colonial New Hampshire and New York, each of which claimed Vermont for its own. Although Vermont ultimately declared itself an independent nation, from 1776 to 1791, Allen and his cohorts diligently participated in the American Revolution by capturing Fort Ticonderoga, across Lake Champlain, without firing a shot. The cave is marked with a carving by the local chapter of the Daughters of the American Revolution. Follow the unmarked Ethan Allen Trail from the Falls of Lana on Route 53 to get to the cave.

Just to the east of the Robert Frost Wayside on the north side of Route 125 in Ripton is an unmarked road leading to the **Robert Frost Cabin,** which the poet used for 23 summers. It lures those who want to poke around his old haunts in hopes of absorbing the enchantment and solitude that no doubt inspired many of his poems. Now owned by Middlebury College, the site has been kept deliberately obscure to prevent the casual passerby from marring its tranquillity.

One-half mile to the east on Route 125 is the sprawl of mustard-yellow buildings that make up the **Bread Loaf Campus** of Middlebury College. The campus's veranda-and-flapping-screen-door country simplicity makes it look like a Shady Acres–type home, but that's the idea. For more than 70 years, these serene meadows, bordered by the national forest, have fostered aspiring writers attending the Bread Loaf School of English and the Bread Loaf Writers' Conference, started by Robert Frost.

NATURE TRAILS AND SHORT WALKS The **Robert Frost Interpretive Trail** (2 mi east of Ripton on Rte. 125) is an easy 1-mi loop through swamps, woods, and blueberry and huckleberry bushes. Plaques along the trail carry smatterings of his writings. The first .3 mi, which runs along a beaver pond, is accessible by wheelchair.

Seven miles to the east across the Middlebury Gap is the **Texas Falls Nature Trail** (3 mi west of Rte. 100 on Rte. 125), an easy 1.2-mi loop along the cascading Texas Brook. The trail begins just across a footbridge near the base of the falls.

A favorite easy hike to a dramatic spot is the one-hour, 1.5-mi round-trip jaunt to **Sunset Ledge.** From Lincoln Gap head south on the Long Trail. It climbs steeply at first, affording fine views to the east, and then levels off fairly quickly, revealing stunning panoramas of the Adirondacks and Lake Champlain to the west.

The **Grout Pond Recreation Area** (12 mi east of Arlington off Kelley Stand Rd.) maintains a series of pleasant, short loop trails totaling about 8 mi. They encircle Grout Pond and access the north end of nearby Somerset Reservoir.

Little Rock Pond, reached via the **Appalachian Trail/Long Trail** (AT/LT), is one of the most popular (i.e., heavily used) trails in the area. (Park in the lot on Forest Rd. 10, east of Mount Tabor on U.S. 7.) Loop back on the **Green Mountain Trail.** It's a moderate 5-mi round-trip hike to the pond.

The **Natural Bridge Trail** begins just west of U.S. 7 at the entrance to Emerald Lake State Park. It passes two old dams, veers right, and begins a short but steep and winding climb before descending to a natural rock bridge spanning a brook's narrow gorge. The round-trip is about 3 mi.

LONGER HIKES The spine of the Green Mountains' main ridge is the national forest's dominant feature, and the **AT/LT** that runs along it offers satisfying long-distance hikes. In addition, a whole network of side trails, some of them loops, provides plentiful options for climbing peaks or traversing the spine and returning to lower elevations. Pick up the AT/LT at any gap crossing and head north or south to the next one; these gap-to-gap jaunts can provide one to three or more days of backwoods repose. Arrange to leave a vehicle at your destination.

Southern Section. More trail networks offer a greater variety of loop options here than in the northern section. From U.S. 7, 2 mi north of Emerald Lake State Park, the **Lake Trail** follows an old carriage path that once brought folks from the valley to an inn on **Griffith Lake.** Two miles up the trail, turn left on the **Baker Peak Trail,** which ascends the peak, providing views of the valley and the marble quarries on Dorset Peak, and meets up with the AT/LT. Take the AT/LT south, back to the lake, and from there take the Lake Trail back to where you started. The whole trip is about 6 mi. For another loop in this area, start at Forest Road 10, just east of a suspension bridge, and take the AT/LT south to Griffith Lake. Return via the **Old Job Trail,** which runs northeast along several old logging roads, past an extensive clearing where the village of Griffith once stood (a shelter occupies the spot now), and back to Forest Road 10.

The **Stratton Pond** area, bounded by Route 11/30 in the north, Stratton Mountain in the east, the Kelley Stand Road in the south, and the Lye Brook Wilderness in the west, has an array of options for long day hikes or extended backpacking trips. Because several trails intersect, many combinations of routes and loops are possible; all are enjoyable, but crowded in the summer. What follows is only a sampling.

If you begin from Kelley Stand Road, you can choose from three northbound trails: the **Branch Pond Trail,** the **AT/LT,** and the **Stratton Mountain Trail** (the most strenuous). The latter two converge at Stratton Pond—the largest body of water on the AT/LT—where you can circle the pond before heading either north on the AT/LT or west toward **Bourne Pond.** There you can continue west into the Lye Brook Wilderness or take the Branch Pond Trail south, passing **Branch Pond** before returning to Kelley Stand Road. (Of course, you can also make the loop in a clockwise direction.)

For a different approach from the north, drive east on Route 11/30 from Manchester Center for 2.5 mi, and turn right on Rootville Road, following it a half-mile to its end, where there's limited parking. (Be careful not to obstruct private driveways.) Ascend about 2 mi along a flumelike stream to a junction with the AT/LT. About 200 ft east via the LT is **Prospect Rock,** an aptly named vantage point towering above Downer Glen, with an excellent view of Mt. Equinox, Dorset Mountain, and the valley below. To make a loop, walk south on the AT/LT about a mile to the Branch Pond Trail, from which you can pick up the Lye Brook Trail north. From its trailhead, just go east on the logging road to get back to your car.

Farther south, a good overnight hike begins from the Route 9 AT/LT parking lot. Hike north to **Glastenbury Mountain** (about 10 mi). You can camp at Goddard Shelter (a quarter mile from the mountain top). To return, take the Bald Mountain Trail to Bolles Brook Road, which will take you back to Route 9.

Northern Section. The summit of **Mt. Abraham** can be approached in two ways: heading north from the Lincoln Gap via the LT or heading east from a trailhead at the end of Mosley Road in the town of Lincoln via the **Battell Trail.** Mt. Abe's rocky summit, well above timberline, boasts some of the best views in the Green Mountains—the panoramic expanse of New York's Adirondacks to the west, the Greens' three ranges stretching to the north and south, and on a clear day, the White Mountains of New Hampshire 80 mi to the east. Either before or after being blown away by the 360° view, look down and take note of the summit's rare and fragile community of arctic-alpine vegetation. Be especially careful to protect this endangered plant life by staying on the marked trail or rock outcroppings when hiking above tree line.

A full-day 12.5-mi circuit into the heart of the **Breadloaf Wilderness**—at 58,000 acres, the largest of the six wilderness areas—begins and ends at the **Cooley Glen** trailhead (Forest Rd. 54 between South Lincoln and Ripton). The trail starts with a gentle climb, crosses a tributary of the New Haven River several times, and intersects the LT. Head south on the LT over the summits of Mts. Cleveland, Roosevelt, and Wilson (the latter two have terrific views to the south and east) before taking the **Emily Proctor Trail** back down to your starting point.

Appalachian Trail. The Appalachian Trail runs for 2,100 mi from Springer Mountain, Georgia, to Mt. Katahdin in Maine. Since it was modeled after the Long Trail, it's curious that today one of its least celebrated sections is the 136 mi in Vermont, including nearly 100 mi along the Long Trail.

From the Massachusetts border, the AT converges with the LT through hollows, brook crossings, and beaver ponds before gaining substantial elevation north of Route 9. It then makes its way across peaks and valleys, skirting Stratton Pond and the northern boundary of Lye Brook Wilderness. Griffith Lake, Little Rock Pond, and Spring Lake beckon the hiker to swim or picnic.

A half-mile north of Sherburne Pass on U.S. 4, the AT diverges from the LT and heads east. A mile later, it enters Gifford Woods State Park, with one of a handful of virgin hardwood stands in Vermont. Next the AT crosses Route 100 and leaves the national forest; for much of the rest of its way in Vermont, it passes along old logging roads and still-used "town highways." (More than half of Vermont's roads are gravel, so it's not surprising that some are designated highways of sorts.) The intrepid traveler may find this part of the AT lacking in awe-inspiring views and challenging terrain, but those looking for gentle hiking options along tranquil backcountry roads will find it pleasant and steeped in the spirit of New England.

OTHER ACTIVITIES **Back-Road Driving.** In addition to those already mentioned, a host of forest roads provide backcountry access. In the southern section, **Forest Road 71,** whose scenery is well worth the rough ride, connects Kelley Stand Road with Somerset Road, Somerset Reservoir, and Route 9. In the northern section, **Forest Road 42** (Bingo Road), off Route 73, is a wooded road. **Forest Road 55,** near Granville, follows the White River's headwaters and gets well up Gillespie Mountain. **Forest Road 32** (Ripton–Goshen Road) runs north–south along the western edge of the mountains' spine and has several scenic spots; a side trip leads to Voter Brook overlook, where you can see to the Adirondacks. Near Forest Road 32's terminus, **Forest Road 224** heads east into open expanses. Several back roads between Lincoln and Ripton, including **Lincoln–Ripton Road, Forest Road 59,** and **Forest Road 54** (Natural Turnpike), are ideal for exploring the woods.

Biking. Thanks to its quiet backcountry roads, rolling countryside, quintessential New England towns, and friendly people, Vermont teems with cyclists during warm weather. They range from muddy, single-track mountain-bike racers to pampered inn-to-inn tour guests. Since the national forest covers the state's hilliest terrain, cyclists should be prepared to sweat at least a little.

Given the shortage of paved roads in the national forest, pedaling on a sturdy mountain bike or hybrid is your best bet. All of the roads listed above under Back-Road Driving are excellent choices. The **Woodford** area, south of Route 9 off Forest Road 273, has an extensive network of ridable roads, and the **Green Peak** area, north of Manchester off Dorset Hill Road, has some challenging rides up to a couple of abandoned quarries. **Forest Roads 25** and **55,** off Route 100 between Warren and Granville, and **Forest Roads 60, 30,** and **279,** off Forest Road 10 between Danby and Peru, access old logging roads and hefty climbs; they're perfect for getting you and your bike as grungy as your soul desires. Please note, however, that none of the trails off these roads are open to mountain bikes.

For those on road bikes, there are countless options just outside the forest's borders. Pick up a copy of *25 Bicycle Rides in Vermont,* by John Friedin (Backcountry Publications), for suggestions.

The **Mad River Bike Shop** (Rte. 100/17, Waitsfield, tel. 802/496–9500) and **Green Mountain Bicycle Service** (Rte. 100, Rochester, tel. 802/767–4464) rent and repair bikes and provide maps and information.

Cycle Inn Vermont (*see* Guided Tours, *above*) leads inn-to-inn tours.

Bird-Watching. With at least 150 species living in and around the national forest, there are plenty of birds overhead. Among them are seven species of hawk, eight sparrows, five owls (including the great horned and long-eared), and at least 15 varieties of warbler. Keep an eye out for nesting loons on quiet, undeveloped ponds, and for turkey vultures and the recently reintroduced peregrine falcon on cliffs at higher elevations. Spring and autumn offer the added bonus of migratory species, the honking of Canada or snow geese flying in formation.

The **Vermont Institute of Natural Science** (Church Hill Rd., R.R. 2, Box 532, Woodstock 05091, tel. 802/457–2779), a nonprofit organization dedicated to environmental education and research, hosts a variety of bird-related workshops and talks, including banding demonstrations. Its **Raptor Center** provides top-quality medical care and rehabilitation for injured birds of prey, with the goal of releasing them into the wild. Permanently disabled birds are kept in spacious habitats accessible to visitors.

Boating. Boating in and around the national forest is best pursued in the southern section, as it has several large lakes and ponds: **Grout Pond** and **Hapgood Pond** are ideal for canoeing; **Somerset, Harriman,** and **Adams reservoirs** are larger bodies of water that have boat launches. Northern options include **Chittenden Reservoir,** east of Pittsford off U.S. 7; **Silver Lake** (which has a mile-long carry from a parking lot); and **Sugar Hill Reservoir,** accessed by Forest Road 32. Canoeing down the **White River** along Route 100 is a popular pastime, too.

Umiak Outfitters (Rte. 100, 849 S. Main St., Lower Village, Stowe, tel. 802/253–2317 or 800/421–5268) has a retail shop and offers customized instruction and tours, including day trips and longer excursions. **Batten Kill Canoe Ltd.** (Rte. 7A, between Manchester and Arlington, tel. 802/362–2800) is a complete paddler's shop with rentals, sales, lessons, tours, and a shuttle service.

Cross-Country Skiing. The 280-mi **Catamount Trail** runs the length of the state on old logging roads, groomed cross-country trails, and snowmobile trails and passes through more than 20 ski-touring centers and by many inns and B&Bs. Much of it traverses the national forest. The **Catamount Trail Association** (Box 1235, 1 Main St., Burlington 05401, tel. 802/864–5794) provides maps and information for self-guided skiing and sponsors guided trips ranging

from day tours on gentle terrain to longer, more challenging backcountry tours. Other trail networks can be found just north of the **Moosalamoo Campground** (near Goshen on Forest Rd. 32), at **Chittenden Brook Campground** (off Rte. 73), and at **Grout Pond Recreation Area** (off Kelley Stand Rd.).

Caroll and Jane Rikert Ski Touring Center (Rte. 125, Ripton, tel. 802/388–2759) has 50 km of varied machine-tracked trails that meander through the forest; instruction, rentals, and repairs are provided. **Blueberry Hill Inn** (Ripton–Goshen Rd., Goshen, tel. 802/247–6735), in the heart of the national forest, has 75 km of trails, 50 of them machine tracked; instruction; rentals; repairs; and dining and lodging in the adjacent country inn. Though outside the national forest, **Camel's Hump Nordic Ski Center** (Handy Rd., R.D. 1, Box 422, Huntington, tel. 802/434–2704) has the most spectacular setting of any Vermont ski center. It's worth the few extra miles to get here. In the foothills under the shadow of the Green Mountains' most distinguished peak, it has 65 km of trails, 40 of which are machine tracked; instruction; rentals; and repairs on premises. **Hermitage Cross-Country Ski Area** (Coldbrook Rd., Box 457, Wilmington, tel. 802/464–3511) has 50 km of trails, 40 of them machine tracked, including a ridge-top trail with spectacular views of the Mt. Snow valley. Instruction, rental, repairs, and excellent dining and lodging in the fine inn are also available.

Fishing. Vermont has ample angling opportunities in mountain streams and undeveloped lakes and ponds. Their limestone bottoms have helped spare them the destruction acid rain wrought on the waters of the nearby Adirondacks. Brook and rainbow trout, landlocked salmon, yellow perch, northern pike, bass, bullhead, and panfish are common catches.

In the southern section, the **Batten Kill,** the state's most well-known trout stream, originates above Dorset and flows for about 25 miles through Manchester and Arlington before emptying into the Hudson River in

New York. Despite many years of heavy fishing, the river's consistently cool waters yield quality brown and brook trout. Access is from Route 313 and River Road just south of Manchester. If you're looking for good backwoods fishing, head for **Stratton, Branch,** or **Bourne Pond** (*see* Longer Hikes, *above*). The nearby **Somerset** and **Harriman reservoirs** offer boating access to both warm- and cold-water species.

Pickings are a bit slimmer in the northern section, although there are many small trout streams with great fish. **Lake Dunmore,** 4 mi long and just west of the forest, produced the state's record rainbow trout. The **Chittenden Reservoir** and beautiful walk-in ponds along the LT have good fishing as well.

The **Vermont Fish and Wildlife Department** (103 S. Main St., Waterbury 05676, tel. 802/241–3700 or 802/241–3703) can supply license applications, a pamphlet outlining fish and wildlife laws, and a list of organizations that provide guided fishing trips. Licenses, required of anyone 15 or older, can also be purchased at local sporting goods and general stores as well as many town clerks' offices.

There are many stores near the forest that supply fishing equipment. Among them is **Bisbee Hardware** (Mad River Green, tel. 802/496–3635).

Horseback Riding. Stratton Stables (behind the base lodge at Stratton Mountain, tel. 802/297–2200) offers mountain trail rides in the national forest. **Icelandic Horse Farm** (Common Rd., Waitsfield, tel. 802/496–7141) offers trail rides. **Firefly Ranch** (R.D. 1, Quaker Rd., Box 152, Bristol, tel. 802/453–2223), a year-round B&B, offers an equestrian package to its guests as well as trail rides for intermediate and expert riders by reservation only. **Kedron Valley Stables** (Box 368, Rte. 106, South Woodstock 05071, tel. 802/457–2734) leads trail rides and can provide information on the weekend or weeklong **Inn-to-Inn Tours** for riders of intermediate or expert ability.

Rope and Rock Climbing. Due to the soft nature of a lot of the rock in the Green Mountains, climbing opportunities are limited. However, if the need to get vertical overwhelms you, contact **Climb High** (U.S. 7, South Burlington, tel. 802/985–5055), where you can buy or rent equipment, use an indoor climbing wall, or get tips on where to find some solid rock.

Snowmobiling. Nearly 2,000 mi of groomed snowmobile corridors and 1,500 mi of secondary trails run along designated unplowed roads and trails as part of an extensive statewide system, developed and maintained by the **Vermont Association of Snow Travelers** (V.A.S.T.; Box 839, Montpelier 05601, tel. 802/229–0005). Within the national forest, snowmobiling is permitted only on these trails, which are marked on the Winter Recreation Map, available at district ranger offices.

Snowshoeing. The trails and roads listed in previous sections are also great choices for winter use, provided you know what you're doing. If you're not entirely comfortable in the woods in the winter, stick to shorter, easier trails close to roads; always carry extra food and clothing and notify others of your whereabouts. The **Valley of the Mad River** (Box 871, Waitsfield 05673, tel. 888/445–3766), an association of lodging places, has developed an extensive network of snowshoeing trails. Many ski centers (*see* Cross-Country Skiing, *above*) rent snowshoes.

Swimming. Just jump in! There are plenty of places to get your feet wet in the national forest. Most of the rivers in and around the forest, including the **White, Mad,** and **West rivers** and the **Batten Kill,** have many a swimming hole. Or try a recreation area: **Grout Pond,** a popular unsupervised swimming and canoeing spot, or **Hapgood Pond** (*see* Camping, *below*), where for a fee you get a full-fledged camping and day-use area with toilets.

Other local favorites include **Bartlett's Falls** (off Rtes. 17 and 116, Lincoln), famous for its numerous cascading pools, and a good **swimming hole** at the edge of East Middlebury (near Rte. 125 bridge, where the road begins to climb).

■CHILDREN'S PROGRAMS■ The national forest doesn't sponsor activities for kids, but many of the state parks' evening events and nature programs are suitable for children (*see* Evening Activities, *below, and* Orientation Programs, *above*). The **Green Mountain Audubon Nature Center** (*see* Orientation Programs, *above*) holds several ecology day-camp sessions as well as preschool programs.

■EVENING ACTIVITIES■ The Vermont Department of Forests, Parks, and Recreation offers **campfire programs** in the state parks. Along with the Vermont Council on the Arts and the Vermont Youth Conservation Corps, the organization sponsors the **Summer Series,** an arts and entertainment program. Performances and workshops, which have included fables, storytelling, puppetry, and folk and jazz music, are hosted at selected state parks bordering the national forest. Shows, for which there's no additional charge, generally begin at 7. Contact the Department of Forests, Parks, and Recreation (*see* Visitor Information *in* Essential Information, *above*) for dates and locations.

DINING

■SOUTHERN SECTION■ Because of the large number of former city dwellers turned innkeepers and restaurant owners, as well as the presence of the New England Culinary Institute in Montpelier, dining in and around the Green Mountain National Forest is about as varied as that in more populated urban areas. You'll find everything from New York City–style pizza to the newest of nouvelle cuisine. Dress is casual, unless noted otherwise. Even where not required, reservations are recommended at most restaurants.

Barrows House. This 200-year-old Federal-style inn, a longtime favorite, was originally built as the home of Dorset's minister, and it has always been a town focal point. Carrying on this tradition, the superb dining draws people from surrounding communities, including many who wish to escape the commercial hustle of Manchester. The deep-red woodwork and library theme of the pub room make it an intimate setting for the elegant country fare, and the greenhouse room, embellished with terra-cotta and deep blue hues, is a pleasant summer eating spot. Breakfast and dinner are served daily. *Rte. 30, Dorset, tel. 802/867–4455 or 800/ 639–1620 outside VT. Reservations essential. AE, D, MC, V. $$$*

Hemingway's. One of—if not *the*—finest restaurants in the state, Hemingway's is a former stagecoach stop built in the 1860s. The fare, described by the owners as "American with classical roots," includes dishes prepared with light sauces and local ingredients. Ernest Hemingway, for whom the restaurant is named, would have approved of the menu's game selections. Diners can choose from three four-course, price-fixed menus, including one that's vegetarian. Two menus include wines selected from the restaurant's extensive cellar. Dinner is served in three areas: a brick-wall, brick-hearth garden room overlooking an herb garden and patio; a peach-tone room with vaulted ceilings, polished wood floors, upholstered chairs, and chandeliers; and the stone-wall wine cellar—a favorite with those preferring an intimate setting. *Box 337, Rte. 4, Killington, 05751, tel. 802/ 422–3886. No lunch. Closed Mon. and mid-Apr.–mid-May. Reservations essential. $$$*

Main Street Café. Since it opened in 1989, this small storefront with polished hardwood floors, candlelit tables, fresh flowers, and northern Italian cuisine has drawn raves. The menu, which changes frequently, might include a dish such as eggplant stuffed with chicken and fontina cheese and topped with a sauce of tomato, horseradish, and Romano and Parmesan cheeses. *Rte. 67A, North Bennington, tel. 802/442–3210. No lunch. Reservations essential May–Nov. AE, DC, MC, V. Closed Mon. $$$*

Simon Pearce Restaurant. Candlelight, sparkling glassware made in the studio downstairs, exposed brick, and large windows overlooking the roaring Ottauquechee River make an ideal setting. Sesame-crusted tuna with noodle cakes and wasabi, and roast duck with mango chutney sauce are among house specialties; more than 700 choices on the wine list complement the cuisine. *Main St., Quechee, tel. 802/295–1470. AE, D, DC, MC, V. $$$*

Bistro Henry. Just outside the town of Manchester, this restaurant attracts a devoted clientele for its updated French bistro fare and attention to detail. The dining room is spacious and open, and a bar sits off in a corner. Recently on the menu were sweet potato risotto, braised lamb shanks, escargots with garlic, sweetbreads with wild mushrooms, and a Moroccan vegetable *tagine* (stew). *Rte. 11/30, Manchester, tel. 802/362–4982. AE, D, MC, V. Closed Mon. $$–$$$*

Alldays and Onions. Ingredients are fresh, recipes are creative, and menus change daily. Innovative dishes include sautéed scallops and fettuccine in a jalapeño-ginger sauce and rack of lamb with a honey-thyme sauce. Pastries and other desserts are baked on the premises. Local musicians perform Wednesday evenings. *519 E. Main St., Bennington, tel. 802/447–0043. Reservations essential for dinner. MC, V. No dinner Mon.–Tues. Closed Sun. $–$$*

Blue Benn Diner. Breakfast is served all day in this authentic diner, which serves down-home eats such as turkey hash. There can be a long wait. The diner closes in the late afternoon most days; Wednesday through Friday it's open till 8 PM. *U.S. 7 N, Bennington, tel. 802/442–5140. Reservations not accepted. No credit cards. No dinner Sat.–Tues. $*

Common Ground. The political posters and concert fliers that line the staircase alert you to Vermont's strong progressive element as you ascend into the loft-like, rough-hewn dining rooms. Owned cooperatively by the staff, this vegetarian restaurant serves the likes of cashew burgers, veggie stir-fries, and the "humble bowl of brown rice." Local suppliers and organic produce are used whenever possible, and there's a great selection of Vermont microbeers. Homemade desserts (sans white sugar, of course) will lure confirmed meat-eaters. Brunch is offered on Sunday. *25 Elliott St., Brattleboro, tel. 802/257–0855. No credit cards. Closed Tues. $*

NORTHERN SECTION **Mary's at Baldwin Creek.** One of the most inspired eating experiences in the state, Mary's is in a roomy 1790 farmhouse on the outskirts of Bristol. The "summer kitchen," with a blazing fireplace and rough-hewn barn board walls, and the lighter, pastel-colored main room provide breathing room; there are many secluded corner tables. The innovative, ever-changing cuisine might include the legendary garlic soup, Vermont rack of lamb with a rosemary-mustard sauce, duck cassis smoked over applewood, and mako shark with a banana salsa. For dessert, the raspberry gratin is a favorite. Sunday brunch is a local ritual. *Rte. 116, north of Bristol, tel. 802/453–2432. Closed Mon. in winter. AE, MC, V. $$$*

Swift House. The white wainscoting, elaborately carved mahogany and marble fireplaces, and cherry paneling lend a formal touch to the dining room in this elegant Georgian inn (*see* Lodging, *below*). An attentive staff serves dishes from a menu that changes seasonally and stresses Vermont ingredients. Entrées might include regional treats like New England seafood pie or beef medallions sautéed with wild mushrooms and fresh apples and flambéed with applejack brandy. The coffee-toffee pecan torte is a standout. *25 Stewart La., Middlebury, tel. 802/388–9925. Closed Tues.–Wed. AE, D, MC, V. $$$*

Georgio's Café. This amiable restaurant occupies two dining rooms in the rustic Tucker Hill Lodge (*see* Lodging, *below*). The more formal room is upstairs; the one downstairs has a bar, open stone oven, and fireplace. Both have a warm Mediterranean feel, the same menu, and the same prices. Selections—mostly northern Italian—change with the seasons and might include *pettini alla Veneziana* (stone-seared scallops with raisins and pine nuts); pasta dishes and pizza round out the menu. *Rte. 17, Waitsfield, tel. 802/496–3983 or 800/543–7841. AE, MC, V. $$*

Storm Café. A black-and-white tile floor, paintings by local artists, and the sounds of the espresso machine working overtime contribute to this café's European feel. The menu changes constantly, but attention to detail never varies, and breads, tortillas, and soups are all homemade. In summer, when the deck that overlooks Otter Creek beckons, local organic produce is featured in innovative salads, sandwiches, and grilled entrées. *3 Mill St., Frog Hollow Mill, Middlebury, tel. 802/388–1063. Closed Sun. MC, V. $–$$*

Miguel's. Subtle flavors, ample portions, and a hopping cantina make this local favorite a good bet when satisfying an appetite is of prime importance. In addition to burritos and the like stuffed with a wide choice of fillings, there are daily specials that might include grilled salmon with mango or black-bean-and-corn salsa. For the faint of heart, there's always a gringo option. Everything's made from scratch, including the chips and salsa. *Sugarbush Access Rd., Warren, tel. 802/583–3858. No lunch. Open Easter–Memorial Day. Closed Sun.–Wed. MC, V. $–$$*

Richard's Special Vermont Pizza (RSVP). Walk through the door and you're immediately transported through time (to the 1950s) and space (to anywhere but Vermont). The pizza—legendary around these parts, with its paper-thin crust and toppings like cilantro pesto, cob-smoked bacon, pineapple, and sautéed spinach—has become known for transport as well: Richard will Federal Express a frozen pie almost anywhere in the world overnight. And there are plenty of takers. Salads and sandwiches are also available, and the salad bar —with local produce

and delicacies such as poached salmon and homemade gravlax, smoked trout, and mozzarella, are not to be missed. *Bridge St., Waitsfield, tel. 802/496–7787. Reservations not accepted. MC, V. $*

PICNIC SPOTS In the southern section, have a picnic at **White Rocks Recreation Area** (follow signs on Rte. 140 in Wallingford) for great views of towering cliffs, or at **Grout Pond Recreation Area** (*see* Nature Trails and Short Walks *in* Exploring, *above*) and explore the trails before, during, or after your meal. For more solitude, just head out on any trail or back road and pick your spot.

There are several picnic areas along Route 100 in the northern section, including **Branden Brook Picnic Area** (8.4 mi west on Rte. 73); **Texas Falls Recreation Area** (3 mi west on Rte. 125), which has a few relatively short trails in addition to tables and a falls observation site; and **Peavine** (near Stockbridge). Picnic facilities under a red-pine grove make the **Robert Frost Wayside** (Rte. 125) a pleasant spot. For a more rugged experience (sans picnic tables), head for **Lake Pleiad** (.5 mi south of Rte. 125 on the LT), **Sunset Ledge** (.5 mi south of Lincoln Gap Rd. on the LT), or **Abby Pond** (2.5 mi west of Rte. 116 on a blue-blazed trail, East Middlebury).

LODGING

Lodging in and around the national forest runs the gamut from chain motels and ski lodges to cozy bed-and-breakfasts and elegant country inns. Availability depends on season and location. Take your pick on a quiet spring weekend, but you'll have to take your chances near a major ski area in February or anywhere during peak foliage time (from late September to early October) without a reservation. Choices are usually plentiful, though, especially in the larger towns, and almost every village, however small and remote, has a generations-old inn or a newly sprouted B&B. Be aware that some lodgings close during the slower seasons, which are April to May and late October to early December.

SOUTHERN SECTION **Windham Hill Inn.** In the converted, turn-of-the-century dairy barn, two rooms share an enormous deck that overlooks the West River valley. Rooms in the main building are more formal. There are personal touches throughout: Cherry pencil-post canopy beds were made by a local artisan, and there's a restored Steinway piano. There are fireplaces in common areas; many guest rooms have gas fireplaces, and several have whirlpool baths or soaking tubs. This is an ideal place to indulge one's craving for the genteel after a long day of hiking or biking on the 6 mi of nearby trails. In winter, equipment and instruction for cross-country skiing are available and you can ice-skate on the pond. *West Townshend 05359, tel. 802/ 874–4080 or 800/944–4080, fax 802/874– 4702. 21 rooms. Facilities: restaurant, bar, pool, tennis court. Closed Apr. and Christmas wk. AE, D, MC, V. $$$*

Nutmeg Inn. This cozy inn has all the Colonial touches you'd expect in a two-centuries-old farmhouse: an old butter churn, antique dressers, rag rugs, mason jars with dried flowers, and hand-hewn beams in the low-ceiling living room; 10 rooms have fireplaces. Three suites in the barn are larger than rooms in the main inn and get less road noise; the king suite has a private balcony with a terrific view of Haystack Mountain. A fabulous gourmet breakfast is included in the room rate. *Rte. 9W, Wilmington 05363, tel. 802/464–3351. 11 rooms, 3 suites. AE, D, MC, V. $$–$$$*

Batten Kill Inn. The hearts carved into the outside trim were the final touches when this 1840 architectural gem was built as a wedding present—the 50 rose bushes on the grounds are a modern-day toast to that romance. Deep red wallpaper with dark green print line the dining and sitting rooms. Original wooden doors and window frames, polished oak floors, and a grand, curving walnut staircase all make up for the small bathrooms—a hindrance that often plagues 1800s farmhouses turned inns. Rooms in the rear have decks that look out toward a meadow and the Batten Kill. Fireplaces in common areas and some rooms add a warm glow in winter. Attentive hospitality and the memorable breakfasts are this inn's trademarks: Raspberry and cream-cheese-filled French toast is a favorite; low- or non-fat ingredients are used when possible. *Box 948, Historic Route 7A, Manchester Village 05254, tel. 802/362–4213 or 800/441–1628. 11 rooms. $$*

Hill Farm Inn. This homey inn right next to the famed Batten Kill still has the feel of the country farmhouse it used to be. The surrounding farmland was deeded to the Hill family by King George in 1775 and is said to be one of the oldest farms in the state. It is now protected from development by the Vermont Land Trust. The mix of sturdy antiques and hand-me-downs, a spinning wheel in the upstairs hall, paintings by a family member, jars of homemade jam, and loaves of fresh-baked bread contribute to a relaxed, friendly atmosphere. Room 7 has a beamed cathedral ceiling and a porch with a view of Mt. Equinox; rooms in the 1790 guest house are very private. Rates include breakfast; dinner is optional. *Off U.S. 7A on Hill Farm Rd., Box 2015, Arlington 05250, tel. 802/375–2269 or 800/882–2545. 13 rooms, 5 share bath; 4 cabins in summer. Facilities: restaurant. AE, D, MC, V. $$*

Molly Stark Inn. Tidy blue plaid wallpaper, gleaming hardwood floors, antique furnishings, and a wood-burning stove in the sitting room's brick alcove add country charm to this 1860 Victorian. Molly's Room, at the back of the building, gets less noise from Route 9 and has a whirlpool bath; the attic suite is most spacious. A new, secluded cottage with a 16-ft ceiling, a king-size brass bed, and a two-person whirlpool bath surrounded by windows that look out to the woods is as romantic as it gets. The innkeeper's genuine hospitality and quirky charisma delight guests, as does the full country breakfast that's been known to feature cinnamon-apple cheddar-cheese quiche. *1067 E. Main St., Benning-*

ton 05201, tel. 802/442–9631 or 800/356–3076. 6 rooms, 1 suite. MC, V. $–$$

Inn at Long Trail. This 1938 skier and hiker lodge is just a quarter-mile from the Pico ski slopes and even closer to the Appalachian/Long Trail. Nature is the prevailing theme in the unusual decor (e.g., massive boulders inside the inn). The suites all have fireplaces. Gaelic charm is on hand with Irish music, darts, and Guinness always on tap. Irish hospitality is extended particularly toward end-to-end hikers, who get a substantial break in the rates (call for details). Rates include full breakfast. Lunch and dinner (weekends only) are available. *Rte. 4, Box 267, Killington 05751, tel. 802/ 775–7181 or 800/325–2540. 14 rooms, 5 suites. AE, MC, V. $*

NORTHERN SECTION **Blueberry Hill Inn.** Here, tucked on a backcountry road in the hushed woods of the national forest, you can pamper yourself while "roughing it." Rooms are available either in the classic 1813 farmhouse or attached working greenhouse. Access to trails doesn't come any easier, and the solarium, swimming pond, and two fireplaces are ideal places to unwind. *Ripton–Goshen Rd., Goshen 05733, tel. 802/247–6735 or 800/448–0707. 12 rooms with bath. Facilities: restaurant, cross-country skiing, sauna, mountain bikes. MC, V. $$$*

Churchill House Inn. First, walk down the road to check out the llamas. Then settle into the sauna or read a book on the screened porch until dinner's ready. With access to 15 mi of trails and homey country decor, this place on the edge of the national forest is very casual—perfect for the outdoor enthusiast. Rooms are furnished with antiques; some have whirlpools. Breakfast and dinner are included in the room rates. *Rte. 73, R.D. 3, Box 3265, Brandon 05733, tel. 802/247–3300. 8 rooms. Facilities: pool, sauna, bikes. MC, V. $$–$$$*

Latchis Hotel. When this Art Deco hotel opened in the heart of Brattleboro's historic district in 1938, it housed the largest ballroom in the state and the elegant Latchis Theatre, with Greek murals and exquisite terrazzo floors. Today the beautifully restored hotel—still in the Latchis family— is on the National Register of Historic Places. Rooms vary dramatically in size and brightness. The standard rooms, with one window, tend to be gloomy while the deluxe rooms, facing the Connecticut River, are spacious and cheerful. If you're traveling with kids, the two-bedroom suites are one of the best buys around. Movie passes are included with the rooms, and even if you don't want to catch the show, you should take a look inside the theater. Muffins are available free of charge in the morning, and the rooms have coffeemakers. *50 Main St., Brattleboro 05301, tel. 802/ 254–6300. 60 rooms. Facilities: restaurant. AE, MC, V. $$–$$$*

Swift House Inn. Just two blocks from town, the main house of this lovely three-building inn on 3 acres of landscaped grounds was built in 1814 and was once the home of Vermont governor John W. Stewart. There's also a turn-of-the-century gatehouse, and a carriage house built in 1886. Furnishings and fixtures include antiques, elaborately carved marble fireplaces, and winding staircases. The bedrooms have oversize four-poster beds and fresh flowers, and each bathroom has either a whirlpool tub or antique footed tub with shower. Some rooms have private balconies. The formal gardens are magnificent. The rate includes Continental breakfast. *25 Stewart La., Middlebury 05753, tel. 802/388–9925. 21 rooms. Facilities: restaurant, sauna, steam room. $$–$$$*

Beaver Pond Farm Inn. A peaceful drive down a country lane lined with sugar maples leads to this small, restored 1840 farmhouse that overlooks rolling meadows, a golf course, and cross-country ski trails. Guest rooms are decorated simply, but bathrooms are ample. The focal point of the inn is the huge deck with mountain and meadow views; another attraction is access to the Long Trail just a couple of miles away. A full breakfast that might include orange-yogurt pancakes is served at a long walnut table; dinner is also offered three nights a week to guests. Favorite dishes are shiitake mushroom soup and chicken stuffed with roasted red peppers and served with a scallion plum-wine sauce. The inn is just down the road from a snow-shoe center, and the owner will take guests fly-fishing on the Mad River. *Golf Course Rd., R.D. Box 306, Warren 05674, tel. 802/583–2861, fax 802/583–2860. 6 rooms, 2 share bath. MC, V. $$*

Lareau Farm Country Inn. Surrounded by acres of pastures and woodland, and just an amble away from the Mad River, this collection of old farm buildings (the oldest part dates from 1790) appeals to outdoor enthusiasts as well as to those seeking rejuvenation in the country. A mile-long stroll following a detailed walking guide takes you through some of the property's history. The furnishings in the inn are an eclectic mix of Victorian sofas and Oriental rugs. There's a whirlpool bath in one guest room and a fireplace and TV in the common sitting room. The many-windowed dining room is the most inviting room, partly because it's where you'll eat breakfast family style. Dinner is served Friday and Saturday in peak season, Friday only in off-season. Sit on the covered porch in an Adirondack chair, explore the large jazz collection, swim in the river, take a horse or sleigh ride, or stroll in the beautiful gardens. And don't miss the delicious American flat bread pizza cooked in a wood-fired stone oven. *Rte. 100, Box 563, Waitsfield, tel. 802/496–4949 or 800/833–0766. 11 rooms with bath, 2 rooms share bath. Facilities: restaurant. MC, V. $$*

Tucker Hill Lodge. Attempts to maintain the 1940s ski-lodge-style ambience of this inn, which opened the same year as Mad River Glen ski area, have been successful. Pine paneling and otherwise simple furnishings suffice, as most guests here are more interested in skiing all day than enjoying in Victorian frills. Georgio's Café (*see* Dining, *above*) occupies two dining rooms. *Rte. 17, 05673, Waitsfield 05673, tel. 802/496–3983 or 800/543–7841. 16 rooms*

with bath, 4 rooms share bath. Facilities: pool, tennis court, hiking. AE, MC, V. $–$$

Long Run Inn. Across the street from the New Haven River and its numerous swimming holes and down the road from the Lincoln Gap and the Long Trail, this inn is just the thing for the outdoors lover who doesn't feel like camping. Sitting on the inn's wraparound porch facing the subdued little town's main street brings to mind lazy summer afternoons spent by generations past. Food is the specialty here: hearty country breakfasts, afternoon hors d'oeuvres, and ample family-style dinners. You can even get a lunch packed. *Lincoln Gap Rd., Lincoln 05443, tel. 802/453–3233. 7 rooms share 2 baths. No credit cards. Closed Nov.–Apr. $*

CAMPING

The U.S. Forest Service allows dispersed camping on national forest lands. Campers are expected to follow strict fire-safety guidelines and "no trace" camping procedures: Sites should be at least 200 ft from any trail, stream, or pond; never use streams or ponds for washing dishes or clothes (water should be used and disposed of well away from a water source); remove all traces of having been at a site, including a fire; and don't camp where someone has clearly camped before, unless it is an established site. In addition, backpackers are urged to use the Long Trail's 70 cabins and lean-tos, each about a day's hike apart, to minimize camping impact. Certain restrictions, which are prominently posted, apply to fires and camping in designated recreation areas.

The national forest campgrounds listed below tend to provide fewer facilities (e.g., no showers or electricity) than private campgrounds, but they offer immediate access to the ruggedness of the forest. Except at Hapgood, camping is on a first-come, first-served basis. Campgrounds are accessible by gravel or paved road, and sites have gravel surfacing that can accommodate RVs up to 18 ft. Water hand pumps and nonflush vault toilets are provided, and fees are $5 at all areas except Red Mill, where donations are welcome, and Hapgood, where the fee is $10 and reservations are accepted.

For a list of private campgrounds and state parks with camping facilities, contact the **Vermont Department of Forests, Parks, and Recreation** (*see* Visitor Information *in* Essential Information, *above*).

Chittenden Brook. There's easy access to the Long Trail via the Chittenden Brook Trail from this campground. *6 mi west of Rte. 100 on Rte. 73, no phone. 17 sites. $*

Greendale. Greendale is near hiking and fishing. *2 mi northwest of Rte. 100 on Forest Rd. 18, near Weston, no phone. 14 sites. $*

Grout Pond Recreation Area. With 1,600 acres of semiprimitive land, a 79-acre pond, and 8 mi of multipurpose trails (*see* Nature Trails and Short Walks *in* Exploring, *above*), Grout Pond is another option. Four of the five designated hike-in campsites are accessible by canoe, and there are three lean-to–type shelters. The water spigots are turned off in winter. *12 mi east of Arlington off Kelley Stand Rd., no phone. 5 sites, 3 lean-tos. Facilities: hiking. $*

Hapgood Pond. This is the most heavily used campground. *North of Peru on Forest Rd. 3, tel. 802/824–6456 for reservations. 28 sites. Facilities: fishing, hiking. $*

Moosalamoo. This is a good choice for people who use wheelchairs: Three sites and a toilet are accessible. For the able bodied, there's great hiking, and it's close to Sugar Hill Reservoir's fishing and canoeing. *About 3 mi south of Rte. 125 on Forest Rd. 32, no phone. 19 sites. Facilities: hiking. $*

Red Mill. This is a good spot if you're arriving late from points south. *North of Rte. 9 on Forest Rd. 274, near Bennington, no phone. 16 sites. $*

Gulf Islands National Seashore

Florida, Mississippi

By Dick Pivetz

Updated by Carol and Dan Thalimer

 amilies and beach bums day-trip to Gulf Islands National Seashore, RVers trek between its Florida and Mississippi districts, and walkers and bird-watchers stroll along the many nature trails. Sometimes it seems as much a beach resort as a national park, except that instead of dense crowds and high-rise hotels you find acres of soft sand and sea oats that wave gently in the breeze.

The park, comprising 11 sections, sprawls along 150 mi of Gulf of Mexico coastline from Ft. Walton Beach in the Florida Panhandle to Gulfport, Mississippi. Six sections are in Florida: Okaloosa (19 acres on Choctawhatchee Bay), Santa Rosa (1,598 acres), Ft. Pickens (1,742 acres), Naval Live Oaks (1,378 acres), Ft. Barrancas and Advanced Redoubt (64 acres), and Perdido Key (1,041 acres). Five sections are in Mississippi: Davis Bayou (401 acres), Horn Island (3,650 acres), Petit Bois Island (1,466 acres), East Ship Island (362 acres), and West Ship Island (555 acres).

Spanish explorers recognized the strategic significance of the islands that are now part of the national seashore. Power changed hands regularly for 300 years, as the land in Florida was claimed alternately by Spain, Great Britain, and France, until 1821, when the United States flag first flew here. Established in 1971, Gulf Islands is a relative newcomer to the National Park Service family.

In the Florida district there are beaches at the Santa Rosa, Okaloosa, Perdido Key, and Ft. Pickens areas. All offer fishing, and rangers at Ft. Pickens can recommend good spots for scuba diving. You can jet-ski in the waters near Okaloosa, Santa Rosa, Ft. Pickens, and Perdido Key. The entire Santa Rosa area was hard hit by Hurricane Opal in 1995 and Florida Road 399, which runs from Navarre to Pensacola Beach, was destroyed. The road reopened in December 1996 (but picnic areas will not be ready until summer 1998). Only Ft. Pickens has camping, but all areas have picnic facilities. History buffs can explore Ft. Pickens and Ft. Barrancas, 19th-century brick fortresses, on their own or on a ranger-led tour. Nature lovers find diverse flora and fauna, and stargazers delight in clear nights: The glare of city lights is absent.

The Mississippi Gulf Coast is a study in contrasts. At one extreme is the pristine beauty of the national seashore. At the other is the explosion of Las Vegas–style casinos and hotels. In between are campgrounds, cozy family hotels and motels, and the tacky souvenir shops that often accompany beach resort towns. In Mississippi the national seashore includes four islands: West Ship, East Ship, Horn, and Petit Bois, each about 12 mi offshore, accessible only by boat. (There were three islands before Hurricane Camille's 240-mph winds cut Ship Island in two in 1969.) West Ship Island, accessible by excursion boats from Gulfport in the spring, summer, and fall, has picnic facilities, 19th-century Ft. Massachusetts, and sandlots of soft, white sand. Ferry service isn't available to the other three islands, two of which, Petit Bois and Horn, were declared wilderness areas by an act of Congress in 1978; to reach them you must have your own boat or charter one licensed by Gulf Islands National Seashore. At the Mississippi section's sole mainland area, Davis Bayou in Ocean Springs, you can camp for a few days amid stands of live oaks. Fishing and boating are also popular, but, with alligators aplenty, swimming is not allowed.

ESSENTIAL INFORMATION

VISITOR INFORMATION Both districts can provide information about the entire national seashore; when contacting the park, be sure to specify the type of information you need.

Florida District. The main contact is the superintendent, **Gulf Islands National Seashore** (1801 Gulf Breeze Pkwy., Gulf Breeze 32561, tel. 850/934–2600). Park information on the **Web** can be found at: www.nps.gov. You can also stop by the **Naval Live Oaks Visitor Center** (on the peninsula between the mainland and Santa Rosa Island, tel. 850/934–2600). It is open March–October, daily 8:30–5; November–February, daily 8:30–4:30. For information about Pensacola, contact the **Pensacola Convention & Visitor Information Center** (1401 E. Gregory St., Pensacola 32501, tel. 850/434–1234 or 800/874–1234, fax 850/432–8211), which is open daily 8–5. Their **Web site** is www.chamber.pensacola.sl.us. The **Santa Rosa Island Authority** (Drawer 1208, Pensacola Beach 32561, tel. 850/932–2259) is open weekdays 8:30–5. The **Pensacola Beach Visitor Information Center** (Box 1174, Pensacola Beach 32561, tel. 850/932–1500 or 800/635–4803, fax 850/932–1551) is open daily 9–5.

Mississippi District. Contact the superintendent, **Gulf Islands National Seashore** (3500 Park Rd., Ocean Springs 39564, tel. 228/875–9057) at the **William M. Colmer Visitor Center** in Davis Bayou, which is open March–October, daily 9–5; November–February, daily 8–4:30. The hours are subject to change, so call first. For information

on coastal Mississippi, contact any of the following. **Biloxi Visitor Center** (710 Beach Blvd., Biloxi 39530, tel. 228/374–3105 or 800/245–6943, fax 228/435–6248), which is open weekdays 8–5, Saturday 9–5, Sunday noon–5. **Mississippi Gulf Coast Chamber of Commerce** (1401 20th Ave., Drawer FF, Gulfport 39502–0950, tel. 228/863–2933). **Mississippi Beach Convention and Visitor Bureau** (135 Courthouse Rd., Gulfport 39506–6128, tel. 228/896–6699 or 800/237–9493), which is open weekdays 8–5.

FEES Admission is free to all park areas except Ft. Pickens and Perdido Key, where entrance fees are $6 for a seven-day permit or $20 for a yearly permit. At press time, fees were scheduled to increase, but the amount had not been set; also, new fees will be charged at other areas of the national seashore.

PUBLICATIONS Free National Park Service site bulletins covering all aspects of the park are available at visitor centers.

Bird-watchers should be interested in *Birds and Birding of the Gulf Coast,* by Judith Toups (University Press, $22.95). Birders in the Florida district will want *The Birds of Escambia, Santa Rosa, and Okaloosa Counties, Florida,* by Robert A. Duncan (published by the author and available from him at 614 Fairpoint Dr., Gulf Breeze, FL 32561; $10.95).

GEOLOGY AND TERRAIN Gulf Islands National Seashore preserves three landscapes: southeastern deciduous forests, bayou marshes, and barrier islands. The barrier islands—West Ship, East Ship, Horn, and Petit Bois islands in Mississippi, and, in Florida, Perdido Key and Santa Rosa Island—which protect the mainland from storms, are made of shifting sand, unstable sand dunes, and salt marshes. Here, the beaches are flat and the soil sandy. Backing the beaches, parallel to the Gulf of Mexico, are the primary dunes, whose vegetation slows wind erosion. Still farther inland is another set of dunes, the so-called secondary dunes, which may stand alone or be connected to the primary dunes. They are anchored by vegetation. As a result of gulf currents that bombard their eastern shorelines and dump sand on their western coasts, the barrier islands actually "move." Over the years, the western tip of Santa Rosa Island has moved 1 mi farther west; more fragile Ft. McRee, which once stood on the eastern point of Perdido Key, has been washed away entirely.

At Mississippi's Davis Bayou, a typical bayou salt marsh, the Mississippi Sound meets the mainland, and shallow water and plentiful vegetation nurture fish, migratory birds, and other wildlife. The soil is more stable than in beach areas and able to support the root systems of the live oaks, magnolias, and pine trees that grow along the bayou shore.

FLORA AND FAUNA Vegetation on the islands and in the bayous and salt marshes is determined primarily by a species' tolerance for salt. The primary dunes support only sea oats and the occasional beach morning glory, beach pea, sea purslane, sea rocket, and pennywort. As primary dunes give way to secondary dunes, more species flourish: jointweed, woody goldenrod, golden aster, rockrose, rosemary, and evening primrose. In summer, look for white arrow-leaf morning glories, yellow St. John's wort, and pink meadow beauties between the dunes and the forest.

Still farther inland are slash pines, scrub live oaks, and palmettos. Near freshwater marshes, cattails and saw grass proliferate. Slash, loblolly, and sand pines dot the landscape, and immense live oaks, many cloaked in Spanish moss, reach towering heights on the mainland. Never touch the moss in summer unless you want to battle the itch of chiggers.

Animal life along the coast ranges from fish and shellfish to the American alligator. In the gulf, Florida pompano, sea trout, red drum, sharks, cobia, redfish, and sheepshead are plentiful. Shrimps, crabs, and southern flounder have found homes in the gentler waters of Mississippi Sound. Bird life includes ospreys, brown pelicans, and great blue herons. Horn Island has a large rabbit population. Watch out for less friendly creatures: Eastern diamondback rattlesnakes, water moccasins, and alligators reside in the area. Although the last are sometimes seen on the barrier islands, they prefer the freshwater of the bayous. Raccoons seem to be everywhere in the park; campgrounds are a favorite target of these bandits.

All plants and animals on the national seashore are protected by law, and to help preserve the natural habitat, visitors are asked to stay on established trails.

WHEN TO GO Gulf Islands National Seashore is popular year-round, so don't think you'll find bargains in the low season at the many beach resorts of the Florida district.

Summers are warm and sunny, and winters are temperate. Summer coastal temperatures creep into the high 80s, and although offshore breezes temper the heat, midsummer can be unbearable for hiking and exploring. Spring and fall are the most inviting seasons, with daytime highs in the 70s and nighttime lows in the 50s. In winter, expect the mercury to dip into the upper 30s to mid-40s at night. This is the season when surf anglers and beachcombers use the beaches. Bird-watchers arrive for the spring and fall migratory periods.

Storms come and go year-round, but early summer through fall is hurricane time. Although such storms are infrequent, you should keep abreast of changing weather patterns if you visit during this time. There isn't a defined rainy season, but brief, heavy rainstorms are common in spring and summer, as pressure systems sweeping across the country pull gulf moisture onshore, and winter is fairly wet.

SEASONAL EVENTS Gulf Islands has no scheduled events of its own, but nearby communities offer plenty. Any celebration related to coastal seafood delicacies is bound to be packed.

Florida District. Mid-May: Spring Fest (tel. 850/469–1069 or 800/874–1234) on Spring

Street in downtown Pensacola features arts and crafts, music, and entertainment for children. **Memorial Day and Labor Day: LobsterFest** (tel. 800/635–4803) at Quietwater Boardwalk on Pensacola Beach offers great food and numerous activities. **June:** The annual **Fiesta of the Five Flags** (tel. 850/932–2259) in early June includes a sand castle contest, children's treasure hunt, parades, a fishing rodeo, and other water-related sporting events. **September:** The **Pensacola Seafood Festival** (tel. 850/433–6512) draws shellfish junkies from around the world midmonth. **November:** The navy's Blue Angels, the famed aerial demonstration team, star in an annual **air show** (tel. 850/452–4784) held midmonth at Sherman Field, near Pensacola's National Museum of Naval Aviation.

Mississippi District. March: Many of the antebellum homes of Ocean Springs and Gulfport open their doors midmonth to visitors during the annual **Historic Home Tours**; for information, call the Harrison County Tourism Commission (tel. 800/237–9493). **May:** Biloxi hosts a colorful **Blessing of the Fleet** (tel. 800/239–9493) early in May. **July:** Gulfport is the center of the action for the annual **Deep-Sea Fishing Rodeo** (tel. 228/388–2271) early in the month. **September:** In the Gulfport area, what is said to be the world's largest **Sand Sculpture Contest** (tel. 228/896–2434) late in the month attracts many teams, who use sand, water, and hand tools to sculpt objects relating to an assigned theme.

WHAT TO PACK Pack for a beach resort—swimsuits, shorts, and T-shirts—because casual wear is the order of the day, even in most restaurants. If hikes are on your itinerary, pack a rain poncho in your knapsack. Don't forget sunscreen and a hat: The sun's rays are especially intense when reflected off the water and sand, and there are few trees for cover. Take comfortable, lightweight walking shoes for climbing around the 19th-century forts or strolling the nature trails. Cool evening breezes on your sun-scorched skin will make you glad to have a windbreaker. If you're camping,

venturing onto Davis Bayou, or fishing from the docks, pack insect repellent.

GENERAL STORES Well-stocked stores are virtually nonexistent within the park boundaries: Only **Perdido Key** and **Ft. Pickens** have snack stores, and they carry a minimal supply of food and beach and picnic supplies—hot dogs, sandwiches, soft drinks, and the like. The **campground store** at Ft. Pickens Campground (tel. 850/934–5691), which is open April–October, daily 9–4, has the best selection. Outside the park boundaries on the Florida side, where park areas are interspersed with bustling beach communities, shopping is not a problem. The Davis Bayou Campground in Mississippi has no campground store, but there's plenty of shopping in nearby Ocean Springs.

ATMS In Florida, look for the Bank of the South on Santa Rosa Island, as well as other banks in Pensacola and Gulf Breeze. In Mississippi there are banks in Gulfport, Biloxi, and other towns and cities along the coast.

ARRIVING AND DEPARTING **By Boat.** West Ship, East Ship, Horn, and Petit Bois islands are accessible only by boat. Most people visit West Ship via **Ship Island Excursions** boats March–October (Gulfport, tel. 228/864–1014). However, there are three different seasons with varying hours. In summer, from the second Saturday in May to the first Saturday in September, boats leave for Ship Island at 9 and noon and return at 3:40 and 6:40. The trip takes 55 minutes from Gulfport. In fall (the first Saturday in September to the first Saturday in October) and spring (the first Saturday in March to the second Saturday in May), the boat leaves at 9 and returns at 2:30. In winter, excursions are by charter only. The regular round-trip excursions to West Ship cost $14 for adults. Excursions to East Ship are by charter and require one-week advance reservations and a minimum of two people at $50 per person.

To reach East Ship, Horn, and Petit Bois and to get to West Ship between December and February, you must charter a boat; contact the **Colmer Visitor Center** (tel. 228/875–9057) for a list of licensed operators.

By Bus. In Florida the **Escambia County Transit System** (tel. 850/436–9383) and **Greyhound Lines** (Pensacola, tel. 850/476–4800) offer fairly extensive service throughout the area. In Mississippi, Greyhound has stations in Biloxi (tel. 228/436–4335) and Gulfport (tel. 228/863–1022) or call 800/231–2222. Mississippi is also served by **Coastliner** (tel. 800/647–3957) and **VIP Mobile Shuttle Service** (tel. 800/738–5466). The **Coast Transit Authority** (CTA; tel. 228/896–8080), the local bus system, serves much of the area.

By Car and RV. From Pensacola, U.S. 98 will take you to Gulf Breeze. The Naval Live Oaks area is just east of Gulf Breeze on U.S. 98. To reach Ft. Pickens and Santa Rosa, take Route 399 from Gulf Breeze to Pensacola Beach. From there, Ft. Pickens is 9 mi west, Santa Rosa 10 mi east. The Okaloosa area is on U.S. 98 east of Ft. Walton Beach. To reach Ft. Barrancas and the Advanced Redoubt, take Route 292 from Pensacola; then turn left onto Route 295, which will lead you to the Pensacola Naval Air Station, in whose confines both areas are located—you must stop at the gate to obtain a pass (free). For Perdido Key, take Route 292; on the island, turn left onto Johnson Beach Road.

In Mississippi take the Ocean Springs exit from I–10; then drive south to U.S. 90, which runs past the park entrance at Davis Bayou. Gulfport and Biloxi are off U.S. 90.

Rental-car companies with offices at Pensacola's airport include **Avis** (tel. 850/433–5614), **Budget** (tel. 850/474–3721), **Dollar** (tel. 800/698–3586), **Hertz** (tel. 800/654–3131), **National** (tel. 800/227–7368), and **Thrifty** (tel. 850/477–5553).

From the Gulfport/Biloxi airport, you can rent a car from **Avis** (tel. 228/864–7182), **Budget** (tel. 228/864–5181), **Hertz** (tel. 228/863–2761), or **National** (tel. 800/227–7368).

By Plane. Pensacola Municipal Airport (tel. 850/435–1745), about 20 mi from the Florida district's Ft. Pickens, is served by most major airlines, including Delta, Northwest Airlink, Continental, and US Airways. You'll probably need to rent a car (*see* By Car and RV, *above*); there's no local bus transportation to the park. Mississippi visitors can fly to **Gulfport/Biloxi Regional Airport** (tel. 228/863–5951), which is served by Delta, NW Airlink, Continental Express, ASA, and Reno Air. *See* By Car and RV, *above,* for rental car information.

By Train. At press time, **Amtrak** (tel. 800/872–7245) still ran the *Sunset Limited* between California and Florida via the southern United States. Three trains per week travel east and three west, stopping at Pensacola, Gulfport, and Biloxi.

By Trolley. Instead of fighting traffic on U.S. 90, ride in style on the trolleys of the **Beachcomber Line,** operated by the **Coast Transit Authority** (tel. 228/896–8080). You can catch the trolley anywhere along 26 mi of beach, from Ocean Springs in the east to Bay St. Louis in the west, and get on and off as many times as you wish for the one-day Coastour Pass price of $4 per day or $40 per month. The pass is also good on all CTA buses (*see* By Bus, *above*).

EXPLORING

To experience Gulf Islands, you can explore on foot or by bicycle, or you may just sit still on a soft spot on the sand. Ft. Pickens, Ft. Barrancas, and Ft. Massachusetts can be visited on foot, either on your own or with a ranger-led tour. The many nature trails are neither long nor difficult. You'll find them in Mississippi at Davis Bayou and in Florida at Ft. Pickens, Naval Live Oaks, Perdido Key, and Ft. Barrancas. You can take a scenic boat ride to West Ship Island and tour Ft. Massachusetts.

THE BEST IN ONE DAY **Florida District.** Ft. Pickens offers a sampling of Gulf Islands activities. You can take a break from sunning or fishing to learn about the national coastal-defense system or stroll along a

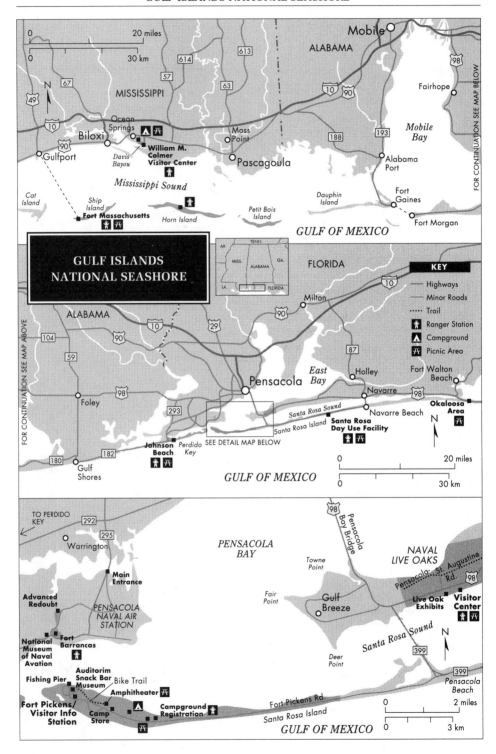

nearby nature trail. Two short trails reveal the diverse ecosystem of a barrier island; a longer trail leads around the western tip of Santa Rosa Island. The small **Ft. Pickens Museum** (tel. 850/934–2635), which is open April–October, daily 9:30–5, and November–March, daily 8:30–4, has excellent dioramas on park wildlife and military history. You can picnic at the beachfront pavilion or in one of the park's shaded picnic areas.

Mississippi District. Taking in this side of Gulf Islands in a day is a little tricky. Catch the excursion boat to West Ship Island (*see* Arriving and Departing by Boat *in* Essential Information, *above*). The 55-minute ride takes you across Mississippi Sound, busy with shrimp boats, intracoastal barges, and oceangoing freighters (some full of chickens and chicken parts bound for Russia); dolphins are often spotted during the ride. Spend some time examining Ft. Massachusetts (*see* Historic Buildings and Sites, *below*) and strolling the island's 7-mi beach. West Ship's snack bar sells hot dogs, sandwiches, fruit, and soft drinks; if you want anything else, pack a lunch. If you like to fish, bring your own tackle and you can go for sheepshead, which are often caught from the dock near the fort. The return ride often includes a view of a lipstick-hued gulf sunset.

ORIENTATION PROGRAMS In the auditorium at the **Naval Live Oaks Visitor Center** (tel. 850/934–2600) you can ask to see a 12-minute slide show on the park. At the **Colmer Visitor Center** at Davis Bayou (tel. 228/875–9057) you can ask to see a video.

GUIDED TOURS Rangers conduct tours of three of the park's forts: **Ft. Massachusetts** (June–Labor Day, daily at 10:30 and 1:30), **Ft. Pickens** (Mar.–Oct., weekdays at 2, weekends at 11 and 2), and **Ft. Barrancas** (June–July, weekends at 2). Candlelight tours are also occasionally scheduled at Ft. Pickens. Confirm schedules for ferries and tours with one of the two main visitor centers before you make plans (tel. 850/934–2600 in Florida or 228/875–9057 in Missis-

sippi). Ranger-led johnboat tours of the marshes around Mississippi's Davis Bayou are scheduled in summer but are heavily dependent on funding and staff availability, so call ahead (tel. 228/875–9057).

SCENIC DRIVES AND VIEWS Driving toward Ft. Pickens on narrow Santa Rosa Island provides a sparkling glimpse of the gulf. Also take in the view from atop **Ft. Pickens** across Pensacola Bay to the naval air station, Ft. Barrancas, and Lighthouse Point; the view of Pensacola Bay from **Ft. Barrancas**; the breezy sea scene from the beaches at **Okaloosa, Santa Rosa,** and **Perdido Key**; and the dramatic boat approach to narrow **West Ship Island** (don't be intimidated by the massive brick fort near the dock—the cannons haven't been fired in years).

HISTORIC BUILDINGS AND SITES Florida District. The **Water Battery of Ft. Barrancas** is the last remaining Spanish fortification overlooking the entrance to Pensacola Bay. Built in 1797, it came under U.S. control in 1821. American engineers built a new fort—today's Ft. Barrancas—into the bluff above the old Water Battery (1839–44) and linked the two with a tunnel. **Ft. Pickens** was built on the western tip of Santa Rosa Island between 1829 and 1834. **Ft. McRee** was built on the eastern tip of Perdido Key between 1834 and 1839. These forts are part of an extensive coastal-defense system launched following the War of 1812. Between 1845 and 1859 the army constructed the **Advanced Redoubt** to protect the mainland flank of Ft. Barrancas; it served in this role in Union defenses during the Civil War.

Historic Pensacola Village. This unique complex uses museums and model historic houses to trace Pensacola's romantic heritage, from the time of Native Americans through that of Spanish explorers and seafaring men to the turn of the century. In addition to the 18th-century French Colonial **Lavalle House,** the 1805 **Julee Cottage,** and the 1871 **Dorr House,** the village contains an 1890s streetscape, the **Museum of Industry,** the **Museum of Commerce,** and the **T. T. Wentworth, Jr., Florida State Museum.** *205 E. Zaragoza, tel. 850/444–8905. Open Mon.–Sat. 10–4; guided tours at 11:30 and 1:30. Admission (good for 2 days): $6.*

The **Pensacola Naval Air Station** (Naval Blvd., off U.S. 98, tel. 850/452–2311) houses about 120 historic aircraft, a spectacular collection that includes planes used by renowned World War II marine Major Greg "Pappy" Boyington, Lieutenant Junior Grade George Bush, and the navy's Blue Angels Aerial Demonstration Team. Exhibits and films document naval aviation. The free 250,000-square-ft **National Museum of Naval Aviation** (Naval Air Station, tel. 850/452–3604), which is open daily 9–5, complements the air station's collection of planes with exhibits and films on aeronautical topics.

Learn about the Civil War's effect on Pensacola and its citizens through artifacts, relics, and life-size dioramas of a Union camp and a Confederate field hospital at the **Civil War Soldier's Museum** (108 S. Palafox Place, Pensacola, tel. 850/469–1900). The museum was created and assembled by a doctor who amassed Civil War–era medical implements to show the desperate inadequacies of medical care during the war. It's open Monday–Saturday 10–4:30. Admission is $3.

Historic Districts: North Hill, Palafox, Seville. Because these three districts are adjacent to one another, they are easily walkable. Historic Pensacola Village comprises the majority of the primarily residential Seville Historic District. The Palafox District, which was the heart of Old Pensacola, is primarily commercial and contains the T. T. Wentworth, Jr., Florida State Museum, the Pensacola Museum of Art, Plaza Ferdinand VII, and the Saenger Theater. Many restored buildings have New Orleans–style ironwork balconies. The 50-block North Hill District is recognized as one of the most intact residential historic districts in Florida. Between 1870 to the 1930s many of the homes were custom

designed for their wealthy owners, so most of the houses are unique. Styles include Queen Anne, neoclassical, Tudor Revival, Craftsman bungalow, Art Moderne, and Mediterranean Revival.

Built in 1832, the **Pensacola Historical Museum** (405 S. Adams St., tel. 850/433–1559) has had a varied life. It was an Episcopal church until 1903 and operated as a library from 1938 to 1957. In 1960 it became a museum where the story of Pensacola is portrayed through exhibits about geology, Native Americans, Colonial Pensacola, and the Civil War. It is open Monday–Saturday 9–4:30. Admission, which also includes admittance to the Research Library on Government Street, is $2.

Once the Pensacola city jail and court, the two-story Mission Revival–style **Pensacola Museum of Art** (407 S. Jefferson St., tel. 850/432–6247) houses permanent collections and traveling exhibits and hosts concerts and lectures. It's open Tuesday–Friday 10–5, Saturday 10–4. Admission is free.

Natural habitats surrounded by botanical gardens permit more than 700 animals in the **Zoo and Botanical Gardens** (U.S 98, Gulf Breeze, tel. 850/932–2229) to wander freely. The zoo's premier attraction is its family of lowland gorillas housed in a multilevel complex. Children love the tall platform from which they can feed the giraffes close up. At the Farm, children can pet and feed smaller animals. The Safari Line is a miniature train that meanders through the 30-acre grounds and permits glimpses of wildlife native to western Florida. A restaurant and a snack bar make it possible to spend the entire day at the zoo. It is open November–March, daily 9–4; April–October, daily 9–5. Admission is $9.25.

Mississippi District. West Ship Island's **Ft. Massachusetts,** never used much militarily, is an excellent example of a restored coastal masonry fort. Begun in 1859, the fort was completed in 1866. Its Rodman cannon and carriage are capable of firing a 15-inch-diameter cannonball weighing more than 300 pounds as far as 3 mi.

After several years of imprisonment following the Civil War, former Confederate president Jefferson Davis spent his retirement at **Beauvoir** (2244 Beach Blvd., Biloxi 39531, tel. 228/388–1313), an antebellum home overlooking the Gulf of Mexico. The Greek Revival, one-story, Louisiana-style raised cottage, which contains furniture and possessions of the Davis family as well as other period furnishings, is open for tours. The **Davis Family Gallery,** in the basement of the house, contains other family memorabilia and Civil War artifacts. After Davis's death, the estate served as a Confederate Veterans Home for 54 years. Buildings and a cemetery remain from that period. A museum in the visitor center chronicles the Confederate experience. It's open daily 9–5. Admission is $6.

Housed in a former Coast Guard station, the **Maritime & Seafood Industry Museum** (Point Cadet Plaza, Biloxi, tel. 228/435–6320) contains photographs, early boat engines, boat models, a lighthouse lens, seafood-gathering implements, and other relics that follow the Mississippi Gulf Coast's seafood industry from the time of the Wetlands Indians through European settlers to the present. Another exhibit traces the history of hurricanes since 1700. It is open Monday–Saturday 9–4:30. Admission is $2.50.

NASA's second-largest space research center, the **John C. Stennis Space Center** (Building 1200, Stennis Space Center, tel. 228/688–2370) in Bay St. Louis, is where large-propulsion space-vehicle engines are tested and flight certified. Among the attractions at the visitor center are the 90-ft Space Tower, a 154-ft Space Shuttle external fuel tank, rockets and rocket engines, a two-person submersible, the Hall of Achievements, films, lectures, and demonstrations. Bus tours of the entire facility are available. Exhibits in the visitor center also showcase the work of the other organizations at the facility: U.S. Navy's Oceanography Command, Naval Research Laboratory, Environmental Protection Agency, National Data Buoy Center, National Marine Fisheries Service, and U.S. Geological Survey. It is open daily 9–5. Admission is free.

The **Mardi Gras Museum** (119 Rue Magnolia, Biloxi, tel. 228/432–8806), housed in the historic antebellum Magnolia Hotel in Biloxi, serves as the headquarters of the Gulf Coast Carnival Association and displays the organization's collection of flamboyant Mardi Gras costumes and memorabilia. Mardi Gras is celebrated in the coastal communities with parades and balls just as it is in New Orleans and Mobile. It is open weekdays 11–3. Admission is free, but donations are appreciated.

The **Scranton Floating Museum** (River Park, Pascagoula, tel. 228/762–2287), a 70-ft retired commercial fishing vessel, shows the decks, galley, bunk room, and wheelhouse as they were before she was drydocked in 1981. Below deck, a museum has aquariums, a wetlands diorama, nature displays, a video presentation, and a hands-on seashore exhibit. It is open Tuesday–Saturday 10–5, Sunday 1–5. Admission is free.

The **J. L. Scott Marine Education Center** (115 Beach Blvd., Biloxi, tel. 228/374–5550) has the largest aquarium in the state and 40 smaller tanks—all of which house marine life, land-based animals, and reptiles of the area—as well as a touch tank, seashell collections, video presentations, and a whale skeleton. It is open Monday–Saturday 9–4. Admission is $3.

The **Marine Life Oceanarium** (Jones Memorial Park, Gulfport, tel. 228/864–2511) has performing dolphins and sea lions as well as underwater dive shows for feeding the loggerhead sea turtles. The facility contains a giant reef tank, a simulated South American rain forest inhabited by exotic birds, a Listening Post where you can hear the dolphins communicating, a touch pool, performing macaws, a narrated Harbor Tour Train, and the S.S. *Gravity,* which investigates the force of gravity. It is open daily 10–3. Admission is $11.75.

The **Ole Biloxi Tour Train** (Biloxi Lighthouse on Beach Blvd., tel. 228/436–0025) winds through Biloxi while a guide identi-fies 75 important sites and describes the history of the seafood industry. It is in fact not a train but a tour bus. Admission is $8.

NATURE TRAILS AND SHORT WALKS Excel-lent trails traverse both districts. When you hike, watch out for fellow travelers—par-ticularly snakes, chiggers, and ticks—as well as cacti and poison ivy.

Florida District. Naval Live Oaks has two short trails and one longer one. The **Visitor Center Trail** winds .7 mi (round-trip) along Santa Rosa Sound and through a forest of Spanish moss–draped live oaks. The mile-long (round-trip) **Beaver Pond Trail** runs along the area's northern boundary, passing a large pond with an active beaver lodge. The 2.2-mi (one-way) **Pensacola–St. Augus-tine Trail,** originally part of the Pensa-cola–St. Augustine Road—Florida's first road, built in 1824—passes through woods of sand pines, longleaf pines, pignuts, south-ern magnolia, and scrub oak. The only inter-pretive trail markers here are along the Visitor Center Trail.

The **Blackbird Marsh Trail** meanders through the marshes and forests behind the campground of the Ft. Pickens unit. The .25-mi (one-way) **Dune Nature Trail** passes through primary and secondary dune sys-tems. Perdido Key's .25-mi (one-way) **John-son Beach Nature Trail** takes you through a marsh on the sound side of the key, where you'll see the short-growth shrub environ-ment typical of maritime forests, with lots of sea oats, palmettos, slash pine, and scrub live oak.

Mississippi District. At Davis Bayou the .5-mi (one-way) **Nature's Way Trail** edges the bayou, leading through dense forests. Stop by the small pond across the street from the trailhead to see the resident alligator.

LONGER HIKES Although there are no des-ignated longer trails at Gulf Islands, you can hike for miles along the beaches. On **Perdido Key** in Florida, the trek from the end of Johnson Beach Road to the jetties on the northeastern tip of the key and back is

12 mi round-trip. There's not a lot to see except surf and sand dunes, but you can count on good surf fishing and plenty of privacy. In Mississippi you can circumnav-igate **West Ship Island**—it's a sandy 7 mi. A shorter, more leisurely hike of 2 mi from the swimming area around the west tip of the island to Ft. Massachusetts takes about 1½–2 hours. Remember to bring water and wear sunscreen and a hat.

OTHER ACTIVITIES Biking. In Florida, Ft. Pickens is popular for cycling. A 2-mi bike path connects Battery Langdon near the ranger station with the fort. Rentals are available for $2 per hour from the **camp-ground store** (tel. 850/934–5691). Pen-sacola Beach has a 4.5-mi trail, and many cyclists ride the highway between the beach and the **bike trail at the Ft. Pickens area.** The **Live Oak Bicycle Trail** in Ocean Springs, Mississippi, goes into the Davis Bayou area; you can get a map at the Colmer Visitor Center (tel. 228/875–9057).

Bird-Watching. Visitor centers in both dis-tricts distribute handouts identifying birds and the best times to spot them. With its diverse habitats, the park attracts an eclec-tic avian population, including more than 280 species. In Florida the Naval Live Oaks area, Ft. Pickens, and Perdido Key (particu-larly the self-guided trail to the overlook above the marsh), and, in Mississippi, Davis Bayou and West Ship Island are on migratory-bird routes. In addition to the ever-present seagulls and terns, you may spot ducks, gallinules, coots, indigo bunt-ings, warblers, and, if you're lucky, nesting ospreys.

Boating. In the Florida district, Pensacola Bay, Santa Rosa Sound, Big Lagoon, and the Gulf of Mexico are favorite cruising grounds; the Okaloosa, Santa Rosa, Ft. Pickens, Perdido Key, and Naval Live Oaks areas are directly accessible by boat. Launch areas on Santa Rosa Sound are on the right side of Ft. Pickens Road, before the Ft. Pickens Area sign, and at the large area on Pensacola Beach Boulevard after the tollbooth at Quietwater Beach on the sound side. There are no launch sites on the gulf side. Several small docks along Pensacola Bay rent and charter boats. **American Boating Club** (Gulf Breeze, tel. 850/470–9771). **Mel's Marina** (Gulf Breeze, tel. 850/934–1005). **Moorings of Pensacola Beach** (Pensacola, tel. 850/932–0305). **The Marina** (Pensacola, tel. 850/932–5700).

In Mississippi you can cruise to all four of the barrier islands, anchoring near beaches on the leeward side. Rangers can tell you where it's safest to anchor; the boat dock at West Ship can be used by private boats during daylight hours. March 1 to October 31 private boaters may tie up to the dock, except at the end, which is reserved for tour boats. You can also anchor at Davis Bayou. Depart from Biloxi or Gulfport for East or West Ship, from Pascagoula for Petit Bois, and from Pascagoula or Ocean Springs for Horn. The **Gulfport Small Craft Harbor** (tel. 228/868–5713), **Biloxi Small Craft Harbor** (tel. 228/436–4062), and **Point Cadet Marina** (tel. 228/436–9312) supply names and numbers of contacts for chartering and renting boats. **Ross Tours** (tel. 228/432–8000) in Biloxi rents boats, as does **Shearwater Charters** (tel. 228/875–7108) in Ocean Springs. **Biloxi Schooner** (tel. 228/435–6320) in Biloxi docks two handcrafted schooners at the Point Cadet Marina behind the Isle of Capri Casino. They're available for charters and tours along the waterfront. Charter prices on the coast range from about $200 for a half-day to $600 for 10 hours, depending on the craft. Only charters licensed by the Gulf Islands National Seashore are authorized to travel to East Ship, Horn, and Petit Bois islands; charters are not permitted to dock at West Ship Island. Contact the Mississippi district office for names and numbers of official charter services (tel. 228/875–9075).

Fishing. You can wet your line from docks, piers, boats, and beaches just about anywhere in the Florida district. You can surf cast off Perdido Key for redfish, blues, pompano, and cobia. The small inlet between the tip of Perdido Key and the mainland is a good spot; the nearest bait and tackle shop is **Gray's Tackle and Guide Service** (Dolphin Square shopping center, 207 Gulf Breeze Pkwy., tel. 850/934–3151). Another good bet is the western end of Santa Rosa Island. At Ft. Pickens you can fish for mackerel, grouper, amberjack, and red snapper, depending on the season; fishing is best in spring and summer. Licenses are available at most bait and tackle shops. For fishing charters try **Moorings of Pensacola Beach** (tel. 850/932–0305) and **The Entertainer** charter boat (tel. 850/932–0305), in Gulf Breeze; charters for as many as six people cost $300–$400 for 4 hours and $600 for 8–10 hours. Your catch may include red snapper, grouper, triggerfish, and amberjack.

In the Mississippi district, Davis Bayou's pier is the hot spot for mullet and blue crabs; get bait and tackle on the mainland at the **Ft. Bayou Bait Shop** in Ocean Springs (tel. 228/875–6252). On West Ship Island you can catch sheepshead and redfish from the dock; buy bait from the Ft. Bayou Bait Shop. Charters take more serious aficionados into the gulf in search of large red snappers, groupers, and amberjack; for information, contact the **Gulfport Small Craft Harbor** (tel. 228/868–5713), **Biloxi Small Craft Harbor** (tel. 228/436–4062), **SeaSpace Dive Center** in Gautier (tel. 228/497–1381), or **Point Cadet Marina** (tel. 228/436–9312).

Gambling. Although they are open 24 hours a day, seven days a week, the Mississippi Gulf Coast's 11 casinos (more are under construction) hop the most at night. All are on the water, and all have slot machines and a variety of wagering games; most have one or more restaurants and some type of live entertainment. The structures range in style from ultracontemporary buildings to paddle-wheel river boats to a gigantic pirate ship attached to a castle. Admission and parking are free. The **Biloxi Grand Theater** (U.S. 90, tel. 800/946–2946) presents a Las Vegas–type show with elaborate songs and dances. For the most up-to-date casino information, call 800/237–9493.

Golf. There are no courses in the park, but the area on both sides of the Florida-Mississippi state line is full of them. Greens fees range from $17 to $45 including cart, and many resorts and motels offer golf packages (tel. 888/218–8463 for information). In Florida a few of the top-rated courses are **Tiger Point Country Club** (tel. 850/932–1333) in Gulf Breeze, **Scenic Hills** (tel. 850/476–0611) in Pensacola, and the **Club at Hidden Creek** (tel. 850/939–4604 or 800/239–2582), 17 mi east of Pensacola on U.S. 98. In Mississippi try Biloxi's **Sunkist Country Club** (tel. 228/388–3961) or **Tramark Golf Course** (tel. 228/863–7808) in Gulfport.

Kite Flying. Wide-open beaches, brisk gulf breezes, and the absence of trees and utility lines make for ideal conditions. You'll see a variety of shapes and styles darting across the sky, especially at Pensacola Beach and the Santa Rosa day-use area. Bring your own kite or try **Alvin's Island** (400 Quietwater Beach Rd. on Pensacola Beach, tel. 850/934–3711).

Sailing. In Florida, sailing to Ft. Pickens, Perdido Key, and Okaloosa is popular, but you can't launch a boat in the park, only at public launches along the beaches. Contact **Perdido Water Sports** (tel. 850/664–7872) at Ft. Walton or **Key Sailing** (tel. 850/932–5520) or **Bonifay Water Sports** (tel. 850/932–0633), both in Pensacola Beach. In Mississippi, rentals are not common, but you can try **Mid South Sailing & Charter** (tel. 228/863–6969) in Gulfport. Sunfish rentals cost $5–$10 per hour, and two hours on a four-person catamaran can cost as much as $60, a little more if you need instruction.

Scuba Diving and Snorkeling. The Naval Live Oaks Visitor Center has handouts covering local diving locations and regulations. The best areas are the grass beds at the Naval Live Oaks area or the end of Shoreline Park in Gulf Breeze (2–5 ft deep) and at the east end of the Big Lagoon (7–10 ft deep) in the Perdido Key area, the diving jetties (15–50 ft deep) at Ft. Pickens. In June and July, Gulf Islands National Seashore sponsors snorkeling programs at **Ft. Pickens;** call 850/934–2600 for tour times. For scuba- and snorkeling-equipment rental and supplies in Florida, try **Gulf Breeze Dive Pro** (tel. 850/934–8845) in Gulf Breeze and **Scuba Shack** (tel. 850/433–4319) and **Gulf Coast Dive Pro** (tel. 850/456–8845), both in Pensacola. In Mississippi call **Sea-Space Dive Center** (tel. 228/497–1381) in Gautier and **Dive Five** (tel. 228/385–7664) in Biloxi for excursions in Mississippi, Alabama, and Florida waters. One-week, accelerated certification courses are available, and scuba-equipment rental costs about $15–$35 per day; charters cost $40–$50 per half-day, $60–$70 per full day, and group dives $30–$60, depending on how far out you go and how many tanks you consume. Fish, particularly red snapper, are abundant throughout the area, and in deep waters you see angelfish, butterfly fish, and other tropical species, as well as the occasional lobster. Sites include wrecks, marine ballast, and artificial reefs.

Shrimping. Learn about shrimping by taking a 70-minute marine adventure ($10): the **Biloxi Shrimping Trip** (Biloxi Small Craft Harbor, tel. 228/385–1182 or 800/289–7908) aboard the *Sailfish*. The process is explained and the entire catch, which includes fish and other sea creatures, is identified. There are five to six departures daily, depending on the weather and the number of passengers.

Water Sports. Swimming, waterskiing, and windsurfing are popular throughout the Florida district and on the Mississippi islands. There is no swimming at Davis Bayou. Lifeguards are on duty in summer at the public beach in Pensacola. Many businesses outside the park rent water-sports equipment, including **Bonifay Water Sports** (tel. 850/932–0633) and **Surf and Sail Windsurfing** (tel. 850/932–7873) in Pensacola Beach, and **Life's a Beach** (tel. 228/385–1488) and **Wet & Wild** (tel. 228/374–7962) in Biloxi.

CHILDREN'S PROGRAMS It won't be easy tearing your kids away from sand castle construction and seaside gamboling. But if they participate in the Junior Ranger program, they'll earn a park button and special certificate. From June through July, in both the Florida and Mississippi districts, park rangers conduct hour-long programs on natural and cultural history for children ages 5–12. Call the visitor centers (tel. 850/934–2600 in Florida, 228/875–9057 in Mississippi) for schedules.

EVENING ACTIVITIES True to the spirit of southern living, evenings along the coast are typically spent perched on the beach lazily watching the sun set over the Gulf of Mexico. In Ft. Pickens, members of the Escambia Amateur Astronomers Association (c/o Dr. Wayne Wooten, Pensacola Junior College, tel. 850/484–1600) gather for **stargazing** on clear evenings; they usually allow nonmembers to gaze through their telescopes. **Ranger programs** on park ecology and history are held in October and March at the Ft. Pickens area (tel. 850/934–2635) and year-round at the Davis Bayou area (tel. 228/875–9057).

DINING

The only places that serve food inside the park are the snack bars at Perdido Key, Ft. Pickens, and West Ship Island, which are open March through Labor Day weekend. Outside the park you'll have no problem finding great food. Shellfish is essential eating. Just about every restaurant serves baked oysters, broiled grouper, and the like, and there are plenty of sandwich shops and pizza joints. On the Mississippi side, creole and Cajun flavors abound. Casual attire is fine in the restaurants reviewed below, unless noted otherwise.

NEAR THE FLORIDA DISTRICT **Boy on a Dolphin.** The Greek-influenced seafood at this popular eatery on the edge of Santa Rosa Sound is among the best in the Pensacola area. Chef Spero Athanasios and his family have been pleasing locals and visitors for three decades with steak, prime rib, and pasta dishes, along with a huge selection of delicious seafood. Whether charcoal-grilled Greek-style or baked in a traditional Athenian marinade, the catch of the day is always superb; it could be grouper, snapper, flounder, or triggerfish. For dessert, try the honey-drenched baklava or *kadaif,* shredded wheat covered with custard and topped with whipped cream, and sprinkled with toasted almonds. *400 Pensacola Beach Blvd., Pensacola Beach, tel. 850/932–7954. Reservations essential for summer weekends. AE, MC, V. $$*

Jubilee Restaurant and BeachSide Cafe. Jubilee, an entertainment complex on the Quietwater Beach Boardwalk, is a total experience, a place where a visitor could spend the whole day—there are many shops, small sailboat rentals, street entertainers, and more. Casual options include the waterfront BeachSide Cafe, with an open-air deck, which serves soups, salads, and sandwiches as well as a few dinner entrées, and has live entertainment nightly. Capt'n Fun is a beach bar and Sweets is Pensacola Beach's only gourmet coffee and dessert shop. For that special evening, there's the formal TopSide Dining Room overlooking Pensacola Sound. Crisp linens, antiques, and contemporary art works compliment a menu described as Florida-style cuisine but featuring many Cajun dishes. Seafood tops the menu, but steak is prominently featured. *400 Quietwater Beach Rd., Pensacola Beach, tel. 850/934–3108 or 800/582–3028. Reservations essential for Top-Side. AE, D, DC, MC, V. $–$$$*

Lighthouse Point. A wall of picture windows at this restaurant, formerly the Pensacola Naval Air Station Chief's Club, allows daytime diners to gaze across Pensacola Bay at Ft. Pickens and Perdido Key. The all-you-can-eat buffet changes daily, but there are always Tex-Mex dishes, build-your-own sandwiches, and gumbos and other soups. The Thursday buffet table is all pasta dishes and salads. On any day, you can also order hot entrées and sandwiches à la carte. *Lighthouse Point, Pensacola Naval Air Station, tel. 850/452–3251. Reservations not accepted. MC, V. Closed weekends. No dinner. $*

Peg Leg Pete's Oyster Bar & Restaurant. Visitors to this easygoing beachside spot on Ft. Pickens Road are in for a treat. For starters, try baked oysters casino or Cajun-style. Chase them down with red beans and rice, jambalaya, or shrimp Orleans (sautéed with rice, onions, and peppers). Or try the Pirate Platter, which includes a little of everything on the menu. Jazz guitarists entertain Thursday, Friday, and Saturday nights from June through September. *1010 Ft. Pickens Rd., Pensacola Beach, Pensacola, tel. 850/932–4139. Reservations not accepted. AE, MC, V. $*

NEAR THE MISSISSIPPI DISTRICT **Blue Rose Restaurant and Lounge.** In an exquisite 1850 West Indies–style house overlooking the Pass Christian Yacht Harbor, the swanky Blue Rose doubles as an antiques shop. Its high-ceiling formal dining rooms are sumptuously decorated with lush floral fabrics and rich jewel tones; an enclosed porch is more gardenlike. The restaurant serves several preparations of alligator in addition to a wide range of seafood, duck, pasta, chicken, pork, and beef dishes. Popular are Sunday brunch and Sunday dinner, when chef's specials such as Hash Christian, sautéed Norwegian salmon hash with poached eggs and lemon hollandaise, or pasta Vieux Carré with Gulf shrimp and tasso are featured. *120 W. Scenic Dr., Pass Christian, tel. 228/ 452–0335. AE, D, DC, MC, V. Closed Mon. No dinner Tues.–Thurs. $$$*

Anthony's. Tucked under the umbrella of a huge, ancient live oak, this restaurant overlooks tranquil Ft. Bayou. Furnished with wrought iron and floral upholstery to resemble a garden room, the many-windowed room has sweeping views of the marshes. Linen tablecloths and napkins add a touch of elegance to such dinner specialties as blackened prime rib, crabmeat au gratin, and red snapper Lafette. The restaurant is noted for its crab and shrimp po'boys served at lunchtime as well as for its sumptuous Sunday brunch. *1217 Washington Ave., Ocean Springs, tel. 228/872– 4564. AE, MC, V. Closed Mon. $$–$$$*

The Chimneys. Long Beach used to be called the Chimneys because of the long line of chimneys on the turn-of-the-century beach homes. The rustic, casual restaurant that now bears the name is one of the few Mississippi Gulf Coast eateries that is actually on the beach overlooking the Gulf of Mexico. Porches, which can be enclosed in bad weather, allow diners to enjoy the sights and sounds of the sea, while the indoor, paneled main dining room is more club-like in atmosphere. True to its location, the restaurant specializes in seafood, although it also offers beef, chicken, and veal dishes. Specialties include sautéed or fried crab claws, soft-shell crabs, and the Cat Island combo—a platter including fried shrimp, oysters, and a fresh Gulf fish. *Long Beach Small Craft Harbor, Long Beach, tel. 228/868–7020. Reservations essential. AE, D, MC, V. $$*

Mary Mahoney's Old French House Restaurant and Complex. Built in 1737 and therefore one of the oldest buildings along the coast, Mary Mahoney's is renowned for its seafood, especially its snapper, lobster, and oyster stew served for lunch and dinner. Furnished with antiques, the restaurant has a graceful Old South ambience. More informal, the adjacent café serves po'boys and other sandwiches. The outbuildings and New Orleans–style courtyard serve as dining areas as well. *138 Rue Magnolia, Biloxi, tel. 228/374–0163. AE, D, DC, MC, V. Closed Sun. $$*

Vrazel's. Hurricane Camille blew away the venerable restaurant here in 1969; the brick building that replaced it gets its charm from soft lighting and dining nooks with large windows facing the beach. Added attractions include the finny fare—red snapper, gulf and sea trout, flounder, and shrimp prepared every which way: amandine, blackened, étouffée, or au gratin à la Cajun (blackened, spicy, and grilled). Seafood à la Vrazel piles crabmeat, shrimp, and scallops over pilaf or spaghetti, and seafood Pontchartrain meunière is sautéed red snapper fillet and soft-shell crabs topped with lemon butter. Snapper Lenwood, another specialty, teams broiled fish with a topping of crabmeat and crayfish in a Cajun sauce. Or try veal Aaron (tender veal medallions in a lemony sauce, chunky with crabmeat and mushrooms). *3206 W. Beach Blvd. (U.S. 90), Gulfport, tel. 228/863–2229. AE, D, DC, MC, V. $$*

Jocelyn's. Locals often celebrate birthdays and anniversaries here. Soft music, bare wood floors, fireplaces, and walls hung with prints by Mississippi son Walter Anderson create a casually refined atmosphere. Specialties include broiled steak, calves' liver, chicken pot pie, baked beans, and baked and broiled seafood served with white sauce, butter sauce, or wine sauce. Every so often Jocelyn adds an idiosyncratic dish to the menu, maybe an entrée of boiled cabbage au gratin or a dessert of cranberry-peach crisp with oatmeal. *U.S. 90, opposite Union Planters Bank, Ocean Springs, tel. 228/875–1925. Reservations not accepted. No credit cards. Closed Sun.–Mon. No lunch. $–$$*

Robby's Seafood. Nautical signs, boating memorabilia, paddles and oars, ship bells, neon seagull signs, running lights, and other nautical trappings decorate this spot, which some might call tacky. But for giant shrimp, oyster, beef, and ham po'boys on thick French bread (9 or 14 inches long), Robby's is tough to beat. Try fried soft-shell crabs or fried oysters your first time around. Regulars know to go for the enormous seafood platters—either of stuffed crab and fried catfish, shrimp, and oysters, or, in season, boiled shrimp, crabs, or crayfish. The gumbo is excellent. *U.S. 49, across from Norwood Village Shopping Center, tel. 228/831–1160 or 228/831–1161. Reservations not accepted. AE, MC, V. $*

PICNIC SPOTS In the **Okaloosa** area, on the shores of Choctawhatchee Bay, a shady picnic area overlooks the bay. The **Santa Rosa day-use area,** on Route 399 between Navarre Beach and Pensacola Beach, and the **Johnson Beach pavilion,** at Perdido Key, offer gulf-side picnic settings. The above-mentioned places were damaged by Hurri-

cane Opal but have been repaired and reopened. **Ft. Pickens** has two wooded picnic groves with views of Pensacola Bay, both well protected from offshore breezes. In Mississippi, **Davis Bayou** has a large picnic area with a playground. But far more scenic is **West Ship Island**'s small pavilion and snack stand. You can bring picnic fixings, but keep things modest, because ferries to and from the island can accommodate only small or medium-size coolers.

LODGING

Although there's no lodging in the park, the surrounding area is full of beach resorts, hotels, and motor lodges. Rooms are more expensive from April through October, high season; a Gulf view will set you back another $10–$15. Because of legalized gambling, once-quiet Biloxi is fast on the way to becoming a neon showcase of bustling casinos and nightclubs. Hotels are shooting up everywhere—and so are room rates.

NEAR THE FLORIDA DISTRICT **Clarion Suites Resort and Convention Center.** Pensacola Beach's newest waterfront property creates a villagelike ambience. Each suite, complete with living and dining area and master bedroom, is furnished in breezy Florida style (mauves predominant) and comes with a queen-size bed, queen-size sofa bed, microwave, refrigerator, toaster oven, coffeemaker, and two TVs. Continental breakfast is included. *20 Via de Luna, Pensacola Beach 32561, tel. 850/932–4300 or 800/874–5303, fax 850/934–9112. 86 suites. Facilities: pool, exercise room. AE, D, DC, MC, V. $$$*

Best Western Pensacola Beach. In this beachside motel, guest rooms are large and brightly decorated in coral and turquoise, with a tropical-fish motif enlivening the bedspreads and watercolors on the walls; windows overlook the Gulf of Mexico or Pensacola Bay. All rooms have one king- or two queen-size beds plus a microwave oven, refrigerator, coffeemaker, and wet bar. Free Continental breakfast is served in the lobby each morning. The pool is a sand dollar's throw from the Gulf and has a cabana bar open on weekends; you can rent beach chairs, umbrellas, and cushions. The clientele includes both families and businesspeople. There's a restaurant next door. *16 Via de Luna, Pensacola Beach 32561, tel. 850/934–3300 or 800/528–1234, fax 850/934–4366. 124 rooms. Facilities: 2 pools, bar. AE, D, DC, MC, V. $$*

The Dunes. This beachfront motel, which looks like a sand castle emerging from the dunes, is close to Ft. Pickens and the Naval Live Oaks Visitor Center and has panoramic views of Santa Rosa Island and the Gulf. The clientele includes businesspeople and families, with some conference traffic. Beach chairs and umbrellas are available for rent. *333 Ft. Pickens Rd., Pensacola Beach 32561, tel. 850/932–3536 or 800/833–8637, fax 850/932–7088. 72 rooms, 4 suites. Facilities: bar, café, pool. AE, D, MC, V. $$*

Holiday Inn Pensacola Beach. This beachfront hotel also offers spectacular Gulf views and is near several park areas. The rooms are done in soft, beachy tones of seafoam green, pale blue, and peach. The ninth-floor penthouse lounge overlooks the Ft. Pickens area to the west and Santa Rosa Sound to the north. The conference center and restaurant were lost to Hurricane Opal and have not been rebuilt. Beach chairs and umbrellas are available for rent. *165 Ft. Pickens Rd., Pensacola Beach 32561, tel. 850/932–5361 or 800/465–4329, fax 850/932–5361. 150 rooms, 1 suite. Facilities: bar, pool. AE, D, DC, MC, V. $$*

NEAR THE MISSISSIPPI DISTRICT **Treasure Bay Resort Hotel and Casino.** This resort is nothing if not eye catching—the casino looks like a huge pirate ship and several of the restaurants, lounges, and the theater are housed in an ersatz medieval castle. Across the street is the hotel, which is decorated in simple, contemporary style. The service is efficient. There's an 18-hole golf course nearby. *1980 Beach Blvd., Biloxi 39531, tel. 228/385–6000 or 800/747–2839, fax 228/385–6067. 260 rooms, 6 suites. Facilities: 3*

restaurants, bar, nightclub, 2 pools. AE, D, DC, MC, V. $$$

Father Ryan House. One of the most gorgeous historic homes on the coast, the Father Ryan House, named for the poet laureate of the Confederacy, was built in 1841. Today it operates as a bed-and-breakfast where several of the antiques-filled guest rooms have private verandas overlooking the beaches and the Gulf; four have whirlpool baths. A full breakfast is included. *1196 Beach Blvd., Biloxi 35630, tel. 228/435–1189 or 800/295–1189, fax 228/436–3063. 11 rooms. Facilities: pool. AE, D, MC, V. $$–$$$*

Harbour Oaks Inn. Adults and families with children over 14 will enjoy this stately 1860 B&B. Overlooking the picturesque Pass Christian Yacht Harbor and sugar-white beaches, it was built when "the Pass" was an internationally known resort. Guest rooms on the first and second floors open onto expansive columned porches shaded by gigantic live oaks draped in Spanish moss. Furnishings are comfortable and are a mix of styles and periods, so each guest room has its own personality. The suite has a two-person whirlpool bath. *126 West Scenic Dr., Pass Christian 39571, tel. 228/452–9399 or 800/452–9399. 4 rooms, 1 suite. Facilities: billiards. AE, MC, V. $$*

Holiday Inn Biloxi Beachfront. Just across the street from the beach, this Holiday Inn is halfway between Gulfport and Biloxi, 6 mi from the Davis Bayou area. There are some 15 types of rooms, from standard doubles and king-size bedrooms with whirlpool baths to bilevel, condominium-like suites with hot tubs and Gulf views. Rooms are decorated in floral patterns of coral, sand, and seafoam green. *2400 Beach Blvd., Biloxi 39531, tel. 228/388–3551 or 800/441–0882, fax 228/385–2032. 268 rooms, 6 suites. Facilities: restaurant, bar, nightclub, pool. AE, D, DC, MC, V. $$*

CAMPING

The park maintains only two campgrounds, one in each district, with 251 sites between them. Both are open year-round; in summer they're especially crowded and fill quickly. However, there are some other options near both districts. No permits or fees are required for primitive camping where it is available.

FLORIDA DISTRICT **Ft. Pickens Campground.** In a grove of tall pines, this campground has picturesque, well-maintained sites that are popular with both tenters and RVers. All sites have water hookups, and 150 have electricity as well; none has a sewage hookup, but there's a dump station near the well-stocked campground store. Sites with electricity cost $20 a night; sites without electricity, $15. The showers are great, with plenty of hot water and good water pressure. The sites are sandy and lightly wooded with scrub pine; some are waterfront. Pets are allowed in the campground, with a 6-ft leash, but not at the beach. Reservations are accepted; walk-ins will be accepted when space is available. *1801 Gulf Breeze Pkwy., Gulf Breeze 32561, tel. 850/934–2621 for 24-hr recorded message. 200 sites. Facilities: picnic area, shop. MC, V. $*

Primitive Camping. Primitive camping is allowed (you must register for a spot) on the eastern end of **Perdido Key,** beginning .5 mi east of the end of Johnson Beach Road. You are asked to avoid the dunes and vegetated areas, and you must pack out what you pack in. Most campers arrive by small boat (land on the northern side of the island). A permit is required if you plan on leaving a vehicle overnight in the parking lot or along the stabilized road shoulder. Only permitted campers are allowed in the area after sunset, when the gate closes.

NEAR THE FLORIDA DISTRICT **Big Lagoon State Recreation Area.** The campground here, just across the Intracoastal Waterway from Perdido Key and a few miles from Ft. Barrancas, has 75 sites, 49 with electric and water hookups. Sites are large, sandy, and lightly wooded with scrub pine. The bathhouses, built of cedar with roomy rest room–shower units, are outstanding. A boardwalk meanders through the lagoon,

where you'll probably see raccoons, opossums, squirrels, rabbits, and a lone resident alligator. The park has an amphitheater and a picnic pavilion. Sites cost $11.02 per night with electricity and water hookups, $8.88 without. *12301 Gulf Beach Hwy., Pensacola, tel. 850/492–1595, fax 850/492–4380. 74 sites. Facilities: grill, picnic area. No credit cards. $*

Gulf State Park. About 15 mi west of Perdido Key, Florida, and 1 mi from the Gulf, this enormous park is one of the best places for camping in the country. Every one of its 468 roomy sites has electric and water hookups, and many have views of freshwater lakes, two of them in the park: It's not unheard of for campers to cast fishing lines from their site's picnic table. The park also offers saltwater angling, golf, and tennis. Campsites cost $11–$25 depending upon location. *22050 Campground Rd., Gulf Shores, AL, tel. 334/948–7275 for information or 800/352–7275 for reservations. 468 sites. Facilities: 18-hole golf course, 2 tennis courts, fishing, shop, coin laundry. AE, MC, V. $*

Navarre Beach Family Campground. This campground is closer to Ft. Pickens and Naval Live Oaks than Gulf State Park. All of its 99 sites have electric hookups, and 60 have full hookups (complete with cable-TV outlets); you'll also find one large fire pit, a pier, and readily available firewood. Fees are $19.95–$35.95 per day depending on hookup and location. *U.S. 98, tel. 850/939–2188, fax 850/939–4712. 130 sites. Facilities: pool, beach, playground, coin laundry. MC, V. $*

MISSISSIPPI DISTRICT **Davis Bayou Campground.** Relatively small, this campground has 51 spacious sites that are protected by live oaks; all have electricity and water hookups, and some have water views. It's first-come, first-served; reservations are not accepted, and there is no waiting list. You will pay $16 for sites with electricity and water, $14 if you're tenting. The showers are hot and have good water pressure. There is a picnic area and a dump station near the bathhouse. *Gulf Islands National Seashore, 3500 Park Rd., Ocean Springs 39564, tel. 228/875–9057. 51 sites. Facilities: coin laundry. No credit cards. $*

Primitive Camping. With their dunes, Gulf surf, slash pines, palmettos, occasional live oak trees, and wax-myrtle bushes, **Horn, Petit Bois,** and **East Ship** islands are popular with primitive campers. On Horn and Petit Bois, permits are not required, but it's wise to check in with the rangers who patrol the islands. Horn Island has a ranger station, but there are no structures on Petit Bois and East Ship islands. On East Ship, you must register, but there are no fees. Only charter captains with permits are allowed to visit the island. Fires are not allowed above the extreme high-tide line, and you must pack out what you pack in.

NEAR THE MISSISSIPPI DISTRICT **Cajun RV Park.** A reliable campground, this RV park is 300 yards off the highway, so it's quiet. Because the beach is across the road, this campground is also convenient. The handful of long-term sites, which have phone hookups, lend a feeling of permanence you don't find everywhere. There are picnic tables, showers, a convenience store, and propane in addition to facilities listed below. Of the 125 sites, 110 are RV sites and 15 are tent sites. Fees are $22.50 for full hookups ($21.40 with electricity and water only) and $16.59 for tents. *U.S. 90, Biloxi, tel. 228/388–5590. 125 sites. Facilities: pool, 9-hole golf course, playground, coin laundry. No credit cards. $*

Casino Magic Campground. All sites have full hookups (including hookups for cable TV) and a general store. There's also a bathhouse. Casino Magic Casino is a three-minute walk from the campground, or you can hop on a complimentary shuttle. The fee for all sites, which are RV only, is $19. *711 Casino Magic Dr., Bay St. Louis, tel. 800/562–4425. 100 RV sites. Facilities: coin laundry. No credit cards. $*

Southern Comfort Camping Resort. One of several campgrounds near the beach in the Biloxi area, Southern Comfort is neat and clean. All 112 sites have water and electricity, and 65 of them have full hookups. Fees are $18–$20 for sites with hookups, $8 for the 25 tent sites. Showers, a game room, picnic tables, and grills are on the premises. *U.S. 90, Biloxi, tel. 228/432–1700. 112 sites. Facilities: pool, hot tub, sauna, coin laundry. MC, V. $*

Hot Springs National Park and Ouachita National Forest

Arkansas, Oklahoma

By Robert S. McCord

Updated by Willard M. Lewis

ong before the spas of California and Florida, there was Hot Springs, a health resort whose main attraction was and is a collection of 47 thermal mineral springs. In the last 50 years, as bath therapy has given way to modern drugs, long-distance travel has become easier, and newer resorts have sprung up, therapeutic baths have become less popular. Recently, however, someone who grew up in Hot Springs became president of the United States, and interest has been rekindled, both in Arkansas and in the Hot Springs area. With its moderate climate and proximity to the lakes, streams, and mountains of the Ouachita National Forest, it's Arkansas's favorite vacation site, drawing visitors year-round.

Though some residents aren't crazy about increased tourism and the crowds and higher prices they bring, travelers are discovering Hot Springs and the nearby Ouachita National Forest in greater numbers. Visitors come to see where Bill Clinton grew up and also to take advantage of the diverse opportunities available where a major national forest is so close to an urban national park. An hour after hiking or canoeing in a wilderness area, you can be eating in a fine French restaurant, watching some of the country's best Thoroughbred racing, or immersing yourself in a hot mineral bath.

Hot Springs the city (population 35,644) and Hot Springs the national park are inextricably linked. Geographically, the city and park are not so much adjacent as they are intertwined; parts of the park are nearly surrounded by city and vice versa.

Functionally, they are interdependent as well. For years each bathhouse had its own spring, but today the National Park Service collects approximately 430 gallons of water a minute from 23 of the spa's 47 springs; it distributes the water to concessionaires, including the bathhouses, a physical medicine center and a hospital that specializes in treating arthritis, and four hotels that operate their own bathhouses. The Park Service also operates thermal jug fountains, from which individuals may carry off as much water as they want at any hour of the day and at no charge.

People have been coming to the area for hundreds of years. The first visitors were Native Americans, attracted by the healing thermal waters that bubbled to the surface of the earth. It is believed by some that Hernando de Soto, on one of his explorations, was the first European here. French hunters and trappers followed, using the springs to ease and rejuvenate their weary bodies.

By the time of the Louisiana Purchase (1803), when the area now called Arkansas became part of the United States, the springs were widely known. In 1832, the federal government designated four sections of land that contained the hot springs as a federal reservation, and soon the sick and the lame were coming in great numbers from all over the country. Regular stagecoaches traveled rough roads beset by bandits, who knew that visitors often carried great amounts of cash. In 1874, the railroad was extended to Hot Springs.

At first the bathhouses were little more than huts open to the public. Later, private bathhouses were built as concessions and operated under the supervision of the federal government. By the early 20th century, Hot Springs's bathhouses were at the height of their popularity, being used to treat almost everything—from arthritis and rheumatism to gonorrhea and syphilis. "The spa," wrote Dee Brown in his book *The American Spa,* "had won wide acceptance among the trend setters of America, travelers who were comparable to the jet set of today. . . . It became fashionable to visit the springs for a series of baths regardless of whether one was ailing or not."

As the springs' popularity grew, so did the town's. Despite being illegal, casinos flourished and generated revenue, while several governors turned a blind eye. Finally, Governor Winthrop Rockefeller shut them down for good in 1967, but Thoroughbred racing remains at Hot Springs's Oaklawn Park, one of America's premier tracks.

With 5,500 acres within its boundary, Hot Springs is the country's smallest national park, it's the only one to include an urban area, and (though it wasn't officially designated until 1921) it also likes to claim to be the country's oldest. Congress "reserved" the springs in 1832, thus planting the germ of an idea for the national parks system that was to follow. (Yellowstone was actually named the first national park in 1872.)

A study in contrasts, nearby Ouachita National Forest is the largest in the South, stretching 1.7 million acres from west-central Arkansas to southeast Oklahoma. It, too, was first explored by de Soto in 1541. In 1907 it was set aside as the Arkansas National Forest and in 1926 was renamed the Ouachita National Forest in recognition of the mountains that run through it. "Ouachita," or "Washita" as it was spelled originally, is a Native American word that some believe means good hunting ground, although this is open to conjecture.

Most of the 66,000 acres of wilderness (defined as any plot of 5,000 or more acres containing no roads) in the national forest are on the slopes of the Ouachita Mountains. In addition to abundant and varied forestland, there's plenty of water, ranging from those intimate little lakes that anglers think of as private ponds to the 48,300-acre Lake Ouachita, one of the cleanest in the United States. As a result, the national forest and its 35 recreation areas offer a wide range of outdoor experiences—camping, canoeing, fishing, hunting, backpacking, crystal mining, swimming, horseback riding, mountain biking, and hiking—as well as historical sites and excavations.

ESSENTIAL INFORMATION

VISITOR INFORMATION For information about the park, contact the superintendent, **Hot Springs National Park** (Box 1860, Hot Springs 71902, tel. 501/624–3383, ext. 620). Also check with the **Fordyce Bathhouse Visitor Center** on Bath House Row in Hot Springs (tel. 501/623–1433 or 501/624–3383, ext. 640). For information on the forest, contact the Public Affairs Office, **Ouachita National Forest** (Box 1270, Hot Springs 71902, tel. 501/321–5202). Information about the city of Hot Springs and nearby areas can be obtained from the **Department of Parks and Tourism** (1 Capitol Mall, Little Rock 72201, tel. 800/628–8725) and the **Hot Springs Advertising and Promotion Commission** (Box K, Hot Springs 71902, tel. 800/772–2489).

FEES There is no entrance fee for the national park. Entry to most of the 35 recreation areas in the national forest costs $2 per vehicle.

PUBLICATIONS The **Hot Springs National Park brochure** is free and lists general rules; it also has a map and information on trails, the Gulpha Gorge campground, and hiking resources. A short (100 pages) and very readable history of Hot Springs is *The American Spa,* sold at the visitor center bookstore and written by Dee Brown, author of the best-seller *Bury My Heart at Wounded Knee.* In addition, special folders on Hot Springs, such as "Tour of President Clinton's Hot Springs," are available from the Hot Springs Advertising and Promotion Commission (*see above*) and the small visitor center in Hill Wheatley Plaza on Central Avenue, the main street. The best publication about the Ouachita National Forest is the *Recreation Area Directory*, a compendium of rules, names and addresses of rangers' districts, campsites, trails, and a map; there is also a trails packet, which describes forest trails in great detail, available from the Office of the Supervisor of Ouachita National Forest at 100 Reserve Street, a block north of Central.

GEOLOGY AND TERRAIN Hot Springs National Park is in a valley formed by four small mountains in the Ouachita range. The springs' water, which averages 143°F, begins as precipitation. Over the course of 4,000 years, it percolates through layers of chert and novaculite (a rock found only in Arkansas, Texas, and Oklahoma) to an unknown depth. It heats up and picks up dissolved minerals and finally rushes back to the surface. Old tufa masses are visible on Hot Springs Mountain and mark the presence of the springs or the paths of past spring flows.

The Ouachita Mountains are the tallest between the Appalachians and the Rockies. The highest point, Rich Mountain, rises to 2,681 ft near the Arkansas-Oklahoma border. The mountains are composed of erosion-resistant sandstone, novaculite, and/or chert that are 300 to 500 million years old. Like many other ranges, they were formed when sediment was deposited in a deepwater setting and then folded and faulted by continental collision. Unlike most others, however, the Ouachitas run east–west.

FLORA AND FAUNA The warmth of the earth's interior, brought to the surface by the springs, allows for the year-round growth of some plants in or near the hot springs. Herbs and ferns live near the two open springs, and Trelease's blue-green algae, found in only a few other places worldwide, exists in the springwater itself. The algae fascinated early scientists, who

could not believe anything could survive in the hot water.

The mountains of the national park are filled with oak, hickory, and pine, and many of the trees are 200 years old or more, despite quite a bit of clearing by homesteaders in the early 20th century. Ozark chinquapin, a native tree made very rare by the chestnut blight, is found in the park. Stately magnolias, introduced along Central Avenue in Hot Springs years ago to mark the border of Bathhouse Row, are most impressive.

The national forest has an interesting mixture of plant life, an estimated 2,500 species. On the northern slopes of these east–west-running mountains, there's a dominance of oak and hickory; on the southern slopes you'll find pines—this is an uncommon combination. Patient visitors can find beautiful orchids and ferns growing out of acid seeps. Two plants, the Cossatot leafcup and Browne's waterleaf, are found nowhere else. The forest contains 60 species of trees, both hardwoods and pines, including the largest expanse of short-leaf pine in the nation. Especially noteworthy is Rich Mountain's elfin forest of 300-year-old, 3-ft-high, lichen-covered white oaks.

Hot Springs National Park is both urban and rural. Within the urban section, which is considerably smaller than the rural part, creatures seen regularly are squirrels, songbirds, armadillos, and, occasionally, wild turkeys. Other fauna once common to the springs, including deer and black bears, are still found in the nearby national forest but rarely in the park itself.

Arkansas used to be known as the Bear State because of the abundance of black bears. Over the years, almost all were killed, but they're now being reintroduced in the Ouachitas. Foxes, white-tailed deer, turkeys, and bobcats roam the forest, but because it is so dense they are seldom seen. Game fish, such as bass, bluegill, sunfish, crappie, catfish, and walleye, abound in lakes and streams, and there are at least three fish—the paleback darter, the Ouachita darter, the Ouachita madtom (catfish), and the Caddo madtom—that are endemic. There are even alligators. Among the forest's endangered animals are the Indiana bat and the red-cockaded woodpecker. The threatened bald eagle also may be spotted around area lakes.

WHEN TO GO The weather in southwestern Arkansas is moderate, though there are four distinct seasons. Many visitors come to see the vibrant fall foliage or the bright profusion of spring wildflowers. Summer is a bit humid; winter is mild and still fine for hiking.

The 30-year average high is 73.1°F and the low is 50°F. The annual precipitation is 56.5 inches. Summer is hot and humid; the average high in July is 93.3°F. Spring and fall are short but very pleasant. The average high and low in April are 74.3°F and 50°F, but it is also a month of thunderstorms and an occasional tornado. The two coldest months are December and January, with lows averaging around freezing and light snow not unusual.

SEASONAL EVENTS Late **January to mid-April:** Hot Springs' Thoroughbred racing season includes Oaklawn Park's popular **Arkansas Derby** (tel. 501/623–4411 or 800/ 722–3652) on the final day of the season. It is second only to the Kentucky Derby in the size of the winner's purse. **May: Celebration of the Visual Arts** includes walking tours of the dozen or so art galleries along Central Avenue, lectures, workshops, and an architectural tour. **June:** The **Hot Springs Music Festival,** classical music performed by chamber players, a festival orchestra, and soloists, offers some two dozen concerts, many free, in venues around the city. **August–November: A Festival of Arts** brings a jazz festival that attracts notables from around the country the second week in September and an acclaimed **documentary film festival** the second week of October. **October:** The **Celebration of the Arts** is very popular. Local and international artisans display and sell their wares, ranging from photographs to sculpture. In the middle of October is **Oktoberfest,** where the large German population re-creates this famed Munich event. The emphasis is being shifted away from beer consumption to family-oriented activities, which include a Volksport Association–sanctioned Volksmarsch, baroque chamber music concerts, Alpenhorn performances, German cooking classes, arts-and-crafts demonstrations, and polka parties. The Mount Ida Chamber of Commerce (Box 6, Mount Ida 71957, tel. 501/867–2723) sponsors a **Quartz Crystal Dig;** amateur miners pay a fee and dig for crystals at any of about 10 commercial mines in the national forest.

WHAT TO PACK If you're heading for the national forest, bring basic outdoor clothes and gear, including first-aid equipment and insect repellent. A good pair of walking shoes and casual clothes are all you'll need to explore the national park. Informal dress is acceptable almost anywhere in town, but during the racing season, men often wear jackets and women dress up more in the evening.

GENERAL STORES There are more than 100 small towns in and around the Ouachita National Forest, and virtually all of them have a service station or a general store that can provide basic supplies. For major purchases, you'll have to travel to Fort Smith, to the northwest, or Little Rock, due east of both the park and the forest. Of course Hot Springs has ample shopping facilities, too. In a pinch, try **Dillard's Department Store** (Hot Springs Mall, 4501 Central Ave., tel. 501/525–4501) or either of two **Wal-Mart** stores in Hot Springs (on the way to Lake Ouachita, 1601 Albert Pike, tel. 501/624–2498, and 3333 Central Ave., tel. 501/623–7605).

As in most other American cities, retailing has moved out of downtown Hot Springs to suburban shopping malls. In the last 10 years, the old Victorian buildings have been taken over by artists, who have added another dimension to the city. Many live and work on the upper floors and display their art in galleries on the first floor. On the first Friday of each month, from 5 to 9 PM, there are gallery walks on Central Avenue, where you can take a self-guided tour of the myriad exhibits.

ATMS Banks with automatic teller machines are located in Hot Springs, Little Rock, Fort Smith, and Mena, Arkansas, and in Poteau, Oklahoma.

ARRIVING AND DEPARTING **By Bus. Greyhound Lines** (tel. 800/231–2222) runs two buses daily between Little Rock and Hot Springs.

By Car and RV. The easiest way to get to Hot Springs from the northeast is to pass through Little Rock on I–30 West, exiting at U.S. 70 West; if you're coming from points south, take the U.S. 270 exit. From here, the Ouachita National Forest is to the north and west. U.S. 270 and 70 both access the forest, and both continue into Oklahoma. North of the forest, I–40 runs from Fort Smith, at the Oklahoma border, east to Little Rock, where you can pick up I–30 West.

By Plane. Hot Springs's **Memorial Field Airport** is served by Aspen Mountain Air/Lone Star Airlines (tel. 800/877–3932) only. Most major airlines fly into **Little Rock National Airport Adams Field** (tel. 501/372–3439), 60 mi northeast. The **Hot Springs/Little Rock Airport Shuttle Service** (tel. 800/643–1505) operates several times daily between the Little Rock airport and downtown Hot Springs and costs $18–$20 per person. All major car-rental agencies can be found at Memorial Airport.

By Train. Amtrak (tel. 800/872–7245) serves Little Rock from Chicago and San Antonio. To get to Hot Springs from Little Rock, take the **Hot Springs/Little Rock Airport Shuttle** (*see* By Plane, *above*).

EXPLORING HOT SPRINGS

Because the national park is so compact, both it and the city can be seen in one day, but two days would be better. Walking is the easiest and best way to explore downtown Hot Springs and its environs as well as park trails. Motorized trolley cars can take you to other places, including the 216-ft mountain tower on Hot Springs Mountain. You'll need a car to drive the mountain roads; see the Lake Hamilton area, which is like another city of hotels, restaurants, marinas, condominiums, and private homes; and take the self-guided Bill Clinton tour.

THE BEST IN ONE DAY A good way to get oriented is to take one of the early morning **Duck Tours** (*see* Guided Tours, *below*). Once back downtown, you might want to visit some of the **art galleries** on Central Avenue. Explore **Bathhouse Row** (*see* Historic Buildings and Sites, *below*), including the outdoor springs behind it. Climb to the **Grand Promenade** (*see* Nature Trails and Short Walks, *below*) for a stroll, and then head north to Fountain Street. Across from the **Arlington Resort Hotel and Spa,** the Park Service allows steaming water to splash down the side of a mountain in an interesting cascade; it's a great spot to take off your shoes and soak your feet. Walk through the historic hotel, and perhaps have lunch there or at the Cafe New Orleans across the street (*see* Dining, *below,* for both). After lunch, sample one of the famous baths. If you're not staying at a hotel with a bathhouse, the easiest way to do this is to go to the **Buckstaff** (*see* Historic Buildings and Sites, *below*). Finish exploring by car. For scenery, drive to the **Hot Springs Mountain Tower** atop Hot Springs Mountain, and, for a glimpse of President Clinton's childhood and an interesting view of the city, take the Clinton retrospective tour (*see* Scenic Drives and Views, *below,* for both). At the end you'll then be in easy reach of restaurants either downtown or in the Lake Hamilton area.

ORIENTATION PROGRAMS The **Fordyce Bathhouse Visitor Center** in the middle of Bathhouse Row in Hot Springs (*see* Historic Buildings and Sites, *below*) runs a 17-minute movie on the park and a 10-minute video on the thermal baths.

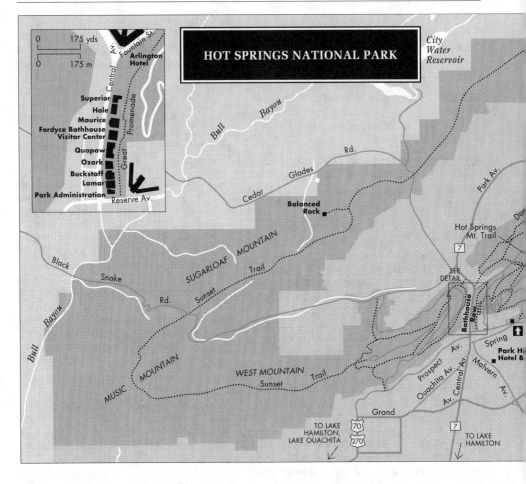

GUIDED TOURS Rangers and volunteers lead 40-minute **walking tours** March to Thanksgiving. These free tours leave the Fordyce Bathhouse Visitor Center and teach visitors about the geology of the cascades and open springs. Schedules for tours vary; check at the information desk when you arrive. Three commercial operators, **Duck Sightseeing** (tel. 501/623–1111), **White and Yellow Duck** (tel. 501/623–1117), and **Duck Tours** (tel. 501/321–2911), use World War II amphibious vehicles known as Ducks to conduct interesting tours of the city and park as well as Lake Hamilton, the resort area 10 minutes from downtown Hot Springs. A motorized—though not guided—trolley service, operated by the city of Hot Springs, provides a good way to see the city. You can get off and on all day for $2.

SCENIC DRIVES AND VIEWS The self-guided **"Tour of President Clinton's Hot Springs"** is the most popular drive in town. Along the way, you'll see the president's two homes and other places from his childhood, including his favorite drive-in, the site of his senior prom, and the hall where his dance band performed. Pick up a map at the Hot Springs Convention Center (134 Convention Blvd.) or at the visitor center at Hill Wheatley Plaza, south of Bathhouse Row.

For more scenery, the National Park Service maintains roads and overlooks on Hot

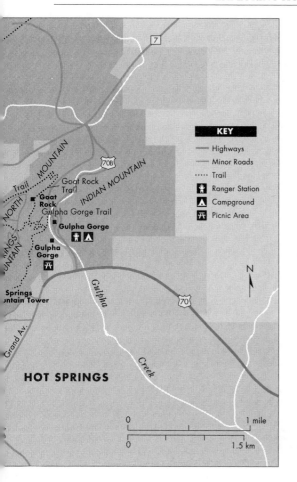

KEY

━━━	Highways
━━━	Minor Roads
·····	Trail
👤	Ranger Station
⚠	Campground
🌳	Picnic Area

the national park's **Bathhouse Row.** Built starting in the late 1800s in the early 1900s to replace earlier ones, they range in style from California modern to Spanish Renaissance. Such notables as F. W. Woolworth, William Jennings Bryan, Andrew Carnegie, Helen Keller, Jack Dempsey, Babe Ruth, and Al Capone were frequent visitors.

Only one of the bathhouses, the handsome neoclassical **Buckstaff** (Bathhouse Row, tel. 501/623–2308), circa 1912, is still operating. For the complete treatment (about $30, with tip) including massage and whirlpool, allow 1½ hours; a bath ($13) takes nearly an hour. It's closed Sunday.

The largest of the bathhouses, the three-story **Fordyce** (369 Central Ave., tel. 501/624–3383, ext. 640) has been turned into the national park's visitor center and museum at a cost of more than $5 million. When built in 1915, it was advertised as the most complete and luxurious bathhouse in the United States. You can take a self-guided tour of the building, which contains bizarre devices once used in "mechanotherapy." The National Park Service is in the process of leasing the other bathhouses to private concerns that will use them for spas, restaurants, clinics, or for other purposes than those for which they were built.

Unfortunately, many of the truly historic buildings in the city have been destroyed or remodeled in the name of progress, but some of the old Victorian mansions remain. **Wildwood 1884 House** (808 Park Ave., tel. 501/624–4267), built in 1884, has a 300-pound front door and is now a bed-and-breakfast (*see* Lodging, *below*). The **Ohio Club** (336 Central Ave., tel. 501/623–4554), across from Bathhouse Row, was one of the original casinos during Hot Springs's gambling days. Supposedly, Harry Truman came by once or twice before he became president to play the piano and a little draw poker. The club has been restored and is now a restaurant and blues club. Evidence of the illegal racing telegraph and bullet holes from a police raid can be seen in the walls.

Springs and West and North mountains with views of downtown Hot Springs and the Ouachita National Forest. The scenery is dominated by short-leaf pine, but flashes of color are provided by oak and hickory in the fall and redbud and dogwood in the spring. Drive up Hot Springs Mountain Road to the Hot Springs Mountain Tower, and take the elevator to the top for a great view of the park, the city, and the national forest.

HISTORIC BUILDINGS AND SITES   There are more than 18 structures in Hot Springs that are on the National Register of Historic Places. The best known are the eight elegant bathhouses facing Central Avenue on

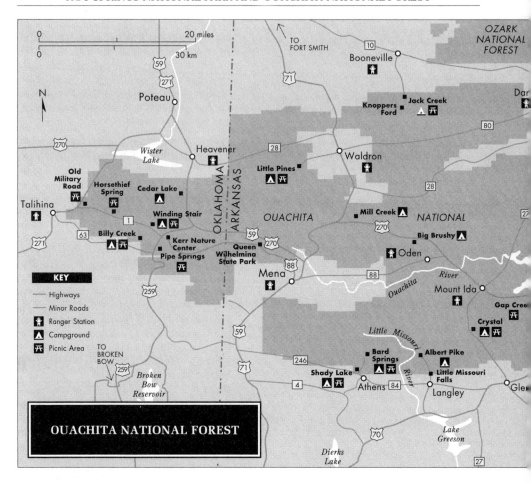

NATURE TRAILS AND SHORT WALKS The very popular and relatively level .5-mi red-and-tan-brick **Grand Promenade** runs behind Bathhouse Row on Hot Springs Mountain. Along this trail you'll walk by stately historic buildings fronted by landscaping and within view of the magnolia trees lining Bathhouse Row.

The park contains several walking trails of varying degrees of difficulty, many of them ending at Hot Springs Mountain Tower. All are listed in brochures available at the Fordyce Bathhouse Visitor Center, where several of the trails begin.

The 3-mi round-trip **Gulpha Gorge** and **Goat Rock trails** start by Hot Springs

National Park campground, where the Gulpha Creek ripples by. Begin on the Gulpha Gorge span; then, after .8 mi, pick up the Goat Rock Trail, which reaches a wildflower-filled meadow. The pinnacle of Goat Rock juts up at the edge of this unusual meadow.

LONGER HIKES There are 28 mi of trails—which all link up with one another—in the national park, leading from downtown to the top of the four Ouachita Mountains that cradle Hot Springs. You can lengthen or shorten just about any hike you embark on—all trail junctions are marked. Most of them pass through dense forests of hickory and short-leaf pine; flowering trees are also

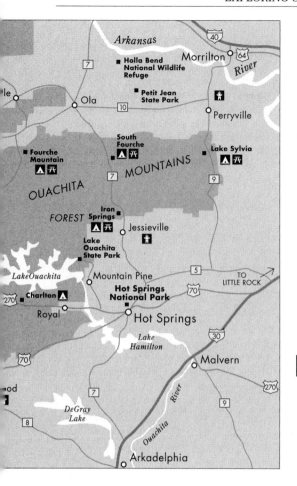

around Sugarloaf Mountain, where Balanced Rock stands precariously before you. This vantage point offers one of the best views in the park. Continue on to Cedar Glades Road, from which it's an easy mile of hiking back to the parking area.

From the Hot Springs National Park campground it's also possible to take the Gulpha Gorge and Goat Rock trails (see Nature Trails and Short Walks, above) and then continue on to the **Dogwood Trail.** The latter runs along the north slope of North Mountain and is blanketed with redbuds and dogwoods, which blossom in spring, and a fair sprinkling of pines mixed in with the predominant hardwoods. The Dogwood Trail hooks up with the Hot Springs Mountain Trail, which loops around Hot Springs Mountain. From this loop, cut down the incline of Gulpha Gorge Trail and return to the creek and campground. The entire hike is about 3.5 mi.

EXPLORING OUACHITA

Ouachita National Forest has six wilderness areas and 35 recreation areas in Arkansas and Oklahoma, accommodating a variety of interests. Trails range from 1 to 192 mi; 31 are for hiking, 8 for horseback riding, 12 for mountain biking, and 3 (Wolf Pen Gap, Bear Creek, and Fourche Mountain) for all-terrain vehicles. Lakes and rivers are popular for canoeing, fishing, and swimming. How long you stay will depend on how much you want to do, but it would take four or five days to really get a feel for the forest, and you will need a car.

THE BEST IN ONE DAY From Little Rock take scenic **Route 10** and stop at the **Winona Visitor Information Center** (north of Perryville) to get maps and information about the forest. Head south on Route 9, and turn on Forest Service Road 324 to reach **Lake Sylvia,** a serene 16-acre mountain lake perfect for swimming and fishing. Hiking and interpretive trails run through the area. Continue west on Road 324 until you reach Winona Forest Drive. The 25-mi route parallels the

common, and successive seasons show off colored leaves and abundant flowers. Redbud and dogwood bloom in the early spring, gracing the understory of the pine and hardwood woodlands. Songbirds and small animals are abundant on these trails.

From the West Mountain Overlook parking area, the 21-mi (round-trip) **Sunset Trail** runs along the rocky ridge that loops around the peak of Music Mountain, at 1,405 ft the highest point in the Zigzag mountain system, a sub-range of the Ouachitas. This is the center of a horseshoe-shape ridge whose ends are Sugarloaf and West mountains. It then heads down a small saddle across Black Snake Road and

Flatside Wilderness Area and provides panoramic views of Lake Winona, Chinquapin and Crystal mountains, the Alum Creek Experimental Forest, and a 1,550-ft rock outcrop. Drive south on Route 7 to the **Iron Springs Recreation Area,** a wooded roadside setting where you can wade in a beautiful mountain stream and walk the 4-mi Hunt's Loop Trail, one of the prettiest in the forest. From here it's a 4.5-mi drive to the **Jessieville Visitor Information Center.** Walk the .7-mi bench-lined, asphalt trail; it's designed for people using wheelchairs but is very popular with all visitors. If you're interested in Ouachita crystals, make your last stop **Ron Coleman Mining** (Little Blakely Creek Rd., off Rte. 7, tel. 501/984–5396) in the town of Jessieville. Here you can see examples of the rocks and crystals found in the forest, including amethysts and agates, and dig for your own in the mine's tailings. From Jessieville you're 19 mi from Hot Springs and 52 mi from Little Rock.

ORIENTATION PROGRAMS Orientation in the national forest is usually provided on an individual basis at the 12 visitor information centers, also called ranger's stations.

GUIDED TOURS Guided tours are available for large groups only through special arrangement with the public affairs office (tel. 501/321–5202) or the district offices.

SCENIC DRIVES AND VIEWS The national forest contains two National U.S. Scenic Byways: **Route 7,** a 60-mi road that passes through some of the most spectacular scenery in both the Ouachita and Ozark national forests, and the **Talimena Scenic Byway,** a 54-mi road that winds along mountain crests between Mena, Arkansas (70 mi west of Hot Springs), and Talihina, Oklahoma. Interesting stops along the latter include the Queen Wilhelmina State Park and the Kerr Nature Center, an interpretive center and outdoor forest laboratory. The forest service has also designated seven scenic areas, most of them accessible by primitive forest roads.

HISTORIC BUILDINGS AND SITES There are many historic sites along the Talimena

byway. The **Queen Wilhelmina Inn** (*see* Lodging, *below*) was built in 1896 for a visit by Holland's queen that never quite materialized and was rebuilt after a 1973 fire. There's a **pioneer cemetery** and the original **survey marker for the Indian Territory,** which became the Oklahoma border. Several Civilian Conservation Corps buildings, dating back to the 1930s, are preserved in the forest. Archaeologists have found evidence of **Caddo Indian villages** in two digs near the Albert Pike and Shady Lake recreation areas, outside Langley. For hundreds of years, Native Americans and mountain people made pilgrimages to what is now the **Bard Springs Recreation Area,** near Mena, for what are believed to be medicinal waters.

NATURE TRAILS AND SHORT WALKS In addition to interpretive trails at Lake Sylvia and Jessieville (*see* The Best in One Day, *above*), try the interesting, pretty, and family-oriented **Serendipity Interpretive Trail,** near the Oden Visitor Information Center on Route 88. Access is easy, the surface is gravel, and it's only .8-mi long.

LONGER HIKES The 4-mi (one-way) **Athens Big Fork Trail** has spectacular vistas but is so rugged that mules had to be used when it was a mail route. Get there by taking Route 246 west from Glenwood to the small town of Athens. The trail is strenuous and passes through some very dense forest; it's best done in fall and winter.

Also difficult and exceptionally beautiful is the 12-mi (round-trip) **Black Fork Mountain Wilderness Trail,** which straddles the Arkansas-Oklahoma border and passes huge rockslides and an elfin forest.

The **Ouachita National Recreation Trail** begins north of Little Rock and extends 226 mi west to Talihina, Oklahoma. Elevation on this trail ranges from 600 to 2,600 ft; the trail passes over the Ouachita Mountains, through valleys, across streams and rivers, and through hardwood and pine forests. Hundreds of old logging roads, which are shown on U.S. Forest Service maps, access the forest, even in areas where there are no formal trails.

OTHER ACTIVITIES **Boating.** Canoeing is very popular on the **Ouachita** and **Little Missouri rivers.** A 45-mi trip on the Ouachita starts at **Shirley Creek Float Camp** (*see* Camping, *below*); it passes narrows, rapids, and rock bluffs. A 3-mi float at a bend in the river here is also possible. Starting at the **Albert Pike Recreation Area** (*see* Camping, *below*) on the Little Missouri River, canoeists can travel 20 mi over challenging rapids past massive bluffs and tree-covered banks. Commercial outfitters in the Mount Ida (Rte. 27 and U.S. 270), Oden (Rte. 88), and Langley (Rte. 84) areas rent canoes.

The **Lake Ouachita State Park Marina** (5451 Mountain Pine Rd., Mountain Pine, tel. 501/767–9366) and **Taylors Water Toys** (on Lake Hamilton, tel. 501/525–4146) rent boats, water-sports equipment, and party barges.

Crystal Hunting. You can look for Ouachita crystals, admired around the world, anywhere in the forest if you aren't going to sell them, but the quickest and easiest way to find some is to go to one of the 30 or so commercial mines in the national forest and dig around in the tailings (*see* The Best in One Day, *above*).

Fishing. The national forest is full of great fishing spots (Lake Ouachita, Cedar Lake, Shady Lake, Lake Sylvia, Lake Hinkle, and the Ouachita and Little Missouri rivers) and fish (*see* Flora and Fauna *in* Essential Information, *above*). Common catches are sunfish, crappies, smallmouth bass, and catfish; Lake Hinkle is stocked by the fish and game department. Oklahoma and Arkansas licenses are required and are sold at most stores and service stations inside the forest and on its borders.

Horseback Riding. The modern, peaceful camping facility at **Cedar Lake** in Oklahoma (*see* Camping, *below*) has a large equestrian camp and more than 200 mi of riding trails around the lake and picturesque Holson Valley.

Swimming. Many of the national forest's lakes and rivers have excellent spots for swimming (*see* Camping, *below*).

EVENING ACTIVITIES During camping season, rangers give free interpretive talks at night at many of the campgrounds (*see* Camping, *below*).

DINING

Neither the national park nor the national forest operates dining facilities, but commercial operations are found in Hot Springs, in the forest, and on its periphery. The Hot Springs restaurant scene is extremely fluid, with openings and closings all the time, but it has some of the best restaurants in Arkansas. Listed below are many of the old standbys, but there are dozens more for the trying. Most have full bars or at least beer and wine, but in rural areas, you'd best bring your own. Dress is informal everywhere, although it gets a little dressier in Hot Springs during the racing season. Reservations are not generally necessary.

IN HOT SPRINGS **Bella Arti.** Atmospheric and balconied, this bastion of Italian cuisine has moved quickly into the forefront of Hot Springs restaurants with offerings of both northern and southern Italian cooking, a very good wine cellar, and a veritable gallery of art that changes every other month. *719 Central Ave., tel. 501/624–7474. AE, MC, V. $$$*

Hamilton House. One of Hot Springs' better restaurants is in the manor house of an old estate, and tables are scattered in rooms and niches on four levels. Situated on a peninsula in Lake Hamilton, it's accessible by boat or car (off Route 7). The extensive menu includes beef and fresh seafood, and one of the most popular dishes is trout Marshall (spicy trout stuffed with crab and baked in parchment). An excellent domestic wine list complements the full bar. *130 Van Lyell Dr., tel. 501/525–2727. AE, D, DC, MC, V. No lunch. Closed Sun. $$$*

Arlington Resort Hotel and Spa. The Venetian Room is the most elegant of the three dining rooms in this, one of the last of the grand hotels. Known for its Sunday brunch and seafood buffets, it has a full menu and excellent service provided by liveried waiters. The informal Captain's Tavern, in the Arlington Mall, serves light meals and sandwiches. *Central Ave. at Fountain St., tel. 501/623–7771. Reservations essential. AE, D, MC, V. $$–$$$*

Cajun Boilers. This roadhouselike restaurant offers little in the way of atmosphere, comfort (the wooden chairs are straight and severe), or amenities, but it certainly knows how to turn out Cajun-influenced seafood, boiled, broiled or—especially—fried. Plump, crusty fried oysters melt in the mouth, and boiled crayfish (in season) are served heaping on trays. *2806 Albert Pike Blvd., tel. 501/767–5695. No lunch. AE, D, DC, MC, V. $$*

La Hacienda. Owned and operated by a Mexican family, this locally popular Mexican restaurant serves standard Tex-Mex fare but does it extremely well, as you'll taste in the green salsa that accompanies every meal. The full bar has many Mexican beers. *3836 Central Ave., tel. 501/525–8203. AE, MC, V. $$*

Mollie's. Since 1946 this has been Hot Springs' favorite deli and kosher-style restaurant. The Reuben is superb, as are the steaks, seafood, and most everything else. Housed in what used to be a private home, it offers dining in an outdoor courtyard in good weather. *538 W. Grand Ave., tel. 501/623–6582. Reservations accepted. AE, D, DC, MC, V. Closed Sun. $$*

Mrs. Miller's. Specializing in home-cooked dishes like fried quail and chicken pot pie, this Hot Springs landmark is where the town folk eat. It is just a block or two from Lake Hamilton in what looks like a white frame country home. *4723 Central Ave., tel. 501/525–8861. Reservations essential Jan.–Apr. MC, V. Closed Mon. $–$$*

Cafe New Orleans. Tourists like this restaurant, with its black-and-white decor, because it's handy, usually filled with characters, and open late. It also serves food that you can't get everywhere: red beans and rice, gumbo, beignets, and café au lait. Most popular are the giant and sloppy po' boys. *210 Central Ave., tel. 501/624–3200. D, MC, V. $*

McClard's. Barbecue aficionados say this white, squat building is the best of the city's many barbecue restaurants, and there are continuing arguments over whether the ribs or the sandwiches are better. Since there's always a line and no one to seat you, you have to jostle the crowd. *505 Albert Pike, tel. 501/625–9586. Reservations not accepted. No credit cards. Closed Sun.–Mon. $*

IN AND AROUND THE NATIONAL FOREST

Mountain Harbor Restaurant. In the rustic registration and office building of Mountain Harbor Resort, 26 mi west of Hot Springs (*see* Lodging, *below*), this restaurant has a commanding view of Lake Ouachita. The fare, which is more varied than what you find at other restaurants near the national forest, consists of salads, sandwiches, steak, and seafood. Weekend buffets are especially popular. *On the shores of Lake Ouachita, 2½ mi off U.S. 270, near Mount Ida, tel. 501/867–2191. AE, D, DC, MC, V. $$*

Chopping Block. A butcher shop for 20 years, this downtown establishment switched gears and became an unusual and popular log-cabin restaurant. Appropriately, steaks are featured; rib eyes are the house specialty. *U.S. 71 S, just south of Mena, tel. 501/394–6410. MC, V. Closed Sun. No dinner Mon.–Tues. $–$$*

Fish Net. The emphasis is on catfish at this restaurant atop a hill near the national forest. Steak is also served, Wednesday there's all-you-can-eat shrimp, and Cajun night is Thursday. *3 mi south of Mena on U.S. 71 S, tel. 501/394–4079. AE, MC, V. Closed Mon. No lunch Tues.–Sat. $–$$*

Crystal Inn. Chicken-fried steak with white gravy is a favorite, catfish is also popular, and prime rib is available several days a week. The breakfast buffet and fruit bar attract a lot of anglers. It's next door to the

Crystal Inn and Motel (*see* Lodging, *below*). *6 mi east of Mount Ida on U.S. 270, tel. 501/ 867–2643. MC, V. $*

Cypress Barn Family Restaurant. As you might expect, this two-story barn in the middle of town is made of cypress. Though the specialty of the house is catfish, many customers prefer the chicken-fried steak. On Thursday night there's a Mexican buffet. *U.S. 71 bypass, Waldron, tel. 501/637– 3369. MC, V. $*

LODGING

Hot Springs has many motels and hotels, and cheaper rates are often available from mid-April to mid-January, when it's not racing season. Since the national forest provides only campgrounds, many visitors to the forest stay in Hot Springs, though lodging is also available along the highways and in the small towns in and around the forest.

IN HOT SPRINGS **Ladies of Court.** Three neighboring two-story shotgun bungalows, built about 1896, have been restored and outfitted with modern kitchens, laundry facilities, whirlpool tubs, and period furnishings. One, dubbed "Miss Fancy," has two bedrooms (one with a double bed, the other with two twins) and a wraparound balcony. "Miss Lilly" and "Miss Scarlett" have three bedrooms each—one queen, one double, and two twins. Maid service is available for an additional charge. *216, 218, and 220 Court St., 1 block from Central Ave., Hot Springs 71901, tel. 888/772–2489. AE, D, MC, V. $$$*

Arlington Resort Hotel and Spa. Since 1875, this landmark has stood at the head of Bathhouse Row. Although accommodations vary from large and elaborate to small and modest, the resort offers all the accoutrements of a grand hotel: a shopping mall, twin cascading swimming pools, dancing to a jazz trio in the lobby bar most nights. Water from the hot springs is piped into the complete bathhouse, and golf and tennis facilities are available to hotel guests at the

Hot Springs Country Club. *Central Ave. and Fountain St., Hot Springs 71902, tel. 501/623–7771 or 800/643–1502, fax 501/ 623–6191. 500 rooms. Facilities: 3 restaurants, bar, 2 pools. AE, D, MC, V. $$–$$$*

Hot Springs Park Hilton. This newest downtown hotel was built in anticipation of a statewide vote to legalize gambling. It didn't happen. (Ask to see where the casino was going to be.) Rooms are small but modern, and the hotel has its own bathhouse with piped-in thermal waters. Waldo Pepper's Lounge, in the lobby, is bustling. *1 Convention Plaza, Hot Springs 71902, tel. 501/623–6600 or 800/844–7275, fax 501/ 623–6600. 200 rooms. Facilities: restaurant, bar. AE, D, DC, MC, V. $$–$$$*

Avanelle Motor Lodge. At the junction of Route 7 and U.S. 70/270, on the way to the national forest, the motor lodge is well known, convenient, and very popular with regular visitors to Hot Springs. Rooms vary in size; some have kitchenettes. The Sirloin Room restaurant has a good reputation for its strip sirloins. *1204 Central Ave., Hot Springs 71901, tel. 501/321–1332. 88 rooms. Facilities: 2 restaurants, pool. AE, DC, MC, V. $$*

Park Hotel. This landmark is popular with Arkansans. Yanni's, a Greek restaurant, is in the hotel and the room rate includes a full breakfast. The location, a block from the start of Bathhouse Row, affords easy access to the promenade behind the bathhouses. Artwork around the hotel is ever-changing and the bar has outdoor seating. *211 Fountain St., Hot Springs 71902, tel. 501/624– 5323 or 800/895–7275. 60 rooms. Facilities: restaurant, bar. AE, MC, DC, V. $$*

Clarion on the Lake. All of the rooms in this high-rise on Lake Hamilton have balconies overlooking the lake. Renovated from top to bottom, this former Holiday Inn has a lakeside pool and boat docks. The restaurant is now dubbed the Sports Grille. *Rte. 7, Hot Springs 71913, tel. 501/525–1391 or 800/ 432–5145, fax 501/525–0813. 151 rooms. Facilities: restaurant, bar, pool, tennis court, playground. AE, D, DC, MC, V. $$*

Wildwood 1884 House. Built in 1884 by a physician who was one of the city's first settlers, this impressive peach-color Victorian mansion with cream and green trim is on the National Register of Historic Places. A full breakfast is included. *808 Park Ave., Hot Springs 71901, tel. 501/624–4267. 5 rooms. Facilities: dining room. MC, V. $$*

IN AND AROUND THE NATIONAL FOREST

Mountain Harbor Resort. The largest facility on Lake Ouachita comprises motel rooms, lakefront cabins with kitchens, and two- and three-bedroom luxury time-share condominiums—all available by the day or week. Campgrounds accommodate tents and trailers. The resort is 3 mi off U.S. 270, 26 mi west of Hot Springs. Recreational facilities range from a game room to a full-service marina with rental boats and marine repair. *On Lake Ouachita, 2.5 mi off U.S. 270 near Mount Ida, Mount Ida 71957, tel. 501/867–2191. 75 units. Facilities: restaurant, 2 pools, 3 tennis courts, playground. AE, D, DC, MC, V. $$–$$$*

Country School Inn. This was the Langley public school until 1987, when falling enrollment forced consolidation with a school in another town. Now it's a bed-and-breakfast: The classrooms are bedrooms with private baths, and the old gym next door is available for guests to use. It's near the Albert Pike Recreation Area and the Little Missouri River. A full breakfast is included. *Rte. 84, Langley 71952, tel. 501/356–3091. 6 rooms. Facilities: dining room, exercise room. D, MC, V. $$*

Queen Wilhelmina Inn. Built in 1896 for the visit of a queen who never came, the inn was rebuilt following a fire in 1973. This modern inn is operated by the Arkansas Department of Parks and Tourism and is situated atop Rich Mountain, 20 mi west of Mena on the Talimena Scenic Byway. Many of the rooms have spectacular views, and two have massive stone fireplaces. Children love the petting zoo and miniature railroad. The restaurant is admired for its catfish and steaks. *Rte. 7, Box 53A, Mena 71953, tel. 501/394–2863.*

38 rooms. Facilities: restaurant. AE, D, MC, V. $$

Beaver Bend State Park. This sprawling compound, 15 mi north of Broken Bow, Oklahoma, consists of rustic cabins, each with a fireplace on the bank of the Mountain Fork River. Canoes can be rented nearby, but entry to the river must be made outside the park. A nine-hole golf course is close by. *Rte. 259A, Box 10, Broken Bow, OK 74728, tel. 405/494–6538. 47 cabins. Facilities: restaurant. D, MC, V. $*

Best Western Lime Tree Inn. The better quarters at this typical chain motel are in the newer addition. Rooms have king-size beds; some have refrigerators and coffeemakers. *U.S. 71 N, Mena 71953, tel. 501/394–6350. 78 rooms, 2 suites. Facilities: restaurant, pool, exercise room. AE, D, MC, V. $*

Charles Wesley's Motor Lodge. Ask for rooms in the newer D section; others at this mid-size motor lodge with western-style cedar decor are a bit drab. *U.S. 259, Broken Bow, OK 74728, tel. 405/584–3303. 50 rooms. Facilities: restaurant, pool. AE, D, DC, MC, V. $*

Crystal Inn and Motel. Close to Lake Ouachita, this small, family-owned motel is operated in connection with the popular restaurant by the same name next door. *6 mi east of Mount Ida on U.S. 270, Mount Ida 71957, tel. 501/394–6410. 12 rooms. Facilities: restaurant. MC, V. $*

Green Country Inn. This motel has no restaurant, but there are several nearby. *U.S. 59, Heavener, OK 74937, tel. 918/653–7801. 27 rooms. AE, D, MC, V. $*

CAMPING

Although backcountry camping is not allowed in Hot Springs National Park, it is a popular pastime in the Ouachita National Forest and is allowed anywhere unless posted.

IN THE NATIONAL PARK **Gulpha Gorge Campground.** Only 2 mi east of Hot

Springs, Gulpha Gorge has 43 paved pads, tables, grills, and a dump, but no showers ($3 showers are available at the Quapaw Community Center, 2 mi away) or hookups. The fee is $8 per night for tents or trailers with stays limited to 14 nights. *Gulpha Gorge Rd., no phone (call the National Forest Service, tel. 501/624–3383 for reservations). 43 sites. No credit cards. $*

IN THE NATIONAL FOREST   Backcountry camping is allowed anywhere in the forest unless posted otherwise. Pack out what you pack in; during hunting season (usually mid-November–early December) wear orange and stick carefully to trails; and use only "dead and down" (fallen) wood to build your campfire. There are more than 30 campgrounds in the forest; three (Charlton, Cedar Lake, and Shady Lake) have sewer hookups and some have electric hookups. Fees range from $8 to $16 per night, depending upon facilities and the season. There are no reservations; it's first-come, first-served.

Albert Pike Recreation Area. In the mountains on the bank of the Little Missouri River, this campground has good fishing and a beach for swimming. It is named for a man who was a widely known mystic, Freemason, soldier, and lawyer, and who holed up here to write *Morals and Dogma,* the compilation of Masonic philosophy. There are showers and drinking water but no hookups. The fee is $8 a night. *6 mi north of Langley, tel. 501/356–4186. 46 sites. Facilities: beach, fishing. $*

Cedar Lake Recreation Area Campground. This campground and equestrian camp in Oklahoma is often booked up way in advance, so call ahead. There's an 86-acre lake for swimming and fishing, but no boat motors over 7.5 horsepower are allowed. A .5-mi interpretive trail and the 2.9-mi Cedar Lake Trail circle the lake, providing views of wildlife. Showers and drinking

water are available, and 25 of the 86 sites have electric and water hookups. The fee is $8 to $14 per night. *Forest Service Rd. 269, 1 mi north of Rte. 5, tel. 800/280–2267, TTY 800/879–4496. 86 sites. Facilities: lake, fishing. D, MC, V. $*

Lake Sylvia Recreation Area Campground. Nestled in the mountains, this campground (which doesn't accept reservations) offers excellent swimming and fishing from the 16-acre lakeshore. No motors are allowed. There are also a number of trailheads (*see* The Best in One Day *and* Nature Trails and Short Walks, *above*). Those of the 19 sites with electric hookups cost $12 per night while those without electricity are $8, and showers and drinking water are available. *Forest Service Rd. 324, 4 mi west of Rte. 9, tel. 501/889–5176. 19 sites. Facilities: lake, fishing. No credit cards. $*

Little Pines Recreation Area. Little Pines is on the 1,000-acre Lake Hinkle, which is run by the Arkansas Game and Fish Commission. Some sites have electric hookups. There are showers and excellent fishing. The fee is $7–$9 per night; reservations are not accepted. *Rte. 248, 11 mi west of Waldron, tel. 501/637–4174. 21 sites. Facilities: lake, fishing. No credit cards. $*

Shady Lake Recreation Area Campground. In a remote mountain area near Langley, this 25-acre lake is great for fishing and swimming: No motors are allowed. A 3-mi interpretive hiking trail is used by mountain bikers, too; and in nearby Caney Creek Wilderness Area, the Tall Peak Trail is a rugged, 3.2-mi climb to an old fire tower. Facilities include showers, drinking water, a beach, and a playground, and the cost is from $8 to $14 a night. No reservations are taken. *Forest Service Rd. 538, north of Rte. 84, tel. 501/394–5313. 96 sites. Facilities: beach, hiking, playground. No credit cards. $*

The Natchez Trace Parkway
Mississippi, Alabama, Tennessee

By Sylvia Higginbotham

Updated by Carol and Dan Thalimer

he Natchez Trace Parkway is unusual in the national park system in that it's a two-lane highway with approximately 400 ft of adjoining timberland, streams, and occasional pastures on either side. It's a long, thin patchwork of forests and fields, hills and vales—a clean, green, historic route that cuts through what may be the most serene and scenic parts of the rural American South. Beginning in Natchez, it crosses Mississippi diagonally from southwest to northeast, touches the northwestern tip of Alabama, and continues through south-central Tennessee before winding up near Nashville. The parkway is currently about 20 mi short of the 445-mi route it will cover when finished.

Visitors on the Trace will appreciate the direct route and the absence of traffic lights, billboards, commercial vehicles, and buildings to obstruct the view. In fact, there's only one gas station on the entire Trace, although it's easy to fill up in nearby towns. Part of the parkway's appeal is that it's unhurried and (usually) uncrowded, as it must have been in earlier times, when it encouraged the exploration and settlement of a vast section of the country.

Long before the Natchez Trace was commemorated with a paved highway connecting Natchez and Nashville, buffalo hooves and Native American moccasins trod pathways through the wilderness. Beginning in the late 1700s, boatmen who arrived in Natchez or New Orleans via the Mississippi River would sell their flatboats and rafts there along with their wares. Then,

instead of attempting a trip upriver, they would use these trails to return to the Ohio River valley states or wherever they had begun their journey.

The Trace became a dangerous route, with bandits waiting to ambush rivermen and other travelers who hadn't lost their holdings at "Natchez-under-the-Hill," the town's notorious red-light district. But it remained a popular route because it saved miles—and time. In 1800 Congress named it a post road for mail delivery. During the War of 1812, General Andrew Jackson marched his troops along the Trace en route from New Orleans, where he had soundly defeated the British and launched his political career. He returned to the Trace many times and married Rachel Robards at Springfield Plantation, which still stands northeast of Natchez. (Jackson defended her "sacred name" by dueling men who questioned her honor because she was divorced.)

Over the years, with so many Native Americans, Europeans, and Americans either walking the Trace or riding it on horseback, the soft loess soil wore down in places, creating deep trenches. The Sunken Trace, near Milepost 41.5, is a good example of the deeply eroded old trail.

In the mid-1930s, a project to create a scenic road in the southeast began. President Franklin D. Roosevelt established the Natchez Trace Parkway in 1938, although work on it actually began the previous year. The National Park Service has done an excellent job of providing Old Trace exhibits, nature trails, picnic areas, campgrounds, and a beautiful 400-plus-mi drive. Bring a camera and lots of film, for in addition to outstanding scenery you'll probably see deer, turkeys, and other wild game. The drive is so peaceful and undisturbed that you may feel as though you discovered it.

ESSENTIAL INFORMATION

VISITOR INFORMATION The **Natchez Trace Parkway Visitor Center** (2680 Natchez Trace Parkway, Tupelo, MS 38801, tel. 601/680–4025 or 800/305–7417), open daily 8–5, provides a good introduction to the parkway and its offerings. The visitor center, at Milepost 266, has a 12-minute audiovisual orientation film, free brochures, information sheets, and a good selection of regional books for sale.

Information on the **Web** about the Trace can be found at http:/www.nps.gov.

FEES There are no entrance fees, user fees, or tolls for National Park Service facilities on the Natchez Trace Parkway.

MILEPOSTS The Trace's mileage from Natchez is posted on the east side of the highway, but the markers can be read from both sides. Sites are commonly referred to in reference to these mileposts. The National Park Service's map shows the location of every tenth milepost.

PUBLICATIONS The visitor center in Tupelo (*see* Visitor Information, *above*) provides free, detailed maps and sells literature pertaining to the Natchez Trace and the region through which it passes. The free "Official Map and Guide," which contains history, a milepost listing, campground locations, a list of facilities, and other general information, is essential. Also at the visitor center are free sheets on hiking trails, bicycling, cultural resources, and foliage seasons.

The center sells a variety of books on the region's architecture, history (including Native Americans and the Civil War), natural phenomena, and cookery. You might want to check out *Devil's Backbone, Story*

of the Natchez Trace ($4.25) or *The Natchez Trace: Pictorial History* ($9.95). For a complete listing and an order blank, contact the visitor center and request the Eastern National's sheet of sale items.

GEOLOGY AND TERRAIN Along its 445-mi route between Natchez and Nashville, the Natchez Trace Parkway—an 800- to 1,000-ft-wide strip of land with a two-lane highway running down its center—winds through six major forest types and eight major watersheds, with elevations ranging from 70 to 1,100 ft. A combination of latitude, soil, and geological formation creates an ever-changing landscape. The Trace crosses flats and ridges, swamps and meadows, encompassing 51,742 acres (81 square mi), with Mississippi claiming most of the land.

From Natchez, which stands on a bluff 100 ft above the Mississippi River, the parkway enters forests draped with swaying Spanish moss, climbs through pine hills, and continues through the lush greenery around the Ross Barnett Reservoir. North of Jackson it passes through the rich alluvial soil of the Black Belt prairie, where agriculture flourishes; then, in northeast Mississippi, through the foothills of the Appalachian Mountains. After traversing the Tennessee River valley of northwestern Alabama, with its red clay soil, the Trace reaches its highest elevation in the oak- and hickory-dominated forests of Tennessee's Highland Rim.

The more fertile lands along the parkway are devoted to milo, soybeans, corn, and cotton, and marginal agricultural lands are used for cattle grazing.

FLORA AND FAUNA Evergreen trees—pine, juniper, magnolia—add luster to the parkway year-round. In May and June the fragrant white magnolias are at their peak. Along the low-lying bayous at the south end of the Trace, cypress trees with their knees and moss-laden limbs cast an air of mystery over lakes and streams. The Trace's thick forests are populated with sycamore, black walnut, and silver maple. To that add 16 different oaks, six hickories, three elms, sweet gums, tupelos, willows, and some

800 other plant species. (One of them is poison ivy, which grows heartily here. Keep in mind the saying "Leaflets three, let it be.")

Expect to see white-tailed deer, armadillos, raccoons, opossums, foxes, squirrels, and rabbits. Don't expect to see black bears, bobcats, or beavers, although they live here, too. Be alert; animals can wander into the path of oncoming cars.

Among the resident reptiles and amphibians, especially in damp forest areas, are alligators, 16 kinds of turtles, and an assortment of lizards and snakes. More than 200 species of birds take wing over the three-state area—among them geese, ducks, hawks, and owls, along with the more common warblers, sparrows, and wrens.

WHEN TO GO Given the moderate year-round climate and lack of seasonal crowds, the best time to go is up to you. Spring offers the pink-and-white blossoms of redbud, dogwood, magnolia, and wild honeysuckle. April and May also bring a sea of red clover and big fields of bright yellow smooth groundsel. Fall is just as colorful, when sumac and red maple turn bright red, red oaks and sassafras turn orange, and hickories become bright gold.

Average temperatures for Mississippi are 44°F in winter (50°F downstate—in other words, south of Jackson), 62°F in spring (64°F downstate), 79°F in summer (81°F downstate), and 63°F in fall (66°F downstate). Summer and early fall seem hotter here because of the high humidity. Temperatures are basically the same in Alabama and a few degrees cooler in Tennessee.

SEASONAL EVENTS The South is a region that celebrates. Most weekends, festivals and fairs are in progress in towns along and just off the Trace. Pilgrimages are a southern tradition during which stately historic homes and their gardens are open for tours. Often there are plays, concerts, balls, and other festivities during them as well. Dates change every year, but the rule of thumb is three weeks in October, two weeks in

December, and three weeks in March and April.

March: Natchez Spring Pilgrimage features tours of the town's grand historic mansions (tel. 601/446–6631 or 800/647–6742). **April: Natchez Trace Festival** is held on the last Saturday in April on the courthouse square of Kosciusko, Mississippi, with big crowds enjoying a fiddlers' contest and children's theater (tel. 601/289–2981). **May: Gumtree Festival,** a juried crafts show and sale in Tupelo, Mississippi, held on the second weekend in May, is also a place for songwriters and short story writers to compete (tel. 601/841–6521 or 800/533–0611). **June:** The **Helen Keller Festival,** held in the Shoals area of Alabama on the last weekend in June, features an outdoor production of *The Miracle Worker,* plus arts, tours, and more (tel. 205/383–0783). **August: W. C. Handy Music Festival,** held the first full week of the month in the Shoals, celebrates the life of this Alabama native (1873–1958), often called the "father of the blues" (tel. 205/760–6434). **October: Canton Flea Market** brings hundreds of dealers in antiques and folk art on the second Thursday of the month to this Mississippi town's courthouse square (tel. 601/859–8055). On the second weekend in October the **Meriwether Lewis Arts & Crafts Fair,** at the Meriwether Lewis Gravesite in south-central Tennessee (Milepost 386), is an interesting display of rural southern crafts (tel. 615/388–1344). The **Pioneer and Indian Heritage Festival** (tel. 601/856–7546), at the Mississippi Crafts Center in Ridgeland (Milepost 102.4 on the parkway), held the third Saturday of the month, offers such collectibles as Choctaw baskets.

WHAT TO PACK Unless you attend a high tea at a Greek Revival showplace in Natchez or go into Jackson for dinner and a concert, dress along the parkway is casual. If it's summer and hiking or bicycling is on the agenda, shorts and a T-shirt will do nicely—and don't forget insect repellent, sunscreen, and water. Winter weather is generally mild, though a "norther" can make the temperature drop quickly. Be prepared with a heavy sweater and a good windbreaker.

GENERAL STORES There's little commercial activity (and no general stores) on the parkway, although supplies are readily available in small towns and cities nearby (there's a camp store at Milepost 193.1). Plot a stock-up stop on your map, and plan to enjoy the many picnic areas and historic sites along the Trace.

ARRIVING AND DEPARTING By Car. An automobile is essential for this 400-mi-plus journey. The major highways near the Trace are I–20 (east–west), at Jackson, Mississippi; I–55 (north–south), also at Jackson; U.S. 78 and 45, at Tupelo, Mississippi; U.S. 72, in the Shoals area of Alabama; and I–40, I–65, and I–24, at Nashville. You probably won't want to spend much time on any of them, though, because highways and interstates are plentiful and common. There's only one Natchez Trace. You must get off the Trace temporarily near Jackson, as this portion is not completed.

If you arrive via commercial transportation, plan to rent a car at the nearest rental counter. At the Baton Rouge Metropolitan Airport, you can rent from **Avis** (tel. 504/355–4721), **Budget** (tel. 504/355–0312), **Hertz** (tel. 504/357–5992), **National** (tel. 504/355–5651), or **Thrifty** (tel. 504/356–2576).

If you're flying into Nashville, rent a car from **Alamo** (tel. 615/275–1050), **Avis** (tel. 615/361–1212), **Budget** (tel. 615/366–0800), **Hertz** (tel. 615/275–2600), **National** (tel. 615/361–7467), or **Thrifty** (tel. 615/275–4257).

By Plane. If you're planning to start at the south end of the Trace near Natchez, consider flying into the **Baton Rouge Metropolitan Airport** in Louisiana (tel. 504/355–0333) on American Eagle, Continental Express, Delta, Northwest, or US Airways Express. Rent a car at the airport and then head to Natchez, 90 mi north, on U.S. 61.

If you're beginning at the northern terminus, fly into **Nashville International Air-**port (tel. 615/275–1675) on Air Canada, American, Continental, Corporate Express, Delta, Midway, Northwest, SkyWays, Southwest, TWA, United, or US Airways.

By Train. Amtrak (tel. 800/872–7245) does not serve Nashville or Baton Rouge, but it does serve Jackson.

By Bus. Greyhound Southeast (tel. 800/231–2222) serves Nashville, Baton Rouge, and Jackson.

EXPLORING

Even with its speed limit of 50 mph (strictly enforced by uniformed park rangers), the Natchez Trace Parkway can be driven in its entirety in one long, long day—but that's obviously not the best way to experience the scenery. Plan on frequent stops to observe and photograph the colorful foliage and wildlife and to explore the many historic sites. Hiking trails, long and short, abound, and there are even trails for horseback riders. Note: Runners and hikers should be aware that there are three different kinds of poisonous snakes along the Trace. Keep to designated paths and trails.

THE BEST IN ONE DAY If you're limited to a single day on the Natchez Trace Parkway, concentrate on the southern end, between Natchez and Jackson. Enjoy a quick drive through the antebellum grandeur of **Natchez,** and then pick up U.S. 61 heading north, which leads you to the parkway. Stop at **Emerald Mound** (Milepost 10.3) to inspect the country's second-largest Native American ceremonial mound. The **Mount Locust Inn** (Milepost 15.5), the last inn left standing on the Trace, is one of the oldest surviving structures in Mississippi. Be sure to stop off at its bookstore, which has a large selection of regional literature. Next, detour into **Port Gibson** to visit a lovely little town full of fine old homes and churches. At the **Sunken Trace** (Milepost 41.5) you can walk on a section of the original Trace that travelers gradually wore down. The **Rocky Springs Site** (Milepost

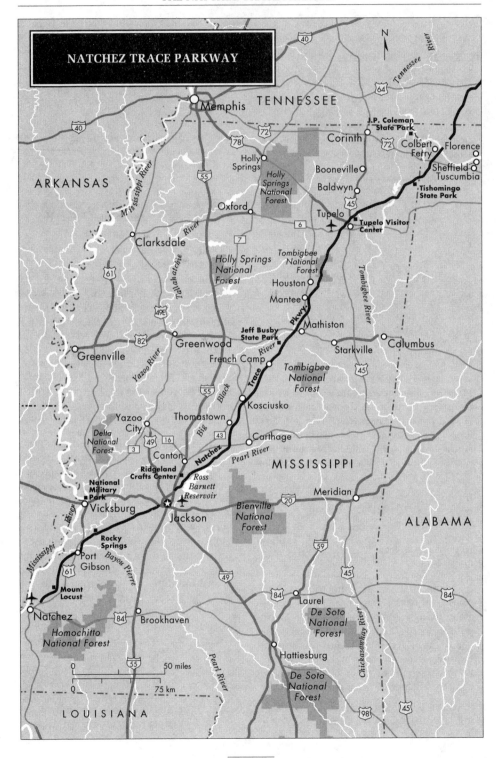

NATCHEZ TRACE PARKWAY

54.8) marks the location of a town that vanished after the Civil War; here you'll find interpretive trails, an information station, campsites, and picnic tables. (For fuller descriptions of all these places, *see* Historic Buildings and Sites, *below.*)

By this time, your day should be about over, and you'll be nearing Jackson. The Trace is interrupted through Mississippi's capital city. You can pick up I–20 east to I–55 north, where you'll find restaurants and accommodations. If you're planning to continue, I–55 will return you to the Trace just north of Jackson at Ridgeland.

ORIENTATION PROGRAMS The **Natchez Trace Parkway Visitor Center,** 6 mi north of Tupelo (*see* Visitor Information *in* Essential Information, *above*), provides the Trace's official orientation. It's also the source for maps, historic and educational literature, artifacts, displays, and a continuously running 12-minute video that depicts the development of the Old Trace and the modern parkway.

GUIDED TOURS There are no officially sanctioned guided tours of the Natchez Trace Parkway, though bus tours (permits are required) are welcome. At Mount Locust (*see* Historic Buildings and Sites, *below*), Park Service employees conduct free tours of the historic property. **Convention and visitor bureaus** in **Natchez** (tel. 601/446–6345 or 800/647–6724), **Jackson** (tel. 601/960–1891 or 800/354–7695), and **Tupelo** (tel. 601/841–6521 or 800/533–0611) can tell you about tour organizers and guides in these Mississippi cities.

In the Alabama portion, contact the **Chamber of Commerce of the Shoals** (tel. 205/764–4661) or the **Mountain Lakes Tourist Association** (tel. 205/350–3500 or 800/648–5381).

SCENIC DRIVES AND VIEWS The entire parkway is a scenic drive replete with pastoral landscapes and seasonal foliage. (In fact, the Natchez Trace Parkway, as a unit of the National Park Service system, will administer the **Natchez Trace National Scenic Trail**—for hikers and horseback riders—which has been legislated, but at press time only portions are in place.) Expect to see rural America the way it was before the days of Styrofoam litter, billboards, and traffic signals. One of the prettiest walks along the Trace is the **Cypress Swamp Nature Trail** (*see* Nature Trails and Short Walks, *below*).

Cypress Swamp is in the **Ross Barnett Reservoir** area. The popular and picturesque 30,000-acre reservoir, built in the early 1960s to prevent flooding in the Jackson area, parallels the parkway for about 8 mi starting north of Jackson at Ridgeland. There's an overlook at Milepost 105 and picnic spots and pull-over places all along the stretch.

The following are among the many other noteworthy overlooks: in Mississippi, **Jeff Busby National Park** (Milepost 193.1), **Black Belt Overlook** (Milepost 251.9), and **Twenty-mile Bottom Overlook** (Milepost 278.4); in Alabama, **Freedom Hills Overlook** (Milepost 317); in Tennessee, **Swan Valley Overlook** (Milepost 392.5), **Baker Bluff Overlook** (Milepost 405.1), and **Water Valley Overlook** (Milepost 411.8).

HISTORIC BUILDINGS AND SITES Natchez, **Mississippi.** The city of Natchez, which marks the beginning of the Natchez Trace Parkway, is a mecca for architectural historians. As you drive in from the Trace on U.S. 61 or U.S. 84 (the two roads merge near Natchez), stay straight as the highways veer left, and you'll be on D'Evereux Drive. On your left you'll soon see **D'Evereux.** The stately antebellum mansion is open for tours only during summer, but many others are open year-round—among them **Auburn, Dunleith, Longwood, Magnolia Hall, Monmouth, Rosalie,** and **Stanton Hall.** Still others can be viewed by appointment, and many offer bed-and-breakfast accommodations. Maps, information, and tour tickets are available from **Natchez Pilgrimage Tours** (200 State St., Natchez, MS 39121, tel. 601/446–6631 or 800/647–6742). The Natchez Convention and Visitors Bureau offers information as well as a handy "Historic Natchez Guide" to attractions, dining, and lodging (422 Main St., Natchez, MS 39121, tel. 601/446–6345 or 800/647–6724).

Grand Village of the Natchez Indians is on the site where the now-extinct Natchez Indians lived from the 1500s to 1729. The matrilineal tribe, which was agriculturally based, was expelled from the area by the French in 1730. Today, in addition to the archaeological relics displayed in the museum, visitors can explore a reconstructed Natchez house, a corn granary, ceremonial plaza, and several earthen mounds. *400 Jefferson Davis Blvd., Natchez, tel. 601/446–6502. Admission free. Open Mon.–Sat. 9–5, Sun. 1:30–5.*

Longwood (Lower Woodville Rd., Natchez) is a stunning, brick octagonal antebellum house with an onion-shape cupola and intricate exterior gingerbread embellishments. However, what makes the house even more fascinating is that it was never completed. Construction was suspended when the Civil War broke out. The family lived in nine rooms in the raised basement during the war and planned to complete the 21 rooms on the upper two floors when the conflict was over. Unfortunately the family was impoverished by the war and never regained enough wealth to complete the structure. Even so, family members continued to live at Longwood until 1970 when it was donated to the Pilgrimage Garden Club. The living quarters, which are open for tours, still contain original family furnishings and artwork. Visitors also get a glimpse of the uncompleted upper stories. *Make arrangements through Natchez Pilgrimage Tours (200 State St., Natchez, tel. 601/446–6631 or 800/647–6742). Admission: $5. Open daily 9–4:30.*

Natchez National Historical Park, established by Congress in 1988, is composed of two historic homes with a third planned to be included. **Melrose,** one of Natchez's grandest homes, is a lavish Greek Revival planter's home from 1845. It features the original furnishings, including rare Victo-

rian pieces. Also a part of the park is the **William Johnson House,** the home of a prominent free black man in antebellum Natchez. It's now a black history museum and is open on a limited basis. *1 Melrose-Montebello Pkwy., Natchez, tel. 601/442–7047. Admission: $5, with guided house tour. Open daily 9–5.*

In the 1800s, the waterfront section of town, known as **Natchez Under-the-Hill** or the Barbary Coast of Mississippi, was a ribald district of saloons, gambling halls, and cheap hotels. Today, the surviving historic buildings on Silver Street have new lives as bed-and-breakfasts, restaurants, saloons, and shops. The ***Lady Luck*** casino boat (tel. 800/722–5825), a replica of a paddle wheeler, is pulled up to the dock. The casino complex has restaurants, lounges, and continuous entertainment on weekends in addition to all the expected wagering games. All these features make the area extremely popular with cruise passengers off one of the Delta Steamboat Company's three steam-powered paddle wheelers as well as with land-based visitors to Natchez.

One of the most palatial mansions in Natchez is **Stanton Hall,** built in 1857. Reminiscent of New Orleans's Garden District mansions, the imposing Greek Revival design adorned with ornate ironwork on the porches and balconies makes the home one of the most-photographed structures in Natchez. A preservation project of the Pilgrimage Garden Club, the exquisitely restored house is filled with some original Stanton family pieces and other antiques from Natchez. The adjacent carriage house operates as a restaurant serving lunch year round and dinner during Pilgrimages. *High and Pearl Sts., Natchez, tel. 601/446–6631 or 800/647–6742. Admission: $5. Open daily 9–4:30.*

On the parkway itself, **Emerald Mound** (Milepost 10.3) is, at nearly 8 acres, the second-largest Native American ceremonial mound in the country (the largest is Monks Mound near Cahokia, Illinois). The flat-topped ceremonial mound was built by a tribe believed to have been the ancestors of the Natchez Indians to accommodate a religious structure or leader's dwelling; it was probably used AD 1250–1600. A trail leads to the top. *West of Natchez Trace Parkway, Natchez, tel. 601/445–4211. Admission free. Open daily dawn–dusk.*

A few miles farther on you'll arrive at the **Mount Locust Inn,** the last remaining inn along the Trace and one of the oldest surviving structures in Mississippi. The house was constructed around 1780 as a family dwelling, but because of its location on the trail used by homeward-bound boatmen, it became a "stand," or inn—one of nearly 50 that stood along the Trace in its heyday. (In the peak year of 1810, some 10,000 travelers headed north on the trail.) It was not uncommon for travelers to sleep on the floor or in the yard; that was preferable to facing the marauding gangs who rode the Trace. After 1812, steamboats from New Orleans and Natchez ferried travelers north, providing a faster and a safer journey. By 1825 the Mount Locust Inn had become a respite for planters who wanted to escape the party circuit in nearby Natchez. Today park rangers offer free interpretive programs from February through November. *Milepost 15.5, tel. 601/445–4211. Admission free. Open daily 8:30–5.*

Port Gibson (Milepost 39.2) is a treasure—a quiet town with a tree-canopied main thoroughfare lined with lovely old homes and churches. During the Civil War, when Union general Ulysses S. Grant was leaving scorched ruins in his wake, he declared that Port Gibson was "too beautiful to burn"; it still is.

At the **Sunken Trace** (Milepost 41.5) you'll see how the old trail looked. It takes about five minutes to walk along this deeply eroded section of the original Trace, worn down over the years by buffalo and Native Americans, settlers and soldiers. It's one of the most beautiful and most photographed spots along the parkway.

Rocky Springs (Milepost 54.8) was once a prosperous community; now it has disap-

peared. Beginning in the late 1790s, settlers drawn by the rich soil and the numerous springs cleared the land, planted cotton, and built homes and an impressive brick church. At the outbreak of the Civil War in 1861, Rocky Springs was a burgeoning rural community of more than 2,600, with a post office, a Masonic lodge, and several stores. The devastation of the war, a yellow fever epidemic, a boll weevil infestation, and land erosion all contributed to the town's demise. Today the only evidence that Rocky Springs existed is the 1837 church, a cemetery, and an old safe that was once filled with the proceeds from the vast cotton crops. The area also includes an information station, 22 campsites, and picnic tables. Supplies are available at either Port Gibson (*see above*) or Utica, both about 15 mi away.

Jackson. You'll have to get off the Trace in the Clinton/Jackson area (take the Lakeland Drive exit from I–55 north) because the highway is not complete here, so take the opportunity to visit the capital city and surrounding area. In addition, Jackson makes an ideal place to break up your trip and spend the night and/or an extra day.

At the Jim Buck Ross Agriculture and Forestry Museum (*see below*) and operated by the Craftsmen's Guild of Mississippi, an organization of juried professional artisans, the **Chimneyville Crafts Gallery** offers original, handmade, traditional, and contemporary crafts. During warm weather, you may be fortunate enough to see members demonstrating their crafts on Saturdays. *1150 Lakeland Dr., Jackson, tel. 601/981–2499. Admission free. Open Mon.–Sat. 9–5, Sun. 1–5.*

The imposing classic Greek Revival **Governor's Mansion** has been continuously occupied by Mississippi's governors since it was built in 1842, making it the second-oldest continuously occupied gubernatorial mansion in the country. Meticulously restored to its original design, it is one of only two state governors' mansions listed as a National Historic Landmark. In addition to the superior architecture, admire the museum-quality antiques appropriate from the 1820s and 1830s and the beautifully landscaped and manicured grounds. *300 E. Capitol St., Jackson, tel. 601/359–6421. Admission free. Open Tues.–Fri. 9:30–11; guided tours every ½ hr.*

The **Jim Buck Ross Mississippi Agriculture and Forestry/National Agricultural Aviation Museum** is a living-history museum that depicts life on a 1920s farm and in a turn-of-the-century small town and includes a general store, a church, and a cotton gin. The aviation museum has very small crop-dusting airplanes. *1150 Lakeland Dr., Jackson, just east of I–55 N, tel. 601/354–6113. Admission: $3. Open Mon.–Sat. 9–5, Sun. 1–5.*

The **Mississippi Museum of Art,** as well as being the state's oldest and largest art museum, also contains a varied collection of 5,000 pieces, including works by and relating to Mississippians, 19th- and 20th-century American landscapes, 18th-century British paintings, Japanese prints, southern photography, pre-Columbian ceramics, and oceanic art. The Impressions Gallery is a stimulating, high-tech, interactive learning experience for children. *201 E. Pascagoula St., Jackson, tel. 601/960–1515. Admission: $3. Open Tues.–Sat. 10–5, Sun. noon–5.*

Greek Revival in style, the capitol was begun in 1833 and served as the statehouse until 1903. Today it's a museum, the **Old State Capitol/Mississippi State Historical Museum,** which contains 30,000 artifacts that trace Mississippi's past from prehistory through the Civil War, Reconstruction, cotton culture, Civil Rights movement, up to the present day. *100 S. State St., Jackson, tel. 601/359–6920. Admission free. Open weekdays 8–5, Sat. 9:30–4:30, Sun. 12:30–4:30.*

The beautiful Beaux Arts **State Capitol,** based on the U.S. Capitol, replaced the Old State Capitol in 1903. When the legislature is in session, you can watch government at work. *400 High St., Jackson, tel. 601/359–3114. Admission free. Open weekdays 8–5; guided tours at 9, 10, 11, 1:30, 2:30, and 3:30.*

Mississippi. The King of Rock and Roll was born in what is now the **Elvis Presley Birthplace and Museum,** a two-room shotgun house, in 1935. The minuscule house, which is furnished as it would have been when the Presleys lived here, was repossessed when Elvis was only three and the family lived in several other houses before they relocated to Memphis when Elvis was 13. Also on the grounds is the **Elvis Presley Memorial Chapel,** which was built with fans' donations, and the **Elvis Presley Museum: Times and Things Remembered,** where Elvis memorabilia, including rare photographs and articles of clothing, are displayed. *306 Elvis Presley Dr., Tupelo, tel. 601/841–1245. Admission: house $1, museum $4. Open May–Sept., Mon.–Sat. 9–5:30, Sun. 1–5; Oct.–Apr., Mon.–Sat. 9–5, Sun. 1–5.*

Tupelo National Battlefield, 1.2 mi east of the Trace at Milepost 259.7, is a 1-acre site that serves as a grim reminder of the July 1864 encounter.

The **Tupelo Museum,** .25-mi west of the parkway, houses artifacts from the Civil War Battle of Tupelo as well as a diorama that depicts the events. Other exhibits chronicle the history of local Native Americans and life in early Tupelo. There's an old-time country store, a sorghum mill, a turn-of-the-century Western Union office, a train depot, and a caboose. *W. Main St. at James J. Ballard Park, Tupelo, tel. 601/841–6438 or 800/533–0611. Admission: $1. Open Tues.–Fri. 8–4, weekends 1–5.*

Exit near Jackson onto I–20 heading west to reach the **Vicksburg National Military Park,** where cannons, graves, and monuments from each of the states that lost soldiers in battle line a 16-mi drive. *The visitor center is 1 mi north of I–20, Exit 4B, 3201 Clay St., Vicksburg, tel. 601/636–0583. Admission: $2 per individual, $4 per carload. Park open May–Aug., daily 8–8; Sept.–Apr., daily 8–5; visitor center open daily 8–5.*

Alabama. In the Shoals section of northwestern Alabama, you can visit **Ivy Green,** the birthplace of Helen Keller and the house where the teacher Annie Sullivan taught the blind and deaf child to communicate. The house and grounds are now a museum. *300 W. North Commons, Tuscumbia, AL 35674, tel. 205/383–4066. Admission: $3. Open Mon.–Sat. 8:30–4, Sun. 1–4.*

Tennessee. Close to the Trace's northern terminus in Leipers Fork, Tennessee, is the charming town of **Franklin,** where the entire 15-block old downtown area is listed on the National Register of Historic Places. **Carnton Plantation,** built in 1826, served as a hospital during the Civil War. *1345 Carnton La., Franklin, tel. 615/794–0903. Admission: $5. Open Apr.–Oct, Mon.–Sat. 9–5, Sun. 1–5; Nov.–Mar., Mon.–Sat. 9–4, Sun. 1–4.*

Several exits from the Trace will take you to **Shiloh National Military Park,** just across the Mississippi state line in Tennessee, where you can take a self-guided auto tour and visit a national cemetery where some 4,000 soldiers lie buried. A film at the visitor center helps explain this supremely important battle *Tel. 901/689–5275. Admission: $2. Open fall–spring, daily 8–5; summer, daily 8–6.*

NATURE TRAILS AND SHORT WALKS There are 23 nature trails along the parkway. Most hiking trails are short by serious hikers' standards, but the longest is 24.5 mi; the next-longest are 14.6 mi, 10 mi, and 4.6 mi. Though comfort stations are available, take water (there are no fountains) and, definitely, insect repellent.

There's much to ponder on the **Rocky Springs** hike around the now-vanished community (*see* Historic Buildings and Sites, *above*). It begins at Milepost 54.8 with a 1.5-mi round-trip trail over the old Trace; a separate trail is the 10-mi route between Rocky Springs and the Owens Creek area (Milepost 52.4), which passes a small waterfall. This hike is on rolling terrain and should take about four hours to complete.

Some 21 mi north of the parkway entrance at Jackson (Milepost 122), the 2,200-ft round-trip **Cypress Swamp Nature Trail** offers one of the prettiest short walks along the Trace. Its 22 interpretive stops explain what's what in a typical cypress swamp. There's a sturdy wooden bridge over the dark water, where cypress knees and Tupelo trees cast an air of mystery. The bridge is a good place to photograph whatever comes up from the glistening water—perhaps an alligator, certainly a turtle or two.

The **Jeff Busby Site** (Milepost 193.1) offers a hiking trail up 600-ft Little Mountain, one of the highest points on the parkway. A scenic overlook is the payoff for the fairly easy mile-long hike from the Jeff Busby Campground. Along the way, markers at 28 interpretive stops draw attention to the importance of protecting the natural environment. (Jeff Busby was the Mississippi congressman who in 1934 introduced a bill authorizing a survey of the Old Natchez Trace; four years later the Natchez Trace Parkway became a reality.) Just completed is the 25-mi **Garrison Creek** hiking and horse trail between Tennessee Route 50 and Milepost 408.

In Tennessee the **Glenrock Branch** (Milepost 364.5) is a 1-mi trail (one-way) along a clear, fast stream. Once you're in Tennessee you'll notice a dramatic change in the terrain. At the **Meriwether Lewis Site** (Milepost 385.9), it's hilly and forested, with less undergrowth than you'll have seen at the southern end of the Trace. The site's namesake—the Lewis of Lewis and Clark (the explorers who first charted the American West)—died in 1809 at Grinder's Inn here. Two-and-three-tenths miles of trails (half on the Old Trace) take you past the grave site to the Little Swan picnic area. There's a ranger station near the grave site.

This is waterfall country, and another trail on the Trace is at **Jackson Falls** (Milepost 404.7). The trail descends steeply to the falls (named for Andrew Jackson), which empty into the Duck River. You can hike to Baker's Bluff Overlook and see a picturesque farm in the distance. The fairly easy trail is less than a .5-mile long one-way. Another trail begins at Fall Hollow (Milepost 391.9S).

OTHER ACTIVITIES **Biking.** Mountain bikes and trail bikes are not allowed on parkway trails. Otherwise, bicycling along the Trace is governed by Title 36, Code of Federal Regulations. Each bicycle must exhibit a white light on the front and a red light or reflector on the rear. Obviously, you need to be extremely cautious about automobiles. Keep to the right, in single file; never carry other riders; use proper hand signals; and be off the parkway by sundown. For further information, contact the visitor center in Tupelo (*see* Visitor Information *in* Essential Information, *above*).

The width of the parkway varies—it is wider at historic and recreational sites. All lands outside the parkway right-of-way (except Tishomingo State Park and Tombigbee National Forest, both in northeastern Mississippi) are privately owned, and it's up to the owners to grant permission for use.

Bird-Watching. Despite the absence of designated observation points for bird-watching, the parkway offers ample opportunities; the variety of environments attracts an equal variety of species. A host of woodland birds perch in the forested areas of the **Meriwether Lewis, Jeff Busby,** and **Rocky Springs** sites (*see* Nature Trails and Short Walks, *above*). During September, the ruby-throated hummingbird makes its annual migration through the **Rock Spring Nature Trail** in Alabama; bluebirds, hawks, and vultures keep their watchful eyes on the parkway's trails year-round. Travelers in northern Mississippi and Alabama are occasionally greeted by wild turkeys feeding along the roadside.

Horseback Riding. Though riding is prohibited along the parkway proper, there are three designated horse trails. The visitor center in Tupelo (*see* Visitor Information *in* Essential Information, *above*) has information on the established trails. The **Tombigbee Horse Trail,** in the Tombigbee National Forest, is an elongated figure eight, 15 mi in length (or just 9 if you stick to one loop). Enter it at the Witch Dance Picnic Area at Milepost 233.2; there's a comfort station nearby. The **Tupelo Horse Trail** at Milepost 260.8 is a 3.5-mi loop; you access it at Route 6. Finally, near the northern terminus of the parkway (Milepost 427.5) is the 25-mi-long **Garrison Creek Trail.** Enter the trail at the comfort station; you'll stay parallel to the parkway until you reach Route 7.

Running. It's permitted, but there are no special provisions or locations. Be careful. Traffic can be heavy, especially near Jackson and Tupelo, and it gets worse during holiday periods and the foliage seasons. Wear colorful, high-visibility clothing. You are required to run against the traffic, on the shoulder (which is mowed and stable). And be prepared for the high humidity from May through September.

Swimming. The beach on the parkway at Colbert Ferry, Alabama, no longer has a lifeguard. Swim with caution.

CHILDREN'S PROGRAMS Park rangers at the **Mount Locust Inn** (*see* Historic Buildings and Sites, *above*) offer projects for children through a Junior Ranger program. The kids, generally ages 8–12, work alongside the rangers with cleanups and other activities and participate in special events, learning about conservation, preservation, and history. At the **Mississippi Crafts Center** (Milepost 102.4, tel. 601/856–7546), open daily 9–5, children enjoy watching artisans at work, especially weavers and quilters. Children are fascinated by the **Cypress Swamp Nature Trail** (*see* Nature Trails and Short Walks, *above*), though parents must watch them carefully, since the place really is a swamp. The **visitor center** in Tupelo (*see* Visitor Information *in* Essential Information, *above*) has a good selection of children's literature, educational games, and hands-on exhibits of Trace-related artifacts.

EVENING ACTIVITIES The Trace is fairly desolate at night. There isn't even much traffic. Campgrounds observe quiet time from 10 PM till morning, so if you're looking for action—such as it is—check out the nearby towns for movie theaters or lounges. Natchez, Jackson, and Tupelo have many more options.

DINING

Those who don't want to leave the parkway had best plan to bring their own food and take advantage of the cook-out grills along the way, for there are no restaurants directly on the Trace. There are, however, some very good restaurants in Natchez, Jackson, and Tupelo. Smaller towns generally have fast-food franchises and a locally owned café or two, though the latter may have limited hours and a menu heavy on fried items—from chicken and catfish to little fried peach or apple pies. The exits are well marked, and except for Jackson, the towns are small enough to get around in easily.

NEAR THE PARKWAY: JACKSON, MISSISSIPPI

Ralph & Kacoo's. This nicely decorated Jackson restaurant uses fresh Louisiana seafood for some of its Cajun specialties. The crayfish étouffée is excellent, shrimp and red snapper are delicious, and the gumbos are the best around. There's steak, too, cooked to perfection. *100 Dyess Rd., I-55 and E. County Line Rd., Jackson, tel. 601/957-0702. Reservations not accepted. AE, D, DC, MC, V. $$-$$$*

Dennery's. Romantic ambience begins with an interior fountain with the Greek goddess of love, Aphrodite, in the center. Greek specialties lead the menu, but you can also choose from steak and seafood entrées. *330 Greymont Ave., Jackson, tel. 601/354-2527. No lunch Sat. Closed Sun. AE, D, DC, MC, V. $-$$*

Primos Northgate. Primos has been serving Jackson families for years. The atmosphere is quiet, somewhat French-country in style; outside there's a patio. Count on fresh seafood, prime rib, and big, delicious salads. *4330 N. State St. (exit I-55 at Northside Dr.), Jackson, tel. 601/982-2064, fax 601/981-8109. Open Mon.–Sat. 7:30 AM–11:30 PM. AE, DC, MC, V. $-$$*

NEAR THE PARKWAY: NATCHEZ, MISSISSIPPI

Monmouth Plantation. Dine in antebellum style at gorgeous Monmouth Plantation, which serves Continental cuisine with a southern flair. The plantation also operates as a bed-and-breakfast and is open for public tours. *John A. Quitman Pkwy., Natchez, tel. 601/442-5852. AE, D, DC, MC, V. Reservations essential. Closed Sun.–Mon. No lunch. $$$*

Natchez Restaurant. The decor is rustic and the ambience casual at Natchez Landing at Natchez-Under-the-Hill; the favorite dining spot is the porch overlooking the Mississippi River. Menu choices include barbecue, ribs, smoked chicken, gumbo, and steaks. *35 Silver Street, Natchez, tel. 601/442-6639. AE, DC, MC, V. Open daily for lunch only during Pilgrimages. $$*

Carriage House. Lunch on the grounds of the magnificent Stanton Hall, one of the grandest antebellum mansions in Natchez, is a true southern experience. This open, paneled restaurant is managed by the same garden club that owns the mansion. The ladies of the club offer such plantation specialties as southern (delicately) fried chicken, baked ham, tiny biscuits with homemade preserves—and mint juleps. *401 High St., Natchez, tel. 601/445-5151. AE, DC, MC, V. No dinner except during Pilgrimages. $*

NEAR THE PARKWAY: TUPELO, MISSISSIPPI

Gloster 205 Restaurant. An elegant and romantic restaurant in an old family home, Gloster has dining rooms with different atmospheres: Garden Room, State Room, Wicker Room, Gaslight Room, Upstairs Room, and Library. There's also a pleasant bar. Menu items are lead by steak and prime rib but also include seafood and pasta. *205 North Gloster, Tupelo, tel. 601/842-7205. AE, D, DC, MC, V. No lunch. $$*

Harvey's. Amid the dark wood enlivened by green plants, you can order grilled chicken and fish along with big, filling salads such as the Southland, an extravagant chef's salad. The dressings are homemade. This innovative Tupelo restaurant now has branches in four cities. *424 S. Gloster, Tupelo, tel. 601/842-6763. AE, D, MC, V. Closed Sun. $-$$*

Jefferson Place. In a superbly restored 19th-century home, Jefferson Place is known for its steaks, although health-conscious items are available as well. Entertainment includes blues, jazz, and rock, and possibly an appearance by a Dr. Nash, who reputedly haunts the restaurant. *823 Jefferson, Tupelo, tel. 601/844–8696, fax 601/842–6026. AE, MC, V. Closed Sun. $*

NEAR THE PARKWAY: KOSCIUSKO, MISSISSIPPI

Redbud Inn. This gracious old Victorian house (circa 1885) is also an antiques shop and a B&B (*see* Lodging, *below*). Every day at lunch the Redbud serves up a chicken or a seafood entrée, with lots of fresh vegetables, salads, and a secret-recipe hot fudge cake. Candlelight dinners may be arranged in advance. *121 N. Wells St., Kosciusko, tel. 601/289–5086. Reservations essential for dinner. MC, V. $*

NEAR THE PARKWAY: ALABAMA **Old Rocking Chair Restaurant.** The down-home country cookin' here—ribs, chicken, steaks, cobblers—fits nicely with the rocking chairs on the front porch. The restaurant, which serves three meals every day, stands across the highway from the Alabama Music Hall of Fame. *800 U.S. 72 W, Tuscumbia, tel. 205/381–6105. AE, D, MC, V. $*

NEAR THE PARKWAY: TENNESSEE **Choice's Restaurant.** This local favorite is housed in an old hardware store. Top lunchtime choices from the eclectic menu include the salad sampler and a vegetarian burrito; at dinner the star is the stuffed chicken breast. Among the popular desserts is the chocolate peanut-butter GooGoo cluster cake with chocolate mousse icing; if you've ever listened to the Grand Ole Opry, you won't need "GooGoo" translated. *108 4th Ave. S, Franklin, tel. 615/791–0001. AE, D, DC, MC, V. No dinner Sun. $$*

Merridee's Bakery-Restaurant. You'll sniff the aroma before you see the place. There are omelets at breakfast and soups, sandwiches, and salads at lunch, but the real star is the baked goods. (Take a loaf with you.) The regulars hang out here for hours at a time. *110 4th Ave., Franklin, tel. 615/ 790–3755. Reservations not accepted. MC, V. Closed Sun. $*

PICNIC SPOTS The Natchez Trace Parkway maintains 34 designated picnic sites along its 435 mi. All have tables; some have grills and rest rooms; all are marked. (*See* Exploring, *above*, for more information on these sites.) The most picturesque and popular sites for alfresco dining are **Rocky Springs** (Milepost 54.8; *see* Historic Buildings and Sites, *above*), the **Mississippi Crafts Center** (Milepost 102.4), **River Bend** (Milepost 122.6), **Jeff Busby** (Milepost 193.1; *see* Nature Trails and Short Walks, *above*), **Witch Dance** (Milepost 233.2), **Colbert Ferry, Alabama** (Milepost 327.3), **Meriwether Lewis** (Milepost 385.9; *see* Nature Trails and Short Walks, *above*), **Jackson Falls** (Milepost 404.7; *see* Nature Trails and Short Walks, *above*), and **Garrison Creek** (Milepost 427.9; *see* Horseback Riding *in* Other Activities, *above*).

LODGING

Because of the isolation, it's a good idea to be off the Trace by dark. There are no hotels or motels directly on the parkway, but accommodations are plentiful within a short distance. You won't find pricey hotels, but you will find chains with reasonable rates.

A more intimate but somewhat costlier alternative is a bed-and-breakfast. For accommodations in an antebellum mansion, expect to pay $85 to $140 for one or two persons. For reservations, contact **Natchez Pilgrimage Tours** (Box 347, Natchez, MS 39121, tel. 601/446–6631 or 800/647–6742) or **Lincoln, Ltd., B&B Reservations** (Box 3479, Meridian, MS 39303, tel. 601/482–5483 or 800/633–6477).

NEAR THE PARKWAY: NATCHEZ, MISSISSIPPI

Monmouth. Gorgeous Monmouth, which was built in 1818, has been called the most romantic place in America by several publications. The mansion is surrounded by 26 acres lush with formal gardens and moss-draped live oak trees. Guest accommodations are in the main house and several out-buildings: The decor of each room varies from very formal to more country casual depending on its location. Many rooms have fireplaces and/or whirlpool baths. In addition to breakfast served to overnight guests, a restaurant serves dinner to the public (*see* Dining, *above*). *36 Melrose Ave., Natchez 39120, tel. 601/442–5852 or 800/ 828–4531. 15 rooms, 14 suites. Facilities: restaurant, pool. AE, D, DC, MC, V. $$$*

The Burn. This elegant 1832 Greek Revival B&B in a residential neighborhood in the downtown district is a treasure trove of 19th-century antiques. The centerpiece of each romantic room is a four-poster bed; four rooms have working fireplaces. The grounds include a garden, a carriage house, and the oldest wrought-iron fountain in Mississippi. *712 N. Union St., Natchez, MS 39120, tel. 601/442–1344 or 800/654–8859, fax 601/957–3191. 7 rooms. Facilities: pool. AE, D, MC, V. $$–$$$*

Dunleith. Imposing antebellum Dunleith was constructed with stereotypical southern design. Built in 1856, the mansion features full-length verandas supported by eight columns on both the first and second stories. The beautiful house, which sits amid 40 superbly landscaped acres, is furnished with elegant French-inspired antiques. You may recognize the estate from its frequent use as a movie backdrop. Some rooms have fireplaces. *84 Homochitto, Natchez 39120, tel. 601/446–8500 or 800/ 433–2445. 11 rooms. D, MC, V. $$–$$$*

Natchez Eola. Built in the 1920s, this gracious, upscale hotel has rooms that are tastefully furnished with period reproductions; many have superb views of the city and the river. *110 North Pearl St., Natchez 39120, tel. 601/445–6000 or 800/888–9140, fax 601/446–5310. 125 rooms, 12 suites. Facilities: 2 restaurants, 2 bars. AE, DC, MC, V. $$–$$$*

Lady Luck Hotel. This modern hotel is close to downtown and the *Lady Luck* dockside riverboat casino. *645 S. Canal St., Natchez, MS 39120, tel. 601/445–0605 or* *800/722–5825, fax 601/442–9823. 141 rooms, 4 suites. Facilities: restaurant, bar, pool, hot tub. AE, D, DC, MC, V. $$*

Ramada Hilltop. This hotel sits high on a bluff overlooking the Mississippi River. *130 John R. Junkin Dr., Natchez, MS 39120, tel. 601/446–6311 or 800/256–6311, fax 601/446–6321. 172 rooms. Facilities: restaurant, bar, pool. AE, D, DC, MC, V. $$*

Weymouth Hall. Among the many B&B treasures, Weymouth Hall is a prize for several reasons—one of which is its incredible view. Built in 1855, the striking Greek Revival home is regally poised on a steep bluff overlooking Natchez Under-the-Hill and the Mississippi River. In fact, it is the only B&B in Natchez with a view of the river. Even if you're not fortunate enough to stay at Weymouth, take the public tour to admire the magnificent architecture, detailed millwork and brickwork, and fine period antiques. *1 Cemetery Rd., Natchez 39120, tel. 601/445–2304 or 800/633–6477, fax 601/445–0602. 3 rooms. AE, MC, V. $$*

NEAR THE PARKWAY: JACKSON, MISSISSIPPI

Fairview. This stately Colonial Revival B&B with a two-story, white-columned portico was built in 1908 and is listed on the National Register of Historic Places. *73334 Fairview St., Jackson 39202, tel. 601/948– 3429 or 888/948–1908, fax 601/948–1203. 2 rooms, 6 suites. AE, D, MC, V. $$$*

Edison Walthall Hotel. This elegant hotel has well-equipped rooms and suites. Amenities include coffeemakers, hair dryers, and dataports; some rooms have minibars and/or whirlpools. There's also an Executive Level with additional amenities. *225 E. Capitol St., Jackson 39201, tel. 601/948–6161 or 800/ 932–6161, fax 601/948–0088. 208 rooms, 6 suites. Facilities: restaurant, bar, room service, pool, whirlpool, exercise room, free parking. AE, D, DC, MC, V. $$–$$$*

Millsaps-Buie House. One of the finest places to stay in Jackson is this elegant, historic B&B that is filled with exquisite antiques and artwork. In the heart of the historic district with a commanding view of the capitol, this imposing three-story Victorian house was built in 1888 and is on the National Register of Historic Places. Amenities include hair dryers, cable TV, dataport, guest lounge, and fresh fruit and flowers. Some guest rooms have terraces, whereas others have refrigerators. *628 N. State St., Jackson, MS 39202, tel. 601/352–0221 or 800/784–0221, fax 601/352–0221. 10 rooms, 1 suite. Facilities: pool. AE, D, DC, MC, V. $$–$$$*

Plaza Hotel. There's usually a convention or two in progress at this popular, relatively new high-rise. *1001 County Line Rd. (at I–55), Jackson, MS 39211, tel. 601/957–2800. 299 rooms. Facilities: restaurant, bar, meeting rooms. AE, D, DC, MC, V. $$–$$$*

Cabot Lodge. This place has a homey, comfortable feel despite its uninspired contemporary decor. *120 Dyess Rd. (off I–55 at County Line Rd.), Jackson, MS 39120, tel. 601/957–0757 or 800/342–2268, fax 601/957–0757. 208 rooms. AE, D, DC, MC, V. $$*

NEAR THE PARKWAY: TUPELO, MISSISSIPPI

Ramada Inn. This Ramada's best feature is its Café Bravo, which has outstanding food and service. *854 N. Gloster, Tupelo, MS 38801, tel. 601/844–4111 or 800/228–2828. 230 rooms. Facilities: restaurant, lobby lounge, 2 pools, exercise room. AE, D, DC, MC, V. $$*

Comfort Inn. This no-nonsense motel emphasizes value; a Continental breakast is included in the room rate. *1190 N. Gloster St., Tupelo, MS 38801, tel. 601/842–5100 or 800/228–5150. 83 rooms. Facilities: exercise room. AE, D, DC, MC, V. $*

NEAR THE PARKWAY: KOSCIUSKO, MISSISSIPPI

French Camp Academy Bed and Breakfast. A B&B formed by joining two log cabins together, this comfortable lodging on the site of an earlier Trace inn has iron beds, handmade quilts, and other rustic amenities. In the fall, they make sorghum here on weekends. The Huffman Cabin visitor center and gift shop stands nearby. French Camp is 21 mi northwest of Kosciusko. *Drawer 120, French Camp, MS 39745, tel. 601/547–6835. 4 rooms, 1 suite. No credit cards. $$*

Redbud Inn. A pretty 1885 Queen Anne house, the Redbud operates as a B&B and also has a popular restaurant (*see* Dining, *above*). Each room is decorated with period antiques. *121 N. Wells St., Kosciusko, MS 39090, tel. 601/289–5086. 5 rooms. MC, V. $$*

NEAR THE PARKWAY: ALABAMA **Holiday Inn.** While this is a standard Holiday Inn, the service here is outstanding. *4900 Hatch Blvd., Sheffield, AL 35660, tel. 205/381–4710 or 800/465–4329, fax 205/381–4710, ext. 403. 201 rooms. Facilities: restaurant, bar, pool, hot tub. AE, D, DC, MC, V. $$*

NEAR THE PARKWAY: TENNESSEE **Holiday Inn Express.** Like most of the others in this chain, this is a comfortable, dependable, and bland establishment. *1307 Murfreesboro Rd., I–65 and Hwy. 96, Franklin, TN 37064, tel. 615/794–7591 or 800/465–4329, fax 615/794–1042. 100 rooms. Facilities: pool. AE, D, DC, MC, V. $$*

McEwen Farm Log Cabin Bed & Breakfast. This is actually a trio of modernized cabins on a farm 2 mi from the Trace, just north of the crossroads community of Duck River. It's popular with Trace walkers and cyclists, and the privacy is splendid. *Bratton La., Box 97, Duck River, TN 38454, tel. 615/583–2378. 3 cabins. MC, V. $$*

Ramada Inn. This link in a chain is standard but comfortable and favored by visitors to the nearby Saturn plant. *1208 Nashville Hwy. (I–65, Exit 46) Columbia, TN 38401, tel. 615/388–2720 or 800/272–6232, fax 615/388–2360. 155 rooms. Facilities: restaurant, bar, pool. AE, D, DC, MC, V. $*

CAMPING

In addition to the numerous private campgrounds near the Trace, there are three campgrounds directly on (and administered by) the Natchez Trace Parkway. The designated campsites are free, available on a first-come, first-served basis, and crowds are almost never a problem. Uniformed parkway rangers patrol the campgrounds periodically. Cutting plants and digging are both prohibited; fires may be built in fireplaces only, with dead or downed wood; pets must be leashed or otherwise restrained. Quiet hours last from 10 PM to 6 AM.

Each campsite is outfitted with a picnic table, a fireplace with grill, and a level tent site. Drinking water and rest rooms are provided at the campgrounds, but there's no hot water or showers, nor electrical or sanitary hookups. RVs will find drive-through spaces but no pull-ins and no hookups at the parkway sites; for other options, *see below.*

Note: Campers should watch out for the poisonous brown recluse spider that is prevalent in this area and usually found near such outdoor facilities as latrines.

Jeff Busby Campground. A concessionaire operates a camp store and service station at this campground. There's a rest room and good hiking on Little Mountain (*see* Nature Trails and Short Walks *in* Exploring, *above*). *Milepost 193.1, tel. 601/387–4365. 18 sites. $*

Meriwether Lewis Campground. There's a rest room at this campground and hiking nearby. Camping supplies and gas can be found 7 mi west of the parkway on Route 20 in Hohenwald. All of the sites are primitive and heavily wooded. *Milepost 385.9, tel. 615/796–2675. 34 sites. $*

Rocky Springs Campground. There are two comfort stations, water, and a hiking trail (*see* Historic Buildings and Sites *and* Nature Trails and Short Walks *in* Exploring, *above*) here. Camping and picnicking supplies are available at Port Gibson or Utica, both about 15 mi away. *Milepost 54.8, tel. 601/535–7142. 22 sites. Facilities: hiking. $*

Tishomingo State Park. For people with RVs: If the drive-through spaces in the public campgrounds are not sufficient, there are other options. Tishomingo, one of Mississippi's prettiest parks, lies in the Appalachian foothills. RV camping (all sites are paved) and tent camping both cost $12 per night here. All sites are heavily wooded. *Box 880, at Exit 304, Tishomingo, MS 38873, tel. 601/438–6914. 62 sites. Facilities: picnic area, playground, coin laundry. MC, V. $*

Okefenokee National Wildlife Refuge
Georgia

By Jeffrey R. Young

Updated by Carol and Dan Thalimer

trip into the refuge feels like you've been transported to another, or at least an earlier, world. Swamp is everywhere—growing out of endless water and hanging in impossibly tall trees with wide, exposed stumps—the heavy canopy of overhanging trees is dripping with Spanish moss. Native Americans named this land Okefenokee ("Land of Trembling Earth") because when they stomped the unfirm peat, cypress trees swayed and shrubs quivered.

Animals, some of which have probably never seen a human, still rule this primitive area. Alligators—about 10,000 strong—reign, and birds representing 235 species wade through flooded marshes and glide from island to island in the muggy air. This is also the land of possums, as anyone familiar with Walt Kelly's comic strip "Pogo" can attest.

The swamp has been marked by human hands, however. Native Americans lived here as early as 2500 BC and remained a presence until the Seminoles were driven out in 1850. Next, the timber industry took an interest in the swamp's giant hardwood forests and cut most of the virgin timber in the early 1900s. Some of the trees taken were as old as 2,000 years and as thick as 18 ft in diameter.

In the 1960s, a dam was built on the swamp's western edge. It was intended to protect the adjacent private timberland from fire by controlling drainage into the Suwannee River and storing more water in nearby areas. In recent years, however, scientists have called into question the wisdom of interfering with the swamp's natural processes; fire, it seems, is necessary to burn away sediment and allow new growth.

Since 1937, Okefenokee has been under the protection of the federal government but as a national wildlife refuge, under the U.S. Fish and Wildlife Service, rather than a national park. As such, it has more restrictions on camping and fewer recreational activities than a national park, but if you plan carefully, these limitations can become advantages. The refuge is less crowded, and fewer people mean less trash and other human evidence. Still, there are plenty of opportunities to explore and camp in this magic country of bogs, islands, and marshes.

Entrances to the swamp are at its northern, eastern, and western edges, and though all enable you to tour the swamp by boat or boardwalk, each provides a slightly different experience. The east entrance, near Folkston, offers the most quiet, undisturbed view of the swamp. For a quick look, your best bet is the north entrance, near Waycross, which has the Okefenokee Swamp Park, a private, nonprofit attraction. The west entrance, outside Fargo, accesses the 80-acre Stephen C. Foster State Park, one of few state parks within a national wildlife refuge.

ESSENTIAL INFORMATION

VISITOR INFORMATION For information about the refuge, contact the refuge manager, U.S. Fish and Wildlife Service, **Oke-fenokee National Wildlife Refuge** (Rte. 2, Box 3330, Folkston 31537, tel. 912/496–7836, fax 912/496–3332). Information about the refuge can be found on the **Web** at: http://www.fws.gov. Contact the park manager at **Stephen C. Foster State Park** (Fargo 31631, tel. 912/637–5274). Or try the manager at **Okefenokee Swamp Park** (Way-cross 31501, tel. 912/283–0583).

FEES Entrance fees for the Okefenokee National Wildlife Refuge are $5 per car at the east and west entrances. Admission at the north entrance's Okefenokee Swamp Park is $8. For canoeing and camping, the fee is $10 per person per night.

The Golden Eagle Pass, Golden Age Passport, Golden Access Passport, and Duck Stamp, valid at all national wildlife refuges, can be used at the east and west entrances but not at the private Okefenokee Swamp Park at the north entrance.

PUBLICATIONS The refuge provides several free, information-packed brochures, including "Okefenokee National Wildlife Refuge," which includes month-by-month listings of the wildlife visible in the swamp. A small hardcover book, *History of the Okefenokee,* by McQueen and Mizell, is the best record of the swamp's past. "The Okefenokee Swamp," a colorful, magazine-size pamphlet put out by Dot Gibson Publications, gives information on swamp wildlife and folklore. These and other publications are available at the visitor centers at all three entrances.

The best canoe trail map is within a canoeing brochure put out by the refuge. This small guide, which includes all public boat trails, is sent out along with overnight canoe permits and is also available at the eastern and western entrances for only $1.

GEOLOGY AND TERRAIN The 396,000 acres (about 620 square mi) of swampland in the Okefenokee, part of the Suwannee and St. Marys river watersheds, make it one of the largest swamps in the United States, but it wasn't always as it is today. During the Pleistocene epoch, the sea level rose and what is now the southeastern United States was covered by ocean, reaching up past the Georgia-Florida state line. When the waters receded a low-level basin was left dry and eventually filled with rainwater and created a large freshwater lake. Gradually, decaying plant material filled it in, producing nutrient-rich soil in which other plants took root.

Nor will the Okefenokee remain as it is. A swamp is an evolving ecosystem, constantly growing and changing, working to complete the transition from water to land. Some areas of the swamp are already mature forests still bounded by water. The swamp as a whole contains examples of almost every in-between stage of the lake-to-forest progression—from open "prairies" of marsh grasses and shrubs to islands clustered with trees.

The swamp has 60 lakes large enough to be named. They are shallow (most only a few feet deep), small (from 100 to 250 yards wide), and teeming with fish. Because of the dark background of decayed plants on the bottom, the tea-colored water looks almost black, and the dark, still waters cast almost perfect reflections of the trees towering above the surface.

Dividing these many lakes are some 60,000 acres of "prairies," so called because of their resemblance to the prairies of the American Midwest. These expanses of tall grasses would more correctly be called marshes. Here, aquatic plants stand on a bed of peat that dislodged from the nutrient-rich bottom to float in 1 to 2 ft of water. Swamp "prairies" are home to such wading birds as herons, egrets, ibises, cranes, and bitterns.

Small clusters of trees and underbrush in the swamp's prairies were called "houses" or "hammocks" by early settlers. Over time, some of these small, isolated groupings grew and combined; they look solid but are not.

There are approximately 70 islands in the Okefenokee, 60 of which are big enough to merit names. They are actually sandy ridges left by receding water. They are higher in elevation than "houses" and support more plant life (e.g., pines, oaks).

FLORA AND FAUNA Whether you're looking at the plants of a lake, a prairie, or an island, you'll notice one striking similarity: Species grow on top of species in an interwoven tangle of life. A giant cypress at the water's edge grows "knees," extra stumps jutting up from the root system. Biologists still don't know what to make of these outgrowths, but plants do, taking root on the raised surfaces, which provide a firm footing out of standing water. Such symbiotic relationships are common in the swamp community, and sometimes it's difficult to see where one plant ends and another begins.

When talking about the teeming swamp life, people generally give numbers instead of names. In addition to the 621 species of plants, there are 39 types of fish, 37 amphibians, 64 reptiles, 235 birds, and 50 mammals. If local naturalists are pressed for names, they sound like they're at an auction, running down lists so fast you can hardly follow them—Fish: bowfin, pickerel, bluegill, mosquito fish, pirate perch, flier, warmouth, largemouth bass, eel, scalyhead darter, swamp darter, brook silverside . . . and they're just getting started. There are hundreds of rare and endangered species; the gopher tortoise, the red-cockaded woodpecker, and the bald eagle are a few of the better-known ones. If you ask the right question, you can get a smaller list; for instance, there are only five species of poisonous snakes.

Since the swamp's sprawling plant growth provides cover for creatures great and small, a quick glance may reveal no animal life at all. You could be a few yards away from a 10-ft alligator and not notice its dark body swimming in the water. It doesn't take long to feel life all around you, however. Frogs, birds, and insects sing together in an unending background accompaniment; fish pop up here and there; and squirrels and other animals rustle in the foliage.

The real action of the swamp occurs at night, though, when predators take advantage of the extra cover darkness brings. Opossums can be seen looking for their dinner on an island, and alligators, bats, raccoons, and foxes also do their hunting.

WHEN TO GO To avoid the bugs and heat, visit between October and mid-May. From June through September, the 90°F heat and high humidity keep even the sun-loving alligators from venturing out into the open. Summer is also the swamp's rainy season, with afternoon rain and thunderstorms typical. Daytime winter temperatures average in the 50s and 60s but can be as low as 40°F or as high as 80°F. Winter nights are much colder, with temperatures dipping below freezing and often accompanied by high winds.

SEASONAL EVENTS **April:** During **National Wildlife Week,** the third week of the month, several educational programs and lectures are given at the east entrance visitor center. Speakers generally bring along rare animals and discuss topics of wildlife preservation. **October:** In the second week of October, the **Okefenokee Festival,** at the east entrance's Chesser Island Homestead, celebrates early swamp settlers. Descendants of the Chesser family lead living-history demonstrations that include wood carving, meat smoking, soap making, and cotton weaving.

WHAT TO PACK If you're just coming for the day, bring along sunblock, a hat or visor to protect against the sun, and plenty of insect repellent. For wilderness camping, add drinking water, mosquito netting, rain gear, a first-aid kit, a flashlight and extra batteries, litter bags, rubber boots, rope for pulling your canoe, a pup tent or jungle hammock, and a sleeping bag. Pack binoculars if you want to benefit most from the observation towers.

GENERAL STORES Basic foods and supplies can be purchased from the concessionaires at any of the swamp's entrances. In Stephen C. Foster Park, the concessionaire is in the same building as the visitor center; at the east entrance, it's adjacent to the visitor center (the only other building). In addition, camping equipment, such as tents, sleeping bags, and portable toilets and stoves, can be rented from the concessionaire at the east entrance.

The town of **Folkston,** near the east entrance, has limited shopping. **Okefenokee Sportsman** (411 N. 2nd St., tel. 912/496–7286) and **Big J. Grocery** (U.S. 301, tel. 912/496–7093) offer some basic food and camping supplies. Fargo has even less in the way of shopping, but **Waycross** has the **Hatcher Point Mall** (off U.S. 1, about 10 mi north of the swamp park, tel. 912/285–1431), with more than 20 stores, and a **Wal-Mart** (2425 Memorial Dr., tel. 912/283–9000) next door. There are also several large grocery stores nearby, including a **Winn Dixie** (1912 Memorial Dr., tel. 912/285–7750) and a **Piggly Wiggly** (1312 Plant Ave., tel. 912/285–7530), both in Waycross.

ARRIVING AND DEPARTING The first decision you have to make is which entrance to go through. All have a visitor center, boardwalks, viewing towers, and boat tours, but each offers distinctive opportunities and styles of viewing the vast swampland. From the east (main) entrance, which has a number of educational and recreational facilities, the artifically created Suwannee Canal reaches more than 10 mi into the swamp, and several canoe trails branch off it. The east entrance is open 7 AM–7:30 PM in spring and summer and 8–6 in fall and winter. The Okefenokee Swamp Park, at the north entrance, is set out like a small amusement park. Containing exhibit pavilions and fenced-in swamp life, it's entertaining, educational, and great for children. There are even reptile shows with live snakes; however, there is only one small canoe trail. Tickets can be purchased between 9 and 5, and the gate closes at sunset. The west entrance's Stephen C. Foster State Park, where the Suwannee River snakes into the center of the swamp, offers fewer interpretive activities but more options for boating and camping, including the only in-swamp campground. Hours for interpretive activities and concessions are Sunday–Thursday 7 AM–6:30 PM and Friday–Saturday 6:30 AM–7:30 PM. The gate closes at 8:30 PM.

By Bus. **Greyhound Lines** (tel. 912/283–7211 or 800/231–2222) serves Waycross. The Waycross depot is downtown, about 8 mi from the swamp park. Taxi service from **Waycross Cab** (tel. 912/283–8889) is available ($15 for the first passenger, $5 for each additional person), as are car rentals through **Hertz** (tel. 912/285–8412), located along U.S. 1 about 1 mi from the bus terminal. It's possible to have a car waiting for you at the station upon your arrival. There is a stop in Folkston at the Shell Station, but there is no car rental or cab company nearby, so you must make your own arrangements to get to the refuge.

By Car and RV. If you're coming on I–95 from either Jacksonville and the south or Savannah and the north, you'll probably want to take Route 40 (Exit 2 off I–95) west to Folkston. From here it's about 8 mi south on Route 121/23 to the refuge's east entrance. The west entrance and the Stephen C. Foster State Park are, quite frankly, in the middle of nowhere and can only be reached by small highways running around the swamp's perimeter. Continue on Route 121/23 past the east entrance to Route 94 west, which cuts through a corner of Florida before reaching Fargo. Route 177, a 17-mi road leads to the state park. To get to the north entrance from Folkston, drive northwest on U.S. 1 to Route 177 (not connected to the west entrance causeway), which runs south to the swamp park.

If you're coming from the north on I–95 and are bound for the north entrance, take Exit 6. U.S. 84 stretches west to Waycross, a little more than 50 mi, from which U.S. 1 heads southeast to Route 177 and the swamp park. If you want to continue to the west entrance from Waycross, drive southwest on U.S. 84 to Homerville and south on U.S. 441 to Fargo and the causeway.

Car rentals at the Jacksonville airport are available through **Avis** (tel. 904/741–2327 or 800/331–1212), **Budget** (tel. 904/720–0246 or 800/527–0700), **Dollar** (tel. 904/741–4614 or 800/800–4000), **Hertz** (tel. 904/741–2151 or 800/654–3131), and **National** (tel. 904/741–4580 or 800/328–4567).

By Plane. Jacksonville International Airport (2400 Yankee Clipper Rd., Jacksonville, FL 32218, tel. 904/741–4902), southeast of the refuge over the Florida border, is the nearest major commercial airport. It is served by Air South, American, Continental, Delta, Gulf Stream, Midway, Northwest, TWA, United, AirTran, and Southwest. From here, the only way to get to the Okefenokee is by car. Take I–95 north to Exit 2, and head west on Route 40 to Folkston. From here, the directions vary, depending on which entrance you'd like to visit (*see* By Car and RV, *above*). Car rentals (*see* By Car and RV, *above*) are available at the airport.

By Train. Jacksonville, Florida, also has the nearest train depot. **Amtrak** (tel. 800/872–7245) runs three trains north and three trains south daily from points along the East Coast, with stops at Savannah and Jacksonville, and three days a week from the West Coast. The station is 6 mi northwest of downtown Jacksonville, about an hour's drive from the swamp.

EXPLORING

There is no single best way or place to see the Okefenokee. Only about 80% of the swamp is within the national wildlife refuge, so you're in the swamp even before you reach the visitor centers. Along large ditches beside the roads, you can sometimes spot alligators and wading birds.

Once you reach one of the visitor centers, the best way to continue into the swamp is by boat. There are few opportunities for hiking, biking, or driving, as the waterlogged "trembling earth" is too unstable. The limited boardwalks, viewing towers, and trails at the visitor centers can all be undertaken in a single day, whereas boat trails are numerous and can take days to

explore. Most trails are only a few miles long, but combinations of trails can pose real challenges to all levels of boaters. Day-use sections average about 5 mi, and a round-trip can be accomplished in about six to eight hours. However, some trails allow you to cross the swamp, which takes from three to four days one-way. While some areas are deep enough for small motorboats, the longer trails can be navigated by canoe only.

THE BEST IN ONE DAY Arrive at one of the visitor centers early in the morning. Start off in one of the museums, and watch any of the short documentaries to learn what to look for in the swamp. Take a guided boat tour to get a full overview of the swamp environment. Then strike out onto the boardwalk and climb an observation tower, binoculars in hand. If you're at the north or east entrance, visit the restored homesteads.

ORIENTATION PROGRAMS Brief films are shown at the east and north entrances. The best is National Geographic's *A Swamp Ecosystem*. The 22-minute film is entertaining and informative and features great nature footage of some truly memorable swamp creatures in action. The Okefenokee Swamp Park generally shows the film at 10:30, 12:30, 2:30, and 4:30; the east entrance visitor center gives screenings on request.

GUIDED TOURS Guided boat tours are offered at all three entrances: At the east entrance, contact the concession manager (Rte. 2, Box 3325, Folkston 31537, tel. 912/496–7156 or 800/792–6796) for information about tours and equipment rentals. For tour and concession information at the other entrances, call or write the park manager (*see* Visitor Information *in* Essential Information, *above*).

At the east entrance, one- and two-hour motorboat tours are led by one of the concessionaire's naturalists. There are no scheduled tours, but guides are generally available between 8 and 4:30 and will take a group out as soon as there are enough people (four are required for a one-hour

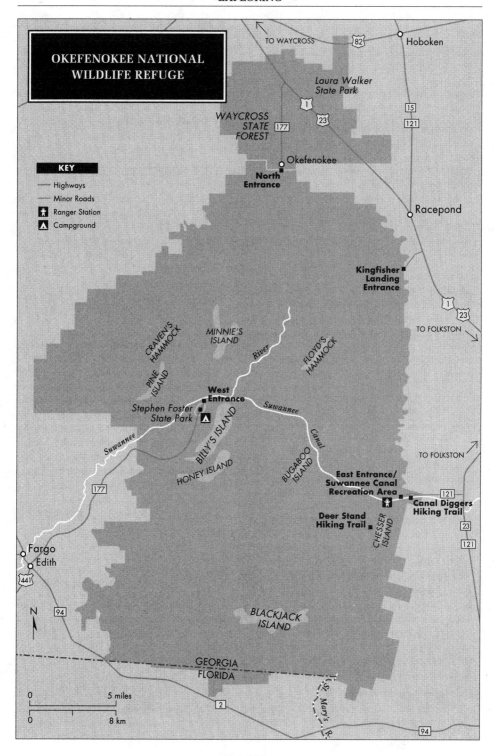

OKEFENOKEE NATIONAL WILDLIFE REFUGE

KEY

— Highways
— Minor Roads
Ranger Station
Campground

TO WAYCROSS

82   Hoboken

*Laura Walker
State Park*

1

WAYCROSS
STATE
FOREST   177   23   15   121

Okefenokee

**North
Entrance**

Racepond

**Kingfisher
Landing
Entrance**

*CRAVEN'S
HAMMOCK*

*MINNIE'S
ISLAND*

River

*FLOYD'S
HAMMOCK*

1   23

TO FOLKSTON

*PINE
ISLAND*

**West
Entrance**

Suwannee

Stephen Foster
State Park

BILLY'S ISLAND

Suwannee

Canal

TO FOLKSTON

HONEY ISLAND

*BUGABOO
ISLAND*

177

**East Entrance/
Suwannee Canal
Recreation Area**

121

**Canal Diggers
Hiking Trail**

**Deer Stand
Hiking Trail**

*CHESSER
ISLAND*

23

121

Fargo
Edith

441

N

94

*BLACKJACK
ISLAND*

GEORGIA
FLORIDA

St. Mary's R.

0   5 miles

0   8 km

2

94

trip, six for two hours). The per-person cost for one hour is $8; for two hours, it's $16. Night tours, by reservation only, are available for a minimum of six people and cost $16 per person. Night tours should be arranged with the concession manager at least a week in advance.

At the north entrance, half-hour boat tours are $12 per person. Park guides, often college students, lead small motorized tour boats with about nine people around a circular boat trail that was artificially deepened to accommodate the boats. Since the swamp park feeds its wildlife, there are always plenty of alligators and other animals en route. Tours start on the hour and the half hour all day long.

At the west entrance, tours of roughly an hour are given at 10, 1, and 3. A pontoon boat takes up to 17 passengers out on Billy's Lake and the Suwannee River. Led by state park rangers, the tours are very interactive, and guides are eager to answer questions or stop the boat to watch alligators or other wildlife. The cost is $8 per person.

Wilderness Southeast (711 Sandtown Rd., Savannah 31410-1019, tel. 912/897–5108), a nonprofit educational organization in Savannah, offers extended tours. A five-day canoe trip takes visitors from the eastern side of the swamp to the western side, beginning at the Suwannee Canal Recreation Area. A less-demanding five-day cabin trip at the Stephen C. Foster State Park lets guests spend their days paddling through the western parts of the Okefenokee and their nights in the comfort of cabins. Offered from October through November and from February through May, both trips are led by trained naturalists and focus on the swamp's wildlife. The cost, $625 per person for a five-day trip and $705 for a cabin trip, includes all entrance and permit fees. The company will also customize trips as long as they include at least four people and are for at least three days.

SCENIC DRIVES AND VIEWS Other than the causeways and roads leading to the swamp entrances, there is little in the way of driving tours. At the east entrance, the 4.5-mi scenic **Swamp Island Drive** leads to the boardwalk and trailheads on Chesser Island, including a path to the Chesser Island Homestead (*see* Historic Buildings and Sites, *below*). The scenery here is not much different from that along the causeway leading up to the refuge, but the 15-mph speed limit allows for a closer look at forests and ditches.

HISTORIC BUILDINGS AND SITES There is no additional charge for visiting any of the following sites inside the refuge. Be aware, however, that Swamp Island Drive, the road you need to use to reach most of these attractions, closes earlier than the main gate. Main gate, east entrance, is open mid-September–February, daily 8–6; March–early September, daily 7 AM–7:30 PM. Swamp Island Drive is open mid-September–February, daily 7–5:30; March–early September, daily 8–4:30.

At the east entrance, **Chesser Island Homestead,** first established in 1858, offers a glimpse of how early settlers lived off the riches of the land. The existing five-bedroom pine-and-cypress main house was built by the Chesser family in the late 1920s. Although you're not allowed inside (except when volunteers or staff are available—daily in spring, weekends the rest of the year), you can peek in its windows to see some of the original furnishings. Walking around the dirt yard, you'll see the large family's grindstone, hog pen, chicken coop, sugarcane mill, and smokehouse. The homestead is accessible by a short path off the Swamp Island Drive. The 4.5-mi scenic drive is the only way to get to the homestead entrance and to the boardwalk–observation tower.

Indian mounds can be found in various spots in the Okefenokee, but the only easily accessible one is a few steps from the Chesser Island Homestead (*see above*). This raised area marks a burial ground once used by the Timucuan people, who were known for their extreme height (up to 7 ft).

The **Pioneer Homestead,** at the north entrance, is a reconstructed pioneer cabin, complete with many of the tools used by early settlers to make their living from the swamp.

Billy's Island, one of the largest islands in the Okefenokee, was once the headquarters for a large timber operation on the west side of the swamp. The Hebard Cypress Company developed the island for its employees, building an office, commissary, barbershop, and even a movie theater. Today the island is abandoned, and fresh timber grows around the ruins of the old company town. It's a short boat ride from the Stephen C. Foster State Park and is open to the public for day use only.

Outside the park, the **Okefenokee Heritage Center Museum** provides a glimpse into the rural heritage of former residents of the swamp and the surrounding area. On display are Native American relics, artifacts from early settlers, and even an old train. *1460 N. Augusta Ave., Waycross 31501, tel. 912/285–4260. Admission: $2. Open Mon.– Sat. 9–5, Sun. 1–5.*

Southern Forest World, next to the Okefenokee Heritage Center Museum (*see above*), tells the dynamic story of forestry in the 13 southern states. In addition to educational exhibits, the facility has a fire tower from which to view the area and several nature trails. *1440 N. Augusta Ave., Waycross 31501, tel. 912/285–4056. Admission: $2. Open Mon.–Sat. 10–5, Sun. 1–5.*

A re-created farmstead at **Obediah's Okefenok** tells the story of Obediah Barber, a 6-ft, 6-inch, 1800s swamper who was known as the King of the Okefenokee or the Southeast Paul Bunyan. Children, in particular, love to hear stories about the pioneer who successfully fought off a huge black bear, married three times, fathered 20 children, aided the Confederacy, and lived as a hunter, trapper, and cattle farmer. The farmstead includes a log home, a dozen historic farm buildings, 50 exhibits of artifacts, a petting zoo, and nature trails. Periodically there are living history demonstrations of swamp life and Native American lore. *500 Obediah Trail off Swamp Rd., Waycross,*

tel. 912/287–0090. Admission: $4.50. Open daily 10–5.

When you're anywhere in the vicinity of the Okefenokee Swamp, it makes sense to combine the trip with a visit to the fabulous **Cumberland Island National Seashore.** On an island off the coast of southeast Georgia, this is one of the best-preserved parks in the national park system because the number of visitors is strictly regulated—300 campers and day-trippers per day. Access to the island is via ferry only, and reservations must be made in advance. The unspoiled island has 20 mi of pristine wide, flat, hard-packed beach; hundreds of acres of maritime forest heavily wooded with live oaks and palmettos; and wildlife ranging from alligators and armadillos to wild horses and sea turtles. Camping is permitted at one small developed campground near the ferry landing and at several primitive sites—some of which are a daunting distance away. No vehicles (except those of the Park Service) are permitted on the island, and there are no stores or snack outlets, so visitors must carry everything they may need. Day-trippers can enjoy the beach, surf fishing, bird-watching, and wildlife observation, as well as hikes to the remains of several Carnegie estates abandoned by the family who once owned the island and donated it to the federal government. It is possible to stay on Cumberland Island without camping; members of the Carnegie family retain one of their estates and operate it as the elegant **Greyfield Inn** (tel. 904/261–6408). For information about Cumberland Island, contact the National Park Service in St. Marys (tel. 912/882–4335). The departure point for Cumberland Island is the town of St. Marys, which has an appealing historic hotel, two historic bed-and-breakfasts, and several interesting historic sites.

NATURE TRAILS AND SHORT WALKS Boardwalks, located at all three entrances, provide one of the best and easiest ways to access the wet swamp. Each boardwalk is less than 1 mi long. The east entrance also offers a few nature trails through drier areas, including the .5-mi **Deerstand** and **Homestead trails.** These easy walks are flat and shaded, winding through forests of pine and palmetto. The .55-mi **Canal Digger's Trail** is slightly more difficult since it runs along uneven terrain. A short portion of it circles around the eastern end of the Suwannee Canal and is accessible from Swamp Island Drive.

OTHER ACTIVITIES **Biking.** Bicycling is allowed on the roads of the east and west entrances. Bikes can only be rented through concessionaires at the west entrance to the park (for about $3.50 per hour, $7 for four hours, and $10 for eight). The beach cruiser-style bicycles are in relatively good shape and allow a calm, leisurely ride through the drier areas of the swamp. Bike rentals are offered on a first-come, first-served basis, but usually there are enough to go around. You may also bring your own.

Bird-Watching. Observation towers at the east and west entrances provide the best perch for bird-watchers. Two photo blinds along the east entrance's boardwalk also have great views over the marshes and prairies (these were closed for repairs at press time), and a checklist of hundreds of swamp birds is available at the visitor center. The best seasons for birders are winter and spring, when migratory birds, both those en route and those arriving to nest, are in the area. The morning is the best time to view pileated and redheaded woodpeckers, as well as egrets, blue herons, and sandhill cranes, from the swamp observation towers.

Boating. You may bring your own boat, to launch it from public boat ramps at the east and west entrances, or rent a small canoe or motorboat for fishing and exploring (about $12 a day for a canoe, $30–$50 a day for a motorboat). Canoes can be rented at the north entrance for $9. Motors above 10 horsepower are prohibited, however, and there's a launching fee of $2.50 at the east entrance and $1 at the west. Contact the concessionaire at the east entrance (*see* Guided Tours, *above*) or the visitor centers (at the manager's address) at other en-

trances (*see* Visitor Information *in* Essential Information, *above*) for more information about boat use and rentals.

Fishing. The swamp's fishing holes, prized by many locals, offer up largemouth bass, warmouth, chain pickerels, bowfins, and sunfish, to name a few. The canal offers the best fishing. A valid Georgia fishing license is required and can be purchased (about $3.50 for a one-day permit) from the concessionaires or at most nearby convenience stores.

Swimming. There is no swimming in the refuge because of the danger from alligators and other creatures. In fact, you should not drag your hands in the water behind your canoe nor trail fish that you have caught.

CHILDREN'S PROGRAMS Unfortunately, there's little in the way of children's activities, though the visitor center at the east entrance does show an upbeat 10-minute film called *Our Untamed Wilderness.* Available upon request, it's a great way to get kids interested in the swamp.

DINING

There are no restaurants in the refuge. For a sit-down meal, your best bet is one of the inexpensive eateries in Folkston or Waycross.

INSIDE THE REFUGE At each entrance, small concessionaire's shops, which sell basic supplies and run the tours and equipment rentals, offer the only food within the swamp. At the east entrance, box lunches, including a sandwich, chips, a dessert, and a drink, are prepared to order and are available for $6.50 each. At the west and north entrances, sandwiches and snacks can also be purchased.

NEAR THE EAST ENTRANCE **Okefenokee Restaurant.** On U.S. 1, Folkston's main drag, this simple, down-home restaurant is the closest eating spot to the east entrance, about 9 mi away. Both locals and tourists flock here for southern-style meals that taste home cooked and especially for the lunch buffet. Although it's best known for steaks and seafood, everything here is good. Booths and hanging plants constitute the basic decor. *103 S. 2nd St., Folkston, tel. 912/496–3263. MC, V. Closed Sun. $*

Tahiti Restaurant. Although this small restaurant has no atmosphere, it is one of the best places in town. Like the Okefenokee (*see above*), it offers real southern cooking and a popular lunch buffet. Specialties include country-fried steak and the Big Mamma Platter, which includes one of the biggest hamburgers you've ever seen. *At the Days Stop/Tahiti Motel, U.S. 301 S, Folkston, tel. 912/496–2208. No credit cards. $*

NEAR THE NORTH ENTRANCE **Whitfield's.** This downtown restaurant bears some resemblance to an English pub, and a varied yet consistently lively clientele is almost always on hand. Its three floors each have a different ambience: a sports bar on the lower level, a casual sunroom and *Cheers*-style bar on street level, and more formal dining on the top level. Grilled and broiled fish, rib-eye steak teriyaki, and fresh pasta are specialties. The "formal" dining area (don't worry; slacks and sport shirt or skirt and blouse are fine) serves only dinner. *514 Mary St., Waycross, tel. 912/285–9027. AE, MC, V. Closed Sun. No lunch. $–$$*

Adolph's. This downtown restaurant's elegant atmosphere includes hunter greens and burgundies and linen tablecloths. The hearty lunch buffet consists of a variety of home-cooking specialties but often includes fried chicken and country-fried steak. The Sunday buffet offers even more choices. *410 Plant Ave., Waycross, tel. 912/283–1766. Reservations not accepted. AE, D, MC, V. No dinner Sat.–Thurs. $*

Blueberry Hill. This Cajun restaurant is truly off the beaten track, but people generally don't mind driving great distances to eat here. It's east of Waycross, hidden in a wooded glen of pines, oaks, azaleas, dogwoods, redbuds, and wild blueberry bushes. The ancient weather-beaten log cabin houses a rustic dining room presided over by an imposing stone fireplace. Try the Lyons' Share, a sampler with shrimp étouffée, shrimp au gratin, crabmeat casserole, and eggplant-shrimp casserole. *Rte. 121/15, Hoboken 31542, tel. 912/458–2605. AE, MC, V. Closed Sun.–Tues. $*

Ocean Galley. This rustic (but modernly built) family seafood restaurant is on U.S. 1, 7 mi from Waycross. The ocean inspires the decor, and the Swamp Platter is the house specialty—a whole catfish, as well as samplings of turtle, crab, gator, frogs' legs, and crawfish. The restaurant is also known for prime rib and rib eye, and all dishes are cooked to order. In keeping with its family-oriented atmosphere, no alcohol is served. *421 Memorial Dr., Waycross, tel. 912/283–8341. AE, D, MC, V. $*

PICNIC SPOTS Since the Okefenokee is a national wildlife refuge, you won't find picnic tables sprinkled in remote locations. Each entrance has a group of tables clustered near the visitor center, usually under a shelter—the only picnic areas in the swamp. If you're taking a boat out, you can enjoy a packed lunch on the calm, secluded swamp waters.

LODGING

There are no accommodations within the refuge itself. Instead, visitors can choose from a number of relatively inexpensive options, mostly motels, nearby. Since there is no real peak season, prices and room availability remain about the same year-round.

NEAR THE NORTH ENTRANCE **Pond View Inn.** A B&B and a casual country retreat on 300 acres, Pond View is several miles outside Blackshear—a suitable base from which to visit the Okefenokee Swamp. The modest, 30-year-old, two-story house sits on a bank overlooking water lilies and a beaver dam in the pond from which the inn takes its name. Decor in this easygoing inn includes leather chairs and sofas, furniture fabrics embellished with hunting and fishing scenes, and handpainted, handcrafted furniture. Each attractive guest room has a ceiling fan, TV, and clock radio. Small but significant touches set Pond View Inn apart from many of its rivals: Surprises are provided for honeymooners or for other special occasions. Dinner is served to the public on Friday and Saturday nights by reservation and can be served to guests any night by reservation at an additional cost. *4200 Grady St., Blackshear, tel. 912/449–3697 or 800/585–8659, fax 912/449–5624. 5 rooms. Facilities: restaurant. AE, MC, V. $$–$$$*

Jameson Inn. This link in a Georgia chain of motels is off Memorial Drive and offers slightly better accommodations than the national chains—usually with friendlier service. A complimentary Continental breakfast is served daily. It is entirely no-smoking. *950 City Blvd., Waycross 31501, tel. 912/283–3800 or 800/526–3766, fax 912/283–9135. 60 rooms. Facilities: pool, exercise room, no-smoking rooms. AE, D, DC, MC, V. $–$$*

Blueberry Hill. Tucked away on 14 heavily wooded acres on Big Creek, east of Waycross, this rustic bed-and-breakfast offers two simple one-bedroom cottages, each furnished with plain semi-antique pieces. Hiking and canoe trails and a Cajun restaurant are on the property. The full breakfast, served on the restaurant's enclosed porch, includes blueberry pancakes or blueberry muffins. *Rte. 121/15, Hoboken 31542, tel. 912/458–2605. 2 cottages. Facilities: restaurant. AE, MC, V. $*

Days Inn. This Days Inn is among the best low-cost accommodations choices in the area. *U.S. 1 S, at 2016 Memorial Dr., Waycross 31501, tel. 912/285–4700 or 800/325–2525, fax 912/283–0971. 56 rooms. Facilities: pool. AE, D, DC, MC, V. $*

Holiday Inn. About 60 percent of rooms here are no-smoking. The game room and pool will keep kids busy. *1725 Memorial Dr., Waycross 31501, tel. 912/283–4490 or 800/322–6866. 148 rooms, 3 suites. Facilities: restaurant, bar, pool, exercise room,* recreation room, no-smoking rooms. AE, D, DC, MC, V. $

Red Carpet Inn. This place has the lowest rates of the several motels in the vicinity of the refuge. The frills are few (the pool is small). *1740 Memorial Dr., Waycross 31501, tel. 912/283–6134 or 800/251–1962. Facilities: pool. AE, D, DC, MC, V. $*

NEAR THE WEST ENTRANCE The **Helmstead.** Roughly equidistant from the north entrance in Waycross and the west entrance in Fargo, this B&B is the classiest accommodation for miles. Bedding varies from twins to doubles, and furnishings are antiques and period reproductions. Let Jane pamper you with afternoon tea, evening turndown service, and a Continental breakfast. *1 Fargo Rd., Homerville 31634, tel. 912/487–2222 or 888/224–3567. 4 rooms, 2 share bath; 1 suite. Facilities: pool, tennis court. No credit cards. $$*

CAMPING

Canoeing offers the only access to camping in the heart of the swamp, and raised platforms for tents and some pit toilets are the only facilities, so full wilderness camping supplies are needed. Reservations and permits, available from the refuge manager up to two months in advance, are required for use of canoe trails, which begin at the east and west entrances and by a small boat-ramp access point at the northeastern corner of the swamp. No more than one party can use each trail at a time. For canoe trail reservations, call 912/496–3331 between 7 AM and 10 AM.

INSIDE THE REFUGE Stephen C. Foster State Park. Aside from the raised wooden tent platforms (*see above*), the only campsites within the swamp itself are in Stephen C. Foster State Park. Of the 68 tent and trailer sites, 66 have water and electric hookups for RVs. There are two picnic shelters. Campsite reservations can be made up to 90 days in advance, and cottages, which are usually full year-round, can be reserved up to 11 months in advance. *Fargo, GA 31631, tel. 912/637–5274. 68 tent and trailer sites, 9 cottages. $*

NEAR THE EAST ENTRANCE **Okefenokee Pastimes.** Just across the road from the east entrance to the refuge, this campground has an arts-and-crafts marketplace as well as a supply store. There are full hookups available, in addition to primitive and tent camping. *R.R. 2, Box 3090, Folkston, tel. and fax 912/496–4472. $*

Traders Hill Park Campground and Recreation Area. This campground has the only camping in the Folkston area. About 8 mi from the visitor center, this 32-acre park along the St. Marys River has 24 tent and trailer sites with water and electric hookups, virtually unlimited walk-in tent sites, a boat ramp, a fishing pier, picnic tables and shelter, and rest rooms. The park is run by the county, and costs per night are $9.50 for sites with hookups and $5 for other sites. There are no reservations, but the park is rarely crowded. *7 mi south of Folkston on Rte. 23/121. For information, call the Board of Commissioners, tel. 912/496–3412. 24 tent and trailer sites. $*

NEAR THE NORTH ENTRANCE **Laura S. Walker State Park.** Just 8 mi from the swamp park, the state park has 306 acres on the outskirts of the Okefenokee Swamp, including a 120-acre lake. Water and electric hookups are available at all sites for $11 per night, and a disposal station, picnic tables, canoe rentals, and a boat ramp are provided. Reservations are not accepted, except during major holidays, but the park is rarely filled to capacity. *5653 Laura Walker Rd., Waycross 31503, tel. 912/287–4900. 44 tent and trailer sites. Facilities: pool, fishing, boating. $*

Shenandoah National Park
Virginia

By Paul Calhoun

Updated by W. Lynn Seldon

henandoah National Park drapes the backbone of Virginia's northern Blue Ridge Mountains like one of the region's famous handcrafted quilts—a patchwork of hardwood and evergreen forest accented by rocky crags, open meadows, crystal streams, and roaring waterfalls.

The birth of the Blue Ridge dates back a billion or more years, when shiftings and upheavals in the earth thrust skyward a granitic ridgeline. Now, trees come up the slopes and claim most of the peaks; only a few rocky summits stand barren.

Shenandoah National Park claims a much shorter history. What is now a scenic and nearly wild landscape was in the 1920s home to some 500 families. Unlike most areas that became national parks, the lands were privately owned, and when Congress authorized creation of the park in 1926, it did so with the stipulation that no federal funds could be used to buy these properties. The parcels were acquired—by sale, donation, and condemnation—with private contributions and an appropriation by the Commonwealth of Virginia. The mountaineers were proud, self-sufficient, and defiant; many of them bristled at the idea of being evicted. Today battle lines still form when anyone mentions expanding the park's 196,000 acres.

Within the park's territory lies an array of historical and recreational enticements. Many are readily accessible from the Skyline Drive, the 105-mi paved roadway that runs the length of the park along the spine of the Blue Ridge. Others require some hiking. Each turn on road and trail reveals stunning scenery, always with the chance of spotting white-tailed deer, black bears, and other wildlife. More than 200 species of birds have been identified in the park. Wildflowers are plentiful.

Unfortunatedly, Shenandoah National Park is not the pristine and ecologically secure preserve that was envisioned when it was established in the 1930s. It is suffering two kinds of degradation. One kind is airborne pollution emitted by and blown into the park by sources as varied as coal-fired fuel power plants and automobiles, from local areas and from hundreds of miles away. This pollution contributes to limited visibility, dangerous ozone levels, and the acid rain that is slowly killing many of the parks streams. The other type of degradation is done by non-native forest pests such as the gypsy moth, a native of France that escaped from a New England silkworm experiment in the 1930s and reached the park in 1983. Damage peaked in the early-1990s. Currently, the hemlock wooly adelgid, an aphid-like insect, is weakening the hemlock trees in the park and may kill all or most of them within 10 years.

ESSENTIAL INFORMATION

VISITOR INFORMATION For general information on the park, including developed campsites and backcountry camping, contact the superintendent, **Shenandoah National Park** (3655 U.S. 211 E, Luray 22835-9036, tel. 540/999–3500). The park's **Web site** is www.nps.gov/shen.

Travel information—reports about weather and road conditions, interesting events, wildlife sightings, and more—is also available at several waysides, campgrounds, an information center, and two major visitor centers along the Skyline Drive.

You can also buy the new 100-minute audiocassette tour, **Auto Tour Along Skyline Drive,** which starts at Front Royal and continues south along the 105 mi of the Skyline Drive. As you drive, the narrator directs you to overlooks where you may see a valley town, a mountain peak, or the snakelike bends of the Shenandoah River. You'll also hear about trails to explore, the families who once lived in the mountains, and the park's plants and animals. The tape, produced by the Shenandoah Natural History Association, is as much a guide to the Shenandoah National Park as it is to the Skyline Drive.

The area surrounding the park is rich in attractions. Contact **Charlottesville/Albemarle Convention & Visitors Bureau** (Box 161, Charlottesville 22902, tel. 804/977–1783) for information about Thomas Jefferson country, including Monticello and the University of Virginia. **Foothills Travel Association** (183-A Keith St., Warrenton 22186, tel. 540/347–4414) covers Virginia's horse country. **Front Royal–Warren County Chamber of Commerce** (414 E. Main St., Front Royal 22630, tel. 540/635–3185 or 800/338–2576) has information on Shenandoah and Skyline caverns and Shenandoah River. **Harrisonburg-Rockingham Convention & Visitors Bureau** (800 Country Club Rd., Harrisonburg 22801, tel. 540/434–2319) can provide information about Central Shenandoah Valley, including Massanutten, Endless, and Grand caverns, Natural Chimneys, and Massanutten Resort. **Lexington Visitors Bureau** (106 E. Washington St., Lexington 24450, tel. 540/463–3777) has information about Civil War history (Robert E. Lee and Stonewall Jackson), the Virginia Horse Center, and Natural

Bridge. **Luray-Page County Chamber of Commerce** (46 E. Main St., Luray 22835, tel. 540/743–3915) can tell you about the Luray Caverns. **Shenandoah Valley Travel Association** (Box 1040, New Market 22844, tel. 540/740–3132) has information on the entire region and Civil War history and battlefield reenactments. **Augusta-Staunton-Waynesboro Visitors Bureau** (1303 Richmond Ave., Staunton 24401, tel. 540/332–3972) covers the area in which you'll find the birthplace of Woodrow Wilson and Cyrus McCormick and the Museum of American Frontier Culture.

FEES Entrance fees are $10 per vehicle and $5 per hiker or bicyclist for a seven-day pass. An annual Shenandoah Passport is $20. Entry is free if you have an Annual Golden Eagle Passport, Golden Age, or Golden Access permit (*see* Planning Your Trip *in the* Essential Information *chapter*).

MILEPOSTS Mileposts—small gray concrete markers with black mileage indicators—are numbered from north to south on Skyline Drive, a 105-mi road. For this reason, most park literature (and this chapter) refers to locations in terms of mileposts (for whole numbers) and miles (for numbers with decimals) from the northern end of the park. In the case of Loft Mountain (Mile 79.5), for example, the designation means this popular area is 79.5 mi from the northern end of the Skyline Drive, but only 25.5 mi from the southern end.

PUBLICATIONS A full-color map and guide labeled simply *Shenandoah* is available for only 50¢ at visitor centers. The text addresses everything from geology to history; the map includes scenic areas, overlooks, and picnic grounds. *Shenandoah National Park Magazine,* a slick, pocket-size, full-color booklet available at park lodges, gives an informative overview. *Shenandoah Overlook,* the park newspaper, can be found at entrance stations and visitor centers; it provides seasonal information about the park, a bit of history, and helpful travel hints. "Exploring the Backcountry," a free brochure available at entrance stations and visitor centers, addresses rules, precautions, and equipment for venturing into the park's remote regions. "Hikes to Waterfalls" and "Birds of Shenandoah" also may be of interest to visitors.

For a comprehensive account of the park's history, trails, and more, read *Guide to Shenandoah National Park,* by Henry Heatwole ($6.50). *Herbert Hoover's Hideaway,* by Darwin Lambert ($4.95), is the story of the tiny cluster of buildings built at the headwaters of the trout-rich Rapidan River as a retreat for the president; at press time Camp Hoover was undergoing restoration. Both books are available from the **Shenandoah Natural History Association** (3655 U.S. 211 E, Luray 22835-9036, tel. 540/ 999–3582; include $3.50 for postage and handling) and are also on sale in park visitor centers and gift shops. So is *Skyland,* by George Freeman Pollock ($5.95), the author's account of arriving in the mountains a half-century before the park was founded and of establishing the mountain resort now known as Skyland. Colorful and dryly humorous, the book provides an account of life in the mountains a century ago.

GEOLOGY AND TERRAIN Underlying the mountains of the park are two types of ancient granite: the rare Old Rag, such as that exposed on the face of Old Rag Mountain itself; and the fairly common granodiorite, visible throughout the park. The granitic core beneath goes back a billion years or more. More recent geologic periods include a time of volcanic eruptions resulting in a dozen or more layers of lava flows, which, compacted with greenstone, still cover much of the park today; a period during which the park was covered with shallow water; and finally the modern era of the past 225 million years, which saw the uplifting and erosion that created the mountains and valleys as they are today.

Today most of the ancient rocks are draped in vegetation, from low-lying ground cover and wildflowers to the shrublike mountain laurel and rhododendron to the mature oak-hickory and evergreen forest. The

rocks here, unlike those in the barren vistas of the West, peer out only on occasion.

The park is composed mainly of highlands and mountain peaks; only occasionally do its lands work their way down toward the more fertile and gentle terrain below. At the heart of the park are the Blue Ridge Mountains, an eastern flank of the Appalachian Mountains, which run from Pennsylvania to Georgia. The park area runs at a southeast–northwest diagonal, from Afton Mountain (just east of Waynesboro) to the northwest terminus at a point just south of Front Royal.

To the east of the park is Virginia's rolling Piedmont. To the west is the Shenandoah Valley, named (like the park) for the Shenandoah River that winds through it. The valley was the setting for several Civil War battles, a history preserved in many of its towns and museums. On the western horizon, far across the Shenandoah Valley, are several prominent Appalachian peaks. Closer, in the valley itself, is the 40-mi-long mountain called Massanutten.

Most of the park's terrain is mountainous, but the extensive flatlands of Big Meadows (Milepost 51) are a rare and interesting exception. The meadow was probably first cleared by fire, set either by lightning or by Native Americans. Subsequent Native American fires, along with grazing by deer, elk, and bison, kept the meadows open until the mountaineers arrived with their cattle. The meadows actually suffered from the decision to return the park to its wild state: Without fire or grazing animals, they succumbed to the encroachments of the surrounding shrubs and forest. Once covering 1,000 acres, they have now shrunk to about 150 acres. Today they're maintained by mowing and occasional controlled burning.

FLORA AND FAUNA More than 95% of the Shenandoah is now covered by more than 100 species of trees, testimony to nature's ability to heal and reclaim the land if given the opportunity. The reclamation has been so successful that in 1976—a mere 40 years after the park's dedication—Congress designated 40% of it wilderness.

The sheltering forest is typical of the deciduous oak-hickory blend that blankets most of the region. A few pockets of unusual or specialized trees are interspersed: Evergreens (such as the hemlock, in wet, cool areas, and pines, mostly on dry slopes) are typically the predominating conifer species. The once towering ancestors were American chestnuts. Black locust, dogwood, sassafras and black cherry are invaders of fields, abandoned farms, and other open areas. Cove hardwoods, including birches, maples, and the tulip poplar, often establish territory at the head of lowland hollows and along low-elevation stream banks.

The abundant wildflowers—200 or more species of interest—are one of the park's most popular attractions. The leafy forest canopy restricts the sunlight that might otherwise contribute to a lavish display, yet the mixture of heavy shade, partial sunlight, and forest fringe fosters a great floral diversity. With the exception of the open fields of Big Meadows, where there can be a veritable blanket of flowers, the sun-loving varieties are easiest to find along trails and roadsides. Furtive species, such as the pink lady's slipper, lurk in the deeper, darker woods. Note that the park rule is very strict: No collecting!

Only a few decades ago postcards depicted the black bear as a playful buffoon, begging for treats or helping itself to a picnic basket while people smiled and watched. Those days have passed, and today's emphasis is on discouraging interaction. Though it doesn't have the size or the reputation of the western grizzly, the black bear is still a powerful and unpredictable creature. And big, strong, wild animals and naive tourists are a bad combination. Although the park has one of the highest concentrations of black bears in the region (approximately 250–300), the animal's natural inclination is to avoid people, lying low during the day and prowling mostly at night. You probably have little to fear from a black bear, but it can harm cars, tents, and people in its quest for food—and it can do a truly serious amount of damage if it sets its mind and muscle to the task. Obey all rules for food storage when camping, and consider yourself fortunate if you do catch a glimpse of a black bear in the wild.

White-tailed deer are likely to be seen at almost any time or place in the park—especially feeding around campgrounds and roadsides where the sun spurs the growth of grasses and shrubs. Although many are used to being around people, they are not tame and should not be fed or approached too closely. It's against park rules and potentially dangerous: Even the most soft-eyed doe can rear and strike unexpectedly with her front hooves. The most common (and dangerous) place to spot a deer is from your car, on the Skyline Drive. Obey the speed limit and immediately slow down if you see a deer, especially at night, when your headlights might blind or confuse it.

Among wildlife you're likely to see during the daytime are chipmunks and groundhogs; at night, the gray fox, striped skunk, and raccoon. Less common are the red fox, spotted skunk, and bobcat.

There are more than 200 species of birds in the park (*see* Other Activities *in* Exploring, *below*). A project on Hawksbill Mountain helped to reintroduce the peregrine falcon to the wilds of the region. Famous as the world's fastest bird (it can dive for prey at more than 200 mph), it was once common throughout the East—before DDT and other pesticides contributed to a decline in its reproduction.

There is also a wide variety of snakes, lizards, frogs, salamanders, and other reptiles and amphibians in the park. Only two of the park's snakes, the timber rattler and copperhead, are poisonous.

WHEN TO GO Autumn, when thousands upon thousands of visitors converge on the Skyline Drive to view the stunning fall foliage (usually at its peak October 10–25), is the most popular season at Shenandoah National Park.

Only winter, which brings limited (only valley) lodging options and the possibility of road closings, could be declared off-season at the park. Startling cold and unexpectedly heavy snowfalls can strike anytime from October to April. But the clear views that the cold, crystal winter skies can hold a special allure for many.

The park's spring arrives in April or May, depending on the severity and stubbornness of winter in the highlands. Early wildflowers bloom during those two months. The green of new foliage charges up the flanks of the mountains at a rate of 100 ft per day, finally reaching the peaks in late May, just in time for the resplendent display of the pink azalea. The tiny white teacup-shape blossoms of the mountain laurel follow in June. Rivaling the spring bloom are the vivid, vocal, fast-flying colors of warblers and other mating songbirds.

Summer is a time of nesting birds, spotted fawns, and an explosion of wildflowers. Summer temperatures range from the 40s to the 90s, and are usually 10°F to 15°F cooler than in the valleys below.

SEASONAL EVENTS **May:** During **Wildflower Weekend** mid-month, the park sponsors walks, exhibits, slide programs, and other activities that draw attention to the spring wildflowers. **August:** On the weekend closest to August 10 (Herbert Hoover's birthday), **Hoover Days** are celebrated with tours and bus shuttles from Byrd Visitor Center to the former president's summer camp at the headwaters of the Rapidan River. **December:** The park's annual bird count takes place the third Sunday in December.

WHAT TO PACK Regardless of the season, you'll probably want sunscreen, sunglasses, a hat or cap, rain gear, and comfortable walking shoes. Long-sleeved shirts and light jackets are often welcome even in July and August. Other handy accessories include field guides and field glasses. The park is relatively pest-free, but pack an insect repellent to ward off ticks and the few chiggers, mosquitoes, or small gnats you might encounter. It's a good idea to bring your own drinks, snacks, and such

for times you are not near park concessions. You might also bring a couple of aerosol tire-inflator cans, should you have a flat you don't want to change on the spot.

GENERAL STORES The park is far removed from malls and grocery stores, though convenience stores are common in the small towns you pass through on your way to the park. The few stores along the Skyline Drive are far removed from each other. Note that schedules are subject to change, because summer hours are often extended. Check the *Shenandoah Overlook* for the current schedule. **Elkwallow Wayside** (Mile 24.1, tel. 540/999–2253) is a camp store with groceries, camping supplies, ice, and gasoline; it's open mid-April–October, daily 9–5:30. **Panorama** (Mile 31.5, at the Thornton Gap entrance at the U.S. 211 interchange, 4 mi east of Luray) is a combination gift-crafts shop and restaurant. **Skyland** (Mile 41.7, tel. 540/999–2211) isn't a general store per se, but this lodge with a dining room has a mountain-crafts shop, a newsstand, touring information, drink machines, and pay phones; most services are open late March–late November, daily 9–8. **Big Meadows** (Milepost 51, tel. 540/999–2251) wayside camp store has food, drinks and ice, a gift shop and newsstand, gasoline, and a short-order snack shop; it's open April–November, daily 9–5:30. **Lewis Mountain** (Mile 57.6, tel. 540/999–2255) has a campground store with wood, ice, food and drinks, and other supplies, as well as showers and washers and dryers; it's open May–October, daily 9–5:30, till 8 June–August. **Loft Mountain** (Mile 79.5; tel. 804/823–4515) offers the same things as Lewis Mountain (*see above*); it is open late May–October, daily 9–5:30.

ATMS There are no ATMs within the park. All towns surrounding the park and all entrances have ATMs at banks. One of the closest is at the **East Luray** branch of Jefferson National Bank (Business Rte. 211 at East Luray Shopping Center, tel. 540/743–6566), approximately 6.5 mi east of the Skyline Drive via U.S. 211. Another close ATM is in **Front Royal,** the South Street branch of Jefferson National Bank (432 South St., tel. 540/635–1952). To get here, take Route 340 north from the park entrance into Front Royal and turn right at the second traffic light on South Street/Route 55; the bank is across from the Kmart.

ARRIVING AND DEPARTING There is no rail or air service into the park itself, but several of the park's gateway communities are accessible by air, rail, or bus.

By Bus. Greyhound Lines (tel. 800/231–2222) serves Charlottesville, Harrisonburg, Staunton, and Culpeper—all of which are convenient to the park. Once you reach any of these towns, though, you'll need to rent a car.

By Car and RV. Shenandoah National Park is readily accessible by motor vehicle, although larger RVs may be challenged by the fairly steep climb to the Skyline Drive. From Charlottesville, take I–64 west to the park's southern entrance at Rockfish Gap; or take U.S. 29 north, then U.S. 33 west to the park's central entrance at Swift Run Gap, a 30-minute drive. From Washington, take I–66 west, then U.S. 340 south through Front Royal to the Skyline Drive access at Dickey Ridge, a 1½-hour drive.

Gasoline is available, but not always conveniently so, in the park. Roadside assistance is even harder to arrange, so make sure your car is serviced and top off the tank before you enter the park. There are two gas stations along the Skyline Drive. **Elkwallow Wayside** (Mile 24.1) is open early April–October, daily 9–5:30. **Big Meadows Wayside** (Milepost 51) is open late March–late November, daily 9–5:30.

You can rent a car at Charlottesville-Albemarle Airport from **Avis** (tel. 804/973–6000), **Budget** (tel. 804/973–5751), or **Hertz** (tel. 804/973–8349).

Shenandoah Valley Airport has desks for **Avis** (tel. 540/234–9961) and **Hertz** (tel. 540/234–9411).

Rental agencies at Dulles include **Alamo** (tel. 703/661–8149), **Avis** (tel. 703/661–3514), **Budget** (tel. 703/437–9373), **Dollar** (tel. 703/661–8823), **Hertz** (tel. 703/471–6020), and **National** (tel. 703/471–5278).

By Plane. Charlottesville-Albemarle Airport (201 Bowen Loop, Charlottesville, tel. 804/973–8341 for Airport Authority Office), 8 mi north of Charlottesville on U.S. 29, is the closest major airport. Airlines serving it include American Eagle (tel. 800/433–7300), Comair/Delta (tel. 800/354–9822), United Express (tel. 800/241–6522), and US Airway Express (tel. 800/428–4322). There are several rental car options at the airport (*see* By Car and RV, *above*). There is no public transportation to the park; a **Yellow Cab** (tel. 804/295–4131) taxi to Big Meadows Lodge runs about $70 one-way.

To get to the park from the airport, take U.S. 29 south and then I–64 west to the park's southern entrance at Rockfish Gap; or take U.S. 29 north and then U.S. 33 west to the park's central entrance at Swift Run Gap. Driving time is approximately 30 minutes either way. The southern access is preferable for a one-way, end-to-end viewing of the park; the central access is the quickest way to the main lodges at Big Meadows and Skyland.

Shenandoah Valley Airport (tel. 540/234–8304), west of Grottoes on Route 256 between Staunton and Harrisonburg, is midway between the Rockfish and Swift Run entrances on the park's west side (*see* By Car and RV, *above,* for rental car information). The much larger **Dulles International Airport** (tel. 703/661–2700), near Herndon, Virginia, and just east of Washington, D.C., is within 1½ hours of the park's Swift Run and Front Royal entrances (*see* By Car and RV, *above,* for rental car information).

By Train. The nearest major station is the one in Charlottesville (600 E. Water St.), served by **Amtrak** (tel. 800/872–7245). There is no public transportation from the station to the park. A **Yellow Cab** (tel. 804/295–4131) taxi to Big Meadows would cost around $100 one-way. A cab to the rental car agencies at the airport (*see* By Plane, *above*) is about $20.

EXPLORING

One of the Shenandoah's best qualities is that it appeals equally to the most and least adventurous of visitors. The best way to experience the park is to combine car tours with short walks from overlooks and trailheads. Serious hikers can explore the expansive backcountry. Bicycling is allowed, but it's difficult for inexperienced riders because of all the climbs and descents and the narrow to nonexistent road shoulders.

THE BEST IN ONE DAY Although the park covers 300 square mi and stretches along the 105-mi Skyline Drive, it is relatively narrow, ranging from 1 to 13 mi in width. By devoting a day (or less) to traveling the drive and stopping at visitor centers and some of the 75 overlooks, motor tourists can learn a lot about the park—and enjoy mountaintop views of most of it—without venturing more than 50 yards from their vehicles. By combining a motor tour with a couple of short-to-intermediate walks, you can see a great expanse of nature from a distance and a fair amount of it up close.

Overlooks along the drive offer short walks, informative exhibits, expansive views, fabulous sunsets or sunrises—and some even have drinking fountains with treated water tapped from natural springs. The visitor information centers at **Dickey Ridge** (Mile 4.6), open daily early April–late November, and **Byrd** (Milepost 51), open daily April–late November, are the park's two major information facilities. They have historical and cultural exhibits, pamphlets and publications, rest rooms, phones, drinking water, picnic areas, hiking trails, and friendly and helpful staffs that can answer just about any question. While at Byrd, take time to view the **Big Meadows** area and the exhibit on the loss of the native chestnut trees that once dominated the region's forests; then consider a short detour to see Big Meadows Lodge, a structure built from these ill-fated trees. When in the park's South District, you can get information and publications mid-May–October at **Loft Mountain Information Center** (Mile 79.5).

Skyland (Miles 41.7 and 42.5) was originally established by George Freeman Pollock as Stony Man Camp, after the mountain that towered over it. Pollock had done much to preserve the beauty of the area, and Skyland had become a popular mountain retreat long before his insistent campaigning inspired the creation of the national park.

ORIENTATION PROGRAMS The **Dickey Ridge Visitor Center** (Mile 4.6) shows, on request, a 12-minute film that is an introduction to the park. Newcomers nervous about rules, animals, trails, and so on may find it informative and reassuring. The **Byrd Visitor Center** at Big Meadows (Milepost 51) shows several alternating films about the park and its wildlife and plants.

GUIDED TOURS There are no commercial tours. Park Service rangers conduct free interpretive walks in season; these vary in time (1–4 hours), attendance (5–100 people), subject, and location, but typically they deal with natural or cultural history, or such current management concerns as air quality and forest health. Details about current and upcoming activities are published in the park newspaper, the *Shenandoah Overlook* (free at park entrance stations and visitor centers).

SCENIC DRIVES AND VIEWS The **Skyline Drive,** from its northern terminus (just south of Front Royal at U.S. 340) to its southern terminus (at Rockfish Gap, at the I–64/U.S. 250 interchange just east of Waynesboro), was created as a scenic drive. It offers outstanding views, from open panoramas of distant peaks and valleys to roadside foliage and wildflowers, throughout its 105-mi length. The following is a list of the most popular vantage points along the roadway.

Shenandoah Valley Overlook (Mile 2.8) provides a soaring view across Shenandoah Valley to Signal Knob, a Civil War communications post on Massanutten Mountain.

Range View Overlook (Mile 17.1) offers a sweeping expanse of the Blue Ridge from a 2,810-ft elevation.

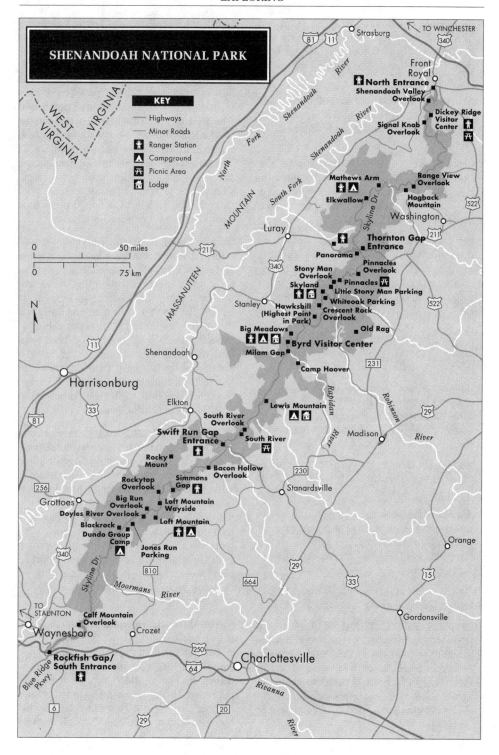

SHENANDOAH NATIONAL PARK

KEY

— Highways
— Minor Roads
👤 Ranger Station
⛺ Campground
🏕 Picnic Area
🏠 Lodge

0 ——— 50 miles
0 ——— 75 km

N

WEST VIRGINIA
VIRGINIA

TO WINCHESTER

Strasburg

Front Royal

North Entrance
Shenandoah Valley Overlook

Signal Knob Overlook

Dickey Ridge Visitor Center

Range View Overlook

Mathews Arm
Elkwallow

Hogback Mountain

Washington

Luray

Thornton Gap Entrance

Panorama

Pinnacles Overlook

Stony Man Overlook
Skyland
Pinnacles
Little Stony Man Parking
Whiteoak Parking

Stanley

Hawksbill
(Highest Point in Park)

Crescent Rock Overlook

Old Rag

Big Meadows

Byrd Visitor Center

Milam Gap

Shenandoah

Camp Hoover

Harrisonburg

Elkton

Lewis Mountain

Madison

Swift Run Gap Entrance

South River Overlook

South River

Rocky Mount

Bacon Hollow Overlook

Rockytop Overlook

Simmons Gap

Stanardsville

Big Run Overlook

Doyles River Overlook

Loft Mountain Wayside

Loft Mountain

Grottoes

Blackrock
Dundo Group Camp

Jones Run Parking

Orange

TO STAUNTON

Calf Mountain Overlook

Crozet

Gordonsville

Waynesboro

Rockfish Gap/ South Entrance

Blue Ridge Pkwy.

Charlottesville

Moormans River

Rivanna River

MASSANUTTEN MOUNTAIN

North Fork
South Fork
Shenandoah River

Rapidan River

Robinson River

Pinnacles Overlook (Mile 35.1) is an overview of many of the park's peaks, including the distant, rock-studded, lichen-covered ridgeline of Old Rag and the valley beyond.

Stony Man Mountain Overlook (Mile 38.6) features a view of Stony Man Mountain to the south and Massanutten Mountain to the west.

Crescent Rock (Mile 44.4) has by far the best view of 4,051-ft Hawksbill Mountain, the park's highest peak. The viewpoint is only 25 yards from the drive, but watch out: Footing can be unstable.

Big Meadows (Milepost 51) is a must-see destination. A walk along the inviting paths in the last of the park's open meadows (*see* Geology and Terrain *in* Essential Information, *above*) puts you among a richness of wildflowers, berries, and songbirds not found in more heavily forested sections. The browsing deer are usually numerous (especially on spring evenings) and uncharacteristically calm and trusting.

Bacon Hollow Overlook (Mile 69.3) has views of two drastically different regions of Virginia—the rolling Piedmont to the east, and 3,000-ft-plus peaks to the north and south.

Rockytop Overlook (Mile 78.1) offers views of the valley and wild backcountry of the Big Run watershed.

Big Run Overlook (Mile 81.2), one of the park's best views, is another perspective on the Big Run watershed, from the cliffs and talus slopes of Rocky Mountain to distant Massanutten.

Calf Mountain Overlook (Mile 98.9) is known for excellent sunsets and 300° views.

HISTORIC BUILDINGS AND SITES Because the park was established to preserve the remaining wilderness and let the elements reclaim what humans had wrought, many structures have been allowed to crumble. There are, however, six preserved historic districts in the park. Two are Camp Hoover and Corbin Cabin.

Camp Hoover, President Herbert Hoover's earlier version of Camp David, was used by Hoover as a retreat until he donated the dwellings to the park in 1933. It's set at the headwaters of the Rapidan River, one of the best trout streams in the park (catch-and-release only), and is maintained much as it was in Hoover's time. The camp can be reached by an easy 2-mi walk on the Mill Prong Trail, from Mile 52.5 on the drive, or by a longer one from Milam Gap (*see* Nature Trails and Short Walks, *below*), and, occasionally, by a special-permission car pool from the Byrd Visitor Center. At press time Camp Hoover was undergoing restoration.

Corbin Cabin is one of only two mountaineer's homes that have been maintained and kept fully intact, its main distinction. Most of the others (including two near Corbin Cabin) have been reclaimed by nature. Access is by a challenging trail from the drive at Mile 37.9. The cabin is intended mainly for the use of those who rent it; when it's occupied, other visitors are encouraged to keep their distance. For rental information, contact the Potomac Appalachian Trail Club (*see* Appalachian Trail *in* Longer Hikes, *below*).

NATURE TRAILS AND SHORT WALKS For taking a break from the driver's seat and stretching your legs, the park has nearly limitless options. The main problem is deciding which trail to take. Contact the park for short hikes in the northern, central, and southern districts (*see* Visitor Information *in* Essential Information, *above*), or Henry Heatwole's wonderful *Guide to Shenandoah National Park* (*see* Publications *in* Essential Information, *above*). Note that pets are not allowed on some trails. The following is an abbreviated list of short hikes.

North Marshall Viewpoint (Mile 15.9; .75 mi, 45 min round-trip). Follow the Appalachian Trail, on the east side of the Skyline Drive, less than 100 yards north of the milepost. The gentle climb, with switchbacks, will bring you to an open ledge with a sheer drop and a fine view. In the distance you can spot the Pinnacle, Marys

Rock, Stony Man, Millers Head, and Pass Mountain.

Limberlost (Milepost 43; 1.3 mi, 45 min). This easy circuit walk along a 5-ft-wide hard-packed greenstone trail starts at the parking area and circles through a section of old-growth hemlock forest that George and Addie Pollock saved by paying a logger not to cut it. Some of the ancient hemlocks, 3 ft or more in diameter, still tower; the fallen and decaying trunks of others make for somber but interesting scenery. Considerable effort has gone into making this an easy trail—a 150-ft-long boardwalk and a 65-ft bridge, for instance—and in late 1997 it will be rededicated as an "accessible" trail.

Blackrock (Mile 84.8; 1 mi, 1 hr round-trip). Parking is on the west side of the Skyline Drive, around 100 ft from the road. Take Trayfoot Mountain Trail (a former fire road) up the ridge; continue on the Appalachian Trail. For .3 mi the path is an easy climb through the forest, followed by a gradual descent of 200 yards or so across an open talus slope of rocks that range from small to car-size. Beyond the slope is a stunning panorama over the Madison Run watershed and Dundo Hollow. The trail loops around Blackrock Summit. (There is no trail to the summit, but you can find your way by scrambling uphill over the rocks.) Return via the same route.

LONGER HIKES Experienced hikers can spend weeks exploring the park's 500 mi of trails and still see only a portion of its backcountry. Carry a copy of Heatwole's *Guide to Shenandoah National Park* (*see* Publications *in* Essential Information, *above*), because it's possible to get turned around on some of the trails and end up well away from your intended destination. The longest trail is the approximately 101 mi of the famous Maine-to-Georgia Appalachian Trail (*see below*). The following are some other popular trails.

Overall Run Falls (Milepost 22.2; 3.8 mi, 3–4 hrs round-trip). It's an easy descent to—but a challenging climb on your return from—93-ft Overall Run Falls, the park's highest waterfall. From the end of Loop B in Mathews Arm campground, take the old Mathews Arm fire road 1.4 mi to Big Blue Trail, and then continue 100 yards and take a left on the Big Blue/Overall Run Trail. After another .1 mi, there's a side trail on the left to the upper falls. Continue down the trail to other side trails to view the falls.

Whiteoak Canyon (Mile 42.6; 4.6 mi, 4 hrs round-trip). This popular but strenuous hike takes you to the first and tallest (86 ft) of Whiteoak Canyon's six noted waterfalls. The trailhead lies on the east side of the Skyline Drive, just south of the south entrance to Skyland. The trail descends through the towering Limberlost hemlocks, along Whiteoak Run (nearly dry in some seasons, torrential in others), into the heart of Whiteoak Canyon, and, finally, to the waterfalls. The first is the highest; there are five more deeper in the canyon, but the trail is very rough and steep.

Camp Hoover via Mill Prong from Milam Gap (Mile 52.8; 4.1 mi, 3¾ hrs round-trip, or well under 3 if you're in practice). If you want just one fairly easy longer walk, here's a great choice. From the south end of the Milam Gap parking lot, follow the Appalachian Trail about 50 yards on the east side of the Skyline Drive; then turn left onto the Mill Prong Trail. The single-track dirt trail skirts an old orchard and then meanders across the fern-carpeted floor of second-growth forest. The trail crosses Mill Prong twice as it follows the small stream to Herbert Hoover's summer retreat. In some places the stream is barely a trickle; in others, the holes are large enough to support brook trout and encourage hot-weather hikers to take an impromptu (chilly) dip.

Pocosin Mission and South River Falls via Pocosin fire road (Mile 59.5; 8.5 mi, 7 hrs). You reach the crumbling ruins of an early 20th-century Episcopal mission and 83-ft-high South River Falls on this challenging circuit hike. Heatwole's book (*see* Publications *in* Essential Information, *above*) describes the rather complex route.

Doyles River/Jones Run/Appalachian Trail (Mile 81.1; 8 mi, 7 hrs). There are three waterfalls, a bunch of tiring climbs and descents, some of the park's biggest trees, and expansive views along this circuit hike. Take the Doyles River Trail downhill from the parking area, crossing the Appalachian Trail and Browns Gap fire road, to the Doyles River Falls. From there, continue descending to the Jones Run Trail; follow it uphill and take a right onto the Appalachian Trail. It's approximately 3 mi back to the parking area. If you can leave one car at the Doyles River parking lot (Mile 81.1) and a second vehicle at the Jones Run parking area (Mile 84.1), you can shorten the hike to 4.8 mi by dispensing with the return leg on the Appalachian Trail.

Appalachian Trail. Some 101 mi of the Maine-to-Georgia **Appalachian Trail** (AT) run within the park's boundaries roughly parallel to the Skyline Drive. The park section of the AT is well maintained by volunteers, with, generally, good footing and even grading; it is marked by white blazes on trees and rocks, which make it easy to follow. Wilderness hikers must possess valid backcountry permits (*see* Visitor Information *in* Essential Information, *above*). The best source of information for AT hikers is the **Potomac Appalachian Trail Club** (118 Park St. SE, Vienna, VA 22180, tel. 703/242–0315), which is open Monday–Thursday 7 PM–9 PM, Thursday–Friday noon–2. The club maintains seven trailside huts and six backcountry cabins, which provide good overnight stops. The huts are basically covered sleeping and lounging areas; the fee is $1 per night. The cabins are better appointed than the huts; each has a table, a fireplace, bunks for up to 11 people, a pit toilet, and a door with a lock, and there is a spring nearby (water should be treated before drinking). They can be reserved through the club.

OTHER ACTIVITIES **Biking.** Experienced bicyclists will delight in the vistas and in the drive's 35-mph speed limit, but they'll be challenged by the narrow road shoulders, the heavy traffic in high season (particularly October weekends), and the climbs to elevations of 3,680 ft. (Amateurs should not attempt it.) Off-road or mountain bikes have the ideal gearing for the steep going, but they may be used only on paved areas. During times of limited visibility or at night, each bicycle must have a white light on the front and a red light or reflector on the back. For additional safety, wear gloves and a helmet at all times.

Bird-Watching. Carry a field guide and binoculars and you can rack up an impressive variety of sightings—more than 200 species of birds have been identified in the park. Novice birders can readily spot ruffed grouse, black vultures, ravens, crows, robins, and blue jays. Students of the hobby will appreciate the way the park's high altitudes and dense cover attract birds that are usually found farther north, such as the woodcock, junco, wood thrush, and some 35 species of warblers.

While a few birds live in the park year-round—notably the ruffed grouse, barred owl, and wild turkey—late spring and summer are the best times to see birds that visit the area for breeding and nesting. The park is also an excellent observation area for watching the thousands of raptors (several types of hawks plus the occasional eagle and falcon) that migrate south along the Blue Ridge every autumn.

The open areas of Big Meadows (Milepost 51) support an outstanding diversity of species, especially small songbirds. The small and furtive warblers, flycatchers, and vireos abound in the forest canopy; sharp-eyed birders are likely to spot them at just about any time and place. The park is also a good place to watch the fall migration of raptors. For a closer encounter with some of the "fighter jets" of the bird world, attend a "Bird of Prey" program, starring injured hawks and owls that have been rescued and rehabilitated. Park bulletin boards and the park newspaper carry the schedule. The publication "Birds of Shenandoah" is helpful.

Fishing. Regulations have changed significantly in order to ensure effective protection and management of the fisheries resources. However, these changes eliminate many of the differences that existed between Virginia fish regulations and park regulations. There are about 25 streams that are open for consumptive fishing; all others are catch-and-release only.

The fishing season is now year-round for both stream classifications. A Virginia fishing license is required for all persons 16 years of age and older ($15 for nonresidents, $6.50 for residents; good for five days). The minimum size limit for trout is 9 inches and the maximum creel limit is six fish. Size and catch limits for other game-fish species coincide with Virginia regulations. Use of single hook (barbed or barbed-less) artificial lures is required.

It's important to handle hooked trout properly. Maintain control of this fish with wet hands; avoid contact or damage to sensitive gills; and minimize the amount of time the fish is held out of water. Experienced and conscientious trout fishers play the hooked fish and release it without ever removing it from the water and also avoid dragging it over rocks. Ethical fishing techniques are critical to sustaining the Eastern brook trout populations in the park. For a list of streams open for harvest and other valuable tips, consult the "Recreational Fishing" brochure that is available at campgrounds, entrance stations, and visitor centers.

Horseback Riding. Horseback riding is allowed on designated trails from April through October. Contact the park superintendent (*see* Visitor Information *in* Essential Information, *above*) for maps and information. **Skyland Stables** (tel. 540/999–2210), near Skyland Lodge (Mile 41.7), offers guided trail rides only, April through October ($20 for one hour, $40 for 2½ hours); pony rides are available for small children ($6 per half hour). Credit cards are not accepted.

Rock Climbing. The most popular routes are on Old Rag Mountain and Little Stony Man Cliff—though the latter may be closed when peregrine falcons are nesting there. You don't need a permit, but you must be familiar with park restrictions: no altering rock faces, no removing plants or lichens, no using motorized drills in designated wilderness areas. The superintendent's office can supply the complete list of regulations.

Swimming. Swimming, at your own risk, is allowed in park streams. However, except during the spring runoff, when they're too cold for comfort, park waters are too shallow for anything but wading. Most streams do have a few small holes that allow for a modest amount of hot-weather splashing—for example, Mill Prong, on the hike to Camp Hoover.

CHILDREN'S PROGRAMS Activities for children from preschool age to early teens fall into two categories—summer interpretive programs and the Junior Ranger program.

The schedule of free summer interpretive programs—nature walks, night-sky observation, and so forth—is published in the park newspaper, *Shenandoah Overlook*. There's also a Junior Ranger program, which involves taking ranger-led walks and buying a book (in park visitor centers and gift shops), completing its puzzles and exercises, and turning it in to earn a Junior Ranger badge.

EVENING ACTIVITIES Park rangers conduct free programs most summer evenings at lodges, campgrounds, and amphitheaters. The programs vary in length and content; most involve slide shows and ranger-led night walks. For a schedule of topics, times, and locations, consult the park newspaper, *Shenandoah Overlook*. Wear comfortable walking shoes and clothes; bring a flashlight and a long-sleeved shirt or jacket. Insects aren't much of a problem in the park, but you might carry bug spray, just in case.

DINING

INSIDE THE PARK The park's six restaurants cater to appetites and attire that suit the outdoors. Meals are filling, the setting casual, the service good, the scenery outstanding. The accent is on local foods: simply prepared fried chicken, grilled fresh trout, fried local catfish, and broiled steaks and chops. In the two larger restaurants (Big Meadows and Skyland) you can get all three meals: Breakfast and lunch are inexpensive, with plenty of selections; dinner is moderate. The dining rooms at Big Meadows and Skyland have good wine lists. Because reservations aren't taken, you should try to have dinner a bit early or late, avoiding the 6:30–7:30 rush. The adjacent taprooms are modest extensions (seating 20–30) of their respective lodges, with sandwiches, snacks, and evening entertainment during peak visitor periods.

In addition to the two large restaurants, there are four inexpensive wayside stops.

Big Meadows Lodge. The rich tones of native American chestnut dominate the interior of this historic structure. The exterior has a multitiered roof and large windows that provide sunset views from the dining room. The homemade breads are excellent, as is the Caesar salad; entrées, although not fancy, are generous and well prepared; and the blackberry ice cream pie topped with blackberry syrup is heavenly. All three meals are served daily in this cozy lodge, which is popular with Europeans. Big Meadows Wayside (*see below*) is nearby. *Milepost 51, Skyline Dr., tel. 540/999–2221 or 800/999–4714. AE, D, MC, V. Closed Nov.–early May. $$*

Skyland. If you can secure a window table in this rustic stone-and-timber setting, you may see deer and rabbits nibbling at the grasses on the narrow strip of lawn between the lodge and a nearby stand of mountain laurel and rhododendron; if not, you can still enjoy the view toward Massanutten Mountain through the expansive glass of the dining room's west wall. Skyland's dining room is bigger and a bit better than the one at Big Meadows. The traditional Southern Highlands menu (the same menu as at Big Meadows) includes fresh Shendandoah trout, broiled with almonds and served with wild rice. Finish off the meal with a scrumptious dessert, such as fresh apple cobbler with caramel sauce. Breakfast is also served. *Mile 41.7, Skyline Dr., tel. 540/999–2211 or 800/999–4714. AE, D, MC, V. Closed late Nov.–late Mar. $$*

Panorama. Panorama is a multilevel concrete-block building with a dining area with waitresses serving lunch and dinner daily, offering pizza and subs. There is no wine list or taproom—just wine by the glass or draft beer. The hours are shorter, though sometimes during peak visitor traffic they're extended. *Mile 31.5, Skyline Dr., tel. 540/999–2265. AE, D, MC, V. Closed mid-Nov.–late Mar. $$*

Big Meadows Wayside. All three meals are served daily at this wayside with waitress service in the dining room; you can also carry out items such as soup, salads, and sandwiches. It's part grocery store, part gift shop, and part dining room. *Milepost 51, Skyline Dr., tel. 540/999–2251. AE, D, MC, V. Closed Nov. 30–3rd wk of Mar. $*

Elkwallow Wayside. This wayside, open daily 9–5:30, has counter service providing sandwiches and grilled items; seating for all three meals daily is outside on the patio or on picnic tables. *Mile 24.1, Skyline Dr., tel. 540/999–2253. AE, D, MC, V. Closed Nov.–early Apr. $*

Loft Mountain Wayside. Open daily 9–5:30, Loft Mountain has counter service and tables and booths inside and picnic tables outside for fast food like hamburgers; all three meals are served daily. At the Loft Mountain Campstore, you can stock up on groceries and camping supplies. *Mile 79.5, Skyline Dr., tel. 804/823–4515. AE, D, MC, V. Closed Nov.–early Apr. $*

NEAR THE PARK The park's gateway communities offer a variety of dining options, from fast to fine. If you're staying the night in the park, the long drive out for dinner may not seem practical. Dress is generally casual, although a jacket for men is advised in very expensive restaurants, even if one is not required.

For other options near the park, *see* the Blue Ridge Parkway chapter.

Inn at Little Washington. You can splurge here on the likes of medallions of veal Shenandoah (with grilled local apples, Virginia apple brandy, and fresh fettuccine) and accompany it with wine from the inn's 8,000-bottle cellar. It's extremely expensive (*see* Lodging, *below*), but for quality it ranks among the best restaurants on the East Coast. *Middle and Main Sts. (13 mi from the Thornton Gap entrance to Skyline Dr.), Washington, tel. 540/675–3800, fax 540/675–3100. Reservations essential. MC, V. No lunch. Closed Tues. except May and Oct. $$$*

Dean's Steakhouse. The understated wood-and-brick exterior sets the casual, friendly tone for the three interior dining areas and outdoor patio. Specialties include locally raised trout, fresh seafood, and baby back and prime ribs. The extensive wine list includes many Virginia and California labels. *701 S. Royal Ave. (¼ mi from the northern entrance to Skyline Dr.), Front Royal, tel. 540/635–1780. AE, DC, MC, V. $$*

Parkhurst Restaurant. The stately white building has the air of a country club. The international specialties include chicken dishes (from fried to cordon bleu), steak, and fettuccine with shellfish. There's an emphasis on Virginia wines. *2547 U.S. 211, W. Luray (2 mi west of Luray Caverns on U.S. 211, 10 mi from Skyline Dr.), tel. 540/743–6009. AE, D, DC, MC, V. No lunch. $$*

Brookside Restaurant. This full-service, home-style restaurant offers homemade breads and desserts, a 30-item salad bar, luncheon and dinner buffets, and such specialties as stove-top pan-fried chicken. The dining room decor is country conservative: country curtains, wood-grain tables, carpeting, wood paneling. There are booths in a separate coffee-shop section, as well as a gift shop. *2978 U.S. 211 E, Luray (4½ mi from Skyline Dr.; 20 min from Skyland), tel. 540/743–5698. Reservations not accepted. AE, D, DC, MC, V. $*

Pano's. The French provincial motif outside belies the cozy wood paneling and bargain prices inside this spacious, family-oriented restaurant. The huge menu offers 65 entrées at lunch, 96 at dinner. *3190 S. Main St., Harrisonburg (just off I–81 at Exit 243; 30 min west of Skyline Dr. via U.S. 33), tel. 540/434–2367. Reservations not accepted. AE, D, DC, MC, V. $*

PICNIC SPOTS Box lunches, including a sandwich, fruit, chips, and cookie for around $6, are available from the Big Meadows Lodge, Panorama, and Skyland dining rooms. You can eat at one of the overlooks (no tables) or at one of the park's picnic areas: Dickey Ridge (Mile 4.6); Elkwallow (Mile 24.1); Pinnacles (Mile 36.7); Big Meadows (Milepost 51); Lewis Mountain (Mile 57.5); South River (Mile 62.8); or Loft Mountain (Mile 79.5). The designated picnic areas have tables, grills, drinking water, and rest rooms; nearby camp stores offer soft drinks, firewood, snacks, and other supplies.

LODGING

There is a multitude of motels, hotels, bed-and-breakfasts, and country inns close to Shenandoah National Park; within the park itself are several suitable options—from lodge rooms to private cabins. Vacancies are hard to come by, especially during the peak summer and fall foliage seasons (when rates are higher—though usually not by more than 10%), so make your reservations as far in advance as possible. Contact the **ARAMARK Virginia Sky-Line Co.** (Box 727, Luray 22835, tel. 800/999–4714, fax 540/743–7883). If all nearby rooms are booked, the next-closest options are the chain motels in Harrisonburg, Charlottesville, and Winchester. For more information call **Virginia's Bed and Breakfast hot line** (tel. 800/934–9184). The **Virginia Division of Tourism** (tel. 804/786–4484) can also assist in finding accommodations.

IN THE PARK **Skyland.** The stone-and-timber dining room here is at the highest point on the drive. The area traces its roots to Stony Man Camp, which George Freeman Pollock established here in 1886. Many guest rooms in the complex overlook the Shenandoah Valley; some have TVs, but none has an in-room phone. Skyland offers a variety of lodging, from rustic cabins to motel-style rooms and suites; everything is within a short walk or drive of the main dining area. Skyland has a taproom, newsstand, and crafts shop. *Mile 41.7, Skyline Dr., Skyland, tel. 540/999–2211 or 800/999–4714, fax 540/999–2231. 177 rooms. Facilities: restaurant, bar, no-smoking rooms, hiking, horseback riding, playground. AE, D, MC, V. Closed late Nov.–early Mar. $$–$$$*

Big Meadows Lodge. Built in 1939 of native stone and chestnut, the rustically elegant main lodge has 20 rooms. In the Great Room and the Dining Room there are huge windows that yield soaring over-the-valley views. Other accommodations within the complex include 62 rooms in six motel-style units and 10 less expensive but fully appointed rustic wood cabins that each sleep two. There are TVs in only 10 rooms and there are no in-room phones. *Milepost 51, Skyline Dr., Skyland, tel. 540/999–2221 or 800/999–4714, fax 540/999–2011. 102 rooms, 99 with bath. Facilities: restaurant, bar. AE, D, MC, V. Closed Nov.–early May. $$*

Lewis Mountain Cabins. The least expensive of the park's lodging options, these 1940s-era one- or two-room housekeeping cabins combine modern baths and sleeping spaces with covered picnic areas and outside fireplaces with grills. Basically they're semimodern motel rooms nestled in an oak forest, with campsite-style cooking facilities—a good way to rough it without making it too rough. There are no TVs or phones. The camp store and laundry are nearby. *Mile 57.6, Skyline Dr., tel. 540/999–2255, fax 540/743–7883. 4 single cabins, 5 double cabins. AE, D, MC, V. Closed Nov.–early May. $$*

NEAR THE PARK For other options, *see* the Blue Ridge Parkway chapter.

Inn at Little Washington. From its white stucco-and-clapboard exterior to the antiques inside, this remarkable inn, on a two-block expanse in a small Virginia town, has the look and feel of an exquisitely elegant English country house. Rates start at $240 per night. The restaurant (*see* Dining, *above*) is one of the best in the country. There are tennis courts nearby. *Middle and Main Sts., Washington 22747 (13 mi from the Thornton Gap entrance to Skyline Dr.), tel. 540/675–3800, fax 540/675–3100. 12 rooms with bath. Facilities: restaurant. MC, V. Closed Tues. except May and Oct. $$$*

Cabins at Brookside. Here is a successful combination of rusticity and luxury, privacy and accessibility. While the milled-log exteriors pay tribute to Blue Ridge frontier cabins, interior amenities such as queen-size beds and modern baths with skylights provide the comforts of a luxury motel—and there's a grassy distance between you and your neighbors. Private decks overlook a small brook, resident peacocks prowl the grounds, and there's fresh-brewed coffee delivered to your cabin every morning. *U.S. 211 (Rte. 4, Box 346), Luray 22835 (4½ mi west of Skyline Dr.), tel. 540/743–5698. 6 1- and 2-bedroom cabins. Facilities: restaurant. AE, D, MC, V. $$–$$$*

Jordan Hollow Farm Inn. At the heart of this 145-acre horse farm is a 200-year-old Colonial farmhouse with four cozy dining rooms, a small pub, and a game room. Guest rooms in the main house or in rustic buildings nearby are decorated with antiques and country artifacts. Some have fireplaces and whirlpool tubs; five have TVs; all have in-room phones. Gentle horses are used for long trail rides in the mountains and carriage rides on the 5 mi of trails on the property. Across the road from the farm is a small town park with a swimming pool; golf and canoeing are also available nearby. Breakfast and dinner are included in room rates. *Rte. 626, Stanley,*

VA 22851 (south of Luray on U.S. 522, 12 mi from the Thornton Gap entrance to Skyline Dr.), tel. 540/778–2209, fax 540/778–1759. 21 rooms, 1 suite. Facilities: restaurant, pub, hiking, horseback riding. D, DC, MC, V. $$–$$$

Quality Inn. This three-level motor inn is very nice by chain-motel standards, from the marble and slate in the lobby to the custom wallpaper and drapes in the rooms. The downtown location is convenient to the Front Royal visitor center and just 10 minutes from the northern entrance to the Skyline Drive. *10 Commerce Ave., Front Royal 22630, tel. 540/635–3161 or 800/228–5151. 107 rooms. Facilities: restaurant, bar, pool. AE, D, DC, MC, V. $$*

CAMPING

CAMPGROUNDS The park has three developed campgrounds (a fourth, Mathews Arm, at Milepost 22.2, is scheduled to reopen in June 1998). Each has a store, rest rooms, showers, and laundry facilities; and each campsite has a table and fire grate. There are no RV hookups, but sewage disposal stations are available at all but Lewis Mountain. Camping is permitted for up to a total of 14 days from June through October. Pets are allowed, as long as they're kept on 6-ft (or shorter) leashes and never left unattended. Expect crowded conditions in peak season.

Big Meadows. The largest (and most popular and crowded) of the park's campgrounds has the most convenient access to facilities. The sites in the new section are closer together; X, Y, and Z loops in the old section are at an access to the Appalachian Trail. Reservations (required) may be arranged up to eight weeks in advance. *Milepost 51, Skyline Dr., tel. 540/999–3231 or 540/999–3500 for park headquarters.*

227 sites: 40 tent, 167 tent or RV. D, MC, V. Closed Nov.–late May. $

Lewis Mountain. A smaller, quieter facility than the other campgrounds, this one is heavily wooded with older-growth timber and staffed mainly by volunteers. The campground, which operates on a first-come, first-served basis, frequently fills up early with overflow campers from Big Meadows. The fee is $14 per night per site. *Mile 57.6, Skyline Dr., tel. 540/999–3500 (park headquarters). 32 sites: 16 tent, 16 tent or RV. Credit cards not accepted. Closed Nov.–late spring.*

Loft Mountain. The elevated views from the hillside location take in the valley and the surrounding mountains; the sites with the best views vary, though, depending on the state of the foliage. This campground, too, operates on a first-come, first-served basis. The fee is $14 per night per site. *Mile 79.5, Skyline Dr., tel. 804/823–4675 or 540/999–3500 for park headquarters. 219 sites: 54 tent, 165 tent or RV. MC, V. Closed late Oct.–late spring.*

BACKCOUNTRY CAMPING Wilderness hikers must possess valid backcountry camping permits, which are free and available in advance from park headquarters or at entrance stations, visitor centers, and park headquarters during normal business hours. Backcountry camping has its own set of rules and responsibilities (camp out of sight of trails; stay at least 250 yards away from paved roads; and so on). The "Exploring the Backcountry" pamphlet, available at entrance and ranger stations and visitor centers, outlines the rules of wilderness etiquette. The Potomac Appalachian Trail Club operates seven trailside huts and six backcountry cabins (*see* Appalachian Trail *in* Exploring, *above*).

Voyageurs National Park
Minnesota

By Gene Rebeck

Updated by Chris Mikko

oyageurs National Park lies at the top of Minnesota, right on the Canadian border and near the internationally renowned Boundary Waters Canoe Area. It's one of the least known, least visited members of the National Park System. Why? For one thing, it's relatively new, having become a national park only in 1975. While it's a jewel of North Woods beauty, it hasn't built up the reputation of a Yellowstone or a Yosemite, and it doesn't have their tourist trappings.

Its interior is also more difficult to get to than theirs. Voyageurs is above all a water park–wilderness locked in by large lakes. Though the four main access points are accessible by car, the bulk of the park consists of the Kabetogama (pronounced kab-uh-*toe*-ga-ma, though some locals elide it to kap-*toe*-ga-ma) Peninsula and four large lakes, none of which can be traversed by car or RV. You have to own, borrow, or rent a watercraft (luckily, that's easy up here), and even then, once you've crossed the lake and reached the peninsula you'll find yourself in a wilderness area with only a few trails, many of them so rarely traversed that they may be partly obscured by grasses and ferns.

So why come here? Precisely because of those broad blue lakes and that wild green peninsula: for good fishing, for wilderness hiking, for motorboating, and for camping. You come because it isn't touristy—at least, not yet.

Though Voyageurs is young as national parks go, its history goes back nearly as far as that of the first European settlement in North America. The most notable—and most colorful—of those early visitors were *les voyageurs,* hardy French Canadians who, during the 17th and 18th centuries, paddled and portaged their great canoes from Montréal to far northwestern Canada, seeking and transporting the pelts of beaver, fox, wolf, and other animals whose fur was in demand among fashionable Europeans. The voyageurs wore rugged, brightly colored clothing festooned with fur and feathers; they could paddle for up to 16 hours a day; and they sang songs that ranged from the high-spirited to the deeply sorrowful.

With the decline of the fur trade, gold miners and lumberjacks came to take their place, seeking new ways to profit from the border lakes region. But soon the gold became too unprofitable to scratch out of the granite, the old forests were clear-cut, and, in the early part of this century, the area became a haven to another type of adventurer—the sportsman.

As walleye anglers and grouse hunters began to flock here, the border lakes region changed. Small resorts and cabins, most of them family-run, sprang up in clusters on the southern shores of the lake to cater to the seasonal visitors. Those who wanted a woodsier stay crossed over the lake and through tortuous narrows to the Kettle Falls Hotel, a loggers' bordello turned respectable hostelry. (The hotel still exists, as do many of the resorts; *see* Historic Buildings and Sites *in* Exploring *and* Lodging, *below.*)

Hunters and anglers weren't the only visitors. On the other side of the peninsula, on the Canadian border, lies Rainy Lake. With its myriad little islands, woods, channels, and secretive coves, the lake became a popular spot for bootleggers during Prohibition. Boats full of Canadian whiskey and other illicit hootch would cross and continue through the American Channel on the eastern side of the peninsula, moving carefully between the fragments of land.

Though the bootleggers, loggers, and fur trappers are gone, the modern-day visitor should come to the park with something of the voyageurs' spirit. Now that the region is a national park you can no longer hunt here, and fishing is regulated; there are cozier accommodations than tents, if you so choose. But otherwise you'll have to contend with many of the same forces the voyageurs did. Whether you see the park on your own or on a naturalist-led group trip, you need a certain sense of history, an awareness that nothing (except perhaps the fish) will come too easy.

ESSENTIAL INFORMATION

VISITOR INFORMATION Contact the superintendent, **Voyageurs National Park** (3131 Hwy. 53, International Falls, MN 56649–8904, tel. 218/283–9821) for an information packet, which includes a general map and description of the park as well as information on boat trips, guided tours, park wildlife, hiking, and lodging. A brochure listing available publications is also enclosed.

Voyageurs Region National Park Association (514 N. 3rd St., Suite 104, Minneapolis, MN 55401-1202, tel. 612/333–5424, fax 612/339–4731) is a nonprofit organization formed in 1965 to establish Voyageurs National Park's development, help attract visitors, and protect its natural resources. The association offers a wealth of information on the park, including listings of places to stay and things to do. Their **Web site** is www.voyageurs.org.

If you're also interested in traveling elsewhere in northern Minnesota, contact the **Minnesota Office of Tourism** (100 Metro Sq., 121 7th Pl. E, St. Paul 55101, tel. 612/ 296–5029 or 800/657–3700).

FEES There are no fees to enter the park. However, boats must be licensed (*see* Other Activities *in* Exploring, *below*).

PUBLICATIONS The nonprofit **Lake States Interpretive Association** (3131 U.S. 53, International Falls, MN 56649–8904, tel. 218/283–2103) sells publications, videos, and educational materials on Voyageurs and on the surrounding natural attractions, specifically the Chippewa, Nicolet, and Superior national forests. You can order the following publications from them by phone, using a credit card (MC, V); you'll also be charged for postage and handling.

The publications available deal mostly with the human history of the park region, though some cover natural history as well. The most notable on both is Greg Breining's *Voyageurs National Park* ($7.95, 56 pages). The text is beautifully written, and the 36 photographs, by J. Arnold Bolz, illustrate it exquisitely. Offering more detail about the park's natural landscape is Jim DuFresne's *Voyageurs National Park: Water Routes, Foot Paths and Ski Trails* ($9.95, 176 pages), which offers such full descriptions of the lakes and trails that it's considered the park bible by many. And for those who want to know more about the colorful men for whom the park is named, Grace Lee Nute's *The Voyageur* ($8.95, 289 pages) offers perhaps the most definitive history. For the definitive low-down on the area's recent past, check out David Perry's *Gold Town to Ghost Town,* which is a history of the gold rush that rocked Rainy Lake in the 1890s.

The Lake States Interpretive Association also sells different maps of the park. (Many are for sale at the park's four visitor centers.) The choice depends in part on how you'll be traveling. The U.S. Geological Survey's Voyageurs map (VNP-1; $6) has a scale ratio of 1:50,000 and shows lake depths. If you want more detail (and more maps), there are USGS topographical maps ($4.50) at 1:24,000, and McKenzie maps ($6.95) at 1:31,680. For boaters, there are five National Oceanic and Atmospheric Administration (NOAA) navigation charts for canoeists, which do not show depths; there are also NOAA charts for Rainy Lake, which do (all $6.50). For anglers who want to know depths for Kabetogama, the Lake States Interpretive Association sells a "Fishing Hot Spots" map of the lake ($8.95).

GEOLOGY AND TERRAIN Writer Greg Breining (*see* Publications, *above*) describes the Kabetogama Peninsula landscape, paradoxically but aptly, as "flat but rugged." Overall, the elevations in the park don't vary as greatly as in many other national parks. But the glaciers that came through here several millennia ago scraped numerous ridges and striations into the land, and these give Voyageurs a remarkable variety.

The park's bedrock is very old—several billion years old. Later volcanic action and glacial movement created the structures that shape the park today. The northern part marks the southern edge of the Canadian Shield, a mantle of rock made predominantly of greenstone, which is volcanic, that extends north to Hudson Bay. Farther south, encompassing most of the Kabetogama Peninsula, a layer of granite and biotite schist lies beneath the bedrock. In some places, the two types of rock intermingle to form a swirled-striped formation called migmatite. South of the peninsula, vermilion granite predominates.

It was the glacier that gave the landscape its rumpled appearance as it receded about 11,000 years ago. During its retreat, rocks and mineral fragments caught in its flow dragged across the land like fingertips across sand. As you walk across the peninsula, you'll see the results of this movement in the great boulders left behind and in the outcroppings of granite and greenstone that continually interrupt the soil line.

FLORA AND FAUNA The last glacier's recession left the peninsula a huge barren slab of rock. Over the succeeding millennia, vegetation slowly reestablished itself, and a thin layer of soil formed over the rock.

While the soil remains shallow—as you'll find out if you try to stake a tent here—it's still deep enough to support a wide variety of trees. Voyageurs falls within the southern boreal forest, what Minnesotans call the "north woods." Trees that make their home here include, notably, black spruce, balsam fir, and northern white cedar, along with hardwoods such as aspen, oak, and paper birch. Red pine, white pine, and jack pine intermingle with these; on some islands, pines are the only trees you'll find.

The wildflowers are those that can tolerate a great deal of shade or water or both, not to mention hardy conditions and short summers. In early summer, white bunchberry flowers can be seen almost everywhere. Less common but even more exquisite are Indian pipe, fond of mossy habitat, and lady's slipper, which grows amid rocks strewn with pine and spruce needles. As summer progresses, nooks and corners of many park ponds and lakes witness an explosion of water lilies. Tiny wild strawberries and succulent blueberries appear, to be plucked by observant visitors.

Then there are the beasts—of the water, land, and air. Northern pike, smallmouth bass, and walleye are the big reason people have come to the region for decades. The great elk and caribou have long since been driven from the area by human encroachment and hunting, but such other north woods denizens as deer, black bear, and beaver remain. There are about 200 bears in the park, and more in the area outside it. They aren't frequently spotted, though careless campers occasionally see their handiwork in the morning when an errant bear has smelled their food. Beavers are easier to spot; they have built lodges in many of the inland ponds and lakes.

Rarely seen but often heard are timber or gray wolves, which number about 30 to 40 in the park. After being nearly wiped out in Minnesota, wolves are making a slow but steady comeback, as human beings realize that Canis lupus poses no threat to them and little to their livestock. Wolves remain shy creatures, and they're very susceptible to canine diseases, which is why dogs and other pets are restricted to certain areas in the park. Other less numerous mammals dwelling in the park include bobcat, mink, and pine marten. Kabetogama has the second-highest population of river otter in the world.

Because of the land's moistness, you'll very likely encounter toads and (nonvenomous) snakes shuffling in the underbrush. The moisture also assures that you'll run into mosquitoes and deer flies (often in clouds), as well as both deer and wood ticks. Be ready for these varmints if you come in late spring and early summer.

Last but not least, there are the birds. The singers you'll hear most are thrushes, white-throated sparrows, and varieties of warblers. Even urban birds like robins and blue jays pipe up. Bald eagles and ospreys also make their home here, special blessings to the visitor who happens to spot either of them. On the water, common mergansers and red-necked grebes are most often seen (and gulls, of course); a few less common ducks, such as goldeneyes, make appearances every now and then. Three birds are worthy of special attention. The common loon (not quite as common as it used to be), Minnesota's state bird, is perhaps the most delightful, and if you pick a campsite with care and a bit of luck, its haunting howls will create a strange, moving lullaby. Out on the big lakes, white pelicans, comical yet dignified, love to cluster on small rocky islands. And if you camp in the middle of the woods, you might hear—and hear, and hear—the monotonous nocturne of the whippoorwill. During the day, fearless Canada jays may stop by your camp to beg. Some especially brazen "whiskey jacks" have been known to make off with morsels when unsuspecting backs are turned.

WHEN TO GO If you're a snowmobiler or cross-country skier, the choice is obvious. January and February are when the snow is at its peak, though it often lasts well into March.

If you're coming up for the fishing, you'll do best in late May and June. The fishing tapers off a bit in July and August, then picks up again in September and October. Many people come up in the winter to ice-fish, which in Minnesota is as much (if not more) about fishing-house camaraderie as actually catching anything. If you're up here to boat or canoe, any time but winter is fine, though mid-summer and early fall probably have the nicest weather, and biting bugs are scarcer then, too.

As for hiking, late summer and early fall are prime time. Spring is too humid, and the mosquitoes and black flies are ferocious. Even if you're lathered with insect repellent, their clouding and buzzing can make your jaunt a minor hell. Deer flies and wood and deer ticks are another summer annoyance; the latter can transmit Lyme disease, though cases in Minnesota are not too common. Summer is also when the park is most crowded with folks as well as bugs. Not that this park gets jammed—and the increased numbers can make it more difficult to get your choice of campsite.

WHAT TO PACK Whatever time of year it is, it's good to have a little more clothing on hand than you think you'll need. While T-shirts and shorts are fine most summer days, the weather up here can turn cool quickly. In the spring and fall the temperature can dip below freezing, so it's best to carry extra warm clothing (long underwear, wool socks). If you plan to hike, bring hiking boots that can keep your feet dry; you may go through grassy trails covered with dew. Summer bugs and ticks make deep-woods types of insect repellent a must. Boaters and all their passengers must wear personal flotation devices (PFDs) when on the water.

GENERAL STORES There are no general stores in the park itself. The store nearest the Kabetogama and Ash River entrances is the **Gateway** (corner of U.S. 53 and Rte. 122, tel. 218/875–2121), which not only has a small but broad selection of foodstuffs, it also sells bait and other fishing-related items. It is open in summer, daily 6 AM–10 PM; fall–spring, Monday–Saturday 7–6, Sunday 7–5. The stores closest to the Rainy Lake Visitor Center are the several grocers in International Falls, among them **Lucca's** (1103 7th Ave., tel. 218/285–7295), **Super Valu** (International Mall, tel. 218/283–4475), and **Super One** (Hwy. 11/71, tel. 218/283–8440).

ATMS There are several automated teller machines in International Falls, about 12 mi from the Rainy Lake entrance to the park, at the **Stop and Shop** on U.S. 53 south of downtown. Downtown there are several more: in the **First National Bank** lobby (419 3rd St.), the **First American Bank** drive-up facility (3rd Ave. between 3rd and 4th Sts.), and the **Boise Employee Credit Union** (601 4th St.); all are accessible 24 hours a day.

ARRIVING AND DEPARTING By far the easiest way to get to any of the visitor centers, which also serve as the points of entry, is by car. The nearest major city with both train and regular air service is Minneapolis, 300 mi to the south—a 5½-hour drive. There's plane service to International Falls and bus service to Duluth, but you'll need to get to the park on your own; it's 12 mi from there to the nearest entrance, Rainy Lake. You can rent a car at the airport (*see* By Car and RV, *below*). Alternatively, you can reserve a limousine from **City Cab** (tel. 218/283–4422); a one-way ride to the Rainy Lake Visitor Center is about $20. If you're staying at a resort in the area, the resort's owner may be willing to shuttle you back and forth to International Falls for an agreed-upon sum.

If you're planning to hike and camp, the best point of entry is probably Kabetogama Lake, the one closest to both the main hiking trail in the park and the Woodenfrog State Campground. Boaters will find launches at any entry point.

By Boat. Though you can get to the park entrances by car, actually getting into this water park is another matter. As part of the deal between landowners and government that established the park, Voyageurs itself does not rent boats; instead it relies on concessionaires and lakeside resort owners to supply water transportation for visitors who haven't brought their own. For information on resorts that rent boats or offer "water taxi" service, contact the resort association nearest the park entrance you plan to use. For Kabetogama, contact the **Kabetogama Lake Association** (9707 Gamma Rd., Ray 56669, tel. 218/875–2621 or 800/524–9085). For Rainy Lake information try the **International Falls Chamber of Commerce** (301 2nd Ave., International Falls, MN 56649, tel. 218/283–9400 or 800/325–5766). The **Crane Lake Visitor and Tourism Bureau** (7238 Handberg Rd., Crane Lake, MN 55725, tel. 218/993–2901 or 800/362–7405) has information on Crane Lake. For Ash River information, contact the **Ash River Commercial Club** (Orr, MN 55771, tel. 218/375–4445 or 800/950–2061). Expect to pay around $60–$75 per day for a 16-ft open boat with a 15-horse-power motor—pretty much the standard item, though there are, of course, many options. The more expensive resorts generally have the nicer boats.

By Bus. There is no bus service to the park. The nearest **Greyhound** (tel. 800/231–2222) station is in Duluth, Minnesota, about 150 mi away. You can rent a car in Duluth to get to the park (*see* By Car and RV, *below*).

By Car and RV. Driving up from the Twin Cities, take I–35 to Route 33; then follow Route 33 17 mi north to U.S. 53. Take U.S. 53 north about 130 mi to Route 122, turn right, and follow the signs to Voyageurs' Kabetogama Visitor Center. If you're coming from International Falls, take U.S. 53 south 25 mi to Kabetogama, or Route 11 some 12 mi east to Rainy Lake. For directions to the other visitor centers in the park, contact the superintendent (*see* Visitor Information, *above*).

Nearby National Park Service areas are Grand Portage National Monument and Apostle Islands National Lakeshore. If you're coming to Voyageurs from Grand Portage, take Route 61 south 90 mi (1½ hours) to Route 1; follow Route 1 north and west 111 mi (2½ hours) to U.S. 53; finally, take U.S. 53 another 70 mi (1½ hours) to Kabetogama.

Car rental agencies at the Twin Cities airport include **Avis** (tel. 612/726–5220), **Dollar** (tel. 612/854–3003), **Hertz** (tel. 612/726–1600), and **Thrifty** (tel. 612/854–8080). At Falls International, there's **Hertz** (tel. 218/283–4461), **Avis** (tel. 218/283–3187), and **National** (tel. 218/283–3471).

By Plane. The nearest big-city airport is the **Minneapolis–St. Paul International Airport** (tel. 612/726–5555). Several nonstop, 75-minute flights each day on Northwest Airlines (tel. 800/225–2525) connect it with **Falls International Airport** (tel. 218/283–4630) in International Falls. You can rent cars at both airports (*see* By Car and RV, *above*).

By Train. The closest **Amtrak** (tel. 800/872–7245) comes to Voyageurs is St. Paul. The **St. Paul–Minneapolis Midway Station** (tel. 612/644–1127) is 275 mi away from Voyageurs. *Empire Builder* trains between Chicago and St. Paul run daily; trains between St. Paul and Seattle arrive and depart Monday, Wednesday, Friday, and Sunday. Rent a car in St. Paul (*see* By Car and RV, *above*).

EXPLORING

In the three warmer seasons, the best way to get around is by boat; in the winter, your only real option is a snowmobile. If you can get over to the hiking trails at Lost Bay on the south-central part of the peninsula, you can also spend a day, or several, on foot. Tour boats are available during the summer. Outside of the Kettle Falls Hotel and what remains of the Little American Island gold mine (both accessible only by boat—

see Historic Buildings and Sites, *below*), there are no "sights" as such beyond the woods and waters.

THE BEST IN ONE DAY The Voyageurs information packet (*see* Visitor Information *in* Essential Information, *above*) contains a schedule of naturalist-guided activities, which are conducted in summer only (usually mid-June to late August). Every day has a slightly different schedule. Four days a week in summer you can take a six-hour pontoon boat trip between the Kabetogama Lake Visitor Center and the historic Kettle Falls Hotel (*see* Guided Tours, *below*). The ride gives you an excellent sense of scenic Kabetogama and Namakan lakes, with their wooded shores, bays, and many small islands.

If you don't want to spend your whole day on a boat, the best option is a 1½-hour sunset cruise or park-sponsored canoe trip during the day and a naturalist program in the evening (*see* Guided Tours, *below*). This combination, under the auspices of the Kabetogama Lake Visitor Center, is usually available four days a week. Similar tour boat, canoe, and nature-walk options are available at Rainy Lake. See the activities schedule for exact times and locations.

ORIENTATION PROGRAMS Each of the visitor centers has an auditorium in which a 15-minute narrated slide show, with lots of beautiful photography, gives an overview of the park and its recreational options. Rainy Lake has the most impressive audio-visual setup, but the show's the same.

GUIDED TOURS Several guided tours—on foot or by boat—are available during the summer at Kabetogama, Rainy Lake, and Ash River visitor centers. Nearly all are led by park naturalists. Because of the size and layout of the park, none can claim to give a "complete" view—there are simply too many nooks and crannies here. Boat tourists departing from Rainy Lake board a 49-passenger double-decker; at Kabetogama, the craft is a 19-passenger pontoon boat.

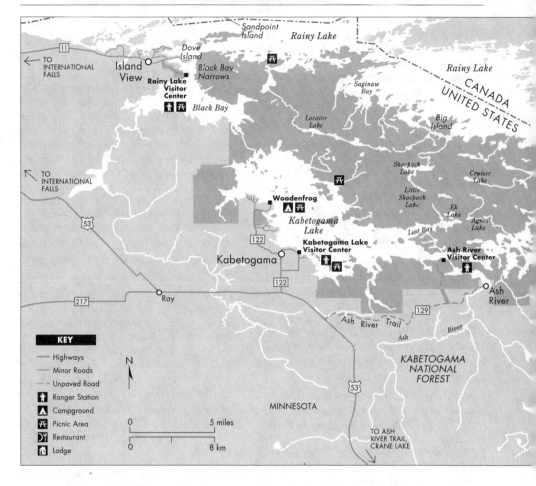

At Kabetogama, the water excursion the rangers recommend is the **Kettle Falls Trip** ($30), which leaves Kabetogama Lake Visitor Center four times a week. It lasts about six hours round-trip, sailing across Kabetogama and Namakan Lakes and anchoring near the historic Kettle Falls Hotel, where lunch is served. As with all Kabetogama boat tours listed here, you should reserve space at the visitor center (tel. 218/875–2111).

But it's by no means the only option. Three different **sunset cruises** are each available once a week. Each explores a different part of the park, and each offers the possibility of glimpsing native bald eagles and osprey.

The Kabetogama Lake Visitor Center also provides canoes for two-hour **guided canoe trips** that travel the waters and explore wooded shores every day except Sunday. These accommodate about 12 people. Both trips are free and are offered on a first-come, first-served basis.

A similar (and longer) trip ($35) to Kettle Falls leaves Rainy Lake Visitor Center once a week and lasts about 7½ hours round-trip. It is run by **Voyageurs National Park Boat Tours, Inc.** (Rte. 8, Box 303, 3017 County Rd. 127, International Falls, MN 56649, tel. 218/286–5470). The same company also offers an overnight trip that includes the tour, lodging at the Kettle Falls Hotel and all meals ($90).

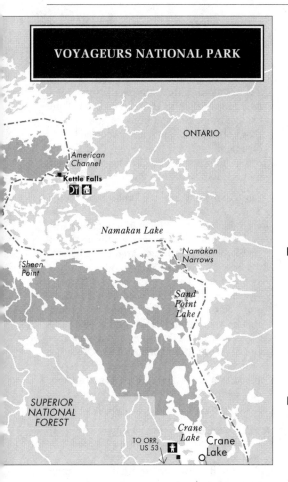

VOYAGEURS NATIONAL PARK

ONTARIO

American
Channel

Kettle Falls

Namakan Lake

Namakan
Narrows

Sheen
Point

Sand
Point
Lake

SUPERIOR
NATIONAL
FOREST

Crane
Lake

TO ORR,
US 53

Crane
Lake

If you come in July or August you can hook up with a two-hour evening cruise departing from the Rainy Lake Visitor Center. The **Starwatch Tour** ($10.75) from Rainy Lake explores the sky above the park—the stars, planets, and (with luck) the northern lights.

For those who prefer nonmotorized transport, there's the 1½-hour park-sponsored **North Canoe Voyage.** Twenty passengers travel with a naturalist aboard a 26-ft *Voyageurs North* canoe copied after the vessels of the original voyageurs. Besides a hearty canoe ride, passengers are treated to talks about voyageur life and even a few of their songs. Equipment and tour are free.

SCENIC DRIVES AND VIEWS For obvious reasons, there are no scenic drives (at least not by car) within Voyageurs. The loveliest approach to the park is on Route 11 from International Falls on to the Rainy Lake Visitor Center. Instead of turning toward the visitor center, you can take Route 11 2 mi east to Dove Island, a pretty little cabin and resort area with some attractive views of the peninsula.

HISTORIC BUILDINGS AND SITES Nearly all of the park is wilderness—second-growth wilderness—but two pieces of the human past do remain. You can reach the **Kettle Falls Hotel** only by boat, and even then it's not easy to get to. Set in the farthest northeastern part of the Kabetogama Peninsula, it's accessible from either Rainy or Namakan Lake. The southern approach through Namakan Lake passes through winding wooded narrows, a route so winding, in fact, that the hotel is one of the few places in the United States where Canada is actually south of the border. It was built around 1940 to accommodate the men working on the nearby Kettle Falls Dam. Its history hasn't always been savory; it once housed a speakeasy and a brothel. But after some years of neglect in the '70s, it has been restored as closely as possible to its 1910 condition (one of the wood floors was kept in its original uneven state). You can still eat and sleep here (*see* Dining *and* Lodging, *below*); tour boats (*see* Guided

There are many guided tours available at Rainy Lake. **The Discovery Cruise** ($15.75) gives its passengers a trip across the wildly beautiful lake and through its forested islands. All Rainy Lake boat tours can be reserved at the tour-boat concessionaire's office (tel. 218/286–5470).

Those who want to see something of the region's history as a gold mining center circa 1893 can take the park's 1½-hour **Gold Mine Tour** ($10.75) to Little American Island, a 3-acre site that includes several deep mine shafts and a huge 500-pound iron wheel that was used for hoisting. Last but not least, a twice-a-week **Grand Tour** ($22.50) combines the Rainy Lake Cruise with the Gold Mine Tour.

Tours, *above*) leave from both Kabetogama and Rainy Lake visitor centers. Contact the superintendent (*see above*). *Admission free. Open Jan.–Mar. and May–Sept.*

Near the Rainy Lake Visitor Center is **Little American Island,** focal point of a brief turn-of-the-century gold rush. There was gold here, but the granite and greenstone in which it was encased made it too expensive to dig out. A few shafts and caverns, plus the odd bit of equipment, are all that remain here, but the island and its surroundings compose the Gold Mine Historic District. It, too, is accessible by boat; a tour boat (*see* Guided Tours, *above*) can take you there.

NATURE TRAILS AND SHORT WALKS Many of the nature trails and short walks at Voyageurs can be traveled with a park naturalist (*see* Guided Tours, *above*). The **Overholzer Trail** (1 mi round-trip) at Rainy Lake and the **Locator Lake Nature Trail** (4 mi round-trip) on the Kabetogama Peninsula can also be done as self-guided tours. Pamphlet guides are available at visitor centers and at the trailheads. Both trails are easy to moderate.

If you have a boat, you can get to the two main hiking trails on the peninsula: **Locator Lake** to the west (*see above*) and the **Cruiser Lake Trail** to the east. The latter comprises the longest trail system in the park, but you needn't hike its entire 15 mi. A pleasant 1-mi (round-trip) jaunt from the trailhead on Lost Bay to Agnes Lake will give you a good sense of the peninsula's terrain. You can also access the trail on Rainy Lake at Anderson Bay and walk the 2-mi Anderson Bay Overlook Loop.

LONGER HIKES The best hiking trail is the park's only hiking trail of any length—the **Cruiser Lake Trail.** It runs about 9 mi from Lost Bay on Kabetogama Lake to Rainy Lake, but there are a number of side loops you can take if you want a longer adventure. It's a good way to see the variety of the park's terrain, from spruce bogs to rocky ridges to tranquil lakes.

The trail is not terrifically challenging, but if you've got a pack on your back, it won't be

a snap, either. Vermilion granite outcroppings pop up constantly, meaning good strong shoes are a must. The little waterways that course through the peninsula create a fair number of hills and valleys. There's more solitude the deeper inland you go, so much that the trail can become all but hidden by grasses and ferns. In other words, it's not the beaten path, and you need to stay observant lest you lose the trail. If you do lose it, don't panic: Stacks of rocks, laid out by park staff, will help guide you back.

The hike is worth its small frustrations. There are several beautiful lakes along the way (all of which have small campsites), and the pine and spruce woods look and smell gorgeous. And you aren't restricted to the trail. If you're handy with a compass and a detailed map, you can walk nearly anywhere on the peninsula. There are several secluded lakes here, many of which also have campsites. One option: Get off the Cruiser Lake Trail system at Jorgens Lake and head to **Little Shoepack Lake.** There's a campsite on the lake, and if you've reserved ahead you can take the Park Service canoe and paddle it out onto Big Shoepack Lake (*see* Boating *in* Other Activities, *below*).

OTHER ACTIVITIES In summer, all park activities are pursued either on foot, by boat, or by floatplane. In winter, skis, snowshoes, and snowmobiles are the only transportation options.

Bird-Watching. The easiest birds to spot in the park are waterfowl. You'll probably see several species of ducks and mergansers on the big lakes, though the roar of motorboats can keep them away. More fearless gulls, cormorants, and pelicans congregate on small stony islands. Your luck will be better in secluded bays and channels protected from the wind. Red-necked grebes and common mergansers are typical sightings, and, in the evening, loons.

On land, the woods and the insects make birding more difficult and less pleasant. City birds such as robins, blue jays, and ravens are remarkably common in the park; in the morning, sparrows and warblers often appear. Bald eagles and ospreys are active throughout the day.

Boating. Boating, for fishing or just for pleasure, is the chief summer pastime at Voyageurs. There are boat launches at all the visitor centers, and private docks at most of the lakeside resorts. Most of these resorts rent boats; the fees vary (see Arriving and Departing by Boat in Essential Information, above). However, only experienced boaters should venture onto the lakes in Voyageurs, since they are filled with small islands and many rocks just below the surface. NOAA depth charts (see Publications in Essential Information, above) can help, but if you think you may be out of your league, find out whether the resort offers a guide service.

While the Park Service leaves most boat rentals to the resorts, it does offer **canoes** on various inland lakes: Locator, Cruiser, Ek, Loiten, Shoepack, and Little Shoepack. Though they are sometimes available the day you come up, it's best to reserve about a week in advance with the Kabetogama Lake Visitor Center (tel. 218/875–2111). The canoes are locked up at shorelines; keys are available at visitor centers. You'll have to hike in on a trail to get one of the boats, but they'll make a delightful addition to your trip.

Motorboaters in the park must make themselves familiar with rules of navigation and the U.S. Coast Guard's numbered buoy system, which is used on the park's lakes. The Park Service's information packet on Voyageurs (see Visitor Information in Essential Information, above) includes a description of the buoy system and a newspaper that outlines rules of navigation, salient hazards, and safety tips. Plan your route in advance and discuss it with a ranger before you set out. Rangers can also advise you on especially scenic routes.

There is yet another boating option here during the May-to-October season: **houseboating.** Large double-decker craft, which have sleeping quarters and kitchens, too, in most cases, combine recreation with lodging. Depending on the number of people in your party and the size of the boat, rates range from about $200 to $500 per day, less if you rent by the week. **Minnesota Voyageurs Houseboats** (10326 Ash River Trail, Orr 55771, tel. 218/374–3571 or 800/253–5475) is near the Ash River entrance. **Voyaguaire Houseboats** (7576 Gold Coast Rd., Crane Lake 55725, tel. 218/993–2333 or 800/882–6287). **Rainy Lake Houseboats** (2031 Town Rd. No. 488, International Falls 56649, tel. 218/286–5391 or 800/554–9188) is near Rainy Lake. **Northernaire Floating Lodges** (2690 County Rd. 94, International Falls 56649, tel. 218/286–5221 or 800/854–7958) is also near Rainy Lake.

Cross-Country Skiing. The park's terrain—generally flat, with a few easy rolling hills here and there—makes it a good place for cross-country skiing. The park maintains the Black Bay Ski Trail, just across the Black Bay Narrows from the Rainy Lake Visitor Center. The looping trail covers about 8 mi. A map of it is available from the park office (see Visitor Information in Essential Information, above) upon request.

Fishing. Fishing is the chief reason people were coming up to the Voyageurs area before there was even a park. It's best during the months of May, June, September, and October. The most common fish here are walleye and northern pike, but the "big lakes" (Rainy, Kabetogama, Namakan, and Sandpoint) also have black crappie, walleye, rock bass, and smallmouth bass. A few inland lakes offer largemouth bass and lake trout, and even the occasional muskie.

In winter, several of the large lakes are popular **ice-fishing** spots. The only way to get to them is by snowmobile, but you can bring and set up your own ice-fishing house. Houses are often equipped with small generators to run boom boxes, heaters, and TVs—which, along with beer, make the time after you've chopped a hole in the ice and dropped your line through pass more pleasantly. You can rent houses from **Red Pine Lodge** (1243 Burma Rd., Ray 56669, tel. 218/875–2441).

All visitors wishing to sink a line in the park lakes need to obtain a Minnesota fishing license. The information packet available from the park superintendent's office (*see* Visitor Information *in* Essential Information, *above*) contains information on fishing and fishing licenses; for more information about licenses, contact the **Minnesota Department of Natural Resources** (500 N. Lafayette Rd., St. Paul 55155, tel. 612/296–4506 or 800/285–2000).

Snowmobiling. This is the park's most popular wintertime sport, and the woodland trails are kept well groomed. The park doesn't rent snowmobiles, but several nearby resorts do, including **Ash-Ka-Nam** (Ash River Trail, Orr 55771, tel. 218/374–3181). Most resorts open during the winter sell snowmobile gas and oil. Snowmobilers should obtain a snowmobile trail map from the park superintendent's office (*see* Visitor Information *in* Essential Information, *above*).

Snowshoeing. Snowshoeing is not discouraged, but the park does not rent snowshoes, and there are no designated snowshoeing trails. The superintendent can, however, recommend places to go (*see above*).

Swimming. The best time for swimming here is mid-June through August, when the water warms up (though it will still be too chilly for some). There are no restrictions, but there are no beaches, changing facilities, or lifeguards, either. (There are leeches in some waters, so you should give yourself a once-over when you come out. If you do find one, pour salt on it to get it off.) A beach with a changing facility is available at Woodenfrog State Campground, about 4 mi from Kabetogama.

CHILDREN'S PROGRAMS Besides its various guided tours (*see above*), Kabetogama Lake Visitor Center also offers a "Northwoods Puppet Show" in summer. The show stars several animals that live in Voyageurs and teaches children how they can help protect their north woods home. Kabetogama Lake Visitor Center's various tours and events also include a once-a-week program called

"Kids Explore Voyageurs," in which children 7–12, led by a naturalist, take a woodland walk and explore a beaver pond, among other outdoor sights.

EVENING ACTIVITIES Voyageurs offers a number of evening cruises and naturalist programs (*see* Guided Tours, *above*). There are no other social activities in the park.

DINING

Dining around Voyageurs is neither gourmet nor ethnic. The food tends toward burgers and chicken, with steak and seafood (especially the locally caught walleye) representing the high end. (Walleye, also known as pickerel, is white and flaky like cod, with a sweet, full flavor. It's often breaded and fried.) Most of the restaurants close by are attached to resorts; if you're staying around Rainy Lake, there are other options in International Falls. If you have a taste for something a bit more unusual, drive the 45 mi south to the Country Supper Club (*see below*). Needless to say, none of these places requires jacket and tie; casual but neat is the style.

INSIDE THE PARK **Kettle Falls Hotel.** Accessible only by boat, the Kettle Falls Hotel has had a long, colorful history (*see* Historic Buildings and Sites *in* Exploring, *above*), and it's still the only place that serves food and beverages inside the park. The restaurant is open for all three meals. The atmosphere is rustic, the food traditional northern Minnesota fare—chicken, hamburgers, and, of course, walleye. Dinners are all-you-can-eat with two entrées available. Even if you're a teetotaler, check out the bar; a large part of the floor still bears the marks of loggers' hobnail boots. *Ash River Trail, Orr, tel. 218/374–4404 or 888/534–6835. Reservations essential. MC, V. Closed Oct.–mid-May.* $$

NEAR THE PARK **Country Supper Club.** Nearly an hour from Kabetogama (1½ hours from Rainy Lake), this is the place for some of the most distinctive food in the area. Chef-owner Bill Clazmer came up north after a long career in the Twin Cities, and he brings to this rural spot an unpretentiously but unmistakably urban sense. Sophisticated examples include Sicilian shrimp stuffed with spinach and basil and topped with Italian cheeses; chicken Joanne, a chicken breast in a Mediterranean-style tomato and mushroom sauce; and tasty homemade pizzas. A simpler lunch is served, too. *9257 Olson Rd. (Hwy. 910), Cook, tel. 218/666–5351. Reservations essential. AE, D, MC, V. $$*

Island View Lodge. Inside this cheerful, woodsy lakeside lodge near Rainy Lake (*see* Lodging, *below*) is a dining room with Diamond Willow furniture and wood paneling. The food ranges from typical Minnesota resort fare (walleye, barbecue) to fancier dishes simply prepared—lobster, shrimp, prime rib, filet mignon. *1817 Hwy. 11 E, International Falls, tel. 218/286–3511. Reservations essential. MC, V. Closed Nov. $$*

Sandy Point Lodge. Inside this lodge—one of the newer ones on Kabetogama Lake (*see* Lodging, *below*)—is what many consider the vicinity's gourmet restaurant. It's gourmet, upper Midwest–style. Sure, you can get burgers and walleye here. But you also get steaks taken from specially raised beef brought in from Iowa. And the lodge loves to use northern Minnesota wild rice. Besides steaks, the house specialty is Voyageurs chicken, sautéed in herbs, served on a bed of wild rice, then further enlivened with a rosemary cream sauce. Breads and rolls are homemade. The ambience here is a cleaner, newer kind of rustic, with log-paneled walls and a big open fireplace. *10606 Gamma Rd., Ray (Kabetogama), tel. 218/875–2615. Reservations essential. MC, V. $$*

Bait & Bite. This spot near Kabetogama is especially popular with locals and regular visitors for its breakfasts, which are hearty in a Main Street, Minnesota-café way. Lunches and dinners are casual, with hamburgers and chicken leading the way. The restaurant's log building also houses a bait-and-tackle shop. *9634 Gamma Rd., Kabetogama,*

tel. 218/875–2281. Reservations not accepted. MC, V. Closed Oct.–Apr. $

LODGING

Before Voyageurs became a national park, the area had long been popular for its fishing and hunting. Numerous mom-and-pop resorts opened to cater to the anglers and hunters and their families. They compose nearly all the lodging around the park. A few inexpensive ones consist of small trailer homes; most of the rest are made up of campgrounds, cottages, and cabins; and a few small lodges round out the selection. Nearly all the places fall into the $ or $$ category; most offer boat rental, a boat launch, and even fishing guides. The park's information packet (*see* Visitor Information *in* Essential Information, *above*) includes a list of resorts, the services they offer, and when they're closed. Most are open only during the May-to-October season.

For visitors looking for something a little different, four vendors offer houseboats for rent (*see* Other Activities *in* Exploring, *above*).

INSIDE THE PARK **Kettle Falls Hotel.** This is the only lodging inside the park, and certainly the most colorful place to stay in the area (*see* Historic Buildings and Sites *in* Exploring, *above*). The exterior is pleasant but unexceptional—something like a barn with a front porch and awnings; the inside is what's special. After closing in the 1970s, the hotel was lovingly taken apart, fixed up, then put back together. Most of the furnishings are early 20th-century originals or reproductions. "Modernizing" has generally been restricted to plumbing and electricity and new mattresses. You can get there only by boat, but boats shuttle back and forth from park visitor centers to the hotel five times a week, and the hotel offers shuttle service from Ash River. There are 10 villas on the "Point" (about a half mile away) overlooking Rainy Lake. These more modern structures include baths, and many have kitchens. All meals are included with all accommodations. *Contact the superintendent (tel. 218/283–9821). 12 rooms share 3 baths, 10 villas. Facilities: restaurant* (see *Dining,* above), *boating. MC, V. Closed Oct.–mid-May. $$*

NEAR THE PARK **Bunt's Bed & Breakfast Inns.** Bunt's is the high-end option around the park. Near the Kabetogama entrance, the complex comprises a four-bedroom B&B, a two-bedroom beach house on the lake, and a four-unit inn. All have kitchens; all are modern, like suburban homes with rustic touches. The B&B is the most private, surrounded by thick woods and connected to the water by a path. The beach house is on the water and has a dock. The four-unit inn is a bit farther away from the park, but its wood-paneled walls offer coziness. Wherever you stay, the rate includes a Continental breakfast. *Lake Kabetogama, 12497 Burma Rd., Ray 56669, tel. 218/875–2691, fax 218/875–3008. Facilities (B&B and inn only): sauna. AE, D, MC, V. $$–$$$*

Island View Lodge. This pleasant little lodge lists its address as International Falls, but it's actually on Dove Island, an old community of summer cabins and resorts beyond the Rainy Lake Visitor Center. The double-decked redwood lodge is agreeably rustic, and it faces onto Rainy Lake, so request a lake view. The rooms are decorated in undistinguished (but still pleasant) motel fashion. *1817 Hwy. 11 E, International Falls 50649, tel. 218/286–3511 or 800/777–7856, fax 218/286–5036. 9 rooms, 12 cabins. Facilities: restaurant* (see *Dining,* above), *beach. AE, D, DC, MC, V. Closed Nov. $$*

Thunderbird Lodge. A somewhat newer resort than Island View (*see above*), the Thunderbird nonetheless goes for the woodsy-rustic look that most of the higher-end Voyageurs lodges pursue. It's close to the Rainy Lake Visitor Center. The comfortable rooms are decorated with a little more warmth than in a good-quality motel, but they don't all face Rainy Lake—so ask. The restaurant and lounge are more elegant than most other area places, with high windows looking out onto a broad expanse of blue water. *2170 County Rd. 139, International Falls 56649, tel. 218/286–3151 or 800/351–5133, fax 218/286–3004. 15 rooms, 10 cabins. Facilities: restaurant, bar, boating. AE, D, MC, V. $$*

Sandy Point Lodge. On a narrow spit of land 5 mi west of the Kabetogama Lake Visitor Center, Sandy Point is one of the newer resorts around Voyageurs. It was built in 1987, but it emulates the old area style with its rustic, log-paneled walls. The log theme is picked up in some of the furnishings, notably the bedsteads. Overall, however, the lodge represents a newer, smoother kind of rusticity. (The resort's housekeeping cabins are some 20 years older, but similar in style.) *10606 Gamma Rd., Ray 56669, tel. 218/875–2615. 8 rooms share 2 baths, 12 cabins. Facilities: restaurant* (see *Dining,* above), *bar, boating. MC, V. $*

Northern Lights Resort. In a heavily wooded area on the shores of Lake Kabetogama, this secluded resort has 10 cabins, each decorated in the knotty-pine style common to the north woods. The spacious cabins, all of which were built between the 1940s and 1960s and refurbished in the mid-1990s, have lakeside decks, queen-size beds, kitchens, and barbecues. The centerpiece of the resort is its log lodge, built in the 1940s, with a massive stone fireplace, satellite television, and a variety of arcade-style games. Northern Lights also is less than a quarter mile from the entrance to a network of fine hiking and cross-country skiing trails. *12723 Northern Lights Rd., Ray 56669, tel. 218/875–2591 or 800/318–7023. 10 cabins. Facilities: beach, boating, playground. $$–$$$*

CAMPING

All camping in the park is tent camping. There are more than 130 developed campsites, most of them accessible only by boat. The exceptions are those on the Cruiser Lake Trail, which can be reached only on foot (but you need a boat to get to the trail itself). There are no camping fees. Campsites can't be reserved, which usually isn't a problem early in the season. In July and August, get there early or on a weekday—or zero in on the Namakan Narrows or Sheen Point. The sites typically have two 12-ft-square sandy tent pads, and each site has a fire grate, a picnic table, and a pit toilet (i.e., without a roof). Many have bear-proof storage lockers. Camping is limited to 14 days at a site. You are not restricted to camping at designated sites, but it's preferred, and it's certainly easier. Some sites may be closed when you visit; check the bulletin boards at park boat ramps.

INSIDE THE PARK All the campsites on the Cruiser Lake Trail are on small, tree-lined lakes—which means great views, a water source (but be sure to filter or boil), and an excellent chance that loons will serenade you to sleep. Don't be alarmed by large splashes; they're far more likely to be caused by beavers or deer than by bears. The campsite on Cruiser Lake itself is on a small island accessible by footboards, hard by a beaver lodge whose residents are fairly unafraid. Pets are not allowed on trails. The trailhead is accessible only by boat.

Boaters have many more choices. All the boat-accessible sites are on the big lakes, many on their own tiny islands or peninsulas. There are clusters of campsites around Sheen Point several miles from the Ash River boat access, and around the Namakan Narrows near Crane Lake. Pets are allowed but must be leashed.

NEAR THE PARK **Woodenfrog State Campground.** Campers with cars and RVs can find a place to stay at this year-round campground, 5 mi from the Kabetogama Lake Visitor Center. Outside of running water and washrooms, it doesn't have a great many services, but it does have a swimming beach and 63 campsites, some of them overlooking Rainy Lake. Reservations are not accepted; the fee is $9 per night. Many resorts near each of the entrances also have campgrounds; the resort listings in the park newspaper (*see* Visitor Information *in* Essential Information, *above*) can tell you which ones. *County Rd. 122, tel. 218/757–3274 for information. 63 sites. Facilities: beach. No credit cards. $*

International Voyageur RV Park. This park near Rainy Lake has a dump station and bathhouse. *U.S. 53, International Falls, tel. 218/283–4679. 60 RV sites. Closed Nov.–Apr. No credit cards. $*

White Mountain National Forest
New Hampshire, Maine

By Tara Hamilton

Updated by Kay and Bill Scheller

Dubbed Aqiochook, "Home of the Great Spirit," by the Abenaki, Sokosis, and Pennacock tribes of the Algonquin nation who inhabited what is now the northeastern United States, Mt. Washington is the centerpiece of White Mountain National Forest. This mammoth, brooding peak—at 6,288 ft the tallest in New England—still evokes a sense of awe. Wind velocities of 231 mph, the greatest ever recorded, were measured at its summit, and its Arctic temperatures are the ultimate lows broadcast to New Englanders every winter. Along with its adjacent brethren in the Presidential Range, Mt. Washington presides over 790,000 acres that spread across parts of central and northern New Hampshire and into a small section of western Maine.

The Presidential peaks extend north and east from Mt. Washington in an arc creating the Great Gulf in the White Mountains. To the southwest of Mt. Washington the mountains rise and fall above tree line several times before finally descending into the woods below Mt. Pierce, forming a ridge that reaches 8 mi to the Webster Cliffs above Crawford Notch. The central region of the White Mountains is also dotted with mountains: Mount Willey and the North and South Twins to the north and east form a giant horseshoe with the Franconia Range to the west. Sharper and craggier than the Presidentials, though slightly smaller, the Franconia Range is no less beautiful.

The most heavily visited areas, Mt. Washington Valley along Route 16, the Kancamagus Highway, and Franconia Notch, are worthy of their popularity because of their spectacular terrain, but they are by no means the only compelling places to visit in the forest. Within the patchwork of national forest lands, a number of state parks—among them, Crawford Notch and Franconia Notch—preserve stunning natural formations and provide educational information and programs.

The above-tree-line summits offer magnificent views of the lush forest, but it is not until you've descended from their heights that the essence of the vast woodland is revealed. It is an expanse of towering cliffs and steep ravines; of narrow, sheer notches etched between masses of ancient mountains; of surging cascades and swiftly flowing rivers. It is a wilderness of moose and bear; of birch, beech, and spruce; of birdsong and howling wind and silence.

That's not to say that White Mountain National Forest is entirely wild and pristine. Just outside its boundaries lie an abundance of hotels, motels, restaurants, factory outlets, miniature golf courses, and tourist attractions, some of the gaudiest kind. And there's plenty of human activity and enterprise within the forest's boundaries, too. A national forest rather than a national park, the White Mountain National Forest is not maintained solely for preservation but managed for multiple uses. In addition to recreational activities, these include timber production, watershed preservation, and wildlife habitat management. The Forest Service manages logging operations so that trails, streams, campsites, and other significant sites are protected—an effort that often has the organization walking the fine line between community interest in development and jobs and environmentalist interest in leaving the forest untouched.

The Wilderness Act of 1964 designated 15% of the forest for special protection. Low-key recreation is encouraged in these wilderness areas, human-made structures are restricted, and mechanized equipment and vehicles, including bicycles, are prohibited. The Forest Service has also established nine scenic areas in the national forest: Gibbs Brook, Nancy Brook, Greeley Ponds, Pinkham Notch, Lafayette Brook, Rocky Gorge, Lincoln Woods, Sawyer Pond, and Snyder Brook.

ESSENTIAL INFORMATION

VISITOR INFORMATION For detailed information about the national forest, write to forest supervisor, **White Mountain National Forest** (719 N. Main St., Laconia, NH 03246, tel. 603/528–8721, TTY 603/528–8722). Ranger stations can also help you. **Ammonoosuc** (Trudeau Rd., Box 239, Bethlehem, NH 03574, tel. 603/869–2626). **Androscoggin** (80 Glen Rd., Gorham, NH 03581, tel. 603/466–2713). **Evans Notch** (18 Mayville Rd., Box 2270, Bethel, ME 04217, tel. 207/824–2134). **Pemigewasset** (Rte. 175, Box 15, Plymouth, NH 03264, tel. 603/536–1310). **Saco** (Kancamagus Hwy., 33 Kancamagus Hwy., Conway, NH 03818, tel. 603/447–2166, TTY 603/447–1989).

The **Pinkham Notch Visitor Center** (Rte. 16, Box 298, Gorham, NH 03581, tel. 603/466–2725 for recording or 603/466–2727 for reservations), the northern New England regional headquarters of the non-profit Appalachian Mountain Club, is an educational and recreational visitor center operating under a special-use permit with the Forest Service. Open daily 6:30 AM–10 PM, it provides hikers with information on the Appalachian Trail and all other trails maintained by the organization.

White Mountain Visitor Center (Rte. 112, Box 10, N. Woodstock, NH 03262, tel. 603/745–8720 or 800/346–3687, fax 603/745–6765) and **Mt. Washington Valley Chamber of Commerce** (Rte. 16, Box 2300-G, North Conway, NH 03860, tel. 603/356–3171 or 800/367–3364) both provide information about the towns in the vicinity of the forest as well as about the forest itself. The following chambers of commerce can also be helpful. **Franconia/Easton/Sugar Hill Chamber of Commerce** (Box D, Franconia, NH 03580, tel. 603/823–5661 or 800/347–9007). **Lincoln/Woodstock Chamber of Commerce** (Rte. 112, Box 358, Lincoln, NH 03251, tel. 603/745–6621 or 800/227–4191 for lodging reservations). **Northern White Mountain Chamber of Commerce** (163 Main St., Box 298, Berlin, NH 03470, tel. 603/752–6060 or 800/992–7480). **Waterville Valley Region Chamber of Commerce** (Rte. 49, Box 1067, Campton, NH 03223 tel. 603/726–3804 or 800/237–2307).

FEES All cars parked on White Mountain National Forest land must have a pass, which costs either $5 (good for seven days) or $20 (good for a year). Passes are available at all visitor centers and at local vendors (60 in total). If you don't have a pass and your vehicle is spotted, you will have an "invitation to pay" slipped under your windshield wipers. There are admission charges for the state parks, state and national forest campgrounds, and some of the backcountry tent sites and shelters within the forest.

PUBLICATIONS A variety of one-page fact sheets available at the ranger stations and information centers (*see* Visitor Information, *above*) cover such diverse topics as alpine plants, hiking safety, and scenic waterfalls in the national forest. Handouts about many of the hikes in the forest include information on local flora and fauna. Also available here free of charge are various brochures, and regulation sheets pertaining to mountain biking, snowmobiling, and fishing in the forest. The "Forest Recreation Map," topographical maps, and other hiking maps are available for purchase.

Available at most bookstores in the Northeast, the *AMC White Mountain Guide,* published by the Appalachian Mountain Club, is the most comprehensive and useful book on hiking in the White Mountain National Forest.

GEOLOGY AND TERRAIN By geologic time, the White Mountains, at roughly 300 to 400 million years old, are middle-aged younger siblings of the nearby Green and Adirondack mountains and older than the youthful ranges of the western United States. Their origins, though, are similar to those of the East Coast's entire Appalachian family. A series of mountain-building periods caused by tectonic plate collision resulted in a heating, crumpling, and uplifting of the Appalachian geosyncline, sediments piled deep in coastal areas from earlier upland erosion.

Nature's formidable power became evident again during the most recent ice age, when glaciers carved and sculpted the mountaintops and valleys. Jagged peaks were softened, sharp-cut river valleys were rounded, amphitheater-like cirques and ravines were scoured, and, when the ice receded, rocks and boulders were left scattered across the landscape.

Although still among the tallest mountains in the eastern United States—dozens rise over 4,000 ft and a handful over 5,000—these peaks have been trimmed by erosion from what may have been twice their current height. The Presidential and Franconia ranges, the White Mountains' two highest subranges, have many peaks reaching above tree line, and they still maintain a decidedly rugged appearance, with granite cliffs and outcroppings. Below, dense forests hide fast-rushing mountain streams that cascade down from the highlands carrying a cargo of rock and sand to be deposited on the continental shelf in preparation for the mountain building of the future.

FLORA AND FAUNA Steep mountainsides, dense forests, and long, harsh winters determine the forms of wildlife found in the White Mountain National Forest. Black bears and white-tailed deer roam valley floors in spring in search of food, as do bobcats and fishers, which can occasionally be spotted on open ridges. Mink follow watercourses, and beaver ponds dot the forest. Other species include red fox, porcupine, raccoon, snowshoe hare, weasel, and woodchuck.

Weighing in at about 1,000 pounds and measuring up to 6 ft at the shoulder, the largest animal in the White Mountains is the moose. The animal's gangly grace and unpredictability make sighting it an unforgettable experience. Often spotted in the spring at lower elevations and along roadsides, where they seek food and refuge from the black flies, moose tend to be active at night, making car-moose collisions an increasing problem. Visitors to the area are advised to be extremely cautious around these beasts: Do not approach them. Take photographs and view them from a safe distance.

Those who hike in the White Mountain National Forest to any summit above tree line will pass through a succession of ecological zones, from lowland deciduous forest to alpine tundra. Northern hardwoods of American beech, various maples, and yellow and paper birch cover much of the forest at lower elevations, where oaks and white pines may also be seen. Hemlocks dominate in some of the deeper valleys, and red pines often line ledges above 2,000 ft. At 3,000 ft, the forest evolves into a mix of birch, spruce, and balsam fir; and, at 4,000 ft, the trees become twisted and stunted—odd, people-size specimens called krummholz (German for "crooked wood")—and interspersed with dense, low mats of vegetation. Above the timberline, they cease to exist altogether, replaced by the low-lying sedges, grasses, lichens, and mosses that cover the rocky surfaces and isolated patches atop the highest peaks.

With 8 square mi above timberline, this is the largest alpine tundra area in the country east of the Rockies. The alpine vegetation here is well adapted to the harsh wind and cold. Evergreen perennials grow close to the ground and may have leaves that overlap each other or have protective coverings. Often found high up in the Presidential and Franconia ranges, many of these tiny alpine plants flower from early spring to midsummer; they are best seen in late June. Some of the most prevalent are the five-petaled white diapensia, minuscule pink alpine azalea, white Labrador tea, and pink-magenta Lapland rosebay. Common in the White Mountains, mountain avens is found elsewhere only on a small island off Nova Scotia. Robbins (dwarf) cinquefoil, a fuzzy plant with yellow flowers, grows only in a small area in the Presidential Range and is one of the rarest species in the United States.

WHEN TO GO The highlight of any north country excursion is seeing the wildflowers bloom in May and June. Spring, when the national forest is still free of the summer crowds, is an ideal time to explore. Mosquitoes and black flies can be a nuisance, however.

Summer is the most popular season to visit. The national forest is sufficiently vast, however, to absorb the hordes of travelers who flock here, and to afford isolation to those willing to get off the beaten track. If avoiding crowds is a priority, head to the less developed sections of the forest east of Route 16 and north of Route 2, or hike a few mi into the backcountry.

In late September and early October, busloads of leaf peepers can turn the Kancamagus Scenic Byway—arguably the most beautiful, and unquestionably the most popular, foliage road in the Northeast—into a virtual parking lot. Make lodging reservations well in advance if you plan to come at this time. And consider coming during the few weeks between Labor Day and peak foliage; this period can be the most pleasant, with moderate crowds and temperatures.

Although winter in the northeastern mountains is known for its severity, it rivals the other three seasons for beauty. The mountains also provide a perfect setting for winter sports: Downhill and cross-country skiing are ever popular in the White Mountains, and interest in snowshoeing is on the rise.

Be aware, however, that the Presidential and Franconia ranges are subject to some of the worst weather on the planet; Mt. Washington's reputation as the most dangerous small mountain in the world should not be taken lightly. Hurricane-force winds, dense fog, and snow occur even in summer, and sudden and extreme weather is common: Winds of 100 mph blow every month of the year.

SEASONAL EVENTS **June–Columbus Day weekend:** Vendors from northern New Hampshire and Vermont gather to sell their wares Saturday from 8 to 4 at the popular **Bethlehem Flea Market** on the corner of Main and Agazzis streets. **June:** Open-house tours of historic inns and homes, a hot-air balloon festival, an antique auto show, and art shows are all part of **White Mountain Heritage Days** (tel. 800/367–3364) mid-month. Folks either flock to, or flee from, Mt. Washington valley during the annual **Auto Road Hill Climb** (tel. 603/466–3988). Beware: The mufflerless vehicles can be heard from the other side of the Great Gulf Wilderness. For the fleet of foot, there's the **Audi–Mt. Washington Hill Climb** (tel. 603/466–3988). **September:** The **Highland Games** (tel. 603/745–6621) bring fife and drum bands and other music, dance, and athletics to the town of Lincoln at Loon Mountain in the middle of the month.

WHAT TO PACK Mountain weather is fickle, so it's best to bring layers of clothing when visiting the area, no matter what the time of year. Hikers and campers in particular should be prepared for anything, especially at higher elevations. Your day pack should always contain a layer of wool, fleece, or other wicking material; rain gear; spare socks (not cotton); a wool hat and mittens; a flashlight; extra food and water; matches; a first-aid kit; sunscreen; a knife; and a map and compass. Good walking shoes or hiking boots are essential, even for short jaunts into the woods. A pair of binoculars may enrich your hikes and your porch sitting.

GENERAL STORES You can find general stores at all corners of the White Mountains. The larger towns of Berlin, Gorham, Jackson, Glen, North Conway, Conway, Lincoln, North Woodstock, and Franconia all have supermarkets and sporting goods stores on their main streets. **Harman's Cheese & Country Store** on Route 117 in Sugar Hill (tel. 603/823–8000) is open all year and is well stocked. **Crawford Notch General Store** (tel. 603/374–2779) on Route 302 south of Crawford Notch State Park is a good place to pick up such last-minute supplies as fishing hooks and Coleman fuel; it also has a minimal selection of food. **Tripoli Country Store** (tel. 603/745–6421) on Tripoli Road north of Waterville Valley is only open in the summer but has a good selection of sporting goods. **Kancamagus Country Store** on Main Street in Lincoln (tel. 603/745–6601) is open 24 hours. **Mt. Washington Trading Post** (tel. 603/846–5055) on Route 302 in Bretton Woods stays open all year and has a great deli.

ARRIVING AND DEPARTING **By Bus. Concord Trailways** (tel. 603/228–3300 or 800/639–3317 in NH) offers daily service to and from South Station in Boston; one route goes up Route 16 through Conway, North Conway, Jackson, Glen, Pinkham Notch, Gorham, and Berlin; another travels along Route 93, stopping at Woodstock, Lincoln, Franconia Notch, and Littleton. From early June through mid-October, the **Appalachian Mountain Club** (tel. 603/466–2727 for schedules and reservations) operates two shuttle buses for hikers. One bus is based at Pinkham Notch Visitor Center and the other at Crawford Hostel. Both stop at most of the major trailheads within the national forest. Cost is $6 for AMC members, $8 for non-members. Reservations are strongly recommended: Walk-ins are accepted on a space-available basis.

By Car and RV. Running north–south from Massachusetts to Quebec, I–93 and Route 3 bisect the White Mountain National Forest at its western end. Route 16, also running north–south, brings you to the eastern portion of the forest, slicing through the Mt. Washington Valley. The Kancamagus Scenic Byway (Route 112) and Route 2 are the east–west thoroughfares that access the southern and northern regions of the national forest, respectively. Route 302 winds through the central portion of the forest in a southeast–northwest direction.

The official state map, available free from the **Office of Travel and Tourism Development** (Box 856, Concord, NH 03302, tel. 603/271– 2343), has useful directories for each of the tourist areas.

By Plane. Laconia Municipal Airport (30 mi south of southern boundary of the forest, tel. 603/524–5003) only accommodates charters and private planes. **Lebanon Municipal Airport** (35 mi southwest of the southern boundary of the forest, tel. 603/298–8878) is served by US Airways, Northwest, and Delta/Business Express.

By Train. There is no rail service into the White Mountain National Forest or into any of the neighboring towns.

EXPLORING

Without a car, exploring the expanses of the national forest is difficult, if not impossible. But investigating every corner of this large region is not necessarily preferable to immersing yourself in a single area. Pedal a bicycle, paddle a canoe, ride a horse, or take a hike for at least part of your stay to really get a sense of the White Mountains. The time spent outside your car will afford a variety of perspectives on the beauty of the forest.

THE BEST IN ONE DAY Start early from Conway, with breakfast behind you and a picnic lunch in tow, heading north on Route 16; to avoid the congestion caused by the popular outlet stores, take a left off Route 16 onto West Side Road, which runs parallel to the more frenetic route through town. About 4 mi north, turn left for the 1-mi drive up to Cathedral Ledge and a rewarding view of the valley below. Then head east to Route 16 and make a left, heading

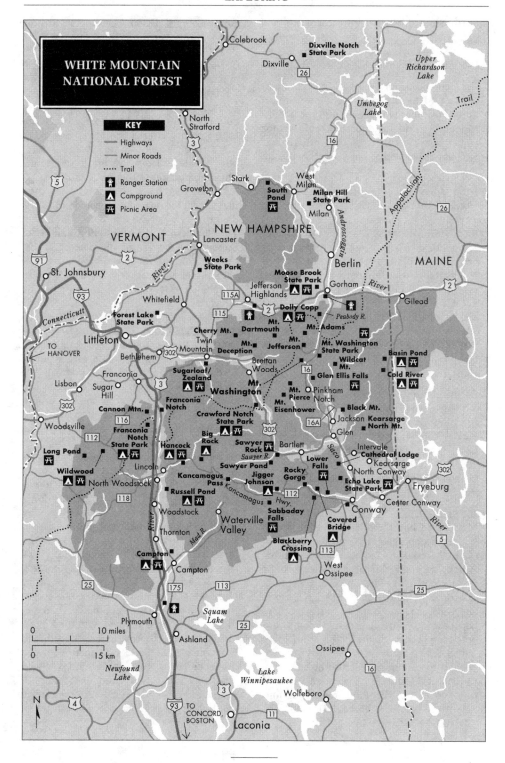

WHITE MOUNTAIN NATIONAL FOREST

KEY

- Highways
- Minor Roads
- Trail
- Ranger Station
- Campground
- Picnic Area

Colebrook

Dixville Notch State Park

Dixville

26

Upper Richardson Lake

North Stratford

3

16

Trail

Umbegog Lake

26

5

Stark

West Milan

South Pond

Milan Hill State Park

Appalachian

MAINE

Groveton

Milan

Androscoggin

NEW HAMPSHIRE

Lancaster

VERMONT

River

Berlin

2

Weeks State Park

Moose Brook State Park

Gorham

River

Gilead

2

91

St. Johnsbury

Jefferson Highlands

115A

115

Dolly Copp

Peabody R.

93

Whitefield

Connecticut

Forest Lake State Park

Cherry Mt.

Mt. Dartmouth

Mt. Adams

Mt. Washington State Park

Basin Pond

Littleton

Bethlehem

302

Twin Mountain

Mt. Deception

Mt. Jefferson

Brettan Woods

16

Wildcat Mt.

Glen Ellis Falls

Cold River

Franconia

Sugarloaf/ Zealand

Mt. Washington

Mt. Pierce

Pinkham Notch

Lisbon

Sugar Hill

3

Black Mt.

Kearsarge North Mt.

302

Cannon Mtn.

Franconia Notch

Mt. Eisenhower

Jackson

116

Crawford Notch State Park

302

16A

Glen

Woodsville

Franconia Notch State Park

Big Rock

Sawyer Rock

Bartlett

Intervale

Cathedral Lodge

112

Hancock

Sawyer R.

North Conway

Kearsarge

302

Long Pond

Wildwood

Lincoln

Sawyer Pond

Jigger Johnson

Lower Falls

Echo Lake State Park

Fryeburg

Kancamagus Pass

Rocky Gorge

Center Conway

North Woodstock

Russell Pond

Kancamagus Hwy.

112

Conway

118

Woodstock

Sabbaday Falls

Covered Bridge

5

River

Thornton

Mad R.

Waterville Valley

Blackberry Crossing

113

West Ossipee

Campton

Campton

25

175

113

25

Plymouth

Squam Lake

25

16

Ashland

Ossipee

0   10 miles
0   15 km

Newfound Lake

Lake Winnipesaukee

Wolfeboro

N

4

93

TO CONCORD, BOSTON

3

11

Laconia

north. Short side trips to the towns of Intervale, Bartlett, and Jackson will provide a more endearing version of small-town New Hampshire than does North Conway.

Continue north on Route 16 into Pinkham Notch and the heart of the White Mountains' Presidential Range. The Appalachian Mountain Club headquarters and visitor center here will help get you oriented. If you are interested in a hike, this is the place to ask for suggestions.

After spending some time in Pinkham Notch, head north to Gorham and turn left on Route 2. In Jefferson, 14 mi to the west, turn left on Route 115 for a cut through to Route 302 in Twin Mountain and an easterly turn to Bretton Woods and Crawford Notch State Park. Or better yet, in Jefferson, take the more adventurous Jefferson Notch Road south between Mt. Dartmouth and Mt. Adams and Mt. Jefferson into Bretton Woods and then Route 302 into Crawford Notch. This serene valley is a good place to break out the picnic lunch and to enjoy a short hike afterward.

Backtrack northwest on Route 302, bearing left onto Route 3 south in Twin Mountain for the 10-mi drive into Franconia Notch State Park, where you might take a dip in Echo Lake. Or consider making a detour via Route 18 to the village of Franconia, renting a bicycle and spending the afternoon riding the 9-mi bike path that slices through the notch.

ORIENTATION PROGRAMS The **Appalachian Mountain Club** offers hundreds of educational programs each year, most of them out of the Pinkham Notch Visitor Center. Among them are day programs covering a wide range of topics, including geology, meteorology, and forest ecology; workshops focusing on outdoor skills, such as backpacking, canoeing, snowshoeing, orienteering, and telemark skiing; and hikes led by skilled guides with extensive knowledge of the natural and cultural history of the White Mountains. For more information, contact **AMC Education Programs** (Rte. 16, Box 298, Gorham, NH 03581, tel. 603/466–2721 or 603/466–2727).

GUIDED TOURS **Great Outdoors Hiking and Walking Vacations** (Stonehurst Manor, Box 1937, North Conway, NH 03860, tel. 603/356–3113 or 800/525–9100) has programs for various ages and abilities. **New England Hiking Holidays** (Box 1648, North Conway, NH 03860, tel. 603/356–9696 or 800/869–0949) offers two- to eight-day inn-to-inn tours. **Hiking Holidays** (Monkton Rd., Bristol, VT 05443, tel. 802/453–4816) offers five- and six-day inn-to-inn tours. The **Appalachian Mountain Club** (*see* Orientation Programs, *above*) publishes a catalogue, which makes choosing from its daunting array of guided hikes a bit easier. The **Northern White Mountain Chamber of Commerce** (*see* Visitor Information *in* Essential Information, *above*) has knowledgeable guides who drive visitors in vans in search of moose, sharing local history along the way.

SCENIC DRIVES AND VIEWS The 34-mi **Kancamagus Scenic Byway** (Rte. 112 east of Lincoln) is the most scenic of the many scenic drives in the national forest. Although it can be overrun with sightseers in summer and fall foliage season, it's a photographer's dream. One of the most stunning vistas in the Mt. Washington valley is from the top of **Cathedral Ledge**, which can be reached via the winding road that heads west off West Side Road, 4 mi north of its junction with Route 16 in Conway. For a tour under a wilderness canopy, take Route 49 east from Campton to Waterville Valley and then **Tripoli Road** back around to I–93. **Routes 112** and **118** in the section of the forest west of I–93 offer panoramic views east toward the higher peaks. **Route 302,** from Glen to Bethlehem via Crawford Notch State Park, affords awesome views of the Presidential Range and makes a convenient loop when combined with the Kancamagus Scenic Byway and **I–93** through Franconia State Park; this section of the interstate is a two-lane, reduced-speed "parkway" that was completed after 25 years of haggling between conservationists and those pushing for a north–south transportation corridor.

The **Mt. Washington Auto Road,** a 16-mi round-trip toll road to Mt. Washington's summit, is open when weather conditions permit. It begins at Glen House, 16 mi north of Glen; there are frequent rest stops. Allow two hours round-trip and check your brakes first. Cars with automatic transmissions that can't shift down into first gear aren't allowed on the road at all. A better option is to hop into one of the vans at Glen House for a 1½-hour guided tour (2 hours if you purchase your ticket before 9:30 AM). *Tel. 603/ 466–3988. Admission: $15 per car plus $6 for each adult passenger; van fare $20. Open mid-May–late Oct., daily (weather permitting).*

Hop aboard the **Mt. Washington Cog Railway** for a three-hour round-trip journey to the summit of Mt. Washington on the second-steepest railway track in the world. Coal-fired steam engines have been hauling passengers up the 2.75-mi route since 1869. It's wise to make reservations and to bring a sweater. *Rte. 302, 6 mi northeast of Bretton Woods, tel. 603/846–5404 or 800/ 922–8825, ext. 7 outside NH. Admission: $35 round-trip. Open May weekends, limited schedule; June–Oct., daily 8:30–4:30, weather permitting.*

In just seven minutes the 80-passenger **Cannon Mountain Aerial Tramway** whisks passengers to that mountain's 4200-ft summit for fabulous views of the White Mountains, Maine, Vermont, and Canada. *Cannon Mountain Ski Area, tel. 603/823–5563. Admission: $9. Open Memorial Day–3rd weekend in Oct., daily 9–4.*

The **New England Ski Museum,** just north of Cannon Mountain at the foot of the tramway, has old trophies, skis and bindings, boots, and ski apparel dating from the late 1800s, as well as a collection of photos. *Tel. 603/ 823–7177. Open Dec.–Apr., Thurs.–Tues. noon–5; Memorial Day–Columbus Day, daily noon–5.*

HISTORIC BUILDINGS AND SITES Just outside the bounds of the national forest, the **John Wingate Weeks Historic Site** on the top of Mt. Prospect, off Route 3 near Lancaster, is the estate and mansion of the former U.S. senator and secretary of war who introduced the legislation to establish the White Mountain National Forest Reserve. The site is on the National Register of Historic Places and is part of the New Hampshire state park system.

Also outside the confines of the forest is the **Robert Frost Place,** home to the poet for many years. Two rooms contain memorabilia and signed editions of his books, and behind the house a .5-mi nature trail is posted with lines of Frost's verse. On summer evenings there are readings by visiting poets. *Ridge Rd., off Rte. 116 in Franconia, tel. 603/823–5510. Admission: $3. Open Memorial Day–June, weekends 1–5; July– Columbus Day, Wed.–Mon. 1–5.*

NATURE TRAILS AND SHORT WALKS The White Mountains offer a staggering number of short hikes that provide everything from panoramic vistas to wilderness solitude. In Franconia Notch State Park, the 1.5-mi loop to **Artist's Bluff and Bald Mountain** is an easy hike that culminates in fine views of Cannon Mountain and the notch; the trailhead is on Route 18, just across from the Peabody Base Lodge. Also in Franconia is a slightly more challenging climb to **Lonesome Lake,** nestled 1,000 ft above the valley floor. It's 1.25 mi to the lake from Lafayette Campground via the Lake Trail.

For a view of the 200-ft drop of **Arethusa Falls,** the highest in the state, take the moderate 1.3-mi trail beginning off Route 302, .5 mi south of the Dry River Campground in Crawford Notch State Park. Return via the same route, or extend the hike into a 3-mi loop past Frankenstein Cliff.

An abundance of short hikes, leading to cascades, rock formations, and other outstanding views, depart from the Kancamagus Scenic Byway. The **Sabbaday Falls Trail** is a .5-mi hike with interpretive signs that leads along a narrow flume; the trail starts at the picnic area 15 mi west of Conway. Five miles east of the picnic area is an easy 3-mi hike to **Champney** and **Pitcher Falls.** And for great views of the Swift River valley, try the 4-mi round-trip to the summit of Mt. Potash. Follow the Downes Brook Trail across from Passaconaway Campground and then veer right onto the **Mt. Potash Trail.**

An easy 20-minute walk partway up the **Tuckerman Ravine Trail,** beginning behind the Pinkham Notch Visitor Center, leads to the Crystal Cascade. Walk just across the road from the visitor center to the trailhead of a half-hour hike to **Lost Pond;** it will take you past beaver ponds, along a mountain stream, and through thick forest.

LONGER HIKES Be sure to choose your route carefully and carry a good map if you plan to take a long hike on the White Mountain National Forest; it's also a good idea to check in with a ranger station before you leave to get information about possible trail changes. Conditions are often not hazardous, but it is *extremely important* when hiking in the high country to be aware of the weather forecast. Stop in at or phone the **Pinkham Notch Visitor** Center (tel. 603/466–2725) for weather information; the line is open 6:30 AM–10 PM. If you hike above the tree line, always stay on the trail. If the weather deteriorates while you are hiking in the Franconia or Presidential Range, turn back; it will not improve.

An easy, well-marked loop, the **Imp Trail** in the Androscoggin ranger district leads to the "Imp Profile," an intriguing, facelike rock formation. The summit of this countenance offers commanding views of the Presidential Range. From opposite the Dolly Copp picnic area (6 mi south of Gorham on Route 16), ascend to the profile, continue another mile to the junction with North Carter Trail, and then continue on the Imp Trail for 3.2 mi to Route 16. It's a 6-mi trip in all.

Crawford Path in the Ammonoosuc District is the oldest continuously used mountain trail in the eastern United States. Ascending first to Mt. Clinton and then across the ridge to Mt. Washington, it is a rigorous trail, 5 mi of it above tree line and exposed to the full force of most storm systems that come through the area. Begin on Route 302 after parking in the lot on Mt. Clinton Road; you'll pass Gibbs Falls and the Gibbs Brook Scenic area, where there is a rare virgin stand of spruce and birch. After passing a junction with the Webster Cliff Trail at the 2.9 mi marker, the Crawford Path traverses several ledges, offering magnificent views on its way from Mt. Clinton to Mt. Eisenhower. At 4.8 mi, the trail begins to ascend Mt. Franklin, passing the summit of Mt. Monroe before reaching the Lakes of the Clouds hut and beginning the final ascent of the cone of Mt. Washington. Those intending to attempt this hike should be well prepared and in good physical condition. Remember, if weather conditions deteriorate, turn back. It is 8.2 mi to the summit of Mt. Washington, so make arrangements to stay at one of the shelters or tent sites in the vicinity; call or write the Pinkham Notch Visitor Center (*see* Visitor Information *in* Essential Information, *above*) for reservations.

Welch Mountain's bold, rocky peak comprises the western wall of the narrow southern aperture through which the Mad River flows out of Waterville Valley in the Pemigewasset ranger district; Dickey Mountain is a short distance to the northwest. Exposed mountain summits below 4,000 ft are rare, but fire bared the tops of these two peaks; as a result, the views from their summits—which are relatively easy to attain—are outstanding. The **Welch/Dickey Mountain Trail** leaves from a parking area on Orris Road (take Mad River Road—reached 4.5 mi from the junction of Route 49 with Route 175—to Orris Road), quickly reaching the ridge of Welch Mountain at 1.3 mi. Waterville Valley can be seen below from ledges here, but the trail climbs farther through contorted jack pine, blueberry bushes, and dwarfed spruce and birch to reach the summit at 2 mi. After enjoying this panorama, continue on the trail, passing through a wooded area and up a natural staircase, toward the exposed summit of Dickey and another chance to touch the sky. This hike is 4.5 mi round-trip.

Outstanding views may be had from the **Roost,** reached by heading east from the Evans Notch Highway (Route 113) at the Evans Brook Bridge, north of Hastings Campground. Follow the trail for .5 mi up moderate to steep grades; then follow the path downhill for a short distance to open ledges that afford excellent views of the Wild River valley, Evans Brook valley, and many mountain peaks. From the Roost continue to follow the trail in a southerly direction along a more gradual grade until it arrives back at Route 113, south of Hastings campground (.7 mi). It's just over .5 mi along the road back to the starting point north of the campground, making it a 1.8-mi hike round-trip.

The hike to Mt. Kearsarge North in the Saco ranger district leads to one of the finest vantage points in the White Mountains. Head out from the parking area 1.5 mi east of Route 16/302 on the north side of Hurricane Mountain Road in Kearsarge, just north of North Conway. **Mt. Kearsarge North Trail** begins on an old logging road, becoming progressively steeper and reaching open ledges that afford views of the Saco River valley and peaks to the west and south; at 2.4 mi, the trail crests the ridge that connects Kearsarge North with Bartlett Mountain and climbs to the summit, which is 3.1 mi from the beginning of the trailhead. To return, retrace your steps back down.

With the passage of the National Trails System Act by Congress on October 2, 1968, the **Appalachian Trail** (AT) became the first federally protected footpath in the United States. The AT traverses the White Mountains for about 150 mi from Hanover, New Hampshire, to Grafton Notch in Maine, crossing many of the major peaks and ranges on the national forest; its most stunning sections are those where it crosses the high ridges of the Franconia and Presidential ranges. For those who would prefer to travel without the weight of a backpack, the Appalachian Mountain Club huts offer a nice alternative to camping: It manages several rustic shelters and tent sites just off

the Appalachian Trail (see Lodging, below). For detailed information, write to the **Appalachian Trail Conference** (Box 236, Harpers Ferry, WV 25425) or **Appalachian Mountain Club** (Pinkham Notch Visitor Center, Rte. 16, Box 298, Gorham, NH 03581, tel. 603/466–2725).

OTHER ACTIVITIES Back-Road Driving. **Cherry Mountain Road** is a dramatic drive on a narrow dirt road that runs for 7 mi from Route 302, about 1 mi west of the Fabyan Motel in Fabyan, to the junction of Routes 115 and 115A, passing through the high notch that separates Cherry Mountain and Mt. Dartmouth and Mt. Deception of the Dartmouth Range. In the same area, and a logical continuation if you're looking to get in some more four-wheel-drive mileage, is **Jefferson Notch Road,** which leads from the Valley Road in Randolph off of U.S. 2 through the mountains to Bretton Woods on Route 302. At more than 3,000 ft, the Jefferson Notch crossing is the highest public road in the state. On the far western edge of the national forest, north of Route 112 and west of Route 116, are several dirt roads worthy of exploration. Forest Service roads 310A and 353 make their way between Cobble Hill and Moody Ledge. There are no views, but the abandoned **South Landaff Road,** off of Route 112, leads to an area strewn with intriguing stone walls, cellar holes, and other remnants of old abandoned farms; this road continues for another 1.5 mi across private land to Mill Brook Road south of Landaff Center. Conditions on all the above-mentioned roads vary with the season and the weather. Although they may be accessible to regular cars with good tires, four-wheel-drive vehicles are recommended.

Biking. Loon, Waterville Valley, and **Bretton Woods** ski resorts (see Skiing, below) open their trails and surrounding logging roads to cyclists in summer and also offer bike rentals and repairs. Miles of the well-maintained cross-country ski trails in the **Whitaker Woods** area are also accessible to mountain bikers. The **Bartlett Experimental Forest** has various graded dirt roads that lead off Bear Notch Road; the terrain is gentle and ideal for beginners. National Forest Service maps of the extensive trail network open to cyclists on federal land can be purchased at the Pemigewasset and Saco district ranger offices (*see* Visitor Information *in* Essential Information, *above*). Also, look for "20 Off-Road and Back-Road Routes in Mt. Washington Valley," a pamphlet available at local sporting goods stores. The five wilderness areas—Caribou-Speckled Mountain, Great Gulf, Pemigewasset, Presidential Range/Dry River, and Sandwich Range—are closed to bicycles.

Opportunities to bike on paved roads are somewhat less plentiful. The **Franconia Notch State Park** bike path runs for 9 mi from the Flume Visitor Center through some of the most inspiring scenery in the state. For riders in top shape, the Kancamagus Scenic Byway affords spectacular views and a 1,200-ft ascent to the top of Kancamagus Pass. Watch out for cars!

Among the many shops that rent and repair bikes are **Franconia Sport Shop** (Main St., Franconia, NH, tel. 603/823–5241), **The Greasy Wheel** (40 S. Main St., Plymouth, NH, tel. 603/536–3655), and **Ski Fanatics** (Campton Plaza, Rte. 49, Campton, NH, tel. 603/726–4327).

Bird-Watching. More than 200 species of birds make their warm-weather home in the White Mountains. A short stroll into the forest may be enough to provide glimpses of gold and purple finch, rose-breasted grosbeak, blackpoll and Canada warbler, scarlet tanager, or wood thrush, and the sound of the hollowed-tree hammering of a yellow-bellied sapsucker or the melody of the song sparrow. At higher elevations, on rock ledges or above tree line, sightings of broad-winged hawks, great horned owls, and other birds of prey are frequent.

Canoeing and Kayaking. Saco Bound (Box 119WM, Rte. 302, Center Conway, NH, tel. 603/447–3801 or 800/677–723 for brochure) specializes in guided family canoe and kayaking trips; rentals are also available here. Also try **Canoe Ring of New England** (1618 White Mt. Hwy., North Conway, NH, tel. 603/356–5280) for rentals and shuttles. In the eastern side of the forest, **River Run** (Brownfield Bridge, Rte. 160, Brownfield, ME, tel. 207/452–2500) offers canoe rentals, shuttles, and camping areas for overnight trips.

Fishing. The White Mountain National Forest supports 750 mi of streams and 50 freshwater ponds that abound with salmon, northern pike, pickerel, black bass, walleye, and lake, brook, and rainbow trout. The **Swift River,** flowing in an easterly direction for more than 20 mi along the Kancamagus Scenic Byway, is a popular and easily accessible spot for nabbing trout. Healthy brook and rainbow trout can also be found on the Ellis, Wildcat, and Saco rivers.

A quieter angling experience, **Big and Little Sawyer ponds**—a hike from either the Kancamagus or Route 302—host brook trout, brown bullhead, American smelt, and creek chub. You can angle for chain pickerel, yellow perch, brown bullhead, and white sucker at Elbow Pond, a 1.5-mi hike from Route 118 near Woodstock.

State fishing licenses are required and available from many area sporting goods and general stores or by writing to the **New Hampshire Fish and Game Department** (2 Hazen Dr., Concord, NH 03301, tel. 603/271–3421) or the **Maine Department of Inland Fisheries and Wildlife** (284 State St., Augusta, ME 04333, tel. 207/289–2043). **Twin Mountain Fish and Wildlife Center** (Rte. 3, Twin Mountain, tel. 603/846–5108) and **Warren Wildlife Center** (Rte. 25, Warren, tel. 603/764–8593) both have helpful fishing-related displays and information.

Horseback Riding. Fields of Attitash (Rte. 302, Bartlett, tel. 603/374–2368) and **Loon Mountain Park** (Kancamagus Scenic Byway Lincoln, tel. 603/745–8111) offer trail rides.

Llama Trekking. Snowvillage Inn (Snowville, tel. 603/447–2818 or 800/447–4345) conducts a guided trip up Foss Mountain. Your elegant picnic will include champagne and gourmet food from the inn's kitchen. The llamas carry the food, the fine china, and the silverware for you. Reservations are required.

Rafting. Saco Bound (Box 119WM, Center Conway 03813, tel. 603/447–3801 or 800/ 677–7238) offers rafting trips down several rivers, including the Swift, Magalloway, and Penobscot, and provides full base facilities (log cabins, campground, restaurant, hotel).

Rock Climbing. The **EMS Climbing School** (Box 514, North Conway, NH 03860, tel. 603/356–5433 or 800/310–4504), in operation for more than 25 years and accredited by the American Mountain Guides Association, offers year-round courses, including those geared specifically for women and adolescents.

Skiing. Opportunities for fine cross-country skiing are abundant. The **Jackson Ski Touring Foundation** (Rte. 16A, Box 216, Jackson, NH 03846, tel. 603/383–9355) offers 155 km of trails that wind through the village and out into the surrounding national forest. Rentals are available. The **Bretton Woods Ski Area** (Rte. 302, Bretton Woods, NH 03575, tel. 603/278–5181 or 800/232–2972) has 100 groomed km with magnificent views of the Presidential Range. There's a rental shop, ski school, and cafeteria. **Franconia Ski Touring Center** (Rte. 116, Franconia, NH 03580, tel. 603/823–5542) connects four inns with Cannon Mountain and Franconia Notch. In **Franconia Notch State Park,** the 9-mi recreation path is open to skiers in the winter. **Loon Mountain** (R.R. 1, Box 41, Kancamagus Scenic Byway, Lincoln, NH 03251, tel. 603/745–6281) and **Waterville Valley** (*see below*) have several challenging routes. You'll also find good cross-country skiing on the extensive hiking trail system of the **White Mountain National Forest.** For details, check with one of the district ranger offices (*see* Visitor Information *in* Essential Information, *above*).

Downhill skiers also have many appealing options. There are eight lift-serviced areas within the White Mountain National Forest. **Attitash** (Rte. 302, Bartlett, NH 03812, tel. 603/374–2368). **Balsams/Wilderness** (Dixville Notch, NH 03576, tel. 603/255–3951 or 800/255–0800) has a huge resort hotel and 13 alpine trails. **Black Mountain** (Rte. 16B, Jackson, NH 03846, tel. 603/383–4490). **Bretton Woods** (*see above*). **Cannon Mountain** (off I–93, Franconia, NH 03580, tel. 603/823–5563 or 800/552–1234) has the highest vertical drop. **Loon Mountain** (Rte. 112, Lincoln, NH 03251, tel. 603/745–8111). **Waterville Valley** (Rte. 49, Waterville Valley, NH 03215, tel. 603/236–8311 or 800/468–2553) has the most trails, the bulk of them intermediate. **Wildcat Mountain** (Rte. 16, Jackson, NH 03846, tel. 603/466–3326 or 800/643–4521). Bretton Woods, Waterville Valley, and Cannon are full-fledged mega-ski resorts with all the trimmings. **Tuckerman Ravine,** the be-all and end-all of skiing in the East, is accessible only by hiking up from the Pinkham Notch Visitor Center on Route 16 and is most popular in late spring. Contact Pinkham Notch Visitor Center (*see* Visitor Information *in* Essential Information, *above*) for details.

Snowmobiling. The national forest is laced by 360 mi of corridor trails. The **New Hampshire Snowmobile Association** (Box 38, Concord, NH 03301, tel. 603/224–8906) can provide maps, snow condition reports, and information on rentals and lodging along these routes.

Snowshoeing. All the trails and roads listed in the hiking, biking, and cross-country skiing sections, *above,* are also great choices for experienced snowshoers. Those not entirely comfortable in the woods in winter should stick to the shorter, easier trails close to the roads. It's important always to carry extra food and clothing and notify others of your whereabouts. Many cross-country ski centers (*see* Skiing, *above*) rent snowshoes.

Swimming. The White Mountains abound in cascades, emerald pools, and brisk mountain water. There are several good swimming spots along Route 302, including the confluence of the **Sawyer** and **Saco rivers;** north of Bartlett on Route 302, follow the well-beaten path that veers left after the bridge over the Sawyer River. Follow Route 16B up the hill past the Wentworth Resort in Jackson to **Jackson Falls;** the large boulders near the many swimming holes here are great for riverside picnics. Other excellent places to get wet are **Profile Lake, Lonesome Lake, Russell Pond, South Pond, Lower Falls,** and the **Peabody River.**

CHILDREN'S PROGRAMS The **Appalachian Mountain Club (AMC)** runs a number of creative programs for children out of the Pinkham Notch Visitor Center and eight backcountry huts; they're a fun way to teach kids about the environment. Contact the AMC Education Department (Box 298, Gorham, NH 03581, tel. 603/466–2725) for a list of current offerings.

EVENING ACTIVITIES The **Appalachian Mountain Club** sponsors lectures, slide shows, and natural history programs at the Pinkham Notch Visitor Center (tel. 603/466–2721) nightly throughout the summer and on weekend evenings the rest of the year. The **forest service** also offers a variety of interpretive programs at the Campton, Russell Pond, Jigger Johnson, and Dolly Copp national forest campgrounds throughout the summer; inquire at any of the ranger stations or write to the forest supervisor (*see* Visitor Information *in* Essential Information, *above*). The **Crawford Notch Hostel** (Rte. 302, Crawford Notch, no phone) occasionally has presentations on outdoor-related subjects such as tracking and hypothermia prevention. Contact the AMC Education Department (*see* Children's Programs, *above*) for times and topics.

DINING

Dining options, from fast-food to four-star, abound around the forest's perimeter. The New Hampshire towns of Conway, North Conway, Jackson, Gorham, Berlin, Bethlehem, Lincoln, North Woodstock, and Campton each offer a range of culinary possibilities. Dress is casual unless otherwise noted.

Horse and Hound Inn. This traditional inn is on 8 acres surrounded by the national forest. The wood-paneled dining room is romantic, with its terrace, roaring fireplace, tables set with dogwood-pattern china, and lawn views. The menu features American cuisine with French sauces, and the chef always prepares something special for vegetarians. *205 Wells Rd., Franconia, tel. 603/823–5501 or 800/450–5501. Reservations essential. AE, D, DC, MC, V. Closed Apr.–early May. Oct. 1–20, dinner weekends only. No lunch. $$$*

Homestead Restaurant. The heavy native timbers and wooden pegs Amos Barnes used to build this old red farmhouse in 1793 are still visible in the Homestead's Colonial-style dining rooms. The Early American tradition is also carried on in such simple yet satisfying fare as New England clam chowder, Cape Cod cranberry pot roast, and oven-broiled scallops. Breakfast is served on weekends. *Rte. 16, south of North Conway, tel. 603/356–5900. AE, D, MC, V. $$–$$$*

Prince Place at the Bernerhof Inn. The chef describes his cuisine as a cross between central European and new American, with emphasis on fresh, local ingredients. On one side of the menu are such Swiss specialties as fondue, Wiener schnitzel, and *delices de gruyère* (a blend of Swiss cheeses breaded and sautéed and served with a savory tomato sauce). The other side of the menu is a changing variety of classic French and American dishes. The wine list favors French and Austrian labels. All entrées in the informal Black Bear Pub are under $10, and there are 85 microbrews to choose from. Ask about the Taste of the Mountains, a hands-on cooking school hosted by some of the region's top chefs. Breakfast is served in summer. *Rte. 302, Glen 03838, tel. 603/383–4414 or 800/548–8007, fax 603/383–0809. AE, D, DC, MC, V. $$*

Scottish Lion Restaurant and Pub. The dining room overlooks meadows and mountains, and the copious Sunday brunch attracts locals as well as visitors. The tartan-papered pub offers more than 50 varieties of Scotch whiskey, and the cuisine, which is mainly Scottish and American, includes hot oatcakes in the evening bread basket. There's also an eight-room B&B. *Rte. 16, North Conway, tel. 603/356–6381 or 888/356–4945. AE, D, DC, MC, V. $$*

Woodstock Station. There are two restaurants in this converted railroad station. It may be hard to choose from the 148-item menu in the informal "station," but once you zero in on something it's bound to be good. Choices include piled-high sandwiches, fajitas, shrimp tempura, pasta dishes, and pub-type food. The upscale Clement Room serves dishes such as roast duckling and chicken with apricots. The Clement Room serves breakfast and dinner; the Station serves lunch and dinner. *Rte. 3, North Woodstock, tel. 603/745–3951. AE, D, MC, V. $$–$$$*

T.H.E. Thompson House Eatery. This rustic restaurant, with a farm produce stand, a bar, and a soda fountain, has been owner-chef operated for 20 years. In nice weather, dine on the outdoor deck overlooking the gardens. The menu of creative country-cooking dishes changes frequently and might include medallions of pork tenderloin piccata and a ham-and-cheddar sandwich laced with apples and maple Dijon. *Junction Rtes. 16A/16, Jackson, tel. 603/383–9341. D, MC, V. Closed Apr. and weekends in Nov. $–$$*

Horsefeathers. This casual neighborhood eatery has been serving good food for more than 20 years. Unfortunately, lots of people know it, so be prepared to wait up to 1½ hours for a seat at busy times. Fresh fish, delivered daily from Portland, Maine, makes the restaurant a haven for seafood lovers, but meat eaters will be happy here as well. House specialties include five-onion soup with puff pastry and gorgonzola cheese and grilled fish with chutney.

Save room for the Lemon Bar Explosion. The kid's menu includes knee-high nachos and free jelly beans. More than 25 wines are offered by the glass, and there's a large selection of regional microbrews. Smokers are welcome to eat in the pub, where there's entertainment four nights a week. *North Conway Village, tel. 603/356–2687. AE, MC, V. $–$$*

Red Parka Pub. Steak—cut and cooked to order—has been the specialty of this popular, family-friendly après-ski spot for 25 years. The prime rib is also marvelous, and sparerib lovers with huge appetites will want to hit the pub on a Monday when seconds are on the house (except holiday weeks). There's a passing nod to seafood (baked stuffed shrimp and scallop pie) and poultry (chicken teriyaki). *Route 302, Glen, tel. 603/383–4344. Reservations not accepted. AE, D, DC, MC, V. No lunch. $–$$*

Polly's Pancake Parlor. You can sample whole wheat, buckwheat, cornmeal, and oatmeal-buttermilk pancakes with real maple syrup, or have a light lunch of baked beans and cob-smoked ham at this extremely popular and venerable establishment. Everything here is homemade, and all the flours and grains are homeground. *Rte. 117, west of Franconia, Sugar Hill, tel. 603/823–5575. D, MC, V. Closed Dec.–Mar., weekdays Apr.–Mother's Day and 1st 3 wks of Nov. $*

Scarecrow Pub & Grill. Here's the place to go if you're looking for the most food for your money. You'll find everything in this rough-hewn, low-lit setting, from "sweet hearts," artichoke hearts in a pesto sauce with melted cheese, to baked, stuffed quahogs and hearty burgers and steaks. *Rte. 16, Intervale, tel. 603/356–2287. Reservations not accepted. No credit cards. $*

PICNIC SPOTS **Long Pond,** a remote body of water on a dirt road off Forest Road 19, is an idyllic spot for an outdoor repast, as is **Beaver Brook Wayside Area,** 4 mi west of Twin Mountain on Route 3. It's an easy walk to the **Basin** in Franconia Notch State Park where the tumbling Cascade Brook and the 20-ft-high Kinsman Falls make two outstanding backdrops for lunch in the woods. **Lower Falls Picnic Area, Rocky Gorge Scenic Area,** and **Sabbaday Picnic Area** are all picturesque places for a meal along the eastern length of the Kancamagus Scenic Byway. On Route 302, **Sawyer Rock Picnic Area,** near Bartlett, and **Crawford Notch State Park** are both ideal for outdoor dining. Two other popular picnic sites are **Jackson Falls** on the Wildcat River in Jackson and the 66-ft-high **Glen Ellis Falls** in Pinkham Notch.

LODGING

Sugar Hill, Lincoln, North Woodstock, Jackson, Bartlett, and North Conway all have country inns and bed-and-breakfasts. For those who prefer anonymity and a remote control TV, motels and hotels are also available, most notably in Franconia and North Conway. In all cases, reservations are a must, especially in foliage season. The state operates a **reservation service** (tel. 800/365–6964). The following are also reservation services. **Lincoln/Woodstock Chamber of Commerce** (tel. 603/745–6621 or 800/227–4191). **White Mountains Attractions** (tel. 603/745–8720 or 800/346–3687). **Mt. Washington Valley Visitors Bureau** (tel. 603/356–3171 or 800/367–3364). **Country Inns in the White Mountains** (tel. 603/356–9460 or 800/562–1300). **Jackson Resort Association** (tel. 800/866–3334).

The **Appalachian Mountain Club** (Box 298, Gorham 03581, tel. 603/466–2727, fax 603/466–3871) operates numerous overnight facilities in the forest that fall in the $–$$ range. MasterCard and Visa are accepted.

Hiking trails start right from the front door of the rustic but immaculate **Pinkham Notch Lodge,** adjacent to the Pinkham Notch Visitor Center. The lodge has private rooms, 23 dorm-style rooms with shared baths, three common rooms, and a restaurant that serves three substantial meals daily. It's open year-round.

The club maintains eight **huts** a day's hike apart high up in the White Mountains. All but one provides bunkroom accommodations, running water, and satisfying meals prepared by the hut staff. If you wish to do your own cooking, Carter Notch Hut offers lodging, a kitchen, cookware, and utensils. The hike to each hut is rated in the AMC's *White Mountain Guide* (available at Pinkham Notch Visitor Center), with some more difficult than others. The operating season for each hut varies.

The clean, self-service, low-cost **Crawford Notch Hostel** has a kitchen stocked with utensils. Two bunk rooms sleep 24, and two adjacent cabins accommodate 8 people each; it's open year-round.

Darby Field Inn. Every room is different at this cozy inn, but what most have in common is a spectacular mountain view. After a day of cross-country skiing, snowshoeing, or hiking (the White Mountain National Forest borders the property), you can warm yourself before the living room's fieldstone fireplace or by the woodstove in the bar, which also has a piano. The suite has a hot tub. Room rates include breakfast and dinner. *Bald Hill, Conway 03818, tel. 603/447–2181 or 800/426–4147. 14 rooms with bath, 2 rooms share 1 bath, 1 suite. Facilities: restaurant, pool, mountain bikes, cross-country skiing. AE, MC, V. Closed Apr. $$$*

Inn at Thorn Hill. One might almost expect Stanford White, the famed architect of the Gilded Age, to turn up at this no-smoking inn, which he designed in 1895: The air-conditioned rooms still have the polished dark woods, rose-motif papers and fabrics, and Oriental rugs that were popular in his day. The casual elegance and romantic ambience make the inn an ideal hideaway for couples. All accommodations have fireplaces and whirlpool baths. *Thorn Hill Rd., Jackson 03846, tel. 603/383–4242 or 800/289–8990. 16 rooms, 3 cottages. Facilities: restaurant, pub, pool, hot tub, croquet, horseshoes, cross-country skiing, tobogganing. AE, MC, V. Closed Apr. $$$*

Mount Washington Hotel & Resort. When this monumental Victorian hotel overlooking the Presidential Range opened its doors in 1902, it was judged one of the most elegant in the world. The "Grande Dame of the White Mountains" has undergone extensive cosmetic surgery and is again looking like a *jeune fille.* An orchestra once again plays for guests as they dine in the octagonal formal dining room with its crystal chandelier, and the 900-ft wraparound veranda, lined with wicker sofas, is once more a favorite place to watch night fall over Mount Washington. The room rate includes breakfast and a four-course dinner (jackets required); guests have the option of dining at several other restaurants, including the small, elegant dining room at the hotel's 1896 Bretton Arms Country Inn, which serves creative new American fare. Ask for a mountain view when making dinner reservations. There are six categories of rooms: Spacious corner rooms are the best bet; some rooms on the lower end are small. There are stables on the property; sleigh and carriage rides are available. *Route 302, Bretton Woods 03575, tel. 603/278–1000 or 800/258–0330 outside NH. 97 rooms, 3 suites. Facilities: restaurant, bar, indoor and outdoor pools, 9-hole and 18-hole golf courses, 12 tennis courts, health club, hiking, horseback riding, shops, children's programs, playground, travel services. AE, D, MC, V. $$$*

Nestlenook Farm Resort. Part of a 65-acre estate, this 200-year-old Victorian gingerbread inn is the perfect place for a romantic getaway or family holiday (if your children are 12 or older). Each of the elegantly decorated guest rooms has a canopy bed and a bath with a two-person whirlpool tub; six have 19th-century parlor stoves and one a Count Rumford fireplace. Winter afternoons are straight out of Currier & Ives: Guests ice-skate on Emerald Lake under the 70-ft arched bridge, cross-country ski, or enjoy a horse-drawn sleigh ride. In summer the gardens are magnificent, the pool delightful, and the hammocks a grand place to rest after a brisk hike. There's a nightly hospitality hour, a game room, and farm animals to pet. Rates include full breakfast. The inn is smoke-free. *Box Q, Dinsmore Rd., Jackson Village 03846, tel. 603/383–9443 or 800/659–9443. 7 rooms. Facilities: restaurant, pub, pool, recreation room, hiking, boating, fishing, ice-skating. D, MC, V. $$$*

Notchland Inn. Gracious accommodations in an 1862 granite mansion, elegantly appointed common rooms, lovely gardens, and a relaxed atmosphere sum up the experience at this no-smoking inn. Each guest room and suite is magnificently decorated and has its own modern bath and fireplace. The spacious Crawford Room, with fabulous mountain views, is a favorite. The best suite has a hot tub and private deck. Rates include a full country breakfast and elegant five-course dinner. There are two great swimming holes across the way in the Saco River, farm animals in the barn, and a justice of the peace on the premises for those in a romantic mood. *Hart's Location 03812, tel. 603/374–6131. 7 rooms, 5 suites. Facilities: hot tub, hiking, baby-sitting. AE, D, MC, V. $$$*

Philbrook Farm Inn. Run by members of the Philbrook family since 1834 and listed on the National Register of Historic Places, this cozy hostelry prides itself on its simple furnishings, a random blending of antiques and practical reproductions meant to give guests a feel for a slower, simpler way of life gone by. Many choose to recapture the feeling, pulling up a rocker after a hearty New England dinner and watching night fall over the Carter, Moriah, and Presidential Mountain ranges. Gramp's Room and the Dodge MacKnight Room are particularly spacious and welcoming. Four cottages have fireplaces. Breakfast and dinner are included in the room rate. *881 North Rd., Shelburne 03581, tel. 603/466–3831. 19 rooms, 7 share baths; 5 cottages. Closed Apr. and Nov.–Dec. 25. Facilities: pool, billiards. $$$*

Bernerhof Inn. This small, Old World hotel, built in the 1890s, is at home in its alpine setting. Rooms eschew the lace-and-doily decor of many other Victorian inns, opting instead for the understated: hardwood floors with hooked rugs, antique reproductions, and large, plain windows. Most rooms have whirlpool baths. Breakfast is included in the room rate; a champagne breakfast is served in bed for guests who stay three days. *Rte. 302, Glen 03838, tel. 603/383–9132 or 800/548–8007. 10 rooms. Facilities: restaurant, pub. AE, D, DC, MC, V. $$–$$$*

Sugar Hill Inn. The old carriage on the lawn and wicker chairs on the wraparound porch embellish the charm of this converted 1789 farmhouse. The old building has begun to tilt and sag over the years, so not a single room in the inn is square or level, and many have rippled antique windows. Climb out of your four-poster, canopy, or brass bed, and set foot on braided rugs strategically placed to show off the pumpkin pine and northern-maple floorboards, some of which are 25 inches wide. Most rooms have a view of Franconia Notch. Also on the property are three country cottages that house two rooms each (a few have fireplaces). The restaurant serves hearty New England fare that includes lamb and beef dishes, homemade chowders, and delicious desserts. Full breakfast and afternoon tea are included; a MAP plan (which includes breakfast and dinner) is available year-round and is required in fall. Guests have golf privileges (complimentary) at a nearby country club. *Rte. 117, Sugar Hill 03585 (mailing address: Box 954, Franconia 03580), tel. 603/823–5621 or 800/548–4748. 16 rooms. Facilities: restaurant, pub, cross-country skiing. AE, MC, V. Closed Apr. and Christmas wk. $$–$$$*

Country Inn at Bartlett. If you're looking for basic, comfortable, no-smoking lodgings, this inn–cottage complex nestled in the forest fits the bill. Accommodations range from single rooms to family-size units; Room 4 is particularly spacious. All 10 of the cottages have a private bath and TV. Some rooms and cottages have fireplaces and cooking facilities; the larger cottages are air-conditioned. The clothes-

optional outdoor hot tub is a favorite year-round gathering place. Owner Mark Dindorf, who worked for the AMC's hut system for six years, knows all of the best places to hike and ski and delights in sharing his knowledge with guests. He also can line up backcountry guides. *Box 327, Rte. 302, Bartlett 03812, tel. 603/374–2353 or 800/292–2353. 1 room with bath, 5 rooms share baths, 10 cottages. AE, MC, V. $$*

Hilltop Inn. It would be easy to imagine staying for a week at this inn, with its front porch overlooking herb and flower gardens, and back deck shaded by a pair of massive black locust trees. In fact, the combination of thoughtfully placed antiques, abundant plump pillows and handmade quilts, Victorian ceiling fans, and the innkeepers' warm hospitality might tempt you to move in altogether. And your pet is welcome. The cottage has a kitchen and fireplace; there are fireplaces in all comman areas in the main inn. Rates include full breakfast. *Rte. 117, Sugar Hill 03585, tel. 603/823–5695. 6 rooms, 1 cottage. MC, V. $$*

Patio Motor Court. Families with small kids and a moderate budget will find these small, rustic one-bedroom, two-bedroom and duplex housekeeping units most welcoming. The complex is set well off the road: There's plenty of room for the kids to run, and loads of activities to keep them amused. All units have baths, color cable TVs, and phones for outgoing calls. There are barbecue grills and carports on the premises. *Rte. 3, Twin Mountain 03595, tel. 800/227–2846. Facilities: pool, recreation room, coin laundry. D, MC, V. $$*

Red Apple Inn. Rooms at this family-oriented, one-story, no-smoking motel are spacious and immaculate. Poolside units have refrigerators and direct access to the playground and picnic areas. There's a game room in the basement with a large-screen TV, VCR, videocassettes, and a fireplace. A Continental breakfast is included in the room rate. *Rte. 302, Glen 03838, tel. 603/383–9680. 15 rooms, 1 suite. Closed 2 wks in Apr., 3 wks in Nov. AE, D, MC, V. $$*

Wilderness Inn B&B. Once a lumber baron's estate (built in 1912), this snug inn has dark wooden beams that create a dramatic backdrop for the comfortable sofas dotted with embroidered pillows. Weather permitting, a bountiful breakfast (included in the rate) is served on the glorious, giant porch framed with plate-glass windows. Rooms are pretty without being fussy and are decorated with exquisite antiques. The honeymoon cottage, with a sleigh bed and gas fireplace, has a private deck overlooking Lost River. The innkeepers offer a sincere, hearty welcome to their guests. Gourmet breakfasts are cooked to order using only fresh ingredients. *North Woodstock 03262, tel. 603/745–3890, 800/945–3200. 5 rooms with bath, 2 rooms share bath, 1 cottage. MC, V. $$*

Wildcat Inn & Tavern. After a day of hiking or canoeing, you can collapse on a comfy sofa by the fire, and maybe even enjoy musical entertainment, in this tavern right in the center of Jackson Village. The entire inn, a small establishment from the 19th century, is full of intriguing furniture and knickknacks. The smell of fresh-baked goods permeates the smallish yet welcoming guest rooms. It's popular with outdoor enthusiasts, partly because frills and Laura Ashley wallpaper are supplanted by a rustic, laid-back atmosphere. A full breakfast is included. *Rte. 16A, Jackson 03846, tel. 603/383–4245 or 800/228–4245, fax 603/383–6456. 14 rooms, 2 share bath. Facilities: restaurant, pub. AE, DC, MC, V. $–$$*

CAMPING

BACKCOUNTRY Backcountry camping is permitted in almost all of the White Mountain National Forest, with the exception of certain fragile Forest Protection Areas (FPA). FPA rules prohibit camping and fires above timberline (where trees are under 8 ft high) and require that visitors set up sites at least 200 ft from certain trails, and from most streams, ponds, and roads. Hikers should contact the **United States Forest Service** (tel. 603/528–8721) or any district ranger office for current information regarding regulations. The Forest Service also expects visitors to abide by "no trace" camping procedures; pick up a copy of the "Backcountry Camping Rules" brochure for details. Although backcountry camping is permitted, and even encouraged, in the national forest, hikers are urged to use existing shelters and established tent sites in popular, heavily used areas, especially along the Appalachian Trail.

NATIONAL FOREST CAMPGROUNDS The many roadside campgrounds that the national forest tend to provide less in the way of such facilities as hot water, showers, and electricity than private campgrounds; most can accommodate small trailers but offer no hookups. **Reservations** (tel. 800/280–2267, TTY 800/879–4496) can be made up to 240 days in advance; however, all have sites available on a first-come, first-served basis. For a complete listing of the 23 national forest campgrounds in the White Mountains, contact the **forest service** (tel. 603/528–8721). Unless noted otherwise, the campgrounds described below—among the most popular—are in New Hampshire.

Basin. The fee for this campground is $12. *Rte. 113, 15 mi north of Fryeburg, ME. 21 sites. Facilities: fishing. $*

Blackberry Crossing and **Covered Bridge.** These campgrounds are across the street from each other; each charges $12 per night. *Kancamagus Scenic Byway, 6 mi west of Conway. Blackberry, 26 sites; Covered Bridge, 49 sites. Facilities: hiking, fishing. $*

Campton. In an area heavily wooded with towering white pines, this campground has a playing field and summer interpretive programs and is the only campground with showers. Vacancies are usually available in the summer season, even on weekends and holidays. The fee is $14. *2 mi east of the city of Campton on Rte. 49. 58 sites. $*

Dolly Copp. As many as 1,000 people may be camped here at one time. There are summer interpretive programs and it is close to many of the popular hiking areas. The fee is $12. *Rte. 16, 6 mi south of Gorham. 176 sites. $*

Hancock. There are 35 sites with trailer space here: It was designed for easy access by trailers or RVs. An appealing swimming hole, Upper Lady's Bath, is a five-minute walk downstream from the campground. The fee is $12. *Kancamagus Scenic Byway, 4 mi east of Lincoln. 56 sites. $*

Russell Pond. This campground is on a particularly scenic pond and offers interpretive nature programs Saturday evening at dusk during the summer; the boat launch and dock are designed for wheelchair access. The fee is $12. *Tripoli Rd., Campton, 13 mi off I–93, Exit 31. 49 tent sites, 38 RV sites. $*

STATE PARKS Several New Hampshire state parks have campgrounds in or near White Mountain National Forest, with fees ranging from $12 to $14 per night. **Reservations** (tel. 603/271–3628) are accepted. Half of the sites are available on a first-come, first-served basis. Campgrounds are generally set up for tent camping; small trailers are welcome where they fit, but no hookups are provided. Call for information on special RV parks. Campgrounds are open from mid-May through mid-October, with the exception of Lafayette Campground in Franconia Notch, which is open year-round, although there is no water in winter. A carry-in, carry-out policy has been established at the state parks: Trash barrels have been removed to provide visitors with a more pristine outdoor experience and to encourage wildlife to remain wild. Contact the **New Hampshire Division of Parks and Recreation** (172 Pembroke Rd., Box 1856, Concord, NH 03302, tel. 603/271–3556) for more information about the campgrounds.

Crawford Notch State Park, on Route 302 and nestled in a stunning mountain pass, is a great base for hiking in the Whites, as well as fishing in nearby streams. The 6-square-mi park has nature trails to scenic waterfalls and picnic areas. The Dry River Campground has 30 tent sites, an information center, a gift shop, and a snack bar, but no showers or hot water.

Franconia Notch State Park, off I–93 between the looming peaks of the Franconia and Kinsman mountain ranges, abounds with dramatic natural wonders, including the Old Man of the Mountain (a great stone face) and the Flume (an 800-ft natural gorge). Lafayette Campground has 97 tent sites, showers, hot water, and a camp store and offers interpretive activities in the summer. An ideal hiking and cycling base, the campground provides easy access to the Appalachian Trail and to a 9-mi paved recreation path.

Moose Brook State Park, off Route 2 near Gorham, is a beautiful, underutilized spot that has 42 tent sites, showers, and hot water. This park is an ideal base for hiking the Crescent and Presidential ranges and for fishing in the heart of stream fishing country.

PRIVATE CAMPGROUNDS For a list of private campgrounds near the national forest contact Ron Brown, **New Hampshire Campground Owners Association** (Box 320, Twin Mt. 03595, tel. 603/846–5511 or 800/822–6764).

Crawford Notch Campground. The only private campground in the national forest, Crawford Notch has 75 wilderness sites, some with river frontage; there's easy access from here to hiking and fishing and swimming in the Saco River. It has showers, a dishwashing station, chemical toilets, supplies, and gas. Twenty sites have electrical hookups. Fees are $18–20 per night; reservations are accepted. *Rte. 302, Crawford Notch, NH, tel. 603/374–2779. 75 sites. Closed Nov.–Apr.*